D1611016

HISTORY AT A GLANCE

The Carnac stones, or megaliths, are erected in rows that stretch for miles in Brittany, France. This remnant of Neolithic culture is the largest megalith site in the world.

HISTORY AT A GLANCE

Illustrated Time Lines From Prehistory to the Present Day

NATIONAL GEOGRAPHIC
WASHINGTON, D.C.

INVASIONS AND ADVANCES: 1000-1500

CONVERGING WORLDS: 1500-1750

Hundreds of thousands of Muslims climax their pilgrimage to Mecca by bowing in prayer at the Great Mosque before the cube-shaped Kaaba, their holiest shrine.

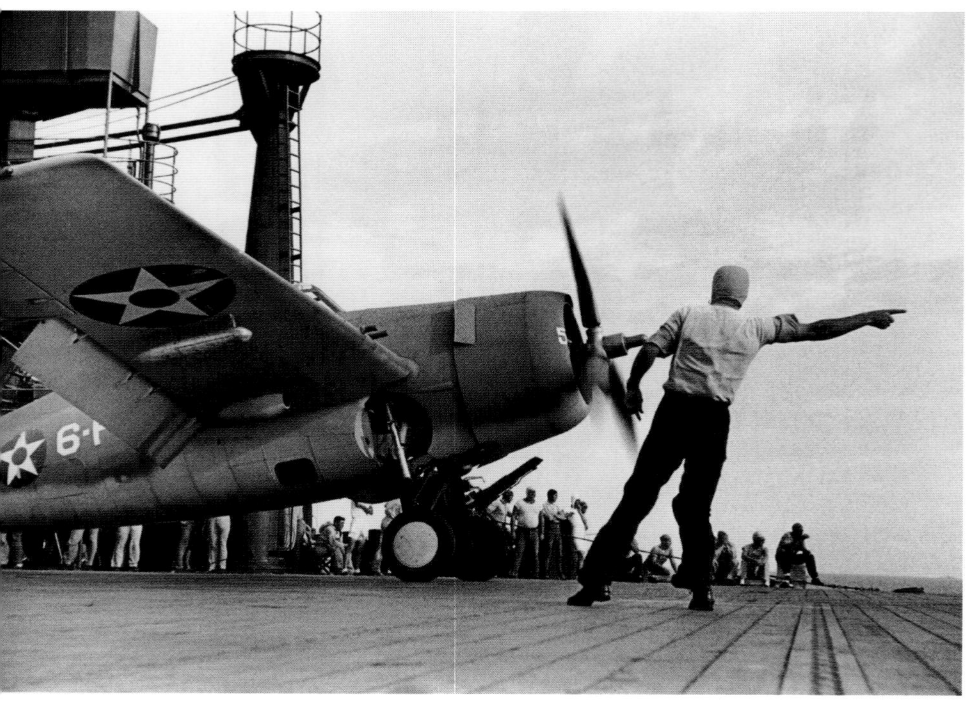

A crewman on the deck of the American aircraft carrier *Enterprise* directs a fighter pilot in the Pacific during World War II, the first major conflict in which air-power played a commanding role.

EMPIRES AND REVOLUTIONS: 1750-1900

GLOBAL CONFLICT:
1900-1950

TOWARD A NEW WORLD ORDER:
1950-2000

GLOBALIZATION AND DISRUPTION:
2000-Present

FOREWORD

In our era of speedy communication, knowing what is happening around the block, around the nation, and around the world is easier than it has ever been. Our smartphones, tablets, and laptops can—in an instant—give us a broad look at people, events, and cultures.

But what about the past?

You may know that "In 1400 and 92, Columbus sailed the ocean blue," but quick! What else was going on in the 15th century?

As it turns out, there was quite a bit: The War of the Roses was raging in Britain, while the Inca were building the magnificent Machu Picchu in the Andes Mountains. Italians in Florence were enjoying Botticelli's "Birth of Venus" for the first time. In West Africa, Muhammad I Askia was usurping the throne of the Songhai Empire and bringing the gold-rich realm to the height of its power.

As we cast our eyes backward, that perspective often narrows, and the picture fragments the further back in time we go. Focus shifts from the world to just one nation, one people, or one event, rather than seeing the whole.

National Geographic History at a Glance changes all that: Covering humanity from the dawn of time up through the modern era, this book puts together the global picture of the past. Going back thousands of years, page after page presents a truly global perspective of history through comparative time lines. Each one highlights the people, places, and things happening all over the world in every historical era. Intriguing artifacts, captivating works of art, and engaging maps create an even more vibrant picture of the inventions, the milestones, the monuments, and the people who lived them.

Turn to page 27 and see what was happening around the world more than 4,000 years ago: Egyptian pharaohs built the first pyramids at Giza, villages were turning into cities along the Indus River in western India, and the Chinese people first began producing silk.

Fast-forward 2,000 years to page 89 to see when the Trung sisters of Vietnam led a rebellion at the same time as Octavian declares war on Cleopatra. Across the Atlantic Ocean, inhabitants of Teotihuacan are constructing massive stone monuments in Mesoamerica as their civilization begins its rise.

Looking back on the history of the world through this approach widens our vision, allowing an immersive view of humanity's rich, shared history. I invite you to get lost in the past, and all that is in it.

— AMY BRIGGS

Executive Editor, *National Geographic History*

The Inca citadel Machu Picchu was erected in the Peruvian Andes around 1450 without the use of metal tools, mortar, or the wheel. The sophisticated city, shown here in a photo illustration, was abandoned during the Spanish conquests of the 16th century and rediscovered by the outside world in 1911.

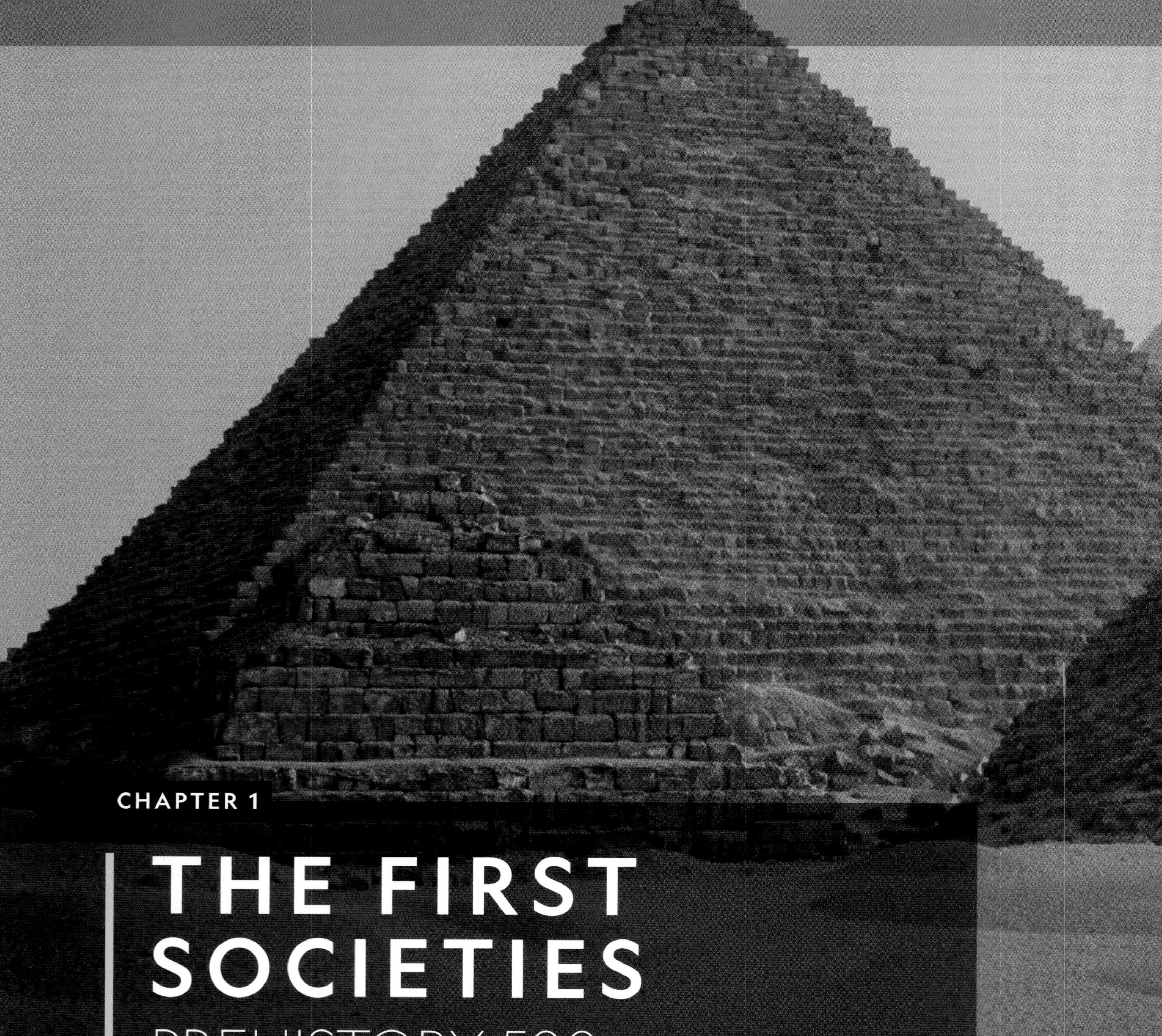

CHAPTER 1

THE FIRST SOCIETIES

PREHISTORY–500 B.C.E.

The Great Pyramid (center) and surrounding monuments at Giza testify to the towering ambitions of the pharaohs who ruled ancient Egypt and conscripted laborers to build these majestic tombs, intended to house their remains eternally and allow their souls to journey to the afterworld.

Human history is the story of a species so skilled at exploiting and altering its environment that it now has the power to create new life forms genetically or destroy life on a vast scale and extinguish many species. As builders, colonists, and conquerors, humans have shown an astonishing capacity to invent, transform, and lay waste. "Wonders are many, but none is more wonderful than man," wrote the Greek playwright Sophocles. "Cunning beyond fancy's dream is the fertile skill which brings him, now to evil, now to good."

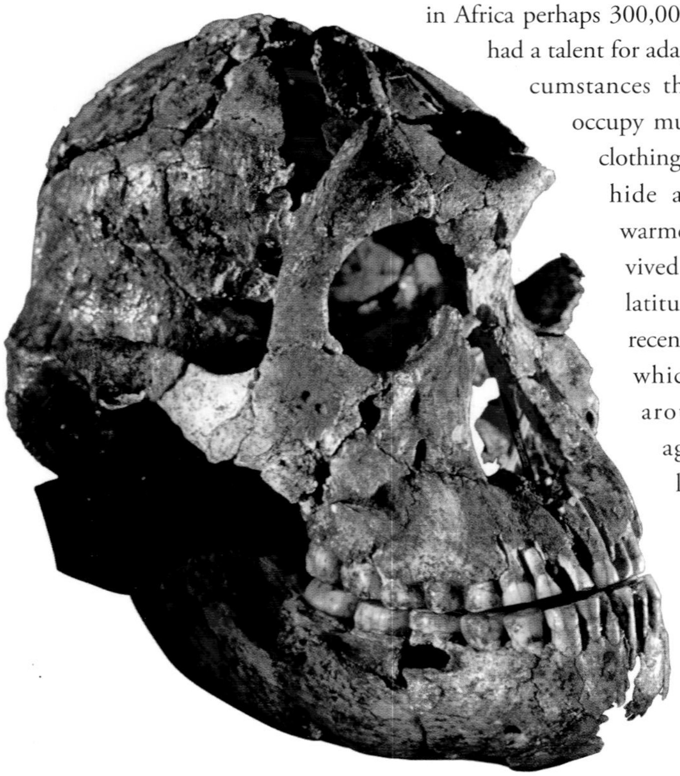

As demonstrated by this two-million-year-old skull, early hominids had a different cranial structure than modern humans, with a smaller brain cavity and a larger jaw. But they shared with modern humans an upright posture that allowed them to carry food, tools, or weapons as they walked.

Humans owe their phenomenal ability to alter the world for good or ill to a process of evolution that began in Africa more than four million years ago with the emergence of the first hominids: primates with the ability to walk upright. Early hominids stood only three or four feet tall on average and had brains roughly one-third the size of the modern human brain, which limited their capacity to reason or speak. But their upright posture and opposable thumbs (used to grip objects between fingers and thumb) allowed them to gather and carry food and process it using simple tools.

Over time, other species of hominids evolved that possessed larger brains and the ability to fully articulate their thoughts, craft ingenious tools and weapons, and hunt collectively. *Homo sapiens,* or modern humans, emerged in Africa perhaps 300,000 years ago, and they had a talent for adapting to changing circumstances that allowed them to occupy much of the planet. By clothing themselves in animal hide and living in caves warmed by fires, they survived winters in northern latitudes during the most recent phase of the Ice Age, which came to an end around 12,000 years ago. That glaciation lowered sea levels and enabled people to walk from Siberia to North America and reach Australia and other previously inaccessible landmasses.

During the Ice Age, humans gathered wild grains and other plants, but they owed their survival and success largely to hunting. So skilled were they at hunting in groups and killing large animals that they probably contributed to the extinction of such species as the mammoth and mastodon. Hunters paid tribute to the animals they stalked in wondrous cave paintings that may have been intended to honor the spirit of those creatures so they would offer up their bounty. From early times, the destructive power of humans as predators was linked to their creative power as artists and inventors.

PUTTING DOWN ROOTS

The warming of the planet that began around 10,000 B.C.E. forced humans to adapt, and they did so with great ingenuity. Many of the larger animals people had feasted on during the Ice Age died out as a result of global warming and over-hunting. At the same time, edible plants flourished in places that had once been too cold or dry to support them. Based on the behavior of hunter-gatherers in recent times, women did much of the gathering in ancient times and probably used their knowledge of plants to domesticate wheat, barley, rice, maize (corn), and other cereals. That allowed groups who had once roamed in search of sustenance to settle in one place.

The domestication of animals also contributed to a more settled way of life. Dogs were probably the first animals tamed by humans. People later succeeded in domesticating other useful creatures such as cattle and sheep, which furnished meat, milk, wool, and hide. This was most likely accomplished by men, who did most of the hunting and learned gradually how to control animals.

That in itself did not cause people to settle down. Nomadic herders continued to follow grazing animals such as sheep and goats from place to place long after other people had settled in villages. The most productive societies, however, were those that practiced agriculture by controlling animals and cultivating plants. Agriculture provided food surpluses that allowed people to specialize in other pursuits and devise new tools and technologies.

Some of the earliest advances in agriculture occurred in the Middle East, where sizable towns such as Jericho developed. By 8000 B.C.E., Jericho had developed into an organized settlement of around 2,000 inhabitants, or more than 10 times as many people as in a typical band of hunter-gatherers. To protect their community from raiders, the people of Jericho built a wall that became legendary. Within Jericho and other such towns lived many people who specialized in nonagricultural trades, including merchants, metalworkers, and potters. The demand for pots to hold grain and other perishables led to development of the potter's wheel, which may in turn have inspired the first wheeled vehicles. Farmers here and elsewhere used wooden plows pulled by cattle or other draft animals to cultivate their fields and exchanged surplus food for clay pots, copper tools, and other crafted items.

By 5000 B.C.E. agriculture was being practiced in large parts of Europe, Asia, and Africa. Few animals were domesticated in the Americas because they had few domesticable species. (Horses had died out and would not be reintroduced until Europeans reached what they called the New World.) But the domestication of corn and other crops in the Americas led to the growth of villages and complex societies, marked by a high degree of specialization.

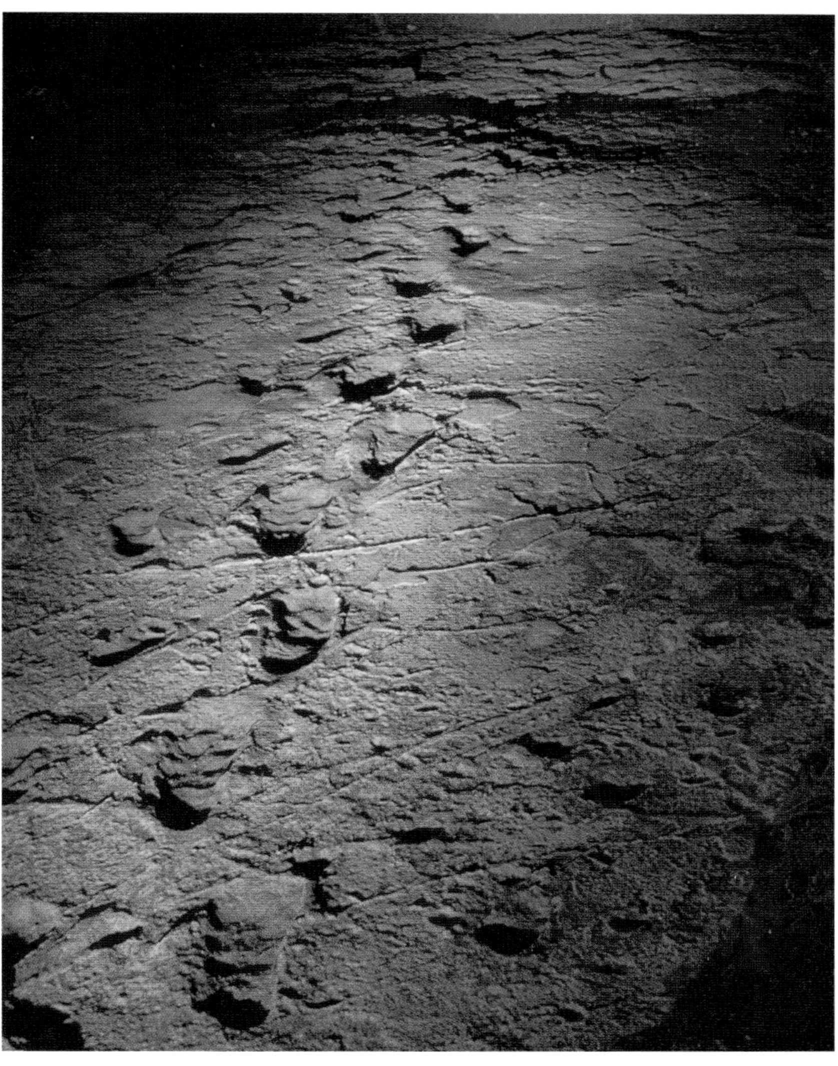

Hominids in Tanzania left these 3.6-million-year-old footprints in volcanic ash that hardened after they passed.

DAWN OF CIVILIZATION

By 3500 B.C.E., the stage was set for the emergence of societies so complex and accomplished they rank as civilizations, a word derived from the Latin *civis,* or citizen. All early civilizations had impressive cities or ceremonial centers adorned with fine works of art and architecture. All had strong rulers capable of commanding the services of thousands of people for public projects or military campaigns. Many but not all used writing to keep records, codify laws, and preserve wisdom and lore in the form of literature.

People in these highly complex societies possessed superior technology, but they were no better or wiser than those in simpler societies. Civilizations embodied the contradictions in human nature. They were enormously creative and hugely exploitative, enhancing the lives of some people and enslaving others. Their cities fostered learning, invention, and artistry, but many were destroyed by other so-called civilized people. The glory and brutality of civilization was recognized by philosophers and poets, who knew that anything a ruler raised up could be brought down. "When the laws are kept, how proudly his city stands!" wrote Sophocles. "When the laws are broken, what of his city then?"

CORRIDORS OF POWER

Several ancient civilizations arose along rivers: the Tigris and Euphrates in Mesopotamia, the Nile in Egypt, the Indus in what is now Pakistan, and the Yellow River in China. People living in these fertile corridors needed

This imposing bronze figure with braided beard represents the ideal Mesopotamian ruler. It may be a likeness of Sargon, who forged the first empire in Mesopotamia by sweeping down from Akkad and conquering the cities of Sumer, on the map opposite.

strong leaders to coordinate irrigation projects or flood-control efforts and collect surplus food for those engaged in public works and other vital tasks. Leaders often demanded heavy sacrifices from people in labor and taxes or required a portion of the harvest, but communities as a whole grew more productive and powerful as a result.

In this way, towns developed into cities that controlled outlying farms and villages. The world's first cities emerged in Mesopotamia around 3200 B.C.E. and grew to contain as many as 50,000 people. Surplus grain was stored at temple complexes, and scribes there developed writing called cuneiform, inscribed on clay tablets, to keep track of goods received and distributed. When conflicts arose with outsiders over access to land or water, the city appointed a chief to wage war. Successful chiefs clung to power and became kings. Some royal families built palaces near temples and demanded human sacrifices. At the Sumerian city of Ur around 2500 B.C.E., some people lost their lives and were buried with deceased rulers to serve them in the next world.

Around 2330 B.C.E. Ur, Uruk, and other prosperous cities of Sumer, situated near the Persian Gulf, fell to a conqueror from northern Mesopotamia named Sargon. His successors lost control of that empire, but the region was later reunited under Hammurabi, who ruled at Babylon. He issued the law of his realm in writing, making it clear and consistent. Writing also enabled Babylonian scribes to transform legends into literature such as the *Epic of Gilgamesh,* the story of a fabled king who sought immortality.

In Egypt cities were slower to develop, but the Nile helped unify the country. People rode boats downstream to the Mediterranean and used sails or oars to travel upstream. Rains falling in the highlands far to the south caused the Nile to overflow its banks in summer and replenish what would otherwise have been a desert. The miraculous emergence of fertile land from the floodwaters helped instill in Egyptians hope that they too might return to life after they died. Their early kings, or pharaohs, who consolidated power around 3000 B.C.E. and ruled at Memphis, were preserved after death through mummification and buried in tombs that grew grander over time. The Great Pyramid of Khufu, built at Giza in the 26th century B.C.E., required tens of thousands of laborers and symbolized the lofty aspirations of Egypt's rulers, who identified with the sun god Re. One text promised that the pharaoh's spirit would rise from the pyramid and "ascend to heaven as the eye of Re" (an image that endures today on the American dollar).

Monumental architecture was not confined to Egypt or other centers of civilization. Construction of the Great Pyramid was preceded by the building of Stonehenge in Britain, which may have been used for religious ceremonies related to phases of the sun and moon. Such massive stone monuments in Europe demonstrate that agricultural societies there were capable of concerted efforts under the direction of priests or other authorities. But Europe had no cities as yet and no rulers who held sway over vast areas and left their mark on history as the pharaohs did. Around 2000 B.C.E. power in Egypt shifted from Memphis to Thebes, whose kings expanded their domain southward into Nubia (present-day Ethiopia).

Along the Indus River and its tributaries, irrigation efforts fed the growth of remarkable cities that were flourishing by 2500 B.C.E. and reflected careful planning, with broad streets, large granaries to store surplus crops, and elaborate sewage systems. The two largest cities were Mohenjo Daro, which had almost 40,000 inhabitants, and Harappa, for which this Harappan civilization is named. Artisans in the cities produced cotton fabric and jewelry, and merchants shipped crafted goods and raw materials to Mesopotamia. Harappan writing has not been deciphered and may have been rudimentary. But this was one of the most-well-organized societies in the world before its cities declined after 2000 B.C.E., most likely as a result of flooding or other natural causes.

In China, agricultural and technological innovation took place in many areas, including the lower Yangzi River, where rice was cultivated as early as 7000 B.C.E. Food surpluses in communities there and elsewhere helped support Chinese artisans skilled at crafts such as pottery, the sculpting of jade objects, and the casting of bronze—an alloy of copper and tin that provided ancient societies in various parts of the world with stronger weapons and tools than those made of copper alone.

Around 2200 B.C.E. crucial political developments occurred along the Yellow River. Villagers there did not have much need for irrigation. They usually received adequate rainfall and raised millet and other grains in loess: fertile yellow soil deposited by winds blowing from the north. That same soil, however, clogged the Yellow River and caused floods. Chinese chronicles credit a legendary king named Yu with taming the river's floods and bringing order to the world. Rulers of the Xia dynasty founded by Yu mobilized laborers for flood-control projects such as dredging the river or building dikes and gained power and prestige in the process.

Around 1600 B.C.E. the Xia dynasty was succeeded by the Shang dynasty, whose rulers built defensive walls of rammed earth around their capitals and raised armies,

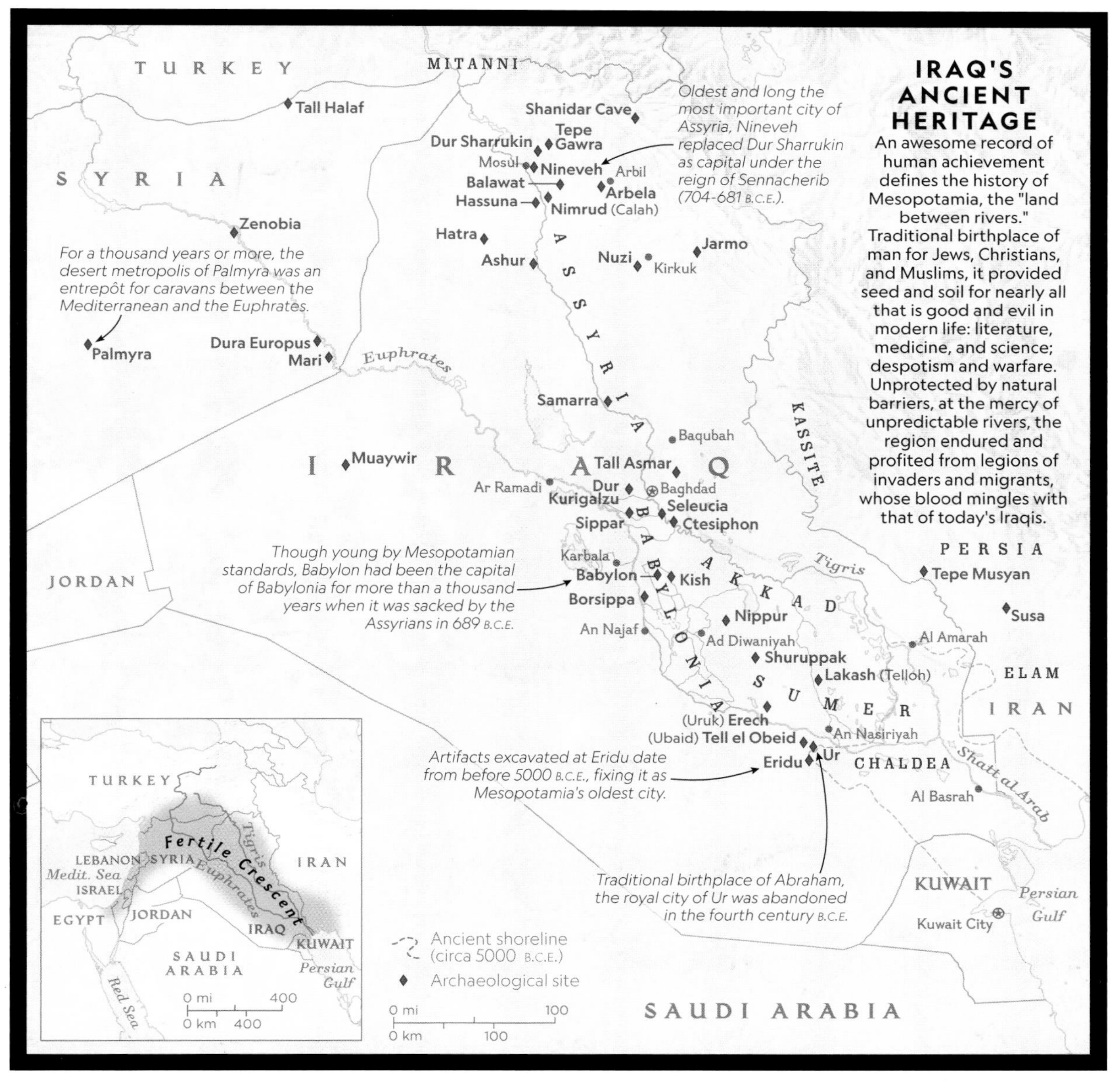

IRAQ'S ANCIENT HERITAGE
An awesome record of human achievement defines the history of Mesopotamia, the "land between rivers." Traditional birthplace of man for Jews, Christians, and Muslims, it provided seed and soil for nearly all that is good and evil in modern life: literature, medicine, and science; despotism and warfare. Unprotected by natural barriers, at the mercy of unpredictable rivers, the region endured and profited from legions of invaders and migrants, whose blood mingles with that of today's Iraqis.
TURKEY
MITANNI
SYRIA
Tall Halaf
Shanidar Cave
Tepe Gawra
Dur Sharrukin
Mosul
Nineveh
Arbil
Balawat
Arbela
Hassuna
Nimrud (Calah)
Oldest and long the most important city of Assyria, Nineveh replaced Dur Sharrukin as capital under the reign of Sennacherib (704-681 B.C.E.).
Zenobia
For a thousand years or more, the desert metropolis of Palmyra was an entrepôt for caravans between the Mediterranean and the Euphrates.
Hatra
Ashur
Nuzi
Kirkuk
Jarmo
ASSYRIA
Palmyra
Dura Europus
Mari
Euphrates
Samarra
Baqubah
KASSITE
IRAQ
Muaywir
Tall Asmar
Ar Ramadi
Dur Kurigalzu
Baghdad
Seleucia
Sippar
Ctesiphon
BABYLONIA
Though young by Mesopotamian standards, Babylon had been the capital of Babylonia for more than a thousand years when it was sacked by the Assyrians in 689 B.C.E.
Karbala
Babylon
Kish
Borsippa
AKKAD
Nippur
An Najaf
Ad Diwaniyah
Tigris
PERSIA
Tepe Musyan
Susa
Al Amarah
Shuruppak
Lakash (Telloh)
ELAM
SUMER
IRAN
JORDAN
(Uruk) Erech
(Ubaid) Tell el Obeid
An Nasiriyah
Eridu
Ur
CHALDEA
Shatt al Arab
Artifacts excavated at Eridu date from before 5000 B.C.E., fixing it as Mesopotamia's oldest city.
Al Basrah
Traditional birthplace of Abraham, the royal city of Ur was abandoned in the fourth century B.C.E.
KUWAIT
Persian Gulf
Kuwait City
Ancient shoreline (circa 5000 B.C.E.)
Archaeological site
0 mi 100
0 km 100
SAUDI ARABIA
TURKEY
Fertile Crescent
LEBANON
SYRIA
Tigris
Euphrates
IRAN
Medit. Sea
ISRAEL
EGYPT
JORDAN
IRAQ
KUWAIT
SAUDI ARABIA
Persian Gulf
Red Sea
0 mi 400
0 km 400

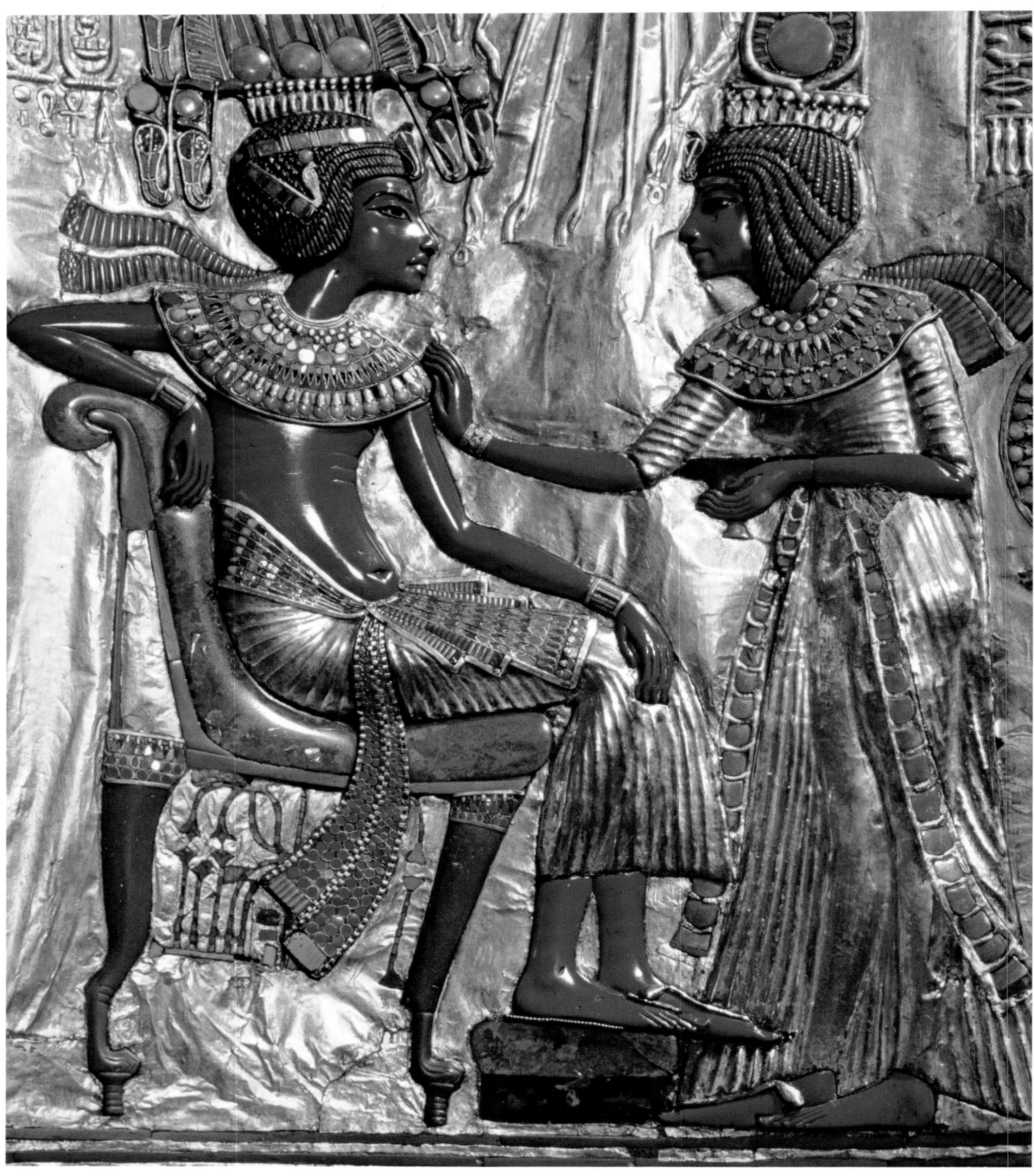

expanding their domain to embrace a large area in northeastern China. Veneration of ancestors was an ancient tradition in China. Shang rulers made offerings to their ancestors in ritual vessels of bronze and tried to divine the future by communicating with their ancestors using oracle bones, which cracked when heated, revealing answers to their questions. Those questions were inscribed on the oracle bones using an elaborate writing system involving thousands of characters. Here as in other ancient civilizations, society became highly stratified, with great differences in wealth and power between rulers or nobles and peasants or slaves. Slaves captured in battle were sometimes put to death and buried with deceased Shang kings in their tombs.

INVASIONS AND INNOVATIONS

Beginning around 1600 B.C.E., invaders from the north swept down into Egypt, Mesopotamia, the Indus Valley, and other parts of the ancient world. Most of these invaders were of Indo-European origin. Over the centuries, wave after wave of Indo-Europeans migrated from the Eurasian steppes above the Black Sea and Caspian Sea, where they were among the first to domesticate horses and use them to haul vehicles. Their horse-driven chariots made them formidable warriors. Through their migrations, they influenced the development of many languages, including Sanskrit (the classical language of India), Persian, Greek, Latin, and English, all of which belong to the Indo-European family of languages.

One group of Indo-Europeans called Mycenaeans had descended into Greece, where they built hilltop fortresses and majestic tombs for their kings, who were buried amid hoards of gold. Before long those restless Mycenaeans took over the island of Crete and ousted its Minoan rulers, who had grown rich through maritime trade and constructed palaces decorated with vibrant wall paintings.

In centuries to come, Celts of Indo-European origin would spread westward across Europe as far as the British Isles, building lofty strongholds like those of the Mycenaeans and burying their nobility amid treasure.

In the Middle East, an Indo-European people called the Hittites invaded Mesopotamia and used war chariots to conquer Babylon in 1595 B.C.E., shattering the empire founded by Hammurabi. Assyrians later dominated the Middle East by adopting chariots and war horses, perfecting the use of cavalry, and crafting sturdy weapons of iron, which was cheaper than bronze and stronger when combined with carbon from charcoal during forging—a process that led eventually to the production of steel. Assyrians boasted of their cruelty to enemies. "I put out the eyes of many of the soldiers," one king proclaimed in writing after a victory. Those who submitted to the Assyrians became part of their empire and provided fresh recruits for their army.

After centuries of conquest, these masters of war were overthrown by Medes and Babylonians, who regained Babylon only to lose that prize to invading Persians in 539 B.C.E. Persian rulers identified with the god Ahura Mazda, a supreme deity engaged in a cosmic struggle with the forces of evil, according to the teachings of the Persian holy man Zarathustra, who inspired Zoroastrianism.

Those Persians descended from Indo-Europeans who called themselves Aryans (noble people) and had occupied Iran (meaning "Aryan") more than a thousand years earlier. Some had remained in Iran while others had swept on through Afghanistan into the Indus Valley, arriving around 1500 B.C.E. By then, Harappan civilization had collapsed. The local villagers were no match for the invaders, who imposed a strict hierarchy in which Aryan priests and chieftains, aided by merchants and landowners, dominated a vast underclass of peasants and laborers. In time, they expanded southeastward toward the Ganges River. Their class system hardened into a caste system, which gave people almost no chance for advancement. Their rituals and teachings, however, were challenged and modified as priests came in contact with beliefs native to the Indian subcontinent. From that great religious ferment arose Hinduism, Buddhism, and Jainism, whose followers practiced nonviolence.

During this tumultuous era in which many kingdoms collapsed, China and Egypt endured, but not without struggle. The Chinese acquired horses and chariots through contact with nomadic people to their north and west and learned to forge iron. These developments spelled trouble for rulers of the Zhou dynasty, which supplanted the Shang dynasty around 1100 B.C.E. The Zhou were unable to prevent local rulers under their authority from amassing iron weapons and other assets. By 700, those lords were rebelling and China

King Tutankhamun of Egypt is anointed with perfume by his wife, Queen Ankhesenamun, in a scene portrayed on his Golden Throne, one of many treasures buried with the young pharaoh when he died in the late 14th century B.C.E.

was fragmenting. But the old ideals of unity and harmony were kept alive by Confucius, a philosopher born around 550 B.C.E. whose teachings inspired later rulers of China.

Egyptian rulers, for their part, overcame a fierce challenge from invaders called the Hyksos by adopting their weapons and horse-drawn chariots. This victory, achieved around 1550 B.C.E., marked the rise of the New Kingdom, during which Egypt reached the height of its power. Some of that authority was exercised by women, including priestesses of the goddess Hathor, who symbolized fertility and motherhood. One Egyptian queen, Hatshepsut, ruled on behalf of her young stepson and clung to power after he reached maturity. But here, as in most ancient kingdoms, men generally dominated society. One ruler who personified this patriarchal trend was Ramses II, who fathered more than 100 children by his various wives and flexed his muscle abroad by leading his forces into Syria, where they clashed with Hittites in an epic chariot battle at Kadesh in 1275 B.C.E.

Among those who came under Egypt's influence or control during this era were Hebrews of nomadic heritage who told in their scriptures of being enslaved in Egypt before Moses led them to the promised land of Canaan, where they forged the kingdom of Israel around 1000 B.C.E. Those Hebrews traced their origins to the patriarch Abraham, from Ur in Mesopotamia, and some of their customs and legends were influenced by Sumerian or Babylonian traditions.

Unlike the Babylonians, however, they rejected all other gods in favor of Yahweh, who entered into a covenant with Abraham and his descendants and revealed his laws to them through Moses. Among those laws, recorded in Hebrew scripture, was the commandment: "You shall have no other gods before me." Theirs was not the first kingdom devoted to monotheism, or the worship of one god. Around 1350 B.C.E., the pharaoh Akhenaten had proclaimed the supremacy of the solar god Aten and outlawed the worship of other deities. But while that cult died with Akhenaten, Judaism endured and inspired both Christianity and Islam.

Egyptians also had a strong impact on the Lybians to their west and the Nubians and other black Africans to their south. Nubians adopted the Egyptian writing system, worshiped Egyptian gods, and built Egyptian-inspired pyramids to house the remains of their kings. Over time, Nubian rulers grew stronger and bolder and stopped paying tribute in gold to Egyptian kings. Around 750 B.C.E., Nubians took power in Egypt and ruled as pharaohs until Assyrians invaded the country in the following century.

AN INCREASINGLY COMPLEX WORLD

Contacts with civilizations sometimes hastened cultural development, but many complex societies evolved largely on their own. Such was the case in Southeast Asia, where prolific rice harvests helped support expert potters and bronze workers employed by nobles who grew rich through trade and warfare.

In the Americas, complex societies emerged in complete isolation from the established civilizations of the Old World. In the Andes, the cultivation of potatoes, corn, and other crops yielded food surpluses that allowed people to devote great energy and skill to building ceremonial centers such as Chavín de Huántar, where work began on temples around 850 B.C.E. Along the Gulf Coast of Mesoamerica, meanwhile, the Olmec people were performing similar architectural feats at sites such as San Lorenzo and La Venta under the direction of strong rulers, whose stern features may appear on the great stone heads carved by Olmec artists. Olmec achievements laid the foundations for Maya civilization.

Some of the world's most dramatic cultural advances occurred where complex societies interacted. Around the Mediterranean between 1000 and 500 B.C.E., Phoenicians from what is now Lebanon and Greeks from rising city-states such as Athens founded scores of colonies and spread literacy through phonetic alphabets consisting of only two dozen or so characters, compared to the hundreds or thousands of characters that scholars elsewhere had to master. This enabled men and women who were not priests, rulers, or scribes to learn to read and write. The growth of literacy helped transform people such as the Romans, who ousted their Etruscan overlords around 500 B.C.E., from subjects into citizens, capable of governing themselves. Literacy did not alter the combative nature of humans, for whom words could be deadly weapons. But it enhanced their capacity to cultivate fields of knowledge and create works of literature, philosophy, and science that would outlast the triumphs of conquering armies. ■

Olmec artists sculpted massive stone heads like this one from huge blocks of basalt transported from distant quarries. The heads probably represent Olmec rulers, who commanded the labor of thousands of people and oversaw the construction of temples and earthen pyramids at ceremonial centers near the Gulf of Mexico.

WORLD AT A GLANCE

PREHISTORY-500 B.C.E.

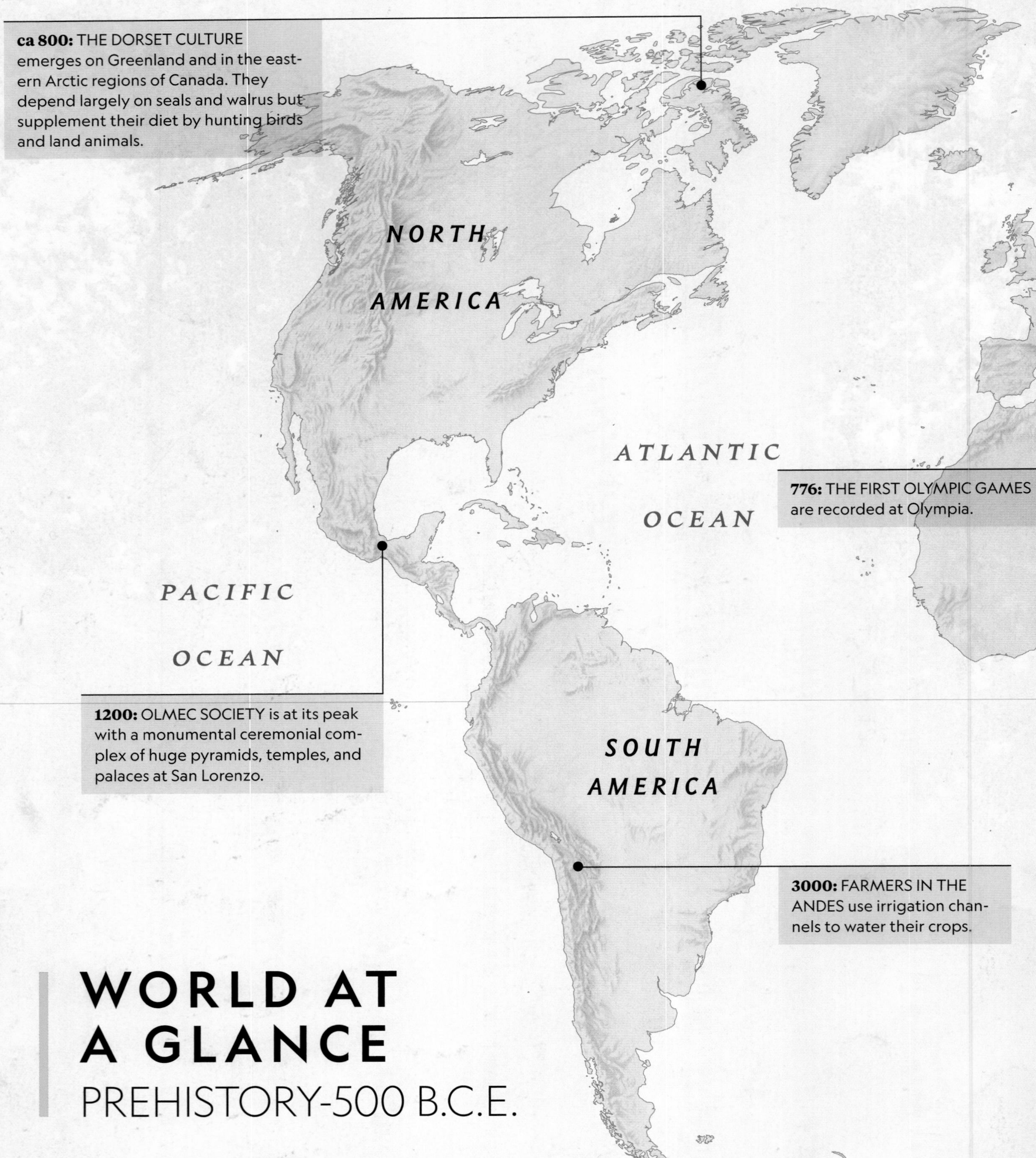

ARCTIC
ca 800: THE DORSET CULTURE emerges on Greenland and in the eastern Arctic regions of Canada. They depend largely on seals and walrus but supplement their diet by hunting birds and land animals.
NORTH AMERICA
ATLANTIC OCEAN
776: THE FIRST OLYMPIC GAMES are recorded at Olympia.
PACIFIC OCEAN
1200: OLMEC SOCIETY is at its peak with a monumental ceremonial complex of huge pyramids, temples, and palaces at San Lorenzo.
SOUTH AMERICA
3000: FARMERS IN THE ANDES use irrigation channels to water their crops.

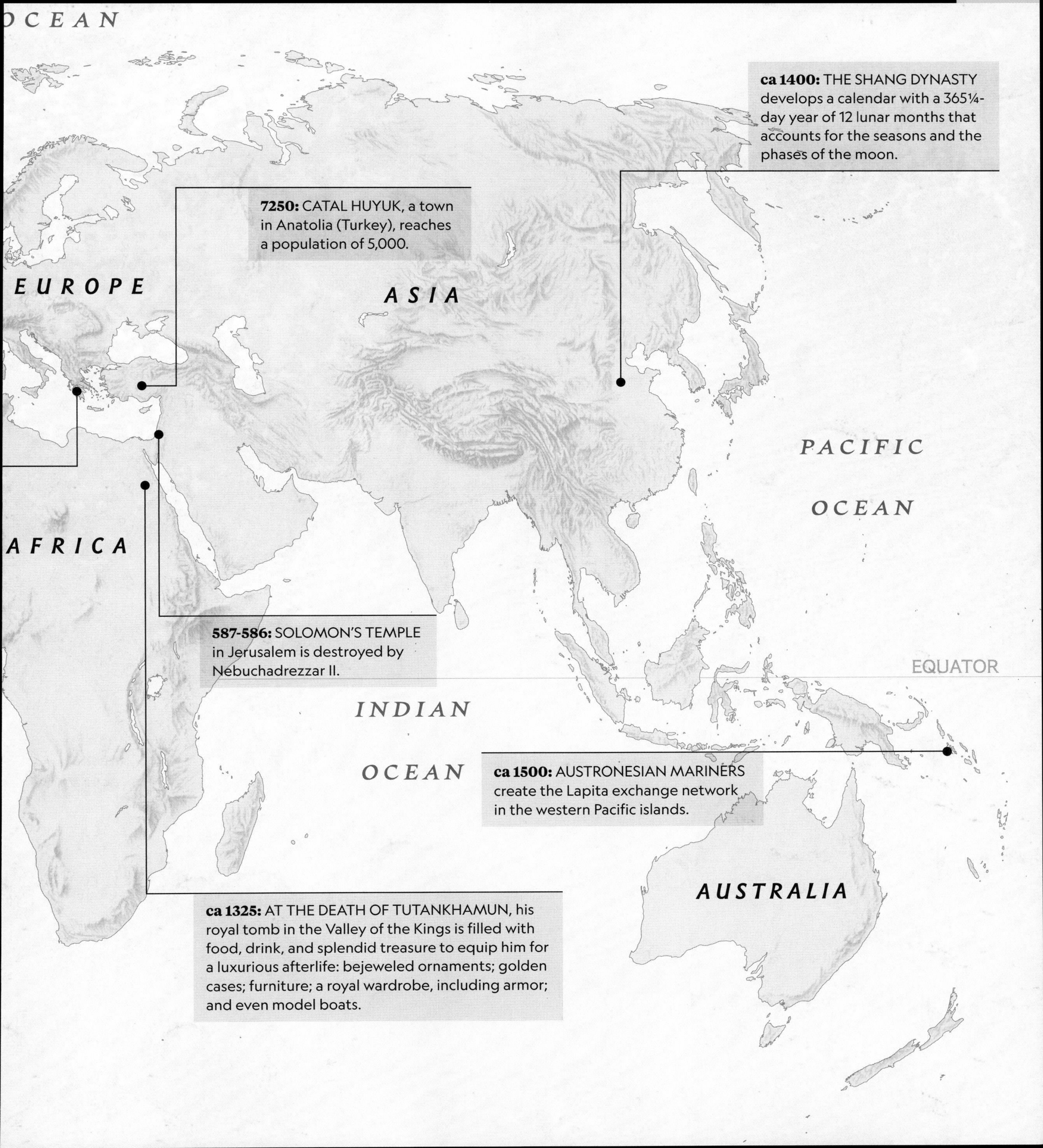

OCEAN

EUROPE

ASIA

AFRICA

PACIFIC OCEAN

INDIAN OCEAN

AUSTRALIA

EQUATOR

ca 1400: THE SHANG DYNASTY develops a calendar with a 365¼-day year of 12 lunar months that accounts for the seasons and the phases of the moon.

7250: CATAL HUYUK, a town in Anatolia (Turkey), reaches a population of 5,000.

587-586: SOLOMON'S TEMPLE in Jerusalem is destroyed by Nebuchadrezzar II.

ca 1500: AUSTRONESIAN MARINERS create the Lapita exchange network in the western Pacific islands.

ca 1325: AT THE DEATH OF TUTANKHAMUN, his royal tomb in the Valley of the Kings is filled with food, drink, and splendid treasure to equip him for a luxurious afterlife: bejeweled ornaments; golden cases; furniture; a royal wardrobe, including armor; and even model boats.

PREHISTORY-3000 B.C.E.

	POLITICS & POWER	GEOGRAPHY & ENVIRONMENT	CULTURE & RELIGION
THE AMERICAS	**ca 16,500-14,500** HUMANS begin to arrive in South America, reaching modern-day Monte Verde, Chile. **ca 12,500** HUMANS begin to inhabit North America. **ca 12,000** THE HEILTSUK CULTURE establishes a settlement on the central coast of Canada's province of British Columbia. **11,500** THE CLOVIS CULTURE, prominent in the Great Plains, spreads across North America.	**ca 11,000** THE LAST WORLDWIDE GLACIATION ENDS, and humans successfully adapt. **ca 4000** THE WOOLLY MAMMOTH goes extinct.	**5700-4300** POTTERY first comes into use in Guyana, South America. **3114** THE FIRST DATE IN THE MAYA CALENDAR, as the later civilization calculates back to the beginning of time.
EUROPE	**500,000** SCIENTISTS think this is the oldest estimate of Neanderthals appearing in Europe. **ca 45,000** MODERN HUMANS—*Homo sapiens*—may have arrived in Europe at this time. They live alongside Neanderthals. **28,000** THE LAST NEANDERTHALS become extinct in Gibraltar. **ca 7000** FARMING TRIBES wander from Anatolia into Greece and farther west into Europe.		**ca 40,000-14,000** HUMANS EXPRESS THEMSELVES WITH CAVE ART in southern Europe. Cave paintings in Lascaux, France, and Altamira, Spain, in particular, have artistic merit. **ca 4500** THE FIRST MEGALITHIC TOMBS are built in western Europe. **ca 4000-1500** MORE THAN 3,000 MENHIRS, or standing stones, are erected in what is modern-day Carnac, France.
MIDDLE EAST & AFRICA	**4,400,000** HOMINIDS begin to appear. **300,000** MODERN HUMANS *(Homo sapiens)* emerge in Africa. **100,000** MODERN HUMANS, subsisting as hunter-gatherers, migrate to the Middle East. **8000** JERICHO in present-day Israel becomes a large city. **7250** CATAL HUYUK, a town in Anatolia (Turkey), reaches a population of 5,000. **ca 3100** MENES unites Upper and Lower Egypt.	**120,000-90,000** HEAVY RAINFALL makes the Sahara in Africa habitable for humans. **12,000** ABUNDANT CROPS of wild cereals grow in the Fertile Crescent, which ranges from Egypt to Iraq. **8000-7700** WHEAT AND BARLEY are cultivated in the Fertile Crescent. Irrigation agriculture begins ca 5000; cattle are domesticated. **ca 6500** UGARIT in modern Syria is settled. **5000** FARMING spreads into the Indo-Iranian borderlands.	**ca 23,000** ROCK PAINTINGS at the Apollo site in Namibia, Africa, can be dated to this period. **ca 4000** SUMERIANS invent a form of writing and numbering called cuneiform, incised in clay, to keep track of trade transactions and taxes. **4000** PEOPLE along the coast of Ghana, West Africa, develop pottery. **3761** THE JEWISH CALENDAR counts the dates from this year on. **ca 3100** HIEROGLYPHIC SCRIPT appears in Egypt.
ASIA & OCEANIA	**100,000-60,000** *HOMO FLORESIENSIS,* a small species of *Homo erectus*, exists in Indonesia. **65,000** MODERN HUMANS reach New Guinea and Australia by boat. **40,000-30,000** ABORIGINAL HUNTER-GATHERERS in Australia develop complex social behaviors, such as cremation and personal ornamentation. **28,000** THE SOLOMON ISLANDS are settled.	**10,000** RISING OCEAN WATERS separate Australia and New Guinea, Korea and Japan. **ca 10,000-8,000** AGRICULTURE develops along the Yellow River and other sites in China. **6500** FARMING BEGINS in the Indus Valley in modern-day Pakistan and western India. **ca 5000** RICE is cultivated as a crop in central and eastern China. **ca 3000** PEOPLE IN NEW GUINEA begin to cultivate yams and taro roots and domesticate pigs and chickens.	▶ **28,000** THE FIRST ROCK ART in Australia is dated to this time. **10,500** JOMON HUNTER-GATHERERS in Japan make the first pottery. "Jomon" means "cord pattern" and describes the ceramic ware.

WHAT LIFE WAS LIKE

In the Stone Age

The Stone Age, the first known period of prehistoric human culture, is so named for the use of stone tools. Striking one stone against another to shape a chopping instrument, early hominids fashioned the oldest known tools more than 3.3 million years ago in Africa. The first stage of tool crafting is characterized by chipping softer stones with harder ones into the desired shape. Their technology advanced over thousands of years and eventually would transition to the Bronze Age of metal tools. The final development of the Stone Age was the Neolithic Period, when hominids learned to raise crops and keep livestock.

SCIENCE & TECHNOLOGY	PEOPLE & SOCIETY
ca 9000 FLINT ARROWHEADS AND SPEAR POINTS, known as Clovis points, are made by the Clovis culture in North America. **8000** THE FOLSOM PEOPLE develop sophisticated tools, enabling them to clean animal hides and make effective weapons. **8000** INDIGENOUS PEOPLE in the Amazon basin domesticate the cocoa tree, rubber tree, brazil nut, and the maripa palm.	
6000 ALONG THE DANUBE in central Europe, people build sturdy huts made of poles thatched with grasses. Plaster floors hold sunken fireplaces.	**ca 5000** SOCIAL HIERARCHIES are evident in varied European burial practices. **ca 4200-500** A PREPONDERANCE OF ROCK ART at the Alta Fjord in modern-day Norway reflects the site's status as an important meeting point north of the Arctic Circle. Among thousands of petroglyphs is a panel depicting skiing.
ca 100,000 MIDDLE STONE AGE flake-tool technology is established in Africa. **35,000** A SIMPLE COUNTING DEVICE is invented in southern Africa. **6000** COPPER SMELTING begins in Catal Huyuk, Anatolia (Turkey). **ca 3500** EGYPTIANS construct the first boats, with oars and a sail, in order to navigate the Nile River. **3800** THE EARLIEST BRONZE WORK is produced in the Middle East, using copper and arsenic.	**ca 3200** THE SUMERIANS, tribes settled between the Tigris and Euphrates Rivers (called Mesopotamia by the Greeks, meaning "land between the rivers"), develop the first civilization. Their fertile valley produces a surplus of food early on, leading to population growth. Cities like Nippur and Ur develop, with leaders organizing large-scale construction projects such as public buildings, temples, and defensive walls. Religion is organized and laws are established, which allow this culture to develop rapidly into a stratified society.
	30,000 HUMANS settle on the archipelago of Japan.

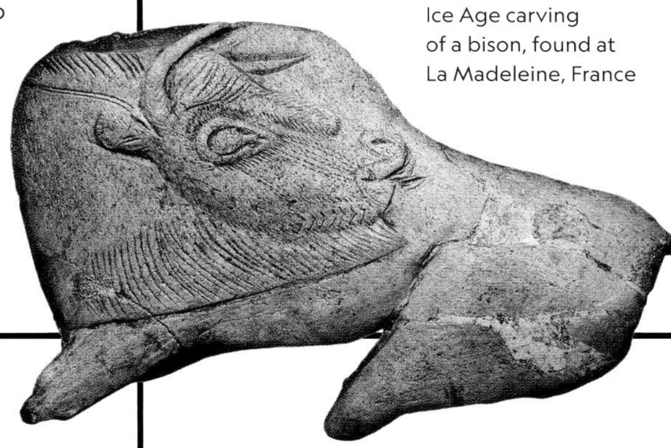

Ice Age carving of a bison, found at La Madeleine, France

Ancient Aboriginal Australian rock painting of Wandjina creator beings

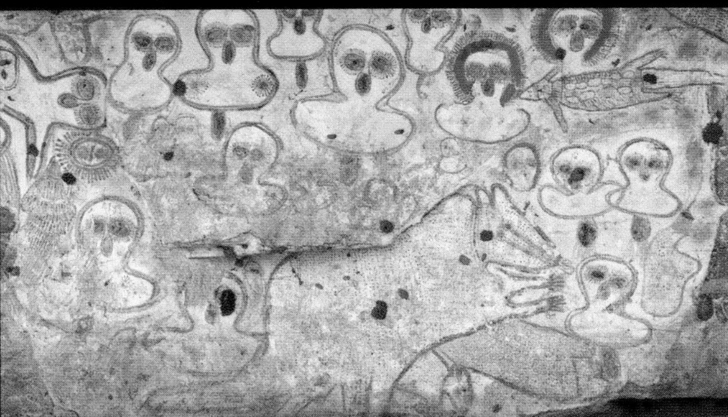

THE ICE AGES

FROM THE FORMATION of the Earth about 4.5 billion years ago to modern times, there have been at least four major Ice Ages, periods when ice sheets covered at least part of the northern and southern hemispheres.

The present Ice Age began 40 million years ago with the growth of an ice sheet in Antarctica and intensified about three million years ago with the spreading of more ice in the Northern Hemisphere. From the south, ice sheets eventually stretched over large parts of South America, covering Patagonia and the Andes; from the north, they reached across Greenland, northern Europe, Canada, and as far south as Pennsylvania, along the Ohio and Missouri Rivers to North Dakota, Montana, Idaho, and Washington. Because the Greenland and Antarctica ice sheets still exist, we are still technically in this Ice Age. During this time, however, the Earth has undergone several cycles of glaciation, where the ice sheets advance, and interglacial periods, where milder climates cause the ice sheets to retreat. These cycles generally occur in 40,000- to 100,000-year periods. The most recent period of glaciation ended about 12,000 years ago, at the end of which the climate was much colder and wetter than at present—as much as 27°F cooler—so that areas that are now desert were lush with vegetation. Large lakes and rivers also formed as ice melted.

This last glaciation made possible the spread of modern humans to all the world's habitats. Because glaciation lowers sea levels, humans were able to move not just from Africa to the Middle East, Asia, and Europe, but also to previously isolated Oceania and North America across temporary land bridges. Once the ice retreated, climate change created favorable conditions for a great variety of foodstuffs, and humans adapted both their diet and lifestyle to this abundance. The beginning of agriculture was soon to come, and with it the development of more permanent human settlements.

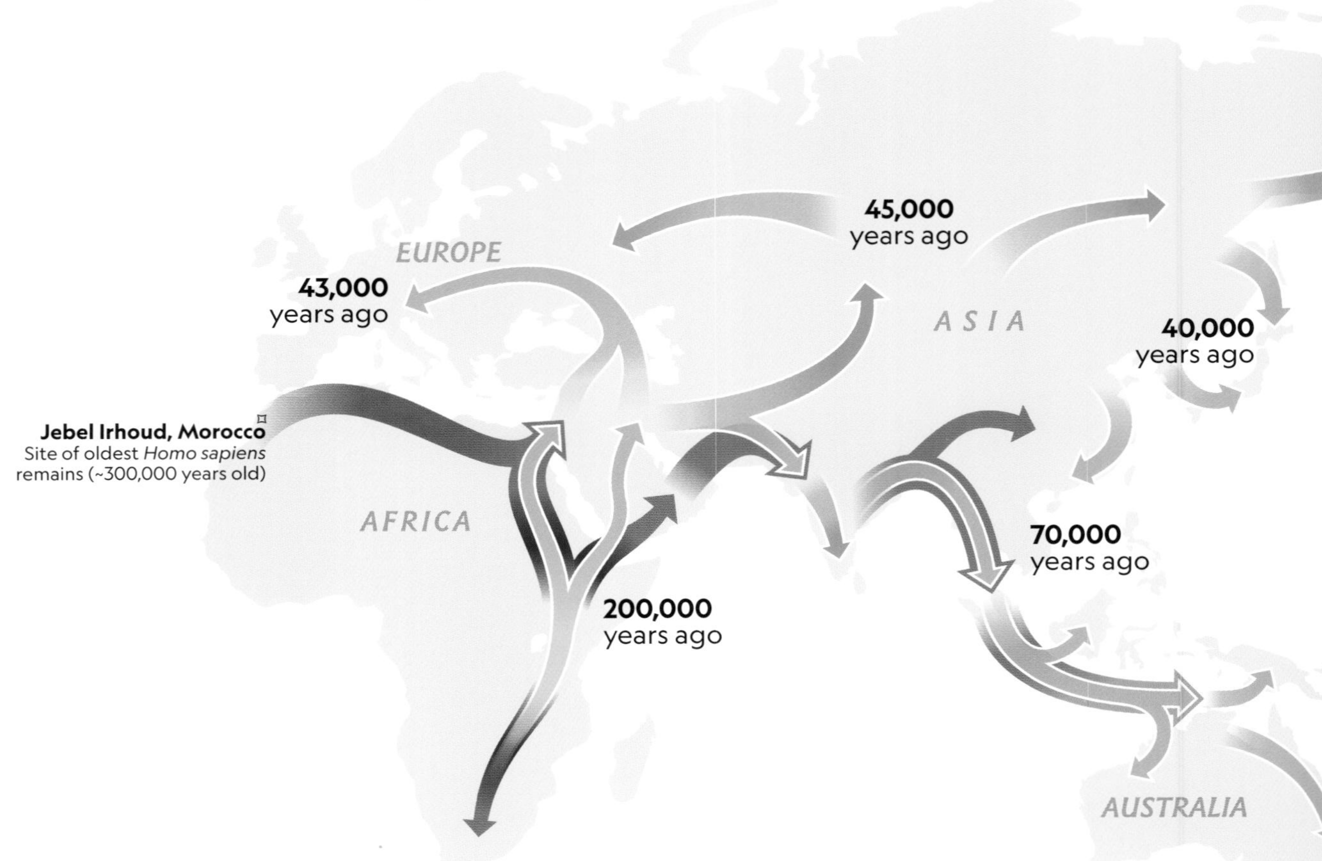

HUMAN MIGRATION

Although the story of human evolution and the peopling of the planet still holds many mysteries, the most widely accepted theory states that modern humans came out of Africa. Piecing together humanity's history from clues found in rocks and bones, paleontologists and archaeologists have come to the general agreement that *Homo erectus,* or upright-walking humans, evolved in Africa from other more primitive ancestors about 1.9 million years ago. From this precursor, modern humans—*Homo sapiens*—evolved about 300,000 years ago and eventually replaced the earlier species.

An increase in population and competition and the ability to shape sophisticated tools, hunt big game, and build permanent shelter may have spurred the first wave of migration of *Homo sapiens* from Africa to the Middle East and onward into Central Asia. This may have occurred 200,000 years ago though most of those migrants would die out. A new push into Southeast Asia occurred about 70,000 years ago, and as Ice Ages cooled the Earth and water

was concentrated in massive glaciers, the Earth's oceans receded and exposed land bridges between continents. Taking advantage of the new routes, humans resumed their migration and established communities along what are now the islands of Indonesia and New Guinea. By 60,000 B.C.E. some groups had also crossed from New Guinea to Australia. *Homo sapiens* began to arrive in Europe about 40,000 years ago, and the temporary land bridge between Siberia and Alaska allowed humans to cross into the Americas around 16,000 B.C.E. By 12,000 B.C.E. humans had reached the southernmost tip of South America.

Adding to these insights is a recent effort by geneticists to trace humanity's ancestry by analyzing changes in DNA. Among them is National Geographic grantee Spencer Wells, who tested blood samples from thousands of indigenous men living in isolated communities around the world and followed the path of the Y-chromosome, which is passed from father to son unchanged. Wells discovered that all non-Africans alive today can be traced back to a single population in Africa. He established a map of the spread of the Y-chromosome and its mutations, mirroring the map of human migration that paleontologists and archaeologists have established.

The Venus of Willendorf, a prehistoric fertility sculpture found in Austria, can be dated to 30,000-25,000 B.C.E.

POLITICS & POWER	GEOGRAPHY & ENVIRONMENT	CULTURE & RELIGION
ca 3000 **ARCHAIC PEOPLE** settle in the Great Lakes region of North America. Others settle near Poverty Point, Louisiana. **ca 3000-2500** **FISHING VILLAGES** become established along the Peruvian coast of South America.	**3000** **FARMERS IN THE ANDES** use irrigation channels to water their crops. **ca 3000-2000** **POTATOES AND QUINOA** become major crops in the Andean highlands of South America.	 Stonehenge, on England's Salisbury Plain
ca 3000 **THE MINOAN CIVILIZATION** on Crete emerges as a leading Bronze Age culture along the Aegean Sea, with rulers organizing the building of palaces and cities.	**ca 3000** **SO-CALLED LAKE DWELLERS** establish settlements along lakes predominantly in Switzerland but also stretching from France to Slovenia.	▲ **ca 3000-2935** **STONEHENGE** is built in Wiltshire, England, a circular earthwork 330 feet in diameter with 56 pits along the edge, known as the Aubrey holes. The site may have been used as an observatory, to follow the positions of the sun and the moon.
ca 3000 **SUMER, THE FIRST CIVILIZATION,** grows in power as Nippur and other city-states begin to form a political federation. **ca 3000** **PHOENICIANS** settle Lebanon and parts of Syria. **ca 2700** **KING ENMEBARAGISI** of Kish in northern Sumer engages in wars against neighbors in the east, the Elamites of present-day Iran. **2650** **PHARAOH SANAKHTE** founds Egypt's third dynasty, beginning the Old Kingdom period.	**ca 3000** **SORGHUM** is cultivated in Ethiopia. **ca 2900** **THE DELUGE OR GREAT FLOOD** described in the Bible and Sumerian epics may have happened at this time. **ca 2500** **AN EGYPTIAN TRADE MISSION** to Punt, recorded in hieroglyphics on the Palermo Stone, exemplifies the robust exchange of goods flowing along the Mediterranean and Red Seas.	**ca 3000** **SUMERIANS** develop a complex society with urban centers built around multilevel temples, known as ziggurats, presided over by priests. **ca 2925-2325** **THE PALERMO STONE** chronicles in hieroglyphics the rulers and major events of Egypt's first five dynasties. **2685** **THE SOPHISTICATED ARTS OF SUMER** include the Standard of Ur, a two-sided mosaic of shell, lapis lazuli, and carnelian, depicting daily life at peace and war.
ca 3000 **AUSTRONESIAN PEOPLE** migrate from Taiwan to the Philippines. **ca 2500** **NEOLITHIC VILLAGES** along the Indus River of modern-day Pakistan and western India develop into large cities.	**2800** **A DROUGHT** hits the Tibetan Plateau.	**3300-2250** **ARTISANS** of China's Liangzhu culture carve smooth jade pieces and place them around bodies in tombs.

SCIENCE & TECHNOLOGY

ca 3000 FARMING GROUPS in the Amazon use fire, manure, and food waste boost the nutritive value of the soil.

ca 3000 COPPER is mined in Cyprus and exported throughout the Mediterranean.

ca 3000 THE EGYPTIANS invent papyrus, a forerunner of paper, made from reeds.

ca 2700 THE SUMERIANS develop a calendar of 354 days.

ca 2650 THE PYRAMID OF DJOSER is built as a royal tomb. This step pyramid is the first of many pyramids built in Egypt, culminating in the massive pyramids at Giza. They are a manifestation of the pharaoh's power as a divine ruler to marshall enormous resources for such building projects.

ca 3000 THE CHINESE develop coal as a fuel.

ca 3000 COTTON FABRIC is first woven by the Harappans of the Indus Valley.

ca 2700 CHINA begins to weave silk.

PEOPLE & SOCIETY

3500-1500 THE VALDIVIA CULTURE flourishes along the coast of Ecuador and establishes trade with Peruvian societies.

3200-2300 THE CORDED WARE CULTURE, named for its simply decorated pottery, occupies northern and central Europe from Ukraine through Scandinavia. It is marked by distinctive burials that place men on their right side and women on their left.

ca 3000 THE CITY OF KISH and other northern Sumerian cities are largely inhabited by Semitic people—Akkadians—whereas the south is populated by Sumerians. Northern Mesopotamia is the land of the Hurrians, and southwest Iran is populated by Elamites.

ca 2650 GILGAMESH rules as the Sumerian king of Uruk.

ca 2550 SNEFERU'S SON KHUFU begins building the Great Pyramid at Giza, which stands 481 feet tall.

ca 3200-2650 PAINTED EARTHENWARE POTTERY is a hallmark of the Majiayao culture that arises along China's Yellow River.

THE BIRTH OF WRITING

THE SUMERIANS' greatest accomplishment was the invention of writing, beginning as early as 3300 B.C.E. Propelled by the need to record business transactions for stored or traded goods or to keep count of numbers of sheep, the Sumerians invented *bullae*—soft clay balls that were hollow inside. Buyers or sellers would press sharp tokens into the clay and place them inside. Deeper indentations meant larger quantities. In case of a dispute, the bulla could be opened and the tokens recounted. This record-keeping rapidly advanced to pictographs—simple representations of the object traded—incised on clay tablets. Merchants used cylindrical clay seals to roll on and impress their signature on a deal.

In time the Sumerians found ways to express more complex ideas by combining symbols, for example, using the pictographs for water and a mouth to express "to drink." Over the centuries the pictographs became ever more abstract and began to express syllables. Working with wedge-shaped reeds, the impressions became known as cuneiform, from the Latin word for "wedge." This form of writing continued to develop and expand and eventually conveyed the first laws and literature.

An account of goats and sheep in Sumerian cuneiform

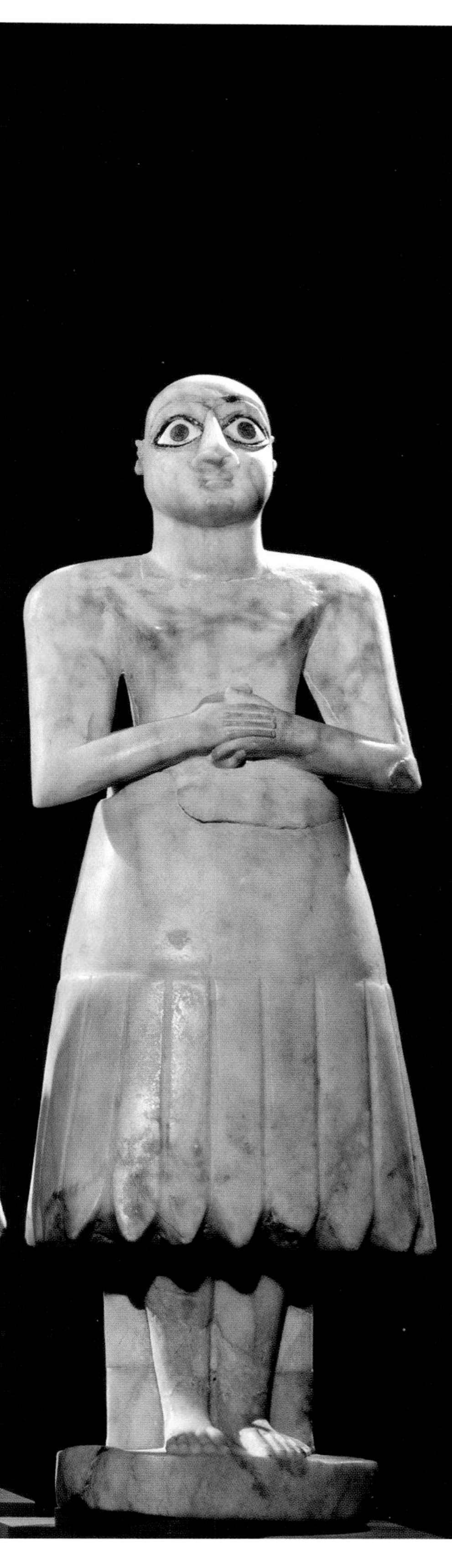

ANCIENT SUMER

The fertile land between the Tigris and Euphrates Rivers, called Sumer in ancient times—or Mesopotamia by the Greeks later on—brought forth abundant crops to support tens of thousands of people. About 5,000 years ago the Sumerians organized life in large cities of mud-brick buildings, surrounded by lush fields and gardens with groves of figs and date palms. Early on they began to settle into an orderly society. As hallmarks of their civilization, they set up a division of labor, marshalled hundreds of laborers for public works, invented a written language, devised a system of laws, educated their young, and prayed to a pantheon of gods. The gods included An of the heavens, Enlil of the air, and Enki of the waters, as well as gods of other natural phenomena, and patron gods for every city.

The Sumerians erected massive temples, topped by a shrine and rising in tiers to 150 feet or more, the most ancient one, shown below, in the city of Ur. These so-called ziggurats were administered by priests, who served the gods and received offerings from the people. Priests also collected food in storerooms surrounding the base of the temple and redistributed the goods, kept tax records, and oversaw the construction of other large-scale works such as irrigation canals. In their appeals to the gods to prevent disasters—flood, fire, or pestilence—people used stand-in figurines in their likeness, shaped of clay or stone, to be placed in the temple to pray for help. The Sumerians also believed in an afterlife, burying their kings with treasures and retainers and everything necessary to carry on the life to which they had grown accustomed.

ABOVE: The massive stepped ziggurat of Ur reaches to the heavens to honor Nanna, the god of the moon.
LEFT: Hands folded in prayer, these statues appeal to the heavens as proxies for ancient Sumerians.

POLITICS & POWER	GEOGRAPHY & ENVIRONMENT	CULTURE & RELIGION
2500 **DORSET PEOPLE** live in the North American Arctic and Greenland, with very little contact or genetic mixing with outside populations.	**ca 2000** **THE PACIFIC COAST** of northern South America boasts 100 permanent settlements with agriculture, crafts, and cultural rituals.	**ca 2500** **PEOPLE IN THE GRAND CANYON CAVES** of North America practice shamanistic magical rituals to boost their success in hunting.
ca 2500 **THE BEAKER CULTURE,** named for its pottery, expands from France to the Low Countries. **ca 2500** **STONE TOOL–USING CULTURES** develop in Scandinavia. **ca 2500** **ALONG THE DANUBE RIVER** and its tributaries in central Europe, people begin to till the soil. When the soil loses its fertility, they move westward.	**ca 2500** **OVERLAND TRADE ROUTES** develop from the Balkans to Spain.	**ca 3000-2200** **ROUND COMMUNAL TOMBS** are built in the Mesara plain of Crete. The snake and the bull are religious symbols. A Nubian archer in Egypt's army
ca 2500 **SEMITIC CANAANITE TRIBES** settle on the coast of Palestine. **2334-2279** **KING SARGON OF AKKAD** conquers Sumer, Syria, and Elam (southwest Iran), and establishes the first empire in history. **2193** **THE AKKADIAN EMPIRE** collapses. **2180** **THE OLD KINGDOM** in Egypt ends in political and social chaos. **2112** **UR-NAMMU** builds the Sumerian Empire in Mesopotamia, centered at Ur. **2008-1957** **MENTUHOTEP II OF EGYPT** reunites the country.	**2180** **DROUGHT** disrupts the seasonal flooding of the Nile, causing famine and anarchy.	**ca 2500** **SUMERIAN ROYAL TOMBS** at Ur hold treasures and human sacrifices. **ca 2500** **EGYPTIANS** begin to mummify their royal dead. **ca 2240** **AKKAD** declares himself a god. **ca 2000** **HEBREW PATRIARCH ABRAHAM** leaves Ur in Sumer with his clan.
ca 2500 **HARAPPAN SOCIETY** in the Indus Valley becomes a full-fledged civilization, complete with civic organization, religion, public works, and a system of writing.	**ca 2500** **THE HARAPPANS** domesticate chickens in the Indus Valley.	**2600-2000** **CRAFTERS** in China's Longshan culture employ a potter's wheel to make a distinctive black pottery.

SCIENCE & TECHNOLOGY

ca 2000 PEOPLE IN THE ARCTIC REGION develop delicate chipped-flint tools, known as the Arctic Small Tool tradition.

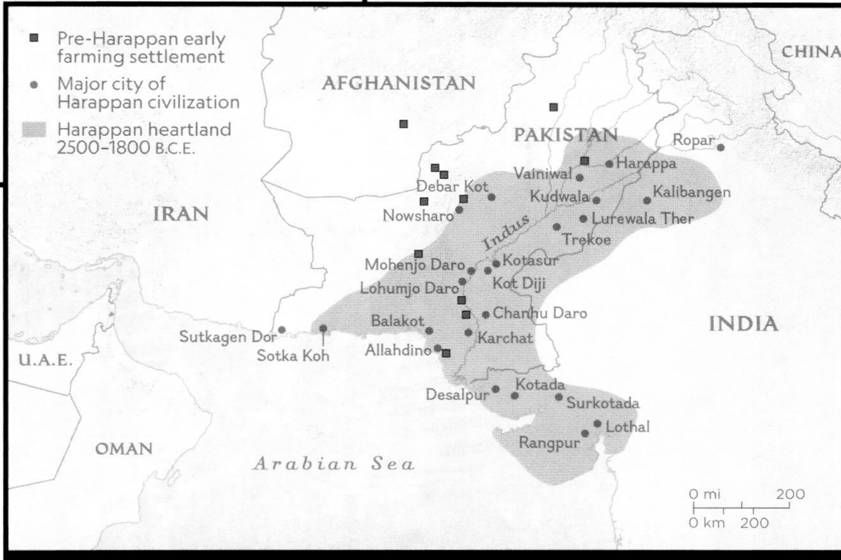

The spread of Harappan civilization in the Indus Valley

ca 2100 SUMERIAN HEALERS prescribe beer and mustard poultices as cures for certain ailments.

◀ **ca 2061-1786** THE MEDJAY PEOPLE OF NUBIA serve as mercenaries in the Egyptian army during the 11th and 12th dynasties of Egypt's Middle Kingdom. They are particularly noted for their archery skills.

ca 2500 ACUPUNCTURE is invented in China.

PEOPLE & SOCIETY

ca 2500 MESOPOTAMIAN SOCIETY is ruled by kings and nobles who win distinction as successful warriors. Priests occupy the next stratum of society, entreating the gods to bring good fortune on their city-state. The priests are supported by offerings from the community; they have authority over large temple complexes and organize community life, agriculture, and the storage and redistribution of foodstuffs. The last rung of society consists largely of commoners, who till the fields, trade goods, and craft items for everyday life. About this time, writing is used for literary as well as economic purposes.

ca 2500 THE HARAPPANS of the Indus Valley build large, well-planned cities indicative of a highly organized government and develop a sophisticated culture, the roots of which can still be seen in Indian and Pakistani society today.

CIVILIZATION IN THE INDUS VALLEY

THE INDUS RIVER VALLEY, located in modern-day Pakistan and western India, attracted herders and farmers as early as 6000 B.C.E. A fertile valley then, its people achieved a surplus in agriculture that gave rise to villages and cities. By 2500 B.C.E. the two largest cities, Mohenjo Daro on the lower end of the valley and Harappa on the upper end, represented the apogee of a highly developed civilization now referred to as Harappan.

The cities were built on a grid of straight, paved streets lined with mud-brick houses, shops, and communal baths that may have served ceremonial purposes. Houses for the elite were larger, often two stories high, built around a courtyard where meals were cooked and served. Each house was equipped with a bathroom, and wastewater flowed into street sewers. The invention of sewers served public hygiene well and allowed for increased population density. The combined population of Harappa and Mohenjo Daro may have reached 80,000 inhabitants. The Harappans created a complex script that has not yet been deciphered and traded widely with Mesopotamia, Iran, and other distant lands. By about 1500 B.C.E. an influx of warriors from the north may have caused the Harappans to abandon the land.

Indus Valley priest or ruler from the ruins of Mohenjo Daro

POLITICS & POWER

1800 ANDEAN PEOPLE of South America build first ceremonial centers of pyramids and temples and shape distinctive pottery.

ca 2000 THE STONE AGE SETTLEMENT of Skara Brae developes on the Orkney Islands.

1800 CRETE'S CENTRAL POSITION in the Mediterranean extends Minoan influence as a trading hub to the south and east.

1600 THE MYCENAEAN CIVILIZATION arises in the south of Greece.

ca 1900 THE AMORITES control all of Mesopotamia.

ca 1915 EGYPT invades Nubia, extending its borders to the second Nile cataract.

1792-1750 HAMMURABI reunites and expands the Babylonian Empire.

1630 EGYPT is defeated and ruled by nomadic Hyksos, marking the end of the Middle Kingdom. Around 1539, Egypt's Theban kings rout the Hyksos and establish the New Kingdom.

ca 2000 THE HARAPPANS of the Indus Valley trade with distant Mesopotamia.

ca 2000 AUSTRONESIANS reach Papua, New Guinea, and slowly move on to other islands.

ca 1920 THE XIA DYNASTY of China is thought to have developed at this time along the Yellow River.

ca 1600 THE SHANG DYNASTY establishes loose control over territory in the lower reaches of the Yellow River Valley and the North China Plain.

GEOGRAPHY & ENVIRONMENT

2000-1000 EASTERN NORTH AMERICANS begin to cultivate summer squash and sunflowers.

1900-1500 POTTERY from the Mokaya cultures of Mexico's Pacific coast reveals traces of cacao, possibly from a chocolate drink.

ca 2000 ARYAN-SPEAKING INDO-EUROPEANS spread into Asia Minor, northern Greece, and Italy.

ca 1900 THE AMBER TRADE ROUTES are established by the Etruscans and Greeks to transport amber and tin from northern Europe.

ca 1700 ARYAN-SPEAKING PEOPLE from northern Turkey and the Ukraine move northwestward to Scandinavia.

1613 A MASSIVE VOLCANIC ERUPTION on the island of Thera (Santorini) disrupts Minoan civilization.

ca 2000 DEFORESTATION of the Indus Valley begins.

ca 1920 LEGENDARY FOUNDER OF THE XIA DYNASTY, YU, is thought to have tamed the flooding of the Yellow River.

CULTURE & RELIGION

ca 1500 COPPER ORNAMENTS from the Old Copper Complex around North America's Great Lakes may indicate the existence of a social hierarchy.

ca 2000 THE LEGEND OF THE MINOTAUR tells of a time when gods begat kings, and a king's daughter begat a Minotaur: half human, half bull. The Minotaur lived in a maze on Crete and required an annual sacrifice of virgins until Theseus of Athens killed him.

ca 1850-1750 THE MINOANS replace an earlier hieroglyphic script with an alphabetic script called Linear A.

ca 2000 THE *EPIC OF GILGAMESH* is composed with king Gilgamesh as its hero. An earlier work of poetry is written by Enheduanna of Akkad.

ca 1792-1750 HAMMURABI compiles a collection of laws, known as the Code of Hammurabi. These laws rely heavily on retaliation, as in "an eye for eye..."

1525-1516 PHARAOH THUTMOSE I begins tomb construction in the limestone cliffs west of Thebes.

ca 1600 THE CHINESE OF THE SHANG DYNASTY develop a writing system, used to record questions asked of the Shang kings' ancestors and the responses given. Known as oracle bone script—because it was used to interpret cracks in burnt bones—these marks are the foundation of the Chinese written script.

ca 1500 INDIA'S ARYANS do not develop an organized political structure, but establish a firm social order. They develop a belief system that is the foundation of Hinduism.

WHAT LIFE WAS LIKE

Hammurabi's Code

Hammurabi's laws empowered men. As heads of households, they represented their families to the outside world. Men could sell their wives and children into slavery to pay for debts. Wives guilty of adultery were condemned to drowning, but men were allowed to engage in sexual relations with concubines, slaves, and prostitutes. A man could divorce his wife but had to return the dowry to her family, who had to take the woman back.

SCIENCE & TECHNOLOGY	PEOPLE & SOCIETY
ca 2000 REED BOATS come into use in Ecuador, Peru, and Chile.	**2000-1500** AS NEOLITHIC PEOPLES SETTLE in villages across the Americas, the skills of weaving, pottery, and stone carving become more widespread.
ca 1800 BRONZE is produced in the British Isles, probably brought in by the Bell Beaker people. **ca 1800** BRONZE CASTING begins in Scandinavia.	**1600** THE MYCENAEANS emerge as the dominant power along the Aegean Sea. Skilled seafarers, they engage in maritime trade with nearby islands and the coast of the eastern Mediterranean and establish trading posts along the way. Their prosperity fuels the building of a tremendous palace and other impressive buildings in their main city of Mycenae.
ca 2000 THE SHADUF, a device for lifting water with a bucket from a pole on a pivot and a counterweight, comes into usage in Mesopotamia. **ca 1650** BABYLONIANS record appearances of Venus. Later, Kassites relay an old text naming constellations and planets. **ca 1600** EGYPTIANS write a medical book showing accurate workings of the heart, stomach, bowels, and blood vessels.	**2100-1570** RULERS AT KERMA IN THE SUDAN become overlords of the lucrative Nile trade. **ca 1900-1700** ASSYRIANS set up a web of trading centers throughout the Near East. While husbands travel and sell merchandise, wives stay home, managing the business of importing, manufacturing, and exporting. **ca 1500** THE MITANNI, a small group speaking an Aryan language, rule northern Mesopotamia, populated mostly by Hurrians. **ca 1500** THE DOMESTICATION OF THE CAMEL in the Middle East transforms the movement of people and goods in the region.
ca 2000-1800 A BRONZE FOUNDRY is established at Erlitou, China, thought to be the early capital of the Xia dynasty.	**ca 1600** THE KINGS OF THE SHANG DYNASTY are supported by aristocrats, who join them in warfare and royal hunts. The masses live in villages outside the royal cities and labor in the fields. The Shang build half-timbered houses over rammed-earth floors, with walls of wattle and daub and thatched roofs. Royal tombs are dug deep into the earth and equipped with splendid pottery and bronze objects, as well as sacrificial royal retainers, who accompany them into the afterlife. Family names carved into bone or brushed onto tortoise shells hint at future ancestor worship.

Minoan fresco

THE LOST WORLD OF THE MINOANS

AN EARLY CIVILIZATION developed on the island of Crete in the eastern Mediterranean. The people were called Minoans, after the legendary King Minos. They fished and sailed and traded widely with Greece, Anatolia, Egypt, and Phoenicia.

About 2000 B.C.E. they built cities and a series of grand palaces on Crete and extended their influence to other islands. The palaces served as administrative centers and storehouses for foodstuffs and trade goods, such as grain, olive oil, wine, and finely crafted pottery. The Minoans also invented a script, called Linear A; although not yet deciphered, it seems to have served for recordkeeping in trade. About 1700 B.C.E. a series of earthquakes disrupted their mode of life, and a cataclysmic volcanic eruption on the nearby island of Thera rained volcanic ash on Crete and destroyed most of Thera.

Eventually the Minoans rebuilt their cities and palaces and added improvements such as indoor plumbing and sewer systems to their houses. But their wealth attracted invaders—most likely the warlike Mycenaeans—and by 1100 B.C.E. the island and their culture lay in ruins. Still, their legacy continued throughout the Mediterranean and among the inhabitants of Greece.

THE JOURNEY TO THE HEREAFTER

The ancient Egyptians believed in resurrection after death, as long as the body was prepared properly. When a person of importance died, the embalmers went to work swiftly on the corpse, discarding the brain as useless and removing the internal organs to be placed in canopic jars. The organs would be reunited with the body upon resurrection. Once the organs were kept safe, the embalmers dried out the body with natron salt and stuffed it with straw or cotton, then coated it with fragrant balm and resin and wrapped it in hundreds of yards of linen strips. When all was wrapped and secured, a process accompanied by chanting of spells and charms, the mummy was placed in a coffin and buried in a well-equipped tomb, provided with all things necessary to start the journey through the underworld.

Beginning with the New Kingdom era, around 1550 B.C.E., royal tombs were cut into the rock of the Valley of the Kings. Consisting of long corridors and multiple chambers, the tombs held veritable treasuries of gifts. The rooms were painted extravagantly with prayers and spells for protection, repeating the person's name many times over in colorful cartouches and portraying the deceased as being received by all the important gods and goddesses. The example at left shows New Kingdom pharaoh Horemheb in his tomb, bearing offerings to Osiris, ruler of the underworld. Osiris is depicted with his royal crook and flail, wrapped tightly in linen, his face and hands the color of death.

The underworld was thought to begin in the west where the sun set each evening, and tombs were usually placed on the west bank of the Nile. According to the *Book of the Dead*—sacred texts compiled significantly during the New Kingdom—the body would travel by boat through the underworld to pass many tests of character. The heart of the deceased would be weighed against the feather of truth, and Osiris would judge whether the person was worthy of eternal life. If judged true, the deceased would be reborn, to rise gloriously the next morning with the sun god Re.

ABOVE: In a tomb painting, New Kingdom Pharaoh Horemheb is received by Osiris to the underworld.
OPPOSITE: The mummy of Pharaoh Seti I was well preserved in its tomb in the Valley of the Kings.

POLITICS & POWER

ca 1500s **AGRICULTURAL VILLAGES** begin to appear in Mesoamerica—the region between central Mexico, Honduras, and El Salvador.

1450 **THE MYCENAEANS** expand their influence beyond mainland Greece, establishing settlements in Anatolia, Sicily, and southern Italy. They also take control of Crete, ending Minoan civilization.

ca 1500 **KASSITES** assert a low-key rule over Babylon, adopting local customs.

ca 1479-1426 **THUTMOSE III OF EGYPT** leads successful campaigns into Syria and Palestine—most notably, Meggido—and presses deeper into Nubia, to the Nile's fourth cataract.

1473-1458 **QUEEN HATSHEPSUT** rules Egypt in her own right. She sends expeditions into Nubia and Somalia.

ca 1500 **THE JOMON PERIOD** in Japan reaches its peak.

ca 1500 **THE SHANG CULTURE** flourishes at Zhengzhou, in China's modern-day Henan Province. The walled city is flanked by large public buildings and a complex of small villages.

GEOGRAPHY & ENVIRONMENT

ca 1400–1250 **MOKAYA VILLAGERS** on Mexico's Pacific coast fish, hunt, and cultivate crops including beans and maize.

ca 1500 **SORGHUM** is cultivated in India.

ca 1500 **AUSTRONESIAN MARINERS** establish settlements in the Fiji Islands.

ca 1500 **AUSTRONESIAN MARINERS** create the Lapita exchange network in the western Pacific islands.

CULTURE & RELIGION

ca 1500 **PEOPLE** in western Mexico begin to bury their dead in early versions of shaft tombs, in which burial chambers are accessed by vertical shafts.

ca 1500 **THE MYCENAEANS** are using a script called Linear B. Artisans create luxury goods out of glass, precious metals, and gemstones.

ca 1500 **THE CULT OF AMURRA,** god of nomads, flourishes in Babylon. He is depicted wearing a long robe and hat, with a crook in his hand and a gazelle by his side.

ca 1500 **UGARIT'S CUNEIFORM ALPHABET** is reduced from 600 signs to 30, although scribes retain the old version as well.

ca 1500 **JAPAN'S JOMON PEOPLE** create human figurines of clay as fertility symbols.

ca 1500-1000 **THE HINDU CASTE SYSTEM** in India is organized into four main varnas:

Brahmins—priests
Kshatriyas—warriors and aristocrats
Vaishyas—farmers, craftsmen, merchants
Shudras—landless peasants

These were followed later by the untouchables—people who do unpleasant tasks, such as burying the dead.

WHAT LIFE WAS LIKE

Egypt's Female Pharaoh

Queen Hatshepsut, widow of Pharaoh Thutmose II and daughter of Thutmose I, seized the role of regent for her young stepson Thutmose III. She was well suited to the role and took the title of pharaoh. To assure her subjects of her legitimacy, she claimed that the god Amun had fathered her and granted her the right to the title. She engaged in impressive building projects, with a mortuary temple near the Valley of the Kings and a sanctuary at Karnak temple for sacred boats. Instead of engaging in further conquests, she encouraged expeditions to foreign lands that expanded trade and brought new treasures into her realm.

SCIENCE & TECHNOLOGY

PEOPLE & SOCIETY

ca 1500 METALWORKING begins in Peru.

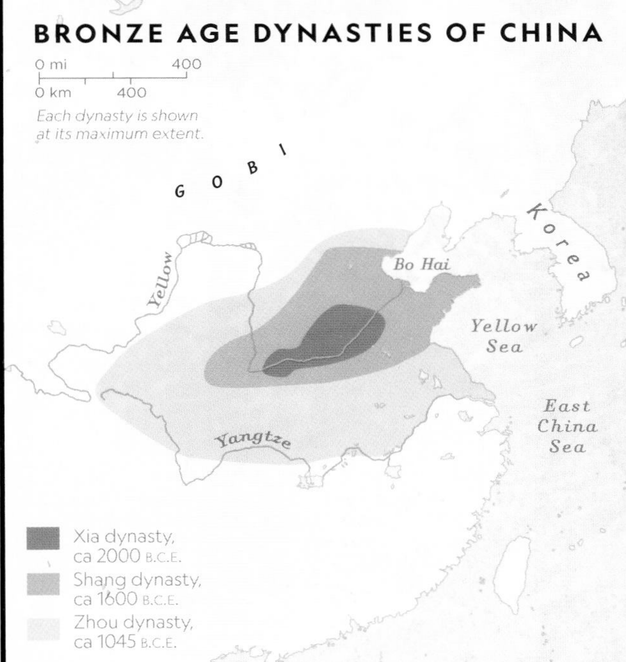

ca 1500 UNETICE CULTURE, near what is now Prague, mines, uses, and trades copper and tin.

ca 1500 EGYPTIANS invent glassmaking.

ca 1500 EGYPTIAN KINGS continue to construct elaborate tombs cut into the mountains west of Thebes—known as the Valley of the Kings—and build grandiose temples in their own name on the east bank of the Nile.

An altar table and intricate wine vessels illustrate the refined decorative artistry of China's Bronze Age.

ca 1500 ARYAN-SPEAKING INDO-EUROPEANS use domesticated horses to migrate out of Central Asia into India. They can transport goods long distances by hitching horses to carts and also use them in warfare.

ca 1400 IN NORTHERN INDIA people begin working in iron, producing implements such as knives and chisels.

CHINA'S ORIGINS UNEARTHED

IN THE PAST 50 YEARS, the rapid pace of archaeological excavations in China has radically revised long-held ideas about the origins of Chinese civilization. Once thought to have begun in the Yellow River Valley, archaeologists have uncovered evidence of Neolithic cultures as early as the sixth millennium B.C.E. in sites from the southern coast to the far northeast. Thus the origins of Chinese civilization are much more varied—regionally, culturally, and ethnically—than previously thought.

According to traditional accounts, sage kings in antiquity like the Yellow Emperor taught the Chinese people the arts of agriculture, writing, and medicine, and early dynasties—Xia, Shang, and Zhou—were founded by virtuous rulers and ended by tyrannical ones. Modern scholarship now views these dynasties as not so much succeeding each other in ever larger geographical zones, but in part co-existing at the same time in different places. Rule in these dynasties evolved from a loose confederation under Shang kings to a decentralized territorial system under the Zhou. At times, archaeology has confirmed the written historical record. For example, the reign of Shang kings in traditional accounts has been verified by inscriptions on oracle bones and bronze vessels. Other bronze work has been discovered as far southwest as Sichuan Province.

POLITICS & POWER

ca 1350 **WHAT MAY BE** Mexico's first public building is constructed in San José Mogote in Oaxaca.

ca 1400 **PEOPLE IN SETTLED COMMUNITIES** all over Europe begin to accumulate material wealth and build fortified villages to defend their possessions.

ca 1400 **THE PHOENICIAN CITIES** Tyre, Sidon, and Byblos thrive as centers of trade, exporting purple cloth and cedars of Lebanon.

ca 1380-1346 **HITTITE KING SUPPILULIUMAS I** ends Mittani power and takes Syria. Ashurballit I regains Assyria's independence.

ca 1335-1325 **TUTANKHAMUN** succeeds to the throne of Egypt as a boy of only nine years old. He dies at 19.

GEOGRAPHY & ENVIRONMENT

1300-600 **REPEATED ERUPTIONS** from Los Humeros volcano in eastern Mexico disrupt local life.

ca 1500-1400 **THE HALLSTATT REGION** of modern-day Austria thrives during the "salt boom" of the Bronze Ages. Road networks, villages, and merchants expand to support the area's flourishing mines.

ca 1400 **FARMERS IN CENTRAL EUROPE** use some metals for making sickles and other tools, and probably rotate their crops.

CULTURE & RELIGION

ca 1400 **AT PASO DE LA AMADA** in Chiapas, Mexico, inhabitants play a ritual ball game on one of the earliest known ball courts.

ca 1400 **CREMATION** rather than inhumation comes into practice, suggesting different ideas about the afterlife.

1353-1335 **PHARAOH AKHENATEN,** for a brief period, establishes a form of monotheism in Egypt.

▶ **ca 1325** **AT THE DEATH OF TUTANKHAMUN,** his royal tomb in the Valley of the Kings is filled with food, drink, and splendid treasure to equip him for a luxurious afterlife: bejeweled ornaments; golden cases; furniture; a royal wardrobe, including armor; and even model boats.

1500-1200 **IN THE LATE BRONZE AGE,** Hindu sages create the Vedas, a collection of hymns, prayers, and liturgy—the earliest Hindu sacred writings.

WHAT LIFE WAS LIKE

The Rebel Akhenaten

Pharaoh Akhenaten inherited the title from his father, Amenhotep III, whose temples and palaces epitomized Egyptian art and luxury. His son, however, eschewed such ostentation and denounced the powerful roles played by the priests. Akhenaten rejected all temple cults in favor of only one god, the sun god Aten. He moved the capital from Thebes to Amarna, where he built a new city with a sun-lit open temple, vastly different from the dark, mysterious older sanctuaries. Art styles changed during this period, too, portraying the king and his family with lifelike expressions. After his death, however, priests reinstated the old order.

SCIENCE & TECHNOLOGY

PEOPLE & SOCIETY

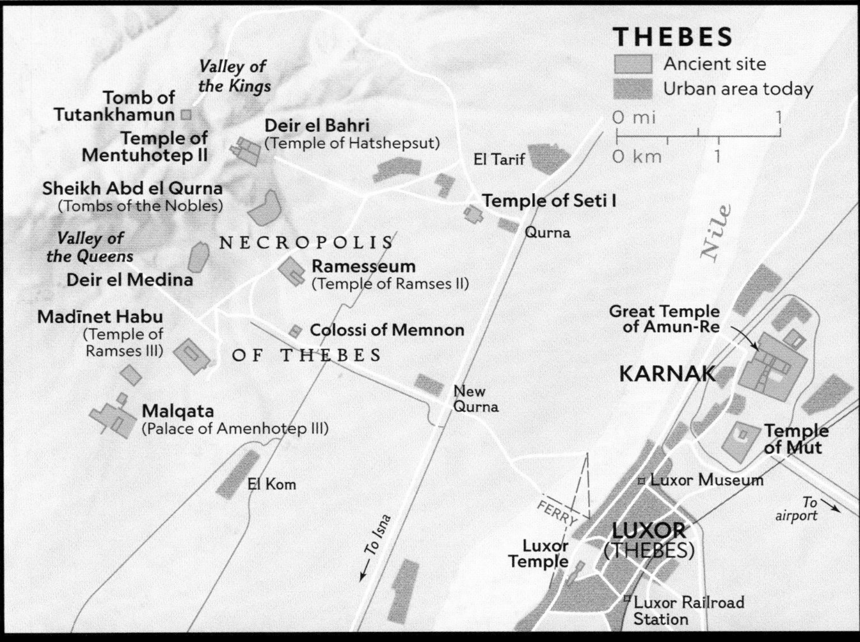

Temple of Thebes in Egypt's New Kingdom

ca 1400 A SHIPWRECK OFF THE COAST OF TURKEY dating to this period, discovered in the 20th century C.E., is loaded with copper, tin, glass, terebinthine resin, ebony logs, ivory, ostrich eggshells, tortoise shells, murex shells, oripiment (yellow dye), figs, pomegranates, grapes, olives, safflower, and coriander.

ca 1400 THE CHINESE PRODUCE STONEWARE POTTERY that is fired at high temperatures—a precursor of porcelain manufacture.

ca 1400 THE SHANG DYNASTY develops a calendar with a 365¼-day year of 12 lunar months that accounts for the seasons and the phases of the moon.

THE TOMB OF TUTANKHAMUN

ALTHOUGH THE BOY KING Tutankhamun had little opportunity to achieve greatness in his short life of 19 years, he is well known to posterity because of his tomb, which was discovered intact in 1922.

As was the custom for pharaohs in Egyptian society, Tutankhamun was buried in the Valley of the Kings. He was embalmed, mummified, and enshrined in a series of coffins, the innermost one of solid gold and an outer sarcophagus of granite. His death mask (below) alone was made of 22½ pounds of gold. Some 50,000 other magnificent grave goods accompanied him to the afterlife, and the contents of the tomb, overflowing with bejeweled treasures, tell much about daily life among the elite in the 14th century B.C.E.

Tutankhamun was probably the son of Kiya, a minor queen, and Pharaoh Akhenaten, who had attempted to supplant the existing priesthood and gods with a single deity, the sun god Aten. After Akhenaten's death, when Tutankhamun was still a child and under the influence of advisers, the priests reinstated the old order along with a pantheon of gods, and moved the capital back to Thebes.

According to artifacts and paintings, Tutankhamun and his young wife, Ankhesenamun, lived a luxurious life and spent their time leisurely. He is shown driving a chariot, swimming and playing other sports, and sometimes hunting and fishing. Although murder was suspected, modern tests showed that he most likely died from a fracture in his left leg that became infected with gangrene.

Death mask of Tutankhamun

1300-1200 B.C.E.

THE AMERICAS

GEOGRAPHY & ENVIRONMENT

ca 1300 **PEOPLE AT POVERTY POINT,** Louisiana, import copper and flint from trading partners in Appalachia and the Upper Mississippi Valley.

CULTURE & RELIGION

ca 1300 **OLMEC** practice ritual bloodletting and ball games, rites that will become characteristics of Mesoamerican civilization.

Minoan civilization on Crete was eventually subsumed by the Mycenaeans, who came to control much of the Mediterranean.

EUROPE

POLITICS & POWER

▶ **1300** **THE MYCENAEANS** of mainland Greece command Crete and numerous colonies along the eastern coast of the Mediterranean established through trade.

MIDDLE EAST & AFRICA

POLITICS & POWER

ca 1285 **ASSYRIA'S KING ADAD-NIARI I** conquers the Mitanni and expands the Assyrian Empire across northern Mesopotamia.

ca 1275 **EGYPT'S RAMSES II** clashes with Hittite King Muwatallis in the Battle of Kadesh, considered one of the greatest military encounters of the ancient world. The outcome is considered indecisive, but Ramses II memorializes it as a tremendous victory.

GEOGRAPHY & ENVIRONMENT

ca 1280 **AN EARTHQUAKE** rocks Phoenician Nineveh and damages the temple of Ishtar.

ca 1279-1212 **RAMSES II** moves his capital to Per Ramessu, in the northeastern delta of the Nile River.

CULTURE & RELIGION

ca 1300 **MOSES** leads the Hebrews in exodus from Egypt to Palestine, according to religious texts. He receives the Ten Commandments at Mount Sinai, in today's Egypt.

ca 1300 **ASSYRIAN KINGS** are responsible to the national god, Ashur, for providing peace, prosperity, and justice to his people.

ca 1300-1100 **THE STORY OF THE TROJAN WAR**—the battle of the Mycenaeans against Troy—is preserved by oral tradition until retold centuries later in Homer's epic the *Iliad*.

ASIA & OCEANIA

POLITICS & POWER

1300 **THE SHANG RULERS** of China move their capital to Anyang.

GEOGRAPHY & ENVIRONMENT

ca 1200 **KOREAN FARMERS** grow rice in dry fields and paddy fields.

CULTURE & RELIGION

1600-1100 **COWRY SHELLS** are used extensively as currency during the middle Shang period.

1500-1200 **SACRED SANSKRIT TEXTS,** the Vedas, are first composed and give their name to India's Vedic period.

SCIENCE & TECHNOLOGY	PEOPLE & SOCIETY
ca 1300 PEOPLE AT POVERTY POINT in modern-day northeastern Louisiana construct a complex of earthworks around a plaza where traders and artisans work and ceremonies are held. The community of about 4,000 to 5,000 people is surrounded by smaller settlements.	**ca 1300** THE POVERTY POINT SOCIETY demonstrates that settlements and the capacity to organize labor are not tied to agriculture. People in this community construct monumental projects, yet they are hunter-gatherers and rely on fishing and trade.
ca 1300 PEOPLE OF THE URNFIELD CULTURE in central Europe use bronze to make weapons and jewelry.	**ca 1300** URNFIELD PEOPLE CREMATE THE DEAD and bury their ashes in urns in cemeteries.
ca 1300-1100 AFTER THE FALL OF TROY, Greek dramatist Aeschylus will report that Queen Clytemnestra of Greece was informed of the victory and the impending return of her husband, King Agamemnon, by a system of signal fires, a forerunner of the telegraph system. **ca 1223** A TOTAL SOLAR ECLIPSE over Ugarit, in modern-day northern Syria, is chronicled in the first reliable account of an eclipse.	**1298-1232** LONG-LIVED PHARAOH RAMSES II of Egypt builds more monuments to himself than any other pharaoh: extensions at the temples of Karnak and Luxor; the Ramesseum on the west side of the Nile; and six temples in Nubia, the most splendid of which is at Abu Simbel. This warrior king fights many battles, but also negotiates for peace. Following the battle with the Hittites, he takes a Hittite princess as one of his many wives. After a reign of 67 years, Ramses dies and leaves 50 sons. The 13th one, Merenptah, becomes his successor.
ca 1200 HORSE-DRAWN CHARIOTS with spoked wheels are in use in Shang China and sometimes included in burials.	**ca 1250** FU HAO, consort of the Shang emperor Wu Ding and a noted general, dies and is buried in a tomb in Anyang along with 271 weapons and precious objects.

Jadeite Olmec statue discovered in Veracruz

THE OLMEC OF MESOAMERICA

AS EARLY AS 2250 B.C.E., people of the lowlands along the Gulf of Mexico planted corn and other crops and exploited the sea for fish and shellfish. They organized into chiefdoms and lived in agricultural communities. By 1200 B.C.E. the Olmec—meaning rubber people, for the rubber trees growing in the region—had organized into Mesoamerica's first civilization.

An authoritarian society with a complex division of labor, the Olmec conscripted thousands of laborers to build elaborate ceremonial centers on earthen mounds with temples, walled plazas, and ball courts. Other workers mined and transported huge boulders of basalt from the mountains to be sculpted into colossal heads, which may have represented leaders or deities. These centers were reserved for the elite and priestly class; ordinary citizens attended only on special occasions. The first center was built at San Lorenzo, followed by a second one at La Venta in 800 B.C.E., and a third at Tres Zapotes in 400 B.C.E. Olmec influence reached far beyond Mexico, and much of their culture, including an early script and calendar, was adopted by later civilizations.

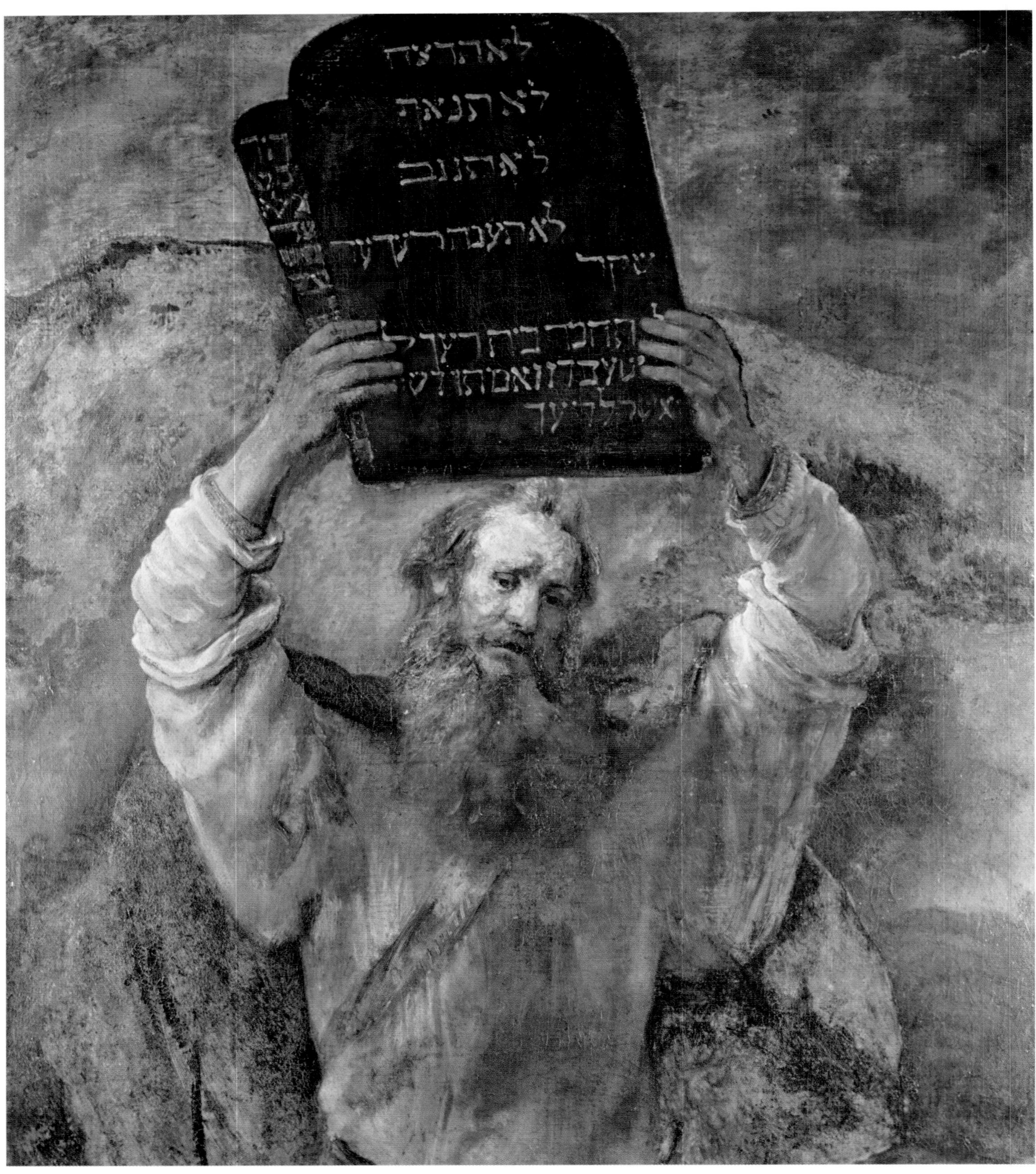

THE BIRTH OF MONOTHEISM

According to the Torah—the Jewish Holy Scriptures, which are also the first five books of the Christian Bible—life on Earth began in the Garden of Eden, a spot from which four rivers sprang. Two of them, the Tigris and the Euphrates, still flow today in Iraq, called Ur at the time. According to religious scriptures, God commanded Abraham in about 2100 B.C.E. to "get thee out of thy country . . . unto the land that I will show thee . . . and I will make of thee a great nation."

As per the Torah, God led Abraham and his clan of nomadic herders to Canaan, the land between Egypt and Lebanon. From that time on, Abraham was connected to God in a personal relationship, following His commands and having his faith tested. He and his people had journeyed from a region where multiple gods were feared and had to be appeased, and yet he began to believe in a single, supreme God, transcendent in power.

Abraham's grandson Jacob had 12 sons, from whom the 12 tribes of Israel are said to be descended. To escape a famine, Jacob and his family migrated to Egypt, where other Hebrews traveled regularly as traders and itinerant metalsmiths. Jacob died there, but the Israelites (so named because God called Jacob "Israel") were enslaved by the pharaoh, possibly Ramses II. Around 1300 B.C.E., Moses delivered them from bondage and led them safely out of Egypt.

At Mount Sinai, Moses received the words of the covenant, the Ten Commandments, written in stone. Stating above all, "You shall have no other gods before me," the Ten Commandments laid the foundation of moral law for Judaism, which eventually became the moral code for Christianity and Islam as well. According to the commandments, idolatry was forbidden; parents were to be honored; murder, adultery, theft, and lying should be punished; and the seventh day of the week should be reserved for rest—a time for prayer and reflection. Virtuous living would be rewarded and wickedness punished.

Upon reaching Canaan, the Hebrews established the kingdom of Israel. Their belief in a single God set them apart from their neighbors and placed on them a heavy burden, but their religion has survived endless trials to this day.

OPPOSITE: In Rembrandt's 17th-century painting, Moses holds aloft the Ten Commandments.

RIGHT: The Torah holds the laws and history of ancient Israel, handwritten on a scroll of parchment.

1200-1100 B.C.E.

	POLITICS & POWER	GEOGRAPHY & ENVIRONMENT	CULTURE & RELIGION
THE AMERICAS	**ca 1200** THE SIOUX PEOPLE live a subsistence existence on the Canadian plains. **1200** OLMEC SOCIETY is at its peak with a monumental ceremonial complex of huge pyramids, temples, and palaces at San Lorenzo. **1200** THE NOMADIC CHICHIMECA PEOPLE expand in northern Mexico.	**ca 1200** MAIZE is a staple crop in Mesoamerica. **ca 1200-200** FOR A THOUSAND YEARS people along the California coast sustain their communities through marine life. While men fish, women grind acorn flour.	**ca 1200** THE OLMEC SCULPT COLOSSAL STONE HEADS, representing aspects of an awesome religion. Their pantheon includes jaguar deities and fertility goddesses. They are also noted for their elaborate serpentine mosaics, some as large as 15 by 20 feet.
EUROPE	**ca 1200** PROTO-CELTIC PEOPLE of Indo-European origin settle in central Europe. **1150** THE MYCENAEAN CIVILIZATION declines on mainland Greece.		**ca 1200** SPIRAL DECORATION STYLES flourish in east-central and central Europe, likely inspired by contact through trade with Mycenaean Greece.
MIDDLE EAST & AFRICA	**ca 1200** ASSYRIA'S KING TUKULTI-NINURTA I defeats Babylon. **ca 1174** THE 12 TRIBES OF ISRAEL, ruled by judges, meet at the sanctuary of Shiloh to agree on a united front. **ca 1119-1098** BABYLONIAN KING NEBUCHADREZZAR I captures the Elam capital of Susa and reclaims the sult statue of the god Marduk. **ca 1115-1077** ASSYRIA'S KING TIGLATH-PILESER extends his influence as far as Lebanon.	**ca 1150** AN EARTHQUAKE hits Nineveh again, damaging the Ishtar temple.	**ca 1200** THE FUNDAMENTAL ARCHITECTURAL STYLE of the four-room house supported by pillars becomes a common dwelling for Iron Age II inhabitants of what is modern-day Israel. **ca 1200** A SAMARIAN HILLTOP SHRINE features a circle of large stones with a standing stone on one side; a bronze figurine of a bull is found on the site. **ca 1100s** THE BABYLONIAN CREATION EPIC, the *Enuma Elish,* is composed. It describes the god Marduk as king of not only all humans, but also of the gods themselve.
ASIA & OCEANIA	**1122-1034** THE SHANG DYNASTY in China shows signs of turmoil.	**ca 1500-1000** A COOLER, WETTER CLIMATE brings Japanese people into coastal settlements, where they develop techniques for deep-sea fishing.	**ca 1100** CHINESE WRITING evolves into the more complex and symbolic form known as *guwen,* inscribed on bronze objects.

CONNECTIONS

The Fall of the Hittites

The Hittite Empire was a blended society of Indo-Europeans of mixed Anatolian, Babylonian, and Hurrian culture living in Anatolia since 650. The empire was known for powerful kings, among them Hattusili I, who abolished most death penalties; Mursili I, who conquered Aleppo and destroyed Hammurabi's Babylon; and Tudhaliya II, who reconquered most of Anatolia and challenged Egypt and the Mitanni in Syria. The Hittites fought Egypt's mighty Ramses II to a draw in the battle of Kadesh, which resulted in a Hittite princess joining Ramses' harem. The Phrygian incursion into Asia Minor circa 1200 caused mass displacement of people into Hittite land, weakening the empire and leading to its downfall.

SCIENCE & TECHNOLOGY

ca 1200 **THE OLMEC** develop a lunar calendar.

1200 **IN AN AREA VIRTUALLY DEVOID OF STONE,** the Olmec move basalt boulders from the northern highlands to their homeland and work the stone without the use of metal tools.

ca 1200 **CRAFTSMEN IN MESOPOTAMIA** perfect iron tools and weapons, although experimentation with iron begins at an earlier date.

PEOPLE & SOCIETY

ca 1200 **OLMEC SOCIETY** is well organized with the elite mobilizing large groups of people for the labor necessary to erect huge structures and monumental sculptures. They develop a far-ranging network of exchange, trading obsidian, jade, and cocoa beans.

Phoenician shipbuilding

PHOENICIAN SEAFARERS

BY THE END of the third millennium, Semiti tribes had settled on the coast of present-day Lebanon and Syria. The Greeks later namec them Phoenicians, from the word "phoinix," o purple, because of their purple cloaks.

The Phoenicians established the cities o Tyre, Sidon, and Byblos at the crossroads o trade and began sailing along the Mediterranean coast. By 1200 B.C.E. they were known a preeminent seafarers, navigating by the star and trading their cedar wood and cloth dyec in a unique purple made from Murex snails They established a trading network tha reached from Spain and North Africa to Turke and Greece and made the first recorded circumnavigation of Africa. To keep track of thei far-flung networks, they devised an alphabetic, rather than a pictorial, system of writing which they passed on to the Greeks and o which the Western alphabet is based.

Never a unified kingdom, Phoenicia consisted of a handful of independent city-states As Assyrian and then Persian power rose i the east, Phoenician cities were invaded. I 332 B.C.E. Alexander the Great destroyed the last one.

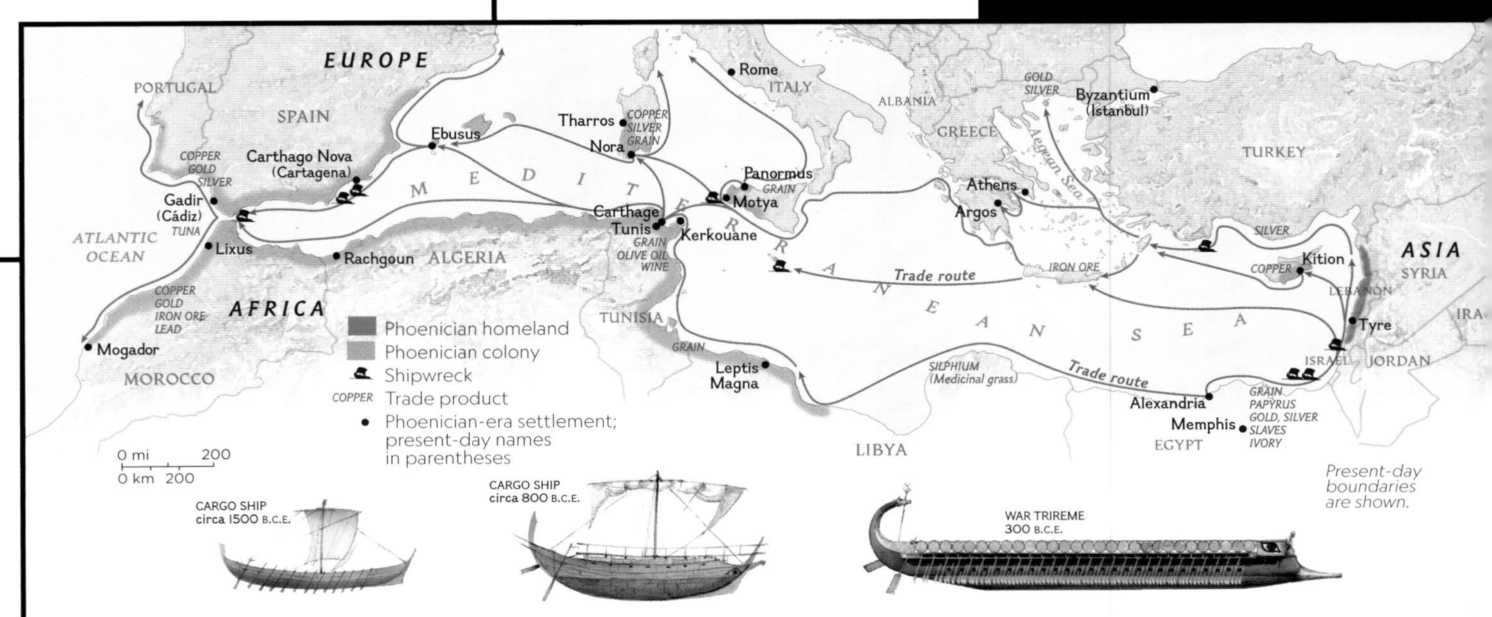

1100-1000 B.C.E.

THE AMERICAS

POLITICS & POWER

GEOGRAPHY & ENVIRONMENT

ca 1000 THE OLMEC manufacture rubber balls from the sap of rubber trees in the tropics to play the famous ball games of Mesoamerica.

CULTURE & RELIGION

ca 1100 ANDEAN SOCIETY in South America is becoming ever more complex. Weavers begin to construct intricately patterned textiles and craftspeople work with gold, silver, and copper to make finely wrought jewelry and sturdy tools.

EUROPE

POLITICS & POWER

1100-1000 DORIAN-SPEAKING GREEKS arrive on the Peloponnese.

CULTURE & RELIGION

ca 1100 AMBER from the Baltic Sea begins to be traded widely in Europe.

MIDDLE EAST & AFRICA

POLITICS & POWER

ca 1100 INCURSIONS BY ARAMAEANS into Assyria and Babylon cause those countries to lapse into a dark age.

1075 CENTRAL RULE is weakened in Egypt and local governments pursue their own interests. A chaotic era begins, spelling the end of the New Kingdom period.

CULTURE & RELIGION

ca 1100 PHOENICIANS standardize the first alphabet of 22 letters, simplifying writing and thus allowing more people to become literate. This alphabet is adapted by the Greeks and is the basis for our modern alphabet.

ca 1100 *THE JOURNEY OF WEN-AMON* tells of an Egyptian official passing through Canaan on his way to buy cedars in Lebanon. He stays for a while with the Sea Peoples, who seem to control the coastal trade.

ASIA & OCEANIA

POLITICS & POWER

1046-1045 THE SHANG DYNASTY is toppled by a challenger from northwestern China, who founds the Zhou dynasty.

GEOGRAPHY & ENVIRONMENT

ca 1100 CHINA cultivates soybeans.

CULTURE & RELIGION

ca 1100 AUSTRONESIAN PEOPLE speak variations of Malayan, Indonesian, Filipino, Polynesian, and other Oceanic languages.

CONNECTIONS

Indo-European Languages

The Indo-Europeans were herders and horse breeders, a hard-charging group of people who exploded out of the Eurasian steppes on horseback and in battle chariots to conquer new lands. Organized into rival tribes, Indo-Europeans spoke a language that gradually branched into many related tongues as groups like the Hittites and the Aryans spread out across a vast area ranging from Asia Minor to India and Europe, losing contact with one another but forming new relationships. Among the linguistic innovations were Sanskrit, the classical language of India, as well as Persian, Greek, Latin, the Germanic and Slavic languages, and the so-called Romance languages, including French, Spanish, and Italian. Today the Indo-European language family is the largest in the world, with more speakers than any other.

SCIENCE & TECHNOLOGY

PEOPLE & SOCIETY

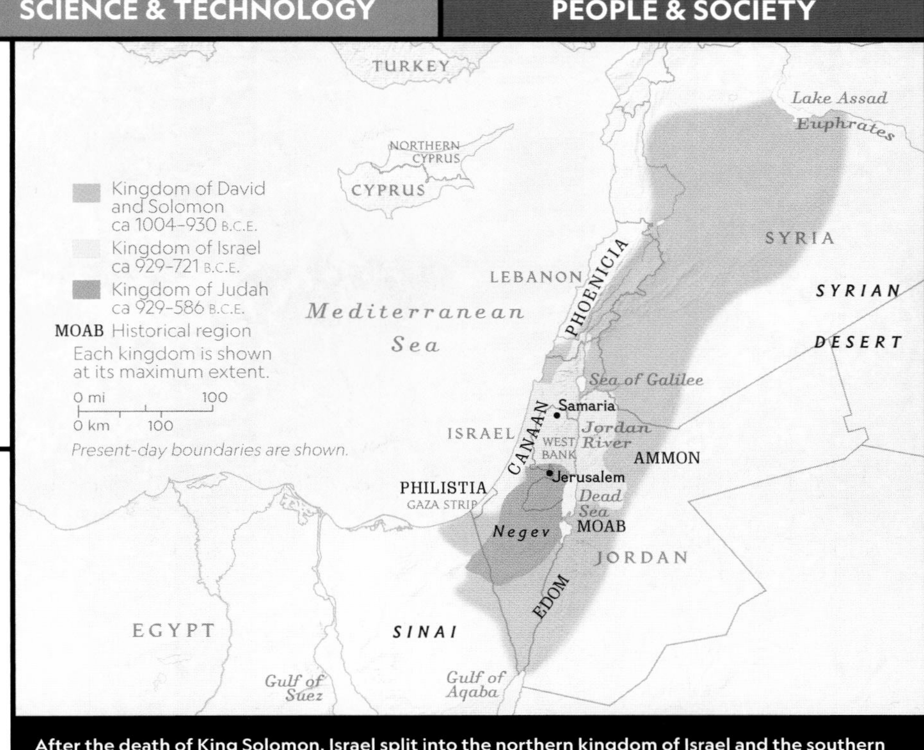

After the death of King Solomon, Israel split into the northern kingdom of Israel and the southern kingdom of Judah.

ca 1100 ESAGIL-KIN-APLI OF BORSIPPA in Mesopotamia puts together a medical diagnostic textbook.

ca 1100 THE LIBRARY of Assyrian king Tiglath-pileser includes manuals for horse training.

ca 1040 DAVID, who defeated the Philistines and the legendary Goliath in battle, unites the kingdom of Israel, according to religious texts.

1045 HORSE-DRAWN CHARIOTS with bronze ornaments were likely used by both armies during the bloody Battle of Muye when the insurgent Zhous defeated the Shang dynasty.

ca 1045 THE ZHOU PEOPLE, ethnically distinct from the rulers of the Shang dynasty, move into Shang territory from the northeast and establish their capital in the Wei River Valley near the modern city of Xi'an.

THE KINGDOM OF ISRAEL

ACCORDING TO TRADITION, the Hebrews left Egypt around 1300 B.C.E. to settle in the uplands of Canaan. The Hebrews originally organized into 12 tribes but, in circa 1174 B.C.E., fear of the warlike Philistines led them to unite into the kingdom of Israel with Saul as their first king. Around 1004 B.C.E. David followed Saul and made Jerusalem the capital of his kingdom. The golden age of a unified Israel lasted 80 years, from David's rise to the death of his son Solomon in 930 B.C.E.—that is, according to the biblical chronology. Archaeologists have found structures from the era, but neither carbon dating nor pottery evidence confirms exact dates, leaving the grandness of David and Solomon's empire open to interpretation.

After Solomon's death, his realm split along tribal fault lines into two kingdoms: northern Israel and southern Judah. Scholars believe that Solomon's policies of coercive tribute and forced labor led to the rift. The rivalry between the northern kingdom and Judah was soon overshadowed by the threat of the Assyrian Empire. Northern Israel became a vassal state of Assyria and was gradually steamrolled by the greater power. The last autonomous city, Samaria, was destroyed circa 721 B.C.E., exiling some 27,000 Israelites by Assyrian records. These survivors, now known as the 10 lost tribes of Israel, were scattered in small populations all over the Middle East.

Though much smaller than the Northern Kingdom and bereft of the ample resources of Israel's valleys, the Southern Kingdom was nevertheless able to survive for two centuries after the fall of the north. One reason may be that, initially, Judah was simply too small and insignificant to play a major role in international affairs. The powerful king Nebuchadrezzar (604-562 B.C.E.), however, destroyed Jerusalem and its Holy Temple during his conquests of the Middle East. The Israelite Kingdom was no more.

POLITICS & POWER	GEOGRAPHY & ENVIRONMENT	CULTURE & RELIGION
ca 1000 **IN THE OHIO RIVER VALLEY,** the Adena people, predominantly hunter-gatherers, live in settled villages and supplement their food stocks by growing squashes, gourds, and sunflowers.	**ca 1000** **INUITS AND ALEUTS,** who have migrated across the sea by boat to the Arctic during the last 2,000 years, have successfully adapted to their polar environment. **ca 900** **THE CHAVÍN CULTURE** establishes itself at Chavín de Huántar, located more than 10,000 feet in the Andes.	**ca 1000** **THE ADENA PEOPLE** of North America carve stone tablets with bold reliefs of birds and geometric designs.
ca 1000 **GREEKS** migrate across the Aegean Sea and colonize parts of Asia Minor.	**ca 1000** **OATS** are cultivated in Europe. **ca 900** **A POPULATION SHIFT** from east of the Adriatic Sea westward into northern Italy leads to the development of the Po Valley.	**ca 1000** **THE VILLANOVAN CULTURE,** considered precursors of the Etruscans, cremate their dead and bury them in terra-cotta urns, sometimes shaped like a house.
ca 1000 **PHOENICIAN CITY-STATES** continue to send out merchant fleets to establish trading posts in Cyprus, Sicily, Malta, and Spain. **1000** **INDO-EUROPEAN MEDES AND PERSIANS** migrate from Central Asia to Iran. ▶ **ca 965-922** **SOLOMON** succeeds his father, David, as king of Israel. He builds a temple in Jerusalem, using Phoenician logs and craftsmen. At his death, his sons split the kingdom in two: Jeroboam becomes king of Israel; Rehoboam king of Judah.	 King Solomon of Israel	**1000** **DAVID** becomes king of Israel, according to religious texts, uniting the states of Judah and Israel. He brings the Ark of the Covenant, containing the Ten Commandments, to Jerusalem.
ca 1000 **ZHOU KINGS** rule the "central kingdom" and apportion rule of outlying territories to their kin, granting titles of nobility as they confer the right to rule.	**ca 1000** **VARIATIONS IN CLIMATE AND FOOD SUPPLY** affect the populations of Jomon Japan, scattered from the northernmost islands of Hokkaido to the southernmost island of Kyushu. **ca 1000** **AUSTRONESIANS** settle the islands of Tonga and Samoa.	**ca 1000** **ZHOU DYNASTY ARTISANS** create richly decorated, spiky bronze vessels to be used in ritual banquets.

SCIENCE & TECHNOLOGY	PEOPLE & SOCIETY
ca 1000 THE OLMEC in Mexico make mosaic mirrors from iron ore minerals.	**900s** THE OLMEC in Tenochtitlán, Mexico, write in symbols on the Cascajal Block, an artifact that archaeologists identify as the earliest example of written language in the Americas.
ca 1000 THE USE OF IRON begins in Greece.	
ca 1000 PHOENICIANS dye fabrics purple with an extract from Murex snails.	
ca 1000 IRON METALLURGY becomes known in China, allowing for a more widespread production of tools, especially weapons. Local governments can arm themselves more cheaply and oppose central rule to follow their own pursuits. **ca 1000** ICE is used in China for refrigeration.	

HINDUISM: AT ONE WITH THE UNIVERSE

OF THE WORLD'S GREAT RELIGIONS, Hinduism may be the oldest, its roots going back to the Indus Valley civilization in Pakistan and western India and mixed with beliefs brought into India by Aryan-speaking Indo-Europeans. Their orally transmitted religious hymns, prayers, and rituals were written down in the Vedas between 1500 and 1200 B.C.E.

As traditions developed further, they were again compiled in the Upanishads around 800 B.C.E. These sacred scriptures hold that everything is part of one cosmic spirit—infusing every living being—called Brahman.

Hinduism venerates thousands of different gods, ranging from household and village protectors to the great Vishnu and Shiva, who have many incarnations. Vishnu, the protector of the world, also appears as Krishna. Shiva—often shown with four arms, indicating his power, and encircled by flames—is the god who destroys ignorance.

The many different gods present different pathways by which a person can approach the divine. Depending on what kind of life a person has lived, he or she will be reincarnated into a better or meaner existence. The ultimate right way of living will lead to liberation from the cycle of birth, death, and reincarnation.

The third-largest religion in the world, with almost a billion followers, Hinduism is unique among world religions in having no single founder.

The Hindu god Shiva, shown in his incarnation as Nataraja, Lord of the Cosmic Dance, dances on a prostrate demon, surrounded by flames.

POLITICS & POWER	GEOGRAPHY & ENVIRONMENT	CULTURE & RELIGION
ca 900 THE OLMEC CAPITAL of San Lorenzo in Mexico is destroyed; a ceremonial complex at La Venta becomes the new focal point of Olmec civilization. **ca 900** PEOPLE ON THE PARACAS PENINSULA of Peru develop ceremonial centers.	 Paracas llama wool textile	◀ **ca 900** THE PARACAS PEOPLE mummify their dead, wrapping them in finely woven cotton fabrics. **ca 800** LA VENTA emerges as the most important ceremonial center of the Olmec. Mound C, a 100-foot-tall adobe pyramid, is considered the first pyramid to arise in Mesoamerica.
ca 900 THE EUBOEANS, Greek traders, found colonies on the west coast of southern Italy. **ca 800s-700s** THE VILLANOVAN CULTURE—a precursor of the Etruscans—flourishes in Italy in settlements ranging from modern-day Bologna in the north to Pontecagnano in the south.		**ca 800** THE GREEKS begin using and adapting an alphabet derived from the Phoenician alphabet.
883-859 UNDER KING ASHURNASIRPAL II, Assyria regains its lost land and again becomes a great power in Mesopotamia. **876-869** KING OMRI rules in Samaria, Israel. **ca 859-824** ASSYRIAN KING SHALMANESER III invades Syria. He is stopped by a coalition including Ahab of Israel. **ca 830s** THE URARTIAN KINGDOM rises to prominence in eastern Anatolia, founded by relations of the Hurrians. Citadels are built on mountain crags. The capital is Van.	**814** CARTHAGE is founded by the Phoenicians on the coast of North Africa, according to legend.	
841 NOBLES in the Zhou court depose Zhou Li Wang and rule until the new crown prince takes over.		

Assyrians assault a well-fortified city with a battering ram.

SCIENCE & TECHNOLOGY	PEOPLE & SOCIETY
ca 800 PEOPLE IN LA MULA-SARIGUA, a settlement in central Panama, use specialized tables and grinding stones to process maize.	**ca 1000** THE OLMEC maintain trade relations as far south as El Salvador. They also trade for jade with the modern-day Mexican state of Guerrero and for obsidian from Oaxaca.
ca 800 IRONWORKING spreads through western and central Europe.	**ca 900-750** HOMER writes the *Iliad* and the *Odyssey*, the epic poems recounting parts of the Trojan War and the journey home for Greek hero Odysseus. Though their authorship is often disputed and their precise chronology uncertain, the two epics are thought to be the oldest literary documents in the Greek language and are considered prototypes for much of Western literature.
◀ **ca 883-681** THE ASSYRIANS develop the battering ram, streamlining it over multiple iterations to be more lightweight, maneuverable, mobile, and replicable.	**883-745** ASSYRIANS bring conquered people to the Assyrian heartland and move Assyrians to the newly conquered territory. All are now considered equal Assyrian citizens. The royal road and postal system is extended throughout the empire.
	ca 800s-500s SCATTERED CLANS in India gradually merge into larger states along the Ganges River.

CELTS: EUROPE'S METALSMITHS

THE PEOPLE KNOWN to the Greeks as Keltoi, or Celts, were settled about 800 B.C.E. in the salt mining region of Hallstatt, in today's Austria. They formed agricultural villages and mined and traded salt, a precious commodity at the time, especially prized for preserving meats. Instead of the draped garments known to the Mediterraneans, Celtic men wore trousers, which the toga wearers viewed as ridiculous.

Of Indo-European origin, the Celts' loose and shifting tribes, united only by language and religious beliefs, spread across central Europe. They brought with them a highly developed skill in bronze work for weapons and functional items. They had horses and four-wheeled wooden wagons, which later evolved into lighter, faster two-wheeled carts. They fortified their villages with huge earthen ramparts but never formed a unified nation. Burial mounds of chieftains held treasures of gold, amber, and other precious goods, indicating trade links to the Baltic and Mediterranean Seas.

With the advent of iron smelting in about 750 B.C.E., the Celts became experts in the technology. Their highly skilled metalsmiths produced hoops for wagon wheels, agricultural tools, functional household items, and brooches and other jewelry, plus swords, lance heads, and shield bosses. Thus well-armed, the Celts swiftly dominated much of Europe. From Austria, they spread into Switzerland—La Tene—Germany, France, and Scandinavia. By 500 B.C.E. they had moved into Spain and Britain, where they thrived for centuries before falling to the Romans.

POLITICS & POWER	GEOGRAPHY & ENVIRONMENT	CULTURE & RELIGION
ca 800 **THE CHAVÍN CULTURE OF PERU** reaches a high point as a religious center and a market center in the long-distance trade network developing in the Andes.	**ca 800** **THE DORSET CULTURE** develops on Greenland and in the eastern Arctic regions of Canada. They depend largely on seals and walrus but supplement their diet by hunting birds and land animals. **ca 800-600** **ARCTIC PEOPLE** begin whaling off the Alaska coast.	**ca 800** **THE PERUVIAN** U-shaped temple at Chavín de Huántar is decorated in elaborate human and animal figures. It faces the rising sun in the east.
800 **THE CELTS,** settled in central Europe, spread westward from the region near Hallstatt, Austria, and move into England. **800** **INDEPENDENT CITY-STATES** develop in Greece; foremost among them are Sparta and Athens. **753** **THE CITY OF ROME** is founded by Romulus and Remus on seven hills in central Italy, according to legend. **ca 700s-600s** **SCYTHIANS,** feared for their military prowess and hosemanship, establish an empire in what is modern-day Crimea.	**ca 800** **THE GREEKS** found colonies around the Mediterranean and Aegean coast. **ca 700s** **ETRUSCANS** develop a reputation for piracy as they force trade links with Egypt, Phoenicia, and the Near East.	**ca 800** **THE CELTS** worship at springs and under oak trees. Druid priests hold rites. **ca 800** **THE SCYTHIANS** of Siberia lead only partially settled lives as herders, but amass vast riches as raiders. They fashion graceful gold objects and jewelry and bury their dead in *kurgans*—large mounds of earth. Kings' burials are accompanied by golden treasures, retainers, and horses to guide them into the next life. **ca 800** **APOLLO** is worshiped at Delphi in Greece. **776** **THE FIRST OLYMPIC GAMES** are recorded at Olympia.
ca 800 **THE ASSYRIAN EMPIRE** encompasses Mesopotamia and conquers Syria and parts of Anatolia. **750** **THE PHOENICIAN COLONY OF CARTHAGE** in North Africa develops into an independent hub of trade for the western Mediterranean. **ca 719-703** **KUSHITE KING SHABAKA** expands upon the conquests of his father and grandfather to conquer Egypt and establish its 25th dynasty.	**ca 800** **NUBIANS** forge iron tools and weapons; the iron industry leads to deforestation. **745** **AGRICULTURAL DEVELOPMENT** is a primary Assyrian aim. New unwalled farming settlements are founded all over the empire. **ca 740** **BABYLONIANS** begin recording celestial phenomena, river levels, commodity prices, and historical events.	**ca 800** **BABYLONIAN** is the lingua franca of the Middle East. It will be supplented by Aramaic in the seventh and sixth centuries B.C.E. ▶**ca 743-512** **PIYE** rules as the first Nubian king of Egypt. The artistic and religious practices of the Nubians and Egyptians, already similar, blend further. A Nubian princess of the 25th dynasty takes on the traditional role as "Wife of Amun," to symbolize the marriage between the ruling family and the deity Amun-Re.
770-476 **WITH THE DECLINE OF THE ZHOU DYNASTY,** China is torn by a power struggle between rival semi-autonomous states in what becomes known as the Spring and Autumn Period.	**771** **NOMADS ATTACK THE ZHOU,** forcing them to move their capital east to Luoyang, and dividing China into Eastern Zhou and Western Zhou kingdoms.	**ca 800** **INDIAN TEACHERS** consolidate Aryan beliefs into scriptures called the Upanishads, which form the basis of Hinduism. **ca 800** **CHINESE POEMS** from this period are later compiled in the *Book of Songs*.

SCIENCE & TECHNOLOGY	PEOPLE & SOCIETY
ca 800 THE SOPHISTICATED ARCHITECTURE at Chavín de Huántar contains more than 1,000 feet of internal draining and ventilation ducts.	**ca 700s** CONSTRUCTION BEGINS on the Zapotec city of Monte Albán, near the modern-day state of Oaxaca in Mexico. The builders create central plazas surrounded by public and religious structures.
800 THE USE OF IRON in England is established. **ca 700s** THE CELTS of the Hallstatt region of modern-day Austria begin commonly using iron to forge such weapons as swords and winged axes.	**ca 800** THE CITY OF SPARTA, situated on the Peloponnese, extends its influence over the entire peninsula. The Spartans develop a highly trained military force—prizing, above all, discipline and an austere lifestyle. Spartan boys enter a rigorous military school at age seven.

Alabaster statue from Karnak depicts the divine Amenirdis I, daughter of Kushite ruler Kashta.

THE NUBIAN KINGDOM OF AFRICA

ANCIENT NUBIA—the area between the first and fifth cataract of the Nile that is today part of Egypt and Sudan—has a history as long as ancient Egypt. Between 3000 B.C.E. and 500 C.E., Nubia was known variously under the names of Yam, Kush, Napata, Meroe, and Ethiopia. Prosperous as a result of agriculture and cattle herding, the Nubians were renowned for their archery skills and often served in the Egyptian armies as mercenaries. In trade they functioned as middlemen, distributing the riches of Africa as far north as Crete, offering much coveted African gold, ebony, ivory, exotic animals, and animal skins.

During Egypt's Middle Kingdom period, various pharaohs pushed into Lower Nubia to the second cataract. Around 1450 B.C.E. Egypt again invaded the kingdom of Kush up to the fourth cataract, and Nubian princes were sent to the court in Egypt, where they adopted Egyptian mores. In the eighth century B.C.E., with Egypt in the throes of anarchy, turnabout was fair play: The Kushite King Piye marched downriver and conquered Egypt. He established a dynasty that would rule Egypt for nearly a hundred years, and the combined kingdom became the largest country in Africa.

In 664 B.C.E. the Assyrians, then the Persians, and finally the Greeks of Alexander the Great and the Romans occupied Egypt. Independent Nubia continued on, building pyramids, smelting iron, and developing an alphabet that has not yet been deciphered.

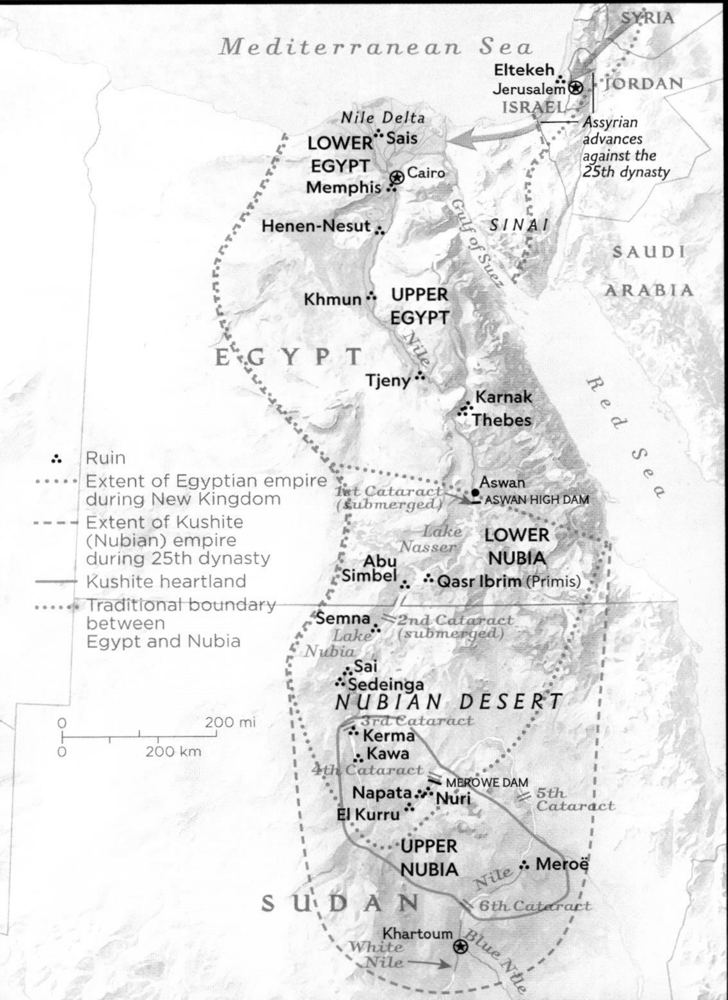

Map showing the comparative extents of the Egyptian and Nubian kingdoms at their respective heights.

POLITICS & POWER	GEOGRAPHY & ENVIRONMENT	CULTURE & RELIGION
ca 700 RELIEFS AT MONTE ALBÁN in what is now Oaxaca state, Mexico, show far-ranging Olmec influence.	**ca 700** DESPITE ONLY A THIN, FERTILE LAYER of earth on top of limestone, the Maya manage to develop settled agriculture in the Yucatán Peninsula.	**ca 650** OLMEC RELIEFS include short hieroglyphs that demonstrate the presence of written language in Mesoamerica.
ca 700 ATHENS AND OTHER GREEK CITY-STATES become centers of learning. Maritime trade brings riches to Athens. **ca 700** ETRUSCANS in northern central Italy become prosperous because of their skill at ironworking and mineral wealth, trading with Egypt, Syria, Asia Minor, and Greece. **616** THE ETRUSCAN TARQUIN becomes king of Rome.	**ca 700** MEDITERRANEAN WINE, and the equipment needed to serve and drink it, is imported into central Europe.	**ca 700s** THE ETRUSCANS excel in fashioning artistic sculpture, particularly their elegant terra-cotta sarcophagi.
ca 700 MOUNTED HORSEMEN—Cimmerians and Scythians—sweep into the Middle East. **672-671** ASSYRIANS drive the Nubians out of Egypt and install Necho I. **646** ASSYRIAN KING ASHURBANIPAL vanquishes the Elamites in southwestern Iran. **625** A NEW BABYLONIAN EMPIRE—the Chaldaean empire—emerges with the ascent, by popular consent, of Nabopolasser to king. **614-609** THE ASSYRIAN EMPIRE is annihilated by the combined forces of King Nabopolasser of Babylon and King Cyaxares of Media.	**ca 704-681** ASSYRIAN KING SENNACHERIB constructs six miles of canals and a massive stone aqueduct to increase the flow of the Khosr River, which he uses to irrigate the multitude of plantations around Nineveh. **ca 700** THE PERSIANS develop an irrigation system of subterranean aqueducts called *qanats*. These channels carry water from the mountains to the desert with a minimum of evaporation.	**ca 650** ACCORDING TO ZOROASTRIANISM, the prophet Zarathustra, born of an aristocratic family, receives a vision and preaches in the region of present-day Iran. He teaches a morality of good versus evil and his apparent belief in monothesim reflects an important pivot from the pervasive polytheistic religions of the time. **ca 600** EGYPTIANS simplify their writing style by using an alphabetic script, called demotic.
685-643 QI HUAN GONG (Duke Huan) of the state of Qi gains power over neighboring territories.	**602** THE MOUTH of the Yellow River changes location to a point on the Yellow Sea.	**ca 600s-200s** CHINESE TEXTS begin to be written with brush and ink on jade, bamboo, wood, and silk.

SCIENCE & TECHNOLOGY

ca 700 THE CHAVÍN OF PERU appear to be the first Americans to develop three-dimensional metal objects through the art of soldering.

ca 700 ROMAN INFANTRY fight with spears, but the cavalry use a long sword likely adopted from the Gallic sword. It will become the standard of the medieval sword.

ca 600 GREEK MILITARY FORCES develop a defensive formation known as the phalanx, a wall of soldiers standing shoulder to shoulder armed with shields and spears.

ca 650-627 ASSYRIAN KING ASHURBANIPAL, the first king to be taught to write, collects copies of all the known scientific, historical, religious, and literary works into a library of more than 20,000 tablets.

ca 700 INDIAN SURGEON SUSHRUTA performs operations on cataracts and creates new noses from skin grafts.

PEOPLE & SOCIETY

ca 600 IN THE ALTIPLANO of modern Bolivia, people live in adobe homes painted yellow and red with thatched roofs and sliding pocket doors.

ca 700 GREEK EPIC POET HESIOD writes about farm life in *Works and Days,* describing the planting of barley, wheat, grapes, and figs and the raising of horses, cattle, goats, sheep, and boars.

ca 600 CELTS begin building *castros,* massive fortified hilltop settlements, in what is modern-day Galicia and Asturias in Spain.

ca 600s THE KINGDOM OF D'MT is established in the northern highlands of the Tigray (modern-day Ethiopia) by a people who speak Ge'ez, a Semitic language. They obtain slaves, ivory, precious metals, and other treasures through trade with South Arabian merchants.

ETRUSCANS: LOVERS OF LIFE

SETTLED IN HILLTOP agricultural villages between the Arno and Tiber Rivers of Italy, the Etruscans rose to swift prominence during the first millennium B.C.E. The mineral wealth of the area—copper, tin, and iron—allowed for lively trade with neighbors and the seafaring Phoenicians. By the eighth century B.C.E. the villages grew into city-states with a stratified society.

The Greeks established colonies near the Etruscan realm and heavily influenced Etruscan arts and culture. Trade brought in luxury goods from Egypt, Syria, Anatolia, and Greece, while Etruscan influence spread north and south. In 616 B.C.E., Lucius Tarquinius Priscus became ruler of Rome. He established a dynasty that transformed Rome into an urban center, constructing monumental buildings, paving the forum, and establishing a sewer system. In 509 B.C.E. the Romans deposed the last Etruscan ruler and formed a republic, and Etruria became part of Rome.

Etruscan sarcophagus

POLITICS & POWER	GEOGRAPHY & ENVIRONMENT	CULTURE & RELIGION

▶ **ca 550** **THE ARCTIC DORSET PEOPLE** begin constructing housing of stone and driftwood and semisubterranean sod shelters around the northern Hudson Bay area, the northern coastal islands of North America, and western Greenland.

The hare, spiritual talisman of the Dorset Inuit

594 **ARISTOCRATIC LEADER SOLON OF ATHENS** introduces reforms that allow all free citizens to participate in government. He is regarded by later generations as "the father of democracy."

509 **THE ROMAN REPUBLIC** is established.

508 **CLEISTHENES OF ATHENS** institutes reforms that shift political organization from the clan to the village by enabling every Athenian citizen to participate in the *demos,* or local village or town council.

ca 510 **THE GREEK HISTORIAN** Hecataeus of Miletus writes the first treatise on geography, which includes a world map.

ca 600 **PEOPLE IN SCANDINAVIA** cast bronze *lurs,* instruments five to eight feet long that are modeled on horns.

581 **PYTHAGORAS,** Greek philosopher and mathematician, begins developing basic principles of mathematics and astronomy.

ca 525 **AESCHYLUS,** considered the first great dramatist of ancient Athens, is born. He writes such plays as *Persians* and *Oresteia* and introduces such innovations as scenery and increasing the cast beyond a solitary actor and chorus.

597 **NEBUCHADREZZAR II** sacks the kingdom of Judah. Many people are carried off to Babylon as captives.

ca 590-529 **CYRUS THE GREAT** rules Elam and Persia and conquers Media, Asia Minor, and Babylon.

546 **WEALTHY CROESUS OF LYDIA** in Anatolia loses his kingdom to the Persian army.

522 **DARIUS I** usurps rule in Persia.

ca 600 **PHOENICIAN SAILORS** in the employ of King Necho II circumnavigate Africa.

ca 546 **CYRUS THE GREAT** captures the Lydian city of Sardis. It becomes the main western terminus of the Persian Royal Road, which originates in the Persian capital of Susa and eventually stretches more than 1,500 miles across Anatolia.

ca 515 **GREEK EXPLORER SCLYAX** of Caryanda is dispatched by Persian king Darius I to explore the course of the Indus River. He becomes the first Westerner to provide an account of India.

587-586 **SOLOMON'S TEMPLE** in Jerusalem is destroyed by Nebuchadrezzar II. In 538, exiled Jews are permitted to return to Jerusalem and begin rebuilding the temple, which is completed in 515.

ca 550 **ZOROASTRIANISM** becomes the official religion of Persia during the Achaemenian dynasty.

ca 550 **THE GAME OF POLO** is developed in the Persian Empire. It is thought to have been part of the training regimen for the imperial cavalry.

ca 600 **IN THE WARS OF EXPANSION** on the Indian subcontinent, several small kingdoms vie for power, but none achieves domination over the others.

520 **PARTS OF NORTHWESTERN INDIA** are conquered by Persia.

ca 543 **THE MAGADHA KINGDOM** in northeastern India begins to rise to power under the leadership of King Bimbisara.

ca 551 **KONG FUZI,** known in the West as Confucius, is born in Qufu, in the modern-day province of Shandong along China's northeastern coast.

SCIENCE & TECHNOLOGY

PEOPLE & SOCIETY

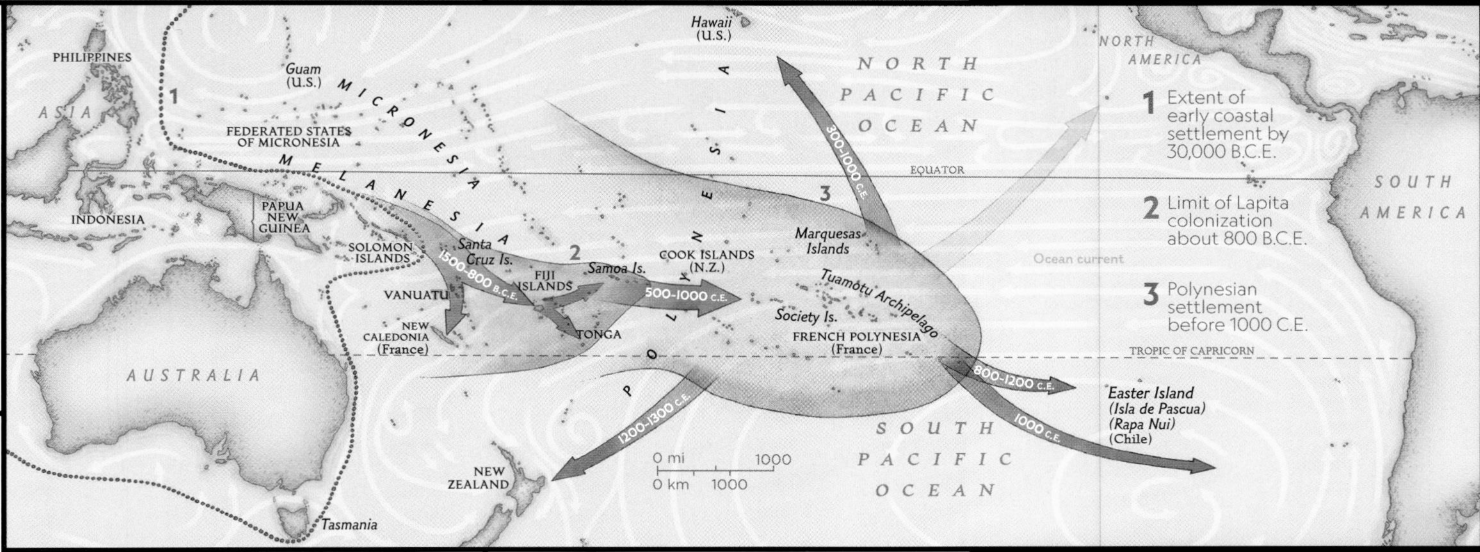

Austronesian mariners established the Lapita exchange network, which spread culture and farming skills throughout the South Pacific.

560 KING CROESUS OF LYDIA in Anatolia mints the first gold and silver coins from gold dust originating from the Patroclus River and ore from mines in Asia Minor.

ca 605-561 NEBUCHADREZZAR II restores Babylon to greatness by rebuilding and embellishing the main temples, creating canals and a great moat, completing fortifications surrounding the city, and paving the Processional Way with limestone. He may have constructed the famous hanging gardens of Babylon, considered one of the wonders of the ancient world.

ca 559-530 ACHAEMENIAN KING CYRUS THE GREAT relies on a vast network of spies throughout the empire to serve as "the eyes and ears of the king."

536 CHIEF MINISTER ZICHAN of China's Zheng state puts forth a code of law inscribed in metal.

EXPLORERS OF OCEANIA

HUMANS MIGRATED to the landmass of Australia and New Guinea and nearby islands around 60,000 B.C.E., arriving from Southeast Asia in simple boats outfitted with sails. Around 8000 B.C.E., rising seas caused by a warming climate separated Australia and New Guinea.

Shortly thereafter, Austronesian seafarers, speaking languages with roots in Malayan, Indonesian, Filipino, Polynesian, and Malagasy, began exploring and trading along the northern coast of New Guinea, introducing the farming of root crops such as yams and taro and the husbanding of pigs and chickens. They sailed the open ocean in outrigger canoes following slight cues such as wind direction, cloud formation, the stars, or the flight of a bird to find the next habitable island. In succeeding waves of discovery, they settled on Fiji in 1500 B.C.E., Vanuatu in 1300 B.C.E., Tonga and Samoa before 1000 B.C.E., the Solomon Islands by 1000 B.C.E., Hawaii about 300 C.E., and finally Easter Island in 500 C.E. and New Zealand by 1300 C.E. Other groups of Austronesians explored Micronesia and Madagascar, introducing crops and farming at each new settlement.

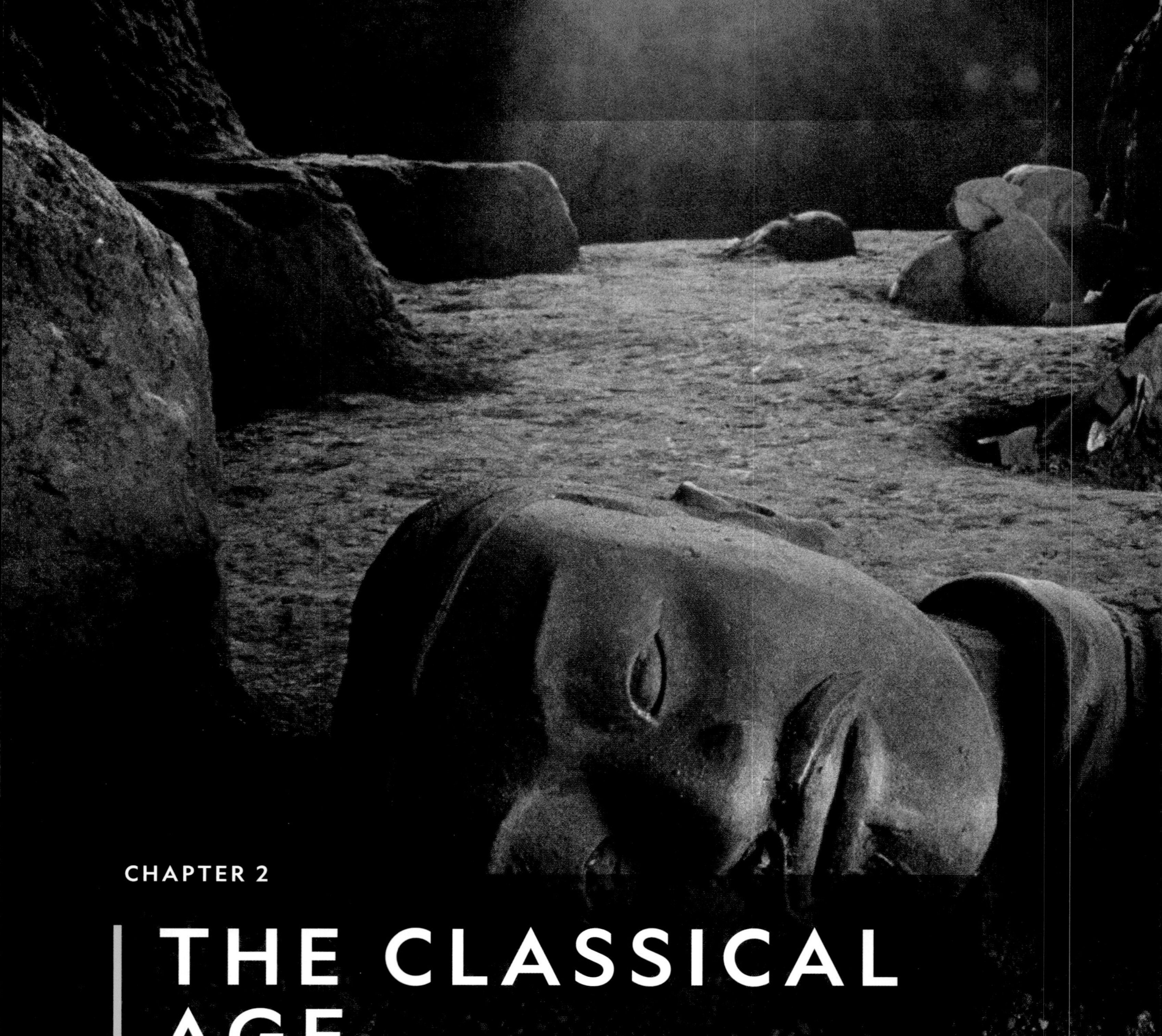

CHAPTER 2

THE CLASSICAL AGE

500 B.C.E.-500 C.E.

The watchful terra-cotta warriors occupying this vault were among thousands fashioned by Chinese artists to guard the monumental tomb of Qin Shihuangdi, an emperor who died in 210 B.C.E.

Beginning around 500 B.C.E., civilizations arose that had such lasting power and influence they were recognized in later times as classical. Much as Greek and Roman civilization influenced later European cultures, classical civilizations in Persia, Africa, India, China, and Mesoamerica had an enduring cultural impact on those areas. Vast empires were forged by brilliant conquerors and held together by shrewd administrators. Travel and commerce increased greatly in scope as roads were built across continents and navigation improved. Merchants, missionaries, and philosophers spread goods and ideas that gave far-flung provinces a common culture. So durable and expansive were these classical societies that they fostered beliefs, customs, and laws that remain in force today.

The Macedonian conqueror Alexander the Great inherited control of Greece from his father, King Philip II, in the fourth century B.C.E. and went on to seize the immense Persian Empire, extending from the eastern Mediterranean to the Indus River.

PERSIAN PRECEDENTS

The dawn of the classical age is often associated with the flowering of Greek civilization. But before Greeks won glory, they had to reckon with the Persians, who ruled the greatest empire the world had yet seen, extending from the Indus River to the Nile and northward to the Black Sea. Much of that was conquered by Cyrus the Great, who took control of what is now Iran around 550 B.C.E. and led his rugged Persian troops against foreigners who could not match their skills on horseback. The Achaemenid Empire won by Cyrus and his son Cambyses was consolidated by Darius I, who divided his realm into

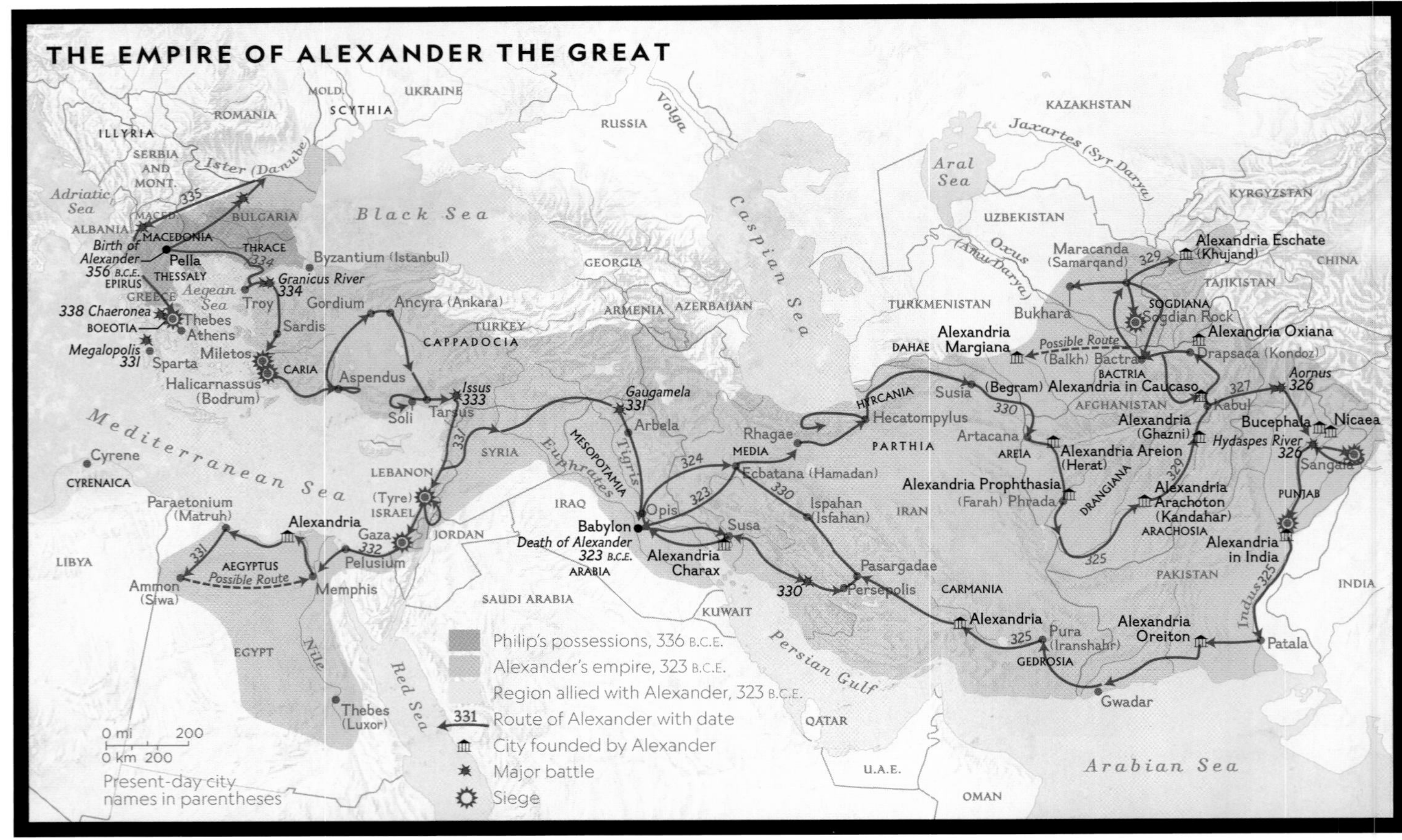

provinces, or satrapies, and appointed men he trusted to govern them. He set tax levies for each province and used the income to build a new capital at Persepolis and a royal road extending to Ephesus on the Aegean Sea, more than 1,500 miles away. That road facilitated trade and tax collection, as did coins Darius issued. Later emperors here and elsewhere would adopt similar measures to govern vast areas.

Around 500 B.C.E., Greeks living on the east coast of the Aegean rebelled against Darius and won support from Greeks elsewhere. Avid seafarers, the Greeks were divided politically into many city-states, including such powerhouses as Athens and Sparta on the Greek mainland and distant colonies around the Aegean, the Mediterranean, and the Black Sea. Greeks sometimes fought each other and vied commercially in marketplaces or athletically at festivals such as the Olympic Games. Thanks to their easily mastered phonetic alphabet, many Greeks were literate and shared the values extolled in epics attributed to Homer. The Homeric hero Odysseus was a cunning warrior guided safely home after the siege of Troy by the goddess Athena, who like other Greek deities shared human attributes and concerns.

Athena was the patron deity of Athens, which led the fight against Darius and repulsed Persian troops at the Battle of Marathon in 490 B.C.E. According to legend, a messenger ran 26 miles from Marathon to Athens to proclaim victory before dropping dead. The actual run was longer—150 miles to Sparta—and occurred before the battle as a plea for help. Darius's son and heir, Xerxes, later renewed the conflict. The Greeks were badly outnumbered, but Persian commanders had trouble supplying and coordinating their diverse forces, which came from many countries. In 480 the Greeks shattered a huge but unwieldy Persian fleet at Salamis and went on to defeat the Persian army at Plataea a year later. This marked the end of Persian expansion and the dawn of a golden age for Greece.

CLASSICAL GREECE

Greek civilization reached its height in Athens after the Persian Wars. "Athens is the school of Greece," boasted the Athenian leader Pericles. Among the geniuses who flourished there were the philosophers Socrates and Plato; the playwrights Sophocles, Aeschylus, and Euripides; the historian Thucydides; the physician Hippocrates; and the sculptor Phidias, whose work adorned the Parthenon, a temple overlooking the city. This burst of creativity coincided with the rise of democracy in Athens. But by allowing male citizens to elect their leaders, Athens set a democratic standard not soon surpassed.

Athenians had joined with Spartans to defeat the Persians, but afterward the two leading city-states in Greece became bitter rivals. In Sparta, all men lived and trained together until they were 30. That made them formidable foes of the Athenians in the Peloponnesian War, an epic conflict that left both the victorious Spartan alliance and their Athenian-led foes weaker. Around 338 B.C.E. Greece fell to King Philip II of Macedon, who swept down from the north with a powerful army. Macedonians had long traded with the Greeks and had adopted their language and culture. Philip's son, Alexander, was schooled in Greek literature and claimed descent from Achilles, hero of Homer's *Iliad.* Having inherited his father's army, he set out to make the Persian Empire his own.

Alexander struck at the right time. Rebellions in Egypt and other provinces had weakened the Persians. They could still muster a huge army, but the Macedonians were better organized and more loyal to their leader, who entered battle with them and was wounded several times. Within a decade, Alexander had conquered the Persians and all they possessed, from Egypt to the Indus River. He died in 323 B.C.E. at 32, a legendary figure of Homeric proportions. Afterward, Alexander's empire was divided among his generals, who founded their own dynasties. Greece and Macedonia were left to Antigonus; Egypt was left to Ptolemy; and the remainder was given to Seleucus, who became the new Persian emperor.

Greek artists celebrated the human form in sculptures like this one portraying a discus thrower, whose skills were tested both in warfare and in athletic contests such as the Olympic Games.

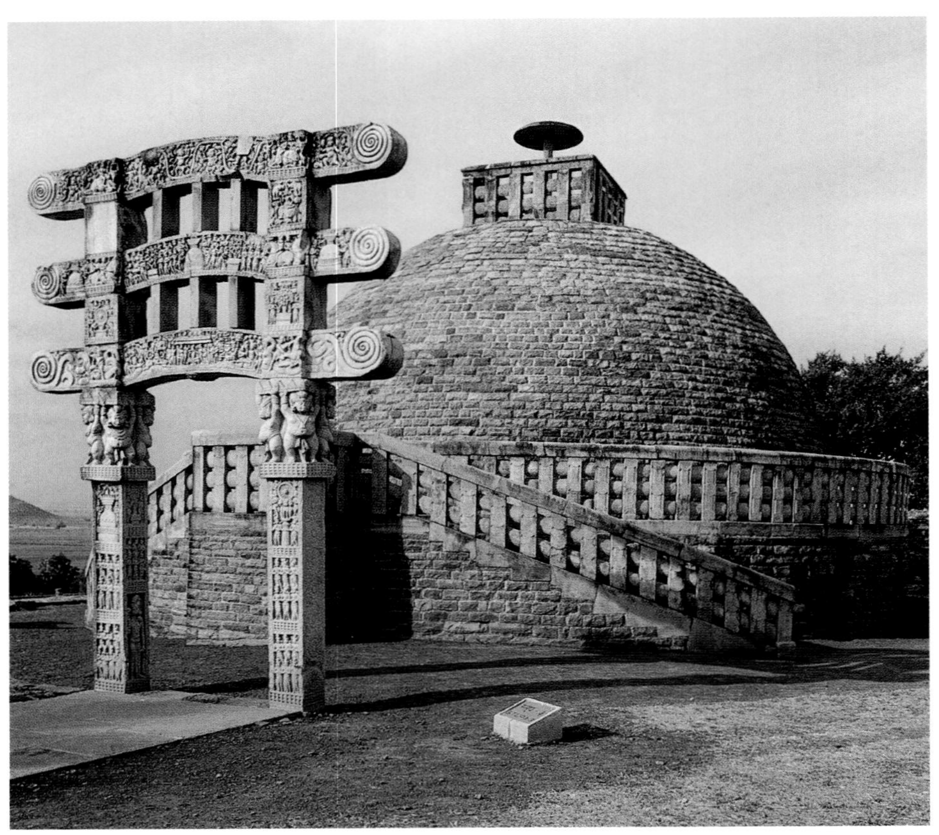

Stone stupa temples in India, such as this structure at Sanchi, date back to a time when Buddhism was developing as the dominant religion. The emperor Ashoka enthusiastically embraced the religion in the third century B.C.E. Meanwhile, the Han rulers in China remained in power with the help of officials guided by the teachings of the philosopher Confucius (opposite).

Greeks spread throughout the lands conquered by Alexander, disseminating their language and culture. Ptolemy built a new capital in Egypt at Alexandria (one of many cities dedicated to Alexander). With its great library and museum, the city attracted scholars from various lands and embodied the cosmopolitan spirit of the larger Greek world.

ASIAN EMPIRES

India was the one land Alexander tried and failed to conquer. After crossing the Indus River, he and his war-weary troops were bogged down by monsoon rains and turned back. But his campaign had a profound impact on India, which was divided into many kingdoms. Before withdrawing, Alexander shattered kingdoms in the Indus Valley, creating a power vacuum that was filled by a conqueror named Chandragupta Maurya, who was from Maghada, along the Ganges River. By 300 B.C.E. he had forged an empire that reached from the Ganges to the Indus. The Mauryan dynasty he founded reached its peak under his grandson Ashoka, who conquered much of southern India. Ashoka then renounced warfare and worked to consolidate his realm by building roads that were used by officials and merchants.

Ashoka's most far-reaching act was to embrace Buddhism, a religious philosophy inspired by the Indian holy man Siddhartha Gautama, who died in the fifth century B.C.E. Known to followers as the Buddha, or Enlightened One, he renounced worldly desires, lived moderately, and meditated intently until he entered nirvana, a perfect state of enlightenment that released him spiritually from all striving and suffering. Buddhism taught that one's capacity to achieve enlightenment had nothing to do with one's place in society. For that reason, it won many adherents among Indian merchants, considered socially and spiritually inferior to the priests and warriors who had long dominated Aryan India. During and after Ashoka's reign, traveling Buddhist merchants served as missionaries and spread their faith from India to Tibet, Southeast Asia, and China.

The Mauryan Empire fractured into competing kingdoms soon after Ashoka's death in 232 B.C.E. Not until the fourth century C.E. did another ruler from Maghada, known as Chandragupta in honor of Chandragupta Maurya, begin reuniting India. The Gupta Empire that he and his successors forged was not as large and cohesive as the Mauryan Empire, but trade and crafts such as weaving flourished, as did science and the arts. By this time, India's dominant faith was Hinduism, whose followers honored many gods and goddesses and believed in reincarnation. Whether one's soul rose to a higher level in the next life or descended to a lower state depended on one's actions. A classic Hindu text called the *Bhagavad Gita* taught that people at all levels of society, from exalted princes and warriors to those of low caste, would be rewarded in the next life if they lived honorably and fulfilled the duties of their caste.

In China, Confucianism came to influence rulers and officials and provided a moral framework for society. The Chinese philosopher Kong Fuzi, or Confucius, who died in 479 B.C.E., had little impact in his own time. China was descending into a violent era called the Warring States Period, and a teacher who advised rulers to rely more on moral authority than on armed force seemed irrelevant.

九月望日和碩果親王

But his principles, set down in writing by his disciples, eventually became the dominant social and political philosophy in China and much of East Asia. Other Chinese thinkers responded to strife and disorder with competing philosophies. Daoists urged people to disengage from worldly ambitions and conflicts and seek harmony with nature. Legalists believed that order could be achieved only through strict laws and harsh punishments imposed by rulers whose authority was absolute. For Confucians, the family was the foundation of society, but for Legalists the state was all important.

Legalism guided the rulers of Qin, the strongest of the Warring States. In 221 B.C.E. China was unified by a conqueror from that state known as Qin Shihuangdi (First Emperor of Qin). As emperor, he was denounced by Confucians and Daoists for ruling with an iron hand, and he executed his critics. He made heavy demands on the populace, drafting millions of laborers for public projects, including work on the defensive barrier that became the Great Wall of China. But like Darius I of Persia and other resourceful rulers of the classical age, he imposed order on his vast realm by building roads, standardizing laws, coinage, weights, and measures, and instituting a common Chinese script that allowed people belonging to many different language groups within the empire to communicate in writing, which helped unify China culturally. At his death in 210, he was buried in an immense tomb surrounded by the bodies of slaves sacrificed for the occasion and thousands of lifelike soldiers, molded of clay with great artistry. Not long after he died, rebellions broke out among the populace, and the government collapsed.

The fall of the short-lived Qin dynasty served as a lesson for the Han dynasty that followed. Han emperors governed China with the help of Confucian officials who believed in leading by moral example. "Approach your duties with reverence and be trustworthy," Confucius advised rulers; "employ the labor of the common people

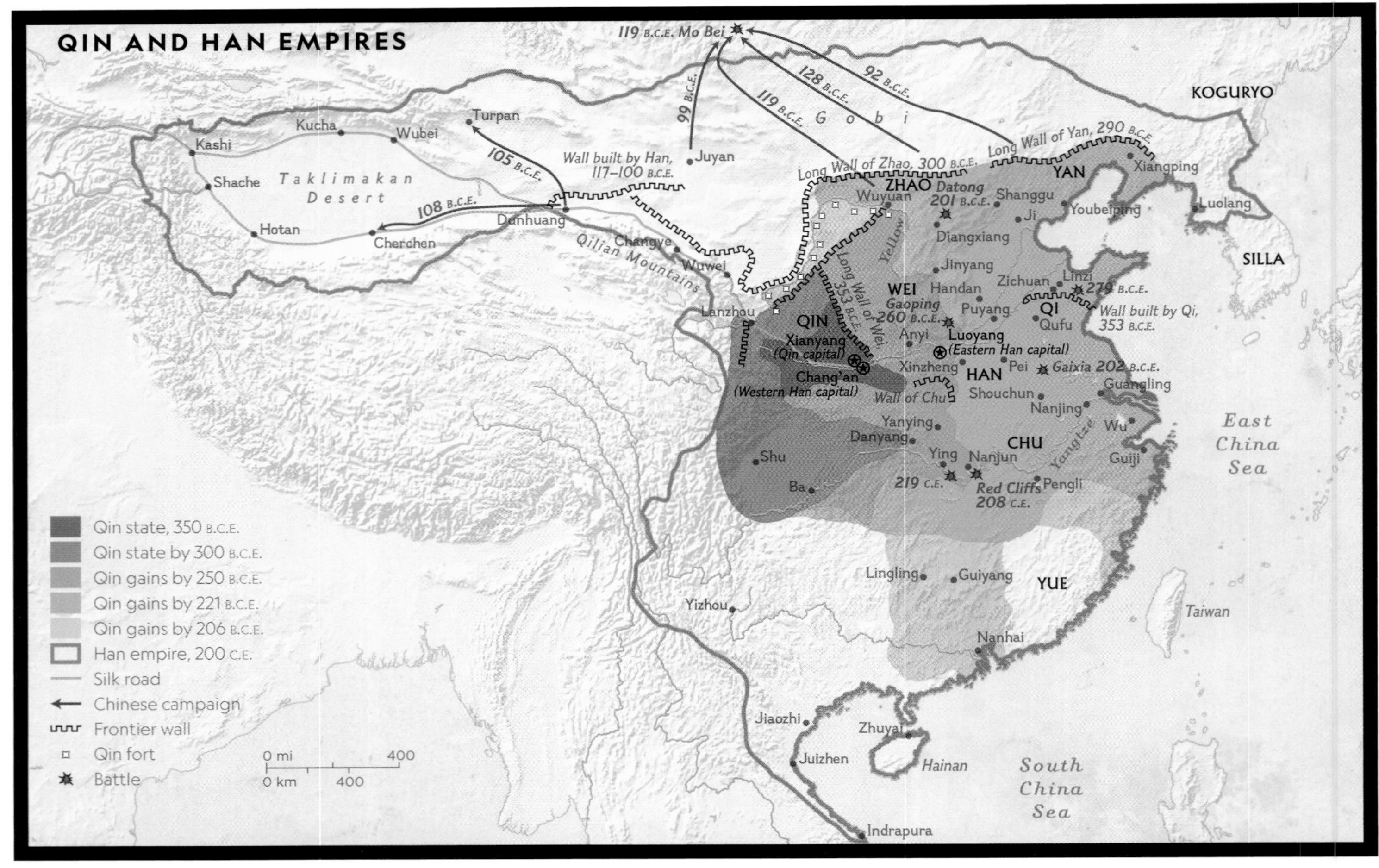

only in the right seasons." Emperors did not always follow that advice. Many were actually Legalists but endorsed Confucian ideals to legitimize and prolong their rule. One such ideal was the mandate of heaven, the belief that rulers were blessed by heaven so long as they governed wisely and justly. The dynasty's strongest emperor was Han Wudi, whose reign began in 141 B.C.E. Under him, Han armies advanced deep into Central Asia, established outposts on the Korean Peninsula, and drove south into Vietnam. As a Legalist, he asserted his authority by conscripting huge numbers of troops and laborers to strengthen the empire, but he allowed Confucianism to prevail among officials educated in the imperial university he created.

The Han capital at Chang'an was the terminus of the Silk Road, which extended to the eastern Mediterranean. That road, which was actually a network of trade routes, brought Chinese silks and other goods to Roman markets and carried ideas and beliefs to and from China. Buddhism came to China as early as the first century C.E. and gained followers as the Han dynasty weakened and ultimately collapsed. One recurring problem Han rulers faced was social strife between wealthy landowners and poor farmers or peasants. Early in the first century C.E., a reformer named Wang Mang redistributed land from the wealthy to the poor, but he and the young emperor he advised were overthrown as a result, and later Han rulers had to contend with peasant rebellions.

In the early third century C.E., the Han dynasty collapsed, and China once again fractured into rival kingdoms. Confucianism lost appeal, and many people turned to Buddhism or Daoism when China was assailed by epidemic diseases and invaders from Central Asia. No walls could fend off such far-reaching agents of destruction and change. They affected Europe as well and contributed to the decline of the Roman Empire and the spread of Christianity.

THE ROMAN WORLD

Rome expanded from a small Italian city-state to a world power not just by conquering other societies but by assimilating them. Romans granted many of those they subdued citizenship and won their cooperation and loyalty, freeing Roman troops to seize more territory or crush rebellions. Roman citizenship gave people legal protection, including the right to confront their accusers in court and maintain their innocence until proven guilty. But it did not give them democratic rights, for Rome was never a democracy. After throwing off Etruscan rule in 509 B.C.E., Romans organized themselves as a republic with a dominant Senate for patricians, or aristocrats, and a subordinate assembly for plebeians, or commoners. Reforms in this system increased the political power of plebeians, but social tensions persisted and gradually undermined the republic.

The political system functioned well enough while Roman power was confined to Italy but came under severe stress after Rome conquered Carthage, an expansive Phoenician city-state on the North African coast. After withstanding an invasion by the Carthaginian general Hannibal, Romans struck back and leveled Carthage in 146 B.C.E. Roman generals gained great power and prestige from such triumphs abroad and began intervening in domestic political disputes between wealthy landowners employing slaves seized in Roman conquests and dispossessed farmers who demanded land reform.

The most imposing of those generals was Julius Caesar, who conquered the Celts in Gaul, in what is now France, and returned to Rome to seize power in 49 B.C.E. As dictator, he took land from the wealthy and gave it to veterans loyal to him. Senators angered by his policies and his refusal to yield power assassinated him, hoping to restore the republic. Instead, they unleashed a tumultuous civil war in which they were crushed by Caesar's nephew Octavian, who then clashed with his co-ruler, Mark Antony. By defeating Antony and his ally, Queen Cleopatra of Egypt, the last ruler of the Ptolemaic dynasty, Octavian won firm control of the Mediterranean world. He took the title Augustus Caesar and reigned supreme as emperor.

Augustus and later Roman emperors were cult figures, worshiped at shrines. Most people under their authority recognized many gods and tolerated that imperial cult. Jews rejected other gods, however, and some hoped for a messiah, or savior, who would end Roman rule and restore the kingdom of Israel. Around 30 C.E., a Jewish visionary named Jesus who promised to restore God's kingdom on Earth was condemned and crucified by Roman authorities who feared he might incite rebellion. His disciples called him Christ, meaning "anointed one," or messiah, and said that he rose from the grave and joined God in heaven. Christianity was inspired mainly by Jewish scriptures, which became part of the Christian Bible, but it was also influenced by Zoroastrianism, which originated in Persia and taught that righteous souls would avoid the torments of hell and enter paradise.

Christians faced persecution as Roman power expanded under such strong-willed emperors as Vespasian, who sacked Jerusalem in 70 C.E. to end a rebellion there; and Trajan, who challenged defiant Parthians in the east and extended the Roman Empire to Mesopotamia before he died in 117. Later emperors consolidated those gains by expanding the network of Roman roads; building defensive barriers such as Hadrian's Wall in Britain; and founding or expanding provincial cities like Lyon in Gaul, which grew to resemble Rome, with fountains and baths fed by aqueducts, and coliseums or circuses to entertain the masses. The poet Juvenal scoffed that Romans who once took an active part in government now cared only for "bread and circuses." But the attractions of urban life helped transform conquered people into grateful Roman citizens. In time, some leading provincial citizens like the North African Septimius Severus became Roman emperors.

During the third century, Roman power declined. Here as in China, epidemics introduced along trade routes ravaged the population and disrupted harvests and shipments of grain on which cities depended. As the empire weakened, Christianity grew stronger by offering those in distress charity and the promise of eternal life. In the early fourth century, the emperor Constantine embraced Christianity and moved his capital from Rome to Byzantium on the Bosporus Strait. Known as Constantinople, that new capital became the seat of the Byzantine Empire, which endured while the old Roman Empire to the west crumbled. In the fifth century, Huns advancing from Central Asia into eastern Europe displaced Vandals, Visigoths, and other nomadic peoples, who then overwhelmed Italy. Rome fell in 476, but the invaders absorbed and perpetuated many elements of Roman culture, including Christianity.

GLOBAL ADVANCES

While empires rose and fell elsewhere, peoples of Oceania, sub-Saharan Africa, and the Americas formed durable and productive societies, laying the foundation for the emergence of strong states or kingdoms there during the classical or later eras. The most adventurous seafarers of classical times were Austronesians (ancestors of the Polynesians), who traveled eastward across the Pacific in outrigger canoes fitted with sails and colonized many Pacific islands, taking with them pigs and chickens and crops such as taro and breadfruit. In later times, their societies grew more complex, and chiefs arose who took control of entire islands or island chains.

Around the fourth century C.E., Malays from Indonesia sailed west across the Indian Ocean and colonized Madagascar, where they introduced bananas. From there, the cultivation of bananas spread to Africa and provided food surpluses that helped sustain populous societies in sub-Saharan Africa, some of which later developed into kingdoms. The societies that preceded those kingdoms were loosely knit politically and held together largely by kinship ties. But long before powerful states emerged in the region, cultures in areas rich in natural resources such as the Niger River Valley were growing more complex and accomplished. As early as 400 B.C.E., people of the Nok culture in what is now Nigeria were forging iron implements and sculpting highly expressive human and animal figures in clay. In North Africa, societies were absorbed by the Roman Empire and transformed by cultural forces such as Christianity that permeated the Roman world.

The massive Pyramid of the Sun looms above the plaza at Teotihuacan, a great commercial and ceremonial center that dominated the Valley of Mexico and reached the height of its power around 500 C.E.

By the fourth century C.E., Christianity was spreading southward from Roman-ruled Egypt to kingdoms in Nubia and Ethiopia.

In North America, the cultivation of corn spread northward from Mexico, allowing hunter-gatherers to begin settling down and building complex societies. In South America, the Moche of Peru carried out massive irrigation projects and disseminated their culture through warfare, trade, and artistry. In Mesoamerica, great cities arose such as Teotihuacan, located in the fertile Valley of Mexico not far from what is now Mexico City. Home to some 125,000 to 200,000 people, this was one of the most impressive urban centers of classical times, with broad avenues, soaring temples, and bustling workshops.

Among those who traded with Teotihuacan were the Maya, who lived around the Yucatán Peninsula. They were divided like the Greeks into rival city-states such as Palenque and Tikal, which grew to a population of more than 50,000. Scribes recorded Maya history in writing, and astronomers charted the heavens and advised kings, who waged so-called star wars based on astrological readings of the planet Venus and other celestial bodies. The main purpose of Maya warfare was to seize captives, whose blood was then offered to the gods. Some captives were forced to compete in ball games, and the losers were beheaded. But the Maya were no more bloodthirsty than the Romans, who watched captives killed in arenas by gladiators or wild animals. People around the world believed that sacrifices were required if societies were to expand and prosper, and they expressed that belief in various religious and civic rituals, from the ball court in Tikal to the Colosseum in Rome.

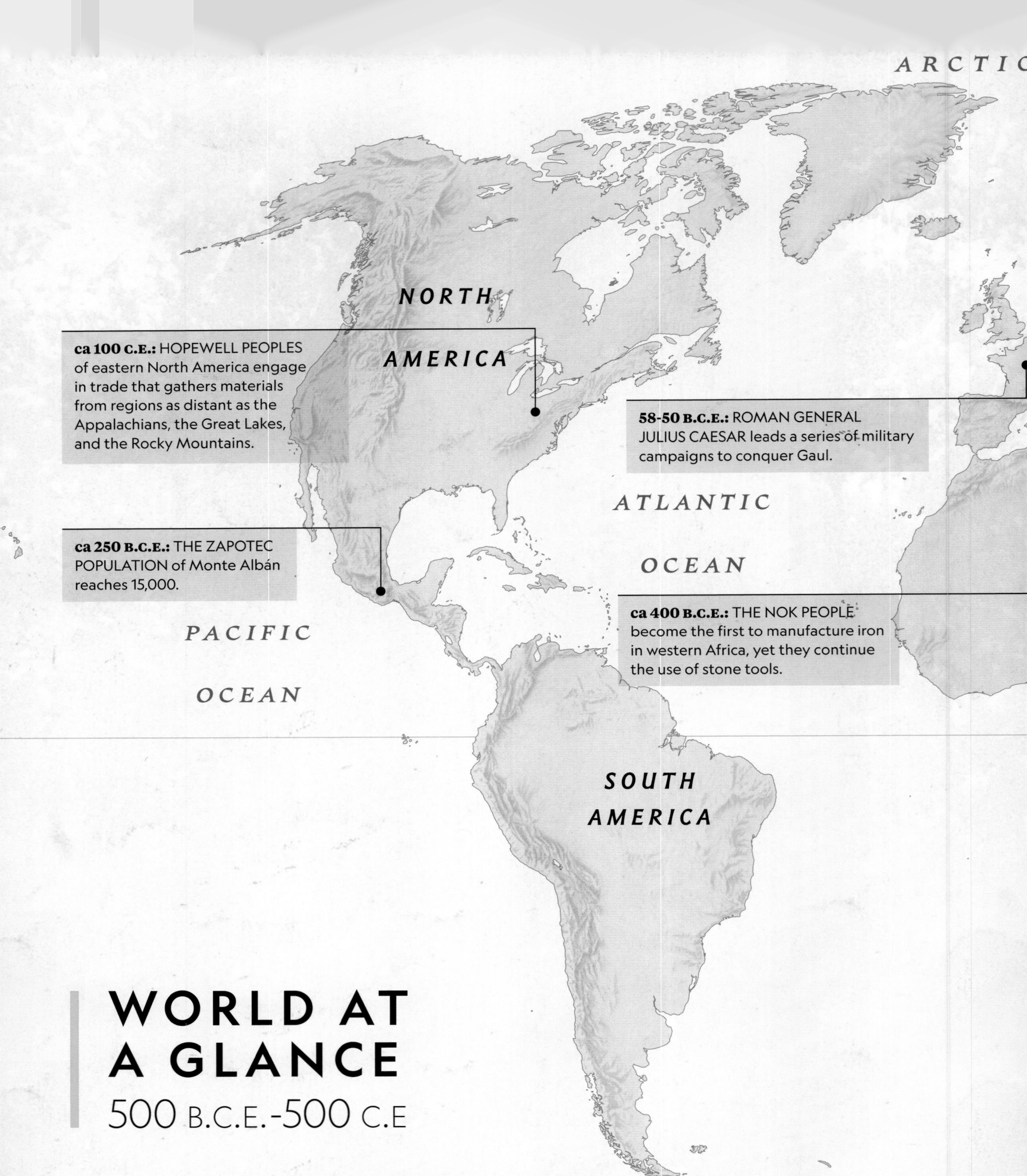
ARCTIC
NORTH AMERICA
ca 100 C.E.: HOPEWELL PEOPLES of eastern North America engage in trade that gathers materials from regions as distant as the Appalachians, the Great Lakes, and the Rocky Mountains.
58-50 B.C.E.: ROMAN GENERAL JULIUS CAESAR leads a series of military campaigns to conquer Gaul.
ATLANTIC
OCEAN
ca 250 B.C.E.: THE ZAPOTEC POPULATION of Monte Albán reaches 15,000.
ca 400 B.C.E.: THE NOK PEOPLE become the first to manufacture iron in western Africa, yet they continue the use of stone tools.
PACIFIC
OCEAN
SOUTH AMERICA

WORLD AT A GLANCE

500 B.C.E.-500 C.E

OCEAN
EUROPE
ASIA
AFRICA
PACIFIC
OCEAN
EQUATOR
INDIAN
OCEAN
AUSTRALIA
ca 80 C.E.: WORK ON THE GOSPELS, accounts of Jesus of Nazareth's life and teachings, is undertaken by members of the new Christian faith.
221 B.C.E.: HAVING SUBDUED RIVAL WARRING STATES to his rule, Ying Zheng, the ruler of Qin, proclaims himself the first emperor of a unified China. He takes on a new title, Qin Shihuangdi, which means "First Sovereign Emperor of Qin."

POLITICS & POWER	GEOGRAPHY & ENVIRONMENT	CULTURE & RELIGION
ca 500 **MONTE ALBÁN** is established in the Valley of Oaxaca, Mexico, on a hill from which leaders can survey their lands.		**400s** **THE OLMEC CULTURE,** which had flourished in Mesoamerica since the 12th century B.C.E., wanes in artistic and cultural dominance. Etruscan fresco from ca 470 B.C.E. in the Tomb of the Diver in Peastum, Italy
490 **GREEK FORCES** prevail at the Battle of Marathon, halting a Persian incursion into the Greek peninsula. **480** **AT KING XERXES' BEHEST,** Carthaginians attack Greek cities in Sicily. Meanwhile, Persian forces are weakened by a small band of Spartans at the pass of Thermopylae. **446** **ATHENIAN STATESMAN PERICLES** avoids a possible war with Sparta and afterward becomes the leading political voice in Athens. **400s** **SPARTA** becomes the most powerful city-state in Greece.	**500** **GREEK TRAVELER AND WRITER HECATAEUS OF MILETUS** details the geography and ethnography of Europe, northern Africa, and Asia in his *Tour Round the World.* **464** **A SEVERE EARTHQUAKE** in Sparta kills an estimated 20,000 people. A serf revolt follows, throwing the city into disarray.	▲ **ca 500** **ETRUSCAN ART** flourishes, inspired by Greek influences to the south. **450** **THE FIRST WRITTEN CODE OF LAW OF ROME,** the Twelve Tables, is placed in the Roman Forum. **447** **ATHENIAN STATESMAN PERICLES** commissions the sculptor Phidias to be artistic director for the construction of the Parthenon. It is finished by 438 B.C.E. and houses the Athena Parthenos, a 30- to 42-foot-tall gold and ivory statue of the patron deity.
500-494 **THE CITIES OF IONIA,** ethnically Greek but located in Asia Minor, rise up in rebellion against Persia in the Ionian revolt, an important precursor to the Greco-Persian Wars that begin just two years later. **480** **XERXES** prepares a huge incursion of an estimated 360,000 troops into the Greek mainland by constructing a floating bridge over the Hellespont, consisting of 676 ships lined up in two rows. **ca 449** **THE PEACE OF CALLIAS** is struck between Persia and the Greek city-states. It will last for most of the next century.	**490** **CARTHAGINIAN NAVIGATOR HANNO** sets sail with 30,000 people on 60 boats with the intent of founding colonies on the Atlantic coast of Africa. He reaches modern-day Gambia, Sierra Leone, and perhaps Cameroon, founding colonies the entire way.	**521-486** **DARIUS I CLAIMS DIVINE RIGHT TO RULE** through Zoroastrianism, a belief system founded between 1200 and 1000 B.C.E. by Iranian prophet and religious reformer Zarathustra. It becomes the state religion of Persia. **459** **THE HALL OF A HUNDRED PILLARS** in Persepolis is completed during the reign of King Artaxerxes I. **445-444** **NEHEMIAH RETURNS TO JERUSALEM** from Susa in Persia with the title of governor of Judah. He rebuilds the city walls and enacts economic reforms.
453 **THE WARRING STATES PERIOD** begins in China, a chaotic and violent era in Chinese history that lasts until 221 B.C.E.	**ca 500** **THE INDIAN STATE OF MAGADHA** emerges as a regional power, favorably located on the Ganges River to control trade and for access to natural resources such as iron. Over ensuing centuries, it will expand control over neighboring states. **ca 500** **MAGADHA KING AJATASHATRU** establishes the city of Pataliputra at the strategic juncture of the Ganges and Son Rivers.	**ca 500** **MAHAVIRA,** also known as Vardhamana, the great teacher of Jainism, abandons all worldly goods to live as an ascetic and preach his doctrine of rigorous austerity to disciples throughout northern India. Jainism's guiding principle of *ahimsa* demands nonviolence toward all living things. **ca 500** **CONFUCIUS** teaches disciples in China the principles of propriety and filial devotion. **ca 460-450** **SIDDHARTHA GAUTAMA,** the historical Buddha, teaches disciples in northern India a philosophy of compassion and wisdom to transcend worldly suffering.

SCIENCE & TECHNOLOGY

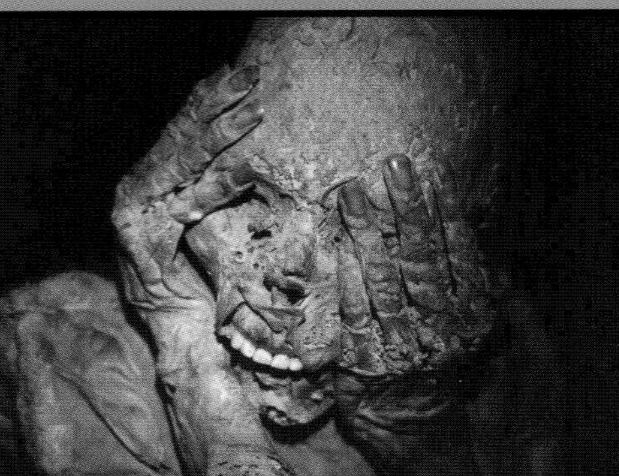

A remarkably preserved Paracas mummy

ca 500 **PYTHAGOREANS** hypothesize from mathematical principles that the Earth is a sphere.

ca 500 **THE CHARIOT** is introduced in Britain.

480 **THE TRIREME,** a light and easily maneuverable boat with three banks of oars, plays a crucial role in the Greek victory in the Battle of Salamis.

ca 450 **MECHANICAL STARTING GATES** for chariot and foot races are employed at the Olympic Games for the first time.

ca 500 **EXPANSION CONTINUES ON PERSIA'S ROYAL ROAD,** which stretches about 1,600 miles, from Sardis in western Anatolia to Susa in western Persia. It is set up with 111 staging posts.

ca 500 **THE IRON AGE** begins in Africa, likely introduced by the Soninke people in West Africa between 500 and 400 B.C.E. for iron agricultural tools and weapons.

480 **DURING A SIEGE OF ATHENS,** the Persian army uses arrows wrapped with fibers that have been soaked in oil—the first known projectile torches.

ca 500 **CONSTRUCTION BEGINS ON THE QI WALL,** a 370-mile rammed-earth wall in the modern-day Shangdong Province of China.

ca 500 **CHINESE PHYSICIAN BIAN QIAO** becomes the first to diagnose disease primarily by pulse and physical examination.

PEOPLE & SOCIETY

ca 500 **THE ADENA CULTURE,** centered in what is now southern Ohio, builds circular houses with conical roofs. They construct earthen burial mounds, which influence the later Hopewell culture.

◀ **400s** **PARACAS MUMMIES** are shrouded in cloaks of a remarkable quality. Their intricate designs will have a strong influence on later Nasca art.

400s **A COMMON PRACTICE** of the Paracas people of Peru is to bind the skulls of infants, resulting in a more elongated, peaked crown.

ca 494 **THE OFFICE OF TRIBUNE** of the plebeians is created in Rome. Also, the ban on marriage between a plebeian and a patrician is lifted.

ca 450 **ATHENIAN STATESMAN PERICLES,** at the height of his influence, broadens opportunities for participation in government, employs thousands in grand building projects, and stongly encourages the arts and sciences.

ca 500 **GIMILLU,** a slave of a temple community in Mesopotamia, is involved in a number of legal cases involving fraud, bribery, and embezzlement. In each case he manages to avoid harsh punishment.

486 **DARIUS I OF PERSIA,** having set up a system of administration that will last for centuries, dies at the age of 64. He is succeeded by his son Xerxes.

ca 500 **HORSE-RIDING NOMADIC GROUPS** are firmly established on the Eurasian steppes.

479 **CHINESE THINKER AND EDUCATOR CONFUCIUS** dies. Having unsuccessfully attempted to become a powerful administrator in his own day, his teachings compiled in the *Analects* will go on to profoundly influence subsequent political and cultural traditions in China.

ca 470-380 **CHINESE PHILOSOPHER MOZI** founds his school of Mohism, based on universal love, the virtues of egalitarianism, and a rejection of war and extravagance.

ZOROASTRIANISM

ZARATHUSTRA, FOUNDER and prophet o ancient Iran's foremost state religion, Zoroastrianism, was born of Indo-European stock, o the same ancestry as polytheistic Etruscans t the west and Hindi to the south. Stories o Zarathustra's early life hold many parallels t familiar motifs. Like Muhammad, he is said t have shone with a radiating light while still i his mother's womb. Like Siddhartha Gautam he was born into a position of considerabl privilege, only to rebuke it all following a transcendent vision. And like Jesus, whose nativit was reputedly visited by three Zoroastria clerics, the Magi, he tested his own fait before embarking on his ministry by wandering into the desert armed only with the wor of Ahura Mazda, the "greatest God."

Elements of Zarathustra's moralistic teachings also resound through several religion that succeeded him, concepts like heave and hell, judgment day, a holy path, and hi timeless credo, "good thoughts, good words good deeds." Greek and Roman philosopher as well held him in high esteem. Unlike man other prophets, however, Zarathustra wa regarded as a great sage and his teaching were widely accepted in his own day. I 522 B.C.E., when Darius I of Persia took the rein of the Achaemenid Empire, the word of Ahur Mazda was spread all the way from the Indu River in the east to the Aegean Sea in th west. Zoroastrianism had become the stat religion of the largest empire the world ha yet known.

Zarathustra speaking to the king of Persia

POLITICS & POWER

ca 400 THE OLMEC CITY OF LA VENTA, after two centuries of waning cultural and trade influence, is completely abandoned and no longer serves as a political or cultural center.

431 THE PELOPONNESIAN WAR breaks out in Greece between two coalitions: the Delian League, led by Athens, and the Peloponnesian League, led by Sparta. After 27 years of civil war, the city of Athens falls to Sparta and its allies in 404 B.C.E.

430 ATHENIAN STATESMAN PERICLES exhorts his countrymen and infantry to remain within the walls of Athens to avoid a battle on land with Sparta. Plague sweeps through the city, killing Pericles the following year.

396 ROME gradually gains control of the Tiber River.

424 IN THE YEAR OF THE FOUR EMPERORS IN PERSIA, King Artaxerxes I dies and is succeeded by his son Xerxes II. Xerxes II is murdered in his bed by his illegitimate brother Sogdianos, who is defeated and put to death by another illegitimate brother, who reigns as Darius II during a period of revolt. Darius II's successor, Ataxerxes II, rules for 46 years.

ca 400 CARTHAGE, a Phoenician colony in modern-day Tunisia, dominates the commerce of the western Mediterranean.

400 THE KINGDOM OF AKSUM is founded in northern Ethiopia.

400s DURING THE WARRING STATES PERIOD, walls are built to repel nomadic Xiongnu tribes to the north. Many of these walls will later be consolidated into the Great Wall.

GEOGRAPHY & ENVIRONMENT

400s THE CULTIVATION OF BEANS spreads from Mexico into the North American Southwest. Together with squash and corn, beans become a staple food in the Southwest.

Zapotec urn recovered from Oaxaca, Mexico

436 A FAMINE STRIKES ROME. It is so severe that thousands commit suicide by throwing themselves into the Tiber River.

ca 400 CELTIC TRIBES known collectively by the Romans as Gauls migrate over several centuries across Europe into northern Italy, France, and Germany.

ca 396 ONCE ROME DRAWS THE ETRUSCAN LANDS of northern Italy into its sphere of influence, it gains access to the large-scale iron industry already in place there.

401 IN THE SEVEN-VOLUME *ANABASIS KYROU (The Expedition of Cyrus),* Xenophon, a Greek mercenary soldier in Persia, records a detailed account of the trek from Babylon to the Black Sea after Cyrus's defeat.

390s THE HANGING GARDENS OF BABYLON are described by Greek physician and historian Ctesias, who had served as a physician in the Persian court.

400s FARMERS in Warring States Period China implement large-scale irrigation and use fertilization to increase their crop yields.

CULTURE & RELIGION

◀ **ca 400 THE BURGEONING ZAPOTEC CULTURE** of southern Mexico uses a calendar and a system of writing.

ca 426 GREEK HISTORIAN HERODOTUS completes his *History*, in which he details the interactions between the Greek world and Persia. Taking a wider view of history than its predecessors, this work garners its author the title "Father of History."

415 ATHENIAN DRAMATIST EURIPIDES produces *Trojan Women*. It is a harsh critique of the cruelty of war.

ca 387 GREEK PHILOSOPHER PLATO founds the Academy, a school of philosophy in Athens.

380 NEKTANEBO I initiates Egypt's 30th dynasty and ushers in a period of prosperity and building, including the earliest temple on the island of Philae, which is now covered by the waters of the Aswan Dam.

ca 400s JAINISM draws many converts in northern India from members of lower castes, who do not derive much esteem from the traditional social order of Indian society. Its ascetic doctrine of surrendering material goods is too demanding to appeal to the masses.

400s BUDDHISM spreads through northern India. Early monks, actively preaching and disseminating the teachings of the Buddha, use the vernacular language of the day, rather than Sanskrit, in order to reach a wider audience.

SCIENCE & TECHNOLOGY	PEOPLE & SOCIETY
ca 400 TREPANATION, a surgical procedure by which sections of the skull are excised, is practiced in the region of modern-day Peru. It is effectively used to treat head injuries, migraines, and seizures.	**ca 400-200** LAPIS LAZULI from the Atacama Desert of Chile appears at Chavín de Huántar in Peru—evidence of an extensive trade network among the Andeans.
ca 440 GREEK MATHEMATICIAN HIPPOCRATES OF CHIOS writes what is considered the first Greek textbook on mathematics. It expounds on the proofs of geometry. **ca 434** GREEK PHILOSOPHER ANAXAGORAS of Clazomenae is banished from Athens for his theory that the sun is a lump of fiery metal. **ca 430** HIPPOCRATES OF COS begins compiling his *Corpus Hippocraticum*, consisting of around 70 works presumably by various authors. It initiates the science of medicine with subjects ranging from pharmaceutical mixtures to a rejection of superstition.	**424** THUCYDIDES is exiled from Athens for a military blunder and starts working on his seminal work, *History of the Peloponnesian War*. **399** SOCRATES is sentenced to death for impiety and corrupting young men. He is credited with establishing the foundations of Western philosophical tradition, along with his successors Plato and Artistotle.
ca 400 THE NOK PEOPLE manufacture iron in western Africa, yet they continue the use of stone tools. **ca 390-340** GREEK MATHEMATICIAN AND ASTRONOMER EUDOXUS OF CNIDUS establishes a school in Cyzicus, Asia Minor. Here he formulates a systematic explanation of the motion of the sun, stars, moon, and planets around the Earth. **ca 383** BABYLONIAN ASTRONOMER KIDINNU improves the astronomical calendar by calculating a more accurate estimate of the length of a lunar month.	**423-404** PARYSATIS, WIFE AND HALF SISTER OF DARIUS II, is an ambitious queen who tries to secure the succession to the throne for her favorite son, Cyrus the Younger, instead of her eldest son, Arsaces. Cyrus dies in battle in 401 B.C.E. while trying to seize the throne. **401** PERSIAN CONQUEROR CYRUS is defeated by his brother at the Battle of Cunaxa. The victor takes the throne under the name Artaxerxes II.
437 THE FIRST KNOWN HOSPITAL is established in Ceylon, modern-day Sri Lanka.	**ca 400** THE USE OF COINS is spread to northern India from Greece via Persia.

The Parthenon atop Athens's acropolis

THE ROOTS OF DEMOCRACY

THOUGH MANY REGARD fifth-century Athens as the birthplace of democracy, this system of governance likely existed in hunter-gatherer societies—well before static communities, which tended toward a more hierarchical social organization, became prevalent. At the very least, Athens reintroduced a primitive idea in an advanced form, coining the term we use today, "democracy," Greek for "rule by the people."

Following a century of aristocratic power mongering, Athenian statesman Cleisthenes in 508 B.C.E. garnered popular support for a series of reforms that would strip hereditary claims of their political clout. He encouraged participation in government by extending the right to participate to all free adult males born into townships. Townships chose representatives by lot to present their constituents' vote at a weekly assembly that met near Athens' acropolis. Though Athens was not a true democracy—only about 15 percent of the populace were adult male citizens, with women, immigrants, and slaves given no voice—it was a step up from tyrannical rule by a small group of aristocrats. A form of democracy continued in Athens until 146 B.C.E., when conquering Romans annexed the city into their growing realm.

THE MIGHT OF PERSIA

What was known as Persia at the beginning of the sixth century B.C.E. encompassed only the southwestern portion of modern-day Iran. In a matter of decades, a dynasty of rulers emerged, known as the Achaemenid dynasty, which would incorporate regions stretching from the Aegean Sea off the coast of Greece to the Indus River of northwestern India, essentially becoming the first of the ancient world's classical societies. Though its borders would expand and contract and its rulers would adopt varying policies, Persia maintained itself as a continual political entity for the entirety of the next millennium and, some would say, to this very day.

The founder and first great ruler of the Achaemenid Empire was Cyrus, whose kingdom could be said to have become an empire in 547 B.C.E., when he conquered the powerful Lydian kingdom in Anatolia. In 539, he seized Babylon and with it large areas of Syria and Palestine. A benevolent ruler, Cyrus allowed his conquered lands to retain their own religions and cultural mores, even releasing Jews captive in Babylon and allowing them to rebuild their temple in Jerusalem. Cyrus took cues from those he conquered, adopting the use of coins from the Lydians and administrative practices from the Babylonians. His empire was further extended by his son, Cambyses, who took Egypt in 525, and by his grandson, Darius I, whose rule reached into northwestern India to the east and into Thrace and Macedonia in the west—easily the largest empire the world had yet known. The forces of Darius's son and successor, Xerxes I, even took Athens for a short time before being turned back.

Though an able military leader, Darius's true greatness was as an administrator. He organized his empire into 20 provinces and fixed the annual tribute due from each; he standardized coinage, weights, and measures; he established Zoroastrianism as the state religion, providing a cohesive Persian identity to his far-flung empire; he built a grand capital of magnificent proportions at Persepolis; he built a system of underground canals to increase agriculture; he started construction on the 1,600-mile Royal Road and equipped it with 111 courier stations at equal intervals; and he kept sedition to a minimum through the use of imperial spies, the "eyes and ears of the king."

Through these measures and a policy of toleration for cultural traditions, Darius saw trade and productivity in his empire increase along with the standard of living, and the stage was set for a long history of Persian rule in the Near East.

A grand decorative stairway ascends to a banquet hall in Persepolis, constructed during the reign of Darius I of Persia to serve as the nerve center of the expanding Achaemenid Empire.

POLITICS & POWER	GEOGRAPHY & ENVIRONMENT	CULTURE & RELIGION
300s **THE CITY** of Kaminaljuyú (in present-day Guatemala) is the largest highland capital of the Maya and is an important trade and cultural center.	**300s** **THE ADENA PEOPLE** of southern Ohio cultivate plants including sunflowers and little barley.	**300s** **THE MAYA** build monumental structures in the city of Calakmul (present-day Mexico). **300s** **MAYA HIEROGLYPHIC WRITING** is in use in Petén, Guatemala.
359 **KING PHILIP II** takes power in the northern Greek state of Macedonia. He assembles a hardy, well-trained army, equipping his infantry with the *sarissa,* a pike 13 to 21 feet long. **351** **A PLEBEIAN** is elected censor in Rome for the first time. **338** **KING PHILIP II OF MACEDON,** after two decades of extending his empire, subdues all of Greece and sets his sights on Persia. **336** **ALEXANDER THE GREAT,** following the assassination of his father, Philip II, inherits his expanding empire at the age of 20.	**334-323** **ALEXANDER THE GREAT** encourages the building of roads and cities throughout his empire, setting a pattern for the later Roman Empire. **300s** **GREEK FARMERS** likely grow more barley than wheat, as the yield is greater on poor soil.	**ca 378** **GREEK PHILOSOPHER PLATO** composes his dialogue, *Republic,* in which he elaborates his notion of the ideal state. **ca 350** **THE "APOLLO BELVEDERE,"** attributed to Greek sculptor Leochares, is made. It is widely considered the ideal form of masculine beauty in the ancient Mediterranean world. **ca 335** **COINS** are introduced into Rome. Around 25 years later, the stores of the Roman Forum are replaced by bankers' quarters.
334 **ALEXANDER THE GREAT** invades Persia with his small but extremely well-trained army of Macedonian soldiers. **331** **ALEXANDER** destroys the Persian forces of the Achaemenid Empire at the Battle of Gaugamela. He then goes on to raze the grand imperial center, Persepolis. **312** **SELEUCUS I NICATOR,** Alexander's general and heir to his Asian empire, enters Babylon and ushers in the Seleucid era, regaining Bactria from Chandragupta Maurya around 306 B.C.E.	**ca 350** **A NEW STRAIN OF WHEAT** is cultivated in Egypt, from which bread can be easily produced. Combined with the Ptolemaic dynasty's support of agriculture, this development helps make Egypt the granary of Rome and the Mediterranean. **332** **ALEXANDER DESTROYS TYRE** and builds Alexandria in Egypt to be the center of Hellenistic commerce. **329** **ALEXANDER** crosses the Hindu Kush into Bactria to defeat its satrap Bessus.	**356** **THE TEMPLE OF ARTEMIS AT EPHESUS** is burned by Herostratus and rebuilt even more magnificently. It is regarded as one of the Seven Wonders of the Ancient World. **ca 332** **AS THEY CAMPAIGN THROUGH THE ACHAEMENID EMPIRE, ALEXANDER'S FORCES** burn many Zoroastrian temples and kill many priests, or magi. Since doctrines of this faith are transmitted orally, many holy verses and hymns are lost to posterity. **324** **3,000 PERFORMERS** arrive from Greece to Ecbatana in northwestern Iran to perform at a feast for Alexander.
390-338 **LEGALIST ADMINISTRATOR SHANG YANG** becomes one of the leading reformers of his age. He centralizes the Qin government and paves the way for a unified China. **327** **ALEXANDER THE GREAT** takes his army across the Indus River into northwestern India. Two years later, he retreats only when his troops threaten mutiny unless they return home. **321** **CHANDRAGUPTA MAURYA** establishes the Mauryan dynasty and becomes the first emperor to unify most of India. He rules until 297 B.C.E.	**327** **ALEXANDER THE GREAT'S** incursion into northwestern India and conquests throughout the Middle East connect the Indian subcontinent to the growing sphere of the Mediterranean basin. Trade will thus be facilitated for centuries to come.	**ca 350** **FORMATIVE DAOIST TEXT** the *Daodejing* is compiled. **ca 350-200** ***THE CLASSIC OF FILIAL PIETY*** is composed in China. It encourages obedience and respect for elders and authorities. **ca 310** **A SCHISM** emerges in Jainism after a 12-year famine prompts Bhadrabahu I and Chandragupta to lead an exodus from the Jain stronghold in northern India.

SCIENCE & TECHNOLOGY	PEOPLE & SOCIETY
300s OHIO'S ADENA CULTURE uses stone axes, hoes, and projectiles and trades for copper ornaments.	**300s** THE JAMA-COAQUE CULTURE of modern-day coastal Ecuador continues to produce a number of clay figurines often with very well-defined features and almost always adorned with headgear and jewelry.
350 ARISTOTLE writes *On the Heavens,* in which he correctly supports the theory that the Earth is a sphere, and incorrectly supports the theory that the Earth is the center of the universe. **312** THE FIRST MAJOR ROMAN ROAD, the Via Appia, is commissioned by censor Appius Claudius Caecus. It initially extends 132 miles from Rome to Capua.	**343** GREEK PHILOSOPHER ARISTOTLE, a pupil and colleague of Plato, travels to Macedonia to become the tutor of the 13-year-old heir to the throne, Alexander. **336** KING PHILIP II OF MACEDON is assassinated. His plans for an invasion of Persia fall to his son Alexander. **323** ALEXANDER THE GREAT falls ill at a feast and dies 10 days later at the age of 32. Theories of the cause of death range from poisoning to malaria or typhoid fever.
ca 331 AFTER ALEXANDER THE GREAT CAPTURES BABYLON, Greek historian Callisthenes sends home to Aristotle accounts of the accomplishments of the Babylonian astronomers.	**ca 350** THE CITY OF ILE-IFE in present-day Nigeria is first occupied. It is described in Yoruba traditions as "the place where the world was created." **338** PERSIAN MINISTER AND MILITARY COMMANDER-IN-CHIEF BAGOAS poisons Artaxerxes III. He is then poisoned in turn by Darius III. **330** AFTER DEFEATING THE PERSIANS, Alexander the Great proclaims himself "Lord of Asia" and soon adopts Persian ceremonial dress and court rituals.
365 CHINESE HISTORIANS believe that ancient astronomer Xi Zezong discovers the existence of Jupiter's moons without the aid of a telescope.	**ca 350** CONFUCIAN THINKER MENCIUS travels extensively through China, extolling the virtue of government through benevolence and respectfulness. **ca 350** LEGALISM appears in China, a system of thought that seeks to strengthen and expand the state at all costs. It strongly emphasizes agriculture and the military and seeks to order society through a rigid set of severe laws.

THE NOK

THE NOK CULTURE of central Nigeria in the fourth century B.C.E. was at the cusp of a revolution in how West African society was organized—the move from the Neolithic to the Iron Age. The Nok were early producers of iron in sub-Saharan Africa, with furnaces dating back to the fifth century B.C.E. Produced by melting and separating the element from chunks of ore taken out of the earth, iron was made into hoes and tools and put to use in clearing lands and growing crops such as yams. The surplus that was created spurred not only the growth of urban centers, but also the development of a sophisticated artistic style.

By firing clay in their furnaces, the Nok created domestic pottery, animal figurines, and stylized human sculptures, which sometimes were just heads. These human figurines show exaggerated facial features, elongated body parts, and abstract geometrical treatments. The Nok's unique style of art is exceptionally preserved and provides testimony to the independent mastery of pottery manufacture in sub-Saharan Africa.

Stylized head of a Nok terra-cotta figurine

POLITICS & POWER

GEOGRAPHY & ENVIRONMENT

CULTURE & RELIGION

ca 300 TIKAL, A CENTER OF MAYA CULTURE located in the lowland rainforest of modern-day Guatemala, moves from a small farming community to a populous ceremonial complex. Around this time, it begins construction on a number of monumental pyramids and temples.

ca 250 THE ZAPOTEC POPULATION of Monte Albán reaches 15,000.

Dancers in Monte Albán's Danzantes relief

ca 300 INHABITANTS OF NAKBE, in modern-day Guatemala, carve a 34-foot-wide, 16-foot-high sculpture of the great mythological bird of the Maya, evidence of the beginnings of the Maya cultural tradition of monumental art.

◀ **ca 250** CARVINGS CALLED DANZANTES at Monte Albán demonstrate Olmec influence on Zapotec art. The friezes are believed to be a public declaration of the political and martial power of the city's elite. It's thought that they may depict slain captives or sacrificial victims.

ca 280-270 ROME becomes the dominant power on the Italian peninsula. Through the establishment of military colonies and equitable treatment of vanquished states, it secures a wide base of political and military authority.

241 THE FIRST PUNIC WAR ends with Rome wresting control of Sicily from Carthage.

ca 310-306 NAVIGATOR PYTHEAS is the first Greek to reach the British Isles and the Arctic Circle. His description of a land where the sea is solid and the sun never sets in summer is ridiculed in his own day.

ca 230 ERATOSTHENES, a geographer in Alexandria, calculates the circumference of the Earth.

ca 294-282 THE COLOSSUS OF RHODES is constructed. This bronze statue of the sun god Helios stands 105 feet tall at the mouth of Rhodes's harbor. It commemorates the end of a long siege by Demetrius I Poliorcetes, king of Macedon.

ca 270-245 APOLLONIUS OF RHODES writes his epic poem, *Jason and the Argonauts*.

305 SELEUCUS I NICATOR consolidates his gains in Babylon. In 280 B.C.E., his son Antiochus I Soter takes the titles "Great King, King of the World, King of Babylon."

ca 245 THE PARTHIAN SATRAP in Iran stages a successful though brief revolt against his Seleucid overlord, starting a 100-year shift in the balance of power between these two forces in the Middle East.

WHAT LIFE WAS LIKE

The Parthians

Originally a group of nomads from the Central Asian steppes, the Parthians gradually settled into an agricultural way of life in modern-day Iran. Without access to conventional feed grains such as those used in more advanced agricultural societies, the Parthians allowed their horses to graze in winter on alfalfa growing naturally on the nearby steppes, a practice which not only made their animals larger than average, but also made them strong enough to support warriors equipped with metal armor. Already skilled in the art of horseback combat, the fully armored and well-trained Parthian cavalry was a formidable match to any rival, and was integral in establishing the Parthian Empire.

ca 300 ARAMAIC AND GREEK are the common languages of newly founded Hellenistic cities in the Middle East.

ca 280 THE MUSEUM OF ALEXANDRIA and Library of Alexandria are founded.

280 THE FIRST FIVE BOOKS OF THE OLD TESTAMENT are translated from Hebrew to Greek.

250 B.C.E. THE DEAD SEA SCROLLS are composed through 70 C.E., expounding the belief system of the Essenes.

ca 300 THE MAURYAN EMPIRE administers trade, agriculture, taxes, and foreign affairs across northern India from the Indus to the Ganges.

260 MAURYAN EMPEROR ASHOKA conquers the Indian state of Kalinga, killing an estimated 100,000 in the fighting. Later, he promotes a Buddhist way of life and gives up hunting.

ca 250 THE YAYOI CULTURE, characterized by advanced skills in metallurgy and wet rice cultivation, becomes increasingly powerful in Japan.

ca 305 UNDER THE PATRONAGE OF EMPEROR CHANDRAGUPTA MAURYA, the city of Taxila in northwestern India becomes a prominent center of learning and commerce.

ca 300 THE CULTIVATION OF WET RICE is introduced into Japan from China.

ca 269-232 MAURYAN EMPEROR ASHOKA founds hospitals in India and supplies them with medicines. He also provides health services for animals.

ca 269-232 WITH THE SPONSORSHIP OF MAURYAN EMPEROR ASHOKA, Buddhism spreads throughout India and to Bactria (modern-day Afghanistan). Mariner merchants take it along sea routes to Southeast Asia.

SCIENCE & TECHNOLOGY	PEOPLE & SOCIETY
200s CRAFTSMEN of the La Tolita culture of modern-day coastal Ecuador continue to produce a multitude of finely wrought gold and platinum pieces that show a skill in casting and overlay that was not found elsewhere in the region.	**ca 250** THE NASCA CULTURE develops in northern coastal Peru. It is characterized by the high quality of its pottery and weaving.
ca 300 BABYLONIAN ASTRONOMER BEROSUS, living on the Greek island of Cos, develops an early form of the sundial to tell time of day. **ca 270** GREEK ASTRONOMER ARISTARCHUS OF SAMOS writes *On the Size and Distances of the Sun and Moon*, in which he employs geometry to estimate the distance of the sun and the moon from the Earth. He also postulates that the Earth revolves annually around the sun and rotates daily about its own axis. **ca 250** GREEK ANATOMIST ERASISTRATUS OF CEOS, considered the father of physiology, explains the functions of the heart's valves.	**ca 300** THREE SCHOOLS of philosophical thought arise in Greece—Epicureanism, which views pleasure as the ultimate good; Skepticism, which values reasoning and inquiry; and Stoicism, which takes as its goal tranquillity of mind by means of a virtuously led life. **264** THE FIRST GLADIATORIAL GAMES, originating from an Etruscan funereal tradition, are held in Rome. Along with chariot races, they will become wildly popular in the Roman world for the next few centuries.
ca 300 PROMINENT MATHEMATICIAN EUCLID, teaching in Alexandria, expounds on the laws of geometry in his *Elements*. **ca 290** HEROPHILUS, considered the father of anatomy, works in Alexandria, practicing human dissection, a research technique banned elsewhere. He recognizes the brain as the center of the nervous system. **ca 280** THE WORLD'S FIRST MONUMENTAL LIGHTHOUSE, the Pharos of Alexandria, begins to be constructed. The light of its fire is reflected out to sea by a mirror.	**ca 300** PERMANENT SETTLEMENT at Jenne-Jeno (modern-day Djenné, Mali) in the Niger delta begins the gradual process of urbanism in West Africa. Rice cultivation, trade, and crafts contribute to this process. **ca 280** ALEXANDRIA becomes the bureaucratic center of the Ptolemaic empire. Its harbor can hold up to 1,200 ships at a time.
ca 250 MAURYAN EMPEROR ASHOKA expands on his grandfather's system of roads to encourage overland commerce and builds an extensive irrigation system to encourage agriculture. **240** THE EARLIEST KNOWN RECORD OF HALLEY'S COMET is made by Chinese astronomers.	**ca 250** CONFUCIAN THINKER XUNZI advocates moral and ritual propriety, a cornerstone of Confucian views on social order, as a means for the state to create order in human society. **ca 250** CHINESE LEGALIST HAN FEIZI formulates views on the state that will influence Chinese politics for centuries.

THE LIBRARY OF ALEXANDRIA

THE HELLENISTIC AGE was characterized by a confluence of ideas and a blending of traditions between the Greek West and the Persian East. Greek merchants poured into the cities recently founded by Alexander the Great, and a cultural interchange of unprecedented proportions ensued.

Nowhere was this more true than in Alexandria, Egypt, one of the most cosmopolitan cities of the ancient world, established by Alexander on the Nile delta in 332 B.C.E. After the partitioning of Alexander's empire following his premature death, Alexandria came under the domain of the Ptolemaic dynasty, which soon established a research library and attendant "museum"—in the original sense of the word, a temple to the muses—the likes of which the world had not yet seen.

Scholars converged from across the Mediterranean world on this burgeoning center of learning, which housed an estimated 400,000-700,000 scrolls, though some were acquired through questionable methods. Prominent geometrician Euclid came to work on his groundbreaking textbook, *Elements*. Physician and anatomist Herophilus came to research human physiology through dissection of cadavers, a practice usually banned elsewhere. Aristarchus of Samothrace set into collated form the various texts associated with Homer. Jewish scholars came to translate from Hebrew to Greek the Old Testament of the Bible.

Libraries subsequently were established throughout the Hellenistic world in emulation of Alexandria's center of scholarship, but until its destruction in the late fourth century C.E. by Christian Roman emperor Theophilus, who was attempting to do away with all remnants of paganism in his realm, few compared.

POLITICS & POWER	GEOGRAPHY & ENVIRONMENT	CULTURE & RELIGION

Map of Hannibal's invasion route from Spain to Italy

ca 200 THE NASCA LINES begin to appear in the arid deserts of southern coastal Peru. Giant geoglyphs created by removing dark, oxidized rocks from the desert surface, some are animal figures, others straight lines emanating from ray centers.

ca 195 GREEK SCHOLAR ARISTOPHANES OF BYZANTIUM introduces accent marks to Greek writing.

▲ **218 CARTHAGINIAN GENERAL HANNIBAL,** at the outbreak of the Second Punic War, crosses the Alps into northern Italy with 40,000 men and 37 elephants. His successful invasion threatens Rome.

ca 225 THE COLOSSUS OF RHODES, one of the seven wonders of the ancient world, is toppled by an earthquake.

214 IN CONSULTATION WITH THE ROMANS, SYPHAX, a Numidian king, leads a short-lived rebellion against Carthage.

202 ROMAN FORCES defeat the amassed Carthaginian forces under General Hannibal at Zama, in modern-day Tunisia. The peace agreement forces Carthage to cede to Rome most of its fleet as well as its holdings in Spain.

189 ROMAN FORCES defeat Seleucid ruler Antiochus III, also known as Antiochus the Great.

ca 200 FLOODING eases and dry conditions appear in the Niger and Senegal valleys, leading to increased settlement.

ca 230 THE "DYING GAUL" is dedicated. This sculpture may commemorate a victory over the Galatians, a Celtic group pushing into Asia Minor. It represents the anguish of war.

196 AN HONORIFIC DECREE by Egyptian pharaoh Ptolemy V is inscribed three times on the Rosetta Stone, once in Greek, once in Egyptian hieroglyphs, and once in demotic script.

221 HAVING SUBDUED RIVAL WARRING STATES to his rule, Ying Zheng, the ruler of Qin, proclaims himself the first emperor of a unified China. He takes on a new title, Qin Shihuangdi, which means "First Sovereign Emperor of Qin."

207 THREE YEARS AFTER THE DEATH OF EMPEROR QIN SHIHUANGDI, civil insurrection breaks apart the Qin dynasty.

206 CHINESE MILITARY COMMANDER LIU BANG establishes the Han dynasty. He becomes known as Emperor Gaozu.

ca 220 CHINESE EMPEROR QIN SHIHUANGDI divides his kingdom into 36 military districts, each governed by a civil administrator and a military commander.

ca 206 THE HAN DYNASTY sets up its capital in Chang'an, near modern-day Xi'an. This cosmopolitan city will serve as an important cultural center for much of Chinese history.

ca 185 THE MAURYAN EMPIRE OF INDIA dissipates, the result of invasions, defections by southern rulers, and disputes over ascension.

ca 220 CHINESE EMPEROR QIN SHIHUANGDI begins construction on a mausoleum spanning 20 square miles and adorned with a pearl-inlaid map of the sky, rivers of mercury, and an army of terra-cotta soldiers.

ca 200-201 THE *BHAGAVAD GITA (SONG OF GOD),* a sacred Hindu text, is further refined. It ruminates on the divine in the form of a dialogue between a warrior prince and his charioteer.

SCIENCE & TECHNOLOGY	PEOPLE & SOCIETY
ca 200 THE NASCA PEOPLE of southern coastal Peru begin constructing a huge network of underground irrigation channels, called *puquios,* many of which are still in working order. They enable the Nasca to make their desert environment arable.	**ca 200** HOPEWELL CULTURE emerges primarily in what is now southern Ohio.
213 GREEK MATHEMATICIAN AND INVENTOR ARCHIMEDES, working in Syracuse, Sicily, creates all manner of military instruments using levers and pulleys, and comes to an approximation of pi. **ca 200** THE ROMANS invent concrete.	**226** A FORCE OF CELTIC GAULS threatens Roman holdings in northern Italy. They are turned away decisively the following year at the Battle of Telamon. **ca 200** LANDS CONQUERED BY ROME largely become property of the wealthy elite, who set up massive plantations, known as latifundia, worked by peasant or slave laborers. These plantations prosper at the expense of their smaller neighbors.
ca 225 APOLLONIUS OF PERGA, while in Alexandria, Egypt, writes *Conics,* a classic Greek treatise on geometry.	**ca 183** HANNIBAL, in exile in Libyssa (in modern-day Turkey), commits suicide rather than submit to the Romans. **ca 171** SOLDIER AND CONQUEROR MITHRADATES I assumes the throne of the Parthian Empire. He will soon rule over lands stretching from India to the Mediterranean.
ca 220 EMPEROR QIN SHIHUANGDI uses a vast force of slave labor to build a system of roads, bridges, and canals across China. He also consolidates the Great Wall. **ca 200** CHINESE MATHEMATICIANS begin using exponential formulas and early forms of scientific notation.	**221-207** CHINA INTRODUCES A STANDARD CURRENCY of round copper coins. Coins of various shapes were used as currency in China during the earlier Warring States Period. **ca 200** CHINESE TRADERS pioneer the Silk Road caravan route. **ca 200** THE XIONGNU PEOPLE OF CENTRAL ASIA form a wide-reaching federation under the ruler known as Maodun. **ca 188** EMPRESS DOWAGER LÜ ZHI becomes the first female ruler in Chinese history to issue imperial edicts.

HANNIBAL

AS A YOUNG MAN in Carthage, Hannibal once asked his father to take him along on a military campaign in Spain. It is said that his father agreed, on one condition: that Hannibal swear never to become an ally of Rome. Hannibal more than held up his end of the bargain, eventually using his military genius to challenge the power of Rome, and very nearly succeeding.

Commander in chief of his own army by age 26, Hannibal pushed Rome into the Second Punic War against Carthage. He then amassed a force of about 90,000 troops, as well as 37 African war elephants, and embarked on an invasion of northern Italy through the Alps that would become legendary. When told it was impossible to cross the Alps with elephants, Hannibal responded, "We will either find a way, or make one." They did, though the feat cost Hannibal half his army.

Hannibal went on to score victories throughout Italy and seriously threatened to conquer Rome. But after the death of his brother and a failed alliance with the Macedonians, Hannibal returned to Africa, where Roman forces were threatening his native city. Carthage was taken and Rome's hegemony in the Mediterranean was firmly established for the next 500 years.

Hannibal's army crosses the Alps.

THE TIGER OF QIN

The first emperor of a unified China, Qin (pronounced Chin) Shihuangdi did far more than lend his name to the modern-day country. He assumed the throne of the state of Qin in 246 B.C.E. at the age of 13, and over the next 25 years would lead Qin armies to defeat all rival states and unify their territory into China's first empire. The ferocity with which he ate up his neighbors earned him the nickname "tiger of Qin." Shihuangdi then set to work reorganizing the political and social structure of the empire with himself at the center; organizing the army; codifying the law; establishing standards for weights, measures, axle lengths, coinage, and a writing system; building new roads, canals, and irrigation systems to crisscross his empire; and even consolidating and enlarging a series of walls built by northern states into what we now know as the Great Wall of China.

Obsessed with immortality, Shihuangdi began work on a mausoleum so elaborate, its construction would last 36 years and required a workforce of slave laborers equal to that used on the Great Wall. The entire complex covered 23 square miles, guarded by a full army of life-size terra-cotta soldiers. According to legend, the mausoleum is equipped with all the accoutrements an emperor might desire in the afterlife, including a scale model of the empire replete with flowing rivers of mercury and a map of the sky with constellations of pearls. So far, only legend qualifies these claims, as Chinese archaeologists hesitate to begin a full-scale excavation until they can be sure of not harming the structure. Through the use of remote sensing survey technology, one very important discovery has been made: the presence of unusual amounts of mercury, up to 100 times above normal.

Beginning with the succeeding Han dynasty, Qin rule was viewed as tyrannical despotism and rejected as the illegitimate wielding of unlimited autocratic power. A famous essay by the noted Han writer Jia Yi (201-169 B.C.E.), "The Faults of Qin," elegantly describes the rise and fall of the Qin state, attributing its demise to the absence of Confucian values in its government. In order to justify their own rule, the founders of the Han dynasty carefully distanced themselves from the Qin and, even though they ruled through the centralized political institutions created by the Qin, they legitimized their power by appealing to Confucian ideals of good rulership.

As Confucian ideas became state orthodoxy during the Han, a bureaucracy of officials evolved who were modeled on Confucian notions of service to a ruler who held the Mandate of Heaven. Under the Han and later dynasties, the Mandate of Heaven became the key source of legitimacy for founders of new dynasties. Like Liu Bang, the founder of the Han dynasty, future dynastic founders also justified their conquest by claiming that heaven had bestowed its mandate on them because they had proven their virtue and ability. From this perspective, Qin Shihuangdi, the first emperor of China, neither sought nor claimed the Mandate of Heaven, ruling instead through the Legalist doctrines of "strict laws and harsh punishments," which served the Qin state so well in its centralization of power, rapid territorial expansion, and unification of the country.

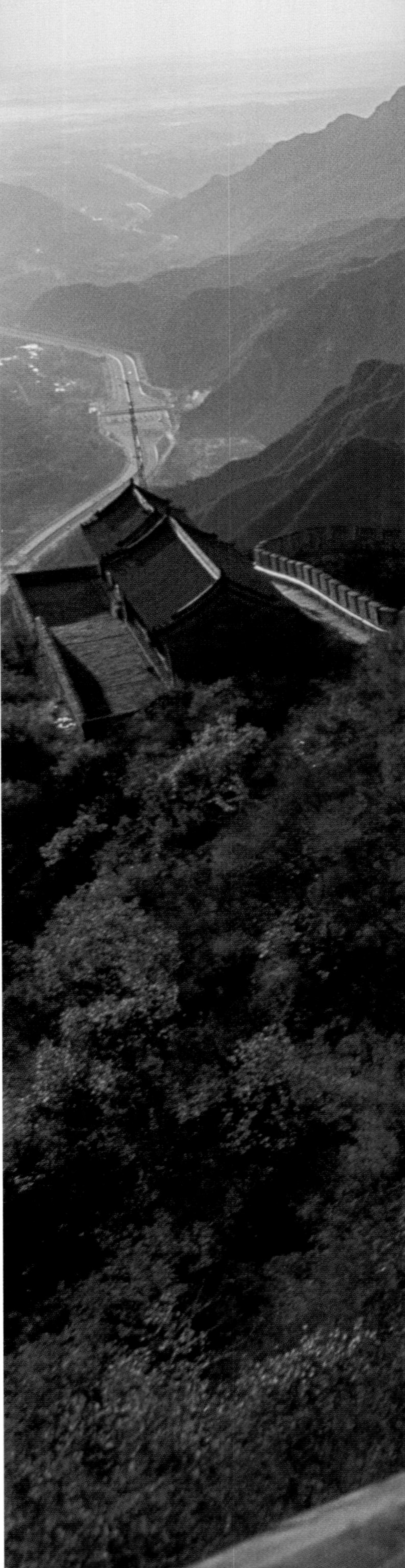

Defenses in northern China were unified into a contiguous structure by Qin Shihuangdi in the third century B.C.E. The Great Wall was reconstructed and refortified by the Ming dynasty in the 15th and 16th centuries C.E.

POLITICS & POWER	GEOGRAPHY & ENVIRONMENT	CULTURE & RELIGION
ca 100 **UNDER A MALE-LED** noble class, the city of Monte Albán begins a period of local conquest.		**ca 100** **IN COSTA RICA,** jadeite stones are worked into pendants and included as funerary offerings.

Brothers Tiberius and Gaius Gracchus

POLITICS & POWER	GEOGRAPHY & ENVIRONMENT	CULTURE & RELIGION
▶ **133** **ROMAN TRIBUNE TIBERIUS GRACCHUS** sponsors an agrarian bill that redistributes land to the poor. He is assassinated in a riot sparked by his opponents in the Senate. **123-122** **ROMAN TRIBUNE GAIUS GRACCHUS, TIBERIUS'S BROTHER,** pushes for land reform and wider distribution of citizenship. Pursued by political enemies, he commits suicide in 121.	**122** **MOUNT ETNA** on the island of Sicily erupts. **113-110** **DROUGHTS** contribute to the migration of the Cimbri and Teutones from the Jutland Peninsula in northern Italy into Roman land, leading to violent clashes with Roman legions.	**166** **LATIN COMIC PLAYWRIGHT TERENCE** produces his first play, *Andria (The Andrian Girl).* **ca 100** **THE SCULPTURE "APHRODITE OF MELOS,"** better known to posterity as the "Venus de Milo," is produced. Nothing is known of its sculptor.
160-152 **PARTHIAN RULER MITHRADATES I** captures the city of Media in today's Iran, expanding Parthian territory and influence in Mesopotamia. **150** **THE CITY OF CARTHAGE,** following incursions by Numidian King Masinissa, violates the terms of peace of the Second Punic War and provides Rome an impetus to begin the Third Punic War in 149. Roman forces led by consul Scipio Aemilianus take the city, raze it, evict the inhabitants, and salt the surrounding earth to hinder agriculture.	**146** **ROME DESTROYS CARTHAGE** and establishes the province of Africa. Rome is now the dominant political and economic force in the Mediterranean. **129** **CTESIPHON,** on the Tigris River, is selected as the winter capital of the Parthian Empire. **125** **A PLAGUE OF LOCUSTS** afflicts Roman areas in northern Africa, raising the price of grain.	**167** **SYRIAN KING ANTIOCHUS IV EPIPHANES** issues a series of decrees against the practice of Judaism in Jerusalem. It sparks a successful revolt by the priest Mattathias and his sons, the Maccabees. In 165, Judah Maccabee rededicates the Jewish temple. **ca 150-100** **JEWISH PHILOSOPHER ARISTOBULUS OF PANEAS** derives Greek philosophy from the wisdom of Moses.
141 **HAN WUDI, THE "MARTIAL EMPEROR,"** begins his 54-year-long reign. Through Legalist principles and an enormous bureaucracy, he seeks to augment the power and sway of the central government. He levies large taxes and establishes imperial monopolies on essential goods. **136** **CHINESE EMPEROR HAN WUDI** declares Confucianism the state ideology. **130s** **WITH THE INVASION BY CHINA** into northern Vietnam and Korea comes the import of Confucianist principles and a Chinese form of government.	**ca 140** **SERICULTURE,** the manufacture of silk, spreads throughout China and India and silk becomes a highly prized commodity, as in Persia, Mesopotamia, and the Roman Empire.	**124** **EMPEROR WUDI** establishes a de facto imperial university to stock his bureaucracy with educated officeholders. Confucian classics are used as the basis of the curriculum. **113** **LIU SHENG, A PRINCE OF THE HAN DYNASTY** in China, dies. A member of the wealthiest class of society, he and his consort are buried in full jade suits threaded with two and a half pounds of gold wire. **108** **SIMA QIAN** succeeds his father as Emperor Wudi's grand historian and assumes the task of completing *Shiji (Historical Records).*

SCIENCE & TECHNOLOGY	PEOPLE & SOCIETY
ca 100 CONSTRUCTION BEGINS on the Pyramid of the Sun and the Pyramid of the Moon at the growing urban complex of Teotihuacan in the northeast portion of the Valley of Mexico.	**ca 100** HOPEWELL PEOPLES, near present-day Toolesboro, Iowa, begin to build conical burial mounds overlooking the Iowa River.
144 ROME'S LONGEST AQUEDUCT, the Aqua Marcia, is built. **142** THE PONS AEMILIUS, Rome's first stone bridge across the Tiber River, is completed. **ca 140** GREEK ASTRONOMER HIPPARCHUS is credited with inventing the astrolabe, which measures the angle of the sun or a star above the horizon. He documents the brightness and position of nearly 850 stars.	**152** GREEK ATHLETE LEONIDAS OF RHODES wins three running events for the fourth straight time at the Olympic Games. **107** GAIUS MARIUS is elected consul in Rome. In order to engage in the ongoing war with Numidian King Jugurtha, Marius recruits an army of landless farmers.
ca 150 GREEK PHILOSOPHER CRATES OF MALLUS, living and working in Asia Minor, develops the first known globe. **100s** GREEK MERCHANT HIPPALUS capitalizes on utilizing monsoon winds to safely sail trade routes between India and the Mediterranean, knowledge likely applied earlier by Arab and Indian seamen. The southwestern wind of summer is later named after him.	**161** ISRAELITE JUDAH MACCABEE establishes diplomatic relations with Rome after the Hasmonean Revolt, spurred by the Seleucids' dedication of the temple to Zeus.
ca 165 THE EARLIEST KNOWN RECORD OF SUNSPOTS is made by Chinese astronomers. **100s** IRON TOOLS, such as shovels, picks, hoes, and sickles, enter into much more widespread use in China under the Han dynasty. The resulting agricultural surplus allows for the specialized manufacture of other crafts.	**138** ZHANG QIAN, an officer in the household of Emperor Wudi, embarks on a diplomatic and cultural expedition that brings him in contact with the Xiongnu, Tibetan, and other Central Asian peoples. **106** CHINESE HISTORIAN AND AUTHOR BAN ZHAO composes her *Admonitions for Women,* claiming fidelity and devotion to husbands as the essential feminine virtue.

THE BROTHERS GRACCHI

IN THE LATTER HALF of the Roman Republic, small landowners, the backbone of Rome's subsistence economy, suffered under a new rule that required every man of age to serve in the army for an entire campaign, regardless of duration. With Rome's manpower extended to its limit, the farms of peasants who were too far from home for too long fell into bankruptcy, only to be snatched up by wealthy aristocrats who were establishing large estates worked by slave labor. The gap between rich and poor was growing exponentially.

Tiberius Gracchus was born into this deteriorating situation. Well connected politically, he was elected in 133 B.C.E. to the tribunate of the plebs—representative of the lower classes of the Roman people—just like nearly every man in his family before him. He proposed a series of reforms to limit the power of large estate owners, which met with fierce opposition from senators with vested interests. Yet Gracchus was able not only to pass his bill, but also to fund it. In doing so, he gained fierce loyalty from masses of plebeians and fierce enmity from powerful patricians. He was clubbed to death in 132 in a riot initiated by the senator Scipio Nasica.

Ten years later another Gracchus, Tiberius's younger brother Gaius, was elected to the tribunate in 123. With the death of his brother, Gaius had inherited not only his family's holdings, but also its strong political views. Gaius turned his attention to both the problem of Rome's landless poor and the maltreatment by Rome of its Italian allies. His proposal to grant citizenship to all Latin-speaking allies led to Gaius's persecution and suicide in 121. A thousand men suspected to have been his supporters were killed soon afterward at the hands of consul Lucius Opimius.

Latin-speaking allies were granted Roman citizenship only 33 years later, in the aftermath of a bloody and unnecessary civil war.

POLITICS & POWER

ca 100 **THE POPULATION OF TEOTIHUACAN** reaches approximately 30,000.

86 **GAIUS MARIUS** returns from exile and marches on Rome. He places the city under military occupation.

83 **THREE YEARS AFTER MARIUS'S DEATH,** his political rival, Lucius Cornelius Sulla, marches on Rome and begins purging political enemies.

49 **JULIUS CAESAR** marches his troops across the Rubicon River into Italy. In 46 B.C.E., he is named dictator for life, an event that, within months, leads to his assassination by a group of senators.

64 **THE REMAINDER OF THE DETERIORATING SELEUCID EMPIRE,** a holdover from the conquests of Alexander the Great, is conquered by Roman forces. This brings Syria into Rome's growing dominion.

53 **THE BATTLE OF CARRHAE,** during which the Parthian forces rout a Roman army in southeast Turkey, prevents the Romans from moving farther east.

87 **EMPEROR WUDI** dies. Though his power is severely weakened by the end of his reign, at its height Han China reaches as far as modern-day Uzbekistan and northern and central Korea.

ca 57-18 **THREE RIVAL KINGDOMS** evolve in the Korean Peninsula: the Silla in 57, the Koguryo in 37, and the Paekche in 18.

GEOGRAPHY & ENVIRONMENT

ca 100 **A MASSIVE LAVA FLOW** covers the town of Cuicuilco and much of its surrounding farmland in the southern portion of the Mexican basin. Refugees flock to nearby Teotihuacan, increasing the extent of the city's regional influence.

58 **JULIUS CAESAR** begins his conquests of Gaul, modern-day France. By the end of the decade, he brings a large number of these Celtic groups into the growing sphere of the Roman world.

111 **CHINESE EMPEROR WUDI** establishes a military command center at the oasis city of Dunhuang, a vital outpost along the Silk Road.

ca 100 **GRANARIES FOR EMERGENCY FAMINE RELIEF** are established throughout China.

CULTURE & RELIGION

ca 36 **THE MAYA** begin to record their history using a base-20 Long Count calendar, the oldest complete record in Mesoamerica.

70s-40s **THE ORATIONS OF CICERO** firmly establish Stoicism in the Roman psyche.

ca 57-56 **CATULLUS,** regarded as the finest lyric poet of Rome, chronicles an intense and unhappy love affair with a woman he names Lesbia in a series of 25 poems.

ca 50s **THE ROMAN USE OF CURSE TABLETS,** dating back to 600 B.C.E., becomes more elaborate, calling for divine actions against rivals in love or business.

42 **CAESAR** is posthumously recognized by the Roman state as a god.

ca 100 **THE ARCHITECTURAL FORM KNOWN AS THE IWAN,** a large room open to one side, develops in Mesopotamia and becomes popular in Parthian and Sasanian construction.

63 **THE JEWISH STATE SHRINKS** when Roman general Pompey storms Jerusalem.

ca 50 **THE ART OF GLASSBLOWING** is refined to a highly advanced level by Syrian craftsmen.

ca 100 **HINDU SCHOLARS** continue to revise and put into writing the two great epic oral poems of India, the *Mahabharata* and the *Ramayana*. They infuse these reworkings with Hindu theology and ethical teachings.

CONNECTIONS

Crossroads of East African Trade

The benefits of widespread trade between far-flung lands, made possible by the administrative policies of imperial states throughout the ancient world, was not lost on cities in sub-Saharan Africa. Mentioned in multiple Greek sources, the East African city of Rhapta came to prominence as a stopping-off point for Arab mariners who traded metal weapons and iron tools for quantities of ivory, coconut oil, tortoiseshell, and rhinoceros horn. Greek and Roman coins unearthed in Tanzania suggest a Mediterranean presence, and a connection to Indonesian seamen has been theorized as well. Though extant until at least the sixth century C.E., no remains of this ancient marketplace have been found, keeping its exact location a matter of dispute.

SCIENCE & TECHNOLOGY	PEOPLE & SOCIETY
ca 100 NASCA PEOPLES of Peru's Ica Valley produce advanced woven textiles, building on the techniques of the earlier Paracas culture.	**ca 50** THE INHABITANTS OF CERROS, on Chetumal Bay of the Yucatán Peninsula, remove prior structures in order to build a civic center dominated by a small pyramid. It is decorated with immense countenances of the sun and Venus.
80 PHILOSOPHER POSEIDONIUS estimates the circumference of the Earth to a high degree of accuracy.	**89** THE SOCIAL WAR IN ITALY ends with Rome granting citizenship to allies on the peninsula. **73** ESCAPED SLAVE SPARTACUS launches a rebellion in Italy that lasts two years and requires eight Roman legions to quell. **46** AS DICTATOR, JULIUS CAESAR extends citizenship to the provinces, begins ambitious building projects to employ the urban poor, and reworks the Roman calendar.
ca 100 THE NABATAEAN CAPITAL OF PETRA, in the Great Rift Valley of modern-day Jordan, prospers. Wealth derived from the incense trade funds the building of remarkably well-wrought tombs and temples directly into sandstone cliffs.	**51** CLEOPATRA inherits control of the Egyptian throne upon the death of her father, Ptolemy XII. In 48 B.C.E. she meets Julius Caesar, becomes his lover, and has his son; later she marries Mark Antony after having twins by him.
ca 100 THE USE OF NEGATIVE NUMBERS becomes standard for Chinese mathematicians.	**ca 100** CHINESE EMPEROR WUDI raises taxes and institutes state monopolies on such commodities as iron and salt in order to finance his military expeditions and other undertakings. **81** "DEBATES ON SALT AND IRON" are held at the Han capital of Chang'an. Confucian arguments to limit government intervention in the economy prevail.

Bust of Caesar, crowned in laurel

JULIUS CAESAR

AT THE AGE OF 30, Gaius Julius Caesar approached a statue of Alexander the Great in tears, weeping that "Alexander at my age had conquered so many nations, and I have all this time done nothing that is memorable." That would not be the case for long. In 59 B.C.E. Caesar was appointed proconsul of three Roman provinces. With legions of the Roman army at his command and considerable political clout in Rome, Caesar was set to pursue his long-held ambition to conquer the known world. Over the course of the next eight years, Caesar would not only extend Roman dominion as far north as Britain, but also pave the way for the transformation of Roman governance from a republic to a dictatorship to an empire.

In 58 B.C.E., Caesar took his troops into Gallia Comata, a vast stretch of land comprising modern-day France. Caesar forced the Celtic tribes there to succumb to Roman domination and sent hundreds of thousands of newly made slaves back to Rome. He then conquered much of Britain in one of the largest naval invasions in history. After subduing 800 cities and 300 tribes, causing the death of over a million Gauls and enslaving a million more, Caesar returned to Rome where he was heralded as a liberator, as dictator for life, and even as a god.

POLITICS & POWER	GEOGRAPHY & ENVIRONMENT	CULTURE & RELIGION
	ca 1 C.E. CORN AND SQUASH are cultivated by people of the southwestern Basketmaker II culture, ancestors to Pueblo Indians.	**ca 1 C.E. CAHUACHI** emerges as the major center of the Nasca culture in southern Peru. With a very small permanent population, it most likely serves as a pilgrimage shrine to host large numbers only for ceremonial events.
32 B.C.E. OCTAVIAN, later known as Augustus, declares war on Cleopatra. The following year, one of his key military commanders, Marcus Agrippa, defeats Mark Antony's forces at the Battle of Actium.	**ca 30 B.C.E. THE POPULATION OF ROME** surges as the state employs hundreds of thousands of workers for numerous building projects of temples, baths, stadiums, and aqueducts. **20 B.C.E. AFTER 17 YEARS OF WORK, MARCUS AGRIPPA** completes a map of the world based on surveys of the Roman road system.	▶ **40-30 B.C.E. GREEK SCULPTORS AGESANDER, POLYDORUS, AND ATHENODORUS** sculpt "Laocoön." The work later influences Renaissance, baroque, and neoclassical sculptors. **29-19 B.C.E. ROMAN POET VIRGIL** composes his *Aeneid,* an epic account of the legendary founding of Rome. **ca 23 B.C.E. ROMAN POET HORACE** publishes his *Odes*.
40 B.C.E. PARTHIANS briefly capture Syria and Asia Minor. **37 B.C.E. THE ROMANS** install Herod, formerly tetrarch of Galilee, as king of Judea.	**19 C.E. AN EARTHQUAKE** in Syria kills more than 120,000 people. **ca 20 C.E. GREEK GEOGRAPHER AND HISTORIAN STRABO** describes the Arabian Peninsula as a land of fabulous wealth, a source of spices and frankincense.	**37-4 B.C.E. KING HEROD** supports Hellenistic culture and begins a massive building program in Palestine. **ca 29 C.E. JESUS OF NAZARETH** begins his ministry in Palestine and attracts devotees through his message of compassion and eternal salvation.
9 C.E. HAN ADMINISTRATOR AND COMMANDER WANG MANG claims the imperial throne as his own. His 16-year reign is the interregnum between the Western Han and Eastern Han periods. **17-23 C.E. THE RED EYEBROW REBELLION** helps to bring down Wang Mang's rule and leads to the restoration of the Han dynasty in China.	**ca 25 C.E. THE CAPITAL OF THE HAN DYNASTY** in China is moved to Luoyang from Chang'an following a rash of damage inflicted upon Chang'an during the previous years of chaos and rebellion.	**ca 1 C.E. CHINESE ARTISTS** produce *mingqi,* realistic earthenware figurines, to accompany the dead in their tombs.

SCIENCE & TECHNOLOGY

The sculpture "Laocoön," depicting the Trojan priest's death in the *Iliad*

ca 36 B.C.E. ROMAN WRITER AND SCHOLAR MARCUS TERENTIUS VARRO proposes the idea that invisible creatures that enter the body through the nose and mouth can cause illness and disease. This is the first known postulation of germ theory.

PEOPLE & SOCIETY

ca 1 C.E. EARLY NASCA PEOPLES settle in villages in the Nazca Valley of Peru.

27 B.C.E. THE ROMAN SENATE grants Octavian the unprecedented title of Augustus, meaning "consecrated," beginning his 41 years of unopposed rule. He ushers in his so-called Pax Romana, an era characterized by increased law, trade, communication, and prosperity throughout the Roman world. He is widely considered the first Roman emperor.

ca 20 C.E. DRUIDISM, A CELTIC RELIGION, flourishes in Britain and Gaul. Attempts at suppression are made by Roman Emperor Tiberius.

30 B.C.E. MARK ANTONY AND CLEOPATRA, on the verge of losing their political power in the eastern Mediterranean, commit suicide. The Ptolemaic dynasty of pharaohs ends and Egypt becomes a Roman province.

ca 30 C.E. JESUS OF NAZARETH, preaching at a time of great tension between Roman overlords and Jewish subjects in Palestine, is crucified by Roman authorities.

39 C.E. SISTERS TRUNG TRAC AND TRUNG NHI lead a rebellion against their Han overlords in what is now northern Vietnam. They briefly establish an autonomous state before being beaten down by Chinese forces and committing suicide in 43 C.E.

WHAT LIFE WAS LIKE

In the Time of Jesus

Judea in the first century C.E. was a land rife with political and social tension between gentiles and Jews, between Roman overlords and subjects, and among various sects of Judaism itself. Any man capable of attracting crowds was viewed as politically dangerous by a number of interested parties, Roman governors and Jewish high priests alike, as there was no dearth of Jews ready at a moment's notice to begin a holy war against Rome. Jesus of Nazareth was never charged in his native region of Galilee with any serious legal offense, but when he entered Jerusalem to observe the Passover and was greeted by a mass of admirers, even his message of compassion became a portent of conflict.

THE REBELLION OF THE TRUNG SISTERS

WOMEN IN ANCIENT Vietnamese society were far from the idealized Confucian wife and mother described by Chinese historian and author Ban Zhao in her *Admonitions for Women*. In Vietnam, women were respected and played active roles in social and economic life. This cultural tradition came into conflict with that of Han China, which had invaded and occupied northern Vietnam in the second century B.C.E. Local resistance built up, and in 39 C.E., two sisters, Trung Trac and Trung Nhi, led a rebellion against Chinese occupation.

When Trung Trac's husband was assassinated for plotting against the Chinese, she took control of the operation. Along with her sister, mother, and members of the aristocracy, she raised a force of 80,000 men and women and marched on Lien Lau, forcing the Chinese general who had killed her husband to flee along with all his troops. Over the next three years, this force of untrained and under-supplied Vietnamese rebels wrested dozens of citadels in northern Vietnam from Chinese rule. In many cases, the leaders of the Vietnamese forces were women, including the Trung sisters' mother.

At Me Linh, on the Red River near modern-day Haiphong, the Trung sisters proclaimed themselves joint queens of an autonomous Vietnamese state extending from southern China to central Vietnam. But when Chinese General Ma Yuan arrived with his battle-hardy and well-trained troops in 43, the sisters and their forces were little match for them. With sure defeat at hand, the Trung sisters threw themselves into the Red River, and the Vietnamese people were once again brought under Chinese dominion. Though their efforts were short-lived, the Trung sisters are still celebrated as heroines and symbols of the first organized resistance against foreign occupation in Vietnam. Their rebellion was certainly not to be the last.

POLITICS & POWER	GEOGRAPHY & ENVIRONMENT	CULTURE & RELIGION
ca 50 HOPEWELL PEOPLES of the east-central area of North America develop increasingly more sophisticated structures made of earth.	 Pliny the Elder, a Roman naturalist and scholar	**ca 50 HOPEWELL PEOPLES** of the east-central area of North America hone their artistic style. As they expand their rituals associated with burial, many finely produced crafts go to the graves of important persons.
60-61 BOUDICCA, queen of the Briton Iceni tribe, leads a rebellion in East Anglia that massacres 70,000 Romans and pro-Roman Britons. After Boudicca's defeat and suicide, her name comes to represent native resistance to Roman occupation. **69 FOLLOWING EMPEROR NERO'S SUICIDE** and the end of the Julio-Claudian line of succession, generals across the Roman Empire vie for the imperial title. At the end of the "year of the four emperors," Vespasian establishes the Flavian dynasty.	**64 FIRE DESTROYS HALF OF ROME.** Emperor Nero blames the Christian community; meanwhile, he undertakes an opulent imperial building project, his Golden House, on the ashes. **79 VESUVIUS ERUPTS,** burying the nearby cities of Pompeii, Herculaneum, and Stabiae under many feet of ash and pumice.	◀ **77 ROMAN AUTHOR AND SAVANT PLINY THE ELDER** completes his *Natural History,* a compilation of 37 books encompassing not only the natural sciences but their application to civilization. He dies of asphyxiation while observing the eruption of Vesuvius in 79. **ca 81-96 EASTERN CULTS** spread in Rome. During Domitian's reign, a temple complex for Isis and Serapis is constructed on Rome's Campus Martius.
66 THE FIRST JEWISH-ROMAN WAR begins with ordinary Jewish priests and renegade high priests leading a successful attack on the Roman garrison in Judaea. The skirmish results in the destruction of Jerusalem and its temple in 70. Roman forces put an end to the Great Jewish Revolt in 72-73 by sieging and overcoming the remaining holdouts of Jewish rebels, some of whom are in the hilltop fortress known as Masada.	**60 AN EARTHQUAKE** destroys the Phrygian city of Laodicea in the Roman province of Asia.	**ca 48 CHRISTIAN CONVERT TURNED MISSIONARY SAUL OF TARSUS** (later known as St. Paul) begins efforts to bring non-Jews into the Christian community. He travels throughout the eastern Roman Empire, corresponding with converts in epistles on matters of faith. **ca 80 WORK ON THE GOSPELS,** accounts of Jesus of Nazareth's life and teachings, is undertaken by members of the new Christian faith.
73 HAN FORCES under General Ban Chao reestablish Chinese control of Central Asia from the nomadic Xiongnu tribes, a pattern that is often repeated during the Han dynasty.	**70 THE COURSE** of China's Yellow River shifts north from its former mouth on the Yellow Sea.	**53 CHRISTIAN APOSTLE AND MISSIONARY THOMAS,** after some initial success converting Indians to Christianity, is martyred in Madras (now Chennai) in northwestern India. **57-75 BUDDHISM** is introduced to China by Han Emperor Mingdi. **68 THE WHITE HORSE TEMPLE,** one of the earliest Buddhist temples in China, is built just outside the new Han capital at Luoyang. **ca 78-102 KANISKA,** during his reign as king of the Kushan dynasty, is instrumental in spreading Buddhism into Central Asia.

SCIENCE & TECHNOLOGY

ca 100 THE PYRAMID OF THE SUN IN TEOTIHUACAN rises 216 feet tall and measures 547,200 square feet at its base. It is one of the largest structures of its type found in the Western Hemisphere.

ca 70 ROMAN EMPEROR VESPASIAN begins construction of the Flavian Amphitheater, better known as the Colosseum. With a 50,000-spectator capacity, it is equipped with underground passageways and trap doors. It can even be flooded to host mock naval battles.

ca 80 GREEK PHYSICIAN PEDANIUS DIOSCURIDES writes his *On Medicine,* a catalog of more than 600 plants and their methods of preparation and medicinal effects.

ca 80 AN ASTRONOMICAL CALCULATOR called the Antikythera mechanism is invented.

ca 62 MATHEMATICIAN AND INVENTOR HERON OF ALEXANDRIA describes mechanical labor-saving devices such as a steam engine, a water clock, a water organ, and an odometer. A world highly dependent on slave labor pays him little heed.

ca 50 CHINESE ASTRONOMERS are established as a skilled professional class.

PEOPLE & SOCIETY

ca 50 THE ZAPOTEC CAPITAL Monte Albán grows and the construction of several temples begins.

40s ROMAN EMPEROR CLAUDIUS creates an imperial bureaucracy of professional administrators, composed largely of former slaves.

ca 89 AFTER EMPEROR DOMITIAN BANISHES PHILOSOPHERS FROM ROME, Stoic philosopher and former slave Epictetus establishes a school at Nicopolis in Epirus that attracts many upper-class Romans.

40-70 THE GREEK MANUAL *CIRCUMNAVIGATION OF THE RED SEA* describes trading in the Red Sea and along the East African coast to India.

ca 100 C.E. INDIAN TEXTILES, Chinese silk, Afghan turquoise, and southeast Asian spices are traded along the Silk Road for Roman gold and silver.

92 BAN GU, author of *The History of the Former Han Dynasty,* dies. His sister, Ban Zhao, completes the work.

MASADA

IN 66 C.E. A GROUP of Jewish rebels took a fortress in the Judaean Desert overlooking the Dead Sea. Known as Masada, from the Hebrew word for fortress, it had been built a hundred years earlier by the Roman-appointed King Herod. This act of rebellion was one of the first of the Great Jewish Revolt that lasted the next seven years and resulted in one of the diasporas that characterize much of Jewish history.

In 72, having already destroyed and looted Jerusalem itself, Roman forces approached Masada with the intention of putting down with finality this local nuisance. The story, as told by Jewish historian Flavius Josephus, is that after an unopposed siege of the fortress, Roman forces knocked through the walls only to find 1,000 dead bodies of men, women, and children, the result of a mass suicide. Archaeological remains tell a slightly different story. Twenty-five skeletons found in a nearby cave hint that some attempted escape. Others, greatly outnumbered, may have fought to the death. In any case, the story of Masada provides a vivid example of the ongoing human struggle for freedom.

Masada, a hilltop fortress in the Judaean Desert

FROZEN IN TIME: POMPEII 79 C.E.

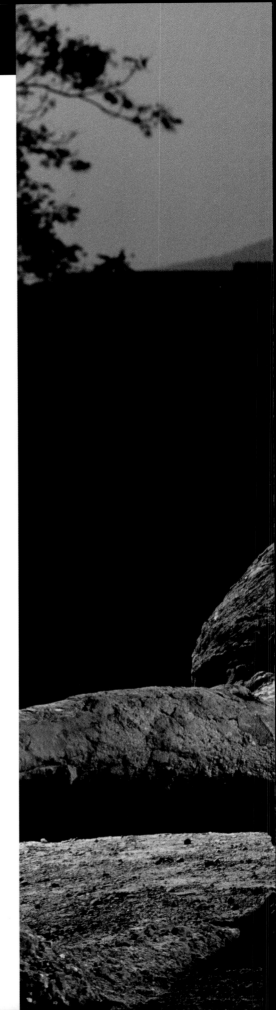

On the early afternoon of August 24, 79 C.E., the cone of Mount Vesuvius erupted 17 miles into the air, sending forth a column of dust, smoke, and pumice, the fallout of which covered a 25-mile span from Mount Vesuvius outward. It buried nearby towns such as Pompeii, Herculaneum, and Stabiae under many feet of ash and pumice, at the same time preserving certain delicacies of their construction, such as the fresco of a young Roman couple (left). Pliny the Elder—statesman, naturalist, and author of *Natural History*—was stationed at the time at the nearby port of Misenum. He ventured into the midst of the destruction out of academic interest and a heroic bent; he never made it out. His nephew, Pliny the Younger, who had stayed behind at Misenum, later wrote a description of the day's events to the historian Tacitus:

> A dense, black cloud was coming up behind us, spreading over the earth like a flood. . . . Darkness fell, not the dark of a moonless or cloudy night, but as if a lamp had been put out in a closed room. You could hear the shrieks of women, the wailing of infants, and the shouting of men; some were calling their parents, others their children or wives, trying to recognize them by their voices. People bewailed their own fate or that of their relatives, and there were some who prayed for death in their terror of dying. . . . I could boast that not a groan or cry of fear escaped me in these perils, but I admit that I derived some poor consolation in my mortal lot from the belief that the whole world was dying with me, and I with it.

In the days and weeks that followed the eruption, former residents along with teams of salvage workers sent from Rome by the Emperor Titus dug out what they could from the buried cities. Residents searched for family members or personal belongings left behind, salvage workers looked for statuary or marble to be shipped back to Rome, looters sought newly buried treasure. Within decades, though, Pompeii and other nearby cities had become the stuff of legend, disappearing completely from maps by the fourth century C.E.

Rediscovered in the late 1500s, the ruins of Pompeii have preserved a glimpse into the daily life of citizens of the Roman Empire that would otherwise be lost to history. The city center, its amphitheater, its shops and sidestreets, its domestic architecture and interior decoration, even the remains of Vesuvius's victims can still be seen as they were, frozen in time, August 24, 79 C.E.

ABOVE: This fresco of a young Roman couple was kept in pristine condition for centuries by Vesuvius's eruption. Much of what is known about Roman wall painting derives from such Pompeiian examples. **RIGHT:** Mount Vesuvius looms in the background over one of its victims. This graphic moment in time has been preserved by plaster poured into the cavity left by a man's decomposed body, a technique developed in 1864 by archaeologist Giuseppe Fiorelli.

100-170 C.E.

THE AMERICAS

POLITICS & POWER

ca 100 TEOTIHUACAN, THE "CITY OF THE GODS," near modern-day Mexico City, rises to prominence over nearby areas through military domination, trade, and cultural influence. By 150, its population nearly triples from its origins.

ca 100 EVIDENCE OF THE ADENA CULTURE of eastern North America gradually dwindles and vanishes, due to their assimilation into the contemporaneous Hopewell culture.

GEOGRAPHY & ENVIRONMENT

▼ **ca 100** HOPEWELL PEOPLES of eastern North America engage in trade that gathers materials from regions as distant as the Rocky Mountains, the Great Lakes, and the Appalachians.

CULTURE & RELIGION

ca 100 MOCHE CULTURE continues to be characterized not only by a high level of agricultural knowledge, but also by advanced metalworking. Artisans master the technique of inlaying turquoise designs on gold plaques and create ornate ceramics.

Hopewell harvest ceremony

EUROPE

POLITICS & POWER

101 ROMAN EMPEROR TRAJAN further extends the boundaries of the Roman Empire beyond the Danube River into Dacia.

161 MARCUS AURELIUS becomes emperor of Rome following the death of his adoptive father Antoninus Pius. Though he espouses the Stoic philosophy throughout his emperorship, he is almost constantly at war.

CULTURE & RELIGION

ca 109 ROMAN HISTORIAN TACITUS writes a history of Rome sharply critical of the emperors following Augustus.

ca 150 GREEK PHILOSOPHER and theologian Justin Martyr reconciles Greek philosophy with Christian teachings and rejects Greek mythology.

MIDDLE EAST & AFRICA

POLITICS & POWER

114 ROMAN EMPEROR TRAJAN conquers Armenia and Mesopotamia.

162-166 WARFARE is renewed between Romans and Parthians over control of Armenia. The result is Persian losses.

GEOGRAPHY & ENVIRONMENT

106 PETRA, in modern-day Jordan, is conquered and subsumed into the Roman Empire.

ca 150 IN *GEOGRAPHY,* Egyptian astronomer, mathematician, and geographer Ptolemy sets out the whole of the world as it is known to the Romans. It stretches from the Shetland Islands in the north to the sources of the Nile in the south, from China and Southeast Asia in the east to the Canary Islands in the west.

CULTURE & RELIGION

132-135 BAR KOCHBA heads a revolt against Rome that leads to the persecution and expulsion of Jews from Jerusalem.

ASIA & OCEANIA

POLITICS & POWER

100s LARGE LANDOWNERS gain an upper hand in the government of Han dynasty China. They evade taxes and burden peasants with the costs of governance, even raising private armies to enforce their interests.

GEOGRAPHY & ENVIRONMENT

116 CHINESE ASTRONOMER ZHANG HENG innovates a grid system for maps.

CULTURE & RELIGION

148 A PARTHIAN MONK, AN SHIGAO, arrives in Luoyang and begins one of the first translations of Buddhist sutras into Chinese. He is instrumental in the establishment of Buddhism in China.

SCIENCE & TECHNOLOGY	PEOPLE & SOCIETY
ca 100 **THE MOCHE** begin construction of the Huaca del Sol, or Pyramid of the Sun, which is one of the largest structures of its day in the Americas.	**ca 100** **EARLY PUEBLOAN PEOPLE** settle into the four corners region of southwestern North America. They weave baskets and sandals for everyday use and supplement hunting and gathering with the cultivation of corn and squash. **ca 150** **THE INHABITANTS OF BECAN,** on the Yucatán Peninsula, build a defensive ditch around their settlement, evidence of the large role warfare played in Maya civilization.
ca 100 **ROMANS** expand their system of roads so they can supply their border forts and move troops more quickly. **ca 100** **MINES IN BRITAIN** supply the Roman Empire with lead and tin. **122** **HADRIAN'S WALL** is constructed in northern Britain to protect the Roman Empire from barbarian invaders. The barrier extends from coast to coast, running for 73 miles.	**ca 100** **MEN FROM THE PROVINCES** join the Roman army in order to gain citizenship and learn the trade of war. **ca 100** **SKILLED CHARIOT DRIVERS** become popular heroes in Rome.
ca 150 **GRECO-ROMAN** Egyptian scientist Ptolemy writes *Mathematike Syntaxis,* later known as the *Almagest,* a book that remains the primary Western text on astronomy until the scientific revolution.	**130** **ROMAN EMPEROR HADRIAN** establishes the city of Antinopolis in Egypt in honor of his companion Antinous, who drowned in the Nile that year.
ca 105 **CHINESE COURT OFFICIAL CAI LUN** describes the modern method of making paper from hemp, bark, old rags, and fishnets. Some sources trace its invention back to 150 B.C.E. **132** **THE SEISMOSCOPE** and armillary sphere are developed by Chang Heng, an astronomer of Han China.	**100s** **MALAY PEOPLE** of Southeast Asia participate in the widespread trade network made possible by classical empires. Due to their seafaring way of life, Malay culture expands throughout the Malay Peninsula and neighboring islands.

ART OF THE MOCHE

HOW DOES AN ANCIENT CULTURE preserve and pass along a history of its leaders, gods, mores, and daily life in the absence of a system of written communication? In the case of the Moche people of coastal Peru, it was through their art.

A people of extremes, the Moche were able to produce pieces breathtaking in their emotional expressiveness or shocking in their gruesome brutality. They used molds to create fired clay for ceramics but worked each piece in an individual way, leaving to posterity a great quantity of unique artifacts. Subjects of their ceramic vessels run the gamut, from portraitures of important people to scenes of mythology, sexuality, or everyday life.

Moche temple complexes were adorned with colorful murals, a common motif of which is a character named the Decapitator, who is often represented with a multitude of arms, always with a knife in one of them and a severed head gripped by the hair in another. Some scenes are so gruesome that scholars assumed them to be hyperbole until archaeological remains confirmed their place in Moche ritual. Through the abundance and remarkable clarity of these pieces of art, a glimpse into the workings of this lost society is made possible.

Victim of the Decapitator, a common Moche motif

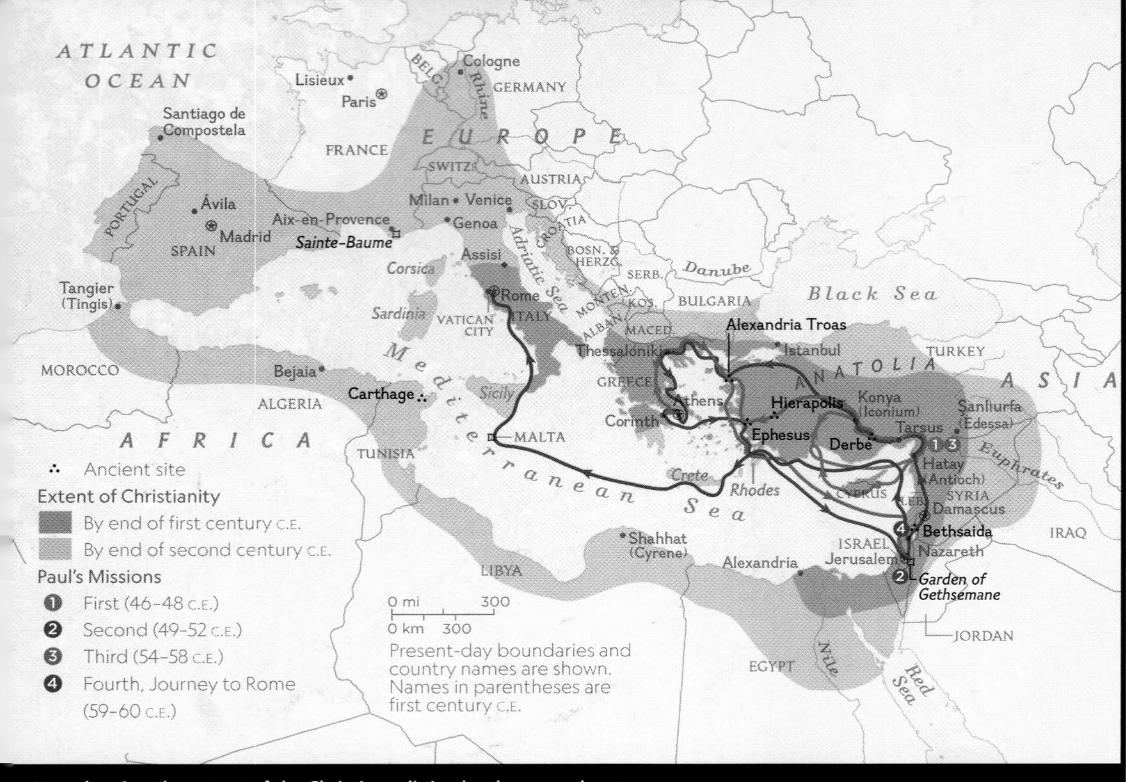

Map showing the extent of the Christian religion by the second century C.E.

POLITICS & POWER

224 THE PARTHIAN EMPIRE, already weakened by internal rebellion, is brought down by the Sassanians of Persia. They will rule Mesopotamia from their capital at Ctesiphon, on the Tigris River near modern-day Baghdad, for the next 400 years.

184 THE YELLOW TURBAN REBELLION erupts in eastern China. Led by Daoist leader Zhang Jue, this peasant rebellion contributes to the weakening state of the Later Han dynasty, requiring a huge army and great expense to suppress.

220-221 AFTER THE COLLAPSE of the Later Han dynasty, China is divided among three territorial states: Wei in the north, Wu south of the Yangtze River, and Shu-Han in the southwest. This is known as the Three Kingdoms period.

GEOGRAPHY & ENVIRONMENT

194 ROMAN EMPEROR SEPTIMIUS SEVERUS divides the Roman province of Syria into two parts, Syria Coele in the north and Syria Phoenice in the south.

▲ **ca 200 THE ROMAN HIGHWAY SYSTEM,** covering some 250,000 miles, facilitated the spread of Christianity as evangelists brought the doctrine into North Africa and across the Mediterranean and Europe.

226 A WU PREFECTURE is established in southern China and named Guangzhou. This port city thrives and grows in both population and wealth.

CULTURE & RELIGION

ca 200 THE MONUMENTAL ARCHITECTURE OF TEOTIHUACAN includes the Pyramid of the Feathered Serpent, Quetzalcoatl, and the 130-foot-wide, 1.5-mile-long Avenue of the Dead. It is one of the architectural masterpieces of Mesoamerica.

203 VIBEA PERPETUA, a young Roman mother, writes an account of her trial and imprisonment for being a Christian. She is later martyred. Her text is one of the few surviving documents written by a woman in the ancient world.

ca 180 CHRISTIAN THEOLOGIAN IRENAEUS writes *Against Heresies,* a refutation of Gnosticism. His writings promote an authoritative canon of Scriptures, the office of the bishop, and the "Rule of Truth," a creed to repudiate heresy.

ca 200 JEWISH SCHOLARS AND RABBIS begin compiling the Mishna, the collection of Jewish legal and moral precepts that serve as the basis of the Talmud.

ca 224-241 KING ARDASHIR I, the first king of the Sasanian Empire in Persia, makes Zoroastrianism the state religion.

ca 175 CONFUCIAN CLASSICS are inscribed on stone stelae at the Imperial Academy in the Han capital of Luoyang.

ca 200 THE PRACTICE OF BUDDHISM undergoes changes that make it more accessible to the layman. Termed Mahayana, this new form of Buddhism reveres the Buddha as divine, allowing for the existence of Boddhisatvas (enlightened beings who delay their entry into nirvana to provide guidance to others).

ca 220 WITH THE DISSOLUTION OF THE HAN DYNASTY, interest in its state ideology, Confucianism, begins to wane.

SCIENCE & TECHNOLOGY

ca 200 STONE-WALLED COMPOUNDS begin to replace the previous, less substantial mud-brick buildings of the city of Teotihuacan in the Mexican basin.

ca 200 THE HOHOKAM PEOPLE develop dry farming techniques to harvest squash, beans, and maize twice a year in the harsh, semiarid environment around the Phoenix basin, in today's Arizona.

ca 216 GREEK PHYSICIAN GALEN OF PERGAMUM dies. In his lifetime he was a prolific thinker and writer, perhaps even developing an early form of brain surgery.

216 THE IMMENSE BATHS OF CARACALLA in Rome are completed. Equipped with an Olympic-size swimming pool, a cold and hot pool room, and space for exercise and games, it can accommodate up to 10,000 people at once.

ca 224 THE CULTIVATION OF EASTERN CROPS such as rice, sugarcane, and eggplant is introduced into Iran by merchants of the newly formed Sassanid Empire, who trade extensively with peoples to both the East and West.

ca 180 THE ZOETROPE becomes popular in China. The slotted rotating cylinder, imprinted with sequential images, gives the impression that the pictures are in motion.

PEOPLE & SOCIETY

100s THE STREET OF THE DEAD, the main thoroughfare of Teotihuacan, is lined with about 100 palaces that house priests and dignitaries. The working populace lives outside of the city.

ca 200 PEOPLES OF COASTAL CALIFORNIA develop advanced fishing skills to extract food from the abundant marine supply. They also engage in long-distance trade that spreads seashells throughout the region.

180 THE POPULATION OF THE ROMAN EMPIRE declines significantly following a 15-year outbreak of the Antonine Plague, thought to perhaps have even claimed Emperor Marcus Aurelius.

229 HISTORIAN DIO CASSIUS retires from politics to finish his *History of Rome*, an effort comprising 80 books, many of which are still in existence.

ca 200 THE NOK CULTURE of West Africa, modern-day Nigeria, fades from the historical record. The clay figures it produced are some of the earliest examples of stylized sculpture in sub-Saharan Africa.

220 CHINESE GENERAL CAO CAO, who put down the Yellow Turban Rebellion, dies at Luoyang. In the last phase of his career, he consolidated power in the state of Wei in northern China.

220 CAO PI, SON OF GENERAL CAO CAO, is crowned the first emperor of the Wei dynasty in northern China.

THE RISE OF CHRISTIANITY

THE CHRISTIAN CHURCH began as a clandestine sect of Judaism that met in homes, as opposed to public centers of worship, and was deemed illegal by the Roman Empire. Around 45 C.E., the freshly converted Paul of Tarsus began a lifetime of missionary work that sought to spread Jesus's message to the non-Jewish world, at the expense of early Christianity's essentially Jewish character and to the dismay of many early Christian conservatives.

Paul traveled throughout the eastern Mediterranean, evangelizing and making converts with whom he corresponded by letter, a corpus of writing that now constitutes a portion of the New Testament. The production of the Gospels soon afterward paved the way for a more structured ministry, and persecution by the Roman Empire served only to strengthen the missionary zeal of the church's faithful. Sympathy for this salvation-based religion continued to increase, culminating in 313 C.E. when Emperor Constantine I extended toleration for Christians throughout the Roman Empire and subscribed to the religion himself.

A great influx of new converts who saw the advantages of adopting the emperor's faith ensued. Though this may have diluted the church's constituency, it did not slow its pace of expansion. Gregory the Illuminator was already converting the kingdom of Armenia, while Nestorian Christians pushed farther into Central Asia, all the way to China. Ulfilas was soon preaching to the Goths and translating the Bible into their language; Martin of Tours found converts in Gaul, Patrick in Ireland, and Frumentius in Ethiopia. A Christian church, which was said to have been founded by the missionary apostle Thomas, was even known to exist in southern India. Indeed, by the close of the fifth century, barely a corner of the Western world was untouched by this religion of humble origins.

POLITICS & POWER	GEOGRAPHY & ENVIRONMENT	CULTURE & RELIGION
ca 250 MAYA SOCIETIES in the southern lowlands of the Yucatán Peninsula enter into what is considered their Classic period, characterized by kings ruling over powerful city-states that conduct their own affairs and carry out their own trade.		**300** JADE is closely associated with ceremonies and burials in Costa Rica. Marble, Mexican ceramics, and obsidian from Honduras and El Salvador are evidence of trade with northern neighbors. Marble sculpture of Roman emperor Diocletian
235-284 TWENTY-SEVEN CLAIMANTS to the imperial throne of Rome successively seize power and hold it briefly. All but four die violently at the hands of either rivals or their own troops. **286** ROMAN EMPEROR DIOCLETIAN splits his empire into two equal administrative units. **293** ROMAN EMPEROR DIOCLETIAN sets up the tetrarchy, a system of deputy emperorship with an Augustus ruling in either half of the Roman Empire and a Caesar assigned to him as collaborator and successor.	**ca 251** THE PLAGUE OF CYPRIAN spreads from Ethiopia to Rome, where it lasts for nearly 20 years and, at its peak, kills 5,000 people a day.	**ca 251-258** DENIS, PATRON SAINT OF FRANCE and reputedly first bishop of Paris, is martyred by either Roman Emperor Decius or Valerian. ◀ **303-304** ROMAN EMPEROR DIOCLETIAN issues four edicts of nontoleration of Christianity. Thus begins the most severe period of Christian martyrdom.
256-260 THE SASSANID EMPIRE under Shapur I defeats several Roman armies, ravages Syria, and captures Roman Emperor Valerian. **272** ROMANS CAPTURE PALMYRA in south-central Syria and its queen, Zenobia. **ca 299** A TREATY is imposed on Persia and Rome, bringing peace to their frontier. Romans build forts and roads for the frontier defense system.	**256** THE PLAGUE ravages Alexandria. Most citizens flee the city, but Christians remain to care for the victims. **ca 300** CHRISTIAN COMMUNITIES flourish in the Middle East and North Africa, as well as in even more distant locales.	**ca 238** GREGORY THE WONDERWORKER makes many Christian converts in central Anatolia. **240** THE PROPHET MANI preaches a new universal religion that blends elements of Zoroastrianism, Christianity, and Gnosticism into a cosmopolitan message. **ca 286** ST. ANTHONY OF EGYPT wanders into the desert, where he remains for about 19 years in solitude and austerity. He is widely considered the founder of Christian monasticism.
238-247 CHINESE HISTORICAL ACCOUNTS describe a female ruler named Himiko, or "sun daughter," in archaic Japan who wielded both political and religious authority.	**233-271** CHINESE GEOGRAPHER PEI XIU is the first to use a system of north-south and east-west parallels.	**ca 220s** DAOISM gains more adherents in China than ever before, thanks in part to less competition from Confucianism and an ideology that seeks inner peace in a confusing world.

SCIENCE & TECHNOLOGY	PEOPLE & SOCIETY
ca 300 THE MOCHE CULTURE has become established in northern coastal Peru. Its pyramid temples are made of adobe bricks and painted with polychrome murals.	**ca 300** PUEBLOAN PATTERNS OF LIFE become widespread on the Colorado Plateau, and in northern regions of modern-day New Mexico.
271 CONSTRUCTION OF EMPEROR AURELIAN'S DEFENSIVE WALL is undertaken in Rome. This massive barricade, 12.5 miles long and about 13 feet thick, is representative of the walls being built around cities throughout the Roman Empire, a trend that continues well into the Middle Ages.	**274** EMPEROR AURELIAN establishes the Sol Invictus cult—which worships a Syrian sun god—as an official cult. It remains the primary imperial worship of Rome until it is displaced by Christianity. **305** FOLLOWING DIOCLETIAN'S RETIREMENT from politics and his own imperial post, the tetrarchy he established to govern the far-flung Roman Empire devolves into a number of factions vying for sole control, and civil war ensues.
ca 275-300 THE MINTING OF COINS is begun in the Ethiopian kingdom of Aksum.	**ca 260** ROMAN SOLDIERS CAPTURED IN ANTIOCH by the Sassanid forces of Shapur I are moved to Iran, where their advanced technical skills are used in building the city of Gondeshapur and a dam at Shushtar, named the Dam of Caesar. Other captives start Christian communities in Iran. **270** PLOTINUS dies, having founded the school of Neoplatonism, which dominates philosophical thinking for centuries and affects Christian and, to a lesser degree, Islamic theological thought.
269 A MANUAL ON ASTROLOGY is composed by Indian scholar Sphujidhvaja. It is based on translations of Greek originals. **ca 300s** A STRONGER VARIATION OF THE SUSPENSION BRIDGE appears in India. It utilizes cables of braided bamboo and, later, of iron chain.	**ca 300** THE TOMB CULTURE OF JAPAN, in which leaders are buried in elaborate sepulchres with clay figurines, flourishes.

THE NASCA LINES

THE NASCA LINES, located in the arid deserts of southern coastal Peru, are a jigsaw puzzle that scholars and conspiracy theorists alike have been grappling with since their shapes were revealed by airline pilots in the 1920s. Visible only from the air, they consist of an immense number of geoglyphs, or markings made in the ground, in a variety of shapes and sizes. Some are strictly geometric—lines, triangles, trapezoids, and spirals—while others are more animated representations of flowers, trees, birds, other animals, and even one peculiar anthropomorphic figure who is referred to as the Owl Man.

The presence of these lines has elicited a number of explanations to justify their presence, some scientifically rigorous, others less so. Since the bulk of the lines were made over an 800-year period from about 200 B.C.E. to 600 C.E., it is reasonable to assume they may have served manifold functions largely associated with rituals, planting, and the extraction of water from a harsh desert environment. We know the Nasca were skilled in irrigation, constructing a network of channels that linked the Nasca River with underground water flowing from the Andes. Just how connected the lines may be to these irrigation channels or other subterranean water supplies remains unknown.

Two workers measure the lines of the Spider glyph.

POLITICS & POWER	GEOGRAPHY & ENVIRONMENT	CULTURE & RELIGION
	ca 300 **LARGE-SCALE EFFIGY MOUNDS** in the shapes of birds, mammals, and reptiles are constructed by American Indians in the upper Mississippi area.	**300s** **DURING THE CLASSIC PERIOD OF MAYA CIVILIZATION,** many intellectual endeavors are pursued, including formulation of a system of writing.
312 **ROMAN GENERAL CONSTANTINE I** marches on Rome and at the Battle of the Milvian Bridge usurps the imperial title from the last aggressivley pagan emperor in the east, his brother-in-law Maxentius. **358** **AFTER CONTINUED RAIDS** and increasing pressure on its borders, the Roman Empire is compelled to abandon the region of modern-day Belgium to the Franks.	**330** **CONSTANTINE I** dedicates the ancient Greek city of Byzantium as his new capital. Fashioning it a "new Rome," he renames it Constantinople. It is located on the European side of the Sea of Marmora, the entrance to the Black Sea.	**313** **THE EDICT OF MILAN** is issued by Eastern Roman Emperors Constantine and Licinius, confirming official toleration by the Roman Empire of Christianity and all other religions.
ca 350 **THE ETHIOPIAN KINGDOM OF AKSUM** invades and brings about the fall of the kingdoms of Meroe in Sudan in the southwestern Arabian Peninsula.		
300s **CHANDRAGUPTA AND HIS SON SAMUDRA** expand dominion throughout most of India through alliances and military force. They create the first centrally administered empire in India since the Mauryan, yet allow local governments to remain intact. **313** **THE CHINESE COLONY OF NANGNANG** in the northwestern portion of the Korean Peninsula is retaken by Korean forces. **316** **THE XIONGNU ARMY** sacks Chang'an, bringing an end to the western Jin dynasty.		**310** **BUDDHIST MONK FOTUDENG** arrives in Chang'an.

Model showing the Colosseum's place amid the monuments of Rome at the time of Constantine I

SCIENCE & TECHNOLOGY

300s MAYA PEOPLE make sophisticated astronomical observations and develop a system of mathematics that incorporates the number zero.

◀ **ca 313** ROMAN EMPEROR CONSTANTINE I undertakes construction on a number of basilicas in Rome, including the Basilicas of St. Peter and of St. Paul.

ca 340 AN ADVANCED CATAPULT DESIGN is developed in Macedonia.

361 THE CITY OF CONSTANTINOPLE passes regulations requiring physicians to receive a license in order to practice.

300s THE KINGDOM OF AKSUM erects immense monolithic granite obelisks, perhaps in memorial to deceased kings. The largest one weighs approximately five tons and stands taller than even the largest Egyptian obelisk.

ca 320 CHINESE RIDERS begin to use paired, full-length stirrups, giving them far greater control of the horse during warfare.

PEOPLE & SOCIETY

300s HOPEWELL PEOPLES continue to build ceremonial mounds, containing beautiful artwork, near present-day Chillicothe, Ohio.

325 ROMAN EMPEROR CONSTANTINE I embraces Christianity and institutionalizes the faith throughout the Roman Empire. He calls bishops to the first ecumenical council, located at Nicaea near Constantinople. At this council, the Nicene Creed is developed, specifying the doctrinal relationship of Jesus to God.

360 MARTIN OF TOURS, a former Roman soldier, founds the first monastery in Gaul, dedicated to spreading Christianity to rural areas.

ca 330 AKSUMITE KING EZANA is converted to Christianity by the Syrian apostle Frumentius. During Ezana's reign, the Ethiopian kingdom of Axum reaches its height, extending its borders west into modern-day Sudan and east into the southern Arabian Peninsula.

300s NOMADIC PEOPLE from the north pour into northern China following the dissolution of the Han dynasty. They establish large kingdoms there that will dominate the region for many successive centuries.

361 FAMOUS CHINESE CALLIGRAPHER WANG XIZHI dies. Even in his own lifetime, his signature is said to be priceless.

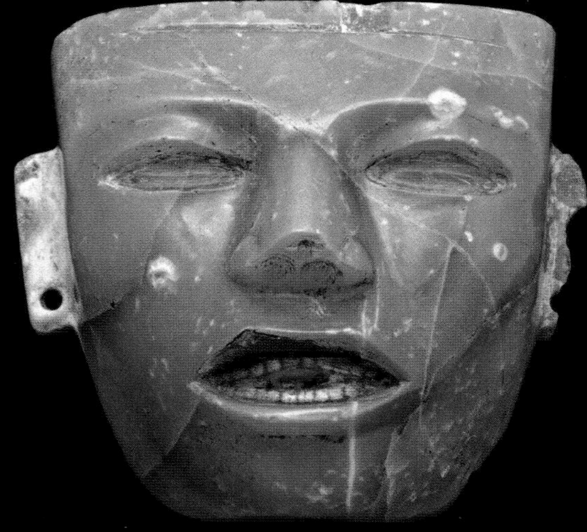

Stone mask unearthed at Teotihuacan

TEOTIHUACAN

TEOTIHUACAN, located in the Valley of Mexico only 30 miles northeast of modern-day Mexico City, was one of the most vital cities of the classical age. At its height, around 400 C.E., it was not only the largest city in the Americas, but one of the largest in the world. Boasting a monumental center that stretched across eight square miles, Teotihuacan housed an estimated 150,000 inhabitants or more—many times the population of London at the time.

Aside from being an important religious center, it was also a hub of manufacturing and economic development, anchoring a trade network that extended throughout Mesoamerica. Its specialty product was green obsidian, a glasslike volcanic stone that was hewn into knives, points, and scrapers; the city also produced a great number of ceramics and votive figurines for export.

Settled by farmers around 400 B.C.E., Teotihuacan began exerting its will over nearby areas around 200 B.C.E., most likely through military force. Its cultural and economic influence outmatched even the later Aztec Empire. Sacked and abandoned sometime in the seventh or eighth century, the city continued to be visited by pilgrims who gave the city the name known to posterity, Nahuatl, for "where men become gods."

POLITICS & POWER	GEOGRAPHY & ENVIRONMENT	CULTURE & RELIGION
378 AN ENVOY NAMED FIRE IS BORN descends from the great city of Teotihuacan into Maya territory in Guatemala. His arrival begins a new dynasty that will lead the Maya Empire to its greatest power. **ca 400 THE HOPEWELL CULTURE** of eastern North America gradually dissipates into less sedentary, more loosely organized groups of people. Mound building declines along with the Hopewell's network of trade.	**ca 400s THE FREMONT CULTURE** in modern-day Utah and the greater Great Basin region of western North America transitions from caves to constructed shelters with storage for agricultural produce.	**ca 400 THE MAYA CITY OF COPÁN** in Honduras becomes an important political and ritual center in the region.
ca 406 GROUPS OF VANDALS and other Germanic people, led by King Gunderic, invade and devastate much of the Roman province of Gaul. **410 VISIGOTHIC FORCES** led by Alaric capture and sack Rome, having laid multiple sieges to it over the previous year. Though it has not been the capital of the empire for over a century, this represents the symbolic fall of the Western Roman Empire. The invaders spare the churches of St. Peter and St. Paul.	**ca 400 GERMANIC TRIBES** invade present-day Switzerland from the north as Roman conquerors enter from the south. The isolation effect of the steep Swiss Alps helps ensure a language divide that lasts to today—northern Switzerland speaks German while Latin-descended Italian and French are the dominant languages in the south.	**381-400 ROMAN GENERAL TURNED EMPEROR THEODOSIUS I** makes Christianity the official religion of the Roman Empire. In 392, he completely prohibits the worship of pagan gods, and in 400, he abolishes the Olympics because of its pagan associations. **428 GREEK THEOLOGIAN** and bishop of Constantinople, Nestorius, emphasizes Jesus's human as opposed to divine nature, sparking much conflict within the Catholic Church.
ca 390 FOLLOWING ROMAN EMPEROR THEODOSIUS I'S OUTLAWING OF PAGANISM, crowds destroy the temple of Serapis in Alexandria and, along with it, Alexandria's great library. **429 THE VANDALS** invade Africa from Spain, capturing Carthage by 439.	**ca 397 NORTH AFRICAN BERBER GENERAL GILDO** attempts, but fails, to break his lands away from the western Roman Empire.	**396 AUGUSTINE OF HIPPO** becomes a bishop in modern-day Algeria. His writings, such as *Confessions* and *City of God,* synthesize Christian theology and Platonic logic and expound on topics such as the "just war" theory. **ca 400 ASHI** is one of the prime movers in the compilation of the Babylonian Talmud, a commentary on the Mishnah. At the same time, rabbis in Palestine compile the Palestinian Talmud, completed around 425.
ca 375 EMPEROR CHANDRAGUPTA II assumes the throne of the Gupta dynasty in northern India. After extending his rule west and south from the Ganges, peace and prosperity are said to grace his lands. **ca 400s THE YAMATO CULTURE** extends its control over rival clans throughout the Japanese archipelago. **424 LUOYANG FALLS** to the Northern Wei, a regime established by Turkic people of northern China.	**402 BUDDHIST MONK FAXIAN** is the first pilgrim to travel from China to India. His vivid writings reveal much about the landscape from scorching deserts in Central Asia to the chiseled pathways and ladders used to cross the Pamir mountains.	**ca 400 INDIAN MONK KUMARAJIVA** oversees Chinese translations of Buddhist texts in Chang'an. **ca 400 SANSKRIT POET KALIDASA** flourishes. His works, especially the drama *Abhijnanashakuntala (The Recognition of Shakuntala),* earn him wide recognition as one of the greatest of Sanskrit poets. **ca 400 THE *BHAGAVAD GITA,*** a discourse on Hindu ethical teachings, takes on its final form after a number of revisions.

SCIENCE & TECHNOLOGY

ca 400 **BY THIS TIME, THE PEOPLES OF MESOAMERICA** have developed the concept of the wheel, but have made no use of it outside of toys produced for children. In the absence of beasts of burden, wheeled vehicles may have served no use.

ca 408-450 **ROMAN EMPEROR THEODOSIUS II** expands the triple walls of Constantinople and builds huge cisterns for water, making the city almost impossible to conquer.

ca 400 **EMPEROR CHANDRA GUPTA II** maintains free rest houses for visitors to his empire, as well as free hospitals for his infirm subjects.

PEOPLE & SOCIETY

ca 400 **TEOTIHUACAN** continues to participate in an intensive trade network that stretches throughout Mesoamerica. It exports ceramics, clay figurines, and its most distinctive wares—knives, points, and scrapers made of green obsidian.

417 **HIEROGLYPHS** in a tomb on the Rio Azul in modern-day Guatemala record this as the birth date of an important Maya ruler; the name is lost to history.

410 **DURING ALARIC'S MULTIPLE SIEGES OF ROME,** many Germanic slaves in the city join his side. In fact, Alaric's forces only enter Rome when a slave opens the gates for them.

415 **THE VISIGOTHS** move out of Italy and into southern Gaul and Spain, where they remain with their capital at Toledo for the next three centuries.

376 **THE HUNS,** a nomadic group of people from eastern Asia, arrive on the frontier of the Roman Empire after defeating Goths living on the Danube River. Over the next seven decades, they will carve out an empire of their own in central Europe.

418 **JEWS** are barred from public office and military service in the Roman Empire.

400s **HINDUISM,** under the patronage of the Gupta Empire, gradually replaces Buddhism as the dominant religious and cultural tradition of India.

ca 414 **FAXIAN,** Chinese scholar and monk, returns from India bringing Sanskrit texts that will become central to Chinese Buddhism. He writes a *Record of Buddhist Kingdoms.*

427 **TAO QIAN,** Chinese Daoist poet, dies.

CONNECTIONS

The Spread of Contagion

The vast network of land and sea routes, known collectively as the Silk Road, that connected distant empires into an integrated web of commerce across the Eurasian landmass, carried not only exotic goods and new ideas, but also infectious diseases hungry for fresh populations of immunity-free victims. In both the Roman and Han Empires, and most likely in the areas between, epidemics ravaged populations in the third, fourth, and fifth centuries C.E., decreasing these empires' ability to maintain their borders against invasions. As trade consequently declined, so did imperial economies, resulting in pockets of regionalized markets that would not again achieve a global level for centuries to come.

Wall mural dated to the Gupta dynasty

INDIA'S GOLDEN AGE

CHANDRAGUPTA II took the throne of the Gupta dynasty in about 375 C.E. and proceeded to usher in an era of cultural and economic prosperity sometimes referred to as the golden age of India. Gupta reestablished traditional Indian mores and administrative practices following an era that had been dominated by Greek influences.

Through a combination of military and marital alliances, Gupta extended his empire from the Ganges to the Indus and north into modern-day Pakistan. This imperial expansion brought an influx of wealth that was lavished in part on science and the arts. Gupta established a circle of poets known as the nine gems of his court, which probably included Kalidasa, the chief figure in classical Sanskrit literature. Astronomy and mathematics also prospered in Gupta's court.

Chandragupta created free rest houses and hospitals, abolished capital punishment, and promulgated a single code of law. The Iron Pillar near Delhi, virtually uncorroded after 1,600 years, commemorates this benevolent ruler.

POLITICS & POWER	GEOGRAPHY & ENVIRONMENT	CULTURE & RELIGION
ca 450 THE ZAPOTEC POPULATION of Monte Albán (today's Oaxaca, Mexico) continues to grow. At its height, it may have had up to 30,000 inhabitants. **ca 450 THE MOCHE CULTURE** of northern coastal Peru further extends its influence over neighboring peoples. It serves as the political and ceremonial nerve center of about 2,500 square miles of river valleys. **500 THE POPULATION OF TEOTIHUACAN** numbers some 125,000 to 200,000 at the height of its prosperity.	**ca 455 THE MAYA CITY OF CHICHÉN ITZÁ** is founded on the Yucatán Peninsula. Over the next millennium it will grow into a major city and temple complex. **ca 500 THE FREMONT PEOPLE** appear in Utah, possibly migrating from the northwestern Plains.	**ca 500 TIWANAKU** rises along the southern shore of Lake Titicaca in the Andes. It becomes known for such architectural splendors as Akapana Pyramid and the rectangular enclosure known as the Kalasasaya.
441 UNDER THE COMMAND OF KING ATTILA, the Huns launch a massive assault on the Eastern Roman Empire, invading the Danubian frontier, then Gaul and northern Italy. Nearly unstoppable, they wreak havoc until Attila's death in 453. **455 VANDALS,** led by King Gaiseric, invade Rome and plunder it of many works of art. **476 GERMAN WARRIOR ODOACER** deposes the final Western Roman emperor, Romulus Augustulus, and is proclaimed king by the barbarian rebels. The western half of the Roman Empire is extinguished.	**480 AN EARTHQUAKE** shakes Constantinople, the capital of the Eastern Roman Empire, for a reputed 40 straight days. **493 THODORIC,** after assassinating Odoacer, establishes an Ostrogothic kingdom in Italy with his capital at Ravenna.	**ca 450 PATRICK,** a Christian bishop from Britain, travels to Ireland as a missionary. He sets up his diocese at Armagh and begins trying to convert the island to Christianity. **451 THE ECUMENICAL COUNCIL OF CHALCEDON** stabilizes the institution of Christianity as set out in the Nicene Creed. It condemns the Nestorian and Monophysite branches of Christianity. **ca 496-498 CLOVIS,** king of the Franks, is baptized a Christian at the urging of his wife, Clothilde.
429 THE VANDALS, a Germanic group of migratory peope, settle finally in North Africa with Carthage as their capital. The Western Roman Emperor Valentinian III recognizes their independence, yet Vandals continue to harass the crumbling Eastern Roman Empire. **484 SASSANID KING PEROZ I** loses his life fighting the Hephthalites. Nobles and Zoroastrian priests become the real power in the Sassanid Empire.	**ca 500 FARMING SETTLEMENTS** with East African and Indonesian origins are established in Madagascar.	**ca 489 NESTORIAN CHRISTIANS** flourish in Persia after being evicted from the Eastern Roman Empire by orthodox Emperor Zeno. **ca 490 THE LYDENBURG HEADS,** life-size terra-cotta masks, are produced. The earliest known sculpture in southern Africa, they are perhaps used in the rituals of agricultural communities.
ca 450-500 THE HEPHTHALITES wear down the defenses of the Gupta Empire in India.	**458 THERE IS EVIDENCE THAT AN EXPEDITION LED BY EXPLORER FU SANG,** a Buddhist monk, crossed the Pacific Ocean from China to America, mapping coastal land that could be anywhere from Mexico to the Aleutian Islands. His travels were reported to the Chinese imperial court. **485 THE WEI STATE** of northern China implements a system of equal land distribution, in which it distinguishes between crop land and orchards.	**ca 440s THE NORTHERN WEI RULERS** build a center of Buddhism and Buddhist art in the capital of Shanxi, a reflection of the spread of the religion among the northern peoples of China. **495 WORK BEGINS** on a series of Chinese cave temples at Longmen, near Luoyang, the new capital of the Northern Wei. **ca 496 THE SHAOLIN MONASTERY** is founded in Henan Province, China.

SCIENCE & TECHNOLOGY

PEOPLE & SOCIETY

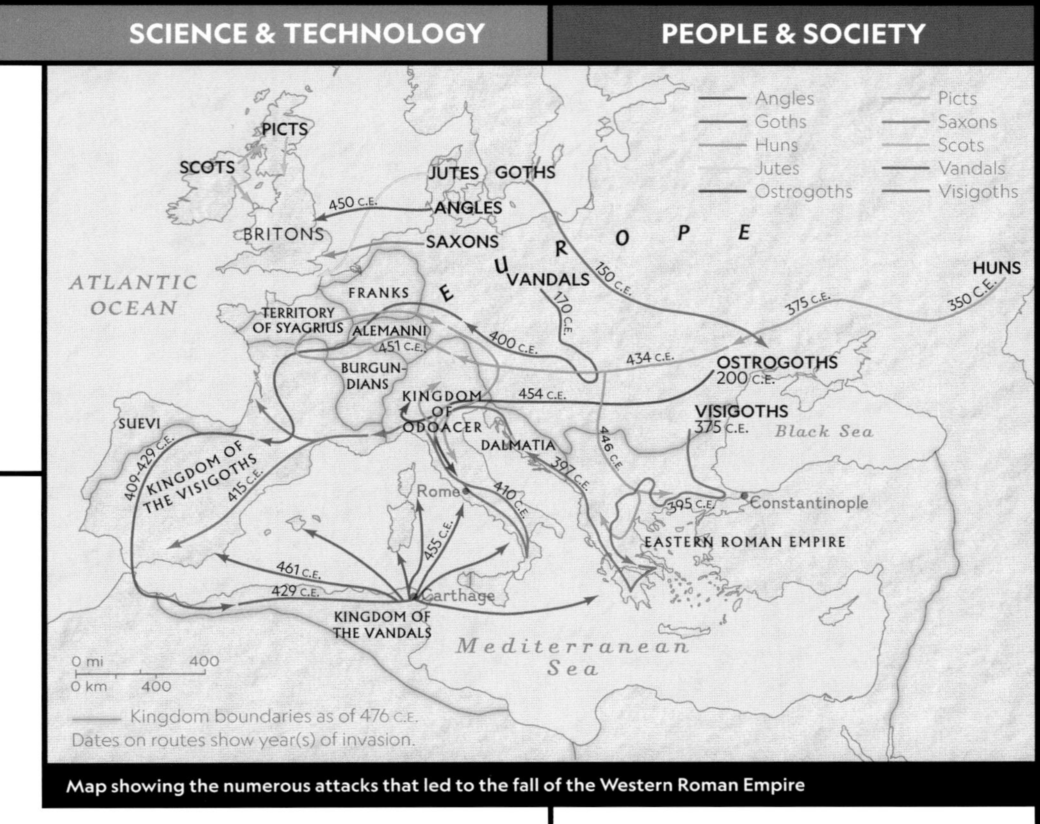

Map showing the numerous attacks that led to the fall of the Western Roman Empire

459 ST. SIMEON STYLITES, famed Syrian monk, dies. From 420 until his death he had lived atop a pillar northwest of Aleppo.

494 AN INNOVATIVE CABLE SUSPENSION BRIDGE of bamboo is used by a Wei general in China to repulse an enemy attack. The bridge crosses a river and is also submersible at will to block ships.

444 DAOISM becomes the official ideology of the Northern Wei kingdom in China.

THE FALL OF ROME

THOUGH GERMANIC PEOPLES had been pushing against the borders of the Roman Empire for centuries, they did not become an acute threat until the fourth century. Rome had been weakened by military usurpers and unqualified leaders for some time, causing emperor Diocletian to split the empire in 286 into two distinct units, eastern and western. Constantine I in 330 moved his capital to Constantinople, modern-day Istanbul, fashioning it a "new Rome"; it would become the center of the Byzantine world. Meanwhile, old Rome and the Western Empire were left in the hands of corrupt and inadequate administrators, managing undertrained and underpaid soldiers.

Around 370, a group of nomadic horsemen known as the Huns rode out of the east. They were skilled archers who could move in tandem in cavalry maneuvers for which the Romans were completely unprepared. From the north came the Vandals, who pushed into Gaul, disrupting Germanic groups that were already established there, namely the Franks, Alemanni, and Burgundians. The Vandals continued into North Africa, where they enjoyed short-lived autonomy and continued to harass the deteriorating Roman Empire. Goths pushed into the Balkans, and after a failed conciliation with Rome, they decimated Roman forces at the Battle of Adrianople in 378. The Goths proceeded into Italy and took the city of Rome by 410.

Meanwhile, Roman forces had abandoned Britain to invading Scots, Picts, Angles, and Jutes, while the Huns of Attila invaded Gaul and Italy, their assault halted only by Attila's death. Finally, in 476, the German chieftain Odoacer deposed the last Western Roman emperor and proclaimed himself king, extinguishing the last sign of life from a once powerful empire.

CHAPTER 3

FAITH AND POWER

500-1000

Millions of Muslims climax their pilgrimage to Mecca by bowing in prayer at the Great Mosque before the cube-shaped Kaaba, their holiest shrine.

With the rise of Islam in the seventh century and the spread of Christianity and other established religions, faith became a more powerful force than ever, inspiring rulers and setting armies in motion. Worldly ambitions combined with religious zeal propelled Arab conquerors across Africa and the Middle East and fueled the expansion of the Byzantine Empire around the Mediterranean and Christian kingdoms in western Europe. These devout societies sought imperial glory and learned lessons from old imperial cultures. Christians in Byzantium were inspired by Greek traditions, while those in western Europe built on Roman foundations, and Muslims inherited the cultural legacy of Persia.

OPPOSITE: Religious fervor and Greek artistic traditions inspired majestic Byzantine icons such as this mosaic of Christ, which survived when the Hagia Sophia in Constantinople (modern-day Istanbul) was transformed from a cathedral to a mosque.

Religion had a profound impact elsewhere as well. Muslims invaded northern India, setting that region apart from Hindu kingdoms to the south. Farther east, Buddhism expanded through the efforts of monks and nuns, much as Christianity did in Europe, and competed with the traditional beliefs of Confucianism and Shinto, the ancestral faith of Japan. In the Americas, rulers among the Maya and other cultures built soaring monuments to their gods and reached new heights of authority. Faith transformed societies, strengthening some and destroying others.

BYZANTINE EXPANSION

When the Roman emperor Constantine moved his capital to Byzantium, or Constantinople, in the fourth century, he laid the foundation for a Greek empire in the east that outlasted the Roman Empire in the west. Greek later became the official language of Byzantium, and Byzantine

BELOW: This map shows the Byzantine Empire at its height during the reign of Justinian in the sixth century. Byzantines regarded Constantinople as the second Rome and carried on Roman imperial traditions by spreading their faith and culture to places as distant as Moscow, later hailed by Russians as the third Rome (inset).

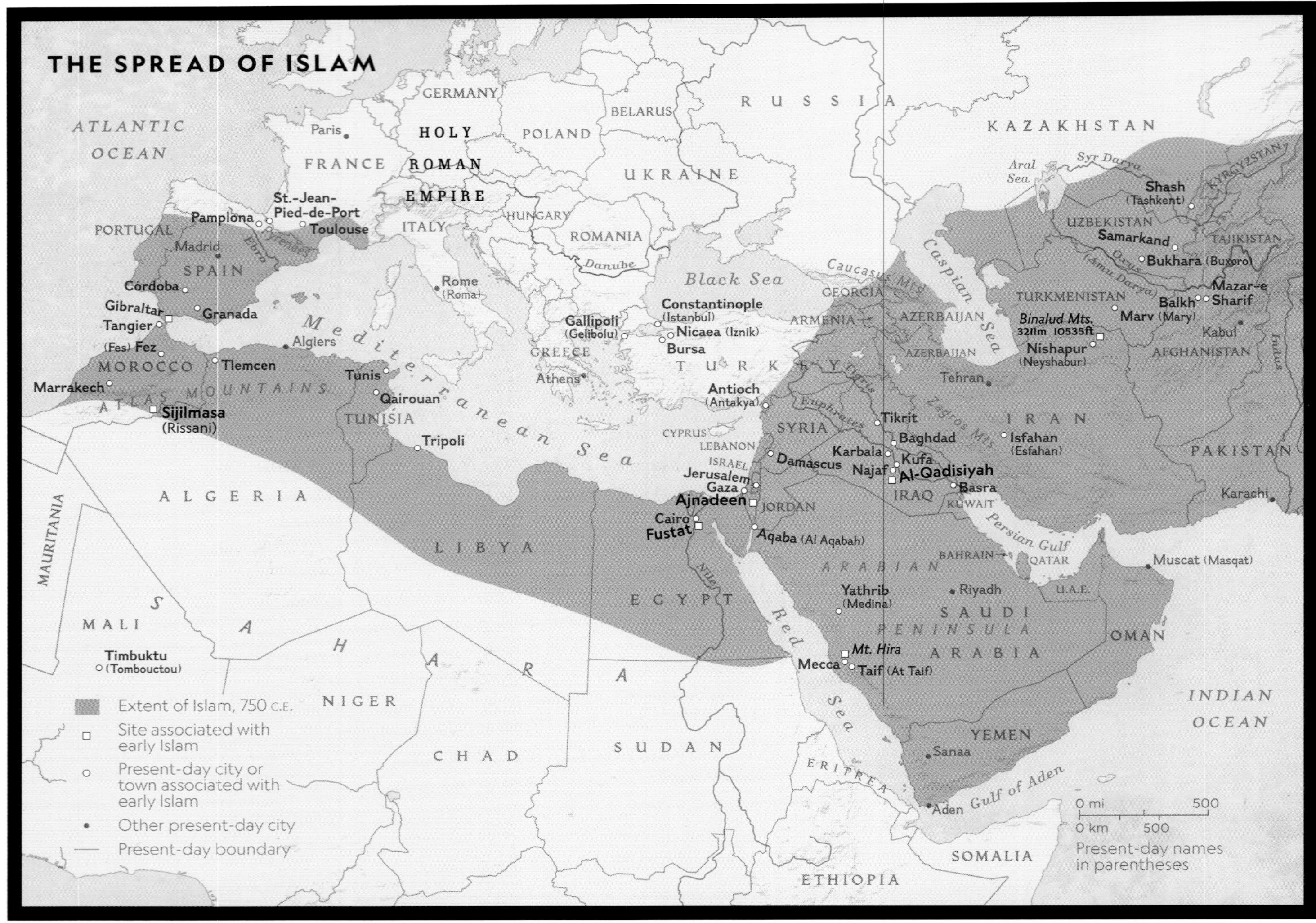

By 750, when the Abbasid dynasty took power in Persia, the Muslim Empire extended all the way from Spain to northern India.

scholars studied the works of Aristotle and other classical Greek authors.

The Byzantine Empire reached its height in the sixth century under Justinian, who raised a great cathedral called the Hagia Sophia and other monuments in Constantinople after much of the city was destroyed by rioters protesting high taxes and food shortages. Those protests nearly drove him from power, but his iron-willed wife, Empress Theodora, persuaded him to hold his ground, and troops crushed the uprising, killing tens of thousands of people. Justinian's forces then embarked on foreign conquests, seizing Italy, northwestern Africa, and southern Spain. At his death in 565, his empire nearly encircled the Mediterranean.

The Byzantine Empire endured for many centuries, but it would never again be as strong as it was under Justinian. His successors lost control of Italy and other western lands, where Christians recognized the bishop of Rome rather than the Byzantine patriarch as their spiritual father, or pope. Within the Byzantine world, a bitter religious dispute arose over iconoclasm—an imperial effort to ban sacred images as idols. Wealthy landowners defied Byzantine emperors by raising their own troops and refusing to pay taxes. But nothing did more to weaken Byzantium than the spread of Islam by Muslim forces, who claimed Egypt, Palestine, and Syria and threatened Constantinople itself.

THE ISLAMIC WORLD

Islam arose in Mecca, an oasis where Arabs gathered to trade and worship at shrines devoted to many gods. The prophet Muhammad was born there around 570 and traveled widely as a merchant, coming in contact with Jews, Christians, and people of other faiths. When he was around 40, he experienced a revelation in which he recognized Allah (God) as supreme and all-encompassing. Muhammad shared his revelation with others and promised salvation to those who embraced Islam, meaning submission to Allah. "There is no God but Allah," Muslims declared ever after, "and Muhammad is his prophet."

Muhammad's message angered those in Mecca who remained devoted to other gods. In 622 he fled Mecca and joined followers in the city they named Medina, where they gained strength. Their ancestors had long engaged in clan warfare, and they were prepared to fight for their beliefs. In 630 they conquered Mecca and made its holiest shrine, the Kaaba, the focal point for pilgrimages to Mecca by devout Muslims in years to come. Muhammad died in 632, but his teachings lived on in the Quran (Koran), inscribed in Arabic not long after his death. His leadership role fell to caliphs, or deputies, who united the Arabian Peninsula under Islam and embarked on far-ranging conquests. By 650 Muslim forces had seized a vast area extending from Egypt to Persia. Over the next century, they expanded southeastward to the Indus River and westward across North Africa, reaching as far as Spain.

During this expansive era, the Islamic world was ruled from Damascus by caliphs of the Umayyad dynasty. One Muslim sect known as the Shiite opposed them because they were not descendants of Muhammad. Other Muslims known as Sunnis accepted their legitimacy, but some Sunnis in conquered lands shared the resentments of Shiites and non-Muslims toward the caliphs. Rebels of various sects in Persia rallied around Abu al Abbas, who ended Umayyad rule in 750-754. He and his Abbasid successors built a new capital at Baghdad, where scholars studied the Quran as well as classical works by Persian, Greek, and Indian sages, including treatises on medicine and mathematics. Arabic numerals and algebra were among the gifts Muslim scholars bequeathed to modern science.

Islamic culture and literature flourished in many cities besides Baghdad. Muslims learned through trade with China how to make paper and produced books in great numbers, kept in libraries like that in Córdoba, the elegant Spanish capital. They did not allow pictures or sculptures in mosques, but their artists were masters of abstract designs and calligraphy. Islamic authorities generally tolerated people of other faiths but required them to pay a special tax. Caliphs recognized leading Jewish rabbis in Persia as *geonim,* or excellencies, and allowed them to resolve all religious issues that arose in Jewish communities under Muslim rule by applying the Talmud, a compilation of Jewish laws and traditions completed in the sixth century. Muslim laws based on the Quran provided protection to women as well as servants and slaves. At the same time, they perpetuated ancient Middle Eastern customs by requiring women to wear veils in public and allowing men to have more than one wife.

FERMENT IN AFRICA

By the ninth century, Muslim traders from North Africa were crossing the Sahara by camel in caravans to seek wealth in West Africa, where prosperous societies had developed along the Senegal and Niger Rivers. Farmers there cultivated rice and other crops in fertile floodplains, providing food surpluses that supported potters, coppersmiths, ironworkers, and other artisans. Here as elsewhere in Africa, long-distance trade was well established before Muslims arrived, fostering the growth of commercial centers such as Jenne-Jeno, a town of more than 10,000 people near the confluence of the Niger and Bani Rivers (today's Djenné, Mali.)

To the west, between the Niger and Senegal Rivers, the kingdom of Ghana developed. Merchants there obtained gold from lands to their south, and that wealth attracted Muslim traders, who also sought ivory and slaves. (West Africa was just one source of slaves—a word derived from "Slav"; many Slavs were seized in eastern Europe and enslaved.) The rulers of Ghana later converted to Islam but were slow to abandon such traditional religious practices as praying to images of their ancestral spirits or nature gods. Trade with the Islamic world brought Ghana wealth and power, and it grew from a kingdom into an empire.

In East Africa, Muslim merchants arriving by sea at busy ports like Mogadishu and Mombasa encountered people who spoke Bantu languages and had long been involved in maritime trade, plying the Indian Ocean and the Red Sea in ships. Referred to by Muslims as Swahilis, or coasters, they incorporated many Arabic words into their dialects and readily communicated with each other and with their Muslim trading partners, to whom they sold gold, ivory, and slaves from the interior. Here as in West Africa, rulers who profited from such trade embraced Islam and grew stronger politically. As East African ports grew into city-states adorned with mosques, Swahili society became part of dar al Islam, or the Islamic world.

With its far-flung trade networks and vibrant markets, this flourishing Islamic world was the envy of rulers in Constantinople and western Europe, where there were no Christian cities to compare with Córdoba or Baghdad.

A DIVIDED WEST

The collapse of the Roman Empire left western Europe divided among various Germanic tribes. Visigoths (western Goths) held Iberia until Muslim forces seized much of what is now Spain and Portugal in the eighth century. Ostrogoths (eastern Goths) dominated Italy until Byzantine forces intervened in the sixth century, followed by Lombards. Britain was occupied by Angles and Saxons from Denmark and northern Germany. But the strongest of the Germanic peoples in Europe were the Franks, whose kingdom expanded far beyond France under the dynamic ruler Charlemagne, who conquered much of Germany and northern Italy. In 800, Pope Leo III crowned him emperor in Rome, rivaling the Byzantine emperor in Constantinople.

Charlemagne's empire fractured not long after he died in 814. His successors could not withstand fierce pressure from invaders, including Magyars advancing from the east and Vikings pouring down from Scandinavia in longships. Vikings pillaged coastal ports and monasteries and surged inland to take control of large areas, including much of Britain, Normandy, Sicily, and parts of Russia, where missionaries from Byzantium later introduced Christianity. Other Vikings sailed westward across the Atlantic and colonized Iceland and Greenland before establishing a short-lived colony in Newfoundland around 1000.

Invasions by Vikings and other marauders left western Europe as divided as ever. In feudal society, serfs toiling on estates owed the lord of the manor rent and other obligations, including labor and military service. Those lords were in turn obligated as vassals to higher nobility and supported them in wars. In some places, kings arose such as Alfred of Wessex, who reclaimed part of Britain from the Vikings; and Otto I of Saxony, who defeated the Magyars and laid the foundation for the Holy Roman Empire. But much of Europe was controlled by nobles and their vassals, who oversaw manors. Those estates were largely self-sufficient, and few traders ventured far from home.

Vikings used their sophisticated shipbuilding and navigation expertise to begin making lightning strike attacks on coastal settlements in Europe from about 800. They would travel as far inland as the Caspian Sea and cross the Atlantic to Newfoundland.

The one great unifying factor in western Europe was Roman Christianity, which was organized hierarchically like the old Roman Empire with local priests supervised by bishops under the supreme authority of the pope. Roman culture endured in churches of classical design called basilicas, in the colorful robes of Roman origin that priests and bishops wore, and in the Latin language, used by priests, teachers, and other literate people. Monks copied Bibles and other books in Latin and lavishly illustrated them. Nuns also copied manuscripts in convents and taught children to read and write. Through the influence of the church, Latin shaped western European culture and gave birth to Italian, Spanish, French, and other Romance languages.

DIVERSITY IN THE EAST

In contrast to Christian Europe, most Asian societies and their rulers allowed for religious diversity. King Harsha, who reunited much of northern India under his rule in the early seventh century after the collapse of the Gupta Empire, was a devout Buddhist, but he did not seek to impose his beliefs on Hindus or those of other faiths. Harsha's empire crumbled after his death, and Muslim forces came down from the north and conquered Sind in 712, embracing the Indus River Valley. Distant caliphs had limited authority over Sind, and not many people in northern India converted to Islam before Muslim Turks invaded the region around 1000. To the south, Muslim merchants settled in coastal towns and attracted some converts, but most people remained Hindus. In the southern Indian kingdom of Chola, donations from Hindus who prospered as traders or manufacturers of trade goods such as cotton cloth supported temples that controlled large tracts of land, just as the well-endowed Christian monasteries in Europe did.

Muslim traders influenced the culture and beliefs of India, but Indian merchants had an even greater impact on countries in Southeast Asia that lay along maritime trade routes between India and China. Rulers of Funan, in southern Cambodia and Vietnam, called themselves rajas, like Indian kings; worshiped Hindu deities; and adopted Sanskrit as their official language. Funan collapsed in the sixth century, and Khmers took control of Cambodia. They too became Hindus but later adopted Buddhism, introduced to nearby Malaysia and Sumatra by Indian merchants.

In China, the Sui dynasty reunified the empire in the late sixth century, ending three centuries of turmoil following the collapse of the Han dynasty. Sui rulers constructed the Grand Canal linking the Yellow and Yangtze

Rivers, a massive project that helped integrate China economically and culturally. Millions of Chinese were conscripted to labor on the canal or serve as soldiers in Korea, where Chinese invasion forces suffered setbacks, triggering a revolt that brought an end to the Sui dynasty in 618 and ushered in the Tang dynasty.

Tang emperors endorsed Confucian ideals of benevolent leadership and claimed the mandate of heaven—a divine right to rule that belonged only to those who governed virtuously, according to Confucius. Office seekers under the Tang had to demonstrate their knowledge of Confucian texts in civil service examinations. The Tang dynasty lasted for nearly three centuries, during which time their capital at Chang'an (Xi'an) grew to a population of nearly one million. Chinese inventors devised the magnetic compass, gunpowder, and porcelain, which became China's most prized export after the secrets of fine silk production reached Byzantium in the seventh century.

Official backing for Confucianism in China did not thwart the spread of other religions or philosophies. Buddhism also received support from Tang rulers and nobility, who sponsored Buddhist monasteries and temples. Chinese Buddhist pilgrims and missionaries journeyed to India to visit sacred sites and spread their faith to Japan and Korea, which reconciled with China after the kingdom of Silla united Koreans against Chinese invaders in the seventh century and induced the Tang emperor to withdraw his forces. In return, the Silla king agreed to acknowledge the emperor as his overlord, but Korea remained essentially independent.

Buddhism, Confucianism, and other cultural influences from China greatly affected the development of Japan, whose emperors claimed their own heavenly mandate by tracing their ancestry to the Shinto sun goddess, Amaterasu. By the ninth century, Japanese emperors were largely ceremonial figures, controlled by regents from the powerful Fujiwara family, which was linked by marriage

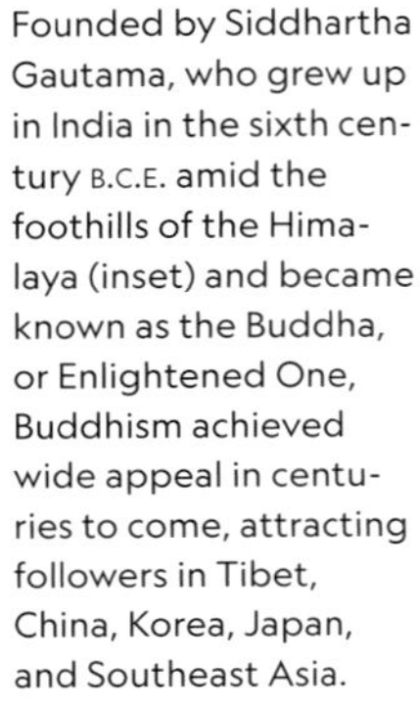

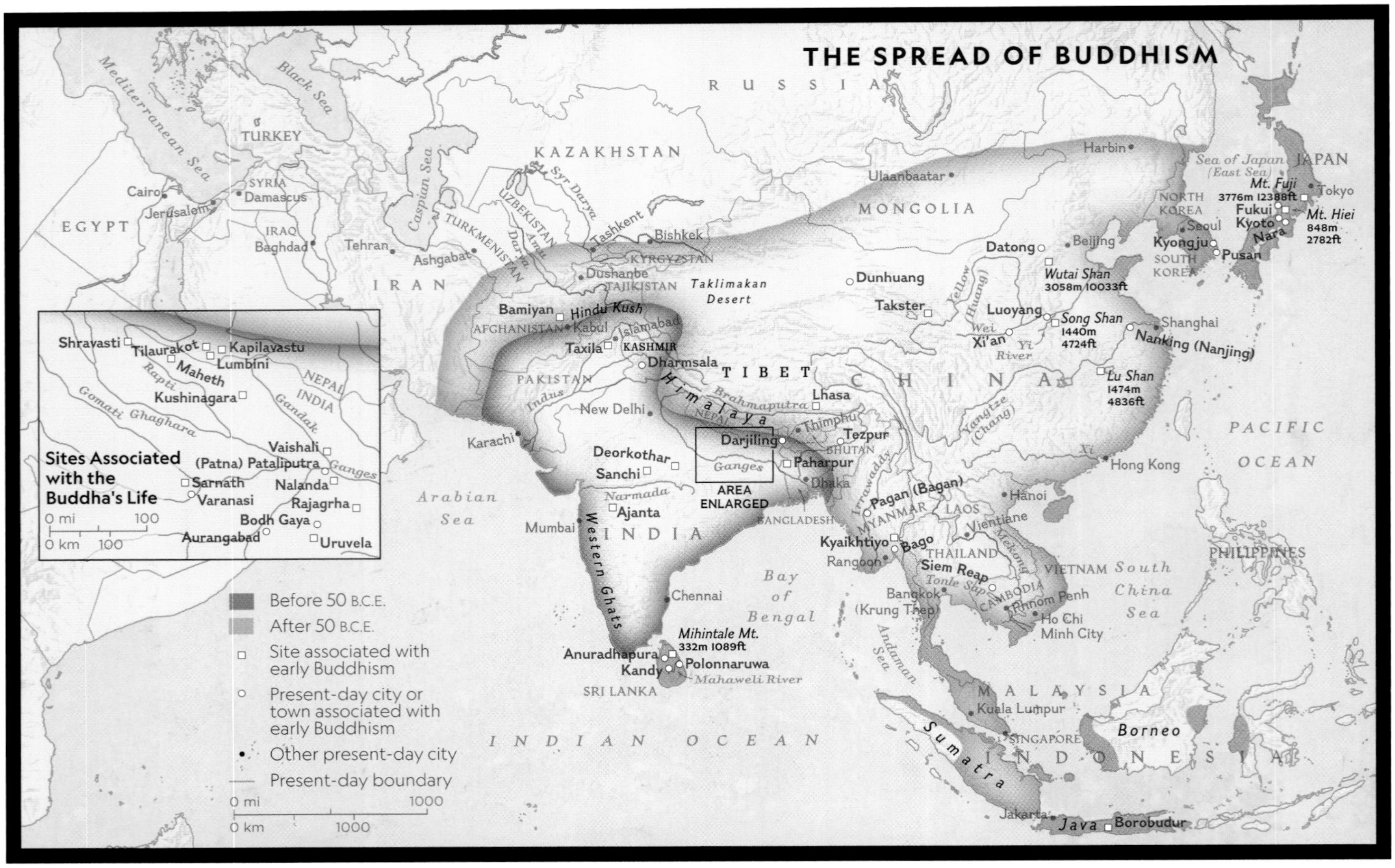

Founded by Siddhartha Gautama, who grew up in India in the sixth century B.C.E. amid the foothills of the Himalaya (inset) and became known as the Buddha, or Enlightened One, Buddhism achieved wide appeal in centuries to come, attracting followers in Tibet, China, Korea, Japan, and Southeast Asia.

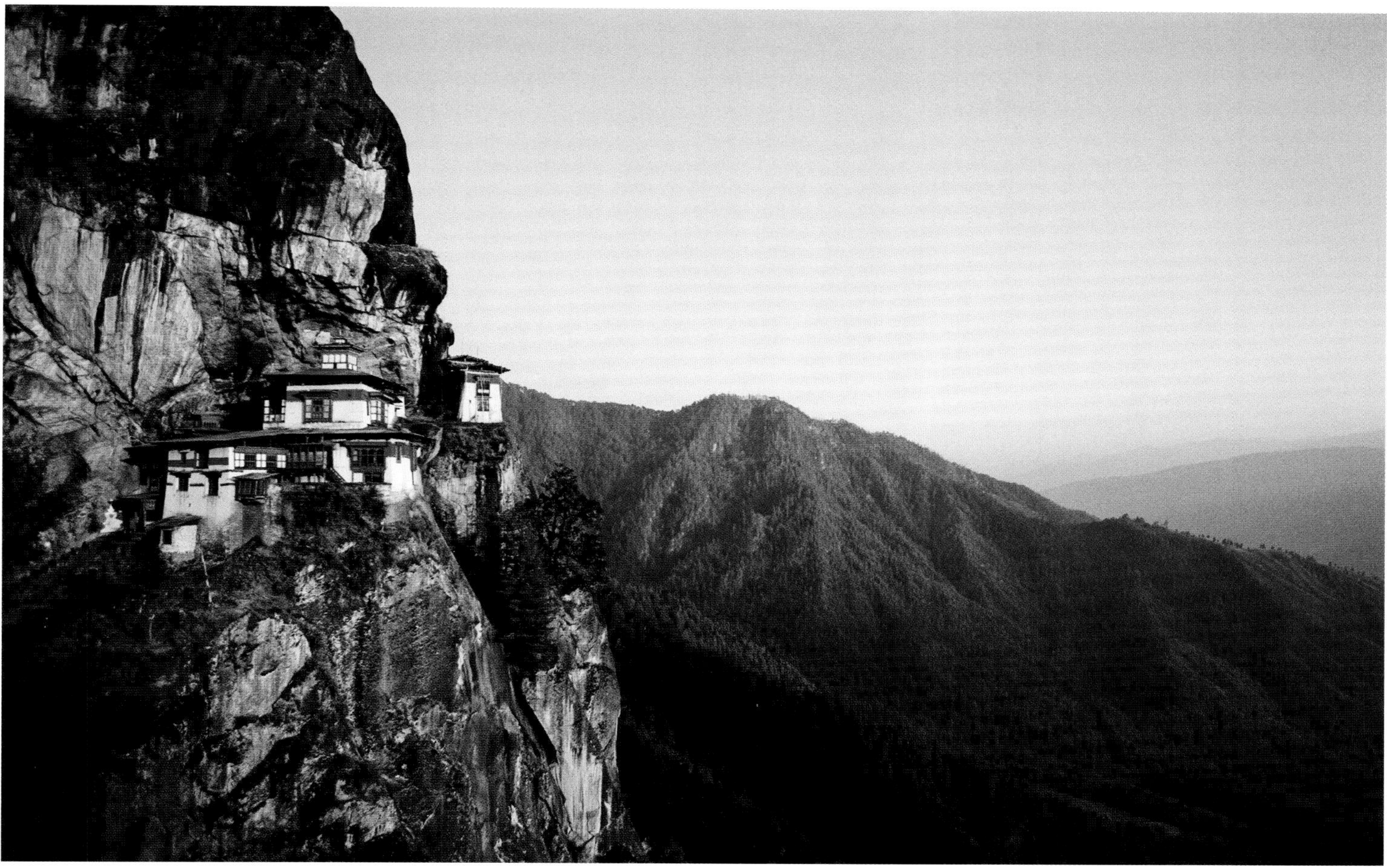

Buddhist monasteries like this one, perched on a cliffside in Bhutan, between India and China, have long offered seclusion to those seeking release from worldly concerns through meditation.

to the imperial family. Literature and the arts flourished at the imperial court at Heian (Kyoto) under Fujiwara Michinaga, who became regent in 995. While men at court wrote in classical Chinese, women wrote in Japanese, using a new phonetic script.

Few rulers around the world claimed direct descent from the gods like the emperors of Japan, but many were sacred figures before whom lesser mortals groveled or kowtowed, as visitors did before Chinese emperors. In Polynesian society, which expanded to New Zealand during this period, chiefs were so exalted that foods they ate and objects they touched were kapu (taboo), or forbidden to common people. Polynesian chiefs and priests made offerings to the gods at temples called *marae,* some of which were shaped like pyramids and rose up to 50 feet high.

In Mesoamerica, Maya rulers offered their own blood or that of captives to the gods at temples set atop pyramids. Soaring Maya pyramids at Copán and Palenque, where King Pacal was buried in splendor in 683 after reigning for 68 years, marked the high point of Maya civilization, which declined in the ninth century as city-states exhausted their resources. By 1000, most lay abandoned like once-mighty Teotihuacan, which suffered a ruinous assault a few centuries earlier. But the feats of those bygone pyramid builders inspired the Toltec—who rose to power in the Valley of Mexico in the 10th century and built an imposing capital at Tula—and they in turn would inspire the Aztec.

In North America, meanwhile, chiefs oversaw the construction of great earthen burial mounds, first in the Ohio Valley, center of the Hopewell culture, and later in the Mississippi Valley, where large towns such as Cahokia grew up around the mounds. Mississippian rulers were buried with offerings that sometimes included human sacrifices. Like other complex societies, these mound builders invested rulers with godlike authority, as long as they retained heaven's blessing and kept the land safe and prosperous. ■

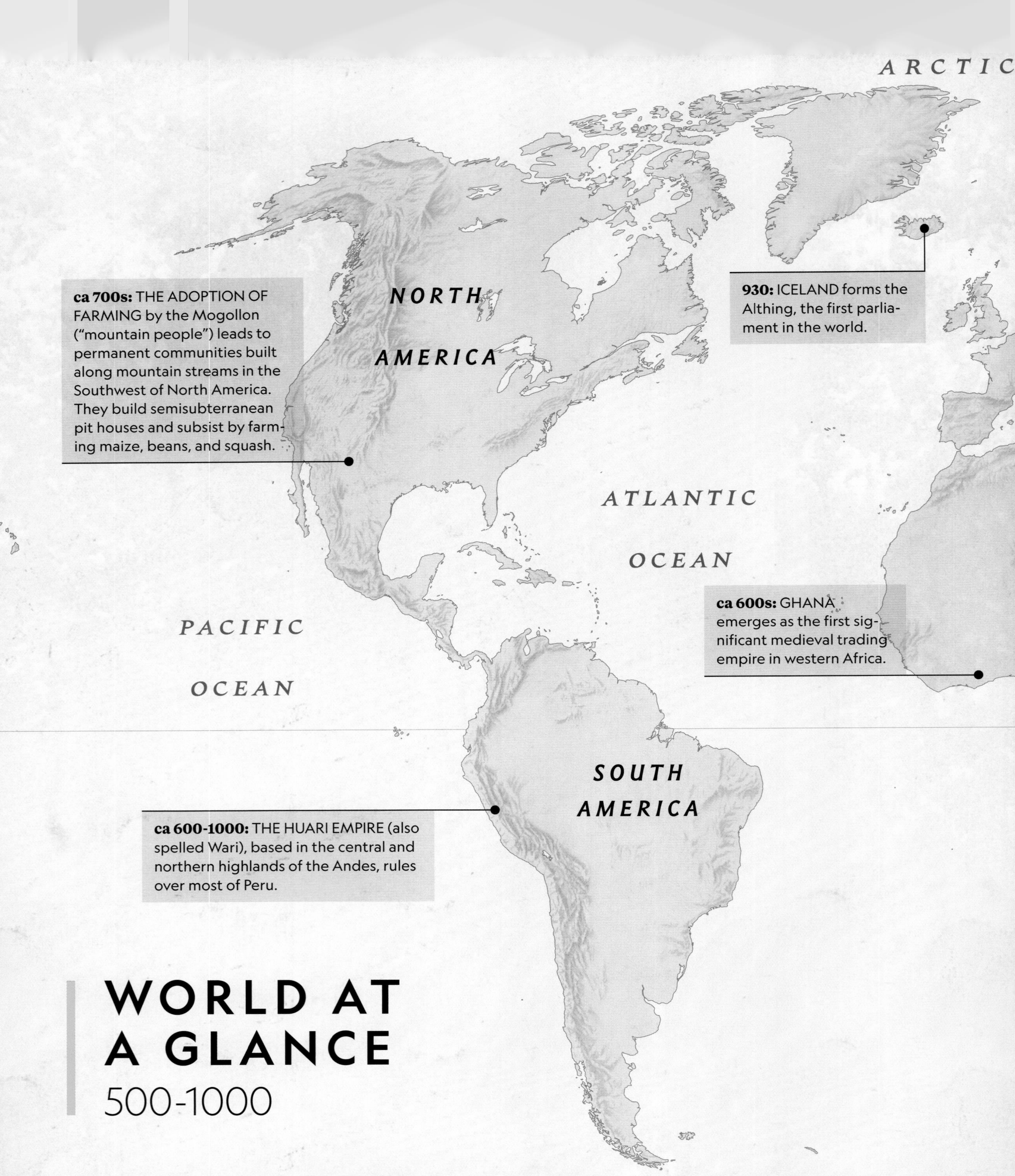
ARCTIC
NORTH AMERICA
ATLANTIC OCEAN
PACIFIC OCEAN
SOUTH AMERICA
ca 700s: THE ADOPTION OF FARMING by the Mogollon ("mountain people") leads to permanent communities built along mountain streams in the Southwest of North America. They build semisubterranean pit houses and subsist by farming maize, beans, and squash.
930: ICELAND forms the Althing, the first parliament in the world.
ca 600s: GHANA emerges as the first significant medieval trading empire in western Africa.
ca 600-1000: THE HUARI EMPIRE (also spelled Wari), based in the central and northern highlands of the Andes, rules over most of Peru.

WORLD AT A GLANCE

500-1000

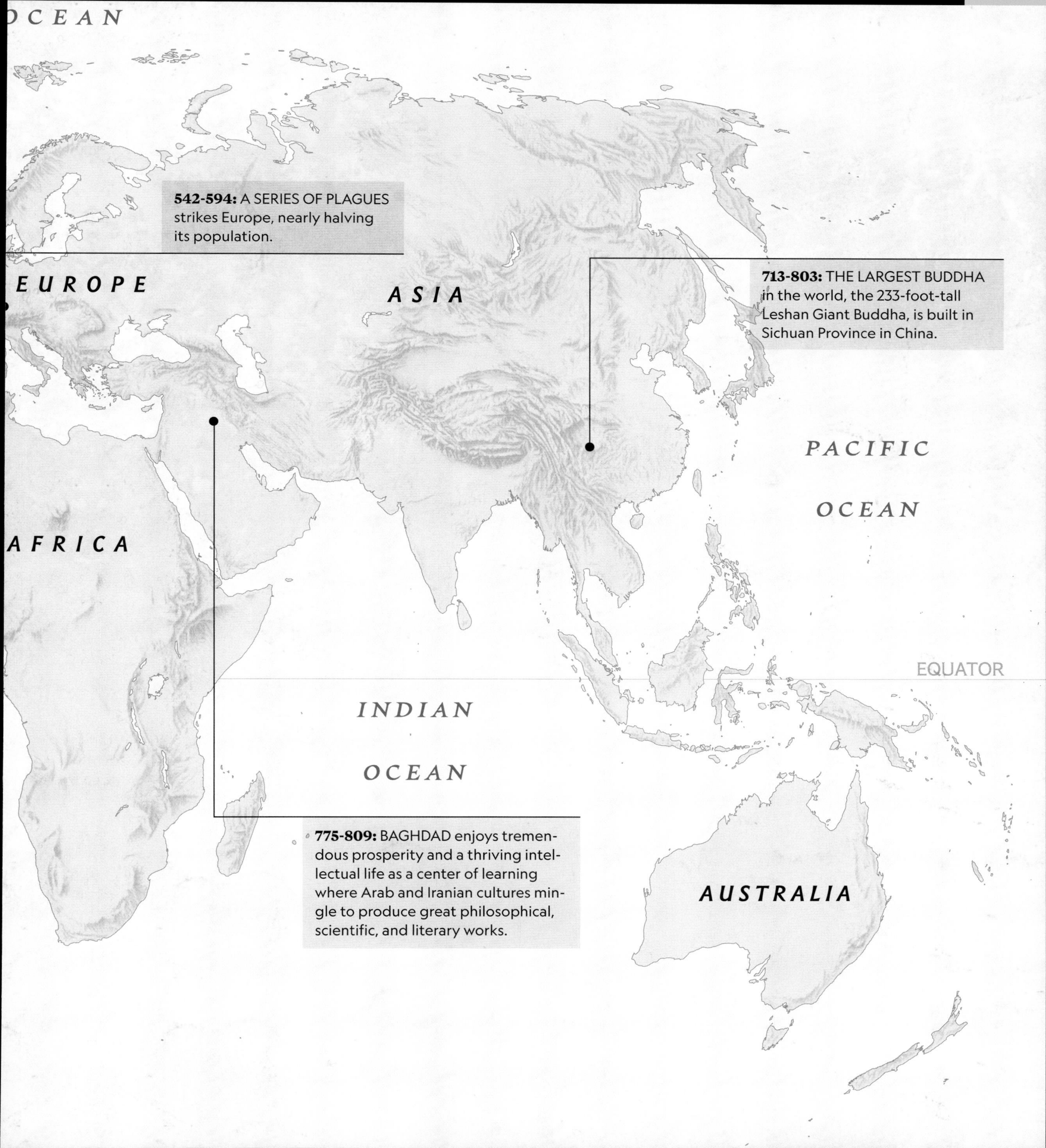

542-594: A SERIES OF PLAGUES strikes Europe, nearly halving its population.

713-803: THE LARGEST BUDDHA in the world, the 233-foot-tall Leshan Giant Buddha, is built in Sichuan Province in China.

775-809: BAGHDAD enjoys tremendous prosperity and a thriving intellectual life as a center of learning where Arab and Iranian cultures mingle to produce great philosophical, scientific, and literary works.

500-540

	POLITICS & POWER	GEOGRAPHY & ENVIRONMENT	CULTURE & RELIGION
THE AMERICAS	**ca 500** THE HOPEWELL CULTURE fades in the Ohio Valley, leaving behind distinctive conical burial mounds. Its westernmost contigent—known as the Kansas City Hopewell—continues to thrive at the junction of the Kansas and Missouri Rivers. **ca 500** MAYA CIVILIZATION on the Yucatán Peninsula flourishes.	**ca 500** THE PUNUK CULTURE, whale-hunting descendants of the Old Bering Sea tradition, develops the Bering Strait area of North America. **ca 500** TEOTIHUACAN, MEXICO, is the largest city in the Americas.	▶ **ca 500** MOCHE PEOPLE in Peru produce spectacular pottery. The pots are painted with intricate scenes of daily life or sculpted as portraits of warriors, kings, and animals.
EUROPE	**500** VISIGOTHS rule Spain from Toledo. **511** CLOVIS I, king of the Franks and ruler of much of Gaul, dies. His kingdom is divided among his four sons. **527-565** UNDER JUSTINIAN, the Byzantine Empire begins to regain lost territory of the once powerful Roman Empire. **530** FRANKISH TRIBES overtake Germany and northern France.	**ca 500s** SLAVS migrate into the Balkans, Hungary, and other nearby regions of Eastern Europe.	**ca 522-524** ROMAN SCHOLAR BOETHIUS writes his celebrated *Consolation of Philosophy* while in prison for treason. He is executed in 524. **ca 525** BRIGID OF KILDARE, a character of Irish legend and a Catholic saint, dies. She is credited with founding a nunnery at Kildare, the first in Ireland. **529** ST. BENEDICT establishes Monte Cassino Abbey in Italy. His rule for monastic life—with vows of obedience, chastity, and poverty—is adopted by other monasteries.
MIDDLE EAST & AFRICA	**ca 523** KING KALEB OF AKSUM avenges the massacre of Christians in Najrab, in the southwestern Arabian Peninsula. Leaving a garrison there, he returns to Africa. **530** GELIMER becomes king of the Vandals in North Africa, a realm reaching from Tangiers to Carthage, Corsica, Sardinia, and Sicily. **531** SASSANID KING KHOSROW I reunites Persia and begins forays west into Byzantium.	**526** AN EARTHQUAKE in Antioch, Turkey, devastates the area, killing some 250,000 people.	◀ **ca 500** JEWISH SCHOLARS compile the Jerusalem Talmud (also known as the Palestinian Talmud), a collection of scholarly tracts of the Bible, law, science, and parables. Talmudic scholars continue to interpret these texts of Jewish law and custom to this day.
ASIA & OCEANIA	**ca 500** THE YAMATO COURT consolidates its rule in Japan. **522** THE HEPHTHALITES reach the height of their power in Central Asia. They rule from northwest India and receive tribute from 40 countries.	**500** TRADE ON THE SILK ROAD continues to connect Asia with Europe in a lively exchange of goods and culture. Two-humped Bactrian camels, uniquely adapted to the extreme cold of the mountains and the heat of Asia's deserts, carry much of the merchandise.	**500s** AFTER THE HUNS destroy numerous Buddhist monasteries in India, Buddhism is revived and flourishes in northeast India. **528** THE BULGUKSA TEMPLE is built in the Silla (Korea) capital, Kyongju. **538** BUDDHISM reaches Japan.

Contemporary artwork in a synagogue in Israel depicts Talmudic teachings.

SCIENCE & TECHNOLOGY	PEOPLE & SOCIETY
 Moche pot with warrior's face	**ca 500** MAYA SOCIETY is organized into city-states covering parts of present-day Mexico, Guatemala, Belize, Honduras, and El Salvador. Priests perform rituals and sacrifices, and maintain calendars for the planting seasons. They grow corn, beans, and chilies, and make land more arable by means of irrigation canals.
ca 500 THE IRON-TIPPED MOLDBOARD PLOW comes into use in east-central Europe, improving agriculture. **ca 530s** BYZANTINE SOLDIERS AND ENGINEERS improve earlier Roman siege machinery. **537** HAGIA SOPHIA in Constantinople is completed, the largest Christian church built at the time, with a main dome spanning 105 feet. It partially collapses in an earthquake in 558.	**529** THE CODE OF JUSTINIAN, including the Codex Constitutionum, is issued for the Byzantine Empire. This codification of Roman law will influence many future European civil law codes.
531 CHOSROES I of Persia builds a palace with the largest iwans ever built. The palace Taq Kisra, near modern-day Baghdad, Iraq, is constructed by a Persian Sassanian ruler around this time. It's known for its iwans, high vaulted halls that serve as a great entrance. Similar portals become architectural features of future mosques.	**ca 531** THE MAZDAKITE MOVEMENT in Iran, which preaches communality of goods and social equality, is persecuted by authorities after the death of its patron, Sassanian king Kavadh I.
ca 500 INDIAN ASTRONOMER AND MATHEMATICIAN Aryabhata I addresses sophisticated concepts in mathematics, including sine tables, and suggests that the Earth rotates on its axis as well as around the sun. **ca 500s** THE GAME OF CHESS is thought to have originated in India or China in this era. It is later introduced to Persia, where it becomes known as *shat-ranj*.	**ca 500** INDIA'S GUPTA KINGS, followers of Hinduism, support the arts and poetry, science and mathematics. Striking murals in the Ajanta caves, depicting court life, musicians, and dancers adorned with pearls and jewels, speak of the wealth and elegance of the period.

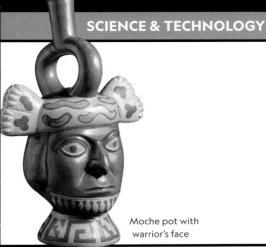

MONASTIC LIFE IN EUROPE

BY THE END of the fifth century, raiding and conquering Germanic tribes had extinguished much of Roman civilization in Europe—a period often referred to as the Dark Ages.

Meanwhile, in Western Europe, the monastic movement took hold and grew and became Europe's intellectual and spiritual bastions. One of the first was the Monte Cassino Abbey founded by St. Benedict of Nursia in Italy in 529. Monasteries remained stable local institutions that provided education for Europe's leaders, scholars, and artists even as Western society grappled with wars and other turmoil. They took up the spread of Christianity and provided isolated centers of calm and learning that preserved Rome's legacy in books. Monks translated and illustrated the Bible, as well as other ancient texts, and upheld moral values. St. Benedict established the Benedictine Rule, which required prayer and work, the two principles that set the standard for the next 600 years. His twin sister Scholastica adapted the rule for nuns.

This rule was carried to England by St. Augustine and his fellow monks, and to the monasteries of the Franks and Lombards. In England, the Benedictine Rule was considered the only true type, whereas in Ireland the earlier Celtic monasticism was firmly established.

In the eighth century St. Boniface converted the pagan tribes in Germany and established the monastery at Fulda, which became the model of all future German monasteries.

One of the first monasteries in Europe, the abbey of Monte Cassino

POLITICS & POWER	GEOGRAPHY & ENVIRONMENT	CULTURE & RELIGION

562 **THE MAYA CITY-STATE OF TIKAL,** in present-day Guatemala, is defeated by rival Calakmul, Mexico.

578 **BUTZ'CHAN,** Smoking Heavens, the 11th ruler of Copán in Honduras, begins his 50-year-long reign.

Contagion spread along trade routes in the sixth century.

546 **ROME IS SACKED** by a new wave of Ostrogoths.

561 **BYZANTIUM AND PERSIA** establish a 50-year peace.

561–584 **CIVIL WARS** break out among the Merovingians in France.

568 **FUGITIVES** from the Lombard invasion of northern Italy settle on the islands in the Venetian lagoon and establish Venice.

▲ **542-594** **A SERIES OF PLAGUES** strikes Europe, nearly halving its population.

568 **THE LOMBARDS,** a Germanic tribe, invade northern Italy.

550 **CHURCH BELLS** come into use in France.

ca 550 **AT THE PERSUASION OF BYZANTINE EMPEROR JUSTINIAN,** two Persian monks are said to have smuggled the secrets of silk-spinning and silkworm culture from China. These first few silkworms signify the beginning of the European silk industry.

573-594 **BISHOP GREGORY OF TOURS** is influential in religious and political matters in the Merovingian kingdom and writes *Ten Books of Histories.*

ca 570 **THE AMHARA** of North Africa establish a protectorate when Abraha, the Yemeni viceroy, marches on Mecca with war elephants, which terrify the Meccans. The period is called the "Year of the Elephant," and many events are dated from this confrontation.

ca 570 **MUHAMMAD,** the Prophet and future messenger of Islam, is born.

575 **THE PERSIANS** overthrow the Abyssinians in Yemen.

551 **BEIRUT IS DESTROYED** by an earthquake; 250,000 lives are lost.

543 **THE FIRST CHRISTIAN MISSION** is established in Nubia. Scholars begin to translate the Bible into the local language.

542 **LY BON** leads the Vietnamese in a successful rebellion against China's occupation. Within five years China retakes the territory.

ca 550 **THE FUNAN CULTURE** loses prominence in the region of the Mekong River.

ca 550 **THE GUPTA EMPIRE** in India breaks up into smaller kingdoms.

577 **THE BEI (NORTHERN) ZHOU DYNASTY,** based along the Wei River, reunifies the splintered kingdoms of northern China.

▶ **552-577** **THE NORTHERN QI KINGDOM** of China adds to and repairs approximately 900 miles of the Great Wall.

Camel and rider, Northern Qi dynasty

SCIENCE & TECHNOLOGY

550 **NATIVE PEOPLE** in southwest Colorado begin building pit houses, roofed with mud and logs.

549 **THE KITE** is invented in China. Although it may have been in use earlier, the year 549 is the first recorded mention of it.

ca 550s **INDIAN ASTRONOMER** and mathematician Varahamihira writes *Five Treatises,* a compilation of Greek, Roman, Egyptian, and Indian astronomy.

PEOPLE & SOCIETY

ca 550 **COAST SALISH PEOPLE** settle along the Duwamish River in what is now Washington State.

571 **THE THREE-STORY MAYA ROSALILA TEMPLE,** Copán's main religious sanctuary, is dedicated.

ca 550 **LEGENDARY KING ARTHUR,** as immortalized in Thomas Malory's *Le Morte Darthur,* leads the Britons against the Saxons in battles and carries the Christian cross. Together with his Knights of the Round Table and their armies, he conquers Scotland, Ireland, Iceland, and Orkney.

ca 540 **THE PEOPLE OF THE ARABIAN PENINSULA** consist of loosely linked nomadic clans—the Bedouin—who herd goats, sheep, and camels in the desert, and settled tribes who are engaged in commerce and long-distance caravan trade.

502-549 **EMPEROR WUDI,** founder of the Nan (Southern) Liang dynasty, reforms the nine-rank system of advancement in China's government. He becomes a devout Buddhist and sponsors construction of numerous temples.

CONNECTIONS

South Asian Hub

India and the Srivijaya kingdom played a major role in keeping trade throughout the Indian Ocean supplied with exotic goods. One geographer from Alexandria, Egypt, Cosmas Indicopleustes—his name translates in Latin to "traveler to India"—explored and later described the world as he saw it when he retired to a Christian monastery. In his book *Christian Topography,* likely written in 547-550, he describes the ships that land in Ceylon, one of Srivijaya's islands. They come from Ethiopia, Persia, India, and China carrying silk, aloe, pepper, sandalwood, musk, and sesame logs and trade for emeralds, elephants, and horses. From Ceylon many of these goods are shipped to more remote ports in the Pacific.

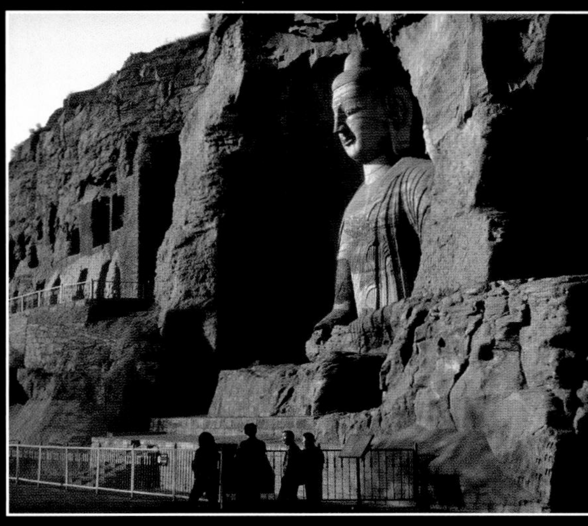

A masterpiece of Chinese Buddhist art, this stone Buddha in the Shanxi Province of China is one of 51,000 statues in a network of 252 caves.

BUDDHISM SPREADS EAST

ARISING IN INDIA about 500 B.C.E., Buddhism slowly gained adherents along the Silk Road. As traders plodded along the trails, monks followed. By the third century C.E. they had founded monasteries at some of the caravan stops in the Kushan Empire of Afghanistan.

In China, Daoism and Confucianism prevailed. After the fall of the Han dynasty—when China split into several warring kingdoms—people may have longed for a religion that offered peaceful meditation and the prospect of personal salvation. Rulers began to support the construction of temples and monasteries, many in caves and on mountainsides. By about 550, China could boast of nearly 14,000 Buddhist temples. In Korea, Buddhism found the support of kings as well. In 538 (or 552 according to another source) the ruler of the Paekche kingdom on the Korean Peninsula sent a diplomatic mission that brought Buddhism to the Yamato ruler in Japan, and the religion gradually developed adherents there, too.

The flow of silk
Colonies
James I of England sent silkworms to Virginia to start a silk industry; the attempt failed.
Americas
Sericulture touched the Americas in 1522, when Cortés had mulberry trees and eggs brought to Mexico.
France
Lyon began to flourish as a silk center in the 16th century. By the mid-18th century nearly a quarter of its population were weavers.
England
French Huguenot refugees carried silk-making skills to 17th-century England, settling in the London district of Spitalfields.
Rome
Silk, exported to Rome by I C.E., was literally worth its weight in gold. Laws tried unsuccessfully to curb the appetite for silk.
Silk Road
Early in the second century B.C.E. caravans linked East and West. Dubbed the Silk Road (red) in the 19th century, the conduit for silk, jade, and spices aided the spread of Buddhism from Central Asia and Islam from Arab countries.
India
Legend traces silk in India to a Chinese princess who smuggled silkworm eggs to Hotan.
Sea Routes
The Silk Road began to decline in the seventh century when sea trade with China developed more fully, and sea routes (blue) proved safer than the treacherous land journey.
London
Lyon
Rome
Antioch
Alexandria
Tyre
Hamadan
Baghdad
Rey
Mary
Bukhara
Samarkand
Kashi
Turpan
Anxi
Gobi
Taklimakan Desert
Hotan
Shache
Xi'an
Kyoto
Barbaricon
Gange
Canton
Quilon

THE SILK ROAD

The fabled Silk Road, a network of footpaths and caravan trails across rugged mountains and barren lands, linked the Mediterranean to China as early as the second century B.C.E. Alexander the Great's army had blazed trails from Greece to the Indus River; Chinese emissaries had scouted the way from the Far East to Central Asia, where they traded for horses from Ferghana to defend against mounted raiders along their northern border.

The main route led from China's capital of Chang'an, modern-day Xi'an, west to the forbidding Taklimakan, or "desert of no return." There the road split into a northern and southern trail, each threading through scarce watering holes. Rejoined at Kashgar (Kashi), the road wound its way through the snow-capped mountains of the Pamirs and the Hindu Kush, skirted the southern coast of the Caspian Sea, and continued via Antioch to the Mediterranean. Most merchants trekked only a short section of the way. The journey took months and was perilous. Sandstorms and mountain passes, marauders and self-appointed taxing agents took their toll.

By the seventh century, though, trade flowed steadily in all directions. China's Tang dynasty expanded far into western lands, setting up protectorates in Sogdiana and Ferghana in Central Asia and eastern Persia. Chinese merchants traded exquisite silks and porcelain for Roman glass, Bactrian gold jewelry, Sassanian bronze and silver vessels, and Indian precious stones. Religion, science and technology, artistic styles, and foods also traveled along the road. Buddhism flowed east from India in the sixth century. A century later Islam began to spread through the Middle East, Central Asia, and far into western China.

This exchange continued well into the 14th century, contributing to a Eurasian culture that was vibrant, luxurious, and complex. Only when trade became more profitable via new sea routes did commerce along the ancient paths began to decline.

Having crossed the most inaccessible regions of the ancient Silk Road, a caravan reaches Jiayuguan fortress in China's Gansu Province. From here traders braved the unknown, conveying goods and ideas to the West.

POLITICS & POWER

ca 600 THE NASCA CULTURE of Peru begins to fade.

▶ **ca 600s** THE MAYA CITY OF PALENQUE flourishes as a powerful regional capital in what is now Mexico's Chiapas state.

ca 600-1000 THE HUARI EMPIRE (also spelled Wari), based in the central and northern highlands of the Andes, rules over most of Peru.

590-604 POPE GREGORY I defends the supremacy of the see of Rome against claims by the Byzantine Empire.

602 PHOCAS overthrows Byzantine Emperor Maurice.

610 HERACLIUS OF CARTHAGE arrives in Constantinople and usurps the throne, executing Phocas. In renewed battles, he regains Syria, Jerusalem, and Egypt.

589 ARABS, KHAZARS, AND TURKS invade Persia, but are repelled.

590-628 CHOSROES II rules in Persia.

ca 600s GHANA emerges as the first significant medieval trading empire in western Africa.

581-604 EMPEROR WENDI reunites a fragmented China and establishes the Sui dynasty.

587 THE SOGA CLAN takes on political power at the Yamato court in Japan.

ca 592 PRINCE SHOTOKU assumes rule over Japan as regent for his mother, the empress, and later his aunt. During his three decades in power, he creates the Seventeen Article Constitution and reinstates the practice of sending envoys to China.

607 KING SONGSTEN GAMPO unifies much of Tibet.

GEOGRAPHY & ENVIRONMENT

ca 600 THE JOYA DE CEREN Maya site in El Salvador is buried under ash from the erupting Laguna Caldera volcano.

ca 600-650 MOCHE SOCIETY is stressed and transformed by decades of El Niño droughts and floods.

Maya maize god

ca 600 AFTER THE REIGN OF JUSTINIAN, the Byzantine Empire begins to lose ground in frequent military clashes with the Avars, Persians, and Muslims.

ca 619 THE SASSANIAN PERSIAN EMPIRE defeats Byzantine forces to temporarily conquer Egypt.

ca 600 THE CULTIVATION OF TARO and construction of the Alekoko fishpond help feed Hawaii's population.

ca 600-630 MON PEOPLE from western China move into Thailand. Thai people from southern China begin to settle among the Mon and form small states.

CULTURE & RELIGION

589 CATHOLICISM is proclaimed the official religion in Spain after King Recared's conversion.

598 THE FIRST ENGLISH SCHOOL is founded in Canterbury.

ca 600 GREGORIAN CHANT is named for Pope Gregory I.

612 THE HERMITAGE at St. Gall, Switzerland, and monastery at Bobbio, Italy, are founded.

ca 610 MUHAMMAD experiences a spiritual transformation and, according to religious texts, begins to repeat a message received from God. When he proclaims in Mecca that there is only one God he is reviled.

ca 600 CHINESE BUDDHIST MISSIONARY Ono no Imoko founds Ikebono, Japan's oldest school of floral arrangement. This classic Japanese art is called ikebana.

618-907 THE TANG DYNASTY ushers in a golden age of poetry and culture in China.

SCIENCE & TECHNOLOGY	PEOPLE & SOCIETY
ca 600 MESOAMERICANS develop amate paper from tree bark. **ca 600s** MAYA STRUCTURES feature a corbel arch, an innovation that uses levels of overlapping stones built into massive walls, instead of a single keystone, to provide the necessary support.	**ca 600-1000** THE HUARI, arising in the region near the modern-day city of Ayacucho, Peru, build elite cities, temples, and palaces and set up a major network of roads and communication that later serves as a model to the Inca.
ca 600-800 DIKES are first built in the Low Countries to protect against floods.	**540-604** AS A YOUNG MAN, GREGORY THE GREAT becomes prefect of the city of Rome, but he abandons that course to become a monk. He sells his family properties in Rome and Sicily and uses the funds to aid the poor and endow seven Benedictine monasteries. In 578 the pope sends Gregory as emissary to Byzantium seeking help against the invading Lombards. Help is not forthcoming, and Gregory returns, convinced that Rome has to become independent of the Church of the East. In 590 he is elected pope and strengthens the papal primacy over the churches of the West.
618 THE CHINESE CAPITAL of Chang'an is the largest city in the world, with a population of one to two million.	**ca 622-623** BILAL IBN RABAH, also known as "The Black," a slave in Mecca, is one of the first people to accept Muhammad's message. Bilal is persecuted for his beliefs but does not renounce Islam. He soon joins Muhammad's forces on campaigns. When Muhammad looks for means to rally people, he turns to Bilal, who has a sonorous voice to call the Muslims to prayer, and thus he becomes the first muezzin.
581-618 DURING THE SUI DYNASTY in China, the emperors undertake construction of palaces and granaries, repair sections of the Great Wall, and complete the Grand Canal. **607** JAPAN'S HORYUJI TEMPLE is completed. The complex has some of the oldest surviving wooden buildings in the world.	**606-647** HARSHA becomes ruler of a large empire in India at age 16, after the assassination of his elder brother, Rajyavardhana. With youthful zeal, he leads his army through northern India and exerts his influence from Gujarat to Assam. As a Buddhist, he is known for his piety and generosity and supports free medical care and hospitalization for his subjects.

The Grand Canal

CHINA'S GRAND CANAL

THOUGH IT TOOK two thousand years for the Grand Canal to reach its full length of 1,100 miles, the largest parts were built during six years of furious building, between 605 and 611, under a mandate from Emperor Yangdi of the Sui dynasty.

Uncounted workers toiled and died undergoing this compulsory labor. They repaired and enlarged an older system of canals that had been started in the sixth century B.C.E. and blazed a new channel for hundreds of miles from Hangzhou to Yangzhou, creating a vital north-south link between the Yangtze and Yellow Rivers. Kublai Khan later extended the canal to Beijing, and the Ming made further improvements.

This monumental feat of engineering—in use to this day—provided a much needed supply route to the agrarian south.

POLITICS & POWER	GEOGRAPHY & ENVIRONMENT	CULTURE & RELIGION
628-695 **SMOKE IMIX,** the 12th ruler of Copán, Honduras, begins his long reign, wielding political control over a wide area of Maya countryside.	**ca 650** **THE PUEBLO CULTURES**—the Hohokam, Anasazi, and Mogollon—develop independently but share a harsh territory extending from northern Mexico to Arizona and New Mexico, southern Utah and Colorado, bounded by desert to the west and grassy plains to the east. They live as hunter-gatherers and begin a settled existence as they develop tenuous agriculture. The development of pottery vessels to store and protect food from mold and pests is an important step in settling permanently.	**628-822** **COPÁN'S ARCHITECTURE AND CULTURAL LIFE** reaches its apogee in Honduras. The city is crowned by a raised platform, now called the Acropolis, with a ballcourt, plazas, temples, and magnificent sculptures.
633 **THE MERCIANS AND WELSH** defeat the Northumbrians at Hatfield in England. **641** **BYZANTINE EMPEROR HERACLIUS** dies. He is eventually succeeded by his grandson Constans II, who repels the Muslim onslaught on Constantinople and defeats the Slavs.	**635** **THE BULGAR PEOPLE,** living north of the Black Sea, unite into the independent Great Bulgaria confederation under their leader Kubrat.	**ca 625** **A ROYAL BURIAL** at the Sutton Hoo site in Suffolk, England, includes a ship equipped for the afterlife and 41 solid gold items. **ca 625** **THE ABBEY OF SAINT-DENIS** near Paris is founded. **630-632** **HERACLIUS** orders the forced conversion of Jews after accusing them of collaboration with Persian invaders.
622 **MUHAMMAD** and his followers flee to Medina. In 630 Muhammad returns and conquers Mecca. **632** **UPON MUHAMMAD'S DEATH,** his father-in-law, Abu Bakr, succeeds him and brings Muhammad's message and Islam to Arabia, Syria, Palestine, and Iraq. **634-644** **UMAR**—successor to Abu Bakr—takes up the sword for Islam and advances into Egypt and other Byzantine territories. **656** **ALI**—Muhammad's son-in-law—becomes the new leader of Islam.	**638** **MUSLIM CAMP TOWNS** spring up, such as Basra and Kufa, where Muslim Arabs begin to assimilate to sedentary lifestyles, farming, and trade.	**624-627** **JEWS ARE EVICTED** from Medina by Muhammad. **638** **ARABS CAPTURE JERUSALEM** and bring Palestine and Syria under Muslim control. Many religious minorities, including Jews, Christians, and Sabaeans, are given protected status *(dhimmi).* **ca 650** **MUHAMMAD'S MESSAGE** from God is written down to form the Quran.
618 **GAOZU,** a Sui official, founds the Tang dynasty. **641** **HARSHA,** ruler of a large kingdom in India, sends an envoy to the Chinese emperor and establishes the first diplomatic relations between India and China. **645** **FOLLOWING A COUP** against the Soga clan in Japan, the imperial court promotes Buddhist doctrines and urges competing clans to overcome their disagreements. **652** **AFGHANISTAN** is conquered by Arabs.	**ca 650** **CHINA** stretches from Tibet to Korea and from Mongolia to the South China Sea. **ca 650** **SRIVIJAYA** on the island of Sumatra establishes itself as a kingdom, a strategic landing point for ships sailing to or from China.	**629-664** **CHINESE BUDDHIST MONK** and pilgrim explorer Xuanzang travels to India and beyond to collect Buddhist teachings. He writes a lengthy account of his journey, entitled *Records of the Western Regions of the Great Tang Dynasty.* Among other things, he describes the giant Buddhas at Bamian, Afghanistan. **ca 650** **KING SONGSTEN GAMPO** introduces Buddhism to Tibet. He builds the Jokhang Temple and Potala Palace.

SCIENCE & TECHNOLOGY

PEOPLE & SOCIETY

ca 650 **THE PUEBLO PEOPLE** of the American Southwest live in pit houses or adobe homes.

Christian Byzantine emperor Heraclius fought a series of wars against Muslim Persians. His crusade became a popular legend in medieval Europe centuries later.

◀ **627** **BY DECREE OF EMPEROR HERACLIUS,** the Greek language replaces Latin as the official language in Byzantium.

635 **AIDAN,** a monk of Iona, establishes a priory, church, and see on Lindisfarne, an island off the Northumberland coast. Lindisfarne flourishes as a spiritual center for more than 150 years and becomes known as Holy Island.

654 **THE VISIGOTHIC LAW CODE** known as Liber Judiciorum becomes the basis of medieval Spanish law.

660 **SYRIAN ASTRONOMER** Severus Sebokht writes *Treatise on the Astrolabe* and *Treatise on the Constellations.*

ca 650 **THE REALM OF ISLAM** becomes a new society, as a rapidly growing number of adherents take inspiration from the words of the Prophet Muhammad.

656 **THE BATTLE OF THE CAMEL,** over succession to the caliphate after the death of Uthman, is attended by Muhammad's widow Aishah on a camel. Her political participation is condemned and leads to the seclusion of women.

ca 632-647 **CHEOMSEONGDAE OBSERVATORY** is built in the Korean kingdom of Silla, the oldest known observatory in east Asia. The outer layer, constructed of 365 stones, denotes one calendar year.

629-649 **TANG EMPEROR TAIZONG,** known for his scholarship, extends the state school system started by his father, Gaozu. He appoints a national academy directorate and establishes prefecture schools—including medical schools—throughout the country.

646 **JAPAN** institutes the Taika reforms, establishing a new government and administrative system. Land is taken over by the state and redistributed among farmers to introduce a new tax system that is adopted from China.

THE RISE OF ISLAM

IN 610 MUHAMMAD of Mecca had a revelation in the desert, when a voice commanded him to pay obedience to the one God, Allah. After further visions, he began to repeat the words revealed to him, later written down in the Quran (below).

His message to the powerful clans of the Arabian desert, bidding them to believe in only one God and to share with the poor, so enraged them that he and his followers were driven from Mecca. On his flight to the town of Medina—the Hegira—in 622, the tenets of his belief crystallized for him, and Muslims ever since have marked the calendar from this date as the year one.

In 630 Muhammad returned to Mecca with a force of men and defeated his opponents. He and his followers smashed the idols in the Kaaba—which had been a holy shrine since time immemorial—but preserved the sacred Black Stone inside. Muhammad spelled out the obligations of the faith by proclaiming the Five Pillars of Islam: belief in one God, prayer, almsgiving, fasting during the month of Ramadan, and performing the hajj (the pilgrimage to Mecca) once in a lifetime or more often if possible.

Muhammad died two years after taking Mecca, but his successors propagated the faith, seeking new converts by word and new territory by sword.

The Quran

POLITICS & POWER	GEOGRAPHY & ENVIRONMENT	CULTURE & RELIGION
682 **MAYA RULER AH CACAO** becomes ruler of Tikal, Guatemala. Temple I on the Great Plaza is built as his funerary monument. **683** **MAYA KING PACAL,** ruler of Palenque in Mexico, dies at age 80, after a long reign, and is buried underneath the Temple of the Inscriptions. **695** **THE 13TH MAYA RULER OF COPÁN,** 18 Rabbit, begins his 43-year-long reign in Honduras.	**600s** **THE MILLER CULTURE** of Mississippi plants maize and hunts with bows and arrows.	**600s** **ANCESTRAL PUEBLOAN** (Anasazi) potters in the American Southwest perfect a distinctive gray ware, suitable for cook pots.
668 **BYZANTINE EMPEROR CONSTANS II** is assassinated. A trio of his sons co-reign for 13 years, until Constantine IV deposes and murders his younger brothers Herakleios and Tiberios to assume sole rule. **681** **BULGARS** settle south of the Danube, establishing their first kingdom. **687** **WITH THE CORONATION OF PIPPIN II,** rule over the Franks passes from the Merovingians to the Carolingians.	**680** **A THREE-YEAR DROUGHT** in England leads to a famine.	**ca 650** **CHRISTIANITY** is disseminated further in Europe. Bishops send missionaries into Celtic and Germanic areas. **664** **AT THE SYNOD OF WHITBY,** the English church decides to follow Roman practices in Christianity instead of Celtic. **697** **THE LAW OF THE INNOCENTS** is passed at the Synod of Birr in Ireland. It punishes those who inflict violence on noncombatants, especially women, children, and clerics.
661 **MUHAMMAD'S FOURTH SUCCESSOR, ALI,** is assassinated in Iraq. Muawiyah declares himself caliph of all Muslim lands and begins the rule of the Umayyad dynasty. He moves the Muslim capital from Iraq to Damascus, Syria. **685-705** **ABD AL MALIK,** fifth Umayyad caliph, adopts Arabic as the language of administration and creates a new Islamic-style coinage with religious quotations instead of pictures.	**661** **CAMEL HERDS OF THE SAHARA** support a nomadic way of life to people in one of the world's most inhospitable environments.	**ca 650** **COPYING THE QURAN** results in ever more artistic forms of calligraphy. **691-692** **THE DOME OF THE ROCK,** one of Islam's holiest shrines, is built in Jerusalem. The rock over which it is built is said to be the one from which Muhammad ascended to heaven. Judaism believes this is where Abraham took his son Isaac to be sacrificed. **ca 699** **THE BERBER WARRIOR QUEEN** and prophet Kahina—regarded as much a mythical figure as a historical one and thought to be Jewish—leads her people in a resistance against the Arab invasion of North Africa.
668 **CHINA** prevails in the 23-year Goguryeo-Tang War with Korea. ▶ **690-705** **EMPRESS WU** of China usurps the throne from her stepson Gaozong and establishes the short-lived Zhou dynasty. She is the only woman in Chinese history to have declared herself emperor.	**ca 660** **SOGDIANA**—in today's Uzbekistan—becomes part of China. **668** **THE SILLA KINGDOM** unites the Korean Peninsula.	**ca 660** **CHINESE ROYALTY** adopts luxury drinking vessels and tableware of silver and gold from Central Asia and greater Iran. **ca 670** **THE FOLDING FAN** is invented in Japan. **676** **EMPRESS WU** supports the construction of the Vairochana Buddha at the Buddhist cave temple at Longmen. **687** **ACCLAIMED CALLIGRAPHER SUN GUOTING** writes a treatise on calligraphy summarizing the aesthetic ideals of Chinese script.

SCIENCE & TECHNOLOGY	PEOPLE & SOCIETY
695-738 DURING THE REIGN of Copán's 13th ruler, 18 Rabbit, architectural and sculptural styles evolve. The chamber of one temple holds a depiction of the cosmos, with a crocodile representing the arc of the night sky.	**679** DOS PILAS, established as an outpost of the powerful Maya city-state Tikal, is forced into allegiance with Tikal's rival Calakmul. Dos Pilas ruler B'ajlaj Chan K'awiil conquers Tikal in a series of battles against his own brother.
678 BYZANTINE WARRIORS successfully use "Greek fire," an incendiary device, against Muslim attackers.	**663-664** HILDA OF WHITBY, an English noblewoman, who governs a double monastery of monks and nuns, advises kings, encourages scholars, and serves as a host of the synod of abbesses of monasteries. **660s** THE UNIFIED BULGAR from the east splinter into five hordes and disperse. One of the hordes, led by Asparukh, engages in skirmishes with the Byzantine Empire. They win territory and settle south of the Danube River in lands of ancient Thrace and Macedonia. Under Khan Asparukh, they establish their first kingdom in 681, which lasts until 1018.
	680 HUSAYN, the grandson of Muhammad, is killed in a power struggle between Sunnis and Shiites.

Empress Wu

THE SPLIT BETWEEN SUNNI AND SHIITE

WHEN THE PROPHET Muhammad died in 632, the Muslim leadership elected his father-in-law, Abu Bakr, to be the first caliph, or temporal leader of the Islamic state. The decision caused a permanent rift between the two major branches of Islam: the Shiite and the Sunni.

Shiites believed that only direct descendants of Muhammad were worthy of the caliphate. Sunnis supported Abu Bakr, as well as two subsequent caliphs who mobilized Arabia with the message of the Prophet and continued Islam's expansion, yet were still considered illegitimate by Shiites.

In 656 Muhammad's cousin and son-in-law, Ali, assumed succession as the fourth caliph—the first caliph recognized by Shiites. But plots against his life finally led to his murder in 661. His successor launched the Umayyad dynasty and moved the Islamic capital from Iraq to Damascus, Syria.

At this point the schism between the factions was complete. When Ali's last heir died, spiritual power according to the Shiites passed to the ulama, a council of 12 scholars who elected a supreme imam. The best known modern example of the Shiite supreme imam is the Ayatollah Khomeini.

Shiite rituals differ slightly from those of the Sunni. Shiites believe that the imam's authority is infallible because it comes directly from God. Imams are often revered as saints, and people make pilgrimages to their tombs.

Sunnis believe that there is no need for a special class of spiritual leaders, nor do they believe that there should be appeals to saints for intercession. They have been willing to accept caliphs who are not of Muhammad's descent as rightful leaders.

Most people do not claim adherence to either group, but simply refer to themselves as Muslims.

POLITICS & POWER	GEOGRAPHY & ENVIRONMENT	CULTURE & RELIGION

ca 700 THE MOCHE SOCIETY in Peru collapses.

ca 700s THE ADOPTION OF FARMING by the Mogollon ("mountain people") leads to permanent communities built along mountain streams in the Southwest of North America. They build semisubterranean pit houses and subsist by farming maize, beans, and squash.

▶ **721-764** MAYA K'INICH AHKAL MO'NAHB III rules Palenque, Mexico.

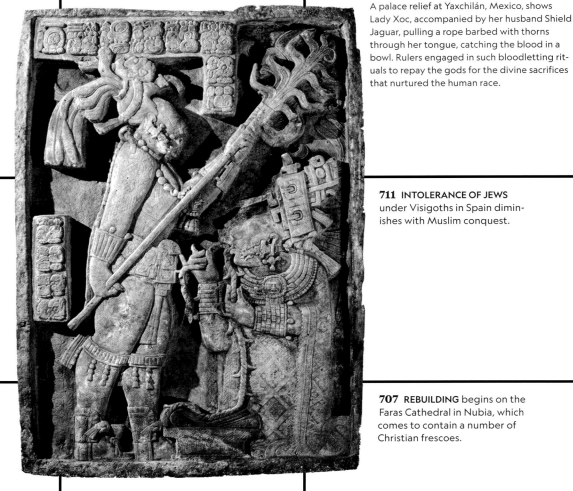

704 KING AETHELRED of Mercia, England, gives up his kingdom to become a monk at Bardney in Lindsey. He is succeeded by Cenred, son of Wulfhere. In 716 Aethelbald takes over.

711 MUSLIM ARMIES invade southern Spain from North Africa.

717 LEO III becomes Byzantine emperor and ends a period of instability. He repels renewed attacks by the Arab Umayyads.

705-715 UNDER CALIPH AL WALID, the Arab Umayyad dynasty extends from the Atlantic Ocean to the borders of China and India.

ca 700s POLYNESIANS settle Rarotonga in the Cook Islands and Tahiti in the Society Islands.

712 SIND IN INDIA is conquered by Umayyad forces.

712-756 TANG EMPEROR XUANZONG assumes his rule. During his reign, Tang China reaches the height of its power.

ca 700 THE UMAYYADS develop desert agriculture in Syria, installing extensive irrigation works around their palaces at the desert's edge.

710-784 NARA, the Japanese imperial capital located on Honshu Island, becomes a prosperous city and the center of Japanese culture. Roads link Nara to provincial capitals, and government agents can collect taxes more efficiently and routinely.

723 THE CITY OF MANJU-PATAN (Kathmandu) is founded in Nepal.

A palace relief at Yaxchilán, Mexico, shows Lady Xoc, accompanied by her husband Shield Jaguar, pulling a rope barbed with thorns through her tongue, catching the blood in a bowl. Rulers engaged in such bloodletting rituals to repay the gods for the divine sacrifices that nurtured the human race.

711 INTOLERANCE OF JEWS under Visigoths in Spain diminishes with Muslim conquest.

707 REBUILDING begins on the Faras Cathedral in Nubia, which comes to contain a number of Christian frescoes.

ca 700-750 SHANKARA, Indian Hindu philosopher, helps revive Hinduism with his writing on the study of the Vedas and combines the many strands into a consistent system of thought.

712 JAPAN'S HISTORY and mythology are recorded in the *Kojiki (Records of Ancient Matters)*. A second chronicle, the *Nihon Shoki (Chronicles of Japan)* is compiled in the year 720.

SCIENCE & TECHNOLOGY	PEOPLE & SOCIETY
700s MAYA astronomers track and chart the movements of Mars in the sky.	**ca 700** PUEBLO PEOPLE in the Southwest of North America live in houses aboveground and embrace farming. **ca 700** THE MISSISSIPPIAN CULTURE emerges in the river valley south of today's St. Louis and spreads throughout the Southeast. It will endure for about five centuries.
725 BEDE THE VENERABLE, monk and scholar at the monastery of Wearmouth-Jarrow in England, finishes *De Temporum Ratione,* a cosmological explanation of the reckoning of time.	**726-727** BYZANTINE EMPEROR LEO III ignites the iconoclasm controversy with a decree outlawing the worship of icons. Western parts of the empire, including popes Gregory II and III, oppose the idea. Leo transfers southern Italy and Greece from the papal diocese to that of the patriarch of Constantinople. An armed uprising in Ravenna, Italy, severs that area from the Byzantine Empire for good.
ca 721 THE PERSIAN ALCHEMIST Abu Musa Jabir ibn Hayyan, sometimes considered a founder of modern chemistry, is born.	**ca 700s** THE AFRICAN SLAVE TRADE, though in progress since antiquity, picks up momentum along with other trans-Saharan trade. Muslim merchants provide access for Indian, Persian, Southeast Asian, and Mediterranean customers.
713 CONSTRUCTION begins on the largest Buddha in the world, the 233-foot-tall Leshan Giant Buddha, built in Sichuan Province in China.	**724** SHOMU TENNO becomes the 45th emperor of Japan. A devout Buddhist, he goes on to build temples and statues and promote Buddhism throughout the country.

Red clay pottery recovered in Aztec Ruins National Monument

TREASURES OF THE DESERT

SINCE EARLIEST TIMES the people of America's Southwest have excelled in their arts and crafts. Paintings on rock walls, baskets woven with geometric designs, jewelry of turquoise, shell and jet beads, and blankets and shawls woven on belt looms attest to their skill.

The first potters learned to roll coils of clay into basketlike shapes and fire them to form crude vessels. By the 10th century these potters had achieved a high level of artistry, moving from simple unadorned jugs to sophisticated polychrome designs and decorations. Each group of people developed its own distinctive shapes.

The Hohokam created pottery with broadline designs. The ancient Pueblo people produced red clay vessels with multicolored geometric designs, embodying mythical concepts sacred to them. The Mimbre people, descendants of the Mogollon, covered their pottery with a white kaolin slip and painted the creatures of their Arizona environment—lizards, turtles, birds, and fish—in black outlines. They attached a particular burial rite to their pottery, ritually piercing bowls and placing them hatlike on the head of deceased family members in their burial pose.

MAYA CHRONICLES

In the ancient New World only the people of Mesoamerica developed a complete system of writing. Though the Olmecs and later the Zapotecs made simple inscriptions in stone, the Maya refined writing into a complex system of 800 pictorial and phonetic hieroglyphs. Inscribed on stelae, altars, and temples, the texts are lined up in a gridlike arrangement or by a linear set of square blocks to chronicle their history, describe the rule of kings, and date important battles. Genealogies and rituals were also recorded, on bark paper.

The Maya were fascinated with tracking the passage of time, and developed several mathematical calendar systems. The Haab cycle has 365 days, similar to the cycle of a full solar year, though the months are not of equal length. In addition, the sacred calendar finished a cycle every 260 days, with periods relating to the growing cycle of maize, the period of pregnancy, and movements of the moon. (Some modern-day Maya still hold a new year ceremony every 260 days.) Both of these systems appear in the Long Count calendar, which tracks days chronologically to mark dates of historical or mythological significance. The Maya also counted time back to the creation of the universe, and arrived at the date of 3114 B.C.E.

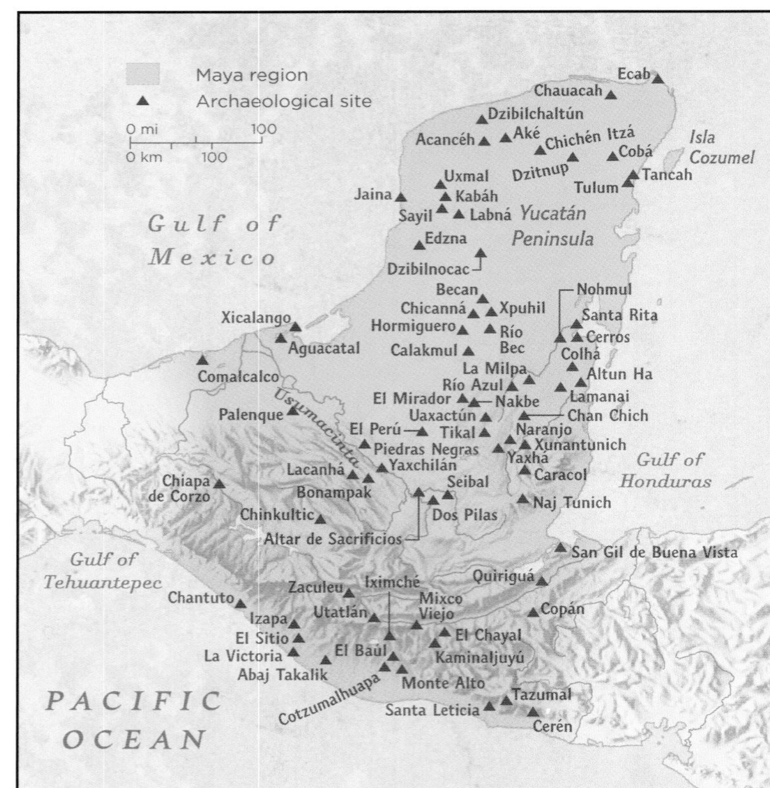

Astronomers charted the movement of the planets and the stars from observatories such as the one at Tikal at right. Built on top of a pyramid, the observatory is sited so that Venus and Jupiter align directly overhead at times of conjunction.

The Maya city-states, each ruled by an independent king who served as an intermediary between gods and the people, created a sophisticated civilization. They played ritual ball games, built pyramids topped with temples, engaged in elaborate rites to appease the gods, and waged war to obtain captives for human sacrifice. Ritual bloodletting was part of the religion; one method entailed the pulling of a thorn-studded rope through the tongue and catching the blood in a bowl, as shown in the relief on page 130. Bloodletting and sacrifice, whether among themselves or using prisoners, was thought to appease the gods, who had used their own blood to create the human race.

By the 10th century this high civilization mysteriously collapsed. People dispersed into the countryside and let the jungle overtake their splendid cities. The demise may have been brought on by a number of factors: endless wars, drought, deforestation, depletion of natural resources, and a reduction of the soil's productivity that could not provide for the increasing population.

Planets align perfectly above the top of the observatory at Tikal in present-day Guatemala, where Maya studied the sky to help predict fortuitous events.

730-760

	POLITICS & POWER	GEOGRAPHY & ENVIRONMENT	CULTURE & RELIGION
THE AMERICAS	**738 THE 13TH RULER,** 18 Rabbit, of the Maya city-state of Copán in Honduras is beheaded by chief Cauac Sky of the neighboring city Quiriguá. Copán does not recover its grandeur until the accession of its 15th ruler, Smoke Shell, in 749. **741 MAYA K'AWIIL CHAN K'INICH** is installed as the last ruler at Dos Pilas, Guatemala. The city-state will be abandoned by 760. **ca 750 THE CITY-STATE OF TEOTIHUACAN** is burned, perhaps during a civil war or uprising.		**751-763 MAYA RULER K'AHK' YIPYAJ CHAN K'AWIIL,** known as Smoke Shell, indulges in a massive building program of temples and monuments in Copán.
EUROPE	**751-768 CHARLES MARTEL'S SON,** Pippin III, rules the Franks. **756 CUTHRED,** ruler of Wessex, England, dies, and Wessex falls under the control of Mercia. **757 AETHELBALD,** king of Mercia, is murdered after ruling for 41 years.		**ca 700-750 THE OLD ENGLISH EPIC POEM** *Beowulf* is composed about this time. **731 MONK AND SCHOLAR BEDE THE VENERABLE** finishes his *Historia Ecclesiastica Gentis Anglorum,* a Latin history of the English people.
MIDDLE EAST & AFRICA	**750-754 ABU AL ABBAS,** founder of the Abbasid dynasty, overthrows the Umayyads and takes up the leadership of the Muslim Empire. **750 PRINCE ABD AL RAHMAN I** flees the massacre of the Umayyads and escapes to Spain, uniting his people there. He makes Córdoba the new capital of the Umayyads. **754 AL MANSUR** becomes second Abbasid caliph, after his brother's death, and founds Baghdad, Iraq, as his capital.	**749 AN EARTHQUAKE** near the Sea of Galilee causes massive damage.	**ca 700s THE LITERARY COLLECTION** known as Muallaqat, meaning "The Suspended Ones," is compiled using elaborate meter and rhyme, expressing universal themes in a few words and setting poetic standards for centuries. **ca 750 JAFAR IBN MUHAMMAD** establishes the Jafari school of Islamic law, the most important in Shiism. **ca 750-759 IBN AL MUQAFFA** translates *Kalila wa Dimna,* an Indian allegory, from the original Pahlavi into Arabic. It becomes a classic work of Arabic literature.
ASIA & OCEANIA	**751 TANG CHINESE** forces are defeated by a coalition of Arabs and Turks at the Talas River in present-day Kazakhstan and in the area of Turkestan. **755-763 CHINESE GENERAL AN LUSHAN** leads a rebellion in Chang'an, modern-day Xi'an. Although he is killed in 757, the rebellion continues until 763 and weakens the Tang dynasty.	**ca 750 IN JAPAN** *shoen* (landed estates) become an important economic institution, as they offer a more manageable form of landholding. Public lands begin to revert to the shoen.	**ca 750 POETRY** flourishes during the Tang dynasty, particularly in the celebrated works of Li Bai (701-762), Du Fu (712-770), and Bai Juyi (772-846). **752 THE STATUE OF THE GREAT BUDDHA** is dedicated at Nara, signaling Japan's prominence as a center of Buddhism in East Asia.

WHAT LIFE WAS LIKE

Maya Cenotes

The Maya of the Yucatán Peninsula believed that to receive the blessings of rain, they should propitiate Chac, the god who lived in the depths of sacred underground pools, called cenotes. These freshwater pools were considered special gifts in an arid region and supplied water to the city-states. The cenotes were used for rites of passage and special ceremonies to benefit the gods. To propitiate the gods and ensure plentiful rain, priests and villagers dropped gifts of pottery—bowls, figurines, and incense holders—into the pools. Skeletal remains suggest possible human sacrifice, or they may indicate accidental drowning.

SCIENCE & TECHNOLOGY	PEOPLE & SOCIETY
700s THE BOW AND ARROW are adopted by people in the American Southeast.	**ca 700s** THE ZAPOTECS of Oaxaca in Mexico begin a period of decline. Outside pressures, predominantly from Mixtec-speaking peoples, lead to the disappearance of Zapotec influence in the region and the abandonment of the main plaza at Monte Albán, their splendid ceremonial center.
700s FARMERS in Europe begin to use a rigid horse collar, allowing them to replace oxen with horses.	**732** CHARLES MARTEL, the mayor of the palace of the Frankish kingdom, achieves his renown for winning the Battle of Tours—also known as the Battle of Poitiers—in central France. This battle is memorialized as "the salvation of Europe," since it preserved western Europe from Muslim conquest. In Arabian history, the battlefield of Tours is called The Pavement of Martyrs, for the numerous prominent men lost in battle. It marks the farthest Muslim advance into Europe and gives Charles's family great prestige.
	750 CALIPH MARWAN II is defeated and killed at the Battle of the Great Zab River, ending the Umayyad dynasty. **ca 750** IBN AL MUQAFFA, a Persian convert to Islam and secretary to early Abbasid rulers, translates much of Middle Persian literature into Arabic and writes advice for Muslim rulers. **ca 750** PERSIANS, SYRIANS, and others under Muslim rule begin to adopt Arabic as their language.
735 THE FIRST RECORDED EPIDEMIC of smallpox in Japan kills almost one-third of the population.	**749** EMPRESS KOKEN (later called Empress Shotoku) takes the throne of Nara period Japan, becoming the last female ruler of the country until the 17th century.

Astrolabes, such as this one from the 10th century, have been used for navigation since the eighth century.

ARAB SEA TRADERS

BY THE MIDDLE of the eighth century, Arab seafarers had mastered the long ocean crossing from the Persian Gulf to the South China Sea. Equipped with compass and astrolabe, they could successfully calculate their route and navigate their sailing vessels across the open sea.

They traveled from ports of the Arabian Peninsula to Quilon in southern India; steered through the Strait of Malacca; called at Quang Ngai in Vietnam; and journeyed as far north as Canton, China. Muslim trading ships carried ivory, pearls, incense, and spices to China and returned with Chinese silk, paper, ink, tea, and porcelain.

The white porcelain from China, difficult to reproduce because the raw material—white kaolin clay—was not available elsewhere, led Arab potters to the invention of lusterware. This pottery was glazed with an opaque white slip and was decorated with designs of an iridescent metallic sheen, a process borrowed from the Islamic glass industry. This new technique traveled along the east coast of Africa and around the Mediterranean and was later adopted by Syria, Spain, and Italy, where it became known as maiolica.

POLITICS & POWER

763 **YAX PASAJ CHAN YOPAAT,** First Dawned Sky Lightning God, the 16th Maya ruler of Copán in Honduras, assumes power.

▶ **776-795** **CHAAN MUAN** reigns over Bonampak in Mexico.

757-796 **OFFA, KING OF MERCIA,** rules parts of England, including Wessex, Sussex, Kent, East Anglia, and parts of northern Wessex.

771 **PIPPIN II'S SON CHARLEMAGNE** assumes sole rule of the entire kingdom of the Franks.

774 **AFTER CONQUERING THE LOMBARDS** in northern Italy, Charlemagne is also crowned king of the Lombards.

775 **EMPRESS IRENE** steps into the role of regent of the Byzantine Empire for her young son Constantine VI after the death of her husband.

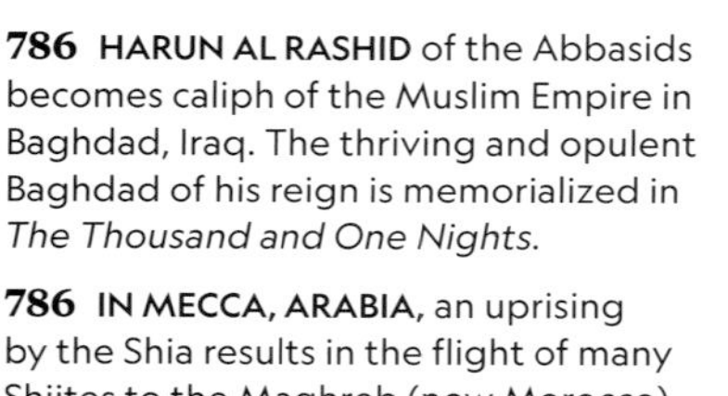

786 **HARUN AL RASHID** of the Abbasids becomes caliph of the Muslim Empire in Baghdad, Iraq. The thriving and opulent Baghdad of his reign is memorialized in *The Thousand and One Nights.*

786 **IN MECCA, ARABIA,** an uprising by the Shia results in the flight of many Shiites to the Maghreb (now Morocco), in North Africa.

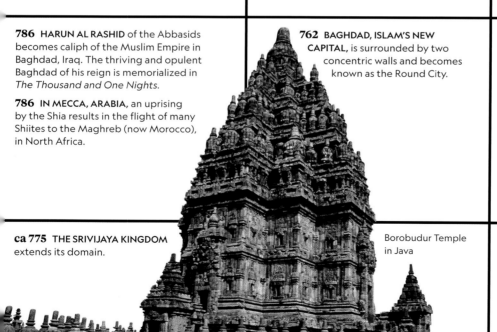

ca 775 **THE SRIVIJAYA KINGDOM** extends its domain.

GEOGRAPHY & ENVIRONMENT

Mural at Bonampak depicting scenes of celebration, battle, and sacrifice

ca 760 **USING IRRIGATION TECHNIQUES,** which enriches the food supply, Muslims introduce cultivation of oranges, lemons, figs, dates, and eggplant in Spain.

762 **BAGHDAD, ISLAM'S NEW CAPITAL,** is surrounded by two concentric walls and becomes known as the Round City.

Borobudur Temple in Java

CULTURE & RELIGION

784-786 **UMAYYAD RULER ABD AR RAHMAN I** begins construction of the Great Mosque in Córdoba, Spain.

ca 760-793 **THE PERSIAN SIBAWAYH** compiles *al Kitab fi an nahw (The Book on Grammar),* the most prominent work on Arab grammar.

775-809 **UNDER ABBASID CALIPHS AL MAHDI AND HARUN AL RASHID,** Baghdad enjoys tremendous prosperity and a thriving intellectual life as a center of learning where Arab and Iranian cultures mingle to produce great philosophical, scientific, and literary works. By the end of Rashid's reign, Baghdad is second only to Constantinople in size.

◀ **ca 778** **CONSTRUCTION** begins on Borobudur Temple, a massive Buddhist monument, built on Java. It requires two million cubic feet of stone and is decorated with 27,000 square feet of bas-reliefs.

SCIENCE & TECHNOLOGY	PEOPLE & SOCIETY
	763-ca 822 YAK PASAJ CHAN YOPAAT, the last of the 16 rulers of Copán, builds onto the lavish temple compound and adds to the complex hieroglyphic chronicle. In one image he receives a baton, referring to the transfer of power from the founder, K'inich Yak K'uk'Mo', who lived some 300 years earlier. **ca 775-975** THE HOHOKAM CULTURE expands its influence across all of what is now the southern half of Arizona.
ca 784 KING OFFA has a dike constructed running north-south, roughly along the border of England and Wales, between the Severn and Dee Rivers. It is the greatest building project of its kind in Europe and involves the deployment of thousands of laborers. A 119-mile-long ditch on the Welsh side of the embankment serves as a territorial boundary marker.	**ca 780** PEASANTS IN EUROPE are generally free in early Germanic society. In the eighth century many begin surrendering their land and person to their lords in return for protection. They become serfs, bound to the land and subject to the lord's control. By 800, about 60 percent of the peasants in western Europe are serfs.
ca 775 YAQUB IBN TARIQ, one of the great astronomers in Baghdad, uses Hindu astronomical measurements in his work.	**786** CALIPH HARUN AL RASHID, who goes out at night in disguise, figures in many tales of *The Thousand and One Nights*. He appoints able administrators to keep his vast empire at peace. He invests much to further the arts while his wife, Zubaydah, is remembered for funding the construction of roads and the drilling of wells. He dies in 809.
ca 768 EMPRESS SHOTOKU of Japan prints one million Buddhist *dharani* (incantations or prayer charms). The collection represents some of the world's earliest printed text.	**763-791** A STRING OF TIBETAN MILITARY VICTORIES weaken the Tang dynasty and dramatically reduce its reach. The Tibetans sack the capital at Chang'an (modern-day Xi'an), cut off China from its Central Asian territories, and dominate the southern portion of the Tarim Basin. Even so, the Tang dynasty continues on until 907, but the population begins to shift from the north to the more fertile south, where abundant production of rice and winter wheat ensures a more comfortable existence.

BYZANTINE EMPRESSES

THEODORA, WIFE OF JUSTINIAN I, served as the Byzantine empress from 527 to 548 and was a valuable adviser to her husband. A former prostitute, she helped pass legislation that empowered and protected women. Conversely, she also conspired against political enemies, sanctioned the massacre of tens of thousands of people, and actively intensified the Christian schism, which her husband had worked hard to reconcile. A partner in power, Theodora was one of the most influential and complex women of the Middle Ages.

The eighth century also witnessed upheaval in Byzantium, despite the empire's gaining in power and influence. Like their Roman predecessors, Byzantine emperors considered themselves God's representatives on Earth. Emperor Leo III (r. 717-741) introduced the religious principle of iconoclasm (from the Greek for "image breaking"), which outlawed the physical portrayal of religious figures. To many, this policy amounted to sacrilege—tens of thousands of monks fled to the Roman church, which was more accepting of physical representations of Christ and the saints. From 741 to 775 Constantine V, Leo III's son, enjoyed a long reign.

Constantine's son Leo IV reigned only five years, but Leo's wife, Irene, ruled for 27. Born an orphan in Athens, Greece, Empress Irene married Leo IV in 769, became empress in 775, and in 780 served as regent for their young son Constantine VI after her husband's death. A strong-willed and ambitious monarch, she restored icon veneration. When Constantine VI came of age, he seized power from his mother in 790, but ended up naming her co-ruler two years later. In 797, Irene conspired against her son, had him blinded, and seized power for herself, becoming the first woman to be sole ruler of the Byzantine Empire. She ruled five more years, ordering the repeal of the iconoclasm decrees and even claiming the title of emperor—not *empress*—until a cabal of generals deposed and exiled her in 802.

POLITICS & POWER

ca 800 THE TOLTEC CAPITAL OF TULA, near present-day Mexico City, becomes a sizable city.

ca 800 MIXTEC ROYAL FAMILIES begin to intermarry with the old Zapotec elite.

ca 800 THE CADDO CULTURE flourishes in Texas and Oklahoma.

ca 800 EL TAJIN emerges as the most important ceremonial center of its time along Mexico's Gulf Coast.

795 VIKINGS appear on the Irish coast for the first time.

797-802 IRENE, widow of Byzantine emperor Leo IV and mother of Constantine VI, has her son blinded so that she can reign alone.

800 POPE LEO III crowns Charlemagne Emperor of Rome.

802-811 NICEPHORUS I becomes Byzantine emperor. He loses territory to the Abbasids but keeps the city of Constantinople safe.

814 CHARLEMAGNE dies. His son, Louis I, becomes emperor.

ca 800 THE CITY OF JENNE-JENO flourishes in the inland Niger Delta. The mud-walled city is a hub of crafts, fishing, farming, and commerce with an estimated population of 10,000.

801 THE BERBERS challenge the rule of the Abbasids by setting up an independent state in North Africa.

809 ABBASID CALIPH HARUN AL RASHID dies.

813-823 AFTER A BATTLE with his brother, which brings on a civil war, Abbasid caliph al Mamun reigns in Baghdad.

794 THE JAPANESE CAPITAL is moved from Nara to Heian (Kyoto).

802 JAYAVARMAN II consolidates small Khmer states into one kingdom in present-day Cambodia.

GEOGRAPHY & ENVIRONMENT

ca 800 FERTILE ALLUVIAL SOIL and abundant springs enable the Caddo people of Texas to develop a rich agriculture that incorporates maize, beans, squash, and pumpkin.

ca 800 THE HOPEWELL of North America spread through the eastern woodlands.

Alcuin, a Latin poet and counselor to Charlemagne

ca 800 THE RADHANITES, Jewish merchants from Iraq, settle in North Africa. These multilingual traders ride with caravans, linking North Africa with Mesopotamia, the Caspian Sea region, and India.

ca 800 PRODUCTION OF IRON TOOLS in the Lake Plateau region of Africa stimulates agriculture and trade but also contributes to deforestation as wood is burned to feed the ironworks.

801 TANG DYNASTY CARTOGRAPHER Chia Tan produces a map of China and nearby areas measuring 33 by 36 feet.

CULTURE & RELIGION

ca 796 THE OTTAWA, CHIPPEWA, AND POTAWATOMI of the Great Lakes region form the Council of Three Fires.

ca 800 CADDO COMMUNITIES build ceremonial mounds and are guided by spiritual leaders called *xinesi* (Mr. Moon).

ca 800 THE HUARI AND TIWANAKU EMPIRES in Peru experience a significant cultural shift, as religious iconography and structures give way to secular themes and usage.

◀ **781-804 ALCUIN,** after serving as Charlemagne's personal tutor, becomes the abbot of the Abbey of St. Martin at Tours. There, he encourages the advancement of the Carolingian minuscule script, a written Latin script that later inspires modern Roman typefaces.

802 ABBASID CALIPH HARUN AL RASHID sends an elephant and other luxuries to Charlemagne as a gift.

ca 815 ABU NUWAS, a poet of Arab and Persian ancestry, dies. One of his verses extols liquor as "hot between the ribs as a firebrand."

815-820 THE THIRD SCHOOL OF ISLAMIC LAW, the Shafi'i school, is established.

ca 800 THE *CI*, a new form of song verse with irregular lines set to a melody, becomes popular in China.

SCIENCE & TECHNOLOGY	PEOPLE & SOCIETY
ca 800-900 NORTHERN FLINT CORN, a variant corn able to withstand lower temperatures, is grown by indigenous people in the northeastern and Great Lakes regions of North America. This corn adapts to the limited growing season of a colder climate than that found farther south.	**ca 800** AMERICAN INDIANS in the Southeast engage in large-scale agriculture and live in settled communities. Men are in charge of hunting, fishing, and defense. Women take care of the fields. **ca 800s** IN CADDO SOCIETY, men assume the physically demanding tasks of turning the soil, while women handle planting the crops. Women also assume control of the lodges that accommodate a number of families related by blood or marriage. However, the role of the caddi, the political head of a community, could be filled by either a man or a woman.
807 EMPEROR CHARLEMAGNE receives an ingenious brass water clock from the Abbasid caliph Harun al Rashid.	**813** THE HERMIT PELAYO believes he has found the tomb of St. James near the *finis terrae*—"end of the known Earth"—in Spain. This discovery results in the annual pilgrimage to Santiago (St. James) de Compostela (alternately "field of stars" or "burial place") by thousands who come to worship at this place of sacred relics.
ca 800 MUSLIM MATHEMATICIAN AND ASTRONOMER Muhammad ibn Musa al Khwarizmi furthers works on algebra. **806** IBRAHAM AL FAZARI is the first Muslim astronomer to construct an astrolabe. **ca 815** ABU MUSA JABIR IBN HAYYAN (GEBER), the first Arab alchemist, dies.	**800** RABIAH AL ADAWIYAH, a Sufi mystic often regarded as the first Islamic saint, dies. **ca 800s** IRON AGE SETTLERS AT SCHRODA, at the confluence of the Shashe and Limpopo Rivers in southern Africa, engage in trade with the coast, as evidenced by glass beads and ivory objects found by archaeologists.
ca 806 A JAPANESE MONK returns from study in China and introduces tea to Japan.	**ca 800** THE POPULATION OF JAPAN reaches approximately four million.

EMPEROR CHARLEMAGNE

ON THE DEATH of Pippin II in 768, the Frankish kingdom was divided between Charlemagne and his brother Carloman. Carloman died three years later, leaving the kingdom to Charlemagne, whose rule would lay the groundwork for the Holy Roman Empire.

Charlemagne enlarged his holdings by beating back numerous Saxon raids from the east. When the Lombards began to invade Italy and threatened to assault Rome, Pope Adrian I summoned Charlemagne for help. Charlemagne successfully restored the pope's control, and in 773 he claimed kingship over the Lombards.

In the year 800, at Mass on Christmas Day in Rome, Pope Leo III crowned Charlemagne Imperator Romanorum (Emperor of Rome). This title was intended to help make western Europe independent of Constantinople and to fix the Catholic Church's role in the secular affairs of Europe's monarchies. Charlemagne, however, did not use the title; he understood the ploy and feared it would create dependence on the pope. Instead he called himself Emperor ruling the Roman Empire.

Although Charlemagne was illiterate himself, he ardently supported scholarship, literature, the arts, and architecture. In fostering a renewal of learning, he called Alcuin to the court to establish a school that became the heart of the Carolingian Renaissance.

Most of the surviving works of classical Latin were copied and preserved by Carolingian scholars who came from all over Europe. This veritable united nations included Theodulf, a Visigoth; Paul the Deacon, a Lombard; and Angilbert and Einhard, both Franks. Alcuin also developed the written Latin script, which is known as the Carolingian minuscule script. The rounded letters were adapted for use in the first printing press and would later become the basis of our modern script.

POLITICS & POWER	GEOGRAPHY & ENVIRONMENT	CULTURE & RELIGION
ca 800-900 **NEWER MAYA CITIES** such as Uxmal and Chichen Itzá emerge in the north, with splendid, ornate architecture surpassing that of the preceding southern Maya capitals.	**800s** **MAYA** clear so much forest for agriculture and construction that the deforestation exacerbates the land's dry conditions, contributing to the collapse of lowland Maya civilization.	**800s** **THE CADDO** in present-day Texas build earthen mounds for political and religious ceremonies and others for burials, which may have been accompanied by sacrifices.
840-843 **AFTER THE DEATH OF LOUIS THE PIOUS,** King of the Franks, his three surviving sons fight for the throne. **846** **ARAB ARMIES** sack Rome.	**843** **WITH THE TREATY OF VERDUN,** the Carolingian Empire is divided among the three sons of Louis: Charles the Bald inherits France; Louis the German inherits the East Frankish Empire, or Germany; and Lothair receives the Low Countries, Lorraine, Alsace, Burgundy, Provence, and most of Italy. This division, without regard to tribal or linguistic adherence, brings about a final separation between France and Germany.	**ca 815-827** **CYRIL AND METHODIUS** are born in Thessaloniki, Greece. Working as missionaries, the brothers introduce the Greek Orthodox faith to the Slavs in 863. **843** **ICONOCLASM ENDS;** images of saints are permitted again in all Christian churches.
833-842 **CALIPH AL MUTASIM** reigns over the Abbasids. **838** **AL MUTASIM** conquers Byzantine Amorium and Ankara in Anatolia.		**830** **CALIPH AL MAMUM** establishes the Bayt al Hikmah (House of Wisdom) in Baghdad. **836** **A BUILDING BOOM** begins in Samarra, Iraq, the new capital of the Abbasids. With some 19 palaces and a huge mosque, known as the Great Mosque, Samarra becomes one of the largest cities in the world.
ca 828 **THE CHONGHAE GARRISON** is built on Wando Island during Korea's Unified Silla dynasty. Commander Chang Po-go is thought to have led a navy of 10,000 men in patrolling the surrounding waters to repel Chinese pirates. **838** **THE LAST OF THE GREAT JAPANESE MISSIONS** leaves for China's Tang court.		**845** **THE TANG GOVERNMENT** destroys 4,000 monasteries as part of a great proscription against Buddhism. An estimated 250,000 Buddhist monks and nuns are either killed or forced to return to secular life.

CONNECTIONS

Africa and China

A vibrant maritime trade connected the Afro-Asian worlds from about the year 800 on. Sailing vessels called dhows from the East African coast traveled across the Indian Ocean to China, carrying gold, ivory, iron, and exotic animals.

Chinese accounts described Bobali, probably a town on the coast of Somalia, where the inhabitants "stick a needle into the veins of cattle and drain blood, which they drink raw mixed with milk"—an accurate account of Masai practices to this day. African traders bartered mainly for cotton, silk, and porcelain objects from the Far East.

SCIENCE & TECHNOLOGY

ca 830 **THE UTRECHT PSALTER** mentions the use of the rotary grindstone to sharpen iron for the first time outside of China.

ca 786-833 **MATHEMATICAN AND ASTRONOMER** Al Hajjaj ibn Yusuf translates Euclid's *Elements* into Arabic.

ca 828-831 **AL MAMUM** builds observatories in Baghdad, Iraq, and Palmyra, Syria.

ca 833 **PHILOSOPHER AL KINDI** writes two works on science and philosophy *De aspectibus* and *De medicinarum,* which greatly influence the West.

PEOPLE & SOCIETY

830-900 **AFTER BEING CONQUERED** by neighboring people, the Maya city Seibal in Guatemala recovers and experiences a resurgence of building and art.

830-846 **PRINCE MOJMIR I** unites two Slavic states into Great Moravia and reigns as its first prince until he is ousted by an ally of Louis the German, king of the East Franks.

ca 847-873 **RENOWNED ARAB SCHOLAR** Hunayn ibn Ishaq translates the work of Plato, Artistotle, Hippocrates, Galen of Pergamum, and other Greek scholars, making their work accessible to Arab philosophers and scientists for the first time.

THE CADDO CONFEDERACY

IN THE EIGHTH CENTURY, the Caddo Indians, who can be traced back to the Woodland period culture groups, settled in the Neches River Valley in eastern Texas. Able farmers, the Caddo were skilled with the land and a new development in maize production led to increased crops and rapidly caused a population growth. At their height, the Caddo numbered more than 200,000 people.

From Texas they slowly spread into Oklahoma, Arkansas, and Louisiana, where they knit together a loose federation of tribes, such as the Pawnee and the Wichita, united by custom and language. They lived in permanent village settlements dotted with distinctive beehive-shaped houses, made of layers of thatch attached to a framework of poles. These houses held multiple families, sometimes as many as 40 people.

The Caddo people developed a sophisticated rural hierarchy that incorporated a chief-priest who combined spectral and temporal authority. Chiefs led important ceremonies and councils for war expeditions and conducted the peace pipe ceremony with visitors to the community. They also provided sustenance and other essential revenue to the population to create loyal followers.

Like the Mississippians, the Caddo were mound builders, constructing civic ceremonial centers on high earthen mounds. Some served as burial grounds for the social and political elite. Others were topped by large temples lit with ceremonial fire. The Caddo were the most southwestern of the mound-building cultures.

Living where the woodlands met the Great Plains, the Caddo developed long-distance trade networks, marketing their surplus corn and other agricultural goods in exchange for buffalo hide and meat. Also in demand were their artistic and functional ceramic wares made for cooking and storage, for which the Caddo were renowned.

Caddo village of grass huts

POLITICS & POWER	GEOGRAPHY & ENVIRONMENT	CULTURE & RELIGION
ca 850 **MAYA SOCIETY** is in full decline as people abandon the cities of the Yucatán Peninsula. The cities revert to jungle and the people disperse into the countryside, though their descendants continue to live in the region to this day.	**ca 850** **MAYA FARMERS** are suffering after a 100-year drought, in which rain has been reduced by as much as 70 percent from previous years.	**ca 850** **ARTISANS** at Chichén Itzá inscribe elaborate scenes onto gold disks imported from Costa Rica and Panama and toss them as offerings into a sinkhole, the Sacred Cenote.
860 **THE RUS,** regarded as Scandinavian Vikings, attack Constantinople. **ca 862** **RURIK,** the semi-legendary leader of the Rus, establishes a capital at Novgorod. **ca 869-870** **UPON KING LOTHAR'S DEATH,** the Treaty of Mersen divides his territories into eastern and western halves. Charles II receives western Lorraine. East Lorraine, Alsace, and north Burgundy are given to Louis II.	**850-950** **VIKING RAIDS** stimulate agricultural production and possibly horse breeding in France. **874** **VIKINGS** settle Iceland.	**865** **BULGARIA ACCEPTS CHRISTIANITY** and follows the Byzantine rites.
847-861 **AL MUTAWAKKIL,** the 10th Abbasid caliph, continues his predecessors' dangerous policy of relying on Turkish soldiers for control. They eventually murder him at the prompting of his eldest son, Al Mutasir. **861-870** **AFTER AL MUTAWAKKIL'S ASSASSINATION,** the Abbasid government descends into chaos. Upon Al Mutamid's ascension in 870 a period of calm is restored. **ca 874** **THE AUTONOMOUS SAMANID DYNASTY** arises in Central Asia, with its capital at Bukhara.	**856** **AN EARTHQUAKE** devastates Damghan, Persia, killing more than 200,000. **861** **THE NILOMETER** is built in Cairo by order of Caliph Al Mutawakkil to measure the annual flooding of the Nile. **872** **IBN WAHAB,** a merchant-traveler of Basra, Iraq, describes a sea voyage to China's capital Chang'an. Among his observations of the capital city, he notes, "The streets were traversed with channels of running water and bordered with trees."	**ca 810-870** **MUSLIM SCHOLAR AL BUKHARI** spends 16 years compiling *Al Jami al sahih (The Authentic Collection),* one of the six canonical books of Hadith (Sayings of the Prophet) published within the next century. **ca 850s-870s** **SCHOOLS OF SUFISM** in Egypt, Iraq, and Iran promulgate such tenets as *ma rifah* (interior knowledge), sobriety and wisdom, and *fana* (annihilation of the self), respectively. **859** **QARAWIYIN UNIVERSITY** opens in Fez, Morocco. It's considered the oldest university in the world.
800-1000 **TAHITIAN SEAFARERS** voyage thousands of miles to populate the island Aotearoa, later renamed New Zealand. These settlers are the ancestors of the Maori people who still reside there today. **ca 850** **THE CHOLA KINGDOM** of southern India keeps to its Hindu roots, beginning a rule of the Coromandel coast that will continue for four centuries. **877-889** **INDRAVARMAN I** of the Khmer in Cambodia builds a temple-mountain (Bakong), a forerunner to Angkor Wat architecture.	**ca 850** **THE MALLA DYNASTY** establishes the town of Bhaktapur in central Nepal.	**868** **THE DIAMOND SUTRA,** the earliest known complete woodblock-printed book with an illustration, is produced in China.

SCIENCE & TECHNOLOGY

ca 875 **ANCESTRAL PUEBLOAN (ANASAZI) PEOPLE** build substantial villages in the central Mesa Verde region of the American Southwest, incorporating masonry blocks.

ca 862-867 **JOHN SCOTTUS ERIUGENA,** an Irish intellectual, writes the *Periphyseon,* a dialogue that attempts to describe the nature of reality and the creation of the universe.

PEOPLE & SOCIETY

Alfred, king of Wessex

▲ **871** **ALFRED THE GREAT** becomes king of Wessex, a Saxon kingdom in southwestern England. He defeats Viking invaders in 878 and establishes a truce with the Scandinavian settlers of the Danelaw.

VIKING RAIDERS

FOR THREE CENTURIES, from about 800, Vikings—or Norsemen from Denmark, Norway, and Sweden—conducted lightning quick strikes on the coasts and rivers of Europe. These former traders found raiding more profitable thanks to formidable sailing vessels whose shallow draft allowed Vikings to beach easily and pillage surprised towns and villages in England, Scotland, Ireland, France, and Germany. They rounded Spain into the Mediterranean, followed the Russian rivers into the Black Sea, and also ventured to new lands to the north and west, settling Shetland, the Faroe Islands, Iceland, and Greenland. They even made a short expedition to Newfoundland in North America.

Eventually the Vikings settled much of the British Isles, clashing with the earlier Anglo-Saxons, and populated the coast of Normandy in France and the northern shores of Russia.

Viking longships with double-ended hulls and pronounced keels—often sporting a carved dragon head—could carry as many as a hundred men across the sea. With a rectangular sail of woven wool, sometimes adorned with red stripes or a diamond design, the ships hugged coastlines, using familiar landmarks as guides. Equipped with only crude instruments, Vikings relied mainly on the position of the sun and the stars for navigation. A helmsman steered the ship with a side rudder and the crew controlled the sail with a network of rigging.

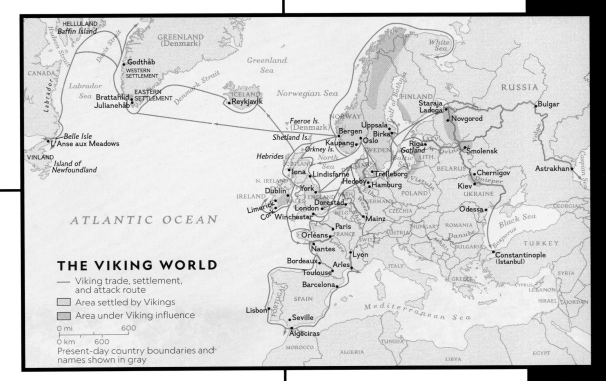

THE VIKING WORLD

— Viking trade, settlement, and attack route

Area settled by Vikings

Area under Viking influence

0 mi 600

0 km 600

Present-day country boundaries and names shown in gray

Superb seamen, the Vikings used ocean and river routes to trade, raid, and colonize from the Caspian Sea to Newfoundland.

POLITICS & POWER	GEOGRAPHY & ENVIRONMENT	CULTURE & RELIGION
ca 900 **TOLTEC** from the north conquer the central valley in Mexico and pillage and burn the great city of Teotihuacán under Chichimeca leader Mixcoatl (Cloud Serpent). His son, Ce Acatl Topiltzin Quetzalcoatl, provides a unified rule. **ca 900** **PUEBLO PEOPLE** in the Chaco Canyon of present-day New Mexico begin building a series of urban communities, sustained by agriculture.	**ca 900** **THE TOLTEC** make the thin, dry soil productive by irrigating their crops.	**ca 900s** **THE FIRST SETTLEMENT ARISES AT ACOMA,** a 600-foot-high pueblo southwest of modern-day Albuquerque, New Mexico. Known as "Sky City," it is considered the oldest continuously inhabited place in the United States.
882 **OLEG OF NOVGOROD** seizes control of Kiev, which he later makes his capital. **885-887** **CHARLES III,** son of Louis the German, briefly unites the West Frankish (France) and East Frankish (Germany) kingdoms. **887** **ARNULF DEPOSES CHARLES III** and is crowned the Carolingian emperor in 896. **899** **KING ALFRED** of Wessex dies. His son Edward takes the throne and continues to battle invaders. **907** **OLEG OF NOVGOROD** leads a successful campaign against Constantinople.	**892-894** **HUNGARIANS** take control of the area of the Carpathian Basin east of the Danube River as they expand their territory in central Europe at the end of the ninth century. **ca 895** **SEVEN MAGYAR TRIBES** and three Khazar tribes form the kingdom of Hungary.	**893-927** **PRESLAV,** capital of the first medieval Bulgarian state, becomes renowned for its artisans and considered a rival to Constantinople. Tile work in the Preslav style is exported to Byzantium and Kievan Rus. **ca 900s** **SAINT CYRIL AND SAINT METHODIUS,** brothers and Eastern Orthodox Christian missionaries, create the Cyrillic alphabet, based on Greek letters. **906** **GREEK LITERATURE** is translated into Slavonic, or Slavic, in Bulgaria.
909 **FATIMIDS**—descendants of Muhammad's daughter Fatima and Ali, and thus Shiite—break away from the Sunni Abbasids to establish their own caliphate and conquer their way to North Africa.	**893** **AN EARTHQUAKE** in Persia causes 100,000 to 180,000 deaths. **ca 900** **AFRICA'S EAST COAST** sees an influx of Arab, Persian, and Indian traders who mix with the native Bantu population. **ca 900s** **ALGIERS** experiences a revival under Berber dynasties.	**882-942** **SAADIAH BEN JOSEPH,** known as the father of medieval Jewish philosophy, writes the *Book of Doctrines and Beliefs* and translates the Old Testament into Arabic. **ca 885** **THE FOURTH SCHOOL OF ISLAMIC LAW,** the Hanbali school, is established. **892** **CALIPH AL MUTADID** moves the Abbasid capital from Samarra back to Baghdad in Iraq and builds the first of a number of palaces known collectively as Dar al Khilafah.
ca 889 **THE KHMER** build a capital city at Angkor, Cambodia. **ca 900** **THE CHOLA KINGDOM,** a Tamil Hindu dynasty, controls all of south India. **907** **THE TANG DYNASTY** in China disintegrates, and the era of the Five Dynasties begins.	**893** **DVIN,** the ancient capital of Armenia, is devastated by an earthquake that kills an estimated 30,000 people.	**ca 900** **A PHONETIC SYLLABARY,** known as the hiragana syllabary, is developed to transcribe the Japanese language, allowing for the expression of native culture in contrast to that of imported Chinese literary forms. **ca 900s** **THE CHOLA DYNASTY** produces some of the most spectacular bronze works of Indian sculptural art to be used in temple processions. As is characteristic of Indian art, the sculptures combine aspects of the sensuous with notions of the sacred.

SCIENCE & TECHNOLOGY	PEOPLE & SOCIETY
ca 900 PUEBLO PEOPLE build a sophisticated road system to integrate all towns in the Chaco Canyon region.	**ca 900s** CONSTRUCTION BEGINS AT PUEBLO BONITO, a village in the Chaco Canyon of modern-day northwestern New Mexico. The settlement will grow to include about 800 rooms and around three dozen kivas (round underground ceremonial chambers). Excavations later reveal a wealth of jewelry, masonry, and pottery.
ca 900s MEDIEVAL WARRIORS, from Vikings to Saracens, begin to use hard, elastic steel swords.	**882-911** RUSSIA IS UNITED by Oleg, ruler of Novgorod. For centuries nomadic horsemen—Cimmerians, Scythians, Huns, Avars, and Khazars—have ridden out of the steppes, often dominating the Slavs, a group of farmers and fur traders living between the Baltic Sea and the Black Sea. Using the Dnieper River, Oleg seizes Kiev in 882 and unites local Slavic and Finnish tribes by delivering them from the Khazars. As leader of the Rus, Oleg in 911 establishes lucrative trade agreements with the Byzantine Empire.
ca 900 A 300-YEAR PERIOD CALLED THE GOLDEN AGE OF SCIENCE ensues in the Islamic world, with scientists such as Isaac ben Solomon Israeli, a Jewish physician from Tunisia, writing treatises on medicine and philosophy and Jewish scholar and physician Dunash ben Tamim, known for his comparative study of the Hebrew and Arabic languages.	**883** THE ZANJ REBELLION OF AFRICAN SLAVES in Iraq against the Abbasid caliphate is suppressed.
ca 900s GUNPOWDER is thought to originate in China during this time, although at first it is used only for fireworks.	**ca 900** ZOROASTRIANS migrate from Persia to northwest India to avoid religious persecution by Muslims. They become known as Parsis (Persians). **ca 910** PAPER MONEY is first used in China.

Saints Cyril and Methodius

THE CYRILLIC ALPHABET

THE BROTHERS CYRIL AND METHODIUS were born in Thessaloniki, Greece, and late served as priests in a monastery along the Bosporus. In 863, having worked as missionaries among the Khazars between the Black Sea and the Caspian Sea, the brothers were called by the patriarch in Constantinople to go to Moravia, beyond the Balkans, where they left a legacy in language.

Moravian Prince Rotislav sought missionaries to teach in the Slavonic, or Slavic, vernacula to forestall further German encroachment in his region. Cyril and Methodius achieved success but aroused hostilities among resentfu visiting clergy. The brothers were recalled to Rome and questioned about their methods but the pope could find no fault with them.

Cyril died in Rome, but Methodius was sent back as archbishop of Sirmium. He spent his remaining years translating the Bible and othe important books into Slavonic, using a specia alphabet that came to be known as Cyrillic after Cyril. It was a version of Greek and Glagolitic, an ancient form of writing that could express Slavonic sounds. The brothers' influence reached into Bulgaria, Serbia, and Ukraine where Slavonic is still the liturgical language

910-940

	POLITICS & POWER	GEOGRAPHY & ENVIRONMENT	CULTURE & RELIGION
THE AMERICAS	**ca 900s** HOHOKAM CULTURE flourishes in modern-day central and southern Arizona. **ca 900s** THE MAYA abandon settlements in the lowlands.	**ca 900s** A NEW PHASE OF BUILDING begins at the Toltec capital of Tula. The original civic-religious center, called Tula Chico by archaeologists, is burned and abandoned. Its much larger replacement, built on a nearby mesa, serves as the main precinct of Tula going forward.	**ca 900** A MILITARISTIC TONE pervades Toltec cities; sculpted, massive stone warriors—complete with armor and feathered headdresses—support a temple's roof.
EUROPE	**ca 913-925** SIMEON OF BULGARIA lays siege to Constantinople. He later annexes Serbia and gives himself the title Tsar of All the Bulgarians. **925** AETHELSTAN becomes the first king to rule all of England. **925** CROATIA establishes its own kingdom. **930** ICELAND forms the Althing, the first parliament in the world. **939-946** EDMUND I succeeds Aethelstan as English king and establishes friendly relations with Scotland and Ireland.	**ca 920s** PERSIAN GEOGRAPHER IBN RUSTAH chronicles his travels to Novgorod (in present-day Russia). He describes the geography of Novgorod (a large, marshy, forested island in a lake), the Rus style of dress (gold armbands and baggy trousers gathered at the knee), and their temperament (hospitable to guests, quarrelsome among themselves).	**922-935** HENRY I OF BAVARIA, Franconia, and Saxony—father of Otto I—builds fortified castles in Germany to guard against marauding Hungarians. These fortifications later become the cities of Quedlinburg, Merseburg, and Nordhausen.
MIDDLE EAST & AFRICA	**930** QARMATIANS, members of a Shiite sect, sack Mecca and carry off the Black Stone of the Kaaba.	**914** ARAB EXPLORER and geographer Al Masudi begins to travel through the Near East, India, and the Mediterranean, which leads him to write a substantial work of history and geography, *The Meadows of Gold and Mines of Gems.*	**917** A BYZANTINE EMISSARY sent by emperor Constantine VII to the court of Caliph al Muqtadir in Baghdad reports on the splendors of 23 palaces there. They describe lavish rooms, a silver tree with moving branches and gold and silver birds, royal stables, zoological gardens, orchards, and gardens of palm trees with a circular pond.
ASIA & OCEANIA	**ca 900** THE KHMER rule an empire based in Cambodia that extends over much of present-day Thailand and Laos. **935** IN SOUTHERN KOREA, the last Silla king surrenders to form the state of Korea. **938** THE KHITAN OF MONGOLIA, founders of the Liao dynasty, establish one of their capitals at modern-day Beijing. **ca 939** VIETNAM regains its independence from China.	**929** THE CAPITAL of Java's Mataram kingdom moves from central to east Java, possibly as a response to the eruption of Mount Merapi.	**ca 935** KOREA'S CULTURE begins an era of high artistic development.

SCIENCE & TECHNOLOGY

Hohokam petroglyph at Saguaro National Park

910 ARAB PHYSICIAN AL RAZI authors more than 200 books on subjects ranging from medical history and astronomy to religion and philosophy. He writes the first account of smallpox and a theory of immunity.

PEOPLE & SOCIETY

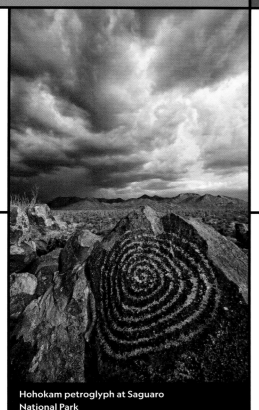

◀ **ca 900s** THE HOHOKAM, masters of irrigation, live in the Sonora Desert of Arizona in villages. The settlement of Snaketown centers on a large ball court for rituals. The items excavated there, including rubber balls and the bones of tropical parrots, seem to indicate Mesoamerican contacts through trade or migration. The Hohokam are probably the ancestors of the modern Pima and Papago.

929 WENCESLAS, a Christian duke of Bohemia, is murdered by his pagan brother on his way to Mass at the door of the church. Shortly thereafter miracles begin to occur at his grave, and he is ultimately canonized as the patron saint of Bohemia. The Christmas carol "Good King Wenceslas," based on the historic duke, is written much later by John Neale and first appears in print in 1853.

929 ABD AL RAHMAN III is caliph in Spain.

CAHOKIA MOUND BUILDERS

THE MISSISSIPPIAN mound builders of North America traded along the waterways of the Mississippi and its tributaries, eventually reaching southeast to Georgia and Florida, north to Wisconsin, and west into Arkansas. They settled in thatch-roofed dwellings, developed a mixed farming and foraging lifestyle, and built earthen mounds for burial and worship.

By the 10th century hundreds of small towns dotted the river valleys, the largest among them Cahokia, near modern-day St. Louis. This early metropolis, surrounded by a stockade and watchtowers, held at least 100 mounds and supported a population of up to 15,000. Several earthen mounds were arranged around a central plaza, rising in steps to four broad terraces topped by ceremonial shrines or houses for chieftains. The largest structure, a pyramid of about 100 feet, covered an area of 14 acres.

At the death of a chieftain, the body, dressed in full regalia, would be carried up to a funerary temple, followed by family and attendants. The chieftain would be interred in the mound, at times accompanied by his attendants.

The populous riverbank city Cahokia near modern-day St. Louis centered on a large plaza and an earthen pyramid about 100 feet tall.

940-970

	POLITICS & POWER	GEOGRAPHY & ENVIRONMENT	CULTURE & RELIGION
THE AMERICAS	**ca 950** CAHOKIA, located near modern-day St. Louis, Missouri, emerges as the most important settlement in the Middle Mississippian culture. **ca 950** MONTE ALBÁN in Mexico is largely abandoned by the Zapotec.	**ca 950** CANTONA, a large fortified city east of the highlands of central Mexico, begins to decline. During its height over the previous three centuries, the settlement had a population of 80,000 to 100,000 residents, 24 ball courts, an extensive road network, and productive obsidian mines that drove trade in the region.	**ca 960** THE TOLTEC AT TULA worship Quetzalcoatl, god of the morning and evening star, at a pyramid temple.
EUROPE	**959-975** EDGAR THE PEACEFUL reunifies the English kingdom. **962** OTTO I OF GERMANY establishes the role of the Holy Roman Emperor, a rival to the papacy as a strong imperial presence in Italy. **965** SICILY falls to Arab conquerors from North Africa.		**961-968** NIKON reconverts the people of Crete to Christianity after the Muslim conquest. **963** THE GREAT LAVRA MONASTERY is founded on the Greek peninsula of Mount Athos. **970** MENAHEM BEN SARUQ of Tortosa, Spain, dies. He composed *Mahberet,* the first Hebrew dictionary.
MIDDLE EAST & AFRICA	**945** ABBASID POWER declines in Baghdad. **946** SAYF AL DAWLAH seizes Aleppo in Syria and becomes emir. **ca 950** ALPTIGIN, a Turkish slave, seizes Ghazna, Afghanistan. His successor, another former Turkish slave named Subuktigin, establishes the Ghaznavid dynasty that is to become the center of Islamic power. **969** THE FATIMIDS conquer Egypt and Syria.		**ca 940** SHANGA RESIDENTS on Pate Island in the Lamu archipelago build magnificent homes of coral and mud, on a site where a small mosque will be constructed later. **945** THE MUSLIM EMPIRE undergoes a significant transformation with the transition of power from the Sunni Abbasid dynasty to the Shia Buyid dynasty.
ASIA & OCEANIA	**955** KING GANDARADITYA rules the Chola kingdom of India. **960** THE SONG DYNASTY reunifies China and ushers in an era of intensive economic, social, political, and cultural change.	**968** DINH BO LINH unites the provinces of Nam Viet (in what is now Vietnam) and declares himself emperor of the new country, Dai Co Viet.	**ca 960** LANDSCAPE PAINTING begins to flourish during the Song dynasty in China.

WHAT LIFE WAS LIKE

Women in China

During the Sui and Tang dynasties women in China moved about easily, even riding horses, elegantly dressed in silks and wearing a veil against the dust. Toward the end of the 10th century the status of women declined as they were more and more confined to the home. "A virtuous woman," it was said, "never takes more than three steps from the threshold." Around 950, during the Tang dynasty, the custom of footbinding began, keeping feet exquisitely small. The painful procedure further restricted women's movements. Fashions changed as well, the slender look of earlier centuries giving way to more voluptuous lines, including blouses, long skirts, wraps, and shawls of patterned silks.

SCIENCE & TECHNOLOGY	PEOPLE & SOCIETY
ca 950 **THE TOLTEC** become skilled in irrigation, tapping the waters of the Tula River.	**ca 950** **THE TOLTEC** protect their empire from invading nomads with a large army and exact tribute from adjoining provinces. They maintain contact with the people of the Gulf Coast and import luxuries, such as jade, turquoise, and exotic bird feathers, from other parts of Mesoamerica. Their artisans excel in weaving, pottery making, and obsidian work.
ca 950 **THE IRON HORSESHOE** comes into use in Europe. **ca 950** **THE MEDICAL SCHOOL AT SALERNO, ITALY,** becomes the first institute of higher education in medieval Europe.	**954** **ERIK BLOODAXE,** last Scandinavian ruler of York, dies. **ca 960** **KING HAROLD I OF DENMARK**—also in control of Norway—is baptized. **966** **MIESZKO I,** first ruler of Poland, is baptized.
ca 964 **PERSIAN ASTRONOMER AL SUFI** publishes *Book of the Fixed Stars,* which describes the Andromeda Galaxy as a "little cloud."	**915-965** **AL MUTANABBI,** regarded by many as the greatest Arab poet, is called the "wandering poet." Born in Iraq, he lives with the Bedouin for a time and later becomes part of the brilliant court of the Hamdanid ruler Sayf al Dawlah in Aleppo, Syria, where he writes many of his elaborate orations. **953** **BUZURG IBN SHAHRIYAR** writes the *Book of Wonders of India,* a collection of stories about travel and adventure.
ca 950 **IN INDIA,** texts about *rasayana,* or alchemy, describe elixirs of immortality and the transmutation of base metals into gold.	**ca 945-960** **GROUPS OF *SOHEI,*** or warrior monks, are organized at Enryakuji temple on Mount Hiei near Kyoto and affiliated temples. Over the next several centuries, these sohei intervene in disagreements between temples, disputes with the imperial court, or on behalf of samurai families.

THE HOLY ROMAN EMPIRE

WITH THE PARTITION of Charlemagne's empire among his grandsons, Germany developed into many small estates ruled by dukes and princes. These estates and their nobles were often in conflict with one another and with the pope in power struggles between church and state.

In 936 Otto of Saxony unified some of the northern regions and was pronounced king of Germany. He was victorious in many military campaigns against the Slavs and Magyars in the areas of present-day Poland, the Czech Republic, and Hungary, and expanded the boundaries of his realm farther to the east. Forays into Italy to keep encroaching tribes away made him the protector of the church.

To show his gratitude, Pope John XII crowned Otto Holy Roman Emperor in 962. The title included rule over the German principalities as well as Lorraine, northern Italy, and Burgundy, and the empire was meant as a Christian revival of the earlier mighty Roman Empire.

This was not to be. The French kings thwarted Otto's efforts to annex any part of France. Germany itself never achieved the political unity that France enjoyed and could not dominate Europe. Relations with the pope proved precarious as well. The pope's authority covered Italy and the church, and he tried to keep the emperor from enlarging his empire.

With mounting disagreements, Otto convoked a synod in Saint Peter's and had Pope John XII deposed and Leo VIII elected. Leo then confirmed Otto's right to a veto in papal elections, which the citizens of Rome had bestowed on him.

Upon Otto's death in 973, his title was transferred to his son Otto II, followed by his grandson. This largely German empire endured for nearly a thousand years, until 1806, waxing and waning at times and ruled by both elected and hereditary emperors.

ISLAMIC ARTS AND SCIENCES

Stretching from Spain to India, the Muslim Empire was a rich amalgam of cultures, held together by its religion and the Arabic language. Deeply influenced by Greek, Persian, and Indian traditions, Muslim scholars combined the latest insights in the arts and sciences and developed them further. Using Hindi numerals, which included the concept of zero—later adopted in Europe as Arabic numerals—they advanced mathematical thought to an understanding of algebra and trigonometry.

Relying again on Hindi and Persian advances in astronomy, they built observatories, computed the movement of the planets, measured the altitude of stars, discovered new stars, and theorized that the Earth rotates on its axis. The use of the astrolabe and compass allowed for fearless navigation across the open sea and thus increased trade.

Arab literature, long honed by a tradition of storytellers, flourished with prose and poetry that rang with musical rhythm in ways no Western translation can do justice. Whether a fable ending in moral advice, an amusing story, or an adventure, the texts—full of puns, sly allusions, and clever metaphors—were meant to be recited. Foremost among the written works is the Quran, which renders the word of Allah in beautiful verse.

An unprecedented building boom—especially of palaces and mosques—occurred after each new conquest. Islamic architecture, sometimes called the "architecture of the veil," concentrates its beauty on interior spaces, with courtyards, gardens, and fountains. Invoking Allah's infinite power, the mosques soar with large domes, minarets, and central prayer halls. The human form and even animals are rarely depicted, because Allah's work is said to be matchless. The decorations therefore consist of geometric patterns and arabesques or quotations from the Quran in calligraphy. Construction of the Great Mosque at Córdoba, left, began in 785 and marks the beginning of Islamic architecture in Spain and northern Africa. The mosque is noted for its striking interior, especially the dome, which is built over 850 columns and 19 aisles, and achieves its elegance through symmetry.

The ceiling of the great dome of Córdoba's mosque is testimony to the elegance of Muslim art and architecture, embellished solely with arabesques and geometric patterns.

970-1000

	POLITICS & POWER	GEOGRAPHY & ENVIRONMENT	CULTURE & RELIGION
THE AMERICAS	**987 THE TOLTEC** capture the Maya city of Chichén Itzá on the Yucatán Peninsula, Mexico. **ca 1000 THE CARIBS** migrate from South America into the islands of the Lesser Antilles. They displace the original agrarian Arawak culture, capturing the women and killing off the men, many by ritual cannibalism.	**ca 1000 CAHOKIA'S LOCATION** along a major tributary of the Mississippi River enables agriculture there to flourish. Residents plant large cornfields in the flood and alluvial plains and multi-crop fields and small gardens within the city boundaries.	**ca 985 ERIK THE RED** and hundreds of other Icelanders name and settle in Greenland. His voyages are commemorated in "Saga of the Greenlanders."
EUROPE	**971 BYZANTINE EMPEROR JOHN TZIMISCES** (John I) beats Russian forces in Bulgaria and fixes the borders of the empire to the Danube. **973 GERMAN KING AND HOLY ROMAN EMPEROR OTTO II** succeeds his father, followed by Otto III in 983. **983 THE WENDS**—Slavic tribes—sack eastern Germany as far west as Hamburg. **987 HUGH CAPET** is elected king of France.	**974 THE EARLIEST DOCUMENTATION** of an earthquake in England is recorded.	**ca 976 CÓRDOBA,** in modern-day Spain, thrives as a center of Muslim culture. The Great Mosque is completed. The town has 70 libraries, the largest one with 500,000 books. About 70,000 books a year are copied by hand. **ca 987 VLADIMIR,** Grand Prince of Kiev, adopts the Christian faith of the Byzantine Church and founds the Russian Orthodox Church. **996 THE CHURCH OF TITHES** in Kiev, Russia, built by Byzantine craftsmen, is completed and dedicated.
MIDDLE EAST & AFRICA	**999 TURKISH GHAZNAVIDS** and Qarakhanids conquer northern India and all of Central Asia, bringing them into the Islamic realm. **ca 1000 KUMBI** is thought to have been the last capital of ancient Ghana, a thriving trading empire. It is split into two cities—one occupied by the king, the other by Muslim traders—and contains stone architecture and an outdoor market on a broad avenue. Its origins predate the spread of Islam.		**971 THE AL AZAR UNIVERSITY** is founded in Cairo, becoming the premier Muslim university. **977 THE SHRINE OF IMAN ALI,** scholars believe, is built in Najaf, Iraq, at the burial site of Ali, son-in-law of the Prophet Muhammad—a holy site for all Shiite Muslims.
ASIA & OCEANIA	**995 THE JAPANESE NOBLE FUJIWARA MICHINAGA** is one of the most powerful statesmen in the Heian period and exercises nearly complete control over the imperial court. **ca 996 UNDER KING RAJARAJA I,** Chola power reaches its zenith in south India. He conquers Kerala and occupies northern Sri Lanka.		**ca 950-1050 A VAST COMPLEX** of about 85 temples arises at Khajuraho, the capital of the Chandela kings in modern-day Madhya Pradesh, India. **ca 1000 CHOLA KING RAJARAJA I** initiates the construction of the Brihadisvara temple at Tanjavur. It is one of three structures referred to as the Great Living Chola Temples, which exemplify the height of Chola architecture, sculpture, painting, and bronze casting.

CONNECTIONS

Salerno Medical School

The medical school in Salerno, Italy, was the first medical school of the Middle Ages and Europe's first university. Constantine the African, a monk and scholar from Tunisia, translated Arabic medical texts there into Latin, which profoundly influenced Western thought. Previously Greek, Salerno was under Norman rule at this time, and Constantine's excellent knowledge of Greek, Latin, Arabic, and several Oriental languages all came in good use in this southern location. The medical school became known for its physicians, who profited from a confluence of Arab, Greek, and Jewish medical thought from around the Mediterranean basin. It was a tolerant and progressive institution, teaching anatomy, dissections of the human body (previously prohibited by the Church), and admitting women as physicians.

SCIENCE & TECHNOLOGY

ca 1000 CAHOKIA enters the period of greatest architectural achievements, as nearly 100 earthen mounds are built, one basketful of dirt at a time, within the five-square-mile settlement near modern-day St. Louis, Missouri. The largest, Monks Mound, stands 98 feet tall and covers around 17 acres.

ca 936-1013 ABU AL QASIM, court physician to the Spanish caliph at Córdoba, writes *The Method,* a 30-part medical volume that includes illustrations of some 200 instruments and the first known description of hemophilia. He is considered Islam's greatest medieval surgeon.

ca 970 SHABBETAI DONNOLO, a Jewish physician in Salerno, Italy, develops new pharmacological prescriptions.

980-1037 AVICENNA, a Persian philosopher and physician, writes more than 450 books on medicine and is considered by many a forefather of modern medicine. Translations of his books exert great influence in Europe.

ca 1000 IRON SMELTING—allowing for better tools—aids the settlement of Bantu speakers throughout sub-Saharan Africa and in the heavily forested areas around the Great Lakes Region.

ca 976 ZHANG SIXUN, a Chinese engineer, builds a large astronomical clock powered by liquid mercury.

PEOPLE & SOCIETY

ca 935-1000 HROSWITHA OF GANDERSHEIM, the abbess of a Benedictine convent at Gandersheim in Saxony, writes six plays, all in Latin, that embody Christian values and are influenced by the Roman dramatist Terence. She also composes poems and a history of the reign of Otto I.

ca 991 THE DANEGELD, a tax to protect against Danish invasion, is levied in England until 1084. English kings use the income to pay off Scandinavian marauders.

998-1030 MAHMUD OF GHAZNA, Afghan ruler and Alptigin's grandson, leads numerous raids into the Punjab of India, looting treasures and laying the foundation for ongoing Muslim rule of the region. His capital, Ghazna, develops into a cultural center on a par with Baghdad.

986 FIFTEEN-YEAR-OLD EMPEROR SHENGZONG of China's Liao dynasty fights off a Song invasion.

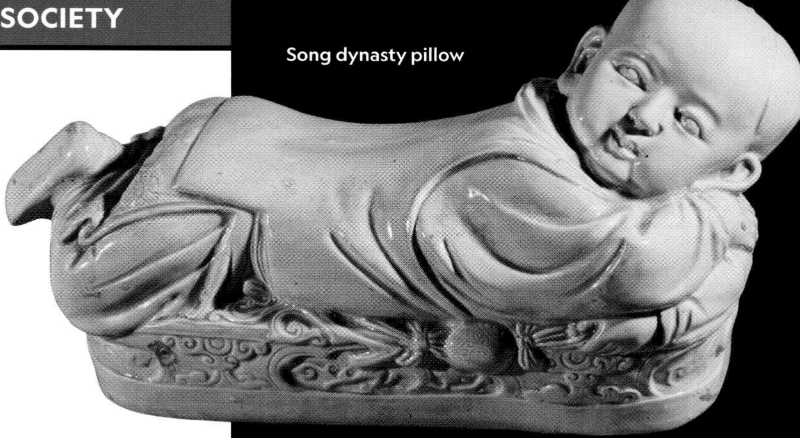

Song dynasty pillow

THE SONG DYNASTY

THE COLLAPSE of the Tang dynasty brought on some 50 years of internecine warfare in China. Finally, in 960, a strong military leader, Zhao Kuangyin, founded the Song dynasty. He reimposed centralized imperial rule and vastly expanded the bureaucracy, though reducing the military. He placed emphasis on civil administration and education instead. With renewed order, Chinese culture underwent another remarkable flowering of the arts and literature, creating ever more artistic porcelains and delicate landscape paintings on paper and silk.

The Song dynasty also saw remarkable improvements in agriculture. A new fast-ripening rice produced two crops a year in the fertile south, which—thanks to the Grand Canal—could be easily distributed throughout the country. Vastly improved, the food supplies in turn supported the expansion of markets, commerce, and a money economy. Cities grew and flourished as both economic hubs and centers of urban and popular culture.

Their reduced military capacity ultimately proved to be the Song dynasty's downfall. Steppe horsemen from the north were a constant threat and demanded heavy tribute. In the early 12th century, the nomadic Jurchen conquered northern China, chasing the Song government to the south of China.

CHAPTER 4

INVASIONS AND ADVANCES

1000-1500

Led by the mighty Kublai Khan, the Mongols completed the conquest of China begun by Genghis Khan. However, their naval expedition to Japan was struck by storms and the diminished forces were beaten back by samurai, a victory commemorated centuries later in this artwork from a volume on the history of Japan.

Between 1000 and 1500, invaders, traders, and explorers crossed continents and oceans and brought societies that were worlds apart into contact and conflict. Christian crusaders from western Europe traveled to Jerusalem to battle Muslims for control of the Holy Land. Turks and Mongols from Central Asia overran vast areas extending from China to eastern Europe. Traffic between Asia and Europe spread a ruinous plague—and sustained a lucrative trade in spices and other goods that spurred advances in navigation. In the late 1400s European mariners seeking new sources of wealth and new routes to Asia rounded Africa and crossed the Atlantic, inaugurating trade and colonization on a global scale. By 1500 few places on Earth were beyond the reach of intruders from distant lands and the unsettling changes they brought about.

TURMOIL IN THE MIDDLE EAST

By 1000 the Islamic world was no longer united. The once-mighty Abbasid caliphs in Baghdad had lost much of their authority, and the rival Fatimid dynasty controlled Egypt, Palestine, and Syria. Divisions within dar al Islam—the house of Islam—allowed outsiders to lay claim to its wealth and holy places. Before the crusaders arrived, Seljuk Turks infiltrated the Middle East from Central Asia, where they had long lived as nomadic herders and clashed with rivals on horseback. They fought for Abbasid caliphs and converted to Islam but preserved their Turkish language and customs. In 1055, a Seljuk Turk named Toghril Beg became sultan (chieftain) in Baghdad. He and his successors left caliphs in place there as figureheads and embarked on conquests, capturing Syria and Palestine from the Fatimids and advancing into Anatolia, or what is now Turkey.

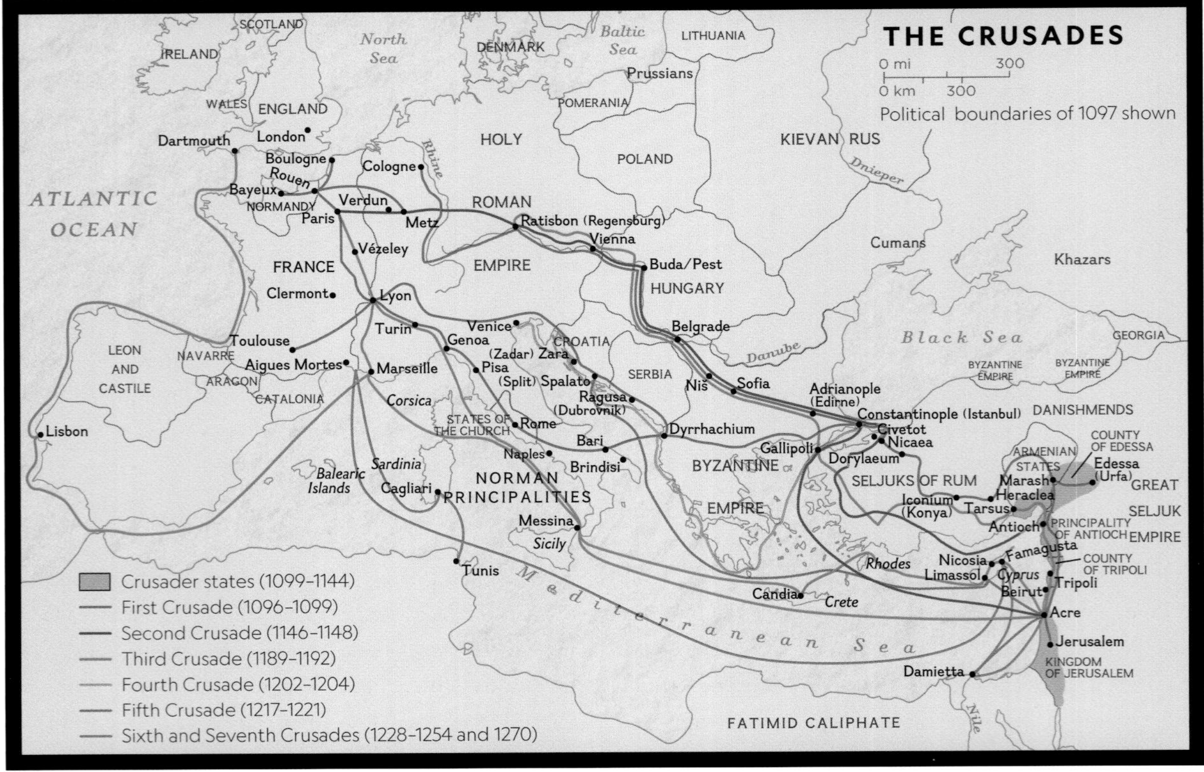

Beginning in 1096, Christians from many parts of Europe joined in crusades aimed at defeating Muslim forces and capturing the Holy Land. Many crusaders marched overland, but some traveled by sea, such as the fleet sailing past an encampment on the Bosporus (opposite).

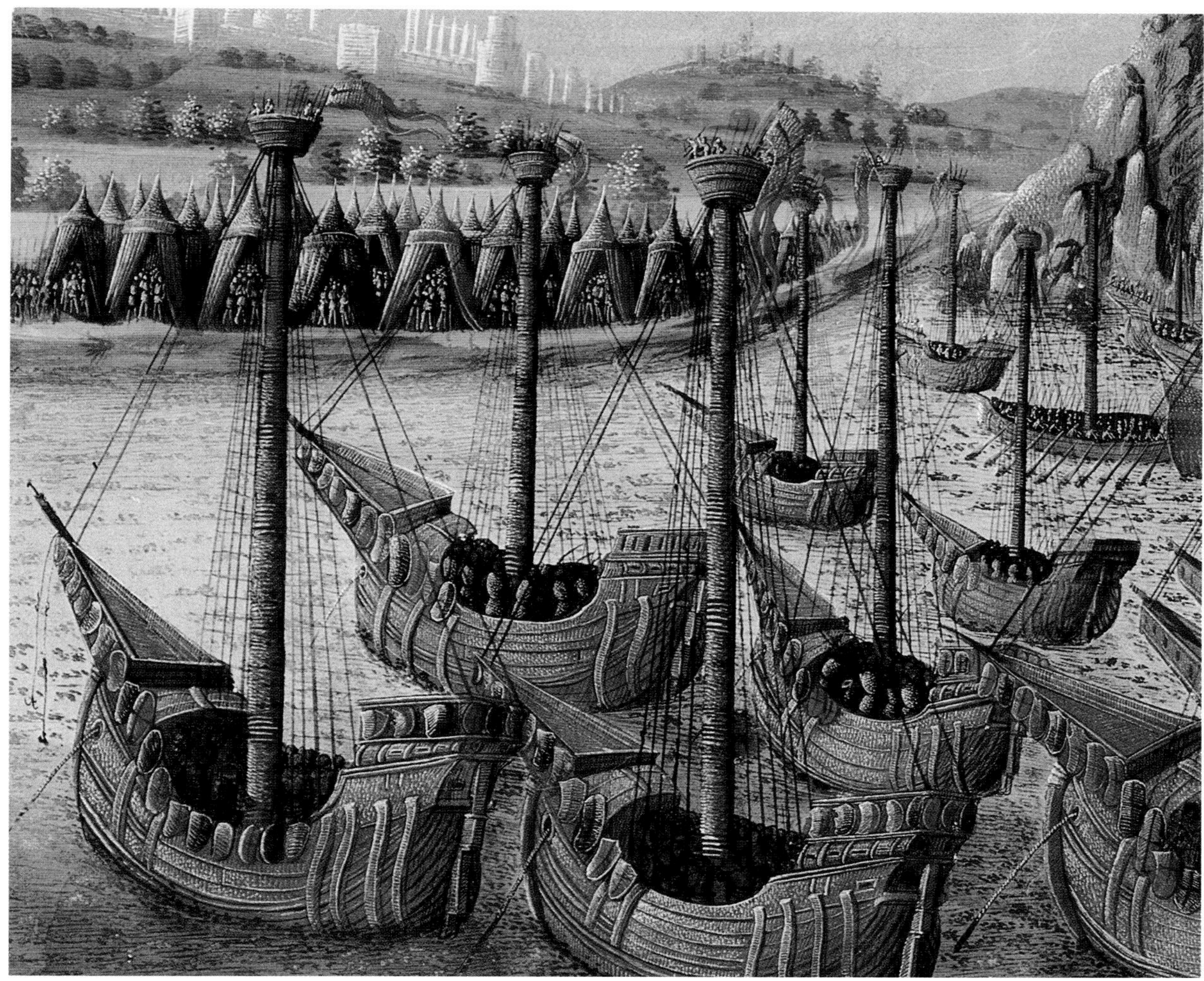

The Turkish advance posed a grave threat to the Byzantine Empire. Under Emperor Basil II, known as Basil the Bulgar Slayer, Byzantine troops had conquered Bulgaria earlier in the century and reached the fertile Danube River Valley. But that gain would be more than offset if Byzantium lost Anatolia, which provided Constantinople with food and trade goods and shielded it from invasion. In 1071 Byzantine forces were defeated in Anatolia by the Turks, who later split into rival camps after their sultan died. Hoping to beat them back, the Byzantine emperor sought help from western Europe, where Christians had their own reasons for opposing the Turks. The Eastern Orthodox Church had recently broken with the Roman Catholic Church, and Pope Urban II in Rome saw a chance to regain authority in the eastern Mediterranean by becoming the spiritual guardian of Jerusalem and other sites in the Holy Land sacred to Christians as well as Muslims. In 1095, he called for a crusade against the Turks to "expel that wicked race from our Christian lands."

The First Crusade, launched in response to the pope's appeal, began badly when a zealot named Peter the Hermit led a motley army to a disastrous defeat. Meanwhile, nobles in France were assembling a stronger fighting force, one that succeeded in capturing Jerusalem in 1099. Bands of crusaders then carved out states along the eastern Mediterranean. The capture of one such state by Turks prompted the Second Crusade in 1146, which ended in failure. In 1171 the Sultan Saladin wrested Egypt from the Fatimids and went on to reclaim Jerusalem for Muslims in 1187. Later crusaders from Catholic Europe were unable to win the Holy Land back and turned against Orthodox Christians in Constantinople, sacking that city in 1204 and leaving the Byzantine Empire vulnerable to future assaults by Turks.

EUROPE GAINS POWER

Although the Crusades accomplished little of lasting value, they exposed Europeans to the larger world and encouraged them to unite under strong leaders. Crusader armies led by Kings Louis IX of France and Richard of England—a successor to William the Conqueror, who had crossed over from Normandy and claimed England in 1066—demonstrated the growing might of European monarchs, whose claims of authority were resisted by some nobles. In England, nobles forced King John in 1215 to sign the Magna Carta, placing legal limits on royal power.

European noblemen were knights, who fought on horseback and were expected to honor the code of chivalry by serving God, obeying their overlords, and honoring and protecting women. Ladies promoted chivalry by patronizing troubadours, who celebrated love, honor, and courtesy in poetry and song. Much the same values prevailed in the courts of Muslim nobles in Spain, whose romantic verses inspired troubadours in France and other Christian countries.

Some knights formed religious orders that fought to spread their faith. Teutonic Knights from Germany invaded Prussia and other countries in the Baltic region

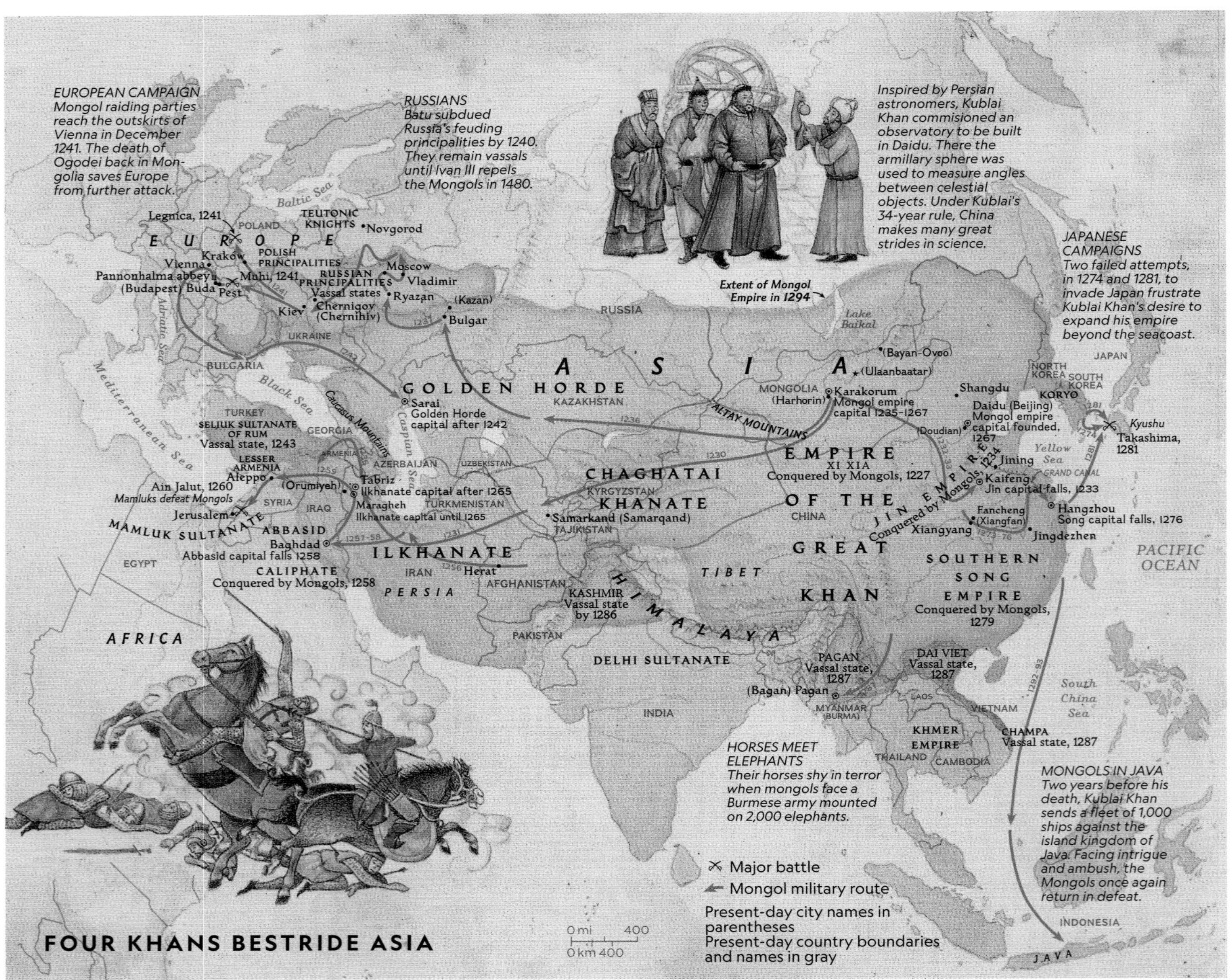

FOUR KHANS BESTRIDE ASIA
EUROPEAN CAMPAIGN Mongol raiding parties reach the outskirts of Vienna in December 1241. The death of Ogodei back in Mongolia saves Europe from further attack.
RUSSIANS Batu subdued Russia's feuding principalities by 1240. They remain vassals until Ivan III repels the Mongols in 1480.
Inspired by Persian astronomers, Kublai Khan commisioned an observatory to be built in Daidu. There the armillary sphere was used to measure angles between celestial objects. Under Kublai's 34-year rule, China makes many great strides in science.
JAPANESE CAMPAIGNS Two failed attempts, in 1274 and 1281, to invade Japan frustrate Kublai Khan's desire to expand his empire beyond the seacoast.
HORSES MEET ELEPHANTS Their horses shy in terror when mongols face a Burmese army mounted on 2,000 elephants.
MONGOLS IN JAVA Two years before his death, Kublai Khan sends a fleet of 1,000 ships against the island kingdom of Java. Facing intrigue and ambush, the Mongols once again return in defeat.
Extent of Mongol Empire in 1294
EUROPE
ASIA
AFRICA
GOLDEN HORDE
Sarai Golden Horde capital after 1242
CHAGHATAI KHANATE
ILKHANATE
EMPIRE OF THE GREAT KHAN
SOUTHERN SONG EMPIRE Conquered by Mongols, 1279
XI XIA Conquered by Mongols, 1227
JIN EMPIRE Conquered by Mongols, 1234
ABBASID CALIPHATE Conquered by Mongols, 1258
Baghdad Abbasid capital falls 1258
MAMLUK SULTANATE
Ain Jalut, 1260 Mamluks defeat Mongols
SELJUK SULTANATE OF RUM Vassal state, 1243
LESSER ARMENIA
Tabriz Ilkhanate capital after 1265
Maragheh Ilkhanate capital until 1265
Karakorum (Harhorin) Mongol empire capital 1235-1267
Daidu (Beijing) Mongol empire capital founded, 1267
Kaifeng Jin capital falls, 1233
Hangzhou Song capital falls, 1276
KASHMIR Vassal state by 1286
PAGAN Vassal state, 1287
DAI VIET Vassal state, 1287
CHAMPA Vassal state, 1287
KHMER EMPIRE
DELHI SULTANATE
KORYO
Kyushu Takashima, 1281
Legnica, 1241
Mohi, 1241
Pannonhalma abbey
TEUTONIC KNIGHTS
POLISH PRINCIPALITIES
RUSSIAN PRINCIPALITIES Vassal states
Novgorod
Moscow
Vladimir
Ryazan
(Kazan)
Bulgar
Chernigov (Chernihiv)
Kiev
Krakow
Vienna
(Budapest) Buda
Pest
Aleppo
(Orumiyeh)
Jerusalem
Samarkand (Samarqand)
Herat
(Bayan-Ovoo)
(Ulaanbaatar)
Shangdu
(Doudian)
Jining
Fancheng (Xiangfan)
Xiangyang
Jingdezhen
(Bagan) Pagan
PERSIA
TIBET
HIMALAYA
ALTAY MOUNTAINS
Caucasus Mountains
Baltic Sea
Black Sea
Caspian Sea
Mediterranean Sea
Adriatic Sea
Yellow Sea
GRAND CANAL
Lake Baikal
PACIFIC OCEAN
South China Sea
JAVA
RUSSIA
UKRAINE
POLAND
BULGARIA
TURKEY
GEORGIA
ARMENIA
AZERBAIJAN
UZBEKISTAN
TURKMENISTAN
KYRGYZSTAN
TAJIKISTAN
KAZAKHSTAN
SYRIA
IRAQ
IRAN
EGYPT
AFGHANISTAN
PAKISTAN
INDIA
MONGOLIA
CHINA
NORTH KOREA
SOUTH KOREA
JAPAN
MYANMAR (BURMA)
LAOS
THAILAND
CAMBODIA
VIETNAM
INDONESIA
Major battle
Mongol military route
Present-day city names in parentheses
Present-day country boundaries and names in gray
0 mi 400
0 km 400

In the 13th century, descendants of Genghis Khan divided the vast area conquered by Mongol forces into four khanates, each with its own leader. Kublai Khan served as the supreme leader, or great khan, and held sway over the Mongolian homeland and China.

and imposed Christianity there. Germany formed part of the Holy Roman Empire, which extended from the Baltic Sea to northern Italy. The first Holy Roman emperor was crowned by the pope in the 10th century, but his successors later clashed with Rome by claiming the right to appoint their own bishops.

Italy, meanwhile, remained divided into many political units, including city-states such as Venice and Genoa, which prospered through trade with the Islamic world. Italian merchants met Europe's demand for eastern goods such as sugar, spices, and silk that became more popular after crusaders encountered them. Marco Polo and other Italian merchants journeyed to China to promote trade. The city-state of Florence emerged around 1300 as a great cultural center, home to the poet Dante Alighieri, the painter Giotto di Bondone, and the scholar Petrarch. Their works drew on classical culture and served as a bridge between Europe's age of faith and the humanism of the Italian Renaissance.

Throughout Europe, the expansion of trade supported the growth of cities inhabited by prosperous merchants and skilled artisans, who organized guilds that controlled production and set prices. Bourse trading and the far-reaching Hanseatic League of German traders were forerunners of the European Common Market. Booming cities such as Paris boasted towering cathedrals and cathedral schools that evolved into universities headed by scholars such as St. Thomas Aquinas, who drew on the works of Aristotle to give Catholicism a strong intellectual foundation.

THE MONGOL INVASIONS

By 1200 various Turkish dynasties ruled North Africa, the Middle East, and northern India. But the Turks would soon be surpassed as conquerors by the Mongols, who occupied what is now Mongolia. They were superb at mounted warfare but lacked political unity until a charismatic chieftain named Temujin created a powerful confederation. He was chosen khan (ruler) at a council of tribal leaders in 1206 and took the name Genghis Khan (Universal Ruler).

His first target as a conqueror was northern China, which had already slipped from the grasp of the Song dynasty. Under Song rule, China remained one of the most accomplished and inventive societies in the world. Printers there invented movable type, and shipbuilders devised rudders to make vessels more maneuverable—breakthroughs that spread to the West along with earlier Chinese inventions such as gunpowder. The printing of paper money stimulated China's economy, and its cities grew larger and wealthier. New techniques of irrigation and fertilization helped feed a population that soared from roughly 60 million in 1000 to nearly twice that two centuries later. Song rulers entrusted their armies to officials who knew little of military matters, however, and lost northern China to invaders called the Jurchens a century before Genghis Khan launched his offensive. The Jurchen put up fierce resistance, but most of northern China was in Mongol hands by 1220.

Mongol warriors like the one portrayed here were expert cavalrymen who used stirrups to steady themselves and could fire arrows with deadly force in any direction.

Heirs to Genghis Khan would later seize all of China, but he himself campaigned westward across Central Asia as far as the Caspian Sea, devastating all who defied him. After Genghis Khan died in 1227, his heirs continued to campaign and divided the vast Mongol Empire into khanates, each ruled by its own khan. Kublai Khan completed the conquest of China and launched large naval expeditions against Japan in 1274 and 1281, both of which were battered by typhoons. The Japanese thanked Shinto gods for sending the kamikaze, or divine wind, that saved them. Those Mongols who made it ashore were beaten back by samurai warriors, whose code required them to commit suicide if they failed to do their duty. Many lost faith in Japan's shogun, or military ruler, when he did not reward them as hoped and raised taxes to pay for the costly defensive preparations.

By 1300 the Mongol Empire extended from China to Russia. Princes in Moscow and other cities were forced to pay tribute to Mongols of the Golden Horde, who pushed eastward into Poland and Hungary. Western Europe escaped invasion, but many there fell prey to an epidemic that Mongols and traders who dealt with them helped convey. The bubonic plague, known as the Black Death, devastated China in the 1300s. Amid the chaos, the Mongols lost power, leading to the resumption of Chinese rule under the Ming dynasty. The plague, carried by fleas that infested rodents, spread from Asia along sea and land routes traveled by merchant ships, caravans, and armies. Most people who became infected died, and outbreaks caused hysteria. In some parts of Europe, Christians blamed Jews for the plague and massacred them.

By 1400 the Black Death had reduced the European population by an estimated 60 percent. The devastation in the Middle East was even worse and caused turmoil in lands ruled by Mongols, allowing Turks to regain control. Forces led by the conqueror Tamerlane, or Timur, seized Mesopotamia, Persia, and northern India and were preparing to invade China when he died in 1405. His empire perished with him, leaving a void that was filled by other Turks, notably the Ottomans in Anatolia. They believed that a warrior who died fighting for Islam gained everlasting glory. "He lives in beatitude with Allah," one poet proclaimed; "he has eternal life." After invading the Balkans, Ottomans shocked Christian Europe by capturing Constantinople in 1453.

By this time western Europe had largely overcome the effects of the plague, and its monarchs were more powerful than ever. In the same year Constantinople fell, an epic struggle between England and France known as the Hundred Years' War came to an end. France succeeded in rebuffing English claims to French territory, but the royal families of both countries grew stronger during the war by raising armies and imposing taxes to finance their campaigns. In Spain the Christian kingdoms of Castile and Aragon, which had earlier reclaimed much of that country from Muslims, were united by marriage in 1469 and went on to conquer Granada, the last bastion of Islam in Spain. Portugal, for its part, became a maritime power under Prince Henry the Navigator, who promoted the study of navigation and sponsored expeditions that colonized the Azores and other islands, where slaves imported from West Africa worked sugar plantations.

Advances in navigation enabled Europeans to bypass Muslim traders and seek maritime routes to Asian markets. In the late 1400s, Portuguese navigators rounded Africa and reached India while the Italian mariner Christopher Columbus opened a transatlantic route for Spain to what he thought were the Indies but proved to be islands in the Caribbean. The stage was set for momentous European ventures that would impact Africa, the Americas, and other regions and disrupt or destroy powerful societies there.

ADVANCES IN AFRICA AND THE AMERICAS

Before Columbus reached the New World or Portuguese traders visited the coast of West Africa, empires had arisen on those continents. The West African empire of Ghana collapsed in the early 1200s under pressure from nomads who swept down from the Sahara, lured by the gold that had long drawn Arab traders. That trade revived with the growth of the Mali Empire, which succeeded Ghana and embraced a wider area. The Mali emperor Mansa Musa dazzled the Islamic world by making a pilgrimage to Mecca in 1324 with thousands of followers and a fortune in gold. Most of Mali's population lived more modestly and adhered to ancestral beliefs. Great artistry and devotion went into crafting masks and other objects they used in rituals honoring their spirits.

On the East African coast, prosperous city-states developed where Swahili merchants imported prized items such as silk, cotton, and porcelain by sea from India and other countries. Inland, the kingdom of Zimbabwe flourished, with impressive stone architecture and an imposing capital that housed between 12,000 and 20,000 people. Like Mali and the Songhai Empire that succeeded it, Zimbabwe prospered by selling slaves as well as gold and ivory. But the slave trade did not become a consuming enterprise until Europeans began sending shiploads of black Africans to colonies across the Atlantic. By the late 1400s, Portuguese traders were exporting a few thousand slaves each year from Africa, and that was a mere trickle compared to the massive transshipments to come.

In the Americas, the period preceding the arrival of Europeans was marked by similar cultural advances. In North America, the mound-building societies of the Mississippi Valley and the Southeast declined in the 1200s as large towns exhausted their natural resources. But tribal societies made up of smaller villages linked by trade and diplomacy flourished throughout the eastern woodlands. In the Northeast, the five tribes of the Iroquois coalesced

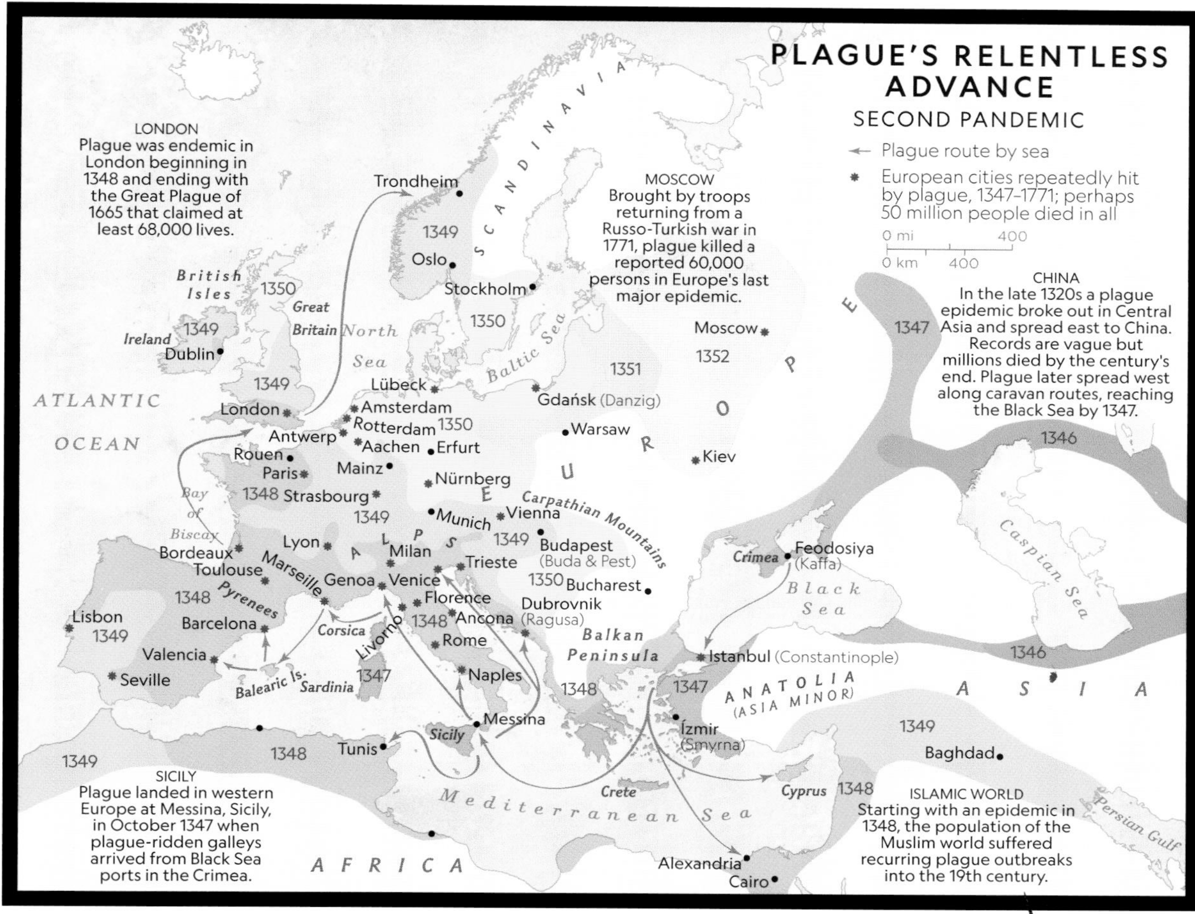
PLAGUE'S RELENTLESS ADVANCE
SECOND PANDEMIC
Plague route by sea
European cities repeatedly hit by plague, 1347–1771; perhaps 50 million people died in all
0 mi 400
0 km 400
LONDON
Plague was endemic in London beginning in 1348 and ending with the Great Plague of 1665 that claimed at least 68,000 lives.
MOSCOW
Brought by troops returning from a Russo-Turkish war in 1771, plague killed a reported 60,000 persons in Europe's last major epidemic.
CHINA
In the late 1320s a plague epidemic broke out in Central Asia and spread east to China. Records are vague but millions died by the century's end. Plague later spread west along caravan routes, reaching the Black Sea by 1347.
SICILY
Plague landed in western Europe at Messina, Sicily, in October 1347 when plague-ridden galleys arrived from Black Sea ports in the Crimea.
ISLAMIC WORLD
Starting with an epidemic in 1348, the population of the Muslim world suffered recurring plague outbreaks into the 19th century.
SCANDINAVIA
EUROPE
ASIA
AFRICA
ATLANTIC OCEAN
British Isles
Great Britain
Ireland
North Sea
Baltic Sea
Bay of Biscay
ALPS
Pyrenees
Carpathian Mountains
Balkan Peninsula
ANATOLIA (ASIA MINOR)
Crimea
Black Sea
Caspian Sea
Mediterranean Sea
Persian Gulf
Corsica
Sardinia
Balearic Is.
Sicily
Crete
Cyprus
Trondheim
Oslo
Stockholm
Dublin
London
Lübeck
Amsterdam
Rotterdam
Antwerp
Aachen
Erfurt
Gdańsk (Danzig)
Warsaw
Moscow
Kiev
Rouen
Paris
Mainz
Nürnberg
Strasbourg
Munich
Vienna
Lyon
Milan
Bordeaux
Toulouse
Marseille
Genoa
Venice
Trieste
Budapest (Buda & Pest)
Bucharest
Florence
Dubrovnik (Ragusa)
Ancona
Livorno
Rome
Naples
Messina
Lisbon
Barcelona
Valencia
Seville
Tunis
Feodosiya (Kaffa)
Istanbul (Constantinople)
İzmir (Smyrna)
Baghdad
Alexandria
Cairo
1346
1347
1348
1349
1350
1351
1352

Bubonic plague, or the Black Death, returned with a vengeance in the 14th century, taking a terrible toll on the Mediterranean world. Later outbreaks were less severe, but the disease remained a dreaded scourge in the 17th century, when a German artist portrayed a physician wearing a mask he hoped would ward off infection (below).

during the 15th century into a strong confederation that would play a major role in the colonial era to come. In the Southwest, the ancestral Puebloan culture reached its peak in the 12th century at Chaco Canyon, a political and ceremonial center linked by roads to outlying settlements. Severe drought later caused the ancient Pueblo villagers to disperse. Some settled along the Rio Grande and inspired the Pueblo society that emerged there.

In South America, the traditions of earlier cultures such as the Moche were carried on by the Chimú, who extended their domain along the Peruvian coast for over 500 miles before they fell to the Inca. Originating in the Andean highlands, the Inca became a great power in the mid-1400s under a ruler who took the name Pachacuti (He Who Transforms the Earth). By 1500 their empire reached from what is now Ecuador to central Chile and included thousands of miles of paved highways, with inns at regular intervals to accommodate traders and officials, who lacked a written language but kept records by tying knots on strings.

In the Valley of Mexico, meanwhile, the Aztec, or Mexica, had forged their own empire centered at Tenochtitlan, a majestic capital built on an island. A plaza nearby housed one of the world's greatest markets, visited daily by tens of thousands of people and filled with alluring items such as jaguar pelts and macaw feathers as well as pottery, cotton fabric, and other crafted goods. Like the Maya, the Aztec had priests who served as astronomers, kept intricate calendars, and preserved their lore in writing. Aztec priests also conducted human sacrifices as offerings to their gods atop the Great Pyramid in Tenochtitlan and other sacred sites. Kings waged wars after their coronations and sacrificed captives by the thousands to seek divine blessings. Aztec demands for tribute from people they ruled caused further resentments that Spanish invaders later exploited to divide and conquer the Aztec Empire. ■

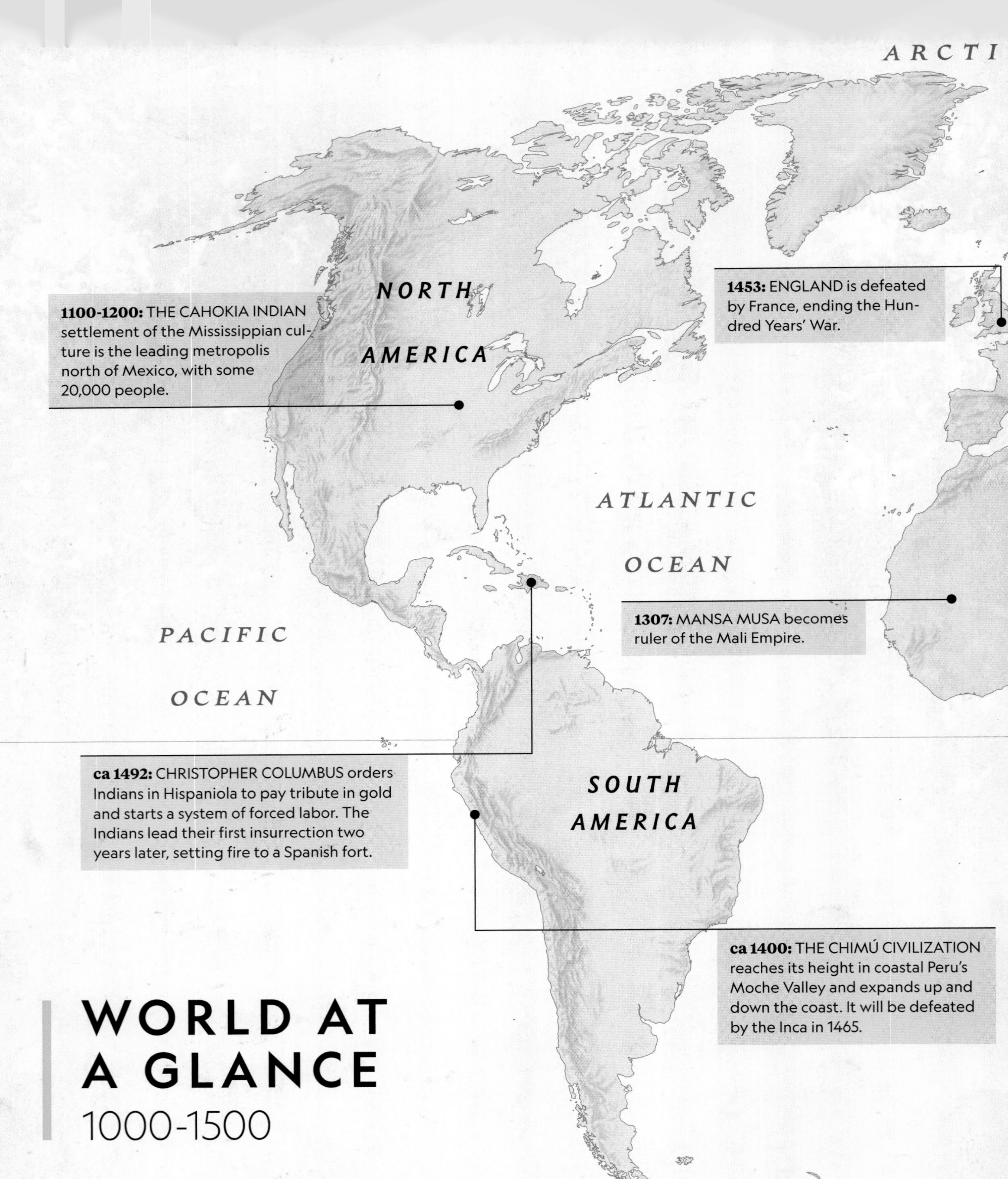
ARCTIC
NORTH AMERICA
ATLANTIC OCEAN
PACIFIC OCEAN
SOUTH AMERICA
1100-1200: THE CAHOKIA INDIAN settlement of the Mississippian culture is the leading metropolis north of Mexico, with some 20,000 people.
1453: ENGLAND is defeated by France, ending the Hundred Years' War.
1307: MANSA MUSA becomes ruler of the Mali Empire.
ca 1492: CHRISTOPHER COLUMBUS orders Indians in Hispaniola to pay tribute in gold and starts a system of forced labor. The Indians lead their first insurrection two years later, setting fire to a Spanish fort.
ca 1400: THE CHIMÚ CIVILIZATION reaches its height in coastal Peru's Moche Valley and expands up and down the coast. It will be defeated by the Inca in 1465.

WORLD AT A GLANCE

1000-1500

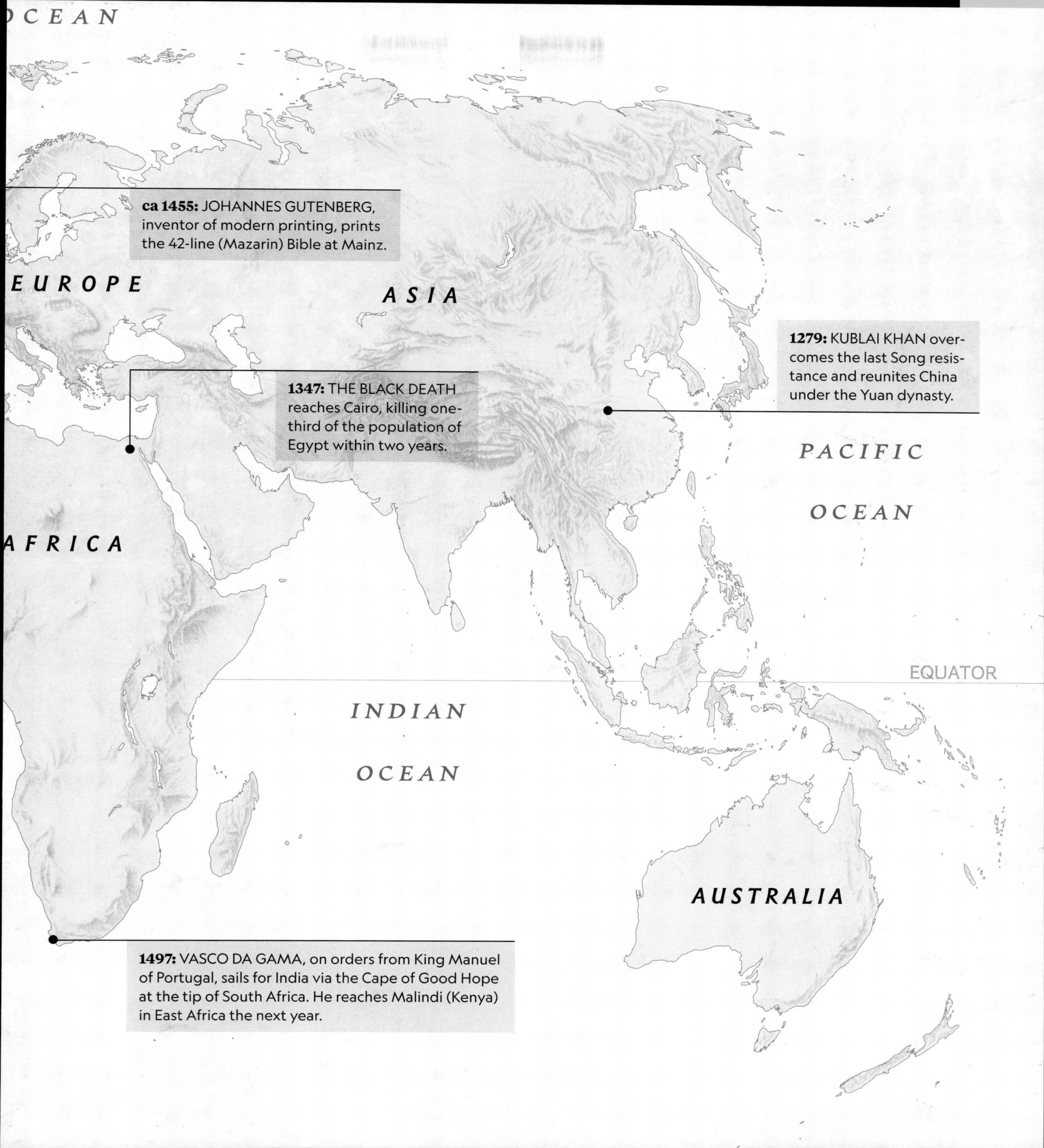

OCEAN

ca 1455: JOHANNES GUTENBERG, inventor of modern printing, prints the 42-line (Mazarin) Bible at Mainz.

EUROPE

ASIA

1279: KUBLAI KHAN overcomes the last Song resistance and reunites China under the Yuan dynasty.

1347: THE BLACK DEATH reaches Cairo, killing one-third of the population of Egypt within two years.

PACIFIC OCEAN

AFRICA

EQUATOR

INDIAN OCEAN

AUSTRALIA

1497: VASCO DA GAMA, on orders from King Manuel of Portugal, sails for India via the Cape of Good Hope at the tip of South Africa. He reaches Malindi (Kenya) in East Africa the next year.

1000-1030

	POLITICS & POWER	GEOGRAPHY & ENVIRONMENT	CULTURE & RELIGION
THE AMERICAS	**ca 1000** THE MULTIETHNIC CITY OF TULA in Mexico is at its height, with a population between 50,000 and 60,000 people living within about six square miles. **ca 1000** THE HUARI EMPIRE of the Highland Andes breaks up. The Chimú Empire is one of several empires that ascend. Its capital is at Chan Chan.	**ca 1000** LEIF ERIKSSON is believed to have discovered North America, visiting the area around the Gulf of Saint Lawrence in modern-day eastern Canada. **ca 1000** THE MANDAN people migrate north along the Missouri River and settle in modern-day North Dakota.	**ca 1000** THE MIXTEC, noted for their mosaic veneers, construct large, beautiful houses, such as the Palace of the Columns, at Mitla.
EUROPE	**1004** ARABS sack Pisa. **1013** THE DANES take England. **1016-1028** THE DANISH KING CANUTE becomes king of England and Norway. In 1028, he appoints his mistress, Aelgifu, and their son Sweyn to be in charge of Norway. **1018** BYZANTINE EMPEROR BASIL II completes his conquest of Bulgaria. **1025** BYZANTIUM begins to decline when Constantine VIII succeeds Basil II at his death.	**1000** SAXONS settle at Bristol. **ca 1016** SOUTHERN AND NORTHERN SCOTLAND are united.	**ca 1000** ICELAND'S PARLIAMENT, named the Althing, adopts Christianity. **ca 1000** THE CENTER OF JEWISH THOUGHT begins to shift from Mesopotamia to Spain. **1021-1036** BERN(O) AUGIENSIS, abbot of Reichenau, compiles his influential book on musical theory titled *Prologus in tonarium*.
MIDDLE EAST & AFRICA	**1009** FATIMID CALIPH AL HAKIM destroys the Church of the Holy Sepulcher in Jerusalem.	**ca 1000** AL MAQDISI, geographer and author of a physical and human geography of the known world, dies.	**1010** FIRDAUSI writes the greatest work in Persian literature, the *Shahnama*. **1021** FATIMID CALIPH AL HAKIM dies after claiming to be the Mahdi (messiah); his followers escape persecution in Egypt to start the Druze religion in isolated areas of Lebanon and Syria.
ASIA & OCEANIA	**ca 1000** SELJUK TURKS rise to prominence in Transoxiana in Central Asia. **1005** THE TREATY OF SHANYUAN between China and Khitan Liao is drawn up. **1008** MAHMUD OF GHAZNA defeats Hindus at Peshawar. **1017-1018** THE SACRED CITY OF MUTTRA is sacked by Mahmud of Ghazna. **1021** CHOLAS invade Bengal in India.	**ca 1000-1500** THE RAPA NUI on Easter Island carve large stone statues known as *moai*. **1011** CHINESE EMPEROR ZHENZONG imports a new variety of drough-resistant rice from Champa, in modern-day Vietnam. Its quick maturation cycle enables farmers to plant two cycles of crops in some areas. The heartier strain is also planted at higher elevations and latitudes.	**ca 1010** JAPANESE AUTHOR MURASAKI SHIKIBU completes *The Tale of Genji,* considered the world's first novel. **ca 1018** MAHMUD OF GHAZNA founds the mosque known as the Celestial Bride at Ghazna in Afghanistan.

SCIENCE & TECHNOLOGY	PEOPLE & SOCIETY
ca 1000 MAYA and most Mesoamerican societies develop two calendar cycles, one of 260 days and another of 365 days.	**ca 1000** IROQUOIS PEOPLES in northeastern North America live in communities and cultivate beans, maize, and squash.
ca 1000 CHAIN MAIL revolutionizes warfare for feudal knights of northern Europe in the Middle Ages.	**ca 1013-1057** SAMUEL HA NAGID serves not only as *nagid* (head of the Jewish community) in Granada but also as an influential adviser and vizier to the caliph. **1015** VLADIMIR, PRINCE OF KIEV, dies after converting to Christianity upon his marriage to Anne, sister of Byzantine Emperor Basil II. His conversion opens Russia to Byzantine influences.
965-ca 1040 EGYPTIAN ASTRONOMER and mathematician Alhacen writes an influential book on optics that theorizes that the reception of light rays makes sight possible. **1012** MOSQUE OF AL-HAKIM is completed in Cairo, Egypt.	**ca 1000** THE YORUBA PEOPLE of Nigeria flourish in the holy city of Ile-Ife, which they believe to be the birthplace of humankind.
ca 1000 EARLY-RIPENING RICE is introduced from the Hindu Kingdom of Champa in Southeast Asia. **ca 1000** THE FEARED SELJUK TURK WARRIORS fight as mounted archers, using the composite bow and lance.	**1006** MUSLIMS settle in northwestern India.

JUDAISM MOVES WEST

AFTER THE ARRIVAL OF ISLAM, Jews lived chiefly in lands that were ruled by Muhammad's followers. Centered in Mesopotamia, the *geonim,* or heads of the academies of learning, held forth as supreme judges of Talmudic law and were consulted on matters both religious and nonreligious by Jews around the world.

One such gaon was Hai ben Sherira of Pumbeditha Academy in Baghdad, considered the last great Babylonian gaon. Hai's reputation for wisdom was such that he received questions from as far away as Spain and Ethiopia. Upon his death in 1038 at the age of 99, the Pumbeditha Academy closed permanently, bringing to an end 600 years of flourishing Babylonian Jewry.

Though some Talmudic academies did remain open in Babylonia and Palestine, the main force of scholarship moved with the Jews, who were relocating to Egypt, North Africa, and western Europe, particularly Spain, where an age of acculturation was beginning because of Islam's toleration of Christians and Jews. Jewish doctors, poets, and scholars were welcomed by the Muslim caliphs into their courts to help spread knowledge. Jews became so influential that in some cases they were appointed viziers to the caliphs.

But this golden age began to crumble when Christians came to power and the Moorish provinces fell to them. Persecution followed persecution, and in 1492 Queen Isabella and King Ferdinand decreed that Jews must convert to Christianity within three months or leave Spain. This decree occurred the same year the Spanish royals financed Christopher Columbus's voyage to the New World, which was also designed to strengthen Christianity. Spanish rulers forbade Jews from going to the Americas, although these areas ultimately offered freedom for those persecuted in Europe and the Middle East.

POLITICS & POWER

ca 1050 **THE TIWANAKU EMPIRE'S** power as a political center of the Andes starts to decline.

1031 **DEPOSITION OF THE LAST UMAYYAD CALIPH,** Hisham III, ends the caliphate of Córdoba.

1037 **FERDINAND I** becomes the first to assume the title of king of Castile in Spain.

1040 **KING DUNCAN OF SCOTLAND** is murdered by MacBeth, who becomes king.

1042 **NORMAN BROTHERS WILLIAM (IRON ARM) AND DROGO DE HAUTEVILLE** come to power in Apulia, southern Italy.

1050 **SELJUKS** seize Isfahan in Persia.

1054-1145 **THE ALMORAVID DYNASTY** in North Africa and Spain reestablishes Sunni orthodoxy.

1055 **SELJUK TOGHRIL BEG** restores the Sunni branch of Islam over the Shiites and installs himself as temporal master of the caliph in Baghdad.

1030-1031 **AFTER THE DEATH OF MAHMUD,** his son Masud blinds his brother Muhammad and seizes the throne in Afghanistan.

1038 **THE TIBETAN-SPEAKING TANGUT TRIBES** establish the kingdom of Xi Xia in what is now Gansu and Shaanxi Provinces in northwestern China.

1040 **THE SELJUK TURKS** defeat Ghaznavid forces in Persia and halt their expansion in the region. Ghanza ruler Masud flees to India.

GEOGRAPHY & ENVIRONMENT

WHAT LIFE WAS LIKE

At a Medieval Trade Fair

Capitalism thrived at international trade fairs held across medieval Europe from Sweden to Germany, France, England, Italy, and into the Middle East. Merchants gathered to buy and sell goods outside a town's walls. A festive atmosphere reigned as clowns, acrobats, jugglers, and musicians strolled among the throngs, performing their arts as fascinated children looked on. Parents were involved in bargaining for a variety of goods, ranging from local wares to exotic silks and spices brought all the way from China. In addition, one might find stalls full of Russian furs, Italian glass, French wines, or Bruges lace, each to be haggled over before a final price was agreed upon. The direct trading of goods would eventually be replaced by currency of coins. Monarchs sometimes waived tolls to encourage a diversity of products, or they levied extra taxes to improve roads and bridges or invest in public works such as an expensive town cathedral.

1033 **A SEVERE EARTHQUAKE** occurs in Palestine.

1047 **NASIR-I KHUSRAU,** Shiite author, traveler, and philosopher visits Egypt.

1049 **ARAB NOMADS** (Banu Hilal) begin to move into North Africa from eastern Arabia in large numbers, a migration that will stretch over several centuries.

ca 1050 **SHEN KUO,** a Song Chinese polymath, includes the first surviving reference of a magnetic compass in *Brush Talks from Dream Brook,* a collection of scientific observations.

1053 **THE ELEGANT PHOENIX HALL** near Kyoto, Japan, is converted from a private summer retreat to a temple.

CULTURE & RELIGION

ca 1050 **TOLTEC ARCHITECTURE** demonstrates a fearsome militant religion, with large snakes and warriors. Chacmools are large reclining human figures on which human sacrifices may have been performed.

ca 1042-1052 **EDWARD THE CONFESSOR** begins building Westminster Abbey in London.

ca 1050 **MUSICAL NOTES** are given time values.

1051 **THE MONASTERY OF THE CAVES** is established south of Kiev. Among its disciples is the founder of Russian monasticism.

1054 **THE SCHISM** between Roman and Eastern churches becomes permanent.

ca 1050-1058 **HILAL AL SABI** writes *Rules of the Caliphal Courts,* and Al Mawardi writes *The Ordinances of Government* to reassert the position of the caliph as the Buyid emirs weaken. Al Mawardi's work is regarded as an influential account of Muslim political theory.

1055 **HANANEL BEN HUSHIEL OF TUNISIA,** who wrote one of the the first Talmud commentaries, dies.

1058 **ABU AL-ALA AL-MA'ARRI,** the last great poet of the classical Arab tradition, dies.

ca 1031 **VIMALA VASAHI,** a Jain temple, is built at Dilwara, Mount Abu, in what is now the northern Indian province of Rajasthan. It is a simpler precursor to the elaborately carved temples that will arise in the area in the following centuries.

ca 1050 **JOCHO** becomes an influential sculptor in Japan.

SCIENCE & TECHNOLOGY

ca 1050 THE TOLTEC use obsidian as an economic mainstay. It is employed for knives, darts, clubs, and decorative votive objects.

ca 1050 PETROCELLUS OF ITALY writes *Practica,* an important early medical work.

1050 THE ASTROLABE arrives in Europe from eastern countries.

1037 AVICENNA, historian, medical scientist, and philosopher, dies.

ca 1040 IBN AL HAYTHAM, astronomer and optical scientist, dies.

ca 1050 HOMING PIGEONS are used by the leaders of Baghdad to deliver messages.

ca 1052 AL BIRUNI, historian and mathematician, dies.

ca 1041-1048 MOVABLE TYPE is invented in China by Bi Sheng.

ca 1044 THE CHINESE MILITARY TEXT *Wu Ching Tsung Yao* describes a floating magnetic compass.

1054 JAPANESE AND CHINESE ASTRONOMERS record the explosion of a supernova, which is still visible and known today as the Crab Nebula.

PEOPLE & SOCIETY

ca 1050 ART AND ARTIFACTS found among remnants of the Mississippian Southeastern Ceremonial Complex dating to this era show evidence of trade exchanges with Mesoamerica.

1051-53 THE POWERFUL EARL GODWINE refuses to obey a command from the king, Edward the Confessor, and is banished. His family restores their position in an invasion led by Godwine's son Harold II. Later, Harold succeeds Edward and serves as the last Anglo-Saxon king of England.

1059 POPE NICHOLAS II decrees that future popes must be elected by cardinals.

WHEN THE MOORS RULED SPAIN

LANDING AT GIBRALTAR IN 711, nomadic Muslims from North Africa invaded the Iberian Peninsula and began their conquest of Spain. Chiefly of Arab and Berber stock, the Moors penetrated all the way to Poitiers, France, before being stopped by Charles Martel in 732. For more than 700 years they would rule Spain to varying degrees, leaving a permanent impression on Spanish culture.

The Moors, whose name probably derives from the Latin "Mauri," the old Roman word for the Berbers of Mauritania (present-day Morocco), made themselves at home in the warm Andalusian countryside, establishing Islamic caliphates throughout the region. Their artistic influence is evident in Spain's mosques and palaces with their bright colors and arabesques. Flamenco music, though considered Spanish, contains the rhythm of medieval Muslim minstrels. And it is said that Arabic poetry inspired European troubadours. By the 12th century, Moorish Spain was a great center of learning where Muslims, Christians, and Jews mingled in study, attracting students from all over Europe.

Little by little, though, Christians retook the region, beginning with Alfonso VIII of Castile, when he drove the Muslims from central Spain in 1212. In 1492 Ferdinand and Isabella finally crushed the Moors' last stronghold in Granada, entering perhaps the most beautiful Moorish edifice of all, the Alhambra, and proclaiming victory.

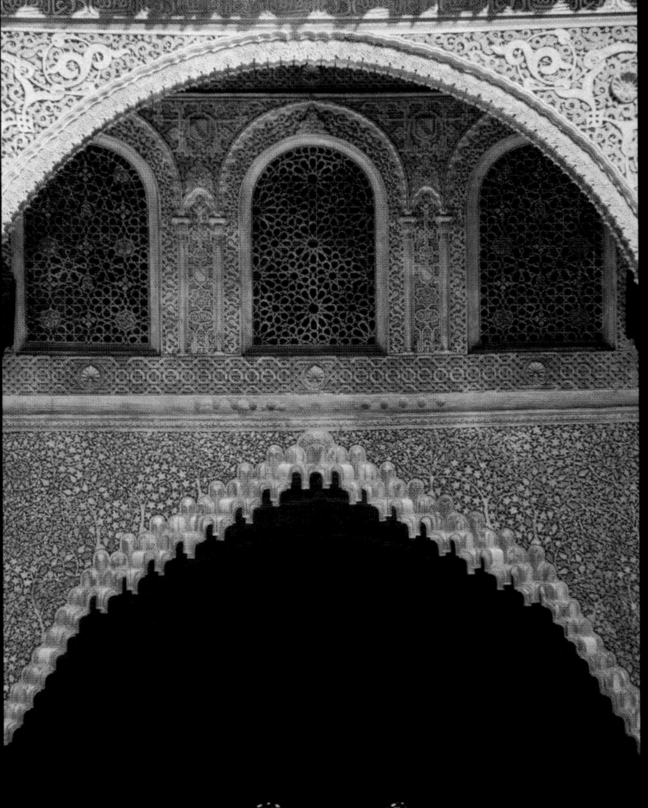

El Patio de los Arrayanes in the Moorish palace of the Alhambra in Granada, Spain

POLITICS & POWER	GEOGRAPHY & ENVIRONMENT	CULTURE & RELIGION

1083 **MIXTEC RULER** Lord Eight Deer Jaguar Claw founds the town of Tututepec in Oaxaca.

1066 **WILLIAM OF NORMANDY** (the Conqueror) defeats King Harold II at the Battle of Hastings and becomes king of England. Harold is killed.

1071 **NORMAN ROBERT GUISCARD** takes Bari, ending five centuries of Byzantine rule in southern Italy.

1084 **GERMAN KING HENRY IV** becomes Holy Roman Emperor.

1094 **EL CID** takes Valencia from the Moors.

1096 **THE FIRST CRUSADE** begins.

1071 **BYZANTINES** are defeated by Seljuk Turks in Anatolia at Manzikert.

1071-1075 **THE SELJUKS** take Jerusalem, Syria, and Palestine.

1092 **THE ASSASSINS,** an Islamic religio-political movement, are thought to have killed Seljuk vizier Nizam al Mulk. The Seljuk realm begins to divide.

1099 **CRUSADERS** take Jerusalem and kill tens of thousands of the city's Jews.

1069 **CHINESE STATESMAN WANG ANSHI** institutes new policies to control economy and government bureaucracy in Song China.

1086 **THE ESTABLISHMENT OF THE "CLOISTERED RULE" SYSTEM** weakens the influence of the powerful Fujiwara family.

WHAT LIFE WAS LIKE

Hunting Buffalo on Foot

Before the Europeans came to America and brought with them horses, buffalo hunting on the plains required ingenuity. In winter a man might stalk buffalo wearing snowshoes, while in other seasons he would sometimes sneak up on them covered in a wolf skin. But the greatest yield occurred when a group of Indians caused a controlled stampede, whereby they channeled a herd toward a cliff, and the bison either died from the fall or were killed by waiting hunters. The Indians built lines of stone cairns that helped guide the bison toward a bottleneck, until at a precise moment people leapt out from their hiding places to begin the stampede. An ideal height for a cliff was one that was tall enough to cause damage to the beasts without crushing them to pieces. And the wind had to be blowing away from the hunters, as buffalo make up for their poor eyesight with a keen sense of smell.

1062 **MARRAKECH** is founded by Almoravids.

ca 1100 **MUSLIM SETTLEMENTS** populate the east coast of Africa and run thriving peaceful trade routes on the Indian Ocean. Swahili, heavily influenced by Arabic, is the lingua franca of the region.

1076 **MAHMUD AL KASHGARI,** a scholar from Kashgar (western China), produces an extensive map centered on Central Asia and including Japan.

900-1100 **ART OF THE SICÁN CULTURE** of coastal Peru includes images of the "Sicán Deity," an icon with a masklike face and, sometimes, avian features. It may represent a god related to life and abundance.

1065 **WESTMINSTER ABBEY** is consecrated.

ca 1066 **NORMAN (ROMANESQUE) ARCHITECTURE** arrives in England.

1075 **CONSTRUCTION BEGINS** on the Cathedral of Santiago de Compostela in Spain.

ca 1080 **THE BAYEUX TAPESTRY** is begun in England, famous for its embroidery at the time.

1094 **ST. MARK'S BASILICA** is consecrated in Venice.

1069-1070 **YUSUF KHASS HAJIB** writes *Wisdom of Royal Glory* for Karakhanids. It is the first major literary work in Turkish.

1076 **KING UMME** of Kanem-Bornu, a trading empire around modern-day Lake Chad, converts to Islam. He later dies on a pilgrimage to Mecca.

ca 1050s-ca 1100 **CHINESE BROTHERS AND PHILOSOPHERS** Cheng Hao and Cheng Yi help to lead a revival of Confucian philosophy in Song dynasty China.

SCIENCE & TECHNOLOGY	PEOPLE & SOCIETY
ca 1085 THULE ESKIMO CULTURE spreads across the North American Arctic to Greenland and Siberia. They develop basic technologies for making kayaks and whaleboats.	**1000s** NORTH AMERICAN PLAINS INDIANS use collapsible tepees and sleighlike travois to break camp easily and follow the buffalo.
ca 1078 CONSTRUCTION BEGINS on the White Tower at the Tower of London. **ca 1080** MUSLIM AND JEWISH ASTRONOMERS complete their compilation of the Toledan Tables, which records the positions of the stars.	**1066** THE PRESTIGE OF THE ENGLISH LANGUAGE is diminished by the Norman invasion. **1075** ADAM OF BREMEN voyages to Scandinavia and records the geography and societies of Thule (now Iceland), Finland, Greenland, and Sweden. **1084** THE FIRST GONDOLAS are recorded in Venice. **1086** COMPILATION OF THE *DOMESDAY BOOK* (a survey for tax assessment) is completed in England.
1067 THE MADRASAH NIZAMIYYAH school for Muslim *ulama* (learned men) is established in Baghdad by Seljuk vizier Nizam al Mulk. **1071** CONSTANTINE THE AFRICAN brings Greek medicine to the Western world.	**1090** THE ASSASSINS are a secret order of the Ismaili religio-political movement of Islam, who hold blind obedience to their spiritual leader and are known for their use of murder to eliminate Sunnis, Shiites, or Franks. **ca 1091** SELJUK VIZIER NIZAM AL MULK writes *Siyasatnama (Book of Government)*, the most representative work of the "mirror for princes" genre in Middle Eastern literature.
1088 A MECHANICAL CELESTIAL CLOCK is constructed by Su Song at Kaifeng.	**1085** SIMA GUANG presents to the throne his *Comprehensive Mirror for Aid in Government*, a history of China from 403 to 959 C.E.

William the Conqueror (on horseback) killing King Harold II during the Battle of Hastings in this detail from the Bayeux Tapestry

WILLIAM THE CONQUEROR

FROM HUMBLE BEGINNINGS in Falaise as the illegitimate son of Duke Robert I, William became duke of Normandy at age seven upon his father's death. Accustomed to the violence of the troubled times in which he developed into a tall, strong man, William quickly found success as a warrior and a baronial leader in France, and soon turned his attention toward tumultuous England.

When William visited Edward the Confessor's court, Edward supposedly named him as his heir. Upon the king's death, however, the Witan, or governing body of England, named Harold as successor, a decision they would soon regret. After building a fleet, assembling an army, and gaining the pope's permission to attack, William was ready to seize his inheritance. On October 14, 1066, William's troops met Harold's at Hastings near England's southern shore, defeating Harold's foot soldiers with a strong cavalry.

A victorious William rode to London, took the city, and had himself crowned King William I at Westminster Abbey on Christmas Day of 1066. He introduced Norman feudalism to the English, which enabled him to bring the country under his control via a monarchy that would last for centuries.

POLITICS & POWER	GEOGRAPHY & ENVIRONMENT	CULTURE & RELIGION

POLITICS & POWER

ca 1100 **CHACO CANYON,** in modern-day New Mexico, is inhabited by more than 5,000 ancient Pueblo settlers.

1100-1200 **THE CAHOKIA INDIAN SETTLEMENT** of the Mississippian culture is the leading metropolis north of Mexico, with some 20,000 people.

1106 **KING HENRY** of England defeats brother Robert at Tinchebrai and reunites England and Normandy, divided since the death of William I.

1126 **ALFONSO I** of Aragon and Navarre raids as far as Granada in Spain.

1128 **HUNGARIANS** are defeated by Byzantine emperor John II Comnenus on the Danube near Haram.

1100 **THE CRUSADERS** kill Jewish defenders of Haifa (Hefa).

1104 **TURKS** defeat crusaders at Harran.

1123 **AN EGYPTIAN FLEET** is defeated off Ascalon by a Venetian crusader fleet.

1125 **THE ALMOHADS,** a Berber Muslim confederation founded by messianic figure Ibn Tumart, seize Morocco.

1100 **NEW CLANS** ruled by chiefs of royal birth are introduced from Tahiti to Hawaii.

1115-1122 **THE JURCHEN** from Manchuria, allied with the Song, overthrow the Khitan Liao and found the Jin dynasty.

GEOGRAPHY & ENVIRONMENT

ca 1100 **CENOTES,** deep sinkholes in lowland Yucatán, are used for sacrifices near monument sites.

ca 1100 **BLACK PEPPER** becomes a major Javanese export.

1100s **TWO-WAY VOYAGING** between Hawaii and Tahiti begins.

CULTURE & RELIGION

ca 1100 **THE HOHOKAM INDIANS** create decorative incised items from cockleshells imported from the California coast.

1100-1350 **TROUBADOUR** and trouvère music begin in France.

1110 **THE EARLIEST RECORD** of a miracle play appears at Dunstable, England.

1122 **THE CONCORDAT OF WORMS** in Germany settles the question of investiture.

1123 **THE FIRST LATERAN COUNCIL** suppresses simony and marriage for priests.

ca 1130 **LA CHANSON DE ROLAND** is written.

1111 **AL GHAZALI,** scholar and mystic, dies. He reconciled mysticism with Islamic orthodoxy.

1122 **AL HARIRI,** who perfected the prose form of the story in his *Maqamat,* dies.

▶ **ca 1100** **THE THAPINYU PAGODA** is constructed in Pagan, Burma. It is one of thousands of Buddhist pagodas constructed by the ruling dynasty between 1057 and 1287.

ca 1120 **OKAGAMI,** or *The Great Mirror,* a history of the Fujiwara family in power at the Heian court between 850 and 1025, is completed by an unknown author.

CONNECTIONS

Spices and Spoilage

Because preservation of food in medieval Europe relied on nothing more than a larder, or storage bin, which usually served only to keep vermin away, herbs and spices were used to enhance or even hide the flavor of some foodstuffs. Meat, in particular, which was liable to rot before it could be eaten, improved with the addition of pepper, nutmeg, and other exotic spices imported from the East, some actually helping to preserve it. Other dishes benefited from local herbs, such as thyme and rosemary from the kitchen garden and plentiful supplies of garlic, salt, and mustard. Sugar, though, was scarce and kept locked up in cone form. Returning crusaders brought it back from the Middle East, along with lemons and melons. Fish was a popular dish, as it was often eaten in observance of church rules on various holy days and every Friday.

SCIENCE & TECHNOLOGY

ca 1100 MISSISSIPPIAN PEOPLE at Cahokia use stone hoes, with chert blades attached to handles, in farming and construction.

1113 ST. NICHOLAS CATHEDRAL, one of the earliest onion-domed churches, is founded in Novgorod.

1123 ST. BARTHOLOMEW'S HOSPITAL is founded in London.

1100 ISLAMIC SCIENCE begins to decline.

PEOPLE & SOCIETY

1115 MIXTEC RULER Lord Eight Deer Jaguar Claw is captured and sacrificed

ca 1100 BRIDGES are early centers of commerce.

1100 MIDDLE ENGLISH supersedes Old English.

ca 1100 THE DIALECT of the Île-de-France becomes the dominant idiom there in the 12th to 13th century.

1124 THE FIRST SCOTTISH COINAGE is made.

ca 1118 THE ORDER OF THE KNIGHTS TEMPLAR is created to protect the road to Jerusalem.

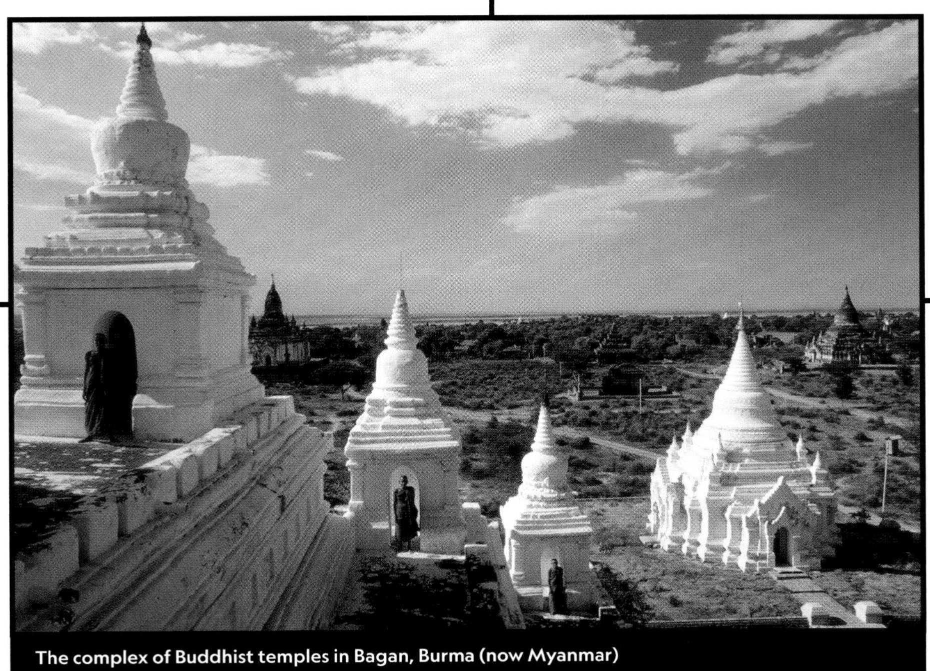

The complex of Buddhist temples in Bagan, Burma (now Myanmar)

THE AGE OF CHIVALRY

THOUGH KNIGHTS EXISTED before the Crusades, these holy wars led to the founding of the first official orders of chivalry, the Hospitallers and the Templars, both pledged to support Christianity's efforts in the Middle East. In France knights were one of the Three Estates, dedicated to the protection of the church and the common man. For assuming the risks of chivalry, knights were rewarded with lordly status and land and the privilege they brought.

The concept of chivalry developed into a code of ideal behavior that offered a sense of certainty in a chaotic and violent period of history. Training for young men born into the class began early and was strenuous. One might be born for knighthood, but one still had to publicly prove one's skills before being anointed. This meant mastering such martial skills as hunting, sword fighting, jousting, wrestling, and falconry.

As a squire, or knight in waiting, a young man was taught to care for his own knight's weapons and spare horse, serve as his valet, help him on with his armor, and attend him at table. After the apprenticeship, the squire was presented with sword, spurs, helmet, and shield. He knelt before his sponsor, who tapped him on each shoulder with a sword, thereby bestowing upon him his well-earned knighthood.

The word "chivalry" itself conjures up mounted men-at-arms, knightly skills, and gallant gentlemen who valued such traits as honor, bravery, and mercy as part of their Christian code. In practice, the code was often neglected, and as the centuries passed, many of the knightly displays became largely ceremonial, another form of showy aristocracy.

POLITICS & POWER | GEOGRAPHY & ENVIRONMENT | CULTURE & RELIGION

POLITICS & POWER

ca 1150 **PUEBLO BONITO,** an ancestral Puebloan site in the valley of modern-day New Mexico's Chaco Canyon, reaches its height.

GEOGRAPHY & ENVIRONMENT

ca 1150 **A DRY PERUVIAN COASTAL CLIMATE** requires elaborate irrigation systems to support Chimú civilization.

CULTURE & RELIGION

1100s **TEAMS IN CAHOKIA** (in present-day Illinois) play chunkey, a game that involves throwing spears at rolling stone disks.

POLITICS & POWER

1138 **CONRAD III** of Hohenstaufen succeeds Lothar III as king of Germany. Civil war ensues when he seizes Saxony and Bavaria.

1146-1148 **THE SECOND CRUSADE** occurs.

1152 **FREDERICK BARBAROSSA** (Red Beard) becomes Holy Roman Emperor upon the death of his uncle, Conrad III.

1152 **ELEANOR OF AQUITAINE** has her marriage to King Louis VII of France annulled and marries the much younger Norman, Henry Plantagenet. Two years later, he becomes King Henry II of England.

GEOGRAPHY & ENVIRONMENT

A later, romanticized view of the monk Abelard reading to his lover, the nun Héloise

CULTURE & RELIGION

◀ **ca 1132** **PETER ABELARD** writes *Historia calamitatum mearum,* a description of his love affair with Héloise.

1143-1153 **ANNA COMNENA** writes *Alexiad,* a chronicle of the career of her father, Byzantine Emperor Alexius I Comnenus.

1144 **GOTHIC ARCHITECTURE** is introduced with the completion of the new abbey church of St. Denis near Paris.

1155 **THE CARMELITE ORDER** is founded.

1156 **CONSTRUCTION BEGINS ON THE KREMLIN,** a wooden citadel in Moscow.

POLITICS & POWER

1130 **ALMOHAD ABD AL MUMIN** is recognized as caliph in North Africa.

1147 **MARRAKECH,** capital of the Almoravid Empire, falls to Almohads under Abd al Mumin.

ca 1148 **MUSLIM ATTACKS** have depleted the joint forces of the Second Crusade by more than half by the time Louis VII and Conrad III reach the Holy Land.

1159 **THE ALMOHAD DYNASTY** conquers Tunisia and reclaims lands taken by Roger II of the Norman kingdom of Sicily.

GEOGRAPHY & ENVIRONMENT

1154 **ARAB GEOGRAPHER ASH SHARIF AL IDRISI,** an advisor to Roger II, king of Norman Sicily, writes a landmark work on medieval geography titled *The Pleasure Excursion of One Who Is Eager to Traverse the Regions of the World.*

CULTURE & RELIGION

1131 **OMAR KHAYYAM,** Persian poet and astronomer, dies. He is best known as a poet for his *Rubaiyat,* a collection of quatrains in which the first, second, and fourth lines rhyme. It is later famously translated into English by Edward FitzGerald.

1146 **ALMOHADS** institute forced conversions of Jews in North Africa.

POLITICS & POWER

1152 **GHURID CHIEF ALAUDDIN HUSSAIN** sacks Ghazna, reducing the Ghaznavids' realm to eastern Afghanistan and northern India.

1160 **THE TAIRA AND MINAMOTO CLANS** of Japan come to blows in the Heiji Rebellion, a precursor of the Gempei War two decades later.

GEOGRAPHY & ENVIRONMENT

1100s **CHINA** experiences unusually warm temperatures during what would come to be known as the Medieval Warm Period.

CULTURE & RELIGION

11456 **CONFUCIAN SCHOLAR KIM PU-SHIK** compiles *Samguk Sagi (History of the Three Kingdoms).*

SCIENCE & TECHNOLOGY	PEOPLE & SOCIETY
ca 1100s SURGEONS in the northern highlands of Peru have become so successful at trephination—a procedure involving drilling a hole in the skull to relieve pressure—that more than 90 percent of their patients survive.	**ca 1150** THE AZTEC, according to legend, leave mythical Aztlan of northern Mexico and begin migrating toward central Mexico. **1150-1300** THE THIRD PUEBLO PERIOD occurs in southwestern North America.
1146 *ANTIDOTARIUM NICLAI,* a treatise on drugs, is written. **ca 1150** MUSLIMS IN SPAIN manufacture paper. **1150-1157** HILDEGARD OF BINGEN writes *Causa at Curea,* a medical treatise in German based on trial, error, and observation.	**1132** HENRY I of France grants charters for corporate towns protecting industry and commerce. **1133** THE FIRST ST. BARTHOLOMEW'S FAIR takes place at Smithfield, London. **1151** THE FIRST FIRE AND PLAGUE INSURANCE is offered, in Iceland. **1151** THE GAME OF CHESS comes to England. **1155** THOMAS À BECKET becomes Henry II's chancellor. **1158** MUNICH becomes center of the salt trade.
ca 1160 ARAB JEWISH SCHOLAR ABRAHAM IBN DAUD writes the influential work of philosophy *ha Emunah ha Ramah (The Exalted Faith).*	**1144** SELJUK TURK ZANGI, the atabeg of Mosul, takes the city of Edessa and pursues jihad against crusaders with similar ideals.
ca 1150 THE TEMPLE OF ANGKOR WAT in Cambodia is completed by Khmer king Suryavarman II as both a Hindu religious complex and his burial site. It is one of the largest religious complexes in the world and a premier example of ancient Khmer architecture. **1151** THE CHINESE use explosives in warfare.	**ca 1132** LI QINGZHAO, considered China's greatest female poet, writes a famous chronicle of her married life and the couple's shared passion for academic pursuits.

THE INVENTION OF GUNPOWDER

LEGEND HAS IT that a Chinese scientist accidentally invented gunpowder while trying to create a potion that would ensure immortality. True or not, this explosive mixture has achieved immortality in its own right. The first mention of a gunpowder formula citing proportions of ingredients is found in a Song dynasty military manual dating to 1044. Alchemists attempting to negate the activity of sulfur by mixing it with saltpeter and other ingredients containing carbon had discovered a new fire compound they called *huoyao.* The nature of the mixture was so violent that the Song manual cautioned against attempting to make it.

Little more than a hundred years later the Chinese were experimenting with gunpowder in warfare, and by 1232 they were using large gunpowder flame-throwers to fight the Mongols at the siege of Kaifeng. These lethal explosives dashed the legend that the Chinese used their new propellant only for fireworks. Later, rockets were launched from huge batteries of racks. But bombs and guns needed a higher nitrate mix, and the Chinese succeeded in perfecting the mix, now known as black powder, by reducing the proportion of saltpeter used in the formula.

The first record of a Chinese cannon dates from 1288, though a carving from a Sichuan cave temple built in 1128 appears to depict a cannon in action. The Chinese apparently had cannons as much as two centuries before Europeans, who probably learned of the new weapons from Muslim traders. Soon the ability to cast cannons in one-piece metal tubes made them strong enough to fire 800-pound balls, making them the main weapon of siege warfare throughout Europe by the 15th century.

Gunpowder remained the only explosive in wide use until the middle of the 19th century, when nitroglycerine-based explosives proved to be more efficiently destructive.

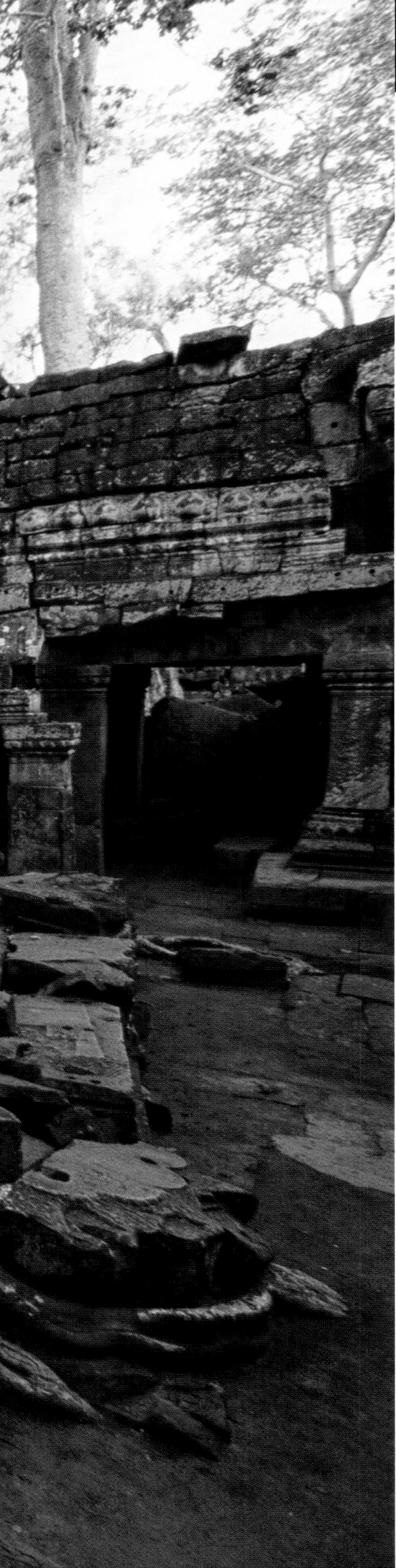

THE GLORY OF ANGKOR

Located at the northern end of the Great Lake, or Tonle Sap, in modern-day Cambodia, Angkor reigned as the chosen site of Khmer capitals from the ninth to the 15th century. The ancient city covered an estimated area of more than 400 square miles, stretching across vast areas of forest and plain, and at its height was home to more than 750,000 people. Here Khmer kings erected some of the world's most spectacular temple complexes, some devoted to Hinduism, others reflecting the kingdom's conversion to Buddhism. The principal complex is Angkor Wat (City Temple), but more than 70 other temples also grace the area.

Angkor Wat was the vision of King Suryavarman II, who ruled in the 12th century and wanted a glorious temple and administrative center for his empire. A full square mile in size, it is perhaps the largest religious structure in the world and is designed to represent the structure of the Hindu cosmos. The outer gate is protected by a moat, suggesting the oceans at the edge of the world. Inside, exquisitely carved bas-reliefs tell the stories of Krishna, Vishnu, and Rama, as well as stories of the Khmer kings. Visitors pass through a rising series of towered galleries and courtyards that lead to the main temple and its central tower, which is shaped like a lotus blossom. The difficulty in reaching this ultimate sanctuary reflects the difficulty in reaching the kingdom of the gods.

Despite this glorious dedication to the Hindu gods, Angkor was sacked by the rival Cham people in 1177, causing the next Khmer king, Jayavarman VII, to look elsewhere for divine protection. He dedicated his own temple complex, Angkor Thom, to Buddhism, and converted Angkor Wat to a Buddhist shrine, replacing many of the Hindu statues. The king's imprint is inescapable here: The central tower of Angkor Thom displays a giant image of Buddha; 50 smaller towers surrounding the complex, however, each feature multiple images of the king as a Buddhist god. As part of a massive building campaign, Jayavarman also built Ta Prohm (left) as a Buddhist monastery and university. Subsequent rulers continued to expand Ta Prohm through the 13th century. The site has become the most popular attraction for visitors because of its picturesque merging with surrounding forest.

Ultimately, Buddhism also couldn't protect Angkor, which was raided and sacked by the Siamese in the 15th century. The Khmer moved their capital to Phnom Penh, where it would remain. Most of Angkor was abandoned, left to be swallowed by the jungle, except for Angkor Wat, which was conserved as a Buddhist shrine by monks who trimmed the vegetation and made repairs. The French, upon colonizing Indochina in the 19th century, rediscovered the "lost city" of Angkor and began the effort to restore this marvelous legacy of the ancient Khmer.

Buddhist monks among the roots of a strangler fig tree that creep over temple walls at Ta Prohm in Cambodia, one of the many magnificent temple complexes built throughout Angkor Wat by Khmer kings.

1160-1200

	POLITICS & POWER	GEOGRAPHY & ENVIRONMENT	CULTURE & RELIGION
THE AMERICAS	**ca 1175** **TOLTEC POWER** ends as the city of Tula falls. The next superpower in Mesoamerica will be the Aztec.		**ca 1190** **ANCESTRAL PUEBLO PEOPLE** construct dwellings into the alcoves of overhanging cliffs in Mesa Verde. They continue to farm on the flat mesa tops that they previously inhabited.
EUROPE	**1170** **THOMAS À BECKET** is murdered at Canterbury Cathedral by Norman knights. **1176** **EMPEROR FREDERICK BARBAROSSA** is defeated by Italy's Lombard League. ▶ **1189** **KING HENRY II** of England dies and is succeeded by Richard I (the Lionheart). **1191** **HENRY VI,** son of Frederick Barbarossa, is crowned Holy Roman Emperor. **1199** **RICHARD I** dies from wounds suffered in France and is succeeded by his brother John.	**Richard the Lionheart leads crusaders in a battle against Muslims at Arsuf.**	**1160** **CELTIC EPIC** *Tristan et Iseult* is written. **ca 1160** **CHRÉTIEN DE TROYES** writes *Lancelot,* a romance of courtly love. **1167** **OXFORD UNIVERSITY** develops rapidly after King Henry II prohibits English students from attending the University of Paris. **ca 1170** **POPE ALEXANDER III** issues rules for the canonization of saints. **1181-1192** **ENGLISH WRITER** Walter Map composes *Courtiers' Trifles,* a Latin text of folklore, legends, and histories of the Anglo-Norman kings.
MIDDLE EAST & AFRICA	**1169** **SALADIN** becomes vizier of Egypt. Two years later, he becomes sultan of Egypt and abolishes the caliphate and reestablishes Sunnism. **1174** **SALADIN** conquers southern Syria. **1187** **JERUSALEM** is reconquered by Saladdin, provoking the Third Crusade, which will begin in 1189. **1191** **RICHARD I** defeats Saladin's forces at Acre but fails to retake any major holy sites.	**ca 1194-1200** **SELJUK POWER** comes to an end in all their territories except Anatolia following the death of the last Seljuk ruler.	**ca 1160** **SELJUK ART** becomes more advanced as inlaid copper, silver, and gold adorn bronze and brass objects inscribed with "animated" Arabic script written to resemble human and animal figures. **1166** **SALADIN** builds Salah El Din Citadel in Cairo. **1180** **MAIMONIDES** completes *Guide of the Perplexed.* **1198** **JEWS IN YEMEN** are forced to convert to Islam.
ASIA & OCEANIA	**1185** **THE PUNJAB** in India is conquered by Muhammad of Ghur. **1185** **MINAMOTO YORITOMO** annihilates the Tairas and sets up a military government at Kamakura in Japan. **1189** **MINAMOTO YOSHITSUNE** commits suicide, along with his monk companion, Benkei, after being defeated by his brother's forces. **ca 1192** **MUHAMMAD OF GHUR** takes Delhi and installs the first Muslim ruler of India. **1192** **MINAMOTO YORITOMO** awards himself the supreme title of *seitaishogun.*	**1177** **KING JAYAVARMAN VII** builds Angkor Thom, a new Khmer capital city, next to Angkor Wat after the Cham invasion. Unlike Angkor Wat, which was dedicated to the Hindu gods, the Angkor Thom complex reflects the king's conversion to Buddhism.	**1191** **THE MONK ELSAI** returns from China, transmitting Rinzai, one of two major Zen Buddhist traditions, and tea drinking to Japan.

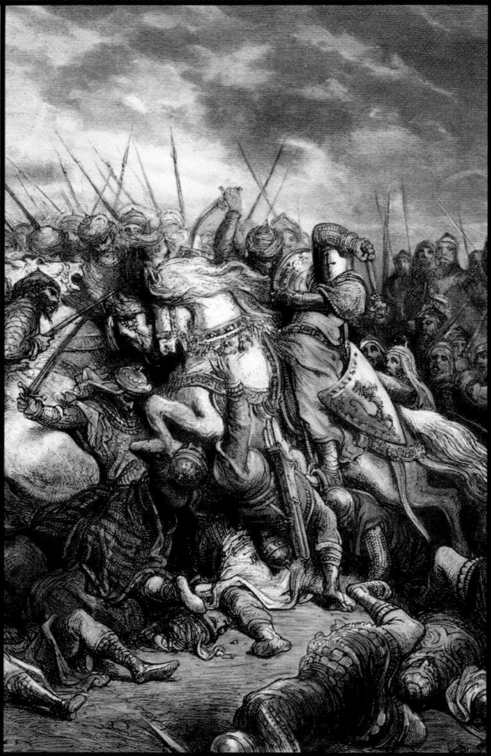

SCIENCE & TECHNOLOGY	PEOPLE & SOCIETY
ca 1200 ARTISANS in Cahokia produce elaborate metal ornaments at a copper workshop and trade them throughout the South.	**ca 1200** THE FIRST INCA PEOPLE settle in Cusco, Peru, establishing a city high in the Andes.
1163 NOTRE DAME CATHEDRAL in Paris is begun. **1173** CONSTRUCTION BEGINS on what becomes known as the Leaning Tower of Pisa. **ca 1175-1183** ALEXANDER NECKAM of England writes *De nominibus utensilium,* the earliest account of a mariner's compass. **1176** LONDON BRIDGE begins to span the Thames River, the first stone bridge to arise over a tidal waterway. **1194** WORK BEGINS on the present Chartres Cathedral in France.	**1100s** WIVES AND SERVANTS often take food to be cooked at the baker's (for example), since most houses do not have ovens. **1100s** AS A RESULT OF THE CRUSADES, Persian and Turkish rugs are seen in English homes. **1180** GLASS WINDOWS appear in English private homes.
	1100s SELJUK SOLDIERS, and later Mamluk soldiers, are expected to play polo in order to keep themselves in shape. **ca 1168** MOSES MAIMONIDES, considered the leading intellectual of medieval Judaism, completes *Mishnah Torah (The Torah Reviewed),* his great law code. ◀ **1193** SALADIN'S DEATH at Damascus sets off years of infighting among his heirs. **1198** IBN RUSHD (AVERROES) dies. His commentary on Aristotle is esteemed throughout Europe and the Muslim world.
	1100s SAMURAI begin to dominate Japanese society. **1100s** A LARGE VARIETY OF PORCELAIN WARES are being produced for functional as well as decorative purposes in China.

Saladin, founder of the Ayyubid dynasty and a Muslim hero

THE LION AND THE SULTAN

THE THIRD CRUSADE brought into confrontation the two most legendary soldiers of these holy wars: England's Richard I (Richard the Lionheart) and Saladin, founder of the Muslim Ayyubid dynasty. Saladin was a scourge to the crusaders, having vanquished them and captured Jerusalem in 1187, ending 88 years of Christian control. The goal of the Third Crusade, charged to Richard, was to win Jerusalem back.

Both men were born into families of power, well educated, and dedicated to spreading their respective faiths. Richard, who was the son of Henry II and Eleanor of Aquitaine, spent only six months of his reign in England. For most of his life he was defending his mother's territories in France, and he spoke French rather than English. Saladin, son of prominent Mesopotamian Kurds, rose to power in a Muslim world fractured by clannish dissension. Given the title of king but known as the sultan, he united Syria, Mesopotamia, Palestine, and Egypt into a spiritual and military force through a combination of diplomacy and military skill.

The talent marshaled by Christendom to recapture Jerusalem only enhanced Saladin's reputation. In addition to Richard, Phillip II of France and Holy Roman Emperor Frederick Barbarossa took part in the Third Crusade. But it was Richard's military genius that was the true threat. His crusaders defeated Saladin's forces on the Levantine coast, taking the city of Acre in 1191. From there he defeated Saladin at Arsuf, giving him control of Jaffa. But Saladin held on to Jerusalem, denying Richard the ultimate prize.

Although Richard and Saladin never actually met each other, each earned the other's admiration as soldiers of the first order. Saladin succumbed to illness in 1193 in Damascus; Richard died as a result of an arrow wound in 1199 while fighting in France.

ANCIENT CITIES IN STONE

In the American Southwest there exists a sweeping panorama that was once home to a progressive group of Indian peoples called the ancestral Puebloans. Known as the Four Corners region—where Colorado, New Mexico, Utah, and Arizona meet—canyons, mesas, plateaus, cliffs, and desert create a dramatic landscape where winters are harsh and where summers offer both dusty drought and violent thunderstorm.

It was into this unfriendly yet beautiful natural environment that the Pueblo people chose to settle at the beginning of the Common Era. Around 1050 they began gathering in large towns, first in a valley called Chaco Canyon (located in present-day New Mexico), and then on the tableland of Mesa Verde to the north, in what is now Colorado. At Mesa Verde they began building elevated shelters for themselves in the cliffs, most likely for protection from the growing threat of Navajo and Apache invasion. The ancient Pueblo people were expert masons, using hand-cut stone building blocks and adobe mortar of exceptional quality to build these terraced apartment-like cliff dwellings, which seem to defy gravity as they cling together in huge crooks and crannies of the canyon walls. Rising as high as five stories, the cliff houses could only be entered by ladders that could easily be pushed away in case of attack. Ground-floor rooms had no doors or windows and were accessible only from within. The largest of these distinctive pueblos, the monumental Cliff Palace, contained about 150 separate rooms measuring about 50 square feet each.

The Pueblo cultures evolved from earlier nomadic tribes of the Basketmaker Period. They turned from basketmaking to building as they began to master dry farming, which allowed them to cultivate maize, squash, beans, and cotton in this arid landscape, and thus settle permanently. In addition to sophisticated irrigation systems, they built subterranean round storage facilities to store grain. These circular pits, or kivas, eventually were adapted for shelters and then gathering places for important ceremonies or communal activities, for which they are still used today. Kivas became the heart of growing Pueblo communities, both symbolically and architecturally. At the Chaco Canyon site known as Pueblo Bonito, two great kivas and 37 smaller ones occupy the central courtyard of an enclosed urban site. Perhaps the largest of all the settlements of this period, Pueblo Bonito housed around 800 separate residences.

By the late 13th century, periods of severe drought, and possible internal conflict in these increasingly crowded towns, forced the Puebloans to abandon their sandstone palaces. Their skill in agriculture, as well as cotton weaving and pottery making, have passed to the current generations of Pueblo people, who still conduct ceremonies in the ancient kivas and look with pride on a rich society that went the way of the winds.

Cliff Palace at Mesa Verde, Colorado, is the largest of the ancestral Puebloan cliff dwellings.

1200-1230

THE AMERICAS

POLITICS & POWER

ca 1200 THE TARASCAN, OR PUREPECHA, STATE is well established at Tzintzuntzan in western Mexico. It is powerful enough to resist all other postclassic empires.

ca 1200 THE TIWANAKU CIVILIZATION in the Andes disappears as the Inca begin to rise.

ca 1200 CHICHÉN ITZÁ'S DOMINANCE ends and Mayapan, a less distinguished city, rises for 250 years.

ca 1200 THE CHIMÚ EMPIRE in coastal Peru begins to expand and flourish.

GEOGRAPHY & ENVIRONMENT

ca 1200 ANCIENT PUEBLO PEOPLE settle in Bandelier, in present-day north-central New Mexico.

ca 1200 CHIMÚ CIVILIZATION extends along more than 621 miles of coastal valleys, between Chancay in the south and Tumbrey in the north.

CULTURE & RELIGION

ca 1200 THE MAYA DRESDEN CODEX contains astronomical information about the cycles of the planet Venus.

EUROPE

POLITICS & POWER

1202 THE FOURTH CRUSADE is led by Boniface of Montferrat.

1215 THE MAGNA CARTA is signed by King John. It subjects the English sovereign to the rule of law and establishes the basis for individual rights.

1217 THE FIFTH CRUSADE is led by Duke Leopold VI of Austria and King Andrew II of Hungary.

1228 HOLY ROMAN EMPEROR FREDERICK II leads the Sixth Crusade.

GEOGRAPHY & ENVIRONMENT

ca 1100-1300 LARGE GERMAN POPULATIONS shift eastward into east-central and eastern Europe in what's called *Drang nach Osten* ("Drive to the East").

ca 1200 PARIS evolves into a modern capital.

1221 DUKE LEOPOLD VI of Austria elevates the status of Vienna and increases its influence as a center of commerce.

CULTURE & RELIGION

ca 1200 JEWISH KABBALISTIC PHILOSOPHY develops in southern Europe.

1204 CRUSADERS capture Constantinople and break their holy oath by destroying holy sites, assaulting women, and pillaging.

1209 FRANCIS OF ASSISI relates the first rules of his brotherhood, the Franciscans.

1215 DOMINIC founds the Dominican Order, whose mission will be to convert heretics.

MIDDLE EAST & AFRICA

POLITICS & POWER

1200 AL MALIK AL ADIL becomes sultan of Egypt.

1204 CRUSADERS seize Constantinople. Byzantines move their empire to Nicaea in Anatolia.

1217-1221 THE CRUSADE against the Egyptian sultanate fails.

1225 ETHIOPIAN EMPEROR LALIBELA dies after moving his capital from Aksum to Lasta and overseeing the building of rock-hewn churches there.

CULTURE & RELIGION

ca 1200 ARTISANS FROM ILE-IFE, in modern-day southwestern Nigeria, become known for their bronze pieces and realistic terra-cotta heads.

1209 NEZAMI, author of the *Khamseh (The Quintuplet)* and regarded as the greatest romantic epic poet in Persian literature, dies.

ASIA & OCEANIA

POLITICS & POWER

1206 QUTB AL DIN AIBAK founds a Muslim dynasty, the Slaves, in India.

1206 TEMUJIN, chief of the Mongol tribes, assumes the name Genghis Khan. He conquers Peking (1214), Persia (1218), and Transoxiana (1220).

1219 HOJOS assume the government of Kamakura in Japan after Sanetomo, the third Minamoto shogun, is murdered.

1227 GENGHIS KHAN dies and his empire is divided among his three sons.

CULTURE & RELIGION

ca 1200 ISLAM begins to replace religions throughout the Indian Ocean, from the Maldives, to Socotora, to the Comoros Islands, due to the influence of Muslim traders.

1227 JAPANESE MONK DOGEN helps transmit Zen Buddhism after returning from China.

WHAT LIFE WAS LIKE

The Way of Tea

Originally imported from China in about the eighth century, tea has been a significant aspect of Japanese culture ever since. Monks made it a part of Zen Buddhist religious ceremony, and merchants, shoguns, and samurai made a ritual of tea drinking as an escape from their busy lives. A formal etiquette of preparing, serving, and drinking tea was developed, based on the virtues of simplicity, gratitude, and solitude. The Way of Tea (Chado) became, as one monk stated, "a religion of the art of life." Tea masters purified their utensils and offered their bitter green tea with modesty and reverence as a way to cleanse one's own thoughts of ego and desire. A form of meditation, the tea ceremony satisfied both the physical and the spiritual thirst.

SCIENCE & TECHNOLOGY	PEOPLE & SOCIETY
ca 1200 **ANCIENT PUEBLO PEOPLE** construct an observatory out of stone slabs and two spiral petroglyphs on the Fajada Butte to record equinoxes, solstices, and the position of the moon. **ca 1200** **ANCIENT PUEBLO PEOPLE** weave yucca plants into sturdy sandals.	**ca 1200** **IROQUOIS IN ONTARIO** live in longhouses warmed by fire pits.
1202 **FIBONACCI** introduces Arabic numerals in Europe. **1210** **THE ORIGINAL REIMS CATHEDRAL** burns. Construction of its replacement begins the next year. **1226** **CAMBRIDGE UNIVERSITY** becomes a more formalized institution, with regular courses of study taught by an organization of scholars.	**1200** **AN ESTIMATED 19,000 LEPROSY HOSPITALS** serve patients across Europe. **1209** **KING JOHN** of England invades Scotland and is excommunicated. **1212** **WOODEN AND THATCHED ROOFS** are outlawed, replaced with tiles, shingles, board, and lead in London houses. **1219** **DENMARK** adopts Danneborg, the oldest national flag in the world. **1228** **JAMES I,** king of Aragon, launches a major offensive against Islam in the Ballearic Islands. He captures Majorca two years later
ca 1206 **AL JAZARI** compiles *The Book of Knowledge of Ingenious Mechanical Devices,* a compendium of automata. **1218-1228** **YAQUT IBN ABDALLAH** writes the extensive Arab geographic dictionary *Mujam al Buldan (Dictionary of Countries).*	**1210** **HASAN III,** chief of the Assassins, converts to Sunni Islam. He becomes known as the *Naw Musulman* ("New Muslim").
1200-1500 **EARLY STAGES** of the construction of stone palaces, temples, and other structures at Nan Madol on the Pacific island of Pohnpei are undertaken. **1227** **JAPANESE POTTER TOSHIRO** returns home after traveling in China and begins to manufacture porcelain.	

JAIN TEMPLES: SANCTUARIES FOR THE NONVIOLENT

FOUNDED BY MAHAVIRA in the sixth century B.C.E., Jainism is the name of a religious movement in India based on the principle of ascetic self-denial. Monks and nuns dedicated their lives to cleansing the soul and embarked on a mendicant's life. By sweeping all living things away before them as they walked, wearing masks over their faces, and blocking their ears, they avoided destroying the souls of all things living, including rocks and other inanimate objects.

The Jain conception of karma, more extreme than what Hindus believe, considers suicide the ultimate sacrifice. Mahavira himself fasted to death at the age of 72, and following his death, the Jain sect grew along caravan routes to the west and south. In their original northern climate near Mount Abu in modern Rajasthan, beautifully carved temples (below) were built as a symbol of their devotion.

The movement today, though less widely practiced, includes prosperous city lawyers and scholars, as well as mendicants, but prohibits farming, as the nature of the occupation requires the killing of living objects.

Thirteenth-century Jain Tejapala Temple at Mount Abu in Rajasthan, India

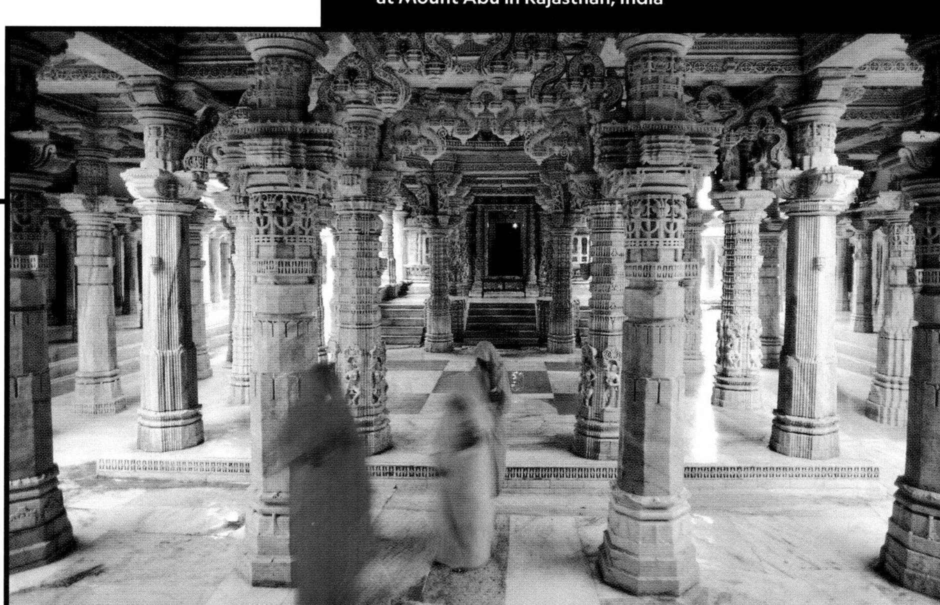

POLITICS & POWER	GEOGRAPHY & ENVIRONMENT	CULTURE & RELIGION
ca 1200 MANCA CAPAC becomes the first emperor of the Inca. **ca 1250 COASTAL PERU'S CIVILIZATION** revives in the Moche Valley. **ca 1250 THE AZTEC,** who call themselves Mexica, arrive in central Mexico. **ca 1250 MIXTEC AND ZAPOTEC** elites intermarry. **ca 1250-1500 THE MOUNDVILLE SETTLEMENT** of the Mississippian culture flourishes in modern-day Alabama.	**1250 CAHOKIA,** the great city of the Mississippian culture, is bigger than London.	**ca 1250 INTRICATE CHIMÚ TEXTILES** incorporate vividly colored patterns and often depict a figure—thought to be otherworldly or revered—capped with a toothed crescent headdress and clutching multiple staffs.
1230 FERDINAND III unites Castile and Leon. **1237 MONGOLS** cross the Volga River, eventually burning Moscow and conquering Russia. **1238 JAMES I,** king of Aragon, reconquers Valencia from the Arabs. **1242 BATU,** grandson of Genghis Khan, establishes the Golden Horde at Sarai in Russia. **1248 FERDINAND III** takes Seville after a two-year siege, and most of its Muslim inhabitants flee to Granada and Tunis.	**1230 PRAGUE'S GROWING IMPORTANCE** is reflected in its elevation to borough status and the completion of a defensive system of walls and fortifications. **1240 THE BORDER** is established between England and Scotland. **1242 THE TOWN OF KIEL** is founded in Germany. **ca 1244 THE CITY OF BERLIN** is first mentioned in historical records. **1253 WILLIAM OF RUBROUCK** travels in Central Asia and reports adventures.	**ca 1230-1276 ITALIAN POET GUIDO GUINIZELLI** is a forerunner of the *dolce stil nuovo* ("sweet new style") form of poetry, of which Dante is the most famous practitioner. **ca 1250 *THE BLACK BOOK OF CARMARTHEN,*** the earliest complete manuscript of Welsh poetry, is transcribed. **1250 THE HIGH GOTHIC PERIOD** in German art begins. **1252 THE INQUISITION** begins using torture instruments.
ca 1230-1255 SUNDIATA KEITA becomes the founder and ruler of the Mali Empire. **1236 THE BERBER KINGDOM** of the Abd al Wadids is founded at Tlemcen. **1243 MONGOLS** conquer Seljuk Anatolia. **1250 MAMLUKS** take power in Egypt and defeat Louis IX of France in the Seventh Crusade.		**1240 IBN AL ARABI,** a Spanish Muslim mystic and cosmologist who believed in the "unity of existence" and analyzed human nature as a microcosm of the natural and divine cosmos, dies. **ca 1250 KONYA,** the capital of Anatolia, flourishes, with impressive buildings such as the Ince Minare and Karaty Medrese rising on the landscape. **1258 SADI,** the Persian poet, writes *The Rose Garden.*
1234 MONGOLS seize Kaifeng in China, completing the destruction of the Jin Empire. **1238 MONGOLS** invade Russia but are repulsed in India.		**1231 LUNA VASAHI,** a Jain temple, is built at Dilwara, Mount Abu, in what is now the northern Indian province of Rajasthan. **ca 1250 THE CHINESE PLAY** *An Orphan of Zhao* is considered a representative piece of *zaju,* or variety play, that evolved into a more complex four-act dramatic form during the Yuan dynasty.

CONNECTIONS

Chinese Living and Dead

Because the Chinese venerated their ancestors, each family had its own household religious hierarchy. The living needed the spiritual assistance of the dead so that they would be able to live a good life on Earth; the dead required the devotion of their living descendants in order to nourish their souls in the afterlife. Death, therefore, signaled the start of a new kind of a relationship. Sons and daughters wore clothes made from uncomfortable sackcloth for 27 months after a parent's death. They were not allowed to use porcelain, have sexual relationships, eat meat, or shave. And every family breathed a sigh of relief when a son was born, since only individuals with sons could require devotion after their deaths.

SCIENCE & TECHNOLOGY	PEOPLE & SOCIETY
ca 1250 THE AUDIENCIA, one of the architectural innovations of the Chimú, is a U-shaped building lined with niches where administrators receive tribute.	**1200s** K'ICHE' MAYA PEOPLE begin to settle in the highlands of Guatemala.
ca 1233 COAL is mined for the first time in Newcastle, England. **ca 1241** THE *DYNAMERON,* an enormous Byzantine volume of pharmaceutical recipes, is compiled by Nichalos Myrepsos. **1248** COLOGNE CATHEDRAL is begun. **1248** THE ALHAMBRA in Granada is begun. **ca 1250** JORDANUS RUFUS writes *De medicina equorum,* a veterinary manual. **1253** THE BASILICA OF ST. FRANCIS OF ASSISI is finished.	**ca 1240** TATAR HORSEMEN place meat under the saddles of their horses, and after a full day's riding it is tenderized and eaten raw. **ca 1250** A TREMENDOUS INCREASE in commerce and industry fuels a widespread growth in prosperity. **1253** LINEN is first manufactured in England by Flemish weavers. **1258** THE PROVISIONS OF OXFORD create a precursor of the House of Commons, enabling landowners and property holders to send representatives to Parliament.
1248 ARAB PHARMACIST Ibn al Baitar dies. He is the author of *The Book of Medicinal and Nutritional Terms,* an encyclopedia of medicinal plants, foods, and drugs.	**1250** SHAJAR AL DURR becomes the queen of Egypt after the death of her husband, Ayyubid ruler Al Salih Ayyubi. She is the second woman in Islamic history to rule in her own right. **ca 1250** THE IRON AGE SETTLEMENT of Great Zimbabwe reaches its height with numerous dry-stone walls and buildings, a vast trade network, and a population of between 12,000 and 20,000 people. **1256** HULEGU founds the Mongol Il Khanid dynasty of Persia and in 1258 seizes Baghdad, overthrowing the caliphate.
1232-1233 CHINESE ARMIES defend the city of Kaifeng from a Mongol attack using gunpowder-filled vessels they called "thunder bombs."	**1236-1240** SULTANA RAZIA becomes the first and only female sultan of Delhi. A well-respected ruler, she is captured and killed by political enemies.

Mask and horned helmet worn by elite samurai—Osaka, Japan

THE WAY OF THE SAMURAI

BY THE 12TH CENTURY an aristocratic class of warriors had begun to wield great power throughout Japan. For nearly 700 years samurai would continue to dominate Japanese society. Their original center, the military government of Minamoto Yoritomo, was located at the coastal town of Kamakura, near modern Tokyo. As power shifted from civil aristocracy to a new bureaucratic regime based on these provincial warriors, the samurai became famous for offering security through military prowess.

Somewhat like knights in medieval Europe, the samurai, who took orders from their lords, valued martial skills, with an emphasis on the ideals of bravery and austerity. In addition, they lived by a code that emphasized loyalty to their lords and honor in defeat. The honorable way to die was called seppuku, literally, "disembowelment," a ritual whereby the defeated warrior would commit suicide with his own sword.

These elite soldiers, wielding swords and wearing terrifying masks and horned helmets, won a number of battles through intimidation alone.

POLITICS & POWER

ca 1260 **THE AZTEC** live in the central Valley of Mexico, where they become over time valuable mercenaries for the Culhuacan, a culture left over from the Toltec Empire. They are called "military maniacs" by the Culhua ruler because of their ferocity in battle and released from their service.

1260 **FLORENTINE GHIBELLINES** defeat the Guelphs at Montaperti.

1283 **THE TEUTONIC KNIGHTS** finish conquering Prussia, which began in 1233.

1284 **GENOANS** nearly destroy the Pisan navy at Meloria, becoming the rival of Venice.

1291 **THE CRUSADES** end. The Hospitallers of St. John of Jerusalem settle in Cyprus.

1297 **WILLIAM WALLACE** leads the Scots in a rebellion against the English.

1261 **MICHAEL VIII PALAEOLOGUS** regains Constantinople.

▶ **1270** **AMHARA PRINCE YEKUNO AMLAK** overthrows the Zagwe dynasty in Ethiopia, which leaves behind a legacy of 11 monolithic Christian churches in what is now Lalibela. Amlak ushers in the Ethiopian Middle Ages, nearly 250 years of tremendous prosperity.

1289 **QALA'UN,** sultan of Egypt, captures Tripoli, leaving Acre the only major Christian stronghold remaining in the Near East.

1291 **THE MAMLUKS** seize Acre.

1279 **KUBLAI KHAN** overcomes the last Song resistance and reunites China under the Yuan dynasty.

1281 **MONGOLS** try for a second time to invade Japan.

1287 **KUBLAI KHAN** conquers Pagan, the capital of Burma.

1290 **KAIKOBAD,** sultan of Delhi, is murdered, then succeeded by Jalal ud Din.

1296 **JALAL UD DIN** of Delhi is murdered, then succeeded by Alauddin Khalji, who controls much of India.

GEOGRAPHY & ENVIRONMENT

ca 1276 **A SERIES OF DROUGHTS** hits the Mesa Verde pueblo in modern-day Colorado and lasts for 23 years, driving the ancient Pueblo people away.

1273 **A SPANISH AGRICULTURAL UNION** is established that grants rights to migratory sheep herders.

1298 **MARCO POLO** returns to Italy and begins to dictate his memoirs in a Genoese jail.

1271 **MARCO POLO** travels to China. In 1275 he is in the service of Kublai Kahn.

CULTURE & RELIGION

ca 1200-1600 **THE MIXTEC** perfect the high style of pictographic writing. Many sacred books that combine pictographs and phonetic symbols commemorate Mixtec rulers; eight of these books survive.

1260 **THE FIRST FLAGELLANT MOVEMENTS** appear in southern Germany and northern Italy.

ca 1266 **THOMAS AQUINAS** begins his *Summa Theologiae*.

ca 1270 **THE ICELAND MANUSCRIPT KNOWN AS *ELDER EDDA*,** a collection of Scandinavian mythology, is compiled.

1276 **ADAM DE LA HALLE** writes *Le Jeu de la feuillée*, a bawdy and satirical work considered a predecessor of comic opera.

ca 1290-1295 **CIMABUE** creates *Madonna Enthroned with St. Francis* at Assisi.

Worshippers at the rock-hewn church of San Giorgio in Lalibela, Ethiopia

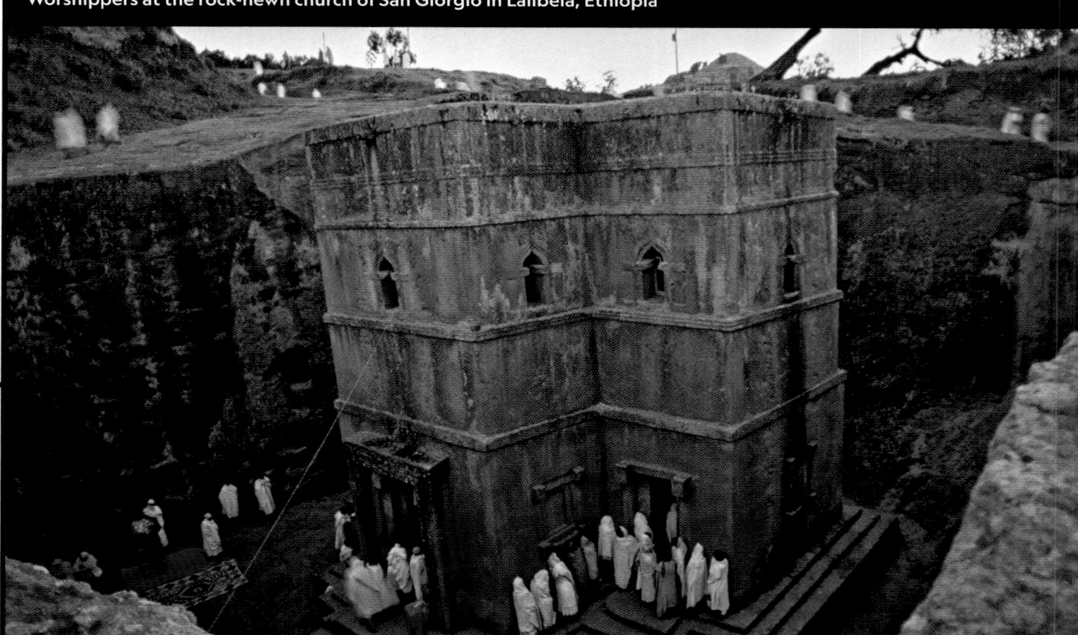

SCIENCE & TECHNOLOGY

1240s-1286 THE KAYENTA BRANCH of the ancient Pueblo people build a 155-room dwelling named Keet Seel in Tsegi Canyon, which is in modern-day northeastern Arizona.

1260 THADDEUS FLORENTINUS, a pioneering medical practitioner, becomes a master at Bologna University.

1264 ROGER BACON writes *De computo naturali.*

ca 1268 ROGER BACON writes *Opus maius.*

ca 1275 THE HOFBURG, originally conceived by Duke Leopold VI, is completed in Vienna.

1296 FLORENCE CATHEDRAL is begun.

1274 NISAR AL DIN AL TUSI, a Persian mathematician, scientist, and philosopher, dies. The observatory at Maragha was built for his use.

ca 1280 MOSES DE LEON is presumed to have composed the *Zohar,* considered the classic text of Kabbala.

1266 THE REBUILT SANJUSANGENDO TEMPLE is completed in Kyoto, Japan.

PEOPLE & SOCIETY

ca 1300 WYANDOT CLANS along the St. Lawrence River unite to form the Attignousntan nation, which French explorers later name the Huron. Extended matrilineal clans live in bark-covered longhouses and depend largely on agriculture, supplemented with fishing and hunting.

1268 ENGLISH SCIENTIST AND PHILOSOPHER Roger Bacon writes the earliest mention of lenses used for optical assistance, an innovation in use in both Europe and China at the time.

1280 THE FIRST GLASS MIRRORS are invented.

1290 JEWS are banished from England.

1200s MUSLIMS make inroads into the African interior by trade as much as by conquest.

ca 1290s PERSIAN VIZIER RASHID AL DIN begins his *Compendium of Histories,* the first broad work of history to include sections on the Islamic dynasties, Indians, Chinese, Franks, Jews, and Mongols.

1200s MONGOLS build circular tents, or yurts, of light wicker frames, which are easy to dismantle when they are ready to move on.

1200s MONGOL SOLDIERS use stirrups and cruppers (leather straps to stabilize saddles). The added stability gives them better aim when shooting with bows and arrows.

ca 1280s FALCONRY is one of the favorite pursuits of Mongol rulers, with Marco Polo later mentioning the falconry of Kublai Khan in his writings.

MARCO POLO

IN 1271 AS A BOY OF 17, Marco Polo set off on a travel adventure that would make his name legendary. Leaving Venice with his father, Niccolo, and his uncle, Maffeo, he finally reached Shangdu, China, the summer home of Mongol ruler Kublai Khan, after traveling four years and 7,500 miles.

When he got word via his pony express that Marco Polo was approaching, Kublai Khan sent escorts to guide him to the court of his shining palace. They became friends, and the Khan employed Polo on several diplomatic missions that added much rich material for the observant Italian's imagination.

When the Polos arrived back home 24 years later, according to legend, their relatives did not even recognize them, as they were dressed in rags and behaved in a foreign manner. Yet all of Venice, it was said, rushed to hear Marco's tales of wonder. His book, *The Description of the World,* relates many fantastic experiences, some so astonishing that they are almost certainly not true. Nonetheless he had made it possible for readers to travel by armchair to exotic places on the other side of the world.

Mosaic of Marco Polo in Genoa, Italy

POLITICS & POWER

ca 1325 **THE AZTEC** found their capital, Tenochtitlan (modern-day Mexico City), on an artificial island in Lake Texcoco.

1304 **BYZANTINE EMPEROR ANDRONICUS II** employs mercenaries to defeat the Ottomans.

1306 **ROBERT THE BRUCE** is crowned king of the Scots and leads successful campaigns against the English.

1315 **ROBERT THE BRUCE'S** brother, Edward, becomes king of Ireland.

1326 **ISABELLA,** wife of Edward II, and her lover, Roger Mortimer, invade England, capturing the king.

1327 **EDWARD III** becomes king of England.

1302 **OSMAN I,** first ruler of the Ottomans, defeats the Byzantines at Bapheus.

▶ **1307** **MANSA MUSA** becomes ruler of the Mali Empire.

1314 **AMDA TSEYON,** powerful king of Christian Ethiopia, solidifies his territorial rule.

1324 **THE OTTOMAN ORHAN** captures Brusa from the Byzantines. Two years later he makes it his capital.

1307 **THE MAHARASHTRA STATE** in western India falls under Muslim control.

1320 **GHIYAS AL DIN TUGHLUQ** establishes the Muslim Tughluq dynasty, which will rule India for nearly a century.

GEOGRAPHY & ENVIRONMENT

ca 1300 **THE MISSISSIPPIAN SITE AZTALAN,** in present-day Wisconsin, is abandoned, possibly because of a shortage of resources.

1312 **UNINHABITED CANARY ISLANDS** in the North Atlantic are discovered.

1314-1322 **ENGLAND SUFFERS FAMINE** and an economic downturn due to a prolonged period of adverse weather influenced by the advance of Swiss glaciers.

ca 1316-1329 **ODORIC OF PORDENONE,** an Italian Franciscan friar, travels extensively throughout Asia, visiting Anatolia, Persia, India, Java, Borneo, and China. His China travelogue enjoys wide popularity.

CULTURE & RELIGION

ca 1325 **THE AZTEC** begin to build the Templo Mayor in Tenochtitlan (modern-day Mexico City). It will be dedicated to Huitzilopochtli, god of war, and Tlaloc, god of rain.

1305-1308 **GIOTTO,** considered the most important Italian painter of the 14th century, paints frescoes in Arena Chapel in Padua.

1307 **DANTE** begins writing *The Divine Comedy.*

1309 **CLEMENT V,** a Frenchman, places the papal residence at Avignon, France. It is the beginning of the "Babylonian Captivity" during which Rome is not the papal seat.

1324 **THE GREAT MOSQUE** in Timbuktu is built by Mali emperor Mansa Musa.

1324 **MANSA MUSA** travels to Mecca.

ca 1300 ***THE CHALK CIRCLE,*** a play written by Chinese dramatist Li Xingfu, is performed in China. It is considered a prime example of *zaju,* or variety play. It is adapted into *The Caucasian Chalk Circle* by German dramatist Bertolt Brecht in 1948.

CONNECTIONS

Changing Climate

The Great Drought of 1276-1299 caused widespread and lasting devastation among the peoples occupying the Four Corners areas of the modern-day American Southwest. Archaeological evidence shows that, as of around 1300, settlements such as Mesa Verde, which at one time had 5,000 inhabitants, were abandoned. The diaspora of inhabitants of the Colorado Plateau area—a migration of tens of thousands of people—disperses largely to the south and east. They settle in Acoma in modern-day New Mexico. They join the Hopi and Zuni in Arizona. And they settle in large villages with the Eastern Pueblo along the Rio Grande River. The ripple effects in social patterns, living arrangements, even symbolism among later Pueblo peoples—such as the stronger affiliation of katsinas with rain-making—last for centuries.

SCIENCE & TECHNOLOGY

ca 1300s **THE SALADO PEOPLE** of the Gila River Valley in modern-day south-central Arizona build Casa Grande (Big House), a four-story walled compound.

1300 **APOTHECARIES** become popular in German cities.

ca 1300 **EXAMINING URINE** as a means of diagnosis is used in medicine.

ca 1301-1320 **INFLUENTIAL FRENCH PHYSICIAN** Henri de Mondeville writes *Anathomia* containing illustrations of human anatomy, and *Chirurgia,* an extensive surgical manual.

1303 **THE SAPIENZA UNIVERSITY OF ROME** is founded.

ca 1325 **ORGAN PEDALS** come into use.

PEOPLE & SOCIETY

ca 1320 **THE AZTEC** develop chinampa gardens around the island in Tenochtitlan to feed their population.

1302 **ITALIAN POET DANTE** is exiled from Florence due to his affiliation with the political faction known as the Whites, which lose control of the city to an opposing faction known as the Blacks.

1305 **EDWARD I** of England standardizes the yard and the acre.

Map of the Mali and later Songhai Empires in West Africa

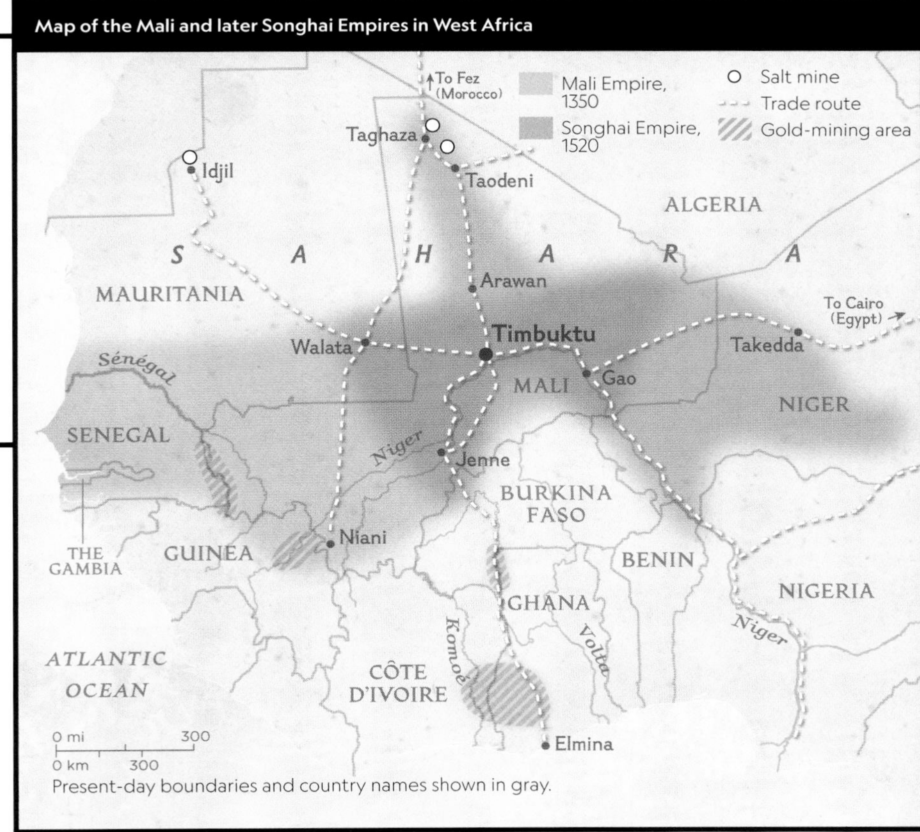

Rose window at Notre Dame Cathedral in Paris

GOTHIC CATHEDRALS

THE 12TH CENTURY in Europe saw the beginning of a soaring architectural style for churches that embodied the exalted place of religion in the Middle Ages. Later called "gothic" by Renaissance artists who viewed the style as barbaric, cathedrals were anything but crude.

Combining pointed arches, flying buttresses, and towering open spaces filled with shimmering light reflected through stained glass, these vaulted masterpieces conveyed a mystical sense of weightlessness, as if one might be able to take flight heavenward.

To Christians cathedrals were cities of God, and with great fervor and sacrifice they undertook the construction of such churches, which often took more than a century to complete. As the seats of bishops, cathedrals were filled with the finest sculptures, relics, and altarpieces to be had. Stained glass windows created atmosphere, and the colorful pictures told Bible stories to illiterate visitors.

A traveler could spot his destination from miles away by the sight of the town's largest and most magnificent edifice, with its towers reaching skyward and serving as a beacon to worshippers far and near. The wayward, lost, and lonely found solace within cathedral walls, as did the more fortunate, who arrived to give thanks. For both rich and poor, the cathedral was the abode on Earth closest to Heaven.

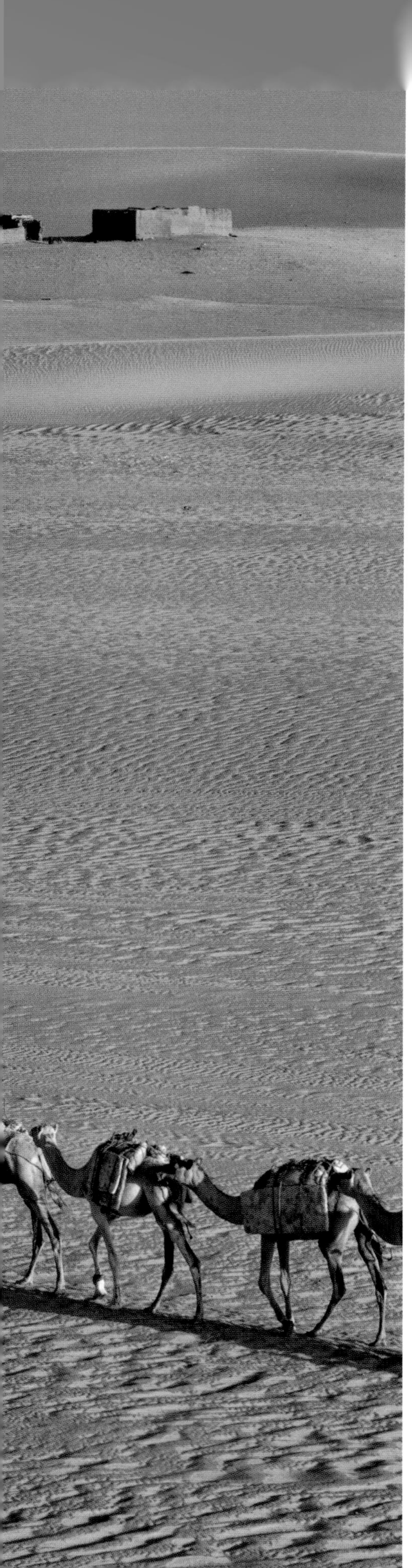

MALI'S KINGDOM OF GOLD

The rich natural resources of West Africa gave rise to great commercial empires beginning in the eighth century and lasting until colonial times. Ghana was the first and Songhai the largest, but Mali achieved legendary status because of its flamboyant ruler, Mansa Musa. Under Musa, who ruled from 1307 into the 1330s, Mali became the largest empire of its day after the Mongol Empire—some "four months of travel long and four months wide," according to an Egyptian sheik. Its actual domain stretched west to east from the Atlantic Ocean to the boundaries of Nigeria, and from the edge of the rainforests in the south to the oasis markets of the central Sahara.

Mali's wealth and power was built largely on gold, for which it was one of the world's chief suppliers. Caravans of Arab merchants braved often dangerous trade routes into the region to acquire the precious mineral, bringing with them salt, luxury goods, and the Islamic faith. Mansa Musa embraced his kingdom's adopted religion, making a 1324 pilgrimage to Mecca that put Mali on the map. Accompanied by a retinue of 60,000 men, each of whom carried a bar of gold weighing 500 *mitqals,* or four pounds, Musa made so many gifts of gold in Egypt along the way that the value of the local dinar was depressed for some 12 years in Cairo.

Mansa Musa made Mali an important center of Islamic scholarship, especially in his capital, Timbuktu. Literate in Arabic, he brought scholars and an Arabic library back from Mecca, and commissioned the famous Arab architect al Sahili to build a palace and a mosque, which served as a university as well. Though the Muslim traveler Ibn Battuta, on a later visit to Mali, complained of the lack of Islamic custom, the durability of Islam here is evident in buildings like the great "mud mosque" in Djenné (above), built on the site of a previous Djenné (then Jenne-Jeno) mosque from the 13th century.

LEFT: Camel caravans still transport goods in West Africa. **ABOVE:** Reconstructed mosque in Djenné, Mali

POLITICS & POWER

ca 1350 AZTEC MILITARY ELITE are at the top of a rigid social hierarchy. They begin to enjoy great wealth and privilege.

1337 EDWARD III, claiming rights to the French throne, assumes the title King of France. The move initiates hostilities that start the Hundred Years' War.

1347 THE BLACK DEATH begins spreading through Europe after arriving in Crimea and Sicily.

1338 OTTOMANS reach the Bosporus in Asia Minor.

1352-1353 ISLAM is seen by Ibn Battuta as only a veneer of the Mali Empire; the underlying substance of Mali culture is a belief in Mande superiority.

1354 OTTOMANS occupy the Byzantine fortress of Gallipoli.

1331 A JAPANESE IMPERIAL SUCCESSION DISPUTE leads to civil war against Hojo regents.

1333 THE EXILED JAPANESE EMPEROR GO-DAIGO returns to power after inciting a rebellion against the Hojo clan that leads to the suicide of the last Hojo regent.

1336 THE HINDU KINGDOM OF VIJAYANAGAR is founded in southern India.

1338 THE ASHIKAGA SHOGUNATE is established in Japan.

1347 ALA AL DIN BAHMAN SHAH begins an independent sultanate in the Deccan.

GEOGRAPHY & ENVIRONMENT

ca 1350-1450 MANY HOHOKAM INDIAN VILLAGES in present-day Arizona are abandoned.

1346 A STRONG EARTHQUAKE hits Constantinople, causing the eastern arch of Hagia Sophia Cathedral to crumble.

1347 THE BLACK DEATH reaches Cairo, killing one-third of the population of Egypt within two years.

1330s BUBONIC PLAGUE (Black Death) originates in Asia.

CULTURE & RELIGION

ca 1350 AZTEC PRIESTS are among the elite, sometimes even becoming supreme rulers.

ca 1350 NAHUATL becomes the dominant language of central Mexico.

1334 GIOTTO begins building the campanile at Florence.

1340 THE FIRST KNOWN LITERATURE in the Cornish tongue is written.

1341 PETRARCH (FRANCESCO PETRARCA) is crowned poet laureate at the Capitol in Rome.

ca 1347-1349 ENGLISH PHILOSOPHER AND THEOLOGIAN William of Ockam dies. He advanced the concept of nominalism and developed what is known today as "Ockam's razor."

1332 AFRICAN SCHOLAR IBN KHALDUN is born in Tunis; he becomes a great philosopher and historian who considers poetry a form of speech that expresses elegance and beauty without excess.

1340 OBEYDE ZAKANI'S SATIRES, especially *The Ethics of the Aristocracy,* explain how the mighty redefine the virtues to suit their own convenience and for their own benefit.

1354 CHINESE PAINTER HUANG GONGWANG, the oldest of the Four Masters of the Yuan Dynasty, dies. The group is credited with pioneering the tradition of *wenrenhua* ("literati painting"), which emphasizes individual expression.

WHAT LIFE WAS LIKE

Ibn Battuta Visits Mali

Moroccan Ibn Battuta traveled the world in his lifetime, recording his observations in his famous memoirs, *Rihla*. Battuta considered himself a citizen of the dar al Islam, the entire "abode" of Islam, and in 1352 visited Mali, the African kingdom made legendary by Mansa Musa's 1324 trip to Mecca. Mali's great wealth was evident, but Battuta was shocked by the lack of Islamic custom. In Walata, the provincial governor offered him a meager calabash of millet, honey, and yogurt and spoke to him only through an interpreter. In Niani, the capital, partially clothed women, subjects who prostrated themselves before the mansa (king), and royal poets who danced in masks all violated orthodox Islam. Mali officially belonged to the Islamic world, which had greatly expanded its trading opportunities, but Battuta suspected the relationship was more a testament to commerce than to faith.

SCIENCE & TECHNOLOGY	PEOPLE & SOCIETY
ca 1350 CITY PLANNERS of Tenochtitlan build a system of canals within the city for transportation and irrigation.	**ca 1350** SLAVES perform labor in both the Aztec and Inca Empires. Aztec slaves work as domesticated servants, while slave cultivators known as *yana* work on lands owned by Inca aristocrats.
1337-1344 WILLIAM MERLE keeps detailed weather records. **1344** ST. VITUS'S CATHEDRAL is begun in Prague by Mathias of Arras. **1348** EDWARD III begins to rebuild Windsor Castle. **1358** THE ALHAMBRA PALACE in Granada is completed.	**1341** THE FIRST RECORD OF ENGLISH PARLIAMENT being divided into two houses occurs. **1350s** BRUGES peaks in importance as a bourse trading center. **1350s** THE HANSEATIC LEAGUE continues to expand the trading interests of German towns throughout northern Europe, eventually securing a trade monopoly in Scandinavia. **1358** TWO GREAT BANKING HOUSES of Florence, Bardi and Peruzzi, go bankrupt.
ca 1300s-1600s METALLURGISTS from the kingdom of Benin in West Africa become known for their bronze and zinc castings. **ca 1350** THE FOUR-LIWAN ARCHITECTURAL STYLE is used to build mosques and schools. It consists of four large vaulted halls opening onto a courtyard in the center.	**ca 1324-1352** THE OTTOMANS establish the timar system, which is a centralized method of allocating land and revenue to military men and requiring regular government surveys of land, crops, productivity, and other revenue sources, such as beehives, fisheries, mills, and industrial and commercial enterprises. **ca 1330** IN THE OTTOMAN EMPIRE, non-Muslims cannot own Muslim slaves. Slaves can only be captured in war or born into slavery.
ca 1340-ca 1425 MADHAVA OF SANGAMAGRAMA of Kerala, India, writes a number of pioneering works on astronomy and mathematics.	**1350s** THE RED TURBANS AND WHITE LOTUS SOCIETY, peasant rebellion movements, lead uprisings in Yuan, China. **1351** FIRUZ III is sultan of Delhi.

Chimú gold funerary mask

THE CHIMÚ SOCIETY OF PERU

BEGINNING IN THE 13TH CENTURY, the Chimú state reigned as the largest and most influential political system in Peru. Its agricultural society thrived along the northern coastal desert, where people raised guinea pigs, llamas, squash, maize, sweet potatoes, cotton, and beans with the help of a sophisticated irrigation system, which also brought water via canals to Chan Chan, their capital and the largest city in ancient Peru.

Chimú society was organized by the governing elite and hereditary rulers, whose burial grounds include 10 royal compounds, each about 20 acres in size. Cities were connected by roads to transport textiles and distinctive pottery made by artisans for a brisk trade industry. Superior metalworking in gold, silver, and bronze was also a feature of Chimú culture.

This high culture impressed the Inca, who conquered the Chimú around 1470 but adopted much of their political organization, irrigation systems, and engineering knowledge for their growing empire.

POLITICS & POWER

1372 ACAMAPICHTLI establishes the Aztec-Mexican dynasty by becoming the first king, known as a *tloatoani* ("he who speaks"). This signals a political change from rule by a confederation of clans to a ruling dynasty.

1371 THE OTTOMAN TURKS defeat the Serbs at the Battle of Marica, paving the way for their eventual conquest of Serbia and Bulgaria.

1371 THE DEATH OF DAVID II in Scotland brings the Stewart dynasty to the throne.

1380 THE DEATH OF KING CHARLES V of France leads to a long uneasy truce in the Hundred Years' War.

1380 PRINCE DMITRY of Moscow defeats the Mongols at the Battle of Kulikovo.

1375 THE MAMLUKS conquer Sis, ending Armenian independence.

1380-1394 THE TURK TAMERLANE (TIMUR) begins successful campaigns in Persia, Russia, Georgia, and Iraq.

1389 BAYEZID I succeeds his father, Murad I, as sultan of the Ottomans.

1396 BAYEZID I conquers the Christian army under Sigismund of Hungary at Nicopolis.

1368 ASHIKAGA YOSHIMITSU is declared the third Ashikaga shogun of Japan.

1368 THE MING DYNASTY begins in China.

1392 GENERAL YI SONG-GYE establishes the Choson dynasty, Korea's last and longest imperial dynasty.

1395 TAMERLANE sacks Astrakhan.

1398 TAMERLANE invades India and sacks Delhi.

GEOGRAPHY & ENVIRONMENT

ca 1400 THE CHIMÚ CAPITAL of Chan Chan, on the northern coast of modern-day Peru, occupies 14 square miles after two and a half centuries of expansion.

1361 THE BLACK DEATH reappears in England.

CULTURE & RELIGION

ca 1375 THE KACHINA CULT, involving ceremonial masked dances and carved figurines, emerges in the American Southwest.

1375 ROBIN HOOD appears in English literature.

1378 THE GREAT SCHISM begins following the death of Gregory XI, whereby two popes are elected, one at Rome and one at Avignon.

1382 THE WORKS OF ENGLISH RELIGIOUS REFORMER John Wycliffe are banned at Oxford.

ca 1387 GEOFFREY CHAUCER begins working on *The Canterbury Tales.*

1397 MANUEL CHRYSOLORAS begins to revive Greek literature in Italy.

ca 1390 HAFIZ, the most important lyric poet in Persia, dies. His poems are still revered in Iran.

1365 INDONESIAN COURT POET AND HISTORIAN Prapanca writes *Nagarakrtagama,* a descriptive poem that captures the culture, legends, history, and politics of life in the kingdom of Java.

1374 NOH THEATER begins in Japan.

ca 1394-1408 THE TEMPLE OF THE GOLDEN PAVILION is built on the outskirts of Kyoto.

CONNECTIONS

Hanseatic League and Trade

German merchant towns joined together in a commercial venture, originated by a group of seafaring traders, that boosted commerce throughout northern Europe beginning in the 13th century. Boycotts and sometimes force were used to control the markets that operated in Hanseatic towns, as well as in far-reaching areas in the North and Baltic Seas. Among the major members were Hamburg and Lubeck. The most important item of trade was textiles, followed by other such popular products as dried or salted fish, grain, beer, wax, and furs. The league reached as far as England before it began to decline in the 16th century, when Dutch sea power surpassed it. The fact remains, however, that the league had succeeded in taking the first step as the forerunner of what would later develop into Europe's Common Market.

SCIENCE & TECHNOLOGY

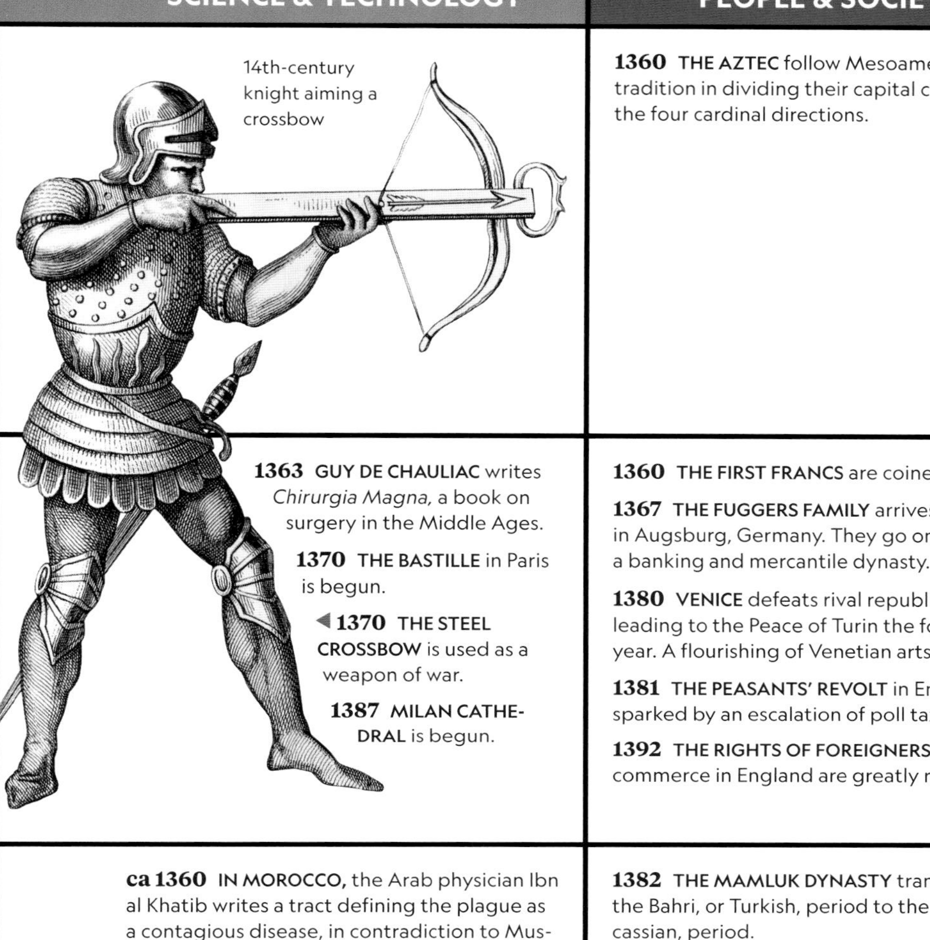

14th-century knight aiming a crossbow

1363 GUY DE CHAULIAC writes *Chirurgia Magna,* a book on surgery in the Middle Ages.

1370 THE BASTILLE in Paris is begun.

◀ **1370 THE STEEL CROSSBOW** is used as a weapon of war.

1387 MILAN CATHEDRAL is begun.

ca 1360 IN MOROCCO, the Arab physician Ibn al Khatib writes a tract defining the plague as a contagious disease, in contradiction to Muslim teachings.

1370 SAMARKAND in Central Asia is reconstructed as Tamerlane's capital. From the 1380s onward, its gorgeous buildings are tile covered and its gardens are irrigated.

1377 KOREAN BUDDHIST TEXT is printed for the first time with movable metal type.

PEOPLE & SOCIETY

1360 THE AZTEC follow Mesoamerican tradition in dividing their capital city by the four cardinal directions.

1360 THE FIRST FRANCS are coined in France.

1367 THE FUGGERS FAMILY arrives as weavers in Augsburg, Germany. They go on to become a banking and mercantile dynasty.

1380 VENICE defeats rival republic Genoa, leading to the Peace of Turin the following year. A flourishing of Venetian arts follows.

1381 THE PEASANTS' REVOLT in England is sparked by an escalation of poll taxes.

1392 THE RIGHTS OF FOREIGNERS to conduct commerce in England are greatly restricted.

1382 THE MAMLUK DYNASTY transitions from the Bahri, or Turkish, period to the Burji, or Circassian, period.

1389-1403 DURING THE REIGN OF OTTOMAN SULTAN BAYEZID I, the Janissaries become a more formalized corps of soldiers by recruiting the fittest non-Muslim youths instead of just relying on prisoners of war to fill the ranks.

1368 ZHU YUANZHANG captures Dadu (Beijing) from the Mongols and establishes the Ming dynasty, with its capital at Nanjing, China.

THE MERCHANTS OF VENICE

FAVORABLY LOCATED on alluvial islets in a lagoon on the Adriatic, Venice is often referred to as the "bride of the sea." By the ninth century an independent republic was founded that during the next 600 years would become the European powerhouse of trade. Incessant fighting with Genoa, the republic's primary maritime rival, ended in 1380 when Venice was victorious in the sea battle of Chioggia.

The strength of Venice lay in its wealth of trade contacts worldwide. In the early years, trade with Constantinople was paramount; Italian merchants frequently moved there, until their population swelled to some 60,000. Eventually, though, Venice began importing the exotic luxuries of the East, such as silk, spices, and perfumes. When trade routes shifted south during the Pax Mongolica in the 13th century, Aleppo in Syria and Alexandria in Egypt became Venice's major trading partners.

This city of sailors also developed its own thriving shipbuilding industry, becoming world famous for its output of trading ships and launching a new galley every 200 days. Some of these same ships would become notorious in the middle of the 14th century for helping transport bubonic plague from Asia to Europe. Some accounts estimate that Venice lost two-thirds of its population to the Black Death.

During the Renaissance, Venice rivaled Florence and Rome in artistic glory, with giants such as Titian and Tintoretto calling the city home. The Turkish capture of Constantinople in 1453, which reduced trade between East and West, and the discovery of the Americas marked the beginning of Venice's decline as a trade power.

1400-1430

	POLITICS & POWER	GEOGRAPHY & ENVIRONMENT	CULTURE & RELIGION
THE AMERICAS	**ca 1400 THE CHIMÚ CIVILIZATION** reaches its height in coastal Peru's Moche Valley and expands up and down the coast. **ca 1400s THE EL VERGEL PEOPLE** (later known as the Mapuche) of the Central Valley of Chile resist being conquered by the Inca. **1418 NEZAHUALCOYOTL,** poet king of the Texcocan, begins his long rule. **1428 ITZCOATL** leads the Triple Alliance to defeat Azcapotzalco.	 **Joan of Arc kissing the Sword of Deliverance in a painting by Dante Gabriel Rossetti**	**1427 AZTEC RULER ITZCOATL** establishes the role of *cihuacoatl,* an adviser position that can only be held by nobility. During certain religious festivals, the adviser dresses as the female goddess for whom the position is named.
EUROPE	**1410 JOHN XXIII** is elected antipope, marking an important phase in the rise of the Medici family, who back him. **1415 HENRY V** of England defeats the French at Agincourt and by 1419 unites all of Normandy except Mont St. Michel. The Treaty of Troyes, negotiated with the Burgundian rulers in 1420, names him heir to the French throne. ▶ **1429 JOAN OF ARC** leads French armies against England.	**1420 PRINCE HENRY OF PORTUGAL** (the Navigator) encourages settlement of Madeira and Porto Santo.	**1408-1415 ITALIAN ARTIST DONATELLO** sculpts "St. John the Evangelist." He later sculpts "David" in 1430-1432. **1413-1414 IN THE DISPUTATION OF TORTOSA,** the differences between Judaism and Christianity are debated over 63 sessions. **1415 JAN HUS** is burned at the stake. **1417 THE ELECTION OF POPE MARTIN V** in Rome brings the Great Schism to an end. **ca 1430 THE LEGEND OF THE PIED PIPER OF HAMELIN** begins.
MIDDLE EAST & AFRICA	**1402 TAMERLANE** defeats Bayezid I, the Ottoman sultan. **1415 KING JOHN** of Portugal seizes Ceuta in Morocco. **1421 OTTOMAN SULTAN MURAD II** resumes the policy of expansion after succeeding his father, Mehmed I, who had united the empire.	**ca 1400 SUCCESSFUL GOLD TRADE** has been developed down the Zambezi Valley to the Sofala coast in Southeast Africa.	**ca 1400 A TIMURID ILLUSTRATED MANUSCRIPT** depicts the story of Alexander the Great. **ca 1403 THE MUSLIM SULTANATE OF MALACCA** in modern-day Malaysia thrives as a center of power, faith, and trade in Asia. **1405 TURKIC LEADER TAMERLANE** is laid to rest in the Gur-Emir (Tomb of the Commander) mausoleum in Samarkand, in modern-day Uzbekistan. The elaborate structure features a blue-tiled dome, gold inscriptions, and turquoise arabesques.
ASIA & OCEANIA	**1403 AFTER A LONG CIVIL WAR,** Zhu Di usurps the throne of the second Ming emperor, Jianwen, to reign as Emperor Yongle in China. **1404 JAPAN** begins trading with Ming China. **1421 EMPEROR YONGLE** of China formally establishes Beijing as the national capital. The secondary capital is Nanjing. **1424 WHEN EMPEROR YONGLE DIES,** his reign is viewed as a "second founding" of the Ming dynasty.	**1405-1433 CHINESE EUNUCH ADMIRAL ZHENG HE** leads seven massive maritime expeditions throughout the Indian Ocean basin. **1421 CHINESE EMPEROR YONGLE** restores the Grand Canal and links it to the Huanghe and Yangtze Rivers.	**1408 THE MULTIVOLUME ENCYCLOPEDIA** *Yongle dadian* is completed under the patronage of Ming Emperor Yongle in China. **1424 JAPANESE PLAYWRIGHT ZEAMI** writes *Kakyo (The Mirror of the Flower),* a formative work in Noh drama.

SCIENCE & TECHNOLOGY

ca 1400 **THE *QUIPU*** is the numeric device used by the Inca for counting and a mnemonic device for recording oral histories. The Inca do not develop a scribal form.

1403 **SEVILLE CATHEDRAL** is founded.

1415 **THE LONGBOW** gives the outnumbered English a strong advantage against the French in the Battle of Agincourt.

1419 **BRUNELLESCHI** designs the Foundlings' Hospital in Florence.

1420 **BRUNELLESCHI** begins construction on the dome of the Cathedral of Santa Maria del Fiore (the Duomo) in Florence. The cathedral is completed and consecrated in 1436.

1406 **IBN KHALDUN,** historian and one of the founders of sociology, dies. He is known for his *Muqaddimah (Introduction),* a study of human history and the decline of civilizations.

1428 **CONSTRUCTION BEGINS** on an astronomical observatory at Samarkand under Ulugh Beg, a Timurid ruler in present-day Iran.

PEOPLE & SOCIETY

ca 1400-1450 **THE MIDDLE MISSISSIPPI** phase of mound builders draws to a close in North America.

1420 **NORTH OF LAKE ONTARIO**, the Attignousntan clan, whose totem is the bear, and the Attingneenongnahac clan, whose totem is the cord, join together to establish the Huron Confederacy.

ca 1400s-1520s **THE GREAT MARKET** in the Aztec city of Tlatelolco, considered Tenochtitlan's "twin city," draws 40,000 to 60,000 people on major market days.

ca 1400 **EUROPE'S POPULATION** falls to roughly 60 million people, but fast-growing towns everywhere are centers of trade.

1401 **THE DOUBLE EAGLE** becomes the symbol of the Holy Roman emperors.

1416 **DUTCH FISHERMEN** are the first to use drift nets.

1420s **COSIMO (THE ELDER)** greatly expands the Medici bank in Florence. It becomes the official bank of the papacy.

ca 1425 **TAROT CARDS** become popular in Europe, thanks to the printing press.

An Aztec priest cuts the heart from one sacrificial victim as another lies below. Human sacrifice atop the great temple was made to appease the tribal god, Huitzilopochtli, and to intimidate foes.

THE AZTEC EM

IN THE 13TH CENTURY a people monly known as Aztec, but who ca selves Mexica, settled in the Valley and quickly developed a reputatic warriors. They provided mercenary the rival city-states that dominatec after the fall of the Toltec Empire.

Around 1325 the Aztec foun capital, Tenochtitlan, now M on an island in Lake Texcoc a strong defensible pos became the heart of an e empire. They erected a wor gious precinct of temples, and palaces, supported paid by conquered foes.

The tribute system, ho the Aztec vulnerable to enemies who could disrup ute and thus, their livelih result, the Aztec joined wi coco and Tlacopan, two potential foes, to form the ance, which, under Moctez II, began conquering trib the valley, expanding the e Central America by the tim ish arrived in the early 16th

Expansion of the Aztec Empire

POLITICS & POWER	GEOGRAPHY & ENVIRONMENT	CULTURE & RELIGION
1433 THE HIGHLAND MAYA establish Utatlan as the capital of their community kingdom. **1438 PACHACUTI** founds Inca rule in Peru. **1463 THE INCA** subdue the Chimú in northern Peru.	**1450-1454 DROUGHTS** and food shortages plague central Mexico.	**ca 1450 VIRACHOCA** is worshipped by the Inca as the creator god. The sun god follows in importance. **ca 1450 THE AZTEC HIGH DECORATIVE ART STYLE** is represented by elaborate headdresses adorned with feathers of the resplendent quetzal, the sacred bird of the Aztecs.
1433 SIGISMUND OF HUNGARY is elected Holy Roman Emperor. **1434 COSIMO DE MEDICI** returns from exile and takes over Florence. **1444-1448 OTTOMANS** conquer Hungarians at the Black Sea, opening their way to Constantinople. **1453 ENGLAND** is defeated by France, ending the Hundred Years' War. **1455 THE WARS OF THE ROSES** begin in England between the Lancasters and the Yorks.	**1443 COPENHAGEN** becomes the Danish capital. **ca 1450 AN ITALIAN CARTOGRAPHER,** Fra Mauro, produces a large and highly detailed map of the known world that is considered one of the greatest works of medieval cartography.	**1430 PHILIP THE GOOD,** Duke of Burgundy, founds the Order of the Golden Fleece, a chivalric order. **1432 JAN VAN EYK** paints "The Adoration of the Mystic Lamb" (also known as the Ghent Altarpiece). **ca 1432-1436 ENGLISH RELIGIOUS MYSTIC** Margery Kempe dictates her autobiography, considered one of the first in English literature. **ca 1455 JOHANNES GUTENBERG,** inventor of modern printing, prints the 42-line (Mazarin) Bible at Mainz.
1450 ALBANIAN LEADER SKANDERBEG fends off the forces of Ottoman Sultan Murad II, propelling him to hero status in the Western world. **1453 OTTOMAN TURKS** under Mehmed II seize Constantinople, bringing an end to the Byzantine Empire and incorporating its last figures into the Ottoman elite. **ca 1470 MUTOTA** is succeeded by his son, Matope, in southeast Africa.	**1434 PORTUGUESE EXPLORER JOÃO DIAZ** rounds Cape Bojador in present-day Morocco. **1435-1455 PORTUGUESE NAVIGATORS** explore the west coast of Africa and reactivate the African slave trade. **1442 AL MAQRIZI,** author of *Admonitions and Observations on the History of the Quarters and Monuments*—which covers the geography, topography, and archaeology of Egypt —dies. **1455 VENETIAN NAVIGATOR CADAMOSTO** explores the Senegal River in Africa.	**ca 1453 MEHMED II** creates a cosmopolitan court culture that draws from East and West. **1453 TURKS** convert Hagia Sophia Cathedral into a mosque, Ayasofya (today a museum).
1434 THE CAPITAL OF THE KHMER KINGDOM moves from Angkor to Phnom Penh after an invasion by the Siamese.	**ca 1453 A MASSIVE ERUPTION** of the Kuwae volcano in Vanuatu releases clouds of particles into the atmosphere and contributes to abnormally cold weather worldwide.	**1438 THE FOUNDATION** is laid for the Jamma Musjid Mosque of Husain in Jaunpur, India.

SCIENCE & TECHNOLOGY	PEOPLE & SOCIETY
1400s THE CORIANCHA (Golden Enclosure, also known as Temple of the Sun) as well as walls and other structures in Cusco, Peru, are built of close-fitted huge stones with little or no mortar between them.	**ca 1450-1500** THE CADDO trade in buffalo meat with the Pueblo Indians in the Southwest and suffer a grievous blow when the Athapaskan arrive in their migration south from present-day Canada. They replace the Caddo as the main source of buffalo meat for the Pueblo.
1443 THE FIRST ORDER CONCERNING QUARANTINE and cleansing is passed in England. **1447-1455** POPE NICHOLAS V assembles a collection of 1,200 Greek and Latin manuscripts that form the foundation of the Vatican Library. **1452** THE FIRST REGULATIONS for European midwives are adopted in Germany. **1455** CONSTRUCTION BEGINS on the Palazzo San Marco (now Palazzo di Venezia) in Rome.	**1431** JOAN OF ARC is burned at the stake in Rouen. **1447** TAPESTRY WEAVERS in Brussels establish their own guild. **ca 1450** MIDDLE ENGLISH gives way to Modern English. **ca 1450** FLORENCE under the Medicis becomes the center of the Renaissance and humanism.
1440s OTTOMAN MILITARY PROWESS advances with the development of enormous cannons and use of the wagon fortress system.	**1450s** THE WOLOF PEOPLE in West Africa sign a treaty to supply the Portuguese with slaves; they provide 200 to 400 slaves a year until around the turn of the century. **1456-1461** THE BAZAAR IN ISTANBUL supports the Ayasofya mosque through its shop rents.
1441-1442 SCIENTISTS IN THE KOREAN COURT of King Sejong build instruments to measure rainfall. They begin a precise systematic record that lasts centuries.	**1446** THE KOREAN SYLLABARY known as Hangul is created by order of King Sejong.

A REVOLUTION IN PUBLISHING

LIKE SO MUCH ELSE, printing with movable type can be traced to China, where Bi Sheng began using movable wood blocks to print in the 1040s. Koreans were using movable copper type to print as early as 1392. But the method developed by Johannes Gutenberg in Mainz, Germany, independent of his Asian predecessors, made printing truly practical and led to a revolution in mass communications. With refinements, Gutenberg's system remained the principal way to print until the late 20th century.

Wanting to mechanically reproduce illuminated manuscripts without losing their beauty, Gutenberg's key innovations involved the making of a punch-stamped mold that could cast large amounts of metal type with precision, a new type of press, and the use of oil-based ink. His masterpiece was the 42-line Bible, printed in Latin in an original edition of about 180 copies no later than 1455. This impressive work with its Gothic typeface represented a quantum advance over the handwritten Bible, which might take a monk 20 years to finish.

Gutenberg's new technology not only spread rapidly (by 1520 more than 200 printed editions of the Bible had been published), but many books were printed in the vernacular rather than in Latin. This made texts available to almost any literate person, not just scholars, which in turn resulted in more people becoming literate. News and ideas spread more quickly and widely, bringing the world closer together.

In his own time, Gutenberg reaped precious little from his invention. Not only did he have financial problems during development, but his backer, Johann Fust, became impatient and successfully sued him, forcing Gutenberg to relinquish all claims to the process. Fust went on to make a fortune with his Bible sales, while Gutenberg died in 1468 in relative obscurity.

POLITICS & POWER	GEOGRAPHY & ENVIRONMENT	CULTURE & RELIGION
1465 THE INCA defeat the Chimú, ending the coastal empire's independence. **1471 TOPA INCA YUPANQUI** becomes emperor after his father, Pachacuti, abdicates to ensure a peaceful succession. **1473 AZTEC RULER AXAYACATL** conquers the neighboring city of Tlatelolco. **1494 INDIANS ON HISPANIOLA** burn a Spanish fort on the Yaque River and kill 10 Spaniards, marking the first local insurrection against the Iberian colonists.	**1492 CHRISTOPHER COLUMBUS,** sailing to discover a western route to the Indies, lands in the Bahamas. **1494 ON HIS SECOND VOYAGE** to the Americas, Columbus lands in Jamaica. **1497 ITALIAN NAVIGATOR JOHN CABOT** explores the North American coastline from Newfoundland to New England. **1499-1502 ITALIAN NAVIGATOR AMERIGO VESPUCCI** reaches the coast of Venezuela and subsequently explores the Brazilian coastline.	**1400s IN ORDER TO ENSURE THE SUN'S DAILY REBIRTH,** Aztec priests sacrifice tens of thousands of people in Tenochtitlan temples. **1400s AZTEC RITUALS FOR NEWBORNS** call for burying a female infant's umbilical cord in a fireplace hearth and a male infant's umbilical cord in a battlefield, to direct the baby to its proper role in the Aztec culture. **ca 1438-1471 MACHU PICCHU** is built in Peru as an estate for the Inca king Pachacuti. **1487 THE TEMPLE OF HUITZILOPOCHTLI,** one of two principal Aztec gods, is dedicated.
1469 LORENZO AND GIULIANO become the Medici rulers of Florence. **1477 MAXIMILIAN I** of Austria marries Mary of Burgundy, making the Habsburgs heirs to one of the most powerful states in Europe. **1485 THE TUDOR DYNASTY** is established in England when Henry VII defeats Richard III at Bosworth field, ending the Wars of the Roses. **1492 THE SPANISH** seize Granada, the last Muslim kingdom in Spain.	**1469 THE MARRIAGE** of Ferdinand V and Isabella entwines the royal houses of Castille and Aragon, establishing a virtually unified Spain. **1492 MARTIN BEHAIM** of Nuremberg constructs the first terrestrial globe.	**1467 THE FIRST BALLAD** relating the story of Swiss legendary hero William Tell appears. **ca 1470 SIR THOMAS MALORY** completes *Le Morte Darthur.* **ca 1473-1492 WILLIAM CAXTON** prints the first book in English and goes on to print more than 100 editions, including *The Canterbury Tales,* before his death. **1483 POPE SIXTUS IV** celebrates the first Mass in the Sistine Chapel in Rome. ▼ **ca 1485 BOTTICELLI** paints "Birth of Venus." **ca 1490 BALLET** begins at Italian courts.
1461 OTTOMAN MEHMED II annexes Trebizond, the last outpost of Byzantine civilization. **1468 MEHMED II** seizes Karaman, the last surviving Turkish emirate. **ca 1469 SONNI ALI BER** leads the Songhai to recapture Timbuktu. **1491 MAMLUKS AND OTTOMANS** make peace in the Near East after six years of war. **1493 MUHAMMAD I ASKIA** usurps the throne of the Songhai Empire. Over the next three decades, he creates the most important state in sub-Saharan Africa.	**1469 SONGHAI KING SONNI ALI** drives Tuaregs out of Timbuktu in West Africa. **1483 THE PORTUGUESE** land in Angola after discovering the mouth of the Congo River. Portuguese missionaries arrive the next year. **1488 PORTUGUESE EXPLORER BARTHOLOMEW DIAS** rounds the Cape of Good Hope. **1497 VASCO DA GAMA,** on orders from King Manuel of Portugal, sails for India via the Cape of Good Hope at the tip of South Africa. He reaches Malindi (Kenya) in East Africa the next year.	 "Birth of Venus" by Sandro Botticelli
1480 RUSSIAN TSAR IVAN III stops paying tribute money to the Mongols. **1495 THE SULTAN OF DELHI,** Sikander Lodi, annexes Bihar.	**1483 RUSSIANS** start exploring Siberia. **1488 KOREAN OFFICIAL CHOE PU** travels to China and chronicles his journey. His diary captures the genial relations and cultural similarities between the two countries. The book becomes widely printed in the 1500s in Japan and Korea.	**1493 THE KOREAN ENCYCLOPEDIA,** *Standard Patterns of Musicology,* is published. **1493 TOSU MITSUNOBU,** founder of the Tosa school of Japanese painting, rises to prominence with his appointment as the head of the court painting bureau.

SCIENCE & TECHNOLOGY

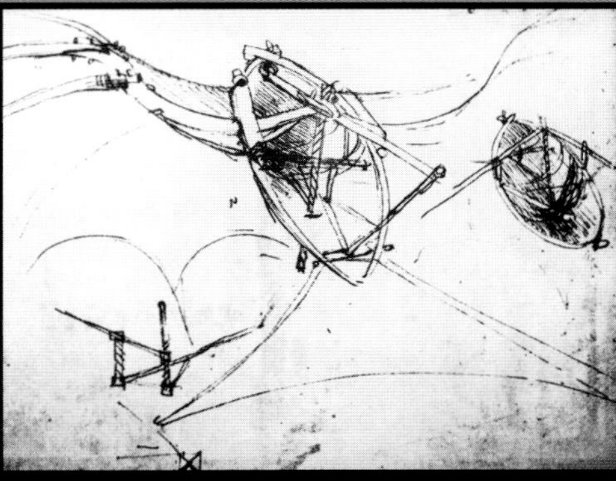

A prototype airplane by Leonardo da Vinci

▲ **ca 1488-1489** LEONARDO DA VINCI draws a flying machine as well as incredibly detailed anatomical drawings.

1489 THE SYMBOLS + (PLUS) AND – (MINUS) are first used. They become common in algebra and arithmetic in the latter half of the 16th century.

1494-1496 ITALIAN MATHEMATICIAN Luca Pacioli writes two volumes that outline the mathematical underpinnings of architecture.

ca 1463 OTTOMAN SULTAN MEMHMED II builds a mosque in Istanbul and surrounds it with eight colleges, forming the pinnacle of the Ottoman Empire's educational system.

1495 CHINESE ENGINEERS divert the course of the Yellow River by closing a channel.

PEOPLE & SOCIETY

1400s KNOWN FOR THEIR ORNAMENTAL USE OF PRECIOUS METAL, the Inca call gold the "sweat of the sun" and silver the "tears of the moon."

1400s THE TAINO of the Caribbean have trading contact with Mesoamericans.

1486-1503 AHUITZOTL, Aztec king, uses merchants to improve trade and spy networks.

ca 1492 CHRISTOPHER COLUMBUS orders Indians in Hispaniola to pay tribute in gold and starts a system of forced labor.

1400s IN FLORENCE, artists have their own guilds and are mentored by wealthy patrons like the powerful Medici family.

1477 MAXIMILIAN OF AUSTRIA gives Mary of Burgundy a gold ring with a diamond, setting the style for the modern engagement ring.

1478 THE SPANISH INQUISITION begins.

1463-1499 THE KINGDOM OF KANO, in northern Nigeria, thrives under Hausa king Mohamman Rumfa. He engages in trans-Saharan trade, builds the Jumaat Mosque and the Kurmi Market, reintroduces Arabic writing, and codifies the administration under Islamic law.

1486 KING OZALUA of Benin welcomes Portuguese traders to his kingdom and exchanges copper, brass, textiles, and glass beads for slaves and cloth.

COLUMBUS DISCOVERS THE NEW WORLD

TOWARD THE END of the 15th century, several elements contributed to the age of European exploration and discovery. Christians were anxious to spread their religion to stop the expansion of Islam. And overland trade routes had been cut off ever since Ottoman Turks had conquered Constantinople in 1453. In order to obtain the spices, silks, perfumes, and other exotic goods in great demand throughout Europe, it was necessary to discover a new way to the Orient.

Christopher Columbus, navigator and agent from Genoa, thought that sailing west across the Atlantic would lead to the East Indies. In 1492 King Ferdinand and Queen Isabella of Spain agreed to outfit him with three ships. From August 3 until October 12 Columbus and his crews were at sea, until with great relief they made landfall on Watling Island in the Bahamas, where they met people whom Columbus called Indians, because he believed he had reached India. His expedition went on to Cuba and Haiti (named Hispaniola by Columbus) before returning to Spain to receive a hero's welcome.

During the course of three more voyages, Columbus reached Central and South America. He died in 1506. His voyage remains one of the most important events in modern history, one that brought the Old and New Worlds together, with devastating consequences to the people of the Americas.

Reconstruction of Columbus's small sailing ships, the *Niña*, the *Pinta*, and the *Santa Maria*

CHAPTER 5

CONVERGING WORLDS

1500-1750

Beginning around 1500, western Europeans greatly expanded their reach by establishing trading bases around the globe and colonizing the Americas. This process transformed both the Old World and the New World as people, plants, livestock, viruses and other pathogens crossed oceans and altered conditions on distant shores. The impact was greatest on the Americas, where native people were devastated by diseases communicated by Europeans. But the Old World also underwent profound changes as new crops and commodities arrived from the Americas, the slave trade destabilized Africa, and societies elsewhere reckoned with colonialism.

REFORMATION IN EUROPE

Colonization of the Americas coincided with revolutionary developments in Europe. The Protestant Reformation began in Germany, where the printing press was devised and knowledge of scripture and other subjects, once confined to priests and scholars, became accessible to literate people. When the German monk Martin Luther launched the Reformation in 1517, he insisted that the Bible, not the pope, was the ultimate religious authority. Luther's protests against controversial church practices such as the sale of indulgences and pardoning people for their sins, were set in print and reached a wide audience, as did his translation of the New Testament. Protestantism was strongest in urban areas in northern Europe, where many people were literate and began to question Catholic teachings. In response, Catholic leaders launched a Counter-Reformation, limiting the sale of indulgences and improving the education of priests, missionaries, and laypersons.

Using a telescope, Italian astronomer Galileo Galilei discovered moons orbiting the planet Jupiter, demonstrating that not all heavenly bodies revolved around the Earth, as once thought.

The struggle between Catholicism and Protestantism often involved political factors. In England, King Henry VIII broke with Catholicism in 1533 after the pope refused to allow him to divorce his wife, who had not provided him with a male heir. Henry then disbanded English monasteries and confiscated their wealth. A fierce rivalry ensued between Protestant England and Catholic Spain, where heretics were tried by the Spanish Inquisition. Henry's daughter Queen Elizabeth I survived a challenge from Spain's King Philip II in 1588 when her navy repulsed the Spanish Armada. Later, radical English Protestants called Puritans opposed their own king, Charles I, who was suspected of plotting to restore Catholicism and executed in 1649. King James II was overthrown in 1688 for similar reasons, and England emerged as a constitutional monarchy.

Dutch provinces joined together to fight for political and religious independence from Spain, which tried to suppress Protestantism. The resulting Republic of the United Netherlands became a world power in the 17th century. In France, by contrast, Catholicism prevailed under King Louis XIV, the so-called Sun King, who controlled the wealth of the Church and reigned in splendor at Versailles.

In central Europe, Protestants rebelled in 1618 when the Habsburg dynasty that ruled both the Holy Roman Empire and Spain tried to enforce Catholicism, unleashing the brutal Thirty Years' War. The combined opposition

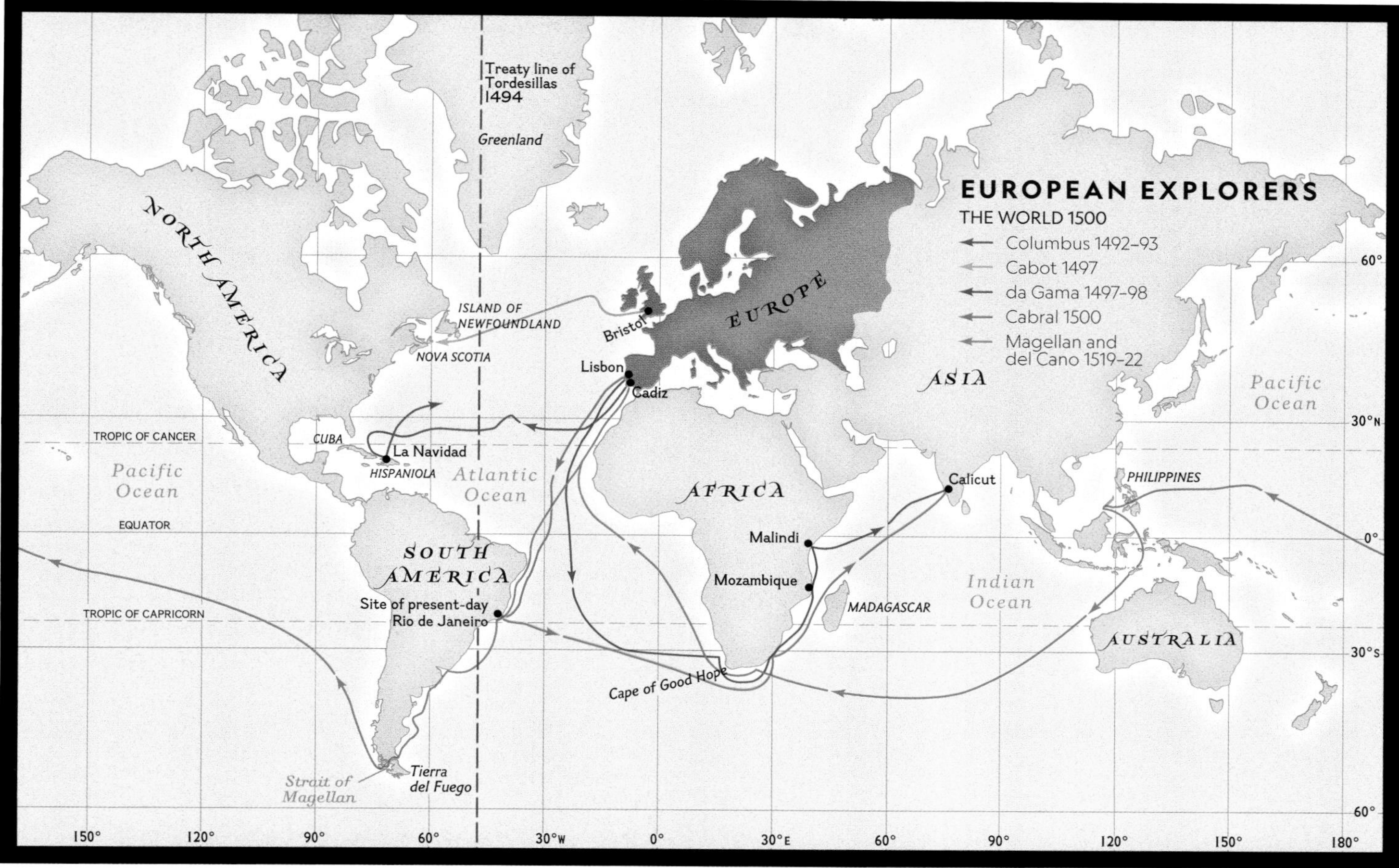

of France, which aimed to weaken the Habsburgs, and Protestant countries such as Sweden and the Netherlands forced the Holy Roman Empire to grant sovereignty to Switzerland and freedom of worship to various Christian denominations in Germany.

In years to come, religious strife receded and Europe prospered. New crops from the Americas improved the diet of Europeans and raised life expectancies. Global trade fostered a wealthy merchant class that patronized musicians and painters such as the Dutch master Rembrandt van Rijn, who drew on the heritage of the Italian Renaissance and portrayed both religious and secular subjects. Scientific inquiry fostered a new view of the cosmos, put forward by astronomers such as Galileo Galilei and the physicist Isaac Newton, who explained gravity in mathematical terms. Advances in science and technology and the rise of corporate capitalism, which encouraged investment and economic risk taking, contributed to European expansion overseas.

COLONIZING THE AMERICAS

Spanish colonization of the New World began in the Caribbean, where Columbus and others founded settlements on Hispaniola (the island shared today by Haiti and the Dominican Republic), Puerto Rico, Jamaica, and Cuba. Spanish settlers demanded labor and tribute from the native people they called Indians, who suffered severely from exploitation by colonists and diseases they introduced. As Indians died out in the Caribbean, Spaniards brought enslaved Africans to labor on plantations, and the population became largely African-American. A similar process occurred in Portuguese Brazil.

In 1519 the Spanish conquistador (conqueror) Hernán Cortés left Cuba with several hundred men to seek fortune in Mexico. Aided by a Tabascan Indian woman called Marina who served as his interpreter and later bore his child, Cortés forged alliances with groups subject to the Aztec, who were devastated by smallpox and other Old World diseases. In 1521 Cortés and his forces razed the

This map charts the pioneering transatlantic voyage of Christopher Columbus, sailing for Spain, and subsequent voyages made by John Cabot for England; Vasco da Gama and Pedro Álvares Cabral for Portugal; and Ferdinand Magellan and Sebastián del Cano, who circumnavigated the globe for Spain.

Aztec capital, Tenochtitlan, and founded Mexico City in its place. In South America, conquistador Francisco Pizarro used similar tactics to divide and conquer the Inca Empire. Spain then took direct control of American colonies and appointed two viceroys, who ruled for the king at Mexico City and Lima, the Spanish capital of Peru. Missionaries introduced Catholicism and Spanish authorities abolished Indian slavery, but many Indians remained bound under forced labor. In the 1500s the Spanish crown profited hugely from silver extracted from Mexico and Peru, but by the 1700s many Spanish-American colonies were a drain on the royal treasury. Spain regarded them strictly as sources of raw materials and discouraged colonists from manufacturing goods or entering into maritime trade.

By 1750 Spain had colonized a broad area north of Mexico, including Florida, Texas, and New Mexico, where colonists relied heavily on the labor of Pueblo Indians. Those frontier provinces were intended as buffers to shield Mexico from foreign intervention. Chief among the rivals to Spain in North America were the English, whose colonies along the Atlantic were prospering and expanding westward. The French also posed a threat to Spanish interests when they ventured south from Canada in the late 1600s and claimed Louisiana, a sprawling territory embracing the Mississippi River and its tributaries.

Blessed with fertile land, English colonies attracted far more settlers to the New World than French or Spanish colonies did. Some immigrants sought religious freedom, like the Puritans who settled Massachusetts and the Catholics who founded Maryland, only to become embroiled in further religious strife. Rhode Island, founded by religious dissidents from Massachusetts, became the first American colony to tolerate those of all faiths, including Jews.

Unlike Spanish or French colonists who intermarried with Indians and formed a mixed race known as mestizos or métis, most English colonists avoided contact with Indians except when trading with them for valued items like beaver pelts or negotiating for land. Colonists sometimes used liquor to extract treaty concessions from Indians and set one tribe against another when conflicts arose. The powerful Iroquois Confederacy was strained to the breaking point when its alliance with English colonists drew it into repeated battles with tribes loyal to the French. English planters who needed laborers relied not on Indians but on indentured servants from Europe, who worked under contract, or on slaves from Africa. By the 1700s ports such as Philadelphia and New York, founded by Dutch colonists but seized by English forces in 1664, had developed into thriving commercial centers, where colonists built ships, engaged in overseas trade, and met in assemblies that prepared them for self-government. Such advances came at a steep price, however, for native people in America, Africa, and other lands impacted by colonization.

AFRICA BESIEGED

Beginning in the late 1400s, Africa underwent wrenching changes as traders and troops from Europe and the Middle East intervened there. Ottoman Turks conquered much of North Africa in the 1500s but failed to take Morocco, which was bolstered by Muslims fleeing persecution in Spain. Moroccans and other North Africans crossed the Sahara in caravans to trade with the flourishing Songhai Empire in West Africa, whose Muslim rulers founded an Islamic university at Timbuktu. Their forces patrolled the Niger River in ships but lacked the firepower of Moroccans, who turned from trading to raiding and inflicted a crushing defeat on Songhai troops in 1591 that led to the empire's collapse. Afterward, power shifted to the coast, where African states like Oyo and Dahomey prospered by obtaining captives from the interior and selling them to Europeans along with gold and other items.

The Portuguese figured prominently in that coastal trade and sometimes used military force to secure their interests. The rulers of Kongo, a well-organized kingdom in the Congo River basin, at first welcomed Portuguese merchants and missionaries and embraced Christianity, only to lose faith in the foreigners when Portuguese slave traders made deals with their enemies. In the 1600s Portuguese troops overran Kongo and killed its king, leaving the country in disarray. The Portuguese also invaded Ndongo, or Angola, following the death of the defiant Queen Nzinga, who allied with Dutch merchants hostile to the Portuguese. The Dutch established a trading post at Cape Town in 1652 and later colonized South Africa, while the Portuguese occupied ports along the East African coast and drew profits and power away from Swahili merchants. By 1700 the Portuguese had been surpassed

In a romanticized 19th-century painting set in Tenochtitlan, the Aztec capital, King Moctezuma II stands beside the Great Pyramid and greets the Spanish conquistador Hernán Cortés, who posed as Moctezuma's friend before taking him hostage.

As diagrammed here, slave traders crammed African captives into the holds of ships bound for the New World. Conditions on some ships were so terrible in the early years of the trade that more than half the slaves died before reaching their destination.

in the slave trade by the French and English, and they too had bases in Africa.

African kingdoms such as Dahomey (now Benin) acquired firearms from Europeans and expanded, selling captives into slavery as conquerors around the world had long been doing. Many African societies benefited from new crops imported from the Americas, including corn, peanuts, and cassava, which flourished in the tropics. But such gains were more than offset by the tragic impact of a slave trade that transported about 12 million Africans to the Americas amid such dreadful conditions that many did not survive the journey. Millions more were sold into slavery in other parts of the world by Christian or Muslim dealers. Some who escaped enslavement were caught up in ruinous wars that were triggered or aggravated by the slave trade and left Africa vulnerable to deeper intrusions by Europeans in centuries to come.

CHALLENGES IN ASIA

In Asia, societies responded in various ways to the challenges of a world in which traders and explorers often served as agents of imperial expansion, sometimes welcoming foreigners within prescribed limits and sometimes keeping them at a distance. China had the potential to dominate maritime trade in Asia, as shown by naval expeditions in the 15th century that involved hundreds of ships and projected Chinese power clear across the Indian Ocean. But emperors of the Ming dynasty grew increasingly concerned with fending off threats from Mongols and other foreigners and sought to restrict foreign trade instead of pursuing it as an instrument of state power, as Europeans did. Smugglers defied restrictions Ming rulers imposed, and pirates made incursions along China's southeast coast.

In the mid-1600s invaders from Manchuria called Manchus joined with Chinese rebels and toppled the Ming, installing their own Qing dynasty in Beijing and prohibiting maritime trade until they secured their hold on the country in the late 1600s. Overseas trade never stopped entirely, for there was strong demand in China for silver bullion, which fueled the economy and was obtained from Japan and Spanish America for Chinese products such as silk and porcelain. Foreigners purchased Chinese goods at the port of Guangzhou (Canton), where officials closely supervised trade, and at overseas ports such as Manila in the Philippines, colonized by Spain and visited by galleons bearing silver from the New World. Chinese merchants had their own district there and were envied and resented for their success. Catholic missionaries brought knowledge of European culture and technology to the Chinese court and sought to ingratiate themselves with the emperor and high officials in order to spread their faith. They succeeded in winning some converts but were barred from proselytizing by the emperor after the pope ruled that Chinese converts must no longer venerate their ancestors.

Japan was less receptive to outsiders. European contact was made when a Portuguese trading vessel blew ashore in 1543 introducing firearms and starting a slave trade of Japanese citizens. The trade would be banned by the end of the century as Japan pursued isolationist policies. The civil strife that wracked the country in the 1500s ended when shoguns (military rulers) of the Tokugawa family took control in the 1600s and pacified Japan's daimyo: lords who wielded great power over their domains and commanded the services of hard-fighting samurai. Tokugawa shoguns required those lords to spend every other year at court in Edo (Tokyo), and greatly restricted contact with foreigners to prevent them from supplying daimyo with firearms or otherwise destabilizing Japan. Christianity was banned, and missionaries and converts who violated the edict were executed. Some Dutch and Chinese ships were allowed to enter the port of Nagasaki and do business, but when Portuguese traders arrived there uninvited in 1640, most of them were killed and the rest deported. Like China, Japan prospered during this period. Merchants, long regarded as socially inferior to samurai and daimyo, gained wealth and influence but were not permitted to seek profit abroad.

In India, Turkish conquerors seized power in the 1500s and established the Mughal Empire. The Mughal emperor Akbar, who reigned for nearly half a century, defeated Hindus in southern India but did not force them to convert to Islam, his own faith and that of many people in northern India. Later emperors were less tolerant, leading Hindus to rebel. Mughal rulers were hard-pressed to finance campaigns in the south while maintaining a large bureaucracy and building costly monuments. Desperate for new sources of revenue, they allowed Europeans to establish fortified trading posts in Bombay, Calcutta, and other Indian ports. The British East India Company recruited its own troops and gained power in India as the Mughal Empire declined.

Matteo Ricci, a Jesuit missionary from Italy, stands at left beside his Chinese convert and disciple, Xu Quangqi, who helped convert others in China to Catholicism in the early 1600s.

Even the Ottoman Turks, once so strong that Christians feared they might overrun Europe, gradually lost power. They reached their peak in the mid-1500s with the conquests of Suleyman I the Magnificent, who extended his realm from Baghdad to Budapest. By the 1600s, Ottoman rulers faced strong opposition both in Europe and in Persia, where Shah Abbas the Great mobilized Shiite Muslims against the Sunni Ottomans. By the 1700s, they confronted an even greater challenge from Russia, where Tsar Peter the Great westernized the economy and military. As the Ottoman Empire declined, fresh opportunities for European expansion emerged in the Middle East and North Africa. ■

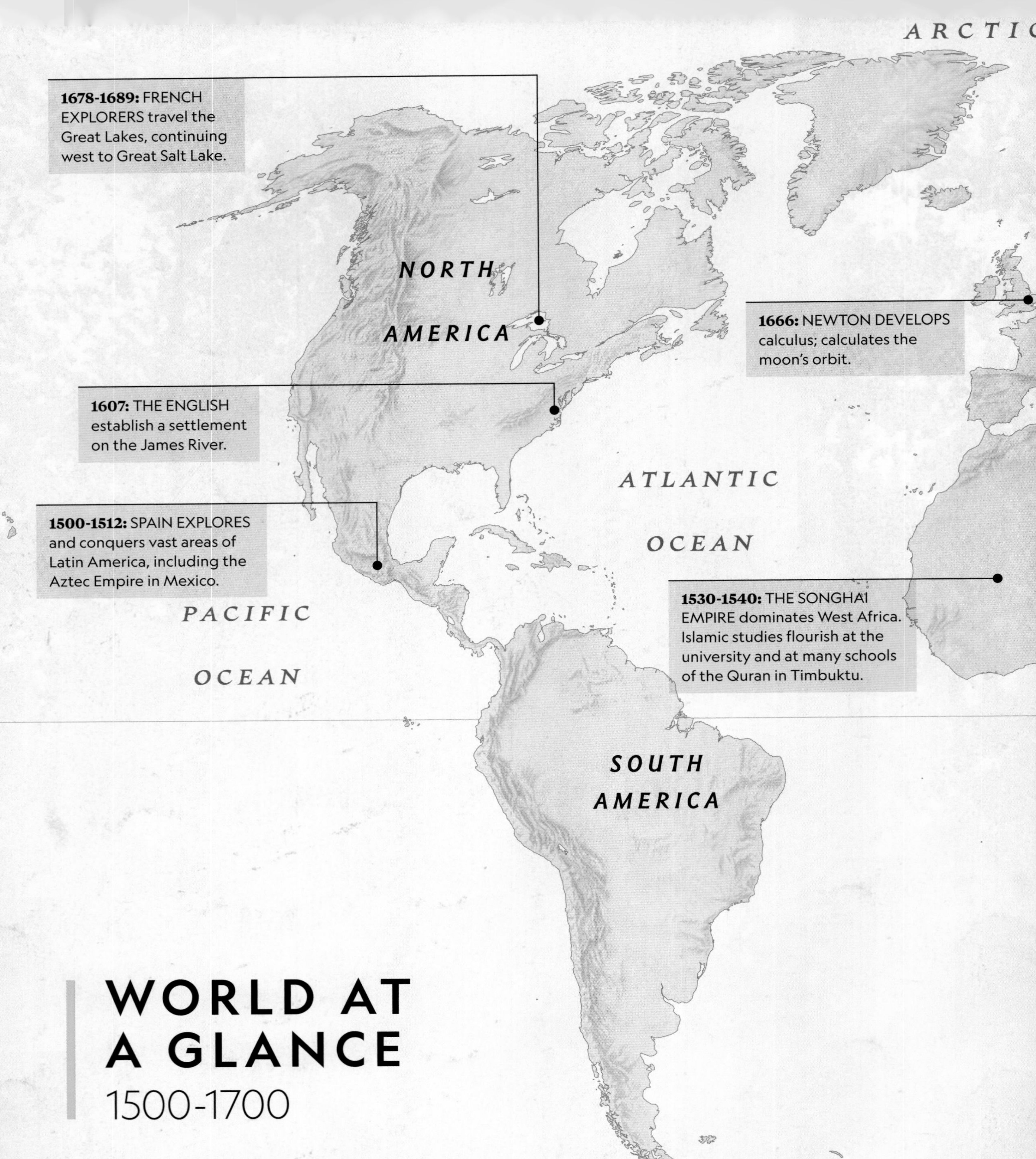

ARCTIC
1678-1689: FRENCH EXPLORERS travel the Great Lakes, continuing west to Great Salt Lake.
NORTH AMERICA
1666: NEWTON DEVELOPS calculus; calculates the moon's orbit.
1607: THE ENGLISH establish a settlement on the James River.
ATLANTIC OCEAN
1500-1512: SPAIN EXPLORES and conquers vast areas of Latin America, including the Aztec Empire in Mexico.
1530-1540: THE SONGHAI EMPIRE dominates West Africa. Islamic studies flourish at the university and at many schools of the Quran in Timbuktu.
PACIFIC OCEAN
SOUTH AMERICA

WORLD AT A GLANCE

1500-1700

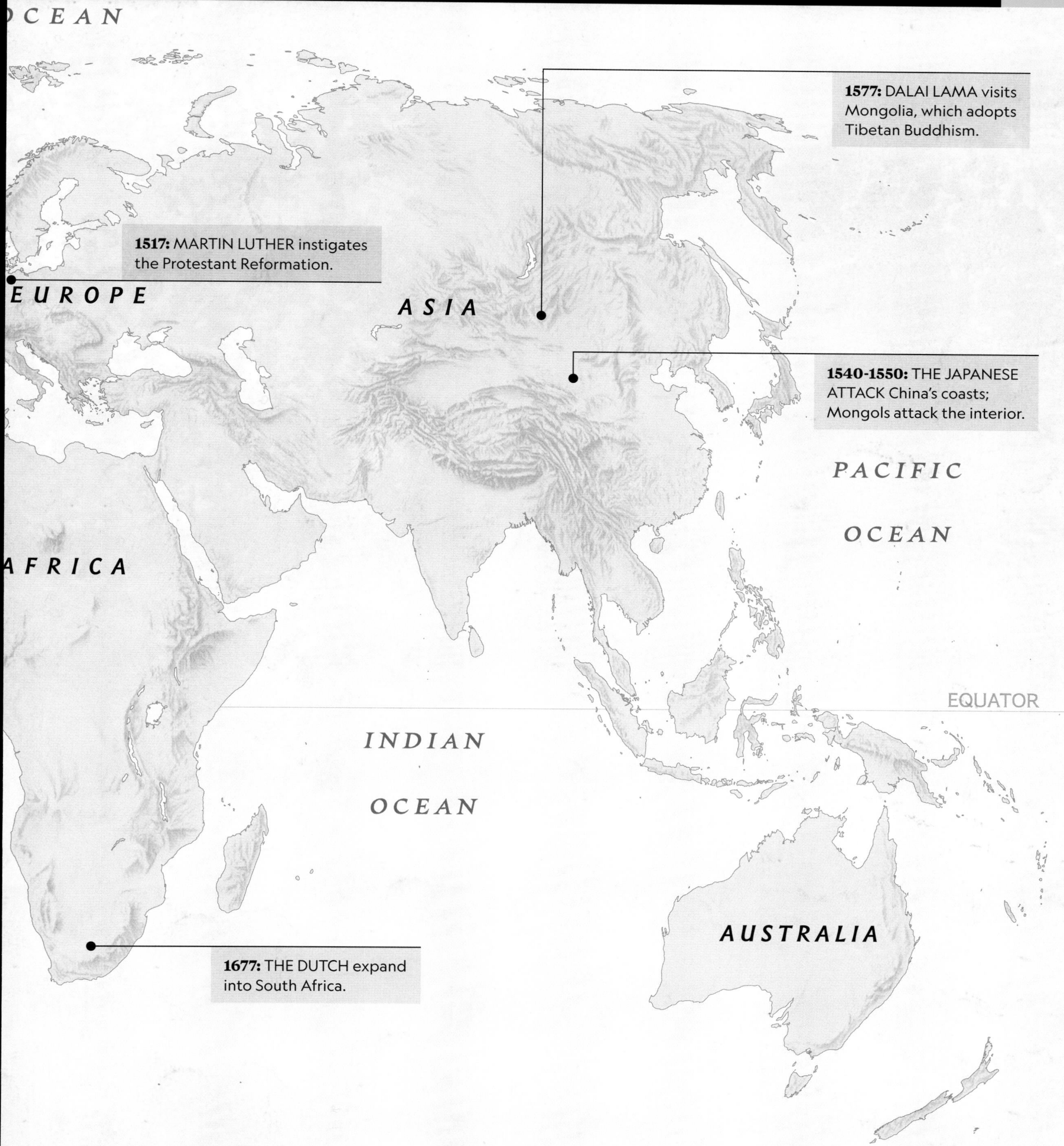
OCEAN
1577: DALAI LAMA visits Mongolia, which adopts Tibetan Buddhism.
1517: MARTIN LUTHER instigates the Protestant Reformation.
EUROPE
ASIA
1540-1550: THE JAPANESE ATTACK China's coasts; Mongols attack the interior.
PACIFIC
OCEAN
AFRICA
EQUATOR
INDIAN
OCEAN
AUSTRALIA
1677: THE DUTCH expand into South Africa.

1500-1515

	POLITICS & POWER	GEOGRAPHY & ENVIRONMENT	CULTURE & RELIGION
THE AMERICAS	**1500s** THE SPANISH REQUERMIENTO demands that indigenous peoples met by the conquistadores submit to the Spanish monarch and to the pope. **1502** MOCTEZUMA II becomes ruler of the Aztec dominions and begins conquests outside the Valley of Mexico. **1509-1511** THE SPANISH invade and conquer Puerto Rico, Jamaica, and Cuba.	**1501** AMERIGO VESPUCCI of Italy makes his second voyage to the New World. **1502** CHRISTOPHER COLUMBUS makes his final voyage to the New World. **1513** VASCO NUÑEZ DE BALBOA crosses the Isthmus of Panama and sees the Pacific Ocean. **1513** JUAN PONCE DE LEÓN explores Florida.	**1508** POPE JULIUS II grants Spain the right to control missionary efforts in the New World. **1511** FATHER ANTONIO MONTESINOS condemns the Spanish settlers on Hispaniola for cruelty toward the Indians and questions Spain's right to rule the natives.
EUROPE	**1500** INVASIONS AND BATTLES are ongoing between France, the Italian principalities, and parts of the Holy Roman Empire. Papal authority intervenes in many of the disputes. **1508** GERMAN KING MAXIMILIAN I becomes Roman emperor-elect; Pope Julius II rules that future German kings will be Holy Roman Emperors. **1509** HENRY VIII becomes king of England and marries Catherine of Aragon, his brother's widow.	 Leonardo da Vinci's "Mona Lisa" with her mysterious smile	**1500-1515** ACTIVE ARTISTS include Cranach, Dürer, Grünewald, da Vinci, Michelangelo, and Raphael. **1501** BOOK BURNING is authorized by papal bull. ◀ **ca 1503** LEONARDO DA VINCI paints "La Gioconda" ("Mona Lisa"). **1508-1512** MICHELANGELO paints the ceiling of the Sistine Chapel at the Vatican.
MIDDLE EAST & AFRICA	**1500s** THE ETHIOPIAN EMPIRE continues its expansion by conquest. **1500s** THE SONGHAI EMPIRE expands in North Africa. **1502** PORTUGUESE EXPLORER VASCO DA GAMA forces the ruler of Kilwa (modern-day Tanzania) to swear loyalty to King Manuel. **1514** OTTOMANS defeat Safavids at Chaldiran in northwest Persia.	**1509** CONSTANTINOPLE suffers a disastrous earthquake.	**1500** IN MANY SCHOOLS in Timbuktu at this time, the Quran is studied. There is also an Islamic university there. **1506** KING AFONSO I of Kongo begins introducing European customs to the country. **1513** PIRI REIS, Ottoman geographer, draws a world map including the Americas.
ASIA & OCEANIA	**ca 1500** JAPANESE DAIMYO LORDS struggle for control as the Ashikaga shogunate weakens. **1505** ZHENGDE becomes emperor of China. **1510** THE PORTUGUESE under Afonso de Albuquerque take over Goa. **1511** THE PORTUGUESE capture Malacca in Malaysia.	**1511** THE PORTUGUESE establish a fortified trading post at Calicut on India's Malabar Coast. **1513** THE PORTUGUESE reach Macau, a peninsula on China's southern coast. **1514** SILVER MINES reopen in western Yunnan, China.	**1509** INFLUENTIAL CHINESE LANDSCAPE PAINTER Shen Zhou dies.

SCIENCE & TECHNOLOGY

ca 1500 THE INCA EMPIRE has about 25,000 miles of roads in the Andes, built using a communal labor system. Their language, Quechua, is widely spoken throughout the region.

1500s IN WHAT IS CALLED THE COLUMBIAN EXCHANGE, New World crops and planting methods begin to be exported to Europe: maize, tobacco, tomatoes, chocolate, potatoes, sweet potatoes, peppers, peanuts, manioc, pineapples, avocados, and vanilla.

1512-1513 HENRY VIII establishes a royal dockyard at Woolwich to build the massive flagship of his new navy, the 1,500-ton *Henry Grâce à Dieu.*

ca 1512 NICOLAUS COPERNICUS first notes his belief that planets revolve around the sun.

PEOPLE & SOCIETY

1500s THE ENCOMIENDA SYSTEM of land grants to individuals, including the right to command native labor, extends across Spanish possessions in the New World.

1501 PORTUGUESE EXPLORER GASPAR CORTE-REAL'S EXPEDITION lands on Greenland. On the return voyage they bring 57 enslaved local Beothuks.

1510 AFRICAN SLAVES are brought to the New World in quantity for the first time.

1505-1506 NICCOLÒ MACHIAVELLI organizes a militia in Florence, Italy.

PORTUGAL SETS SAIL

DETERMINED TO ESTABLISH and control new trade routes, Portugal was exploring the Atlantic by 1420. Prince Henry the Navigator's center at Sagros collected information; supervised mapmaking; designed ships; and adapted the cross-staff, quadrant, and mathematical tables. By 1444 Portugal had reached West Africa. By 1482 they had a fort on the Gold Coast (Ghana) and commanded traffic in ivory, gold, pepper, and slaves.

From there, navigators such as Bartolomeu Dias and Vasco da Gama explored Africa's east coast, India, and southeast Asia, often impressing the locals by slaughtering them. Once new forts were established, priests followed to spread Catholicism.

Successful Portuguese and Spanish expansion in the 1500s signaled a new direction for European interests: outward into the Atlantic and the unknown. The colonial era was just beginning.

This map highlights the explorers and trade routes that made Portugal the first European country to establish an overseas empire.

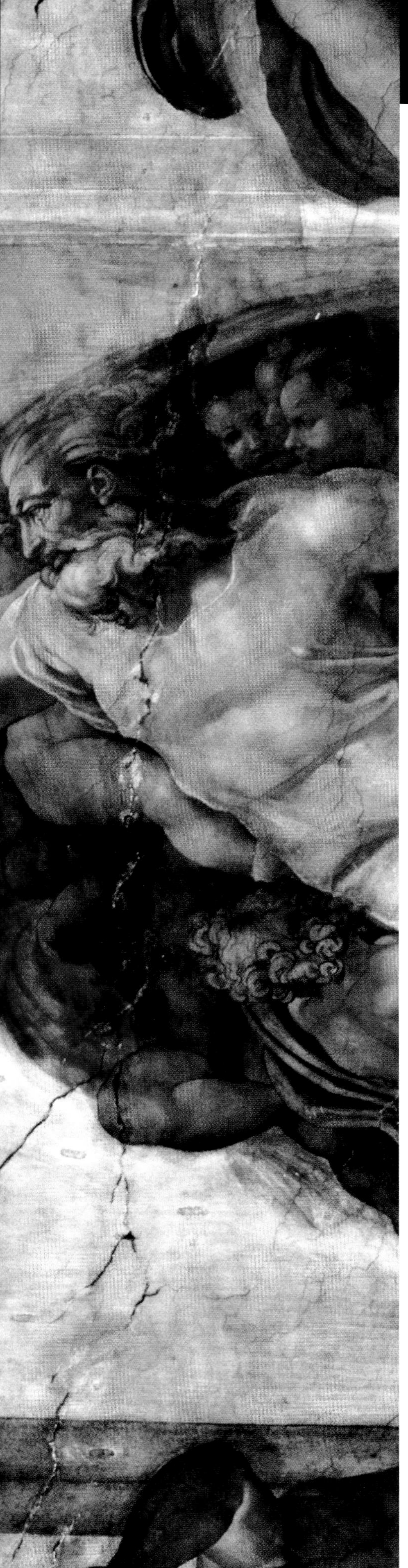

THE GENIUS OF THE RENAISSANCE

During the Renaissance (approximately 1300-1600) the cultural orientation of Europe changed from a focus primarily on religious goals and values to one that blended Christianity with the classical past and direct observation of the world. Traditions of the Greco-Roman world were rediscovered as the works of authors like Plato, Pliny, and Cicero emerged from monastic libraries or were translated out of Arabic to circulate among the wealthy bankers and merchants of 15th-century Italy. The classics valued reason and visual evidence over belief and imagination as sources of truth. To understand the world as the ancients had, it was clearly necessary to look inward at oneself—inward examination set parameters for viewing from a verifiable, human vantage point. This new perspective was reflected throughout the arts, first in literature, then in painting and architecture.

In the 1400s Italian masters codified principles of representing three-dimensional objects on a flat surface by the use of perspective and foreshortening. In the 1500s Michelangelo, Mantegna, and Tintoretto used these techniques to produce emotional, convincingly realistic images. Da Vinci noted that the far distance was bluer in color than the near; his manipulated tones and lines achieve panoramic landscapes such as appear in the background of "Mona Lisa." As three-dimensional painting became more accomplished it introduced a new element: strong sensory appeal. By the later 1500s artists were working not merely to educate, but also to entertain. Contrasts and textures, shapes elongated and emphasized to create pleasing rhythms within compositions, studied repetitions of color that led the eye across an area—these became familiar components of successful paintings. In sculpture, artists made fresh use of exaggeration and a preference for dramatic moments. Both portraits and scenes abandoned the static; 16th-century figures seem arrested in the midst of vigorous action.

Interior decoration became popular, too. Following examples of excavated Roman rooms, the interior walls of palaces and public spaces were painted with lavish decorations ranging from charming domestic scenes to the sublime illusion of the ceiling of the Sistine Chapel at the Vatican.

Celebrated artists not only painted and carved, but also made dining vessels, jewelry, and other objects. Unlike medieval painters and sculptors, often identified only by the pieces they had painted or the churches they embellished, artists of the Renaissance were international stars—Michelangelo was known as Il Divino among contemporaries. In constant demand, engaged by emperors and popes, painters and sculptors documented themselves enthusiastically. Dürer painted himself repeatedly; Ghiberti and Michelangelo set their own recognizable features into their masterpieces. The printing press enabled important artworks to become popular: Paintings, statuary, and even architectural drawings, reproduced as wood block, prints, and engravings, spread Renaissance visions rapidly across the known world.

One of the masterpieces of Western art, Michelangelo's Sistine Chapel ceiling chronicles biblical history, including the creation of Adam.

1515-1530

THE AMERICAS

POLITICS & POWER

1519-1520 **HERNÁN CORTÉS** lands on the coast of Yucatán and marches to Tenochtitlan, the Aztec capital; Moctezuma is killed.

1520s **THE SPANISH** take over Colombia, El Salvador, and Guatemala.

1521 **CORTÉS** defeats the Aztec and claims Mexico for Spain.

1524 **SPAIN** establishes the Council of the Indies for colonial affairs. Viceroys based in Mexico City and later in Lima, Peru, rule under the council.

GEOGRAPHY & ENVIRONMENT

1515 **SPANISH NAVIGATOR** Juan Díaz de Solís reaches the mouth of the Rio de Plata on the Argentine coast.

1523 **THE SPANISH** establish their first permanent settlement in Venezuela at Cumaná.

1524 **ITALIAN GIOVANNI DA VERRAZANO** explores the North American coast and discovers New York Bay.

1527-1528 **ÁLVAR NÚÑEZ CABEZA DE VACA** and his companions, shipwrecked on the Texas coast, wander for nine years through the Southwest before reaching Mexico.

CULTURE & RELIGION

1524 **FRANCISCAN MISSIONARIES** arrive in Mexico from Spain. Franciscans are the main chaplains of the Spanish exploring North America.

1529 **BERNARDINO DE SAHAGÚN,** Franciscan missionary, arrives in New Spain. In the later 1530s he begins recording oral histories of Aztec life and culture. Eventually his work appears as 12 volumes called *A General History of the Things of New Spain.*

EUROPE

POLITICS & POWER

1515 **FRANCIS I** becomes king of France.

1516 **ARCHDUKE CHARLES** becomes King Charles I of Spain.

1518 **THE TREATY OF LONDON** formalizes a rapprochement between England and France.

1519 **MAXIMILIAN I** dies and Charles I of Spain becomes Charles V, Holy Roman Emperor. The Habsburgs begin to consolidate power across Europe.

1520 **CHRISTIAN II,** king of Denmark and Norway, defeats the Swedes in battle and becomes king of Sweden as well.

GEOGRAPHY & ENVIRONMENT

1519 **FERDINAND MAGELLAN** takes his expedition across the Atlantic, suppresses a mutiny, and navigates through a dangerous passage at the tip of South America into the Pacific Ocean. He is killed in a native dispute and only one of his expedition's five ships returns in Europe in 1522.

German monk Martin Luther's criticisms of the Catholic Church incited the Protestant Reformation.

CULTURE & RELIGION

1516 **SIR THOMAS MORE** writes *Utopia.*

◀ **1517** **MARTIN LUTHER,** Augustinian monk, priest, and teacher at the University of Wittenberg, sends 95 theses questioning church doctrine to the Bishop of Mainz.

1519 **ULRICH ZWINGLI** preaches reformation of the church in Switzerland.

1520 **POPE LEO X** excommunicates Martin Luther.

1521 **LUTHER** begins translating the Bible into German. It is completed in 1534.

MIDDLE EAST & AFRICA

POLITICS & POWER

1517 **OTTOMAN TURKS** defeat Mamluk forces in Egypt, take Cairo, and establish suzerainty over Egypt and the Hejaz (Arabian Peninsula).

1520 **SULEYMAN I (THE MAGNIFICENT)** assumes the throne of the Ottoman Empire.

1521-1522 **SULEYMAN'S FORCES** capture Belgrade, then Rhodes. In 1526 he defeats the Hungarians at Mohacs.

CULTURE & RELIGION

1526 **THE MUSLIM STATE OF ADAL** declares a jihad on Christian Ethiopia.

ca 1530 **IBN KEMAL** writes a multivolume history of the Ottomans and standard works on religious sciences.

ASIA & OCEANIA

POLITICS & POWER

1526 **BABUR,** a descendant of Genghis Khan in Central Asia, invades India, occupies Delhi and Agra, and founds the Mughal dynasty.

1527 **THE MAC FAMILY** establishes its dynasty ruling the Tonkin area of northern Vietnam.

GEOGRAPHY & ENVIRONMENT

1518 **THE PORTUGUESE** establish a trade foothold in Colombo, Ceylon.

CULTURE & RELIGION

ca 1516 **ZHOU CHEN,** a painter of street characters, is active in China.

ca 1520 **THE NEO-CONFUCIAN THINKER** Wang Yangming is influential in Ming China.

1521 **THE PEOPLE OF GUAM** have what is believed to be their first encournter with a European visitor, Ferdinand Magellan.

SCIENCE & TECHNOLOGY

1519 INDIANS encounter horses brought to the New World by Hernán Cortés. In time, using and riding horses will transform Indian economies, politics, and lifestyles.

1517 POPE LEO X uses concave lenses to aid his vision while hunting.

1523 MICHELANGELO designs the Laurentian Library in Florence for Cosimo de Medici.

1526-1527 THE OTTOMANS provide military aid in the form of cannon and harquebuses, shipbuilders, and captains to Egypt (1511), Mecca (1517), and Abyssinia (1526), and even send gunmakers to Babur in India (1526).

PEOPLE & SOCIETY

▼ **ca 1515 BARTOLOMÉ DE LAS CASAS,** now in holy orders as a Dominican friar, campaigns in Spain for freedom and better treatment for the indigenous peoples of the Americas. He proposes that Spanish farmers should come to colonize and work alongside the Indians.

ca 1520 A TABASCAN WOMAN MALINTZIN, later named Marina, becomes the mistress and interpreter of Hernán Cortés. She will later be welcomed in the Spanish court

1519 VASCO NUÑEZ DE BALBOA is tried in Spain for rebellion and treason. He is convicted and beheaded.

1528 HENRY VIII of England seeks a divorce from Catherine of Aragon.

1518 KHAYR AL DIN (BARBAROSSA), a North African pirate, receives Ottoman aid against the Spanish.

Spanish friar Bartolomé de las Casas (center, in red) traveled to the New World with conquistadores and attempted to advocate for the indigenous Americans they subjugated.

CORTÉS THE CONQUEROR

HERNÁN CORTÉS WAS BORN in Spain in 1485, raised in a harsh region with a tradition of peasant hardiness and religious warfare. At the age of 19 he sailed for Hispaniola, where he became a farmer and town official before accompanying Diego Velásquez in the invasion of Cuba in 1511.

In 1518 Velásquez appointed Cortés to settle a colony on the American mainland, after previous efforts had failed. Cortés assembled a powerful invasion force and landed on Yucatán with 11 ships, hundreds of armored men, cannon, and horses. He left no doubt as to his resolve by ordering his ships burned, committing his men to conquest with promises of gold and blessings from God.

Intimidating the Indians with his cannon and horses, Cortés sowed favor and admirers before marching toward the Aztec capital of Tenochtitlan (Mexico City). He was aided by Aztec legends that foretold of a white conqueror and by the diplomacy of a Tabascan Indian woman, Marina, who negotiated for him. Welcomed to the capital by its ruler, Moctezuma, who soon submitted to Cortés's authority, the Spanish were amazed by the splendor of the Aztec Empire, and they were eager to plunder it.

In 1520 Velásquez sent a force after the renegade Cortés, who sped to the coast and convinced his would-be arrestors to join him. But in his absence, the Aztec revolted. Moctezuma was killed, and 10 months later, with a powerful army of Spanish and Indian allies, Cortés retook Tenochtitlan. He ordered the looting and wrecking of cities throughout the Aztec Empire, believing it was God's work to destroy this pagan culture.

This extraordinary conquistador had conquered an empire of 11 million people with just a few hundred men. But Cortés was beset by intrigue from jealous compatriots. He died in Spain at the age of 62, disillusioned and embroiled in litigation.

POLITICS & POWER

1532-1533 FRANCISCO PIZARRO invades Peru and kills Inca ruler Atahualpa.

1535 MANCO INCA founds the state of Vilcambamba in the Peruvian highlands. It survives until 1572.

1535 THE FIRST VICEROY of the New World arrives in Mexico City.

1536 INCA INSURGENTS besiege Pizarro's forces in Cusco, but are defeated.

1540 FRANCISCO VÁSQUEZ DE CORONADO defeats Indians in an area north of Mexico.

1530 CHARLES V, Holy Roman Emperor, is crowned king of Italy.

1530 GERMAN PRINCES form the Schmalkaldic League to oppose Charles V and his threats to Lutheranism. Under the league's protection, the Reformation spreads through Germany.

1544 SWEDISH SUCCESSION is attached to the hereditary male line.

1533 KHAYR AL DIN (BARBAROSSA) is made admiral in chief of the powerful Ottoman fleet.

1538 ADMIRAL BARBAROSSA defeats Charles V's fleet at Preveza. The Ottomans now rule the eastern Mediterranean region. Ottomans gain Basra.

1543 THE OTTOMAN FLEET winters in Toulon due to the Ottoman-French alliance against the Habsburgs.

1530 HUMAYUN becomes the second Mughal ruler of India upon the death of his father, Babur.

GEOGRAPHY & ENVIRONMENT

1533 THE PORTUGUESE give individuals land grants in Brazil and extensive power to develop them.

1534 JACQUES CARTIER of France explores Labrador and the St. Lawrence River as far as the site of Quebec.

1540-1541 FRANCISCO VÁSQUEZ DE CORONADO crosses southwestern North America in search of reputed cities of gold. He encounters the Grand Canyon of the Colorado.

The Copernican world system challenged the traditional view of the solar system by placing the sun at the center; the Earth and its moon, along with the planets, revolve around it.

1543 THREE PORTUGUESE MERCHANTS, blown off course, reach the southern tip of Japan in the first encounter between the two cultures.

CULTURE & RELIGION

1531 INDIAN CONVERT JUAN DIEGO has visions of the Virgin Mary at Guadalupe near Mexico City. A popular shrine develops at the site.

1532 FRANCOIS RABELAIS publishes the bawdy satire *Pantagruel*.

1534 IN THE ACT OF SUPREMACY, the British Parliament recognizes Henry VIII as the "Supreme Head of the Church of England."

1534 IGNATIUS LOYOLA founds The Society of Jesus (Jesuits) in Paris. The order is officially recognized by Pope Paul III in 1540.

1535 ANGELA MERICI founds the Ursuline order.

ca 1535 MATRAKCI NASUH compiles a description of towns along the road from Istanbul to Baghdad after the Mesopotamian campaign, illustrated with miniatures of the major towns.

1543 THE FIRST *SOWON,* or private academy, is founded by the Yi dynasty in Korea. It is patterned on the Chinese academies of earlier times that taught neo-Confucianism.

SCIENCE & TECHNOLOGY	PEOPLE & SOCIETY
1532 SUGAR CANE is first cultivated in Brazil. **ca 1535** DON ANTONIO DE MENDOZA, first viceroy of New Spain, sets up a printing press in Mexico.	**1535** FRENCH EXPLORER JACQUES CARTIER encounters the Iroquois along the St. Lawrence River near Quebec. **1539** HERNANDO DE SOTO'S expedition commits rape and murder as the force travels through Indian lands in the American Southeast. **1542** THE NEW LAWS OF THE INDIES regulate Spanish activities in the New World. They set limits on Indian tribute, restrict Indian enslavement, and prohibit forced labor, reducing the power of the encomiendas.
1536 GERMAN-SWISS PHYSICIAN PARACELSUS publishes the first modern manual of surgery. **1543** ANDREAS VESALIUS, a Flemish professor at the University of Padua, publishes human anatomical studies based on dissections. ◀ **1543** NICOLAUS COPERNICUS publishes his treatise on the heliocentric universe, *De Revolutionibus,* and dies shortly thereafter.	**1532** EMPEROR CHARLES V enacts the Constituto Criminalis Carolina, a criminal and procedural code for the Holy Roman Empire. **1536** JOHN CALVIN, becoming an influential Protestant leader, writes *The Institutes of the Christian Religion.* He settles in Geneva. **1542** POPE PAUL III begins the Inquisition in Rome.
1543 THEOREMS IN MATHEMATICAL ASTRONOMY and the description of the circulation of the blood, developed by Arab scientists and contained in Arabic and Byzantine manuscripts in European libraries, are employed by Copernicus.	**1539** MIMAR SINAN, the greatest Ottoman architect, designs his first nonmilitary structure. He will eventually create 79 mosques, 34 palaces, 55 schools, and many other public buildings. His great ambition is to create a domed structure in which all the parts work together and which surpasses in size the dome of Aya Sofia. He finally achieves this in the Selimiye mosque in Edirne.
1543 FIREARMS are introduced to Japan when a Japanese feudal lord buys guns from Portuguese sailors.	**1545** SHER SHAH OF SURI dies. An Afghan emperor of North India, he was an able administrator and road builder who took over the Mughal Empire.

Torture forced Inquisition victims to recant heresy.

THE SPANISH INQUISITION

THE INQUISITION WAS A JUDICIAL process to investigate heresy, sorcery, or other deviations from the Catholic faith. Ferdinand and Isabella were granted an Inquisition in 1478 to quell civil conflicts between conversos (Jewish and Muslim converts) and Christian Spaniards. Eventually the Inquisition operated in Spanish colonies as well as Spain itself. The system relied on local courts and traveling inquisitors; a High Council of five members ruled over the local courts.

Individuals were accused, anonymously, of heretical behavior. Defendants had lawyers, and two impartial priests were present at examinations. But defendants were presumed guilty, and torture was sometimes used to extract confessions. If there was evidence of heresy, defendants were urged to recant or convert anew. Those who did so convincingly were freed. Civil authorities executed others, usually by burning at the stake.

Vatican records indicate that the courts sentenced a relatively small number of accused heretics to death over the 356 years of Inquisition but the widespread persecution and expulsion of non-Catholics devastated the lives of many more.

POLITICS & POWER

1549 **JOHN III** of Portugal names a governor-general of Bahia.

1555 **FRANCE** establishes a settlement in Brazil at the site of Rio de Janeiro.

1547 **IVAN IV (THE TERRIBLE)** becomes tsar of Russia.

1547 **HENRY VIII** of England dies, succeeded by his nine-year-old son Edward VI.

1553 **EDWARD VI** dies; his Catholic half sister Mary becomes queen.

1556 **CHARLES V,** Holy Roman Emperor, abdicates in favor of his brother, Ferdinand I. His son becomes king of Spain.

1558 **QUEEN MARY** dies; Elizabeth I becomes queen of England.

1546 **SONGHAI FORCES** overrun Mali.

1549 **ASKIA DAWUD** becomes emperor of Songhai.

ca 1550s **THE TUTSI** establish the kingdom of Rwanda.

▶ **1551** **THE OTTOMANS** conquer Tripoli.

ca 1556 **THE WOLOF EMPIRE** in West Africa dissolves.

1556 **WAR** breaks out between Kongo and Ndongo (Angola). The Portuguese lend support to Kongo.

1550 **THE MONGOLS** cross the Great Wall and attempt an unsuccessful siege of Beijing.

1550s **JAPANESE PIRATES** launch repeated attacks on the Chinese coast.

1556 **AKBAR** becomes emperor of India. He introduces sweeping reforms of the military and of revenue collection.

GEOGRAPHY & ENVIRONMENT

1550s **THE SPANISH** introduce European cattle to the pampas areas of Argentina.

ca 1554-1557 **SIDI ALI REIS,** Ottoman admiral, writes books on the Indian Ocean, his travels in the Ottoman Empire, astronomy, and mathematics.

1555-1564 **ISTANBUL'S AQUEDUCT SYSTEM** is rebuilt and expanded to meet the demands of an increasing population.

1556 **A DISASTROUS EARTHQUAKE** in northwest China kills 830,000 people.

CULTURE & RELIGION

1549 **MANOEL DA NOBREGA** founds the first Jesuit mission in Brazil.

1550-1551 **IN THE VALLADOLID DEBATE** before the Spanish court, Dominican missionary Bartolomé de las Casas and attorney Juan Ginés de Sepúlveda deliberate "the capacity of Indians to Christianize and westernize."

1551 **THE NATIONAL AUTONOMOUS UNIVERSITY OF MEXICO** and Main National University of San Marcos of Lima are founded.

1545 **CATHOLIC CLERGY** convene at the Council of Trent to discuss strategies to counter the Reformation.

1548 **JESUIT MISSIONARIES** arrive in Kongo at the invitation of the king.

1549 **A NEW PRAYER BOOK** is made official in England, solidifying Protestant practice.

1558 **GIOSEFFO ZARLINO** defines the modern major and minor musical scales.

1543 **ETHIOPIA** defeats Adal and remains Christian.

1545-1574 **EBUSSUUD EFENDI,** Ottoman chief religious authority, reconciles Islamic and Sultanic law codes, especially criminal and land law.

1555 **TURKISH POET BAKI** writes an ode that gains him entry to the court circles of Ottoman sultan Suleyman I.

1557 **ARCHITECT SINAN** completes Suleyman I's mosque complex, including a university, hospital, and soup kitchen.

1550 **TANG XIANZU,** Ming playwright and author of *The Peony Pavilion,* is born.

1556-1605 **AKBAR,** Mughal ruler of India, conquers nearly the entire subcontinent, creates an integrated Muslim-Hindu society and culture, and encourages literature in Persian and a flourishing climate for art. He also reforms taxes and encourages religious tolerance.

CONNECTIONS

Riches of the North

The first treasure Europeans found in the American north was the North Atlantic codfish swimming in vast schools off Greenland and Newfoundland, discovered by far-traveling Basque whalers. The dried, salted cod they brought home became popular in Europe, but the Basques guarded its source. In 1497 John Cabot, exploring for England, reported that cod filled the northern waters. Jacques Cartier noted 1,000 Basque vessels there in 1535. English, French, and Portuguese fishermen began competing with the Basques and in the 1600s the powerful fleets of England and France claimed possession of the North Atlantic fishing grounds.

SCIENCE & TECHNOLOGY

1545-1546 **SILVER MINING** begins in Potosí, Bolivia, and Zacatecas, Mexico.

1557 **THE PATIO PROCESS** is invented, facilitating the separation of silver from raw ore and boosting the New World mining industry.

1558 **THE VALENCIANA MINE** opens at Guanajuato, Mexico.

1545 **ITALIAN MATHEMATICIAN** Girolamo Cardano publishes solutions of cubic and quartic equations.

1546 **FLEMISH GEOGRAPHER** Gerardus Mercator describes Earth's magnetic poles.

1551 **GERMAN MATHEMATICIAN** Georg Rheticus publishes trigonometric tables.

1553 **SPANISH PHYSICIAN AND THEOLOGIAN** Michael Servetus publishes the first description of pulmonary circulation

PEOPLE & SOCIETY

ca 1550 **AN INDIAN FISHING VILLAGE** on the northwest American coast at Ozette is buried by a mud slide, preserving artifacts of a typical Makah settlement of this time.

1550 **PORTUGUESE PLANTERS** begin importing large numbers of African slaves as laborers in the sugar fields.

1554-1558 ***POPUL VUH,*** the Maya creation story, is written down for the first time in the Maya language K'iche'.

1549 **IVAN IV** calls together Russia's first national assembly.

1552 **THE GOLF COURSE AT ST. ANDREWS, SCOTLAND,** opens.

1553 **RICHARD CHANCELLOR** leads an English expedition to find an overland route to China. He establishes trade relations between England and Russia.

From its beginnings in Anatolia, the Ottoman Empire expanded around the Mediterranean over the course of a few hundred years.

MINING THE NEW WORLD

SPANISH CONQUERORS in America produced immense wealth for the Spanish crown, who claimed rights to one-fifth (the Quinto Real) of all gold and silver mined from Mexico and Peru. Pirates preyed on the galleons that carried the precious metals back to Europe (a primary cause of the wars between England and Spain) and fueled the economy of northern ports with captured silver and gold. The flow of metals into Europe boosted supplies of coins, stimulated urban mercantile society, and made trade possible with India and China, who were not attracted by most European goods.

In 1545 the vast Andean silver deposits of Potosí were discovered, followed by mines in Zacatecas, then Guanajuato, Mexico. To get workers for the mines, the Spanish adopted the mita, an Inca tax in the form of prescribed days of labor that took one worker from every family. Avoiding the mita, many fled from their homelands to distant areas, destroying village society.

The mines killed men quickly. Separated from their families, they suffered in the camps and boom towns from polluted water, inadequate shelter, and rampant disease. Narrow shafts pierced the great hill of Potosí; inside, the mines were stiflingly hot and subject to disastrous cave-ins. Miners crept along tunnels in almost total darkness before reaching the workable silver vein; many hours later they crawled out again, exhausted, carrying baskets of ore on their backs. By the mid-1600s mine operators were using mingas, paid laborers deployed in smaller mining camps that moved from place to place when lodes became depleted.

As New Spain developed a culture of its own, colonial governments retained silver to pay salaries, decorate churches, and defend borders. The flow of silver to Europe lessened as Spanish power in the Old World declined and the Americas established the beginnings of autonomy.

THE OTTOMAN EMPIRE

The Ottoman Empire was born as Muslim horsemen from Anatolia raided neighboring towns and brought them under their administration. A dynasty of leaders passed control to their sons, beginning with Osman I in the late 13th century. The empire developed siege craft that overcame fortified Byzantine cities, and it grew through both conquest and negotiation. The Ottomans crossed the Bosporus into the Balkans with mercenary troops and settlers in 1346.

Bayezid I (r. 1389-1402) expanded eastward into Anatolia, provoking an invasion by Tamerlane, who dismantled the administration of the Ottomans and restored the power of local rulers. Bayezid's son Mehmed I reestablished control and expanded the empire further. For years the Ottomans bypassed Constantinople, the great walled capital of Byzantium in the Bosporus. Mehmed II laid siege to it in 1453 with 80,000 men, a fleet of galleys, and one of the earliest and largest cannons ever used. He took the city and renamed it Istanbul. It became his capital, and he refurbished it and encouraged industry, trade, and the mingling of people from across his domains. Selim I (r. 1512-1520) doubled the size of Ottoman territories, adding Syria and Egypt. Suleyman I (r. 1520-1566) took Belgrade and won much of modern Hungary at the Battle of Mohacs in 1526.

The Ottomans were tolerant of different cultures and never imposed a single language or religion on their subjects. But the sultan's hold on power was absolute. The brothers of each new sultan were sometimes executed, along with their families, to avoid disputed successions. Boys were drafted from across the empire to serve in the sultan's *kapikulu,* or slave army. The sultan's slaves enjoyed prestige and the best were educated with the princes in the palace school, often becoming officials, administrators, and learned men.

Suleyman I, called the Magnificent, ruled Hungary, the Crimea, Iran, Arabia, Greece, and North Africa. But the empire felt increasing strain. European sea routes threatened trade, precious metals from America devalued coinage, and the empire failed to match western Europe's military modernization, in part because the janissaries, elite corps of soldiers, stifled military innovation until their removal in 1826. The Ottomans were outmaneuvered on the sea at the Battle of Lepanto in 1571, marking a decline in their naval power. And their failed siege of Vienna in 1683 provoked further assaults by emboldened European armies. Nevertheless, a smaller Ottoman Empire survived into the 20th century, when an alliance with the Central Powers in World War I led to final defeat. The sultanate was abolished in 1922.

ABOVE: Suleyman I raised the Ottoman Empire to the height of its glory. Known to Europeans as the Magnificent and to his subjects as the Lawgiver, he was both brilliant strategist and equitable administrator. **OPPOSITE:** A stylized painting depicts Suleyman I and his troops riding into the Battle of Mohacs on August 29, 1526.

1560-1575

THE AMERICAS

POLITICS & POWER

1565 **ST. AUGUSTINE** is founded by the Spanish. The city strengthens Spanish claims to Florida against the rival French.

ca 1570-1600 **THE IROQUOIS CONFEDERACY** unites the Mohawk, Oneida, Onondaga, Cayuga, and Seneca in a common council created to advance peace and law among its members.

1572 **THE SPANISH** capture and behead the last Inca leader, Tupac Amaru, who had ruled from Vilcabamba.

GEOGRAPHY & ENVIRONMENT

1562 **JOHN HAWKINS** sails from Guinea to the West Indies, carrying a cargo of slaves.

1567 **TYPHOID** kills two million Indians.

An illustration from the Florentine Codex documents an Aztec harvesting amaranth.

CULTURE & RELIGION

1569-1571 **KING PHILIP II** establishes offices for the Inquisition in Mexico City and Lima, Peru.

1572 **JESUITS** arrive in New Spain to begin missionary activity. Franciscans forced out of Mexican missions move to the frontiers, where they are successful converting Indians in Florida and New Mexico.

◀ **1577** **THE INQUISITION** condemns Franciscan priest Bernardino de Sahagún for recording pre-Columbian history. His manuscript becomes known as the Florentine Codex.

EUROPE

POLITICS & POWER

1560s **FRANCE** suffers periodic episodes of civil war over religion.

1562 **HOLY ROMAN EMPEROR FERDINAND I** signs a truce with Ottoman emperor Suleyman I.

1564 **FERDINAND I** dies; his son Maximilian II succeeds him as Holy Roman Emperor.

1564 **IVAN IV** abandons Moscow during a power struggle with the boyars.

1568 **THE EIGHTY YEARS' WAR** begins as the Dutch fight for independence from Spain.

CULTURE & RELIGION

1564 **THE POPE** approves the publication of an Index of Prohibited Books.

1572 **THREE THOUSAND FRENCH HUGUENOTS** are massacred on St. Bartholomew's Day.

MIDDLE EAST & AFRICA

POLITICS & POWER

1560s **IN THE JAGA INVASION,** Imbangala forces from what is now modern-day Angola attack the kingdom of Kongo. King Alvaro I appeals to the Portuguese for arms and troops.

1568 **THE PORTUGUESE** influence pervades the affairs of Kongo (until 1622).

1571 **THE OTTOMAN FLEET** is destroyed by the Spanish at the Battle of Lepanto.

1573 **OTTOMANS AND VENETIANS** sign the Peace of Constantinople.

GEOGRAPHY & ENVIRONMENT

1574 **THE PORTUGUESE** establish a colony in Ndongo (today's Angola).

CULTURE & RELIGION

1568 **SHAH TAHMASP OF PERSIA** sends Selim II, Ottoman emperor, an illustrated copy of the *Shahname (Book of Kings),* containing 258 miniatures, as a coronation gift. It is perhaps the most magnificent Islamic manuscript ever created.

ASIA & OCEANIA

POLITICS & POWER

1571 **JAPAN** opens the port of Nagasaki to Western traders.

1573 **JAPANESE WARRIOR** Oda Nobunaga overthrows the Ashikaga shogunate. He takes decisive military action against the feuding daimyo lords and, by the time he dies in 1582, unifies half of Japan's provinces under his rule.

GEOGRAPHY & ENVIRONMENT

1567 **ÁLVARODE MENDAÑA DE NEIRA,** Spanish explorer sailing from Peru, discovers and names the Solomon Islands.

ca 1574 **THE CHINESE** first plant New World crops: sweet potatoes, maize, and peanuts.

CULTURE & RELIGION

ca 1575 **JAPANESE CASTLE ARCHITECTURE** and the related arts associated with powerful daimyo like Nobunaga and Hideyoshi reach the height of their development.

SCIENCE & TECHNOLOGY	PEOPLE & SOCIETY
1563 MERCURY is discovered at Huancavelica in Peru. It is used in a cheaper amalgamation process for refining silver ore. Spanish silver remittance begins a steady increase over the next 30 years.	**1561** SPANISH EXPLORERS to the Chesapeake Bay kidnap an Algonquin boy Opecancanough, brother of the chief Powhatan. He is taken to Spain but brought back to Virginia in 1570 to interpret for a Jesuit mission. Opecancanough returns to his people and leads an attack on the Spanish settlers, who never establish a colony in the region. **1569** SPANISH VICEROY Francisco de Toledo arrives in Peru. He is credited with stabilizing the government but also represses the native populations.
1561 COINS are first produced by a screw mechanism mill in England. **1569** GERARDUS MERCATOR makes a map using a cylindrical projection system to transcribe shapes from a globe to a flat surface. **1572** DANISH ASTRONOMER Tycho Brahe discovers a new star—a supernova in Cassiopeia. **1573** A SUGAR REFINERY opens in Augsburg, Germany	**1560** CATHERINE DE MEDICI becomes regent of France. The mother of three French kings, she controls France until 1574, attempting to control religious factions. **1564** GALILEO GALILEI, Christopher Marlowe, and William Shakespeare are born.
1569 OTTOMANS attempt to dig a canal between the Don and Volga Rivers, which would create a passage from the Black Sea to the Caspian.	**1560** THE SLAVE TRADE is well established in Central Africa. **ca 1560** DONA GRACIA NASI, a wealthy Jewish businesswoman, moves to Istanbul with her nephew Don Joseph. She helps Jews settle in the Ottoman domains, vastly increasing the Jewish community there. She and Don Joseph become involved in state finances through their widespread family and economic connections.
1575 ODA NOBUNAGA makes innovative use of Western firearm technology to defeat a rival Japanese warlord in the Battle of Nagashino.	**1565** SPANISH GALLEONS begin annual voyages between Manila and Acapulco.

GERM WARFARE

EARLY EXPLORERS from Columbus to John Smith reported thriving, populous societies in the Americas on their first visits. Just 20 years later the picture was very different: Epidemic disease brought by Europeans devastated native civilizations. During the first 130 years after contact, diseases like smallpox, typhus, diphtheria, influenza, and measles wiped out perhaps 95 percent of the indigenous people.

The Arawaks of Hispaniola, severely afflicted by illness since 1495, were all dead by 1552. The loss of Indian workers encouraged the Spanish to import African slaves as replacements, establishing a new economy with far-reaching cultural consequences. In Peru, recurrent waves of smallpox quickly killed half the population, setting off a civil war among the rulers and enabling Pizarro's tiny force of fewer than 200 men to overthrow the vast Inca Empire.

The rich Indian settlements of New England lost 90 percent of their people between 1606 and 1620, probably due to viral hepatitis. The busy urban centers of the Caddo culture dwindled to widely scattered small villages by the mid-1600s as their populations dropped from 200,000 to 9,000.

Many factors contributed to the disaster. Above all, the pathogens were new to Native American immune systems; with no antibodies protecting any individuals, communities died en masse. Pigs introduced by De Soto in 1539 ran wild through the South from Florida to Texas and may have transmitted anthrax, trichinosis, and tuberculosis to wildlife through the food chain. Although Native Americans had many palliative medicines, few could combat the new European diseases.

Lands left empty or weakly defended made colonization easier. In 1763, Sir Jeffrey Amherst, an officer in the British Army, suggested giving Indians blankets infected with smallpox, a vicious policy that institutionalized what had begun as a tragic side effect of mingling people with diverse backgrounds and medical histories.

POLITICS & POWER	GEOGRAPHY & ENVIRONMENT	CULTURE & RELIGION
1580s SPAIN conquers Argentina. Buenos Aires, once abandoned, is now resettled. **ca 1581** THE PORTUGUESE CROWN is annexed to the Spanish crown in the reign of Philip II. Philip's political struggles against the Dutch in Europe lead to clashes between the Portuguese and Dutch in Brazil. **1584** SIR WALTER RALEIGH sends an expedition to scout the North American Atlantic coastal area. They claim it for England and name it Virginia in honor of Queen Elizabeth I.	**1578** SIR FRANCIS DRAKE sails up the west coast of North America to the area of Vancouver. He claims the land for England. **1585** SIR RICHARD GRENVILLE plants 108 colonists at Roanoke Island, where they found the "city of Raleigh." Sir Francis Drake removes the colonists the next year. **1587** JOHN WHITE brings 177 colonists, including women and children, to Roanoke Island. He returns to England for supplies.	**1580s** THE SPANISH CROWN depends on missionaries and the Catholic Church to bring the Indian peoples under Spanish control. Missionaries cost less than soldiers, and their impact is longer lasting. **1587** MANTEO, a Roanoke Indian, converts to Christianity.
1576 RUDOLF II becomes Holy Roman Emperor. He will reign until 1612. **1579-1580** THE UNION OF UTRECHT allies seven northern provinces of the Low Countries against Spain. They later form the Netherlands. **1588** THE SPANISH ARMADA battles the English and is defeated; Spanish power declines.	**1577-1580** FRANCIS DRAKE of England circumnavigates the globe.	**1575** THE UNIVERSITY OF LEIDEN is founded. **1576** JAMES BURBAGE, the father of actor Richard Burbage, builds the first public theater in London. **1577** EL GRECO begins painting his most important works; this period continues until the 1590s. **1580-1581** EDMUND CAMPION starts a Jesuit mission in England. He is quickly arrested, tried for treason, and executed. **1582** THE UNIVERSITY OF EDINBURGH is founded.
1578 MOROCCAN SULTAN ABD AL MALIK defeats the invading Portuguese forces of King Sebastian and deposed Sultan al Mutawakkil in the Battle of the Three Kings. **1588** SHAH ABBAS becomes ruler of the Safavid Empire. He begins rebuilding and enlarging Isfahan and reforms the Persian military and government.		**ca 1570** THE KABALISTIC SCHOOL in Safed started under Moses ben Jacob and Isaac ben Solomon Luria is now at its height. **ca 1582** THE FIRST VOLUME of *Shahinshahname* is composed. It describes important events in the reign of Ottoman sultan Murad III, particularly the circumcision festivities of his son Mehmed.
1581 RUSSIA launches its occupation of Siberia. **1585** HIDEYOSHI carries out a survey to establish control over the Japanese economy.	**1584** THE DUTCH establish a trading post in Arkangel'sk (Archangel), Russia.	**1580s** MATTEO RICCI brings Jesuit missionaries to China. **1584** THE CHINESE define their tempered musical scale.

CONNECTIONS

Queen Versus Queen

Mary, Queen of Scots (1542-1587), only child of James V, was raised a Roman Catholic in France and returned to rule Scotland in 1561. An accomplished, educated woman, she nevertheless badly misjudged Scottish affairs and the power of the nobility. She made two unpopular marriages in succession, alienating powerful nobles and the Presbyterian populace and leading to a civil rebellion that left her faction defeated. Imprisoned in England for 19 years, Mary became the focus of several Catholic plots against Queen Elizabeth I, who finally had her tried for treason and beheaded in 1587. Mary's son, James, inherited the English throne upon Elizabeth's death.

SCIENCE & TECHNOLOGY

1585 THE FIRST VERIFIED SHIPMENTS of chocolate from Mexico are sent to Europe.

1581 ITALIAN GALILEO GALILEI investigates the properties of the pendulum. In 1589 he is appointed to teach mathematics at the University of Pisa.

1582 POPE GREGORY XIII adjusts the Julian Calendar to reflect a more correct year length. The Gregorian Calendar is quickly accepted in Catholic countries, but more gradually throughout Protestant Europe.

1589 WILLIAM LEE invents the first English knitting machinery.

1577-1580 THE ASTRONOMER TAQI AL-DIN IBN MA'RUF founds the Istanbul observatory of Galatu. Using advanced instruments, he corrects astronomical tables.

PEOPLE & SOCIETY

1584 WANCHESE AND MANTEO, Indians from Roanoke Island, sail to England with Sir Richard Grenville.

1586 BRITISH PRIVATEER Sir Francis Drake attacks the Spanish settlement of St. Augustine and burns it to the ground.

1583 LIFE INSURANCE POLICIES are first issued in London.

1589 THE FRENCH COURT begins using forks as eating implements.

1582 MALI'S SONGHAI KINGDOM enters a turbulent period upon the death of its ruler Askia Daoud.

1589 THE OTTOMAN JANISSARIES mutiny over inadequate pay.

1581 THE SINGLE-WHIP TAX SYSTEM is established in Ming China; silver is used as a value base for the monetary system.

1588 UNDER A REORGANIZED JAPANESE SOCIETY, only samurai are privileged to carry weapons.

THE ARMADA'S LAST STAND

BY THE LATE 1500S, Spain was facing a growing challenge to its trade routes with the New World. English merchantmen were making their own voyages to America, and Spanish sanctions provoked costly reprisals from the English corsair Francis Drake. King Philip II become exasperated with these provocations and with English anti-Catholic politics. Supported by the pope, he planned to defeat England using a fleet of 130 ships carrying 30,000 men against the English navy, adding an invasion army of 30,000 men under the Duke of Parma from across the Channel.

For her part, Queen Elizabeth of England authorized Drake to conduct a series of preemptive raids on the Spanish preparations. Philip's armada put to sea in May of 1588 and sailed into English waters in July. The English met them with a comparable number of warships and armed merchantmen commanded by Lord Howard. Winning engagements off Portsmouth, Plymouth, and the Isle of Wight, the English used superior maneuvering, gunnery, and fire ships to harry the Spanish along the length of the English Channel as they made for the French coast.

Parma's army never had to confront an invasion. Unfavorable winds and an English blockade at Calais forced the Spanish to retreat by sailing completely around the British Isles. Water and food supplies ran out and storms wrecked most of the remaining fleet. Survivors who struggled ashore were slaughtered.

The consequences were momentous. Although the Spanish mounted further attacks, their reputation of invincibility had been shattered while the English began their ascent as a major sea power. The outcome stimulated naval technology, secured the Protestant Reformation in England, and broke the Spanish and Portuguese monopoly on world trade. As Spanish power waned, the English, French, and Dutch advanced their own interests in the New World.

POLITICS & POWER

1598 AUTHORITIES IN MEXICO CITY send Juan de Oñate with hundreds of people to colonize the area north of El Paso.

1598 THE SPANISH enslave the Indians of the pueblos.

1598 THE EDICT OF NANTES grants civil as well as religious liberties to French Protestants.

1603 QUEEN ELIZABETH of England dies, leaving her throne to James VI of Scotland. He will reign as James I.

1603 JAMES I orders Sir Walter Raleigh, fashionable favorite of Queen Elizabeth I, arrested for treason and imprisoned in the Tower of London, signaling a new climate at the English court.

1591 MOROCCANS conquer the Songhai kingdom. Songhai's subject states break away.

▶ **1598 ISFAHAN** becomes the capital of the Safavid Empire in Persia.

1600s THE OROMO of Ethiopia expand and raid southward.

1591-1592 TOYOTOMI HIDEYOSHI completes the unification of Japan and begins successive invasions of Korea.

1595 EMPEROR AKBAR of India conquers Afghanistan.

1600 IEYASU, founder of the Tokugawa shogunate, defeats rival daimyo in the Battle of Sekigahara to become undisputed ruler of Japan.

1603 EDO (TOKYO) serves as the seat of government under the Tokugawa shogunate.

GEOGRAPHY & ENVIRONMENT

1590 JOHN WHITE, returning to Roanoke Island with supplies, finds it deserted.

1595 SIR WALTER RALEIGH leads an expedition that penetrates 300 miles up the Orinoco River in Venezuela.

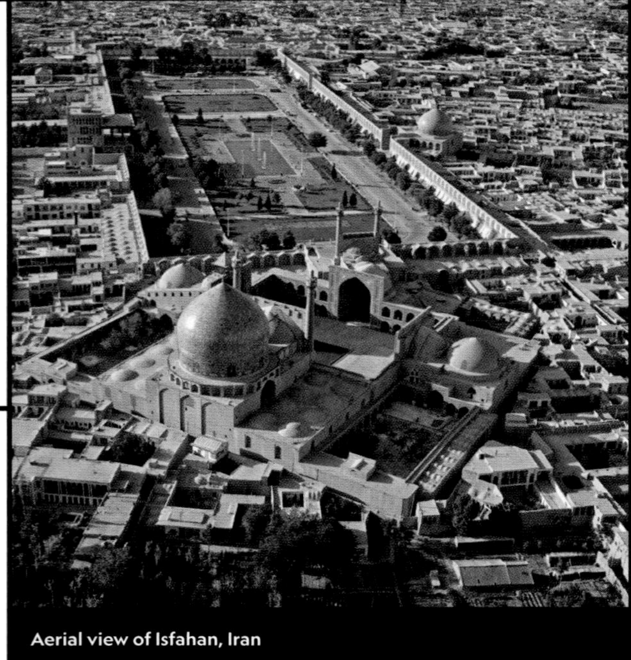

Aerial view of Isfahan, Iran

ca 1592 PORTUGUESE TRADERS settle in Mombasa.

1592 SIR JAMES LANCASTER sails around the Malay Peninsula in the Indian Ocean.

1602 JAPAN invites Spain to conduct trade in the country.

1604 THE COSSACKS found a settlement at Tomsk in Siberia.

CULTURE & RELIGION

1595 THE INQUISITION condemns many conversos (converted Jews) to death at a public sentencing in Mexico City.

1600s FRANCISCAN MISSIONARIES in Florida and New Mexico teach Catholic doctrine and liturgy to Indians, encouraging European culture in dress, food, and farming practices.

1591 WILLIAM SHAKESPEARE'S CAREER as a London playwright begins. After 1593, he produces a new work almost every year.

1593 HENRY IV of France converts to Catholicism. In later years, he reconciles his differences with the pope to end the French religious wars.

1599 THE GLOBE THEATRE is built in London.

1602 PERSIAN PORTRAIT ARTIST Riza yi-Abbasi begins his career as a miniaturist.

1592 THE CHINESE NOVEL *JOURNEY TO THE WEST* is published, describing the pilgrimage of a monk in search of Buddhist scriptures.

1600 TUNG CH'I-CH'ANG, famous artist, critic and scholar, works in China.

1600s STATUE BUILDING ON EASTER ISLAND dies out. Incomplete statues are left in place.

1601 MATTEO RICCI, Italian Jesuit missionary, settles in Beijing.

SCIENCE & TECHNOLOGY

1600 **SYSTEMIC PLANTATION SLAVERY** is well established in Brazil. Slaves learn to manage production of export sugar in factories.

1592 **SAWS** powered by windmills are used in Holland.

1592 **DOMENICO FONTANA** discovers the ruins of the Roman city of Pompeii.

1595 **GERARDUS MERCATOR'S ATLAS** is published.

1600 **TYCHO BRAHE AND JOHANNES KEPLER** begin working together at Brahe's observatory near Prague.

ca 1600s **TOBACCO** is introduced into the Ottoman Empire.

ca 1591 **KOREAN COMMANDER** Yi Sun-shin develops the *kobuson,* or turtle ship, thought to have been the first ironclad battleship in history.

PEOPLE & SOCIETY

1600 **THE POPULATION OF THE AMERICAS** begins to show evidence of a century of intermingled peoples. There are many children of mixed indigenous and European blood, especially in Latin America.

1600s **RUNAWAY SLAVES** begin to form *quilombos,* free communities, in remote areas of Brazil.

1601 **HARSH CONDITIONS** in the New Mexico colony under conquistador Juan de Oñate compel many colonists to abandon the settlement.

1593 **ITALIAN PHILOSOPHER GIORDANO BRUNO,** supporter of Copernicus, is imprisoned by the Vatican. He is executed in 1600.

1597-1598 **THE ELIZABETHAN POOR LAWS** are enacted, providing relief for indigent children and the elderly and employment for able-bodied people in parish workhouses. In effect, these laws set up an early social welfare system.

1600s **THE ENGLISH EAST INDIA COMPANY,** the French East India Company, and the Dutch VOC all trade avidly with the Safavid Empire.

THE EMERGENCE OF RUSSIA

IN 1480 IVAN III, Grand Duke of Moscow, freed Muscovy from the Golden Horde of Tatars that had defeated the city-states of Rus in the mid-1200s and exacted heavy tribute from Russian princes ever since. Ivan IV, called Ivan the Terrible, consolidated Ivan the Great's gains and formally took the title of tsar. Ruthless and unpredictable, he conquered even more land.

In the mid-1500s Russians started to move east. Cossacks sailed north-flowing rivers across the continent, attacking and spreading fear as they created settlements along the way, eventually reaching the Pacific Ocean.

Civil conflicts and foreign invasions, called "the time of troubles," followed until Romanov rule began in the early 17th century. Peter I (the Great) became tsar in 1682, reforming and reorganizing the government, adopting the Gregorian calendar, building bridges, roads, canals, and factories, and bringing European craftsman and doctors to Russia. Peter's reign linked Russia's future to the nations of Europe.

This map documents the expansion of Russia from a small principality in 1462 to a major power in 1796.

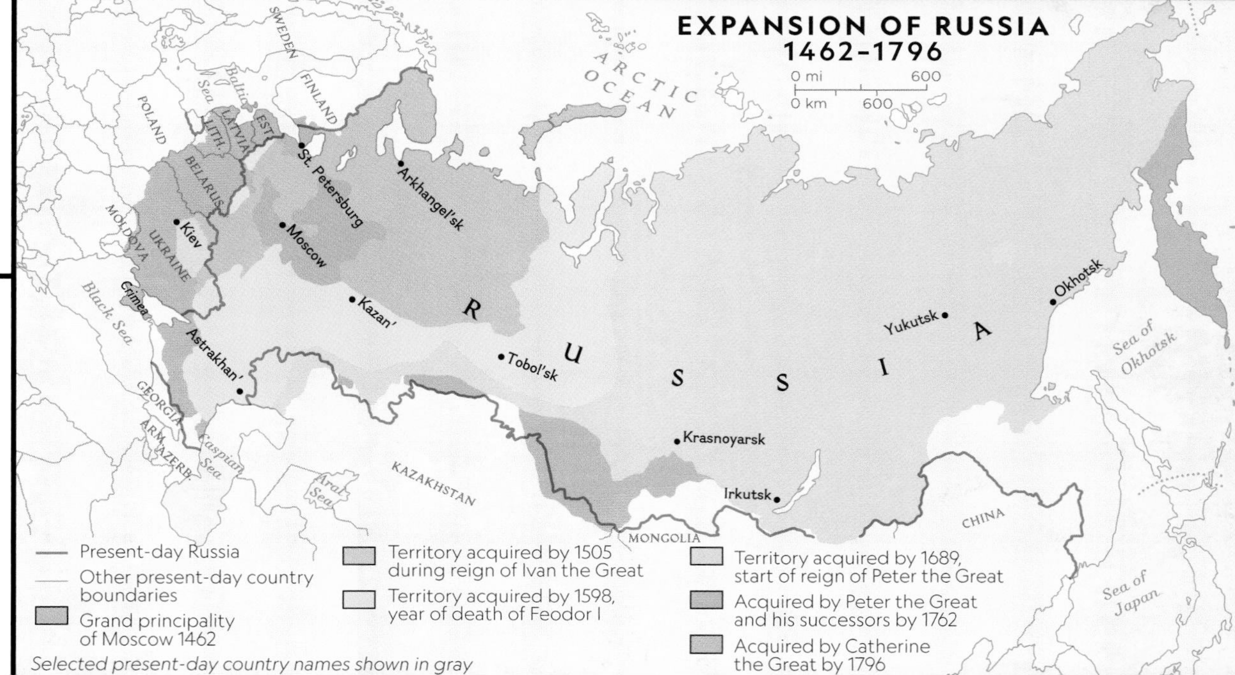

POLITICS & POWER	GEOGRAPHY & ENVIRONMENT	CULTURE & RELIGION
ca 1607 APPROXIMATELY 30 ALGONQUIN TRIBES unite to form a confedercy led by Wahunsenacawh, chief of the Powhatan. **1615 SAMUEL DE CHAMPLAIN** attacks the Oneida peoples of the Iroquois Confederacy. **1619 THE FIRST VIRGINIA COLONIAL ASSEMBLY** meets.	**1608 FRENCHMEN SAMUEL DE CHAMPLAIN** establishes a trading fort that will become Quebec. **1610 THE CITY OF SANTA FE** is founded. **1616 WILLIAM BAFFIN,** searching for a northwest passage to China through Canada, discovers Baffin's Bay. **1616 SIR WALTER RALEIGH** is released from prison to lead an expedition in search of El Dorado. William Shakespeare	**1607 LEADING COLONIAL PAINTER** Baltasar de Echave Orio paints "The Martyrdom of Saint Ponciano," considered among the best of his works he creates for churches throughout New Spain. **1612 FRANCISCO DE PAREJO'S** Castilian-Timucuan catechism is published. It is the first translation of a Native American language.
1605 ENGLISH CATHOLIC CONSPIRATORS, including Guy Fawkes, set explosives in Westminster, but their Gunpowder Plot is discovered. **1608 THE O'DOHERTY REBELLION** in Ireland against the English authorities collapses. **1611 KING JAMES I** discontinues a session of Parliament; disagreements between the kings and Parliament will continue for the next 50 years. **1613 MICHAEL ROMANOV** is chosen tsar of Russia. His descendants will rule until 1917.		◀ **1605-1612 SHAKESPEARE** writes his masterpieces *King Lear, Macbeth, The Winter's Tale,* and *The Tempest.* **1605-1615 MIGUEL DE CERVANTES SAAVEDRA** publishes *Don Quixote* in two installments. **1610 JEANNE DE CHANTAL** and Francis de Sales found the Order of the Visitation. **1611 A NEW VERSION OF THE BIBLE** is published in English, authorized and patronized by King James I. **1612 HERETICS** are burned in England by the authorities for the last time.
1600s THE LUBA-LUNDA PEOPLES move into northern Zambia. Torwa and Mutapa grow as prominent Shona states on the Zimbabwe plateau. **1606 THE OTTOMANS** sign the Peace of Zsitvatorok with the Habsburgs, acknowledging another ruler's equal status.	**1600s THE TIMAR SYSTEM** of landholders supplying military forces, especially cavalry, to the Ottomans declines. Tax farming, as practiced in France, eventually replaces it.	**1609-1615 THE BLUE MOSQUE,** an enormous, elaborate shrine in Constantinople, is built under Sultan Ahmet I. **1611-1616 THE SHAH MOSQUE** is constructed in Isfahan, in modern-day Iran. It becomes known for its towering 170-foot-high domed chamber and vivid polychromatic tiles.
1605 MUGHAL EMPEROR JAHANGIR becomes ruler of India. Intellectual and tolerant, he follows both the teachings of Muslim saints and those of the Hindu yogis. **1612 SAFAVIDS** retake Azerbaijan and parts of the Caucasus. The border is restored to its 1555 position. **1615 TOKUGAWA IEYASU** issues Codes of the Military Houses to regulate lines of the samurai, or warrior class.	**1617 MUGHAL EMPEROR JAHANGIR** grants Sir Thomas Roe the right to maintain trade warehouses (factories) in port cities. This is the start of the English trading advantage in India.	**1609 THE ILLUSTRATED ENCYCLOPEDIA** *San-ts'ai t'u-hui* is published in China.

SCIENCE & TECHNOLOGY	PEOPLE & SOCIETY
1607 THE FIRST AMERICAN SHIP is built, in Sagadahoc, Maine. **1612** VIRGINIA COLONISTS first grow tobacco as a commercial crop. **1619** VIRGINIA COLONISTS build the Falling Creek ironworks. It is later destroyed during conflicts between the colonists and the Powhatan. **1620** HISPANIC ATLANTIC TRADE begins to decline in both volume and value.	**1607** ENGLISHMEN under the command of Capt. John Smith build a small settlement on the James River in Virginia. **1613** POCAHONTAS, daughter of the Powhatan chief, intercedes in favor of John Smith, captured during a dispute. **1616** POCAHONTAS sails for England with her English husband, John Rolfe. She dies in 1617. **1619** THE FIRST SHIPLOAD of African slaves reaches the Virginia colony, where indentured servants provide much of the labor.
1609 THOMAS HARRIOT discovers sunspots. **1610** GALILEO GALILEI uses a telescope he has built to observe the satellites of Jupiter. **1614** SCOTTISH MATHEMATICIAN John Napier publishes tables of logarithms, arithmetical functions he invented. **1618-1619** ENGLISH PHYSICIAN William Harvey describes the circulation of the blood. **1618-1621** JOHANNES KEPLER, German astronomer, publishes *Harmonies of the World* (which contains Kepler's third law) and *Epitome of Copernican Astronomy.*	**1607** THE EARLS OF TYRONE AND TYRCONNELL, with some family friends, abruptly flee Ireland in an event known as the "Flight of the Earls."
1600s OTTOMAN MEDICINE incorporates European medical science published by followers of German-Swiss physician Paracelsus.	
1606 *JIHE YUANBEN,* a Chinese edition of Euclid's *Elements* (a compilation of geometrical knowledge), is published.	

THE NORTHWEST PASSAGE

WHEN EUROPEANS understood that Columbus had not reached Asia, efforts began to find a sea route through the American landmass to China. Magellan found a way to the Pacific, but only by sailing to the stormy southernmost tip of South America. Explorers hoped to find an easier route in the north.

As early as 1497, England's King Henry VII directed John Cabot to seek this Northwest Passage across the Arctic Ocean north of Canada. Many explorers would try and fail: Jacques Cartier, Francis Drake, Martin Frobisher, James Cook, and William Baffin. Humphrey Gilbert drowned in the attempt in 1583. Henry Hudson was set adrift by his mutinous crew in 1611 when they realized that Hudson Bay was an ice-bound trap. John Franklin and 129 men vanished on two ships in 1845. Robert McClure was locked in the ice for two winters, then sledged overland to complete the passage in 1854. These expeditions were not total losses—Europeans established trade with Indians and claimed the rich Mississippi River Valley.

A passage did exist, threaded through the Arctic islands, but it was so challenging that it would be hundreds of years before it was transited. Thick pack ice chokes the sea throughout most of the year; the winds and water are lethally cold; visibility vanishes in whiteouts, fog, and arctic darkness; and a compass is useless so close to the magnetic pole.

The passage was finally negotiated in 1906 by Roald Amundsen, later the first person to reach the South Pole. More recently, the mammoth icebreaker *Manhattan* completed the trip in two weeks, smashing through 650 miles of pack ice in 1969.

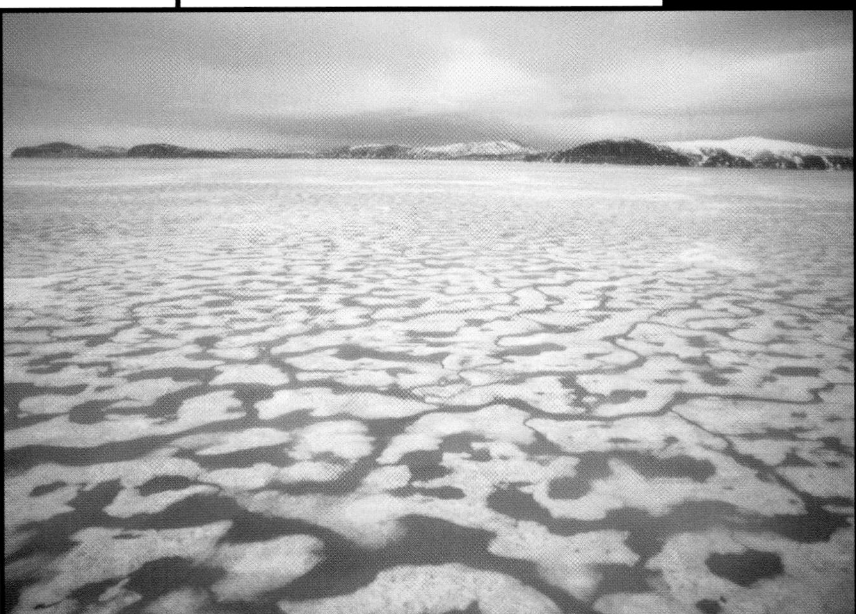

Thawing sea ice on Baffin Bay near Nunavut, Canada

POLITICS & POWER

1621 THE DUTCH WEST INDIA COMPANY is founded.

1622 THE POWHATAN WAR breaks out, leading to 14 years of intermittent warfare by Powhatans against settlements around the Chesapeake Bay and Virginia.

1622 JAMES I is the first king to reign over both England and Scotland.

1624 CARDINAL RICHELIEU becomes first minister in France.

1625 JAMES I dies; his son Charles I becomes king of England.

1629 CHARLES I dissolves the English Parliament. No Parliament will now be held in England until 1640.

1630s SWEDEN becomes heavily involved in the Thirty Years' War.

1622 OTTOMAN SULTAN OSMAN II is deposed and assassinated and succeeded by Murad IV (1623-1640).

ca 1625 THE KINGDOM OF DAHOMEY is established.

1631 ENGLISH TRADING POSTS are established on the Gold Coast (Ghana). The Dutch expel the Portuguese from the Gold Coast.

ca 1620 KHMER KING CHEY CHETTHA II forges an alliance with the Vietnamese.

1632 MUGHAL ARMIES drive the Portuguese out of Bengal.

GEOGRAPHY & ENVIRONMENT

1626 THE DUTCH barter for rights to Manhattan Island.

1630 A LARGE GROUP OF ENGLISH PURITANS sets up a colony at Massachusetts Bay.

1632 ENGLISH KING CHARLES I issues a charter to Cecilius Calvert, who founds a colony near the Chesapeake Bay. It is called Maryland in honor of Charles's consort, Queen Henrietta Maria.

1634 JEAN NICOLET of France explores Wisconsin and Green Bay.

1626 ENGLISH FENS are first drained for farmland.

ca 1620 THE DUTCH establish a city, Batavia, on the island of Java.

1624 THE DUTCH establish trading posts on the coast of Taiwan.

1626 A POWERFUL EARTHQUAKE shakes Beijing.

1633 THE ENGLISH establish a trading post in Bengal.

CULTURE & RELIGION

1630 JOHN WINTHROP, leader of the Puritan colonists at Massachusetts Bay, inspires his people with a sermon on the purpose of their enterprise: to set an example of community to the world, to be "a city on a hill."

1630s FRENCH MISSIONARIES begin work among the Wyandot people, who they call the Huron.

1632 JOHN ELIOT begins establishing villages of Christian Indian converts in New England; he preaches in Algonquian.

1627 HEINRICH SCHÜTZ writes the first German opera, *Dafne*.

1632 DUTCH PAINTER REMBRANDT VAN RIJN paints "The Anatomy Lesson of Dr. Nicolaes Tulp," one of his best-known group portraits.

1633 JUDITH LEYSTER, Dutch painter, becomes the only female member of the Haarlem Painters' Guild.

1633 VINCENT DE PAUL founds the religious Order of the Sisters of Charity.

1632-1635 MURAD IV'S MORALITY CAMPAIGN leads to a ban on tobacco and coffee and the closure of coffeehouses.

1629 THE TOKUGAWA SHOGUNATE forbids women to perform in Kabuki theater because of its origins in prostitution.

ca 1630 LANDSCAPE PAINTER Dong Qichang is active in Ming China.

WHAT LIFE WAS LIKE

In Fabulous Isfahan

When Shah Abbas (1587-1629) of Persia rebuilt Isfahan, south of Tehran in present-day Iran, he created one of the most beautiful cities of its time. At its center was a vast courtyard anchored by mosques and lofty ceremonial gates, and rimmed with two-story buildings ornamented by recessed arches. Wide, tree-shaded avenues featuring fountains and watercourses gave access to the city, which earned lavish praise from visitors. In the 1660s Isfahan boasted 162 mosques, 48 schools, 273 bath houses, and nearly 2,000 hostels. Much of the city was destroyed when Ghilzai Afghans invaded in 1722.

SCIENCE & TECHNOLOGY

1620s THE DUTCH build the first sawmill in the New Amsterdam colony.

1629 SALEM, MASSACHUSETTS, imports shipwrights to establish a shipbuilding center.

1620 CORNELIS DREBBEL, a Dutchman living in England, invents a human-powered submarine. It travels 12 to 15 feet below the water, providing its sailors air through snorkel tubes.

1622 WILLIAM OUGHTRED of England invents a slide rule for making calculations.

1629 GIOVANNI BRANCA invents a design for a steam turbine.

ca 1631 MIR DAMED, Iranian philosopher and metaphysician, dies.

1633 THE ENGLISH open their first factory in Bengal, India.

1621 A TREATISE ON MILITARY ARTS, *Wubei Zhi*, is published in China.

PEOPLE & SOCIETY

1621 SAMOSET, TISQANTUM, AND MASSASOIT meet *Mayflower* voyagers on the coast near Cape Cod.

1623 MYLES STANDISH kills Massachusetts Indian leader Witawanet.

1626 FRANCE institutes the death penalty for duelists who kill their opponents.

1633 GALILEO GALILEI is convicted of teaching the Copernican doctrine.

1633-1637 "TULIP MANIA" rages in the Netherlands.

1623 DEPOSED PROVINCIAL GOVERNOR Abaza Mehmed Pasha leads a rebellion against the Ottoman bureaucracy.

1625 INFLATION reaches its high point in the Ottoman Empire.

ca 1620 DONGLIN ACADEMY achieves its peak of influence in Ming politics.

1624-1627 EUNUCH WEI ZHONGXIAN reaches his highest position at the Ming court.

THE WARRIOR QUEEN OF NDONGO

SEEKING MINERAL WEALTH, salt deposits, and slaves in the mid-1500s, the Portuguese moved into Ndongo, a federation of villages on the Lunda plateau of southwest Africa. The land was held by the Mbundu people under their ruler, known as the *ngola*. Dealings with the ngolas broke down over time under Portugal's increasing demand for slaves, and finally in 1621 the ngola sent his sister, Nzinga, to parlay on his behalf with the Portuguese.

A confident and clever woman, Nzinga entered the council chamber to find only one seat, which was occupied by the Portuguese governor. She motioned an attendant down on hands and knees, creating a living throne for herself, and proceeded to negotiate very favorable terms for the Mbundu. She forged a special connection to the Europeans by requesting Christian baptism, with the governor himself serving as her godfather.

By 1624 relations had once again deteriorated. Queen Nzinga organized an army, fought the Portuguese, and withdrew into the interior. She cast off Christianity to ally with the fierce Jaga raiders. A gifted guerrilla strategist, she took the hill country of Matamba as a Mbundu stronghold, welcomed runaway slaves to her ranks, and gave special inducements to recruit renegades from the Portuguese forces. She established a corps of *kilombo*, men who gave up ties to family and lived together in militia groups, totally dedicated to her army. Queen Nzinga led warriors herself until she was over 60, destroying the slave trade and diverting Portuguese energy into military forays that laid waste to the countryside. Only after her death in 1663 were the Portuguese finally able to penetrate the southwest interior, securing the country they called Angola until 1975.

POLITICS & POWER

1638 NEW SWEDEN (Delaware) is established on the Delaware River.

1639 THE FUNDAMENTAL ORDERS of Connecticut are written for settlers on the Connecticut River.

1640s THE SEIGNEURAL LANDHOLDING SYSTEM controls settlement in New France. Jesuit missionaries at Huronia extend the French influence throughout Indian tribes.

1641-1679 NEW HAMPSHIRE COLONY comes under the administration of Massachusetts

1640 FREDERICK WILLIAM, the Great Elector, becomes the elector of Brandenburg. He is influential in European politics until 1688.

1641 A CATHOLIC REBELLION breaks out in Ireland and Protestants are massacred in Ulster.

1648 THE PEACE OF WESTPHALIA concludes the Thirty Years' War. The period of the Frondes (rebellions against royal authority) begins in France and lasts until 1653.

1645 THE CRETAN WAR begins between the Ottomans and Venetians for possession of Crete.

1648 OTTOMAN MEHMED IV becomes sultan at the age of six.

1644 THE MANCHUS invade from the north, overthrow the Ming ruler, and conquer China. They establish the Qing dynasty.

1645 THE MANCHUS massacre the population in the Chinese city of Yangzhou.

GEOGRAPHY & ENVIRONMENT

Anne Hutchinson

1641-1648 THE DUTCH capture Angola from the Portuguese, before surrendering to Brazilians seeking to restore their supply of slave labor.

1635 RAJASINHA II of Ceylon requests assistance from the Dutch fleet in reclaiming territory from the Portugese.

1637 ENGLISH TRADERS set up a station in Canton (Guangzhou).

1638 THE DUTCH settle in Mauritius.

1639 COSSACKS advance to the Pacific coast.

1639 THE ENGLISH settle in Madras, India.

1642 ABEL TASMAN, Dutch navigator, sails along the coast of Australia, discovering Tasmania, New Zealand, New Guinea, and the Fiji Islands.

CULTURE & RELIGION

1636 ROGER WILLIAMS, expelled from Massachusetts Bay Colony for advocating religious freedom, founds a colony in Rhode Island.

1636 HARVARD COLLEGE is founded in Massachusetts

◀ **1638 ANNE HUTCHINSON,** a Puritan spiritual leader who defied restrictive gender roles, is banished from Massachusetts Bay Colony and moves to Rhode Island.

1640 THE BAY PSALM BOOK is the first book published in the English colonies.

1637 THE INTRODUCTION OF A NEW PRAYER BOOK in Scotland incites violence, precipitating the Covenanter rebellion against state authority.

1641 FRENCH PHILOSOPHER RENÉ DESCARTES writes *Meditations.*

1642 PURITAN INFLUENCE in England closes the theaters of London.

1642 MOLIÈRE founds a theater group in Paris that eventually evolves into the Comedie Française.

1642-1666 SHAH ABBAS II reigns in Persia (Iran), the last great builder and arts patron of the Safavid dynasty. After his death, clerics gain importance in politics and culture.

1637-1638 THE SHIMABARA REBELLION, fueled by Christian converts and socioeconomic ills, leads to the expulsion of the Portuguese and the banning of Christianity in Japan.

1645 THE QING GOVERNMENT forces the Han Chinese to wear the queue—a shaved head with single braid behind.

SCIENCE & TECHNOLOGY

1639 THE FIRST PRINTING PRESS is set up in North America.

1644 THE FIRST IRON FURNACE in the British colonies is built at Braintree, Massachusetts.

1637 RENÉ DESCARTES publishes *La Géométrie,* a work on analytical geometry.

1639 QUININE, an Indian remedy derived from South American tree bark, is first used as a medication against fever in Europe.

1639 ENGLISH ASTRONOMER Jeremiah Horrocks predicts and observes a transit of Venus.

1642 BLAISE PASCAL, French philosopher, invents an adding machine.

1637 *TIANGONG KAIWU* is published, an encyclopedia of Chinese technology.

▶ **1644** THE CHINESE adopt a Western calendar, introduced by the Jesuits.

PEOPLE & SOCIETY

1637 THE ENGLISH begin restricting immigration to their colonies in the Americas.

1645-1654 BRAZILIANS attack the Dutch settlers and finally force the Dutch from colonial Brazil.

1647 MASSACHUSETTS establishes the first public school system in America.

1635 A POSTAL SERVICE unites London and Edinburgh.

1637 RENÉ DESCARTES writes in *Discourses on Method,* "I think, therefore I am."

1642-1649 THE ENGLISH CIVIL WAR rages between armed supporters of Parliamentarians, led by Oliver Cromwell, and supporters of Charles I. The conflict ends with the execution of the king.

1642-1674 KROTOA, OR EVA, a Khoekhoen woman, translates for the Dutch. Her life shows the complexity of the emerging South African community.

A German Jesuit missionary to China

IRELAND INVADED

THE KINGS OF IRELAND were subdued by a Norman invasion in the 12th century. From then on, the incremental shift of land and power from the native Gaelic lords into the hands of foreign overlords fueled resistance that continues in Irish affairs today. To replace the ancient system of elected clan chiefs with hereditary barons answerable to the king, the Normans created earls who ruled Ireland throughout the Plantagenet era, separating the Gaelic population from political affairs. The Tudors later began the wholesale system of plantations—granting Irish land to English landholders to develop and administer in the English manner.

When the English church split from Rome, further divisions appeared. The Catholic Counter-Reformation encouraged Irish clergy to spread hostility against the English. In 1601 the pope supported a Spanish invasion of Ireland that England defeated at great cost. Royal favors to English landlords caused Catholics in the northern province of Ulster to emigrate; many Presbyterian Scots moved there as tenants. Local resentment boiled over in a bloody uprising in 1641 where thousands of colonists were killed.

Incursions of the Parliamentary and royalist forces during the English civil war traumatized Ireland. The victorious Cromwell's soldiers were granted land there and persecuted Catholics. After 1660 Catholics were forbidden to live in towns, all municipal power passed to Protestants, and Catholics claimed a mere 22 percent of Irish land.

By the early 1700s the Test Act prevented Catholics from holding office, the British House of Lords became the supreme court for Irish legal matters, and Irish Catholics owned only 14 percent of their homeland. This relentless genocide by bureaucracy, depriving the Irish of political and economic resources, ensured grievances that were soon emboldened by revolutionary examples in America and France.

POLITICS & POWER

1651-1652 THE DUTCH incite Mohawks to attack the Swedish-allied Susquehannocks.

1663 CHARLES II of England issues land grants for settlements in the Carolina colony.

1664 THE ENGLISH annex New Netherland. The area is renamed New York.

1653 THE ENGLISH AND DUTCH begin sporadic fighting after the English Navigation Act (1651) restricts foreign trade.

1653 OLIVER CROMWELL becomes Lord Protector of the English Commonwealth. He reorganizes England into districts ruled by military governors.

1661 LOUIS XIV reasserts lawful royal government in France.

1650 VENETIANS blockade the Dardanelles.

1654 MEHMED KOPRULI, Ottoman grand vizier, breaks the Venetian blockade.

1656-1702 THE KOPRULI FAMILY of grand viziers reforms the Ottoman state.

1659 THE DUTCH defeat the Khoekhoen in a fight over territory in southern Africa.

1665 AFTER THE PORTUGUESE WIN THE BATTLE OF MBWILA, Kongo no longer functions as a unified kingdom.

1656 THE DUTCH take Colombo (Ceylon) from the Portuguese.

1661 KANGXI becomes emperor of China; his 61-year reign is one of prosperity and stability.

1661 THE QING order an evacuation of the Chinese coast in response to pirate attacks. It will continue for more than 20 years.

GEOGRAPHY & ENVIRONMENT

ca 1650 INDIGO becomes one of the most important exports of Mexico and Cental America.

1652 THE DUTCH EAST INDIA COMPANY establishes a station near the Cape of Good Hope.

1664 THE DUTCH allow individual farmers to plant at the Cape of Good Hope.

1660s THE MUGHAL EMPIRE attains its widest extent in the Indian subcontinent.

1668 THE ENGLISH EAST INDIA COMPANY controls Bombay.

CULTURE & RELIGION

1657 JEWS in New Netherland (later New York) are granted the rights of burghers (English citizens), but are not permitted to worship in public.

1661 JOHN ELIOT translates the Bible into Algonquian.

1670s MISSIONARIES begin losing power over Pueblo peoples, unable to protect them from Apache raids, recurrent drought, or epidemic disease. Sexual exploitation of Pueblo women by missionaries also contributes to discontent.

1651 PHILOSOPHER THOMAS HOBBES publishes *Leviathan,* a defense of monarchy and political absolutism.

1656 BRITISH PLAYWRIGHT William Davenant stages the first opera in London.

1660 THE FIRST FEMALE PLAYERS appear on stages in England. German theatrical companies follow suit later in the decade.

1660 SAMUEL PEPYS of London begins writing his famous diary.

1650 MUSLIMS begin settling among the Fulani in West Africa.

1665 NATHAN OF GAZA proclaims Chabbetai Zevi the Jewish messiah, attracting many Jews, Christians, and Muslims as followers. Arrested for sedition, Zevi converts to Islam, as do many of his disciples, forming the Donme sect in Turkey.

1670s THE FULANI mount jihads against their non-Muslim neighbors in West Africa.

1600s NOH THEATER is officially cultivated by Japan's samurai class, whose high-ranking members are trained in Noh dancing and chanting.

1650 JESUIT MISSIONARY Adam Schall von Bell receives permission from Qing emperor Shunzhi to expand an earlier private chapel and create the first public Roman Catholic church in Beijing.

CONNECTIONS

The Jewish Diaspora

With the fall of the Roman Empire and the rise of Islam in the Middle East, the Jewish people dispersed: One group moved west into the Iberian Peninsula (the Sephardim); the other north into Germany and Eastern Europe (the Ashkenazi). During the Middle Ages, Jews retained a religious and cultural identity in spite of separation by studying the same teachings: the Torah (Hebrew scripture) and the Talmud—commentaries on the Torah. Expelled from Iberia in 1492, many Sephardim immigrated to England and Holland and formed the first Jewish communities in the Americas. Later, thousands of Ashkenazi joined them, fleeing recurrent waves of persecution in eastern Europe.

SCIENCE & TECHNOLOGY

1664 JOHN WINTHROP, JR., governor of Connecticut and talented amateur scientist, reports seeing the fifth moon of Jupiter through his telescope.

1651 ITALIAN ASTRONOMER Giovanni Riccioli publishes a map of the moon.

1654 FRENCH SCIENTISTS Blaise Pascal and Pierre de Fermat formulate a theory of probability.

1656 DUTCH SCIENTIST Christian Huygens discovers the rings of Saturn.

1662 KING CHARLES II charters the Royal Society of London to promote the sciences.

1662 ENGLISH CHEMIST Robert Boyle publishes a description of the relationship between the pressure and volume of a gas; this is known as Boyle's law.

Portrait of Emperor Kangxi in court dress inked onto a silk hanging

PEOPLE & SOCIETY

1650 PORTUGUESE JESUIT ANTONIO VIEIRA is renowned for his writings and sermons in Brazil.

1655 HOPI INDIAN JUAN CUNA, accused of idolatry, is burned to death by a Spanish priest.

1665 CALEB CHEESHATEMAUK attains a Bachelor of Arts degree at Harvard College. He is the first Indian college graduate.

1662 CHRISTOPHER WREN, professor of astronomy at Oxford, designs his first building.

1665 JEAN-BAPTIST COLBERT becomes controller general of finance for King Louis XIV of France. His subsequent economic reforms help make France the dominant power in Europe.

1667 MARGARET CAVENDISH speaks to the Royal Society of London but the members trivialize her ideas. No other woman will be a member until the mid-20th century.

1650s SLAVERY exists in the Dutch Cape colony. It will continue there until the 1830s. The Dutch obtain slaves from West Africa, then from Mozambique, Madagascar, Indonesia, and India.

1652 TARHONCU AHMED PASHA, Ottoman grand vizier, is the first to prepare a budget in advance of the fiscal year.

1652 OMAN intervenes in East African politics and trade, evicting Portuguese colonists at the behest of the local leaders.

◀ **1661 QING EMPEROR KANGXI** is interested in science, music, and poetry, and is a patron of Chinese scholarship. He reigns until 1722.

1662 KOXINGA (ZHENG CHENGGONG), who rebelled against the Manchus and successfully fought against them in Taiwan, dies.

Isaac Newton discovered that white light is composed of every color of the spectrum.

SIR ISAAC NEWTON

ISAAC NEWTON was born in 1642 to a humble Lincolnshire farming family.

He was a sickly baby and not expected to live. As a child, he proved inept at farm chores. Raised by his grandmother and encouraged by a teacher and his uncle, he entered Cambridge a year later than most students. It was only when the university was closed in 1665 due to plague that Newton had his annus mirabilis. In the course of about one year, at the age of 23, he formulated principles that would change science forever.

Newton sought precise mathematical principles by which Nature functioned. He examined the reaction of bodies to forces and proposed the fundamental laws of motion that are the basis of mechanics. He not only formulated the law of gravitation, but also developed a new mathematical method known as calculus to compute his findings.

Newton's work was an astounding demonstration of precise physical laws governing universal phenomena and the power of mathematics to provide testable predictions. He established the scientific method and provided the intellectual impetus that has driven our scientific development ever since.

THE SPLENDOR OF THE MUGHALS

From the early 1500s to the mid-1700s, Mughal emperors ruled an area that expanded from Kabul, Afghanistan, to modern-day Pakistan and Bangladesh in the east, and down across the Deccan to Calicut on the west coast of India. Though they were aggressive in war, it was the Mughals' talent for alliance with enemies that cemented their amazingly diverse empire.

The Mughal period in India is especially noted for flourishing arts, agriculture, economic development, and religious tolerance. The epitome of Mughal culture, wealth transmuted into beauty, is the glorious Taj Mahal, tomb of Shah Jahan's beloved wife. Constructed of marble that reflects changing tones of light throughout the day, the beauty and serenity of this monument are overwhelming. No one knows who designed the tomb, but it was completed between 1632 and 1643. The central dome with mausoleum beneath is 23 stories high, guarded at the corners by four minarets. Workmen from Persia and Central Asia created its intricate flower inlays of semiprecious stone, religious inscriptions, and lavish gardens.

The Mughal Empire began with Babur, a Central Asian Muslim descended from both the Turk Tamerlane and the Mongol Genghis Khan. Hindustan, ruled by Muslim sultans since the 1200s, was rumored to be a land of gems and gold, but poorly defended. Babur marched down from Afghanistan and took Delhi with artillery in 1526. The personable leader quickly established a kingdom that expanded and prospered under seven generations of his heirs.

Babur's grandson, Akbar (r. 1556-1605), ruled as a philosopher king. He founded cities across his land, attracting hundreds of architects, craftsmen, artists, poets, and merchants. In his new capital of Fatehpur Sikri near Agra, he built the Ibadakhana, or House of Worship, as a place for religious debate. Akbar himself often presided over the Hindus, Muslims, Sufis, Parsis, Jains, Jews, and Christians discussing their faiths there. To further intercultural understanding, he commissioned translations of Hindu epics into Persian. His personal library held 24,000 volumes, and classics of literature, philosophy, and history were read aloud to him throughout his day. Hired painters followed his campaigning armies, documenting the action. To gain the support of fierce Rajput warlords, Akbar married Rajput princesses, respected their Hindu faith, and installed their relatives in positions at court. He took Hindus into the civil service and abolished taxes levied on non-Muslims and pilgrims.

Akbar's son Jahangir's passion for art brought European and Chinese treasures into India. Jahangir (r. 1605-1627) built the pleasure gardens of Shalimar and Nishat in Kashmir, where streams ripple across pierced marble screens to create tinkling water music. His son Shah Jahan secured his throne through a bitter rebellion and died a prisoner of his own son, Aurangzeb. Religious and ethnic divisions splintered the empire under Aurangzeb, a strict and doctrinaire Muslim. Persians invaded from the north, the Rajput alliance fractured, and by the mid-1700s European militaries were seizing power in India.

Light and shadow paint the Taj Mahal at sunrise in Agra, India.

POLITICS & POWER

1675-1676 KING PHILIP'S WAR begins when Metacomet, called King Philip by the English, attacks English settlers after the execution of a Wampanoag tribesman. King Philip is killed.

1677 THE ENGLISH sign a treaty guaranteeing autonomy to the Pamunkey and Mattaponi of Virginia. This treaty is honored for the next 300 years.

▶ **1680 RELIGIOUS LEADER POPÉ** leads the Pueblo Revolt, an indigenous uprising that drives the Spaniards out of their settlements in New Mexico.

1674 JOHN III becomes king of Poland after victorious military campaigns against the Turks and Cossacks.

1675-1679 FREDERICK WILLIAM, Elector of Brandenburg, fights the Swedish in Germany.

1685 CHARLES II of England dies, succeeded by James II, known for Catholic sympathies.

1688 JAMES II is deposed in favor of his Protestant daughter Mary and her Dutch husband, Prince William of Orange, in the Glorious Revolution.

1673-1677 THE DUTCH AND THE KHOEKHOEN fight a second war. After a negotiated peace, the Khoekhoen cooperate with the Dutch.

1680-1690 ASANTE CLANS unify on the Gold Coast of West Africa.

1683 THE OTTOMANS besiege Vienna fruitlessly for the last time. They lose much European territory in a war that lasts until 1699.

1673 A REBELLION arises against the Qing; southern Chinese provinces break away from Qing control, and China is engulfed in the War of the Three Feudatories.

1683 THE QING occupy Taiwan and consolidate their conquest of China.

1689 THE TREATY OF NERCHINSK defines the border and trading rights between Russia and Qing domains. It is the first diplomatic agreement between China and a European power.

GEOGRAPHY & ENVIRONMENT

Taos Pueblo, center of a 1680 anti-Spanish revolt

1679 THE EARLIEST NAUTICAL ALMANAC is published in Paris.

1671-1672 OTTOMAN ADMINISTRATOR Eliya Chelebi writes *Travels,* a detailed chronicle of the geograpy, buildings, people, and legends he encountered during his extensive journeys throughout the Ottoman Empire.

1688 FRENCH HUGUENOTS come to settle in Cape Colony at the southern tip of Africa.

1674 THE FRENCH establish a trading station at Pondicherry, India.

1685 THE CHINESE reopen ports to European trade.

CULTURE & RELIGION

1680s JESUIT MISSIONARIES arrive in the Southwest.

1688 ALGONQUIN TRIBES ally with the French against the English and Iroquois in what is later called King William's war, an extension of wars of European alliances.

1670s CHRISTOPHER WREN begins his most active period as an architect. He designs more than 50 London churches and many other buildings, including St. Paul's, Christ Church, Trinity College, Cambridge, and Chelsea Hospital, London.

1670s PLAYWRIGHT APHRA BEHN is the first Englishwoman to make her living by writing.

1678 BRITISH AUTHOR JOHN BUNYAN, a Puritan, publishes the first part of *The Pilgrim's Progress.* The second part is published in 1684.

1684-1686 ETHIOPIAN EMPEROR Iyasu I arranges councils to reconcile opposing Christian religious forces.

1680 BASHO, the Japanese master of the haiku, writes his first poem in what will become his signature 17-syllable format.

1682 IHARA SAIKAKU writes *The Life of an Amorous Man,* an example of the literature of "the floating world" of Osaka and other urban centers. In the 1680s the art of the woodblock print first shows "the floating world."

SCIENCE & TECHNOLOGY	PEOPLE & SOCIETY
ca 1670 NEW SPAIN begins to take the lead from Peru in the production of silver. **1673** THE BOSTON POST ROAD links settlements down the east coast of North America between Boston and New York City. **1686** RICE is first planted in coastal South Carolina.	**ca 1680** DISEASE reduces the Pueblo population from 60,000 to 17,000. **1680s** SOR JUANA INÉS DE LA CRUZ of Mexico is at the height of her intellectual power. A prodigy of learning, she debates with university professors, writes poetry, composes music, and is sent to live in a convent for daring to challenge church authorities. **ca 1688** SMALLPOX first hits the island of Guam, leading to an epidemic that decimates the native Chamorro population.
1675 THE GREENWICH OBSERVATORY is established outside London. **1675** LEIBNIZ describes integral and differential calculus. **1679** FRENCH ENGINEER Denis Papin invents a high-pressure steam boiler, forerunner of the steam engine. **1687** ISAAC NEWTON publishes *Philosophae naturalis principia mathematica,* using mathematics to describe the shape of the Earth, the tides, and the movement of heavenly bodies.	**1670s** PUBLIC COFFEEHOUSES open in France and Germany. **1673** THE TEST ACT bans Catholics from holding office in England. **1685** LOUIS XIV revokes the Edict of Nantes; thousands of Huguenots leave France. **1687** A TURKISH BOMBARDMENT damages the Parthenon in Athens.
ca 1681 PERSIAN PHARMACIST Muzzafar ibn Muhammad al-Husayni Shifa'i's book of remedies is translated into Latin and published in Paris as *Pharmacopoea Persica.*	**1670s** OSEI TUTU of the Asante battles his way to power. He is installed as the Asantehene and founds the Asante Empire.

THE ASANTE UNITE

IN THE LATE 1600s Asante prince Osei Tutu escaped from service as shield-bearer (hostage) at the court of a powerful Denkyira overlord. He fled to Akwamu, a state on equal footing with the Denkyira confederacy. There he planned a union of the small Asante settlements, one that would be welded firmly enough to stand against Denkyira domination and could be defended by an effective army.

When Osei Tutu came home to his throne at Kumasi he brought Okumfo Anokye, an Akwamu adviser and high priest, with him. According to legend, Anokye received a miraculous gift—a Golden Stool, which he announced had descended from heaven in a cloud and come to rest on the knees of Osei Tutu, sanctifying his rule. Anokye interpreted the Golden Stool as more than a symbol of kingship: It was the embodiment of the spirit of all the Asante.

Osei Tutu and Anokye understood the use of such symbols, and they also comprehended the art of war. The Kumasi army made marching ants its model; savagery and surprise were its signature tactics. Osei Tutu purchased guns from European traders, and in the late 17th century his forces defeated the inexperienced new ruler of Denkyira. Osei Tutu's army gathered the prizes of war and slave trade profit, including an immense amount of gold.

Using gold-bought weaponry, the Asante took over West Africa's Gold Coast, what is now Ghana. Osei Tutu became Asantehene, the overall king, and produced a constitution for his union of peoples. The Asante consider him the legendary founder of the empire. His centralized state and patronage of artistic traditions from the various groups within its borders helped create a cohesive Ghanaian identity. Today, the Golden Stool remains the symbol of the spirit of the Asante and is protected by the Asantehene in the modern nation of Ghana.

The traditional Asante flag pictures the Golden Stool, a symbol of the ruler's throne and the unity of the Asante people.

POLITICS & POWER	GEOGRAPHY & ENVIRONMENT	CULTURE & RELIGION
1700 **IN THE AWAT'OVI MASSACRE,** traditional Hopi kill Spanish missionaries and Hopi who had converted to Christianity. **1702** **THE ENGLISH, FRENCH,** and their respective Indian allies begin fighting Queen Anne's War. The conflict continues until 1713.	**1699** **FRENCHMAN PIERRE LE MOYNE D'IBERVILLE** establishes Fort Maurepas on the Gulf Coast of Mississippi, near modern-day Biloxi. **1700s** **A DIVERSE AND INTERMINGLED POPULATION** grows in Spanish America, comprising Indians, Spanish, Africans, and people with mixed bloodlines. **1702** **THE FRENCH** explore and settle in Alabama.	**1692** **WITCH TRIALS** in Salem, Massachusetts, convict and execute 19 people accused of trafficking with Satan. In 1697 the trial findings are repudiated by judge Samuel Sewall. **1701** **THE COLLEGIATE SCHOOL,** the precursor of Yale University, is founded in Saybrook, Connecticut. **ca 1701-1703** **DOMINICAN FATHER FRANCISCO XIMÉNEZ** translates the K'iche' text of the Maya creation story *Popul Vuh* into Spanish.
1690 **WILLIAM III** of England invades Ireland to quell a rebellion by supporters of James II. **1696** **PETER THE GREAT,** after sharing power with his brother, becomes the sole tsar of Russia. **1700** **PHILIP V** becomes king of Spain. **1701** **FREDERICK III,** Elector of Brandenburg, is crowned as King Frederick I of Prussia. **1707** **IN THE ACT OF UNION,** parliaments of England and Scotland unite to form Great Britain.	**1697** **BRITISH BUCCANEER** William Dampier publishes *A New Voyage Round the World* about his circumnavigation of the globe. **1703** **PETER THE GREAT** begins building a new city at St. Petersburg on the Neva River. St. Petersburg becomes the capital of Russia in 1712.	**1699** **PETER THE GREAT** decrees that Russia will recognize January 1, not September 1, as the beginning of the New Year. This is part of his program to westernize and modernize Russia. **1700** **JOHANN SEBASTIAN BACH** publishes the first volume of his cantata libretti. His composing career will last until the mid-1740s. **1709** **AN ITALIAN HARPSICHORD MAKER,** Bartolomeo Cristofori, invents the pianoforte.
1699 **OMAN** controls much of the East African coast. **1700** **THE OYO EMPIRE** flourishes in what is present-day southwestern Nigeria.	**1694-1696** **DROUGHT, FAMINE, AND PLAGUE** strike Egypt. Rioters loot granaries in Cairo.	**1699** **THE TREATY OF CARLOWITZ** removes Muslim-inhabited territory from Ottoman control, greatly reducing Turkish influence in east-central Europe.. **1706** **DOÑA BEATRIZ,** leader of the Kongolese Antonians, is arrested on charges of heresy. She is convicted and burned to death, for which she becomes known as the "Kongolese Joan of Arc."
1696 **THE RUSSIANS** invade and conquer Kamchatka.	**1699-1700** **WILLIAM DAMPIER** of England sails to northwest Australia and New Guinea. **1707** **MOUNT FUJI,** near Tokyo, Japan, erupts.	**1700** **THE GENROKU ERA** of popular culture in Osaka and other urban centers flourishes. **1700** **AN ESTIMATED 196,000 CHRISTIANS** are in China.

SCIENCE & TECHNOLOGY

1690 A PAPER MILL is built in Pennsylvania.

ca 1700 JESUIT PRIEST Louis Nicholas writes *Codex canadensis*, an illustrated manuscript about the flora, fauna, and peoples of the New World.

1702 TO FUND ITS PARTICIPATION IN QUEEN ANNE'S WAR, Massachusetts begins issuing paper currency. Other New England colonies soon follow suit.

1702 FORMS OF STREET LIGHTING appear in many German cities.

1704 ISAAC NEWTON publishes *Opticks*.

▼ **1705** EDMUND HALLEY, English astronomer, predicts that the comet of 1682 will return in 1758. He will not live to see his prediction confirmed, but the comet is named after him.

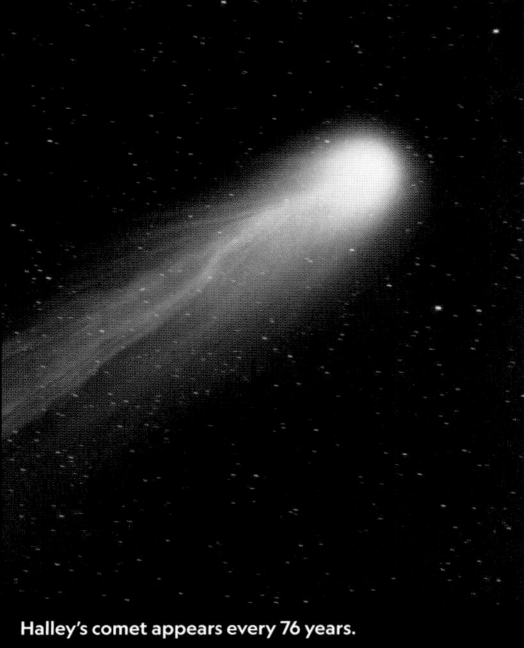

Halley's comet appears every 76 years.

PEOPLE & SOCIETY

1699-1700 SMALLPOX AND YELLOW FEVER epidemics devastate Indians of the Carolinas; many survivors move west. When the elders die, people lose knowledge of important ceremonies, rituals, and traditions.

1704 *THE BOSTON NEWS-LETTER* begins publication.

1707 HENRIETTA DEERING JOHNSTON begins drawing pastel portraits of people and scenes in South Carolina.

1696 ISAAC NEWTON is made director of the English mint after reforming the currency. He is knighted in 1705.

1697-1698 PETER THE GREAT travels through Prussia, the Netherlands, England, and Sweden incognito, observing European life.

1700s PERIODICALS, both news and commentary, increase in popularity throughout Europe.

1703 MERCHANTS AND ARTISTS join Janissary fighters in a revolt in Constantinople, resulting in the dethroning of Ottoman sultan Mustafa II, who had abandoned the capital.

1709 THE "SIBERIAN SYSTEM" begins, with large numbers of Russians being exiled to the remote region.

THE SALEM WITCH TRIALS

BY THE LATE 1600s, as European witch trials were winding down, witch hunt fever was just beginning in the New World. Rumors of witchcraft in Puritan Massachusetts started in 1692 among the prosperous farmers of Salem, a village north of Boston. Quarrels over inheritances, lifestyles, and church affairs, anxiety over a frontier war just 70 miles away, and teenage boredom probably contributed to witchcraft hysteria.

In January 1692, several young girls began jerking spasmodically in public, shrieking that they were being tortured by witches. They accused three women, including the minister's slave, Tituba. A court convened by local magistrates investigated, while the numbers of "possessed" girls increased and accusations multiplied. In May, Governor Phips appointed a new court to take over the cases, including famous witch hunters William Stoughton and Cotton Mather.

The defendants had no legal counsel, and hearsay, gossip, and supposition were admitted as evidence. A skeptical tavern keeper, an elderly women who argued with neighbors, a former minister of Salem church, and a four-year-old child were among the hundreds accused of witchcraft. By October 1692, 19 people had been convicted and hanged, one had been pressed to death, and several had died in prison. Two dogs were executed as accomplices.

In 1693 the remaining defendants were pardoned. Judges regretted their parts in the trials; jurors admitted that they had made mistakes, and the minister of Salem preached repentance. In 1706 Ann Putnam, one of the afflicted girls, confessed that her accusations had in fact been false.

POLITICS & POWER

1710 ENGLISH FORCES invade Acadia in Canada and take Port-Royal from the French.

1710 THREE MOHAWK AND ONE MOHICAN travel to England and ask Queen Anne to support them against their enemies.

1715-1716 THE YAMASEE WAR in South Carolina between British colonists and local Indians, mostly Yamasee, leads to the collapse of Indian control of that area.

1722 SETTLERS IN NORTH CAROLINA attack the Tuscarora. Remnants of the tribe move north and join the Iroquois Confederacy.

1711 THE SOUTH SEA COMPANY, a British colonial investment scheme, begins operations, but goes bust due to fraud in 1720, ruining investors.

1715 LOUIS XV becomes king of France.

1715 JAMES EDWARD, the Old Pretender, son of the deposed James II, enters Scotland in an attempt to regain the British throne, but his attempt fails.

1722 THE GHILZAY AFGHANS, led by Mahmud, invade Iran and seige Isfahan, from which the city never fully recovers.

1724-1727 THE ABOMEY KING AGAJA conquers Allada and Whydah in West Africa (modern-day southern Benin). He renames his enlarged kingdom Dahomey.

1729 THE PORTUGUESE are permanently driven out of Mombasa in eastern Africa (modern-day Kenya).

1720 TIBET becomes a Chinese protectorate.

1720s ECONOMIC, SOCIAL, AND POLITICAL REFORMS are enacted under Shogun Tokugawa Yoshimune in Tokugawa Japan.

1723 EMPEROR YONGZHENG tightens imperial control in China. He abolishes hereditary servitude.

GEOGRAPHY & ENVIRONMENT

1713 THE PEACE OF UTRECHT cedes Newfoundland and other French colonial territory to Britain. Britain receives the exclusive right to bring African slaves to the Spanish colonies.

1718 FRENCH EXPLORER Jean-Baptiste Le Moyne de Bienville establishes the city of New Orleans.

1723 AFTER JOCKEYING with France for control of Florida's Pensacola Bay for three years, the Spanish build a fort called Presidio Isla de Santa Rosa.

1720s-1730s THE CITY OF JAIPUR, INDIA, is planned out on a geometric grid.

1722 DUTCH EXPLORER JACOB ROGGEVEEN discovers Easter Island.

WHAT LIFE WAS LIKE

During the Slave Trade

At the height of the slave trade between Africa and the Americas, most people in Central and West Africa lived in small hamlets, often as extended family groups. Men typically led the family, though inheritance might depend on women. Slash-and-burn agriculture at the forest fringes supported millet, yams, and many cultivars of bananas; there was trade in iron, copper, salt, and shells. Disease was endemic and populations grew slowly. The removal of healthy men, women, and children by slavers crippled both the economy and social custom. Communities where only the sick and the old remained fell into disorder and never recovered.

CULTURE & RELIGION

1711 JOHN V, KING OF PORTUGAL, bans all religious orders from the gold fields of Minas Gerais, Brazil.

1716 THE FIRST THEATER in the English colonies opens in Williamsburg, Virginia. It closes in 1723.

1718 THE ALAMO, a Franciscan mission, is completed in San Antonio, Texas.

1724 THE MONASTERY OF CORPUS CHRISTI, the first convent for indigenous women, opens in Mexico.

1710 GOTTFRIED WILHELM LEIBNIZ, German rationalist philosopher, publishes *Theodicy.*

1717 THE UNITED GRAND LODGE OF ENGLAND is established in London. Freemasonry begins to spread though Europe and North America.

1726 BRITISH AUTHOR Jonathan Swift publishes *Gulliver's Travels.*

1728 THE SPANISH INQUISITION suppresses the Freemasons' Lodge in Madrid.

1718-1730 THE "TULIP PERIOD" occurs in the Ottoman Empire. People experiment with European manners, tastes, and fashion.

1724 IMPERIAL EDICT completely bans Christianity in China. Christian missionaries are expelled from the country.

1725 ISHIDA BAIGAN founds Shingaku, a Japanese religious movement built on Shinto, Daoism, Buddhism, and Confucianism.

1726 *GUJIN TUSHU JICHENG (COLLECTION OF PICTURES AND WRITINGS)* is published by order of Emperor Yongzheng. It fills more than 750,000 pages and attempts to summarize the entirety of Chinese cultural heritage.

SCIENCE & TECHNOLOGY

1715-1716 **SYBILLA MASTERS** of Pennsylvania invents a corn mill and a hat weaving process.

1720s **THE PRINCIPIO COMPANY** builds Accokeek Furnace in Virginia and exports iron to England.

1724 **THE FIRST LEVEES** are built along the banks of the Mississippi River in Louisiana to protect against damaging floods.

1728 **JOHN BARTRAM** purchases 102 acres in Philadelphia for his eventual botanical garden and begins collecting specimens for his vast collection of North American plants.

1710 **JAKOB CHRISTOF LE BLON,** a German engraver, develops a three-color printing process.

1721 **BUBONIC PLAGUE** occurs for the last time in Europe.

1721 **LADY MARY WORTLEY MONTAGUE** encourages inoculation against smallpox in Britain after observing its use in Turkey.

1725 **CATHERINE I OF RUSSIA** opens the St. Petersburg Academy of Science.

1728 **A TREATISE ON DENTISTRY** is written in France.

1729 **OTTOMAN DIPLOMAT AND PRINTER** Ibrahim Muteferrika publishes descriptions of European governments, military organizations, and geography. He also prints maps.

1720s **MAHARAJA SAWAI JAI SINGH II** begins construction of the Jantar Mantar astronomical observatory in Jaipur, India.

PEOPLE & SOCIETY

ca 1715 **THE GOLD FIELDS** of Minas Gerais in Brazil are worked by 30,000 slaves.

1718 **EUROPEANS** describe the game of lacrosse as played by the Ottawa and Potawatomi in Detroit.

1720s **EPIDEMICS** severely reduce the population of Peru.

1710 **REGULAR MAIL SERVICE** begins between London and New England.

1719 **DANIEL DEFOE** anonymously publishes his greatest novel, *Robinson Crusoe.* In 1722 *Moll Flanders* follows.

1720s **FRENCH PHILOSOPHER VOLTAIRE,** exiled in England, is influenced by English thought and scientific inquiry.

1727 **THE SOCIETY OF FRIENDS (QUAKERS)** in England advocates the abolition of slavery.

1713 **A SMALLPOX EPIDEMIC,** originating on a Dutch ship, sweeps through the Cape Colony, killing both whites and Africans.

1721 **OTTOMAN SULTAN AHMED II** opens the empire to Western culture.

1720 **THE TOKUGAWA SHOGUNATE** lifts the ban on foreign books; Dutch learning begins to enter Japan.

1724 **THE KAITOKUDO,** a school for merchant youth, is founded in Osaka, Japan.

1729 **EMPEROR YONGZHENG** prohibits the sale and smoking of opium in China.

THE CASTE SYSTEM

LIGHT-SKINNED ARYAN invaders introduced castes to India in ancient times as a way of ordering society among the darker-skinned natives of the subcontinent. A form of the system survives today, with variations in Nepal, Sri Lanka, Pakistan, and Bangladesh. Caste is hereditary. One is born into a particular relationship with the rest of the world. Caste is related to religious purity as well: Priests are born into the highest caste. Although rooted in Hinduism, caste structure has also developed within Muslim, Sikh, Christian, and Buddhist traditions in Asia.

Caste rules social behavior. One must marry within one's caste, eat particular foods and only in allowable company, and assume specific obligations in business. The four original castes, called varnas, from a word meaning "colors," are Brahmans, the priests; Kshatriyas, the kings, nobility, and warriors; Vaishyas, the merchants and farmers; and Sudras, or the peasants and laborers. Below all these are the people who perform the most menial and religiously impure duties, like garbage collection, sweeping, and cleaning latrines—the so-called untouchables. Within these groupings there are many special positions and levels, so that a person of a low caste may still be a person of great importance and influence locally, though he is deferential in his attitude to higher caste individuals.

Social caste in India often dictates profession, such as these Dhobi women born into a family of launderers.

POLITICS & POWER

1732 **KING GEORGE II** grants James Oglethorpe a charter for a colony south of the Carolinas. Oglethorpe establishes Georgia, named for the king, as a refuge for poor and debtors.

1737 **IN A LAND SWINDLE CALLED THE WALKING PURCHASE,** Pennsylvania authorities seize about 1,200 square miles of territory from the Delaware, claiming it was ceded in a lost treaty from 1686.

1736-1737 **BRITAIN** sends troops to defend the Georgians against an attack from Spain.

1730-1743 **RUSSIA AND PERSIA** engage in wars against the Ottoman Turks.

1740 **FREDERICK WILLIAM I** of Prussia dies, succeeded by his son Frederick II (Frederick the Great).

1740 **HOLY ROMAN EMPEROR CHARLES VI** dies, succeeded by daughter Maria Theresa, who gains a reputation for diplomacy.

1745 **CHARLES EDWARD, THE YOUNG PRETENDER** (Bonnie Prince Charlie), grandson of the deposed King James II, enters Scotland to regain the British throne but is defeated.

1750 **THE KINGDOM OF DARFUR** (in modern-day western Sudan) expands to the south and east.

1739 **PERSIAN FORCES** under Nadir Shah sack Delhi. Shah loots Mughal palaces and steals the Peacock Throne and Koh-i-noor diamond.

1746 **JOSEPH-FRANÇOIS DUPLEIX,** governor-general of French holdings in India, captures the region of Madras in an action against the British during the War of the Austrian Succession.

1748 **THE AFGHAN-SIKH WARS** begin when Afghani leader Ahmad Shah Durrani and his forces conquer Lahore in present-day Pakistan.

GEOGRAPHY & ENVIRONMENT

1742-1743 **THE FRENCH** explore westward, passing through South Dakota.

1748-1749 **THE FRENCH AND BRITISH** vie for control of the Ohio River Valley. The Ohio Company is established to secure English control of the valley, while Pierre-Joseph Céloron de Blainville leads an expedition down the Ohio River to claim the valley for France.

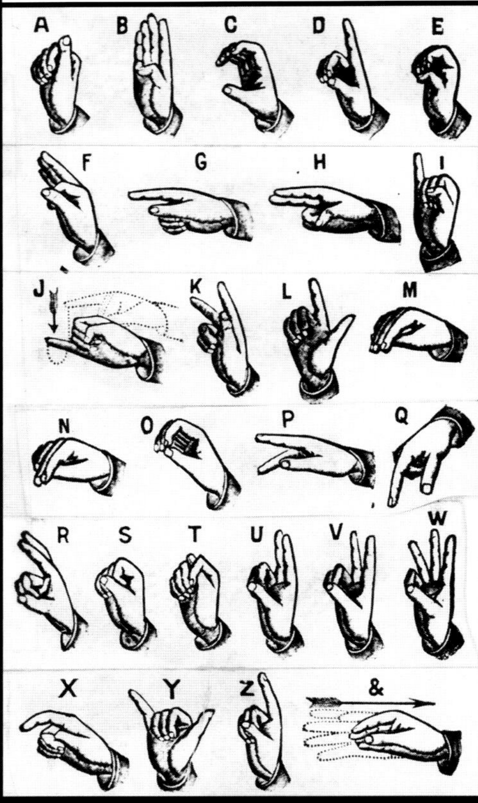

The sign language alphabet

1733 **THE GREAT NORTHERN EXPEDITION** begins. Led by Danish explorer (and Russian naval officer) Vitus Bering, it maps much of the Arctic coast of Siberia.

CULTURE & RELIGION

1730s **THE GREAT AWAKENING** sweeps through the British colonies in North America. During this period of religious fervor, traveling preachers stress the individual's relation to God as being all-important and question established authority.

1730s-1740s **PORTRAITURE** flourishes with the work of John Smibert in Boston and Jeremiah Theus in Charleston.

1740 **MORAVIANS** establish settlements at Nazareth and Bethlehem, Pennsylvania, and later, in North Carolina.

1730s **FRANÇOIS BOUCHER,** Jean-Baptiste-Siméon Chardin, William Hogarth, and Canaletto (Giovanni Antonio Canal) are all actively painting.

1734 **GEORGE SALE** translates the Quran into English.

1734 **EMANUEL SWEDENBORG,** Swedish scientist, writes on the natural world and attains a great following as a philosopher and mystic.

1738 **POPE CLEMENT XII** issues an edict against Freemasonry.

1730s **FRENCH COMTE DE BONNEVAL,** a convert to Islam, brings European expertise to modernizing the Ottoman artillery corps and founding a military engineering school.

1740s **BUNRAKU PUPPET THEATER** flourishes in Japan's urban centers.

1748 **THE KABUKI DRAMA** *Copybook of the Treasury of Loyal Retainers* is written. The story of 47 ronin who avenge their lord is thought to have been based on events from 1701-1703.

ca 1750 **WU JINGZI** writes *The Scholars,* a novel satirizing the examination system in China.

SCIENCE & TECHNOLOGY

1730 THE FIRST SUGAR REFINERY is built in New York.

1738 ANDREW DUCHÉ of Savannah, Georgia, produces the first porcelain in colonial America—six years before the first porcelain made in England is registered.

1739 CASPAR WISTAR opens a glassworks in New Jersey.

1742 ELIZA LUCAS PINCKNEY of South Carolina develops and markets indigo as a useful crop.

1744 BENJAMIN FRANKLIN develops the Franklin stove.

1735 SWEDISH NATURALIST Carolus Linnaeus publishes *The System of Nature*. It establishes the framework of taxonomy by including all known organisms in a single classification system.

1736 THE FIRST SUCCESSFUL APPENDECTOMY is performed in France.

1736 CAOUTCHOUC (RUBBER) is first imported to Europe from South America.

1738 EXCAVATIONS begin at the Roman city of Herculaneum, buried by a volcanic eruption in 79 C.E.

PEOPLE & SOCIETY

1733-1743 COOSAPONAKEESA interprets for James Oglethorpe with the Creeks in Georgia.

1739 THE PEOPLE OF VENEZUELA, Colombia, and Ecuador come under the viceroyalty of New Granada.

1739 IN THE STONO REBELLION, slaves in South Carolina revolt and kill 20 white residents.

1746 THE ACT OF PROSCRIPTION, including the Dress Act, aims to weaken Gaelic culture in Scotland and dismantle the clan system. Many Scottish Highlanders emigrate as a result.

◀ **1749 SPANIARD GIACOBBO RODRIGUES PEREIRE** demonstrates a system of sign language he developed for those who can neither hear nor speak.

1730 THE REBELLION OF PATRONA HALIL in Istanbul protests war taxes and the growing economic divide among the classes.

1740s THE CHINESE CIVIL SERVICE EXAMINATION SYSTEM comes under attack.

1747 JESUITS begin the design of The Garden of Everlasting Spring, one of three gardens at the Summer Palace in Beijing, for Emperor Qianlong.

WHAT LIFE WAS LIKE

On the South African Frontier

In 1652 the Dutch East India Company built a fort and farms at the Cape of Good Hope to resupply ships. By 1700 Cape Town had 3,000 settlers, and pastoral farmers called Trekboers were grazing sheep and cattle in outlying areas, occupying lands of the indigenous African herders. As European disease devastated native peoples, Trekboers spread to the Orange River, 300 miles north of Cape Town. The ethnically European society of this frontier adopted a rugged life of hunting, herding, and trading, hostile to the indigenous population and government restraint. Eventually, patriarchal Dutch Calvinists claiming racial and religious superiority organized armed militias to defend their settlements from attack.

INDIAN WARS

WHEN EUROPEANS AND INDIANS shared a landscape, the first friendly contact and cooperation seemed inevitably followed by misunderstandings and conflict as cultures clashed. European technology enabled conquest everywhere, but land rights and the Indians' indifference to colonial law brewed perennial trouble. Disease weakened native groups and many fell prey to slave hunts in the south; the English sold Indian slaves throughout the colonies and down to the Caribbean plantations. As late as 1730 a quarter of the slaves in South Carolina were Indian.

As European demand for fur grew, planting and fishing were neglected by Indians, disease and alcoholism spread, and hostilities developed between native hunting groups. The Iroquois attacked the Hurons in 1649 to secure fur routes in the north and west. Recurrent warfare sparked by European trade favors displaced tribes and disrupted traditional ways throughout the colonial period.

By 1675 English encroachment on Indian lands had ruined the good relations Massachusetts settlers had established with the Wampanoags. Metacom, known to the English as King Philip, led attacks that spread across New England, burning 52 towns. Six hundred English and 3,000 Indians died before Philip was killed and his tribal alliance broken.

French, English, and Dutch authorities recruited Indian allies for colonial wars, too. Fur trade rights, land claims north and west of New England, and control of the West Indies trade were causes for King William's War (1689-1697), Queen Anne's War (1702-1713), and King George's War (1744-1748). The Hurons and related tribes fought for the French; the Iroquois Confederacy fought for the English, and frontier settlements suffered. In 1754 French, English, and Iroquois all laid claim to the riches of the Ohio country, precipitating the French and Indian War, a conflict that trained leaders like George Washington for the American Revolution.

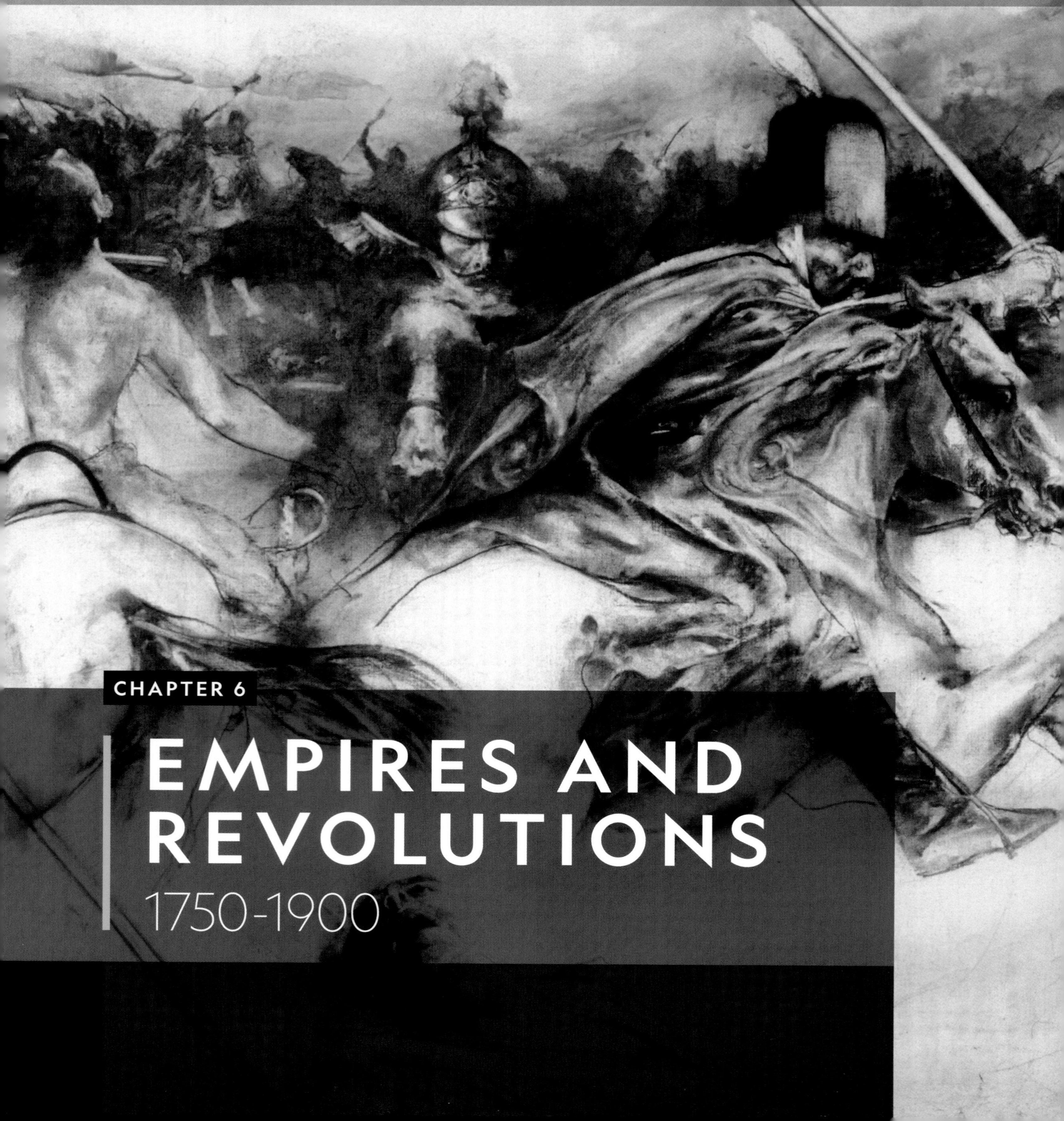

CHAPTER 6

EMPIRES AND REVOLUTIONS

1750-1900

A bare-headed Simón Bolívar battles on horseback against Spanish royalists in a modern depiction of the struggle for independence from Spain launched by Bolívar in South America in 1810.

Beginning in the late 1700s, political and technological advances gave highly industrialized countries a huge advantage over less-developed countries. The industrial revolution began in Great Britain and spread across western Europe along with nationalist fervor and demands for popular sovereignty, or government responsive to the will of the people. Revolutionary France abolished its monarchy, and some other European nations limited royal power by forming legislatures.

In the Americas, many countries rebelled against European rule and achieved political independence, but only the United States, Canada, and a few Latin American nations moved toward economic independence by industrializing. By the late 1800s, most countries in Latin America, Africa, Asia, and the Pacific had come under the economic influence or political domination of the world's major industrial powers, whose ranks grew to include the U.S., Japan, and Russia as well as Britain, France, Germany, and other western European nations. This new imperialism, based on industrial development, set the stage for worldwide convulsions in the 20th century as imperial powers battled for supremacy and developing countries struggled for independence.

AMERICAN REVOLUTIONS

As of 1750, the New World remained divided into European colonies. Conflicts between colonial powers there proved costly for winners as well as losers. In 1763 France conceded defeat to Britain in the French and Indian War—linked to the Seven Years' War in Europe—and surrendered Canada. But Britain, in seeking to recover the costs of war, antagonized its American colonists by imposing new taxes on them without granting them representation in Parliament. In 1775 rebels in Massachusetts launched the Revolution by clashing with British troops. A year later, colonial delegates met in Philadelphia and declared independence. Thomas Jefferson of Virginia made popular sovereignty the cornerstone of the Declaration of Independence when he wrote that governments derived "their just powers from the consent of the governed" and should be altered or abolished if they denied people liberty and other "inalienable rights."

In 1781 the American commander George Washington won a decisive victory over the British at Yorktown with help from French forces, who intervened to strike a blow against Britain. The British recognized American independence, and in 1789 Washington became the first president of the United States under a constitution that reserved many powers to the states. Most states originally restricted the right to vote to white male property owners, and slavery became entrenched in southern states and persisted until the mid-1800s in some northern states.

Rebellions against colonial rule soon erupted in the Americas. In 1791 slaves and free blacks led by one of their own, Toussaint-Louverture, rose up against French rule in Haiti. In 1804 Haitians declared independence. Meanwhile Napoleon Bonaparte, having sold the Louisiana Territory to the U.S., decided to concentrate his resources in Europe against rivals such as Britain and Spain. In 1808 he intervened in Spain and placed his brother on the throne there, triggering revolts in Latin America by colonists who saw Spanish authority eroding.

In 1810 a priest named Miguel Hidalgo y Costilla launched the Mexican war for independence by leading an uprising against Spanish authorities and landowners. Wealthy Mexicans turned against the rebels, and Hidalgo was executed, but the struggle continued. In 1821 a conservative general, Agustín de Iturbide, won independence for Mexico and became emperor. He soon fell from power, and Central American states broke away from Mexico, which reorganized as a republic in 1824.

In South America, Simón Bolívar of Venezuela led a rebellion against Spanish rule in 1810 and went on to become president of a state embracing Venezuela, Colombia, Panama, and Ecuador. Elsewhere, the Argentine rebel leader José de San Martín helped free his own country and neighboring Chile from Spain. He then led his forces into Peru, where he gave way to Bolívar, who took power in Lima. Bolívar went on to defeat Spanish royalists in the southern Peruvian interior, which became known as Bolivia in his honor. He hoped to hold the lands he liberated together as

Welts cover the back of an African American who fled brutal whippings as a slave and joined the Union Army during the American Civil War.

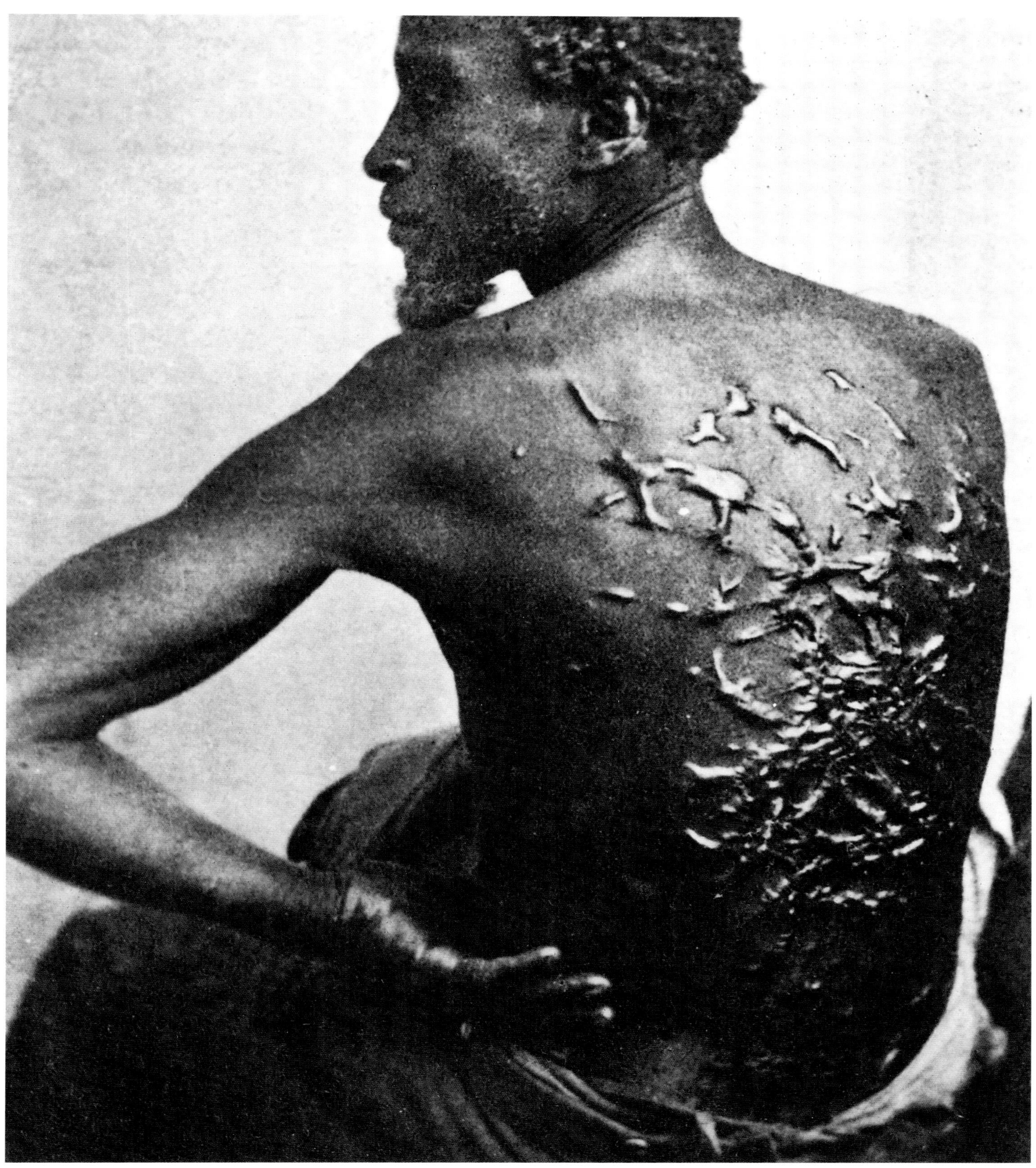

one nation, comparable in size to Brazil, which won independence from Portugal in 1822. But opponents assailed him as a dictator and pressured him into yielding power, and his confederation broke up into smaller, weaker states.

Unlike the U.S. and Canada, which as British colonies had formed their own assemblies and developed economically through trade, Latin America had few sources of wealth other than agriculture and precious metals, much of which had been extracted in colonial times. Poor and politically unstable, many Latin American countries modeled self-government on the traditions of their Iberian colonizers and fell under the control of military rulers, or caudillos. One caudillo, Antonio López de Santa Anna of Mexico, was defeated by Anglo-American insurgents in Texas, who then declared independence. The U.S. was intent on territorial expansion at this time, and the annexation of Texas by the U.S. in 1845 led to war with Mexico, which lost New Mexico and California.

Westward expansion caused bitter discord in the U.S. over the issue of slavery in western territories. After Abraham Lincoln, who opposed extending slavery, was elected president in 1860, southern states seceded and formed the Confederacy. Lincoln gave the ensuing Civil War new meaning in 1863 by issuing the Emancipation Proclamation, which freed slaves in areas currently in rebellion against the Union. This discouraged Britain, which had abolished slavery but still imported cotton from the slaveholding South, from aiding the Confederacy. The Union had a larger population and a stronger industrial base than the Confederacy and won the war in 1865. Reunited, the nation was ready for wholesale industrialization, a process that was well under way in Europe.

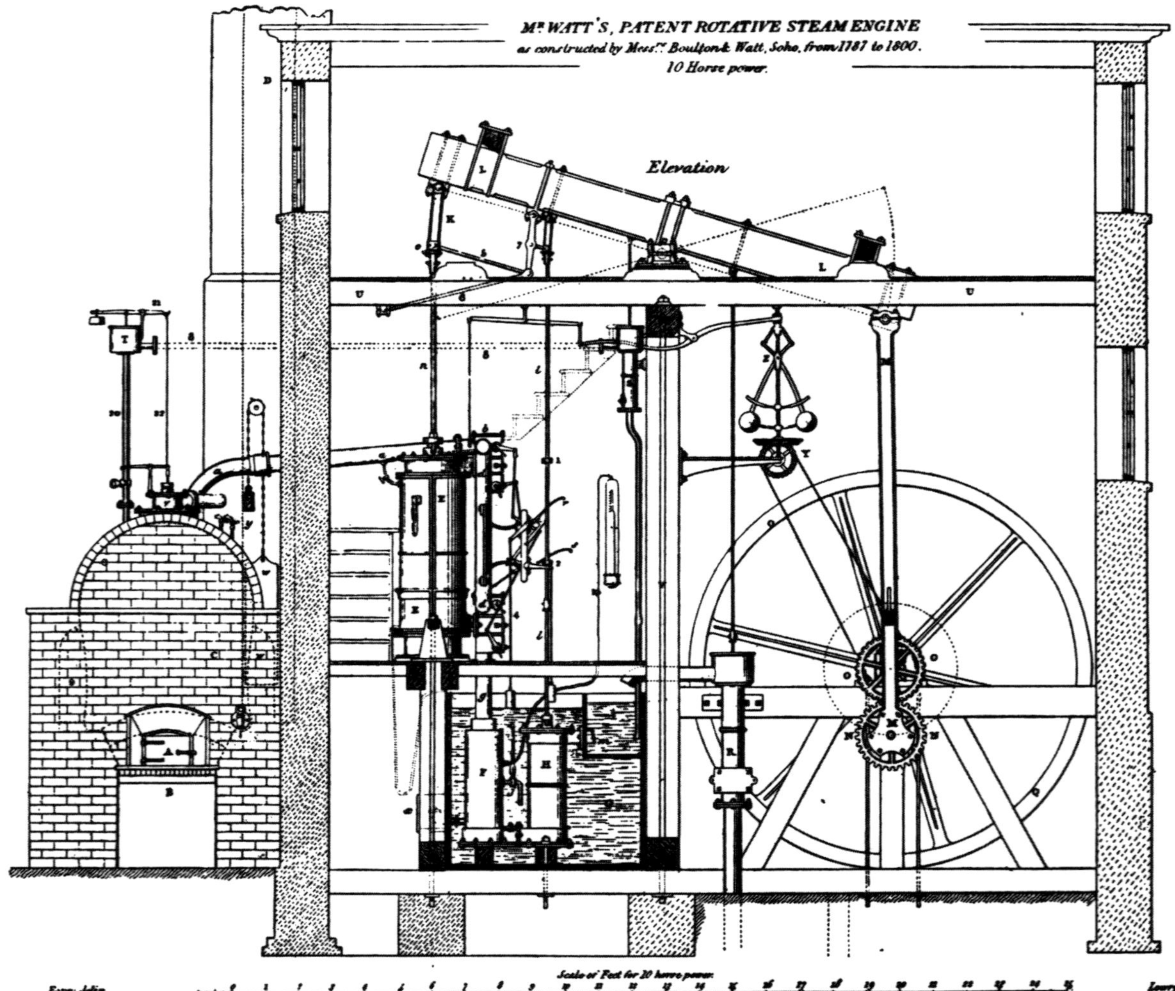

The industrial revolution in Britain received impetus from the steam engine, invented by James Watt, which used steam produced in a boiler to drive a piston and turn a wheel.

EUROPE'S INDUSTRIAL POWERHOUSES

In 1866 the first transatlantic telegraph cable was laid, allowing messages to be sent across the ocean in an instant. Much of the credit went to American financier Cyrus Field, but his Atlantic Telegraph Company was organized in Britain, where the industrial revolution had ignited a century earlier, yielding huge profits that were invested in new technologies in Britain, Canada, the U.S., and many other countries.

Several factors helped make Britain the birthplace of industrialism, including large deposits of coal and iron ore and a political system that encouraged private enterprise and investment. Britain already had a thriving cottage industry, involving workers who spun and wove wool and cotton by hand at home. When James Watt perfected the steam engine in 1765 and steam power was applied to spinning and weaving, the textile industry boomed. Cottages gave way to factories, and the productivity of workers soared, lowering the cost of their products. Steam-powered locomotives, introduced in the early 1800s, linked factories by rail to cities, ports, and coal mines. For laborers, the industrial regime was grueling, and protesters called Luddites sabotaged machinery. But working conditions slowly improved as trade unions gained bargaining power and Parliament enacted labor laws.

Other western European countries followed Britain's path toward industrial development by creating political conditions that favored capitalism, or control of the economy by private interests rather than the state. Prior to the French Revolution, economic policy was set by the king. King Louis XIV and his successors were absolute monarchs, whose counselors could advise but not dictate. But the French rulers undermined their authority by spending heavily on wars and increasing tax burdens on peasants and the bourgeoisie, or middle class, who grew increasingly resentful of royalty and aristocracy. Unlike the American Revolution, the French Revolution that began in 1789 was a radical effort to transform society, inspired in part by ideas of equality and natural rights advanced by Jean-Jacques Rousseau and other Enlightenment philosophers. The execution of King Louis XVI and Queen Marie-Antoinette in 1793 led Britain, Spain, and other countries to oppose the revolution, and France was in turmoil until Napoleon took power in 1799.

As emperor, Napoleon made French society more equitable and enterprising by reforming the tax system and legal code and by instituting public education, but he was a nationalist rather than a revolutionary. His troops were devoted to him, but they were even more devoted to France and demonstrated their patriotic fervor in one punishing campaign after another. Through conquest, Napoleon helped create a new Europe where patriotism, militarism, and capitalism combined to create nations of enormous power whose imperial ambitions were shared by many citizens who fought or worked for their homeland.

Napoleon met with defeat in 1812 when he invaded Russia and most of his army froze or starved to death. At the Congress of Vienna in 1815, the allied nations that opposed him tried to restore the old order in Europe by agreeing to put down uprisings that threatened established monarchies. But nationalist fervor could not be suppressed. Even conservatives were pleased when Greece rebelled against its Ottoman rulers and won independence, but when Belgium broke free of the Netherlands in 1830 defenders of the old order were appalled. Revolutionary passions overflowed in 1848 when demonstrators in Paris restored the French Republic while protesters in Vienna, Berlin, and other cities demanded constitutional government.

Some radicals were inspired by the *Communist Manifesto,* published in 1848 by Germans Karl Marx and Friedrich Engels, but nationalism proved much stronger than communism. Germany was unified by the Prussian statesman Otto von Bismarck, who said that the fate of nations would be decided not by speeches or votes but by "blood and iron." True to his words, he drew on the industrial might of the Krupp family, producers of munitions, and launched wars of expansion that produced a second German reich, or empire, in 1871. (The first reich was the Holy Roman Empire.) Germany's emperor allowed for the establishment of a parliament, or Reichstag, as did the king of newly unified Italy. Reforms were introduced even in the Austro-Hungarian Empire, where the Habsburg dynasty endured, and in imperial Russia, where Tsarina Catherine the Great had ceased efforts to liberalize the political system in reaction to the French Revolution. Serfdom was abolished in Russia under Tsar Alexander II in 1861, and peasants there took part in local elections.

The population of Europe soared during the 1800s as industrial development and improvements in sanitation and public health raised standards of living. Tens of millions of Europeans immigrated to the U.S., Canada, and Latin American countries like Argentina. European investment

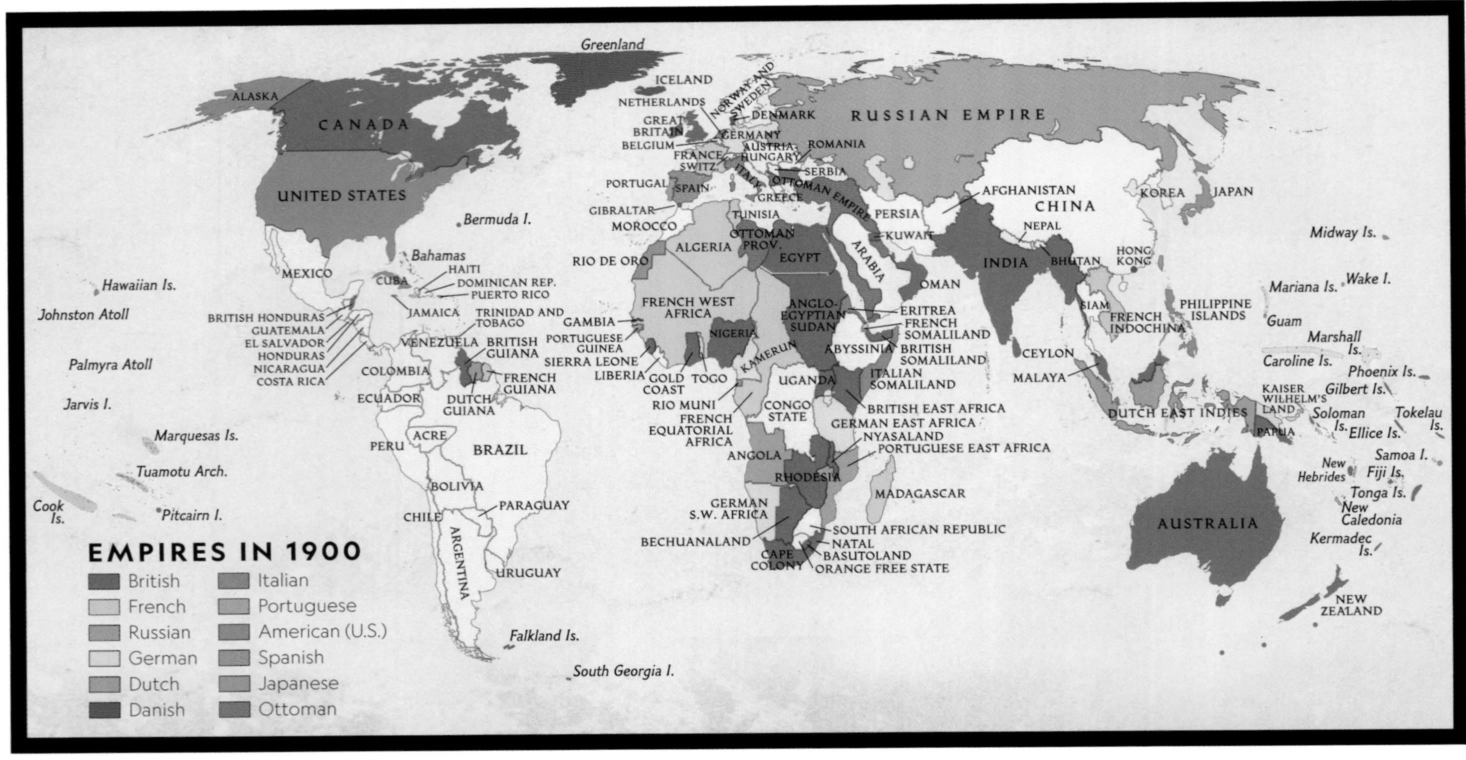

By 1900 Britain, France, and other industrial powers dominated much of the world and had economic influence over China and Latin American countries that were not under their direct control. The once-mighty Spanish and Ottoman Empires had lost territory, while Germany, Japan, Russia, and the United States had recently gained ground.

helped build railroads across North America and provide electrical power to cities, and European immigration contributed to soaring agricultural and industrial productivity in the U.S., which emerged with the world's strongest economy by 1900. Canada became a British dominion in 1867, independent in all areas except foreign policy. But elsewhere, Britain and other industrialized nations tightened their grip on less-developed countries as military advances such as steam-powered, steel-clad battleships allowed them to project power around the globe swiftly and surely.

GLOBAL IMPERIALISM

British domination of India began in the mid-1700s when the East India Company established forts and trading posts there and recruited Indian troops called sepoys to bolster British forces. The Mughal Empire was fracturing, leaving local rulers to contend with the British. In 1757 the ruler of Bengal punished the British for violating trade restrictions by seizing their garrison in Calcutta and, according to one account, confining prisoners to the "black hole," where many died. In retaliation, British forces seized Bengal and replaced its defiant ruler with a compliant one, setting a precedent for the takeover of other Indian states. In 1858 the British Army took control of India following a mutiny by sepoys and imposed direct imperial rule. India became the jewel in Britain's crown, prized as a source of cotton and other raw materials and as a lucrative market for British manufactured goods such as cotton fabric, exported to India in such quantity that its native textile trade withered.

Among the items they exported from India was opium, which was sold illegally in China. When China tried to halt that trade in 1839, British forces intervened and forced China to legalize opium, open coastal ports to foreign trade, and grant Britain control of Hong Kong.

This was a humiliating blow for China's Manchu rulers. In the 1850s their Qing dynasty was nearly toppled by the Taiping Rebellion, an egalitarian movement inspired by Christianity that challenged China's social and political order by advocating that all property be held by the people in common. Government forces massacred the rebels in 1864, but calls for reform persisted. In 1898 reformers at court won support from the young Emperor Guangxu. His aunt, the Empress Dowager Cixi, soon usurped power and executed or exiled the reformers. She then encouraged the ongoing Boxer Rebellion, a popular uprising against foreigners and foreign influence. Foreign troops helped put down the uprising, and China was forced to pay an indemnity to nations that sustained losses. Afterward, many in China began to agitate for the overthrow of the Manchus.

With China debilitated, European powers were free to occupy Southeast Asia and exploit its resources. Britain took Burma and Malaysia, France claimed Indochina, and the Dutch extended their control over the East Indies. Japan escaped foreign domination by becoming an imperial power itself. Shocked when American warships entered Tokyo Bay in 1853 to demand trade rights with Japan, the Japanese overthrew the Tokugawa shogun and restored imperial rule under Emperor Meiji. He presided over a program of modernization in which Japan adopted a constitution, embraced foreign trade, industrialized, and built powerful armed forces that defeated China in 1894 and took control of Korea, Taiwan, and other territories.

In the Middle East, rulers of the Ottoman Empire made efforts at reform but failed to modernize sufficiently and lost much of their territory in the Balkans and North Africa to stronger powers. France first sent troops to Algeria in 1830 and went on to claim most of northwest Africa. In 1859 Britain bought into the ongoing Suez Canal project to secure a shorter maritime route to India and later seized control of Egypt and Sudan to protect that investment.

By 1880 many imperial powers were caught up in a scramble for Africa, where the ruinous transatlantic slave trade had come to an end only to be replaced by new forms of exploitation. Some of the worst abuses of African laborers occurred in the Belgian Congo, but conditions were little better in colonies ruled by other countries. Meeting in Berlin in 1884, delegates from more than a dozen nations, including the U.S., an emerging world power, drew up boundaries for existing colonies and rules for claiming new ones. That did not prevent Europeans from fighting over Africa. Conflict persisted in South Africa between British occupiers and Dutch colonists of longer standing called Boers ("farmers"). Advances inland by Boers in the 1830s had triggered the first Anglo-Boer War, which was in fact a three-way struggle between Boers, British forces, and Zulus, who fought mightily against both European factions. The last Anglo-Boer War broke out in 1899 and ended in 1902 with an agreement that confirmed British rule but made some territorial concessions to the Boers. When South Africa later became a self-governing British dominion, the white minority there took control and instituted the policy of apartheid, or strict racial segregation and discrimination.

The imperial land grab that convulsed Africa extended even to remote Pacific islands such as Tahiti, where Polynesians had welcomed Europeans in the 1700s. Most of those islands were too small for major colonization efforts such as Britain undertook in Australia, settled as a penal colony in 1788. But they were coveted by various nations as naval bases and as sites for plantations and proselytizing. American missionaries and sugar planters established a strong presence in Hawaii, where U.S. Marines came ashore in 1893 and deposed Queen Liliuokalani after she vowed to resist foreign domination. The annexation of Hawaii five years later coincided with the Spanish-American War, during which American forces seized Cuba and the Philippines. When the U.S. entered the imperial contest, it came full circle. A nation that began by throwing off colonial rule was now acquiring colonies of its own. ■

Queen Victoria sits for a portrait on her ivory throne upon being named Empress of India on January 1, 1877. The title was intended to give notice that the British were in India to stay—a commitment imperialists regarded as in the best interests of Indians and Britons.

WORLD AT A GLANCE

1750-1900

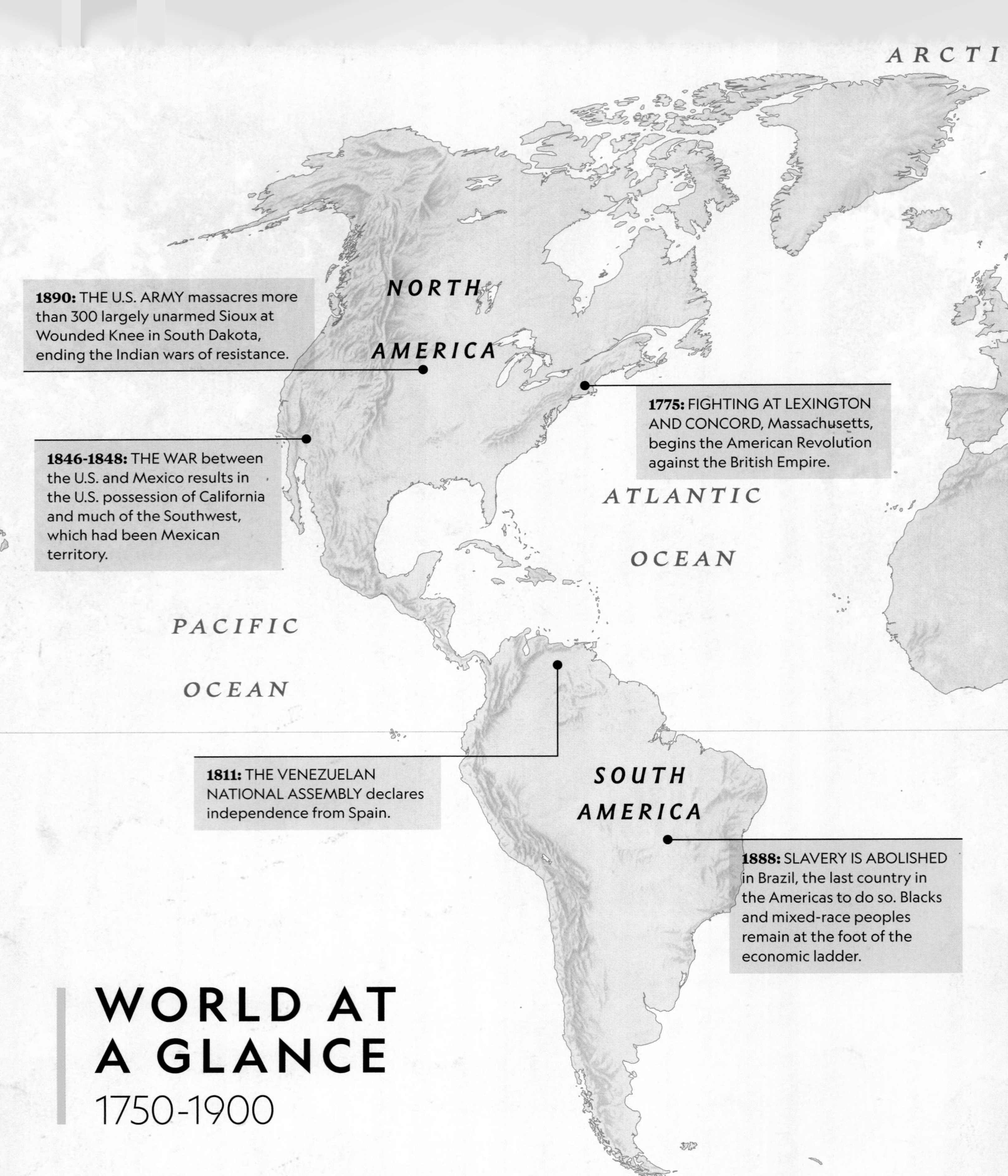

ARCTIC
NORTH AMERICA
ATLANTIC OCEAN
PACIFIC OCEAN
SOUTH AMERICA
1890: THE U.S. ARMY massacres more than 300 largely unarmed Sioux at Wounded Knee in South Dakota, ending the Indian wars of resistance.
1775: FIGHTING AT LEXINGTON AND CONCORD, Massachusetts, begins the American Revolution against the British Empire.
1846-1848: THE WAR between the U.S. and Mexico results in the U.S. possession of California and much of the Southwest, which had been Mexican territory.
1811: THE VENEZUELAN NATIONAL ASSEMBLY declares independence from Spain.
1888: SLAVERY IS ABOLISHED in Brazil, the last country in the Americas to do so. Blacks and mixed-race peoples remain at the foot of the economic ladder.

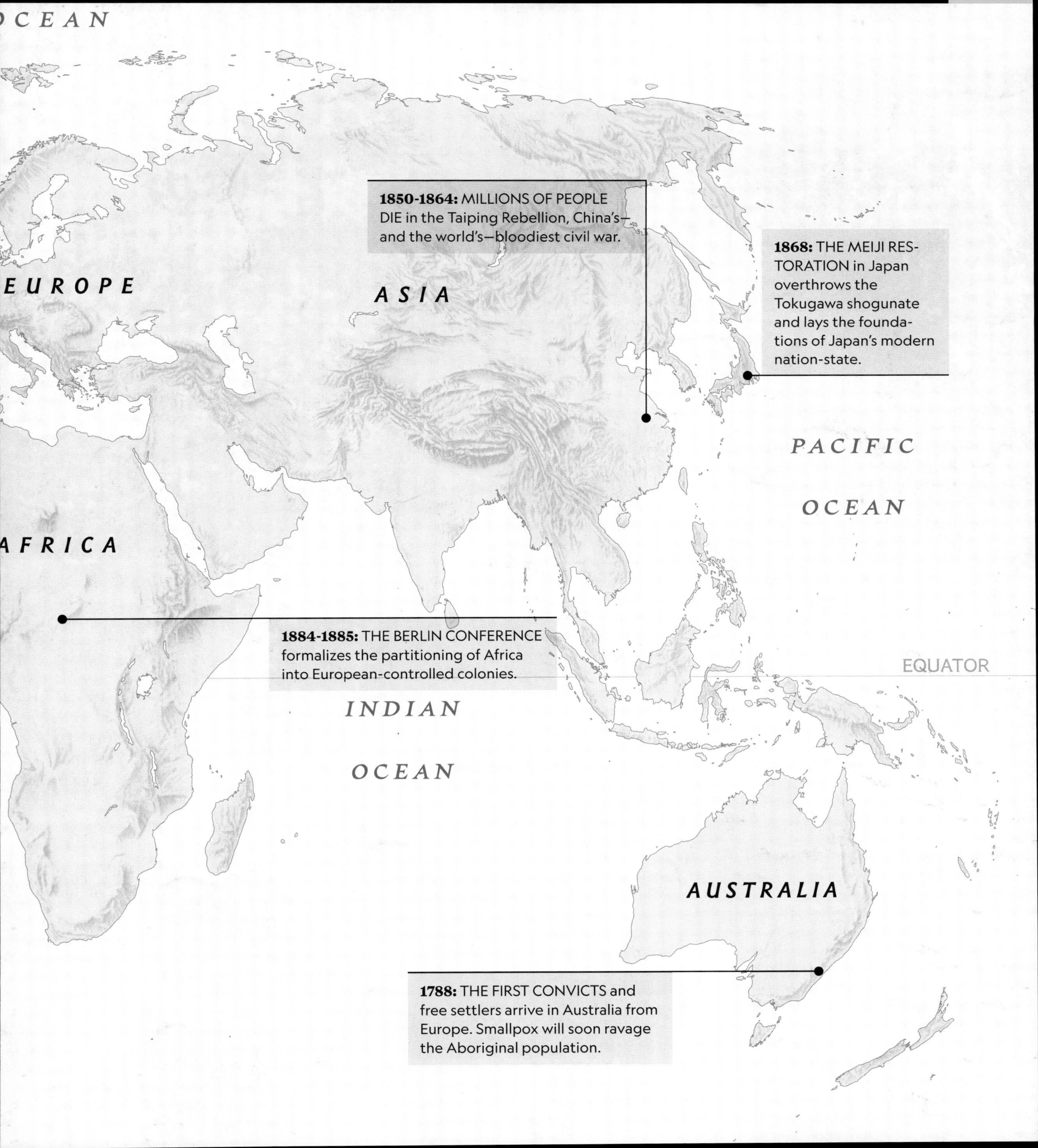
OCEAN
1850-1864: MILLIONS OF PEOPLE DIE in the Taiping Rebellion, China's—and the world's—bloodiest civil war.
1868: THE MEIJI RESTORATION in Japan overthrows the Tokugawa shogunate and lays the foundations of Japan's modern nation-state.
EUROPE
ASIA
PACIFIC OCEAN
AFRICA
1884-1885: THE BERLIN CONFERENCE formalizes the partitioning of Africa into European-controlled colonies.
EQUATOR
INDIAN OCEAN
AUSTRALIA
1788: THE FIRST CONVICTS and free settlers arrive in Australia from Europe. Smallpox will soon ravage the Aboriginal population.

1750-1760

	POLITICS & POWER	GEOGRAPHY & ENVIRONMENT	CULTURE & RELIGION
THE AMERICAS	▶ **1750** FRENCH AGENTS AND TRADERS establish control over trade in the Mississippi Valley. **1754** THE FRENCH AND INDIAN WAR breaks out on the North American continent between the European powers Britain and France. **1759** THE BRITISH CAPTURE QUEBEC from the French.	**1750s** THE OHIO VALLEY has become home to numerous Indian peoples, such as the Shawnee, Delaware, Wyandot, and Miami.	**1759** JESUITS ARE EXPELLED from Brazil because of their work on behalf of political rights for Indians.
EUROPE	**1750** MARQUÉS DE POMBAL becomes a minister of Portugal and implements reforms. He will be instrumental in helping Lisbon recover from the 1755 earthquake that destroys the city. **1756** THE SEVEN YEARS' WAR begins, uniting France, Austria, Saxony, Sweden, and Russia on one side versus Prussia, Hanover, and Great Britain on the other. **1759** CHARLES III becomes king of Spain and intensifies Bourbon colonial reforms. **1760** KING GEORGE III ascends the English throne.	**1750** HALF OF ENGLISH FARMLAND is enclosed by this date. Enclosed farming allowed large landowners to buy out small holders and common lands then lease them back to the displaced laborers. **1755** MORE THAN 60,000 PEOPLE die in a huge earthquake in Lisbon, Portugal, estimated at a magnitude between 8.7 and 9 on the Richter scale.	**1751** FRANCE BEGINS PUBLICATION of the *Encyclopédie*, a leading volume of the Enlightenment. **1754** THE ROYAL AND ANCIENT GOLF CLUB OF ST. ANDREWS is formed. **1755** MOSCOW STATE UNIVERSITY Russia's first university, is founded. **1759** VOLTAIRE publishes *Candide*. **1759** THE BRITISH MUSEUM opens in London.
MIDDLE EAST & AFRICA	**1757** MUHAMMAD III becomes sultan of Morocco. **1757-1774** THE REIGN OF MUSTAFA III maintains peace in the Ottoman Empire until 1768. **1758** THE BRITISH CAPTURE SENEGAL in West Africa from the French.	**ca 1750** ZAHIR AL 'UMAR begins planting and exporting cotton from Tiberias.	**1750-1779** KARIM KHAN ZAND institutes a reign of justice in Iran after the tyranny of Nadi Shah. **ca 1757** MEHMED RAGIB PASHA, Ottoman grand vizier, encourages diplomacy with Europe, and undertakes such military reforms as reorganizing the artillery corps and reopening an engineering school.
ASIA & OCEANIA	**1756** ALAUNGPAYA founds the city of Yangon in Burma. **1757** AHMAD SHAH DURRANI, founder of the state of Afghanistan, plunders the Indian cities of Delhi, Agra, Mathura, and Vrindavan. **1757** ROBERT CLIVE defeats the French-supported Siraj-ud-Daula at the Battle of Plassey, laying the foundation for the British Empire in India. **1760** CANTON becomes the only Chinese port authorized to trade with other countries.	**ca 1750** CHINA'S POPULATION reaches close to 215 million.	**ca 1750** *THE SCHOLARS* is published, a satire of the Chinese civil service examination system.

SCIENCE & TECHNOLOGY

1752 THE LIGHTNING CONDUCTOR is invented by Benjamin Franklin, whose experiments with lightning include flying a kite in a thunderstorm.

1754 THE OUTBREAK OF THE FRENCH AND INDIAN WAR results in many Indian peoples becoming even more reliant on the French and British for vital supplies. Once the war ends these resources vanish, with calamitous results for the Indians.

ca 1755 IN THE AFTERMATH of its devastating earthquake, Lisbon builds Europe's first quake-proof buildings.

PEOPLE & SOCIETY

1754 TWENTY-TWO-YEAR-OLD GEORGE WASHINGTON, commanding British troops from Virginia, ambushes a Canadian reconnaissance party near Fort Necessity in Pennsylvania during the French and Indian War.

1755 EDWARD BRADDOCK is mortally wounded leading British troops and Virginia militia during an attack on the French at Fort Duquesne.

1750 EUROPE'S POPULATION reaches about 140 million.

In the mid-18th century, European claims in North America ranged from the French in Canada, the British along the eastern seaboard, and the Spanish in the Southwest. Russian fur traders had recently colonized coastal Alaska.

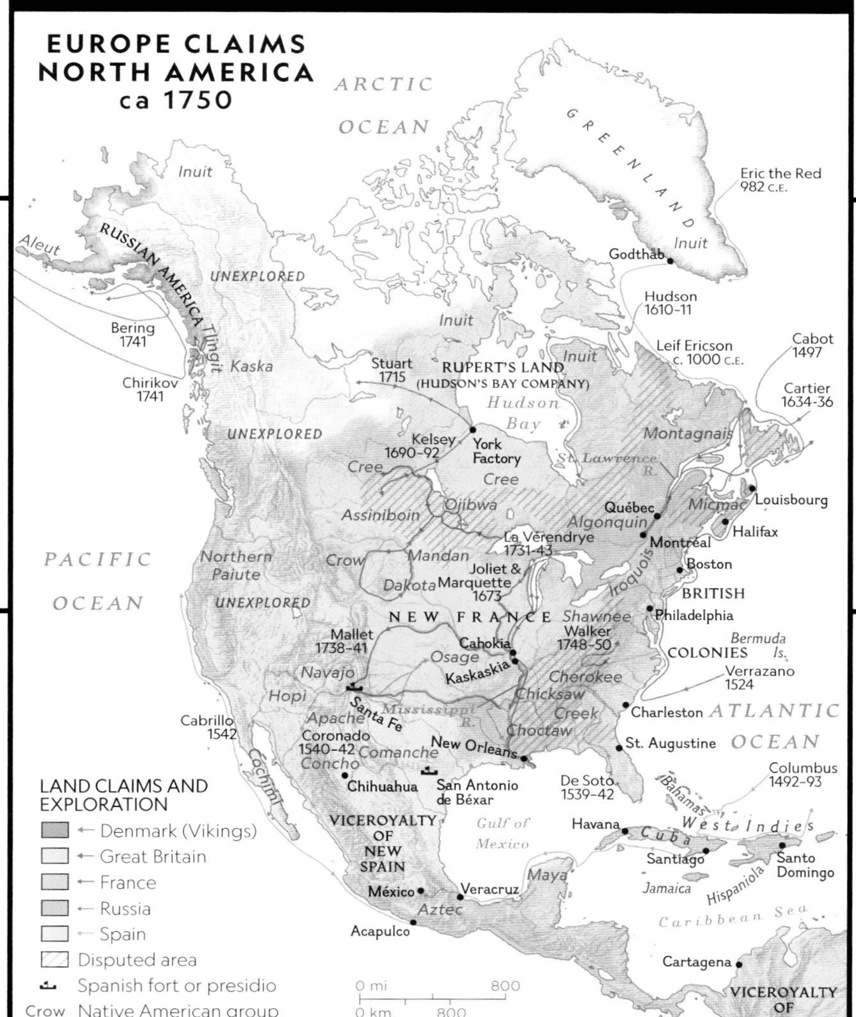

THE AGE OF REASON

BY THE MID-18TH CENTURY, writers and scholars all across Europe and even in the Americas were challenging traditional certainties about the authority of kings, the structure of the universe, and the temporal power of organized religion. Unquestioning obedience to religious, political, and social authority began to be supplanted by the scrutiny of ideas under the penetrating light of reason. If there were natural laws that governed the physical world, might there also be natural laws that applied to the social world—to the world of human activity and government? For many, the answer was a resounding yes.

This period in history became known as the Age of Reason. It has also been called the Enlightenment, because so many thinkers believed that reason could illuminate truth. Nowhere was this spirit of enlightenment more evident than in France, the most powerful country in Europe. The French leaders of this movement, the philosophes, came from a variety of backgrounds and traditions. They included Jean-Jacques Rousseau, a watchmaker's son; Montesquieu, a nobleman and magistrate; and Voltaire, who emerged from the ranks of the wealthy bourgeoisie.

Knowledge, the philosophes said, was the path to happiness. And in 1751 one of their number, the writer Denis Diderot, published the first installment of a 35-volume compendium that contained entries on everything from mathematics, politics, and music to rope-making, tennis, and horsemanship. For the compendium had a simple, if perhaps unattainable, goal: to impart all knowledge. The work was referred to as the *Encyclopédie.*

Diderot published 27 more volumes over the next 20 years. The *Encyclopédie* caused an immediate stir. France's religious and political leaders condemned it, and the police banned it. But the public loved the *Encyclopédie* and bought every one of the 4,000 sets printed.

POLITICS & POWER

1762 **THE SPANISH** temporarily lose control of Havana to the British in the Seven Years' War. The experience encourages them to rebuild defenses in the Caribbean.

1763 **PONTIAC,** an Ottawa Indian chief, leads a rebellion against British settlers in and around Detroit.

1763 **THE SEAT OF BRAZILIAN COLONIAL GOVERNMENT** is shifted south to Rio de Janeiro.

1763 **THE TREATY OF PARIS** ends the French and Indian Wars. Britain gains French Canada and territory east of the Mississippi.

1762 **CATHERINE THE GREAT** becomes empress of Russia.

1768 **WAR BREAKS OUT** between Russia and the Ottoman Turks, imperial rivals for dominance of the Balkans and the Black Sea region.

1769 **MAMLUK LEADER ALI BEY** takes control of Egypt away from the Ottoman governor.

1770 **THE OTTOMAN ARMY** is destroyed in the Russo-Turkish War.

1761 **WITH THE CAPTURE OF PONDICHERRY,** the British destroy French power in India.

1765 **MANCHU CHINESE** invade Burma.

GEOGRAPHY & ENVIRONMENT

1760s **RICE CULTIVATION** fuels the economic growth from colonial North Carolina to Florida.

1769 **SPANISH BEGIN TO SETTLE** in southern California; the San Diego mission is founded, one of a string of missions throughout New Spain.

1763 **FREDERICK THE GREAT** promotes agricultural reconstruction in Prussia after the Seven Years' War.

1768 **BRITAIN'S CAPTAIN JAMES COOK** begins exploring the Pacific, putting ashore at such places as New Zealand and Australia.

CULTURE & RELIGION

1763 **TOURO SYNAGOGUE** opens in Newport, Rhode Island, the first major Jewish center in North America.

1767 **THE SPANISH GOVERNMENT** expels Jesuits from New Spain.

1768 **WESLEY CHAPEL,** the first Methodist center in the North American colonies, opens in New York as the first permanent home of America's oldest continuous Methodist congregation.

1762 **JEAN-JACQUES ROUSSEAU** publishes *The Social Contract,* a representative work of the European Enlightenment.

1762 **SANDWICHES ARE INVENTED** in England and named after the Earl of Sandwich.

1768 ***ENCYCLOPEDIA BRITANNICA*** is first published.

1770 **LUDWIG VAN BEETHOVEN,** broadly considered the greatest composer who ever lived, is born.

1760 **SULTAN MUSTAFA III** begins building the Laleli Mosque in Istanbul, a classic of baroque Ottoman architecture.

1760 **KATSUSHIKA HOKUSAI** is born in Edo, Japan. He will become one of Japan's most celebrated painters and printmakers.

1763 **CAO ZHAN,** also known as Cao Xueqin, author of the Chinese novel *Dream of the Red Chamber,* about an aristocratic family in decline, dies.

WHAT LIFE WAS LIKE

Captain Cook Visits New Zealand

Before Captain James Cook, few outsiders had ever seen the Maori islands of New Zealand. According to oral history, the Maoris had arrived in what they called the Land of the Long White Cloud sometime around 1300 C.E., making the long voyage from other parts of Polynesia in just seven canoes. They adorned themselves with distinctive facial tattoos and clothed themselves in cloaks of woven flax and the feathers of native birds. Excellent hunters and fishermen, the Maoris carved wood, bone, and jade for tools and for weapons of war. Neighboring Maori tribes fought each other over territory or for revenge, with the losers ending up as slaves or, worse, as food.

SCIENCE & TECHNOLOGY

1760s RICE PLANTERS in the American South introduce threshing machines to facilitate rice production.

▶ **1760** BIFOCAL SPECTACLES are invented by Benjamin Franklin.

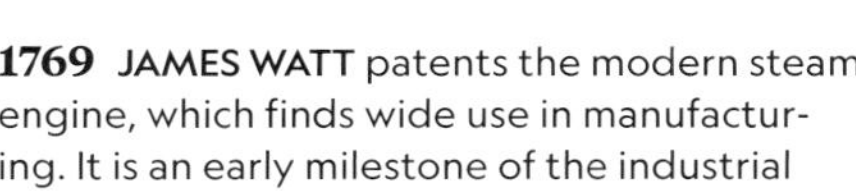

Benjamin Franklin

1769 JAMES WATT patents the modern steam engine, which finds wide use in manufacturing. It is an early milestone of the industrial revolution.

1769 RICHARD ARKWRIGHT patents a water-powered spinning frame, the first machine capable of producing cotton thread of the firmness and hardness required in the warp.

1765 TURKISH MATHEMATICIAN Ismail Effendi translates texts on logarithms into Turkish.

1769 CAPTAIN JAMES COOK and naturalist Joseph Banks observe the transit of Venus across the sun from Tahiti.

PEOPLE & SOCIETY

1761 JAMES OTIS challenges British-imposed writs of assistance and coins the phrase "taxation without representation is tyranny."

1765 CHARLES III allows commerce and trade to flow more freely between the Spanish colonies.

1760s-1770s GERMAN JEWISH PHILOSOPHER Moses Mendelssohn urges that Jews be given civil rights.

1762 THE FRENCH GOVERNMENT opens manufacturing to rural areas.

1767 CATHERINE THE GREAT commissions a new code of laws for Russia, but the effort goes nowhere. Although Catherine sees herself as a monarch of the Enlightenment, serfdom increases in severity in Russia during her reign.

1763 THE OTTOMAN AMBASSADOR visits Frederick the Great in Berlin. After his return to Istanbul (Constantinople), he recommends important changes in the military and relations with Europe.

PONTIAC'S WAR

AMERICAN INDIANS in the 18th century maintained a delicate status quo by playing the two rival colonizing powers—the British and the French—against each other. That changed at the end of the Seven Years' War when France ceded its Great Lakes forts to the British. The British commander in North America, Gen. Jeffery Amherst, took a new approach toward the subjects he viewed as "the Vilest Race of Beings that Ever Infested the Earth." Amherst cut off the French practice of offering trade goods and gifts in exchange for friendly relations around the forts.

Chiefs among the Ottawa, Mingo, Wyandot, Ojibwe, Huron, Choctaw, Peoria, and many others conspired to plan a resistance. The first to strike was the Ottawa chief Pontiac in the Ohio Valley. Within weeks every British post west of Niagara was destroyed, and the settlers of Pennsylvania, Maryland, and Virginia were in a state of terror, but still the strongest forts, including Detroit, Niagara, and Fort Pitt, held out. British reinforcements came to the relief of the beleaguered forts, and Amherst infamously used smallpox-infected blankets in germ warfare against the American Indians. Pontiac hoped the French would come to his aid, but it became clear this was not going to happen. Britain accepted that soft power was a better approach to resolve the embarrassing war and signed several peace treaties in 1764 and 1765 that recognized Indian sovereignty. The role of the war's namesake, Chief Pontiac, is disputed by historians because there are scant details on his biography, but the chief was among those officially pardoned by the British. The anxious American colonists had hoped for harsher repercussions, and it contributed to their growing disillusionment with the empire.

Pontiac recruits neighboring Native American nations to join his uprising against the British in April 1763.

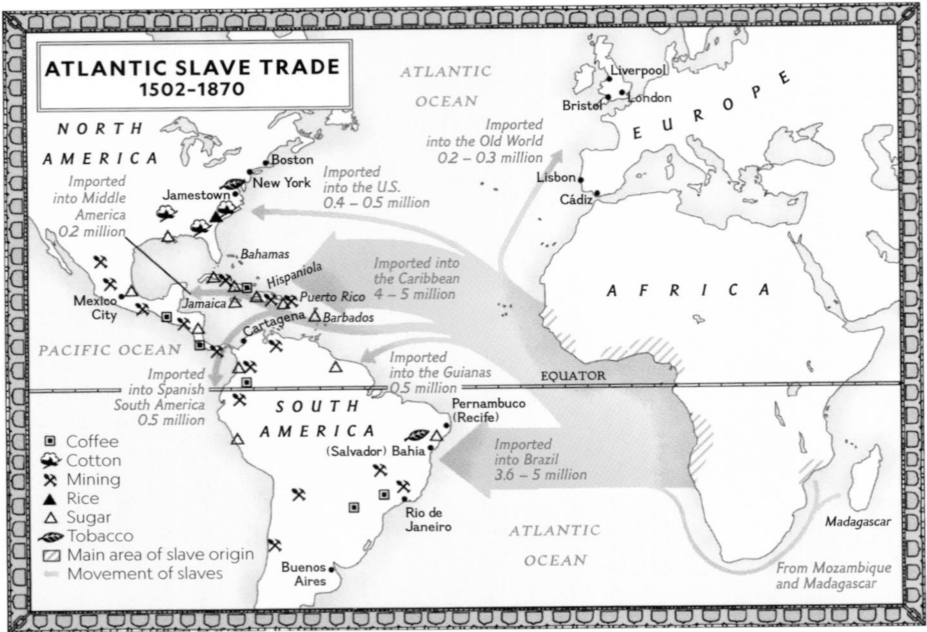

THE TRADE IN HUMAN FLESH

By the 18th century, slavery had existed in Africa for many hundreds of years. Some enslaved Africans were kept locally; some were sent to Muslim lands to the east; and increasingly, some were lashed together by ropes, marched to the Atlantic coast, and inhumanely packed into ships bound for the West Indies or the Americas.

The transatlantic slave trade had begun with the Portuguese and the Spanish, who brought Africans to work on the sugar plantations of Brazil and the Caribbean as well as in the gold and silver mines of Mexico and Peru. But as other Europeans powers, such as the British, the French, and the Dutch, claimed colonies in the Americas, they too joined this terrible and increasingly global human commerce.

In the second half of the 18th century, when the transatlantic slave trade reached its peak, British merchants transported more slaves than any other European nation. Most slaves were taken to Britain's sugar plantations in the Caribbean. The rest traveled on to the colonies in North America. By 1860, one-half of the New World's slaves lived in the United States.

Slaves sent to the Caribbean and to South America often did not live long. A harsh climate, disease, poor nutrition, and the brutality of slave owners led to a high mortality rate. Many Africans resisted their captivity, though, and runaway freedom fighters called maroons helped fuel resistance and sometimes succeeded in establishing their own communities. Despite the odds, some Africans did survive, transmitting their cultural values to new generations of African Americans.

The triangular trade between Europe, Africa, and the Americas (shown on the map above) enriched European industrialists and American plantation owners at the expense of African slaves like these.

1770-1780

	POLITICS & POWER	GEOGRAPHY & ENVIRONMENT	CULTURE & RELIGION
THE AMERICAS	**1775 FIGHTING AT LEXINGTON AND CONCORD,** Massachusetts, begins the American Revolution. **1775 THE CONTINENTAL CONGRESS** appoints George Washington head of the Continental Army. **1776 THE CONTINENTAL CONGRESS** adopts the Declaration of Independence. **1776 VICEROYALTY OF LA PLATA** in Argentina is established. **1778 FRANCE** enters the American Revolution as an American ally.	**1770s COFFEE** grown in Venezuela and Cuba becomes one of the major export crops of the Caribbean along with sugar and cacao.	**1770s FRANCISCAN MISSIONARIES** who followed the Spanish into New California baptize thousands of Indians. **1779 THE FIRST SCHOOL OF FINE ARTS** in the New World is established in Mexico City.
EUROPE	**1772 THE FIRST PARTITION OF POLAND** by Russia, Prussia, and Austria is enacted. (The second and third partitions were in 1793 and 1795.) **1773 THE PUGACHEV REBELLION** of Cossacks in Russia occurs.	**1770s RUSSIAN MERCHANT IVAN LYAKHOV** explores Russia's New Siberian Islands, hoping to collect mammoth bones and ivory. **1770s AGRICULTURIST ROBERT BAKEWELL** gains fame for selective livestock breeding on his farm in England.	**1770 CHRISTIAN EVANGELIST GEORGE WHITEFIELD** dies. He is credited with inspiring the foundation of 50 colleges and universities in the United States. **1773 POPE CLEMENT XIV** suppresses the Jesuit order. **1774 MARIA THERESA** establishes compulsory elementary education in Austria. **1776 ADAM SMITH** publishes *The Wealth of Nations,* which lays the foundation for free-market capitalism.
MIDDLE EAST & AFRICA	**1771 ALI BEY OF EGYPT,** in alliance with the Russians, revolts against Ottoman rule; the revolt is suppressed in 1773. **1774 THE RUSSO-TURKISH WAR ENDS;** Ottomans lose Crimea and lands around the Black Sea where Muslims live. **1779 KARIM KHAN,** who had managed to unite Persia under his rule, dies. The country disintegrates into anarchy again after his death.	**1770 SCOTTISH EXPLORER JAMES BRUCE** encounters the source of the Blue Nile.	**1773 ISTANBUL TECHNICAL UNIVERSITY** is founded in Turkey.
ASIA & OCEANIA	**1779 CAPTAIN JAMES COOK** dies during a skirmish in Hawaii.	**1771 THE GREAT YAEYAMA TSUNAMI** and an earthquake hit Japan's Ryukyu Islands, killing more than 10,000.	**1772 QIANLONG,** the fourth emperor of the Qing (Manchu) dynasty, launches the *Complete Library of the Treasuries* project to compile the entire literary heritage of China into one massive collection.

SCIENCE & TECHNOLOGY

1773 **THE COLOMBIAN BOTANIST MUTIS** is charged with heresy for giving lectures on Copernican theory in Bogotá.

1770s **WILLIAM AND CAROLINE HERSCHEL** build telescopes that will be used in their later study of planets, comets, and nebulae.

1772 **JOSEPH PRIESTLY** discovers the process of photosynthesis.

PEOPLE & SOCIETY

1770s-1780s **LABOR STRUGGLES** break out in Mexican mines over working conditions.

1774 **ANN LEE, KNOWN AS MOTHER ANN,** founds the American Shakers.

1775 **ABOLITIONIST ANTHONY BENEZET** and other fellow Quakers in Philadelphia found the Society for the Relief of Free Negroes Unlawfully Held in Bondage.

1776 **NATHAN HALE** is caught spying on the British on Long Island and hanged, supposedly saying on the gallows, "I only regret that I have but one life to lose for my country."

1780 **BENEDICT ARNOLD** betrays West Point to the British.

THE AMERICAN REVOLUTION

FOR A DECADE, tension had been increasing between Great Britain and the American colonies over British control of colonial governments and over taxation of colonists without their consent. In 1775, Britain's Parliament declared Massachusetts, the center of most of the protests, to be in rebellion. And on April 19 of that year, the American War for Independence began with the battles of Lexington and Concord.

The Continental Congress appointed George Washington commander in chief of the Continental Army and, on July 4, 1776, adopted the Declaration of Independence. Great Britain, with its huge army and navy, launched a land and sea effort to crush the revolution. But the British had to transport and supply their army across the Atlantic. The British won many battles during the war but gained little from their victories, while the Americans, despite hardships that led to frequent desertion, always managed to form new forces and continue the fight.

Washington, with the help of French allies, scored a decisive victory at Yorktown, Virginia, and in 1783 the Treaty of Paris forced Great Britain to recognize the independence of the 13 colonies. The birth of a new and united nation would soon follow.

Marquis de Lafayette, a French ally, stands to the left of Gen. George Washington as they confer at Valley Forge, the main camp of the Continental Army from December 1777 to June 1778. The harsh winter there severely depleted the morale and number of troops.

POLITICS & POWER	GEOGRAPHY & ENVIRONMENT	CULTURE & RELIGION
1781 **AMERICAN AND FRENCH FORCES** bottle up Lord Cornwallis's army of 7,500 men at Yorktown, Virginia; Cornwallis surrenders. **1783** **BY THE TREATY OF PARIS,** Britain accepts American independence. **1788** **THE U.S. ADOPTS A CONSTITUTION.** It establishes the structure of the three branches of federal government, including a bicameral legislature of the Senate and House of Representatives.	**1780s** **SPANISH OFFICIALS** in Louisiana and Florida, desperate to increase the population, entice Americans with offers of land. **1781** **SPAIN** captures western Florida from Britain.	**1780-1781** **JESUIT FRANCISCO CLAVIGERO** writes his *History of Ancient Mexico* from exile. **1789** **FORMER SLAVE OLAUDAH EQUIANO** publishes his memoirs, and he travels in Britain lecturing against slavery.
1781 **JOSEPH II** abolishes serfdom in Austria and grants civil rights to Protestants and Jews. **1783** **RUSSIA** annexes the Crimea, a strategic peninsula in the Black Sea. **1789** **THE FALL OF THE BASTILLE** marks the beginning of the French Revolution.	**1789** **CHRYSANTHEMUMS** from Asia are first introduced to France. **1790** **EUROPE'S POPULATION** reaches about 190 million.	**1788** **CHARLES WESLEY** dies, author of several thousand hymns, including "Hark, the Herald Angels Sing" and "Jesu, Lover of My Soul." **1789** **THE DECLARATION OF THE RIGHTS OF MAN AND THE CITIZEN** is issued in France. **ca 1790** **MOZART, HAYDN, AND BEETHOVEN** dominate the mature Classical period of European orchestral music.
1786 **MOROCCO** agrees to cease raiding U.S. ships in the Mediterranean in return for $10,000. **1787-1792** **THE OTTOMAN WAR** with Russia and Austria proves financially devastating.	**1780s** **DROUGHTS IN WEST CENTRAL AFRICA** accompany increased slave exports, which reach a peak of about 80,000 per year during this decade. **1787** **THE FIRST FREED SLAVES** from Britain settle at Freetown, Sierra Leone.	**1782** **LONDON DEVELOPS A BAND TO PLAY JANISSARY MUSIC** in imitation of those already established in Poland, Russia, and Austria. This so-called Turkish music becomes the rage in Europe, and Ottoman coffeehouses, slippers, dress, and carpets also become popular. **1790** **JEWS ARE PERSECUTED IN MOROCCO** as a reaction against the policies of the former king, who had favored them.
1782 **RAMA I** assumes the throne of Siam (Thailand) and moves the capital to Bangkok. **1787** **RIOTING BY TOWNSPEOPLE** in the city of Edo, Japan, breaks out in protest of economic exploitation.	**1788** **THE FIRST CONVICTS** and free settlers arrive in Australia from Europe. **1790** **MUTINEERS FROM THE *BOUNTY*** settle on Pitcairn Island.	**1782** **THE *SIKU QUANSHU,*** an encyclopedic library of Chinese literature, is compiled by more than 300 scholars commissioned by the Qianlong emperor.

SCIENCE & TECHNOLOGY

The Montgolfiers' first balloon takes to the air near Paris.

▲ **1783** THE FIRST PILOTED FLIGHT in a hot air balloon is made by the Montgolfier brothers.

1785 EDMUND CARTWRIGHT patents a water-powered loom that revolutionizes the production of textiles and helps the growth of the factory system.

1788 ENGLISH NATURALIST SIR JOSEPH BANKS founds the African Association to further exploration and scientific knowledge of the interior of Africa.

1780s HYDER ALI, ruler of southern India's kingdom of Mysore, and his son develop iron-cased rockets that he later uses against the British East India Company.

PEOPLE & SOCIETY

1780-1781 TUPAC AMARU II leads an indigenous revolt in the Peruvian highlands; the Comuneros revolt in New Granada.

1789 GEORGE WASHINGTON becomes the first president of the United States of America.

1786 FREDERICK THE GREAT, king of Prussia, dies. He was a military genius as well as a social reformer.

1781 A CONTINGENT OF BOER SOLDIERS under the command of Adriaan van Jaarsveld kills hundreds of Xhosa and steals thousands of their cattle in the ongoing dispute over territory in the eastern frontier of South Africa.

1789 SMALLPOX ravages Aboriginals of coastal New South Wales in Australia.

REVOLUTION IN THE ARTS

IN LATE 18TH-CENTURY EUROPE, a revolution began to sweep the arts that gave birth to what is now known as the Romantic Era.

The word "romantic" harks back to medieval tales of adventure, fantasy, and high emotion. These attributes gained a renewed importance in literature, painting, and music, eclipsing earlier classical concerns with balance and restraint. During the Romantic Era, expression became everything.

Romanticism stressed the importance of nature and reacted against the Enlightenment and 18th-century rationalism. It emphasized the individual, the subjective, the imaginative, the personal, and the spontaneous.

In music, Romanticism led to looser and more extended musical forms, with melody its dominant feature. No one exemplified these characteristics more than Ludwig van Beethoven, who published his first works in 1783. Although his earliest compositions were very much in the Classical tradition, he soon began to write more daring and expressive compositions. The first composer to earn his living directly from his work without patronage, Beethoven was free to give vent to his extreme individualism and challenged the public to follow him.

Ludwig van Beethoven

POLITICS & POWER	GEOGRAPHY & ENVIRONMENT	CULTURE & RELIGION
1793 IN ACCORDANCE WITH THE U.S. CONSTITUTION, the Fugitive Slave Act of 1793 prevails, providing for the return of slaves who escape from one state into another state or a federal territory. **1800 WASHINGTON, D.C.,** becomes the home of the U.S. government.	**1790s YANKEE SHIPS** increase trade between the newly formed United States and Latin America, especially with the Caribbean. **1790s THE EMBRACE OF SUGAR AND COTTON** in the lower Mississippi Valley moves the region from a marginal place in the production of staples to the very heart of the "plantation world." **1790 THE FIRST CENSUS** in the U.S. counts a population of 40 million, of which 20 percent are black slaves. **1793 ALEXANDER MACKENZIE** completes the first east-west crossing of Canada.	**1790s-1800s THE VIRGIN OF GUADALUPE CULT** in Mexico is transformed from a movement encouraged by the Catholic Church to induce piety in lower classes to a symbol of the Mexico City region to a symbol of Creole nationalism. **1790s THE METHODIST AND BAPTIST CONGREGATIONS** in the Chesapeake who had once embraced black members disavow their commitment to abolition and equality. **1793 FORMER SLAVE KATY FERGUSON** opens an integrated school for poor children in New York.
1790s CHARLES IV of Spain increasingly comes under the influence of his inept minister and adviser Manuel de Godoy. **1792 THE FIRST REPUBLIC** is proclaimed in France. **1793 KING LOUIS XVI** of France is executed. **1793 THE COMMITTEE OF PUBLIC SAFETY** launches France's Reign of Terror in an effort to rid France of all "enemies of the Revolution." **1799 NAPOLEON BONAPARTE** becomes first consul and seizes power in France.	**1791 THE ORDNANCE SURVEY** is founded to map the landscape of Britain.	**1791 THEOBALD WOLFE TONE,** James Napper Tandy, and Thomas Russell form the nationalist Society of United Irishmen, which appeals to both Protestants and Catholics to rid themselves of English rule. **1792 MARY WOLLSTONECRAFT** publishes *Vindication of the Rights of Woman*. **1793 FRANCE** introduces the decimalized currency system. **1798 THOMAS MALTHUS** publishes *Essay on the Principle of Population,* arguing that population will always grow faster than the food supply.
1793 SAUDIS CONSOLIDATE their occupation of Riyadh in the Arabian Peninsula; Wahhabi clerics fill judicial and teaching posts. **1797-1834 THE SECOND QAJAR SHAH OF IRAN,** Fath Ali, establishes dynastic legitimacy. **1798 NAPOLEON INVADES EGYPT** and defeats Egyptians at the Battle of the Pyramids. He is soon forced to abandon his army and return to France with few gains to show.	**1795 SCOTTISH EXPLORER MUNGO PARK** embarks on his expedition up the Niger River. **1800 MAROONS (RUNAWAY SLAVES)** deported from Jamaica settle in Sierra Leone. **ca 1800 THE OTTOMAN POPULATION** is 25-32 million.	**1793-1796 THE FIRST PERMANENT OTTOMAN EMBASSIES** are founded in London, Vienna, Berlin, and Paris. ▶ **1799 THE ROSETTA STONE** is discovered by Napoleon's soldiers in Egypt, allowing historians to translate ancient Egyptian hieroglyphs.
1796 THE BRITISH conquer Ceylon, now known as Sri Lanka. **1796-1804 THE WHITE LOTUS REBELLION,** an uprising against the Qing dynasty, occurs in China.	**1792 MOUNT UNZEN** erupts in Kyushu, Japan, unleashing a landslide and tsunami and killing approximately 15,000. **1798 BRITISH EXPLORERS** George Bass and Matthew Flinders circumnavigate Van Diemen's Land (Tasmania) in the sloop *Norfolk*.	**1797 THE FIRST CHRISTIAN MISSIONARIES** reach Tahiti.

SCIENCE & TECHNOLOGY

1794 ELI WHITNEY patents the cotton gin; cotton becomes the chief crop of the American South.

1796 WILLIAM TUKE opens Britain's first humane sanatorium for the mentally ill in York.

1796 EDWARD JENNER develops a smallpox vaccine using cowpox.

1800 ALESSANDRO VOLTA invents the battery.

The Rosetta Stone shows text in three versions: hieroglyphic, demotic, and Greek, enabling J.-F. Champollion and Thomas Young to decode the previously indecipherable Egyptian hieroglyphics.

1793 LORD MCCARTNEY'S MISSION to China fails to impress the court of Emperor Qianlong. McCartney had brought British goods such as clocks and Wedgwood porcelains, not realizing that "we possess all things," according to the emperor, "and have no use for your country's manufactures."

PEOPLE & SOCIETY

1790s RESENTMENT OF CREOLES against *peninsulares* (Spanish-born Spaniards) increases under the restrictions of the Charles IV regime.

1792 THE COINAGE ACT OF 1792 establishes a mint and regulates the coins of the United States.

1791 JOHN WESLEY, founder of Methodism and 18th-century Protestant revivalism, dies.

1800 THE POPULATION OF CHINA reaches 300 million.

Execution of King Louis XVI

THE FRENCH REVOLUTION

AFTER YEARS OF dissatisfaction with royal and aristocratic rule, the people of France took their first steps toward self-government on June 17, 1789, with the formation of a national assembly. Civil unrest soon followed, and less than a month later, a crowd stormed the Bastille prison in Paris, whose fall marked the beginning of the French Revolution.

After two years of detention, King Louis XVI attempted to flee France but was captured and returned to the capital. The king agreed to a constitution, but as the Revolution faced defeat at the hands of foreign armies, extremists pushed to rid the country of all opponents, and this included the monarchy. The Reign of Terror was unleashed, and in 1792 the French Republic was created. The following year, both the king and his wife, Queen Marie-Antoinette, were guillotined.

Maximilien Robespierre and his Jacobin allies in the Committee of Public Safety plunged France into even more bloodshed. Thousands of people were denounced as antirevolutionary traitors; as many as 40,000 may have died during the Terror. Robespierre was eventually overthrown and then executed in the Coup de Thermidor in 1794.

POLITICS & POWER	GEOGRAPHY & ENVIRONMENT	CULTURE & RELIGION
▶ **1801 FORMER SLAVE TOUSSAINT-LOUVERTURE,** leader of the Haitian independence movement, takes command of the entire island of Hispaniola and declares himself governor-general for life. **1807 THE PORTUGUESE ROYAL FAMILY** flees to Brazil for safety during the Napoleonic War.	**1803 FOR $15 MILLION,** Napoleon sells all the prairie lands between the Mississippi River and the Rocky Mountains to the U.S. The Louisiana Purchase nearly doubles the nation's land area. **1804 MERIWETHER LEWIS AND WILLIAM CLARK** begin to explore the Louisiana Purchase and the Pacific Northwest.	**1804 TRYING TO REDUCE THE CHURCH'S INFLUENCE,** the Spanish government requires church institutions in Mexico to call in all their loans. The near bankruptcy of many businessmen forces reconsideration of the policy. It causes the financial ruin of many criollo elites. **1805 *DIARIO DE MÉXICO,*** the first Mexican daily newspaper, is published. **1809 EDGAR ALLAN POE,** creator of the detective story and known for his gothic tales, is born.
▶ **1805 NAPOLEON** defeats Russians and Austrians at the Battle of Austerlitz; the French ruler stands poised to dominate Europe. **1805 BRITAIN'S LORD NELSON** defeats the Franco-Spanish fleets at the Battle of Trafalgar. Lord Nelson is killed, but his victory ends Napoleon's power at sea and makes a French invasion of Britain impossible. **1807 SERFDOM** is abolished in Prussia. **1808 NAPOLEON** installs his brother as king of Spain.	**1807 THE SLAVE TRADE IS ABOLISHED** within the British Empire. **1809 SWEDEN** cedes Finland to Russia.	**1804 NAPOLEON'S CIVIL CODE** confirms the legal equality and property rights for men that emerged from the French Revolution; the code is adopted in many countries around the world.
1801 SERBIANS REVOLT against rebellious Janissaries, who kill the governor and take control of Belgrade. **1807 SELIM III** is overthrown by a coalition of Janissaries and clerics in Istanbul, but the rebels in turn are overthrown by provincial notables who put Selim's nephew Mahmud II on the throne in 1808.	**1808 SIERRA LEONE** becomes a British colony.	**1803-1808 USMAN DAN FODIO,** a Fulani religious leader from Nigeria, leads his followers in a jihad against Hausa rulers and is later proclaimed "Commander of the Faithful."
▶ **1801 RANJIT SINGH,** the Lion of the Punjab, declares himself maharaja of the Sikh state of Punjab in India at age 21. **1802 THE NGUYEN DYNASTY** is established by Emperor Gia Long in Vietnam after suppressing the Tay Son Rebellion. **1810 KING KAMEHAMEHA I** unites the Hawaiian Islands and establishes the Kamehameha dynasty.		 **1807 ROBERT MORRISON** of the London Missionary Society arrives in Canton to begin Protestant missionary work.

François-Dominique Toussaint Louverture led the Haitian Revolution against France and freed the slaves.

Ranjit Singh consolidated the Punjab with a pluralistic army composed of Sikhs, Muslims, and Hindus as well as European officers.

SCIENCE & TECHNOLOGY

PEOPLE & SOCIETY

1804 GERMAN NATURALIST ALEXANDER VON HUMBOLDT and French botanist Aime Bonpland conclude their five years of groundbreaking fieldwork in Central and South America.

1807 ROBERT FULTON develops the first practical steamboat, known later as the *Clermont*, which sails from New York City to Albany and back.

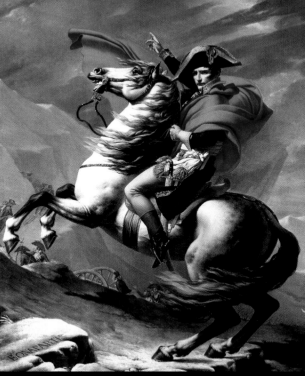

Napoleon Bonaparte is shown crossing the Alps in Jacques-Louis David's famous portrait.

1801 JÉRÔME LALANDE, a French astronomer, publishes a catalog listing 47,390 stars.

ca 1800–1806 OTTOMAN SULTAN SELIM III introduces modern weaponry and military methods to his army.

1805 JAPANESE DOCTOR SEISHU HANAOKA uses general anesthesia for the first time.

1804 THE SANDALWOOD TRADE begins in the Pacific islands.

THE CONQUESTS OF NAPOLEON

AFTER THE EXECUTION of its king and the beginning of the Reign of Terror, revolutionary France found itself at war with its neighbors—Austria, Prussia, Spain, and Britain. A young artillery officer named Napoleon Bonaparte rose quickly through the ranks, capturing the hearts of his countrymen as completely as he overwhelmed his enemies on the field of battle. Napoleon was quick to capitalize on his popularity.

In 1804, in a grand ceremony in Paris's Notre Dame cathedral, he was crowned emperor of the French. During the coronation, just as the pope was about to place the crown on Napoleon's head, Napoleon took the crown out of the pontiff's hands and placed it on his head himself.

No longer at war to defend the Revolution, imperial France now went on the offensive. Napoleon scored a succession of impressive victories, among the greatest the Battle of Austerlitz in 1805, after which much of Europe lay at his feet. However, two countries continued to resist him: the island kingdom of Great Britain and the huge nation of Russia.

To invade Britain, Napoleon needed command of the seas. But the Royal Navy's victory at Trafalgar robbed him of that, and so disappeared any hope of crossing the Channel to England. Instead, Napoleon marched his Grand Army all the way across Europe to invade Russia. This fateful decision would lead to the emperor's downfall and the defeat of France. For although the French managed to fight their way deep into Russia and capture Moscow, they were unable to remain there during the winter of 1812. The army had no choice but to trek back, through freezing temperatures and Cossack attacks. Estimates vary, but of the 600,000 or so who invaded, 40,000 or fewer returned.

Napoleon's hopes for a comeback were crushed in the Waterloo campaign, and he spent his last years in exile.

POLITICS & POWER	GEOGRAPHY & ENVIRONMENT	CULTURE & RELIGION
1810 MIGUEL HIDALGO Y COSTILLA calls for revolution against the Spanish on September 16, the date now celebrated as Mexican Independence Day. **1811 THE VENEZUELAN NATIONAL ASSEMBLY** declares independence from Spain. **1812-1815 THE WAR OF 1812** between the United States and Great Britain is fought. **1813 PARAGUAY** is formally declared an independent republic. **1814 THE BRITISH ARMY** burns down the White House in Washington, D.C.	**1812 THE RUSSIAN-AMERICAN COMPANY** establishes a settlement along California's Sonoma Coast. **1814 THE DEFEAT OF THE CREEKS** by Andrew Jackson leads to the Treaty of Fort Jackson, which requires the Creeks to cede 23 million acres of land in Alabama and Georgia.	**1810-1820 THE LIBERALS AND SEPARATISTS** in the Mexican independence movement raise the standard of the Virgin of Guadalupe, revered as patroness throughout the territories of New Spain. **1818 THE FIRST PUBLIC HORSE TROTTING RACE** in the United States takes place.
1812 NAPOLEON invades Russia; he captures Moscow, but unable to spend the winter there when the city catches fire, he marches his army back to France. **1814-1815 THE CONGRESS OF VIENNA** restores the Bourbon monarchy in France. **1815 AN ALLIED ARMY** led by Britain's Duke of Wellington defeats Napoleon at the Battle of Waterloo.		◀ **1812-1815 THE BROTHERS GRIMM** publish their volumes of *Fairy Tales*. **1813 ENGLISH NOVELIST JANE AUSTEN** publishes *Pride and Prejudice*, anonymously, in three volumes. **1814 THE WALTZ** becomes a popular dance.
1810 MAURITIUS AND SEYCHELLES are annexed by Britain. **1811 MUHAMMAD ALI'S MASSACRE** of the Mamluks of Cairo permits a recentralization of state finances in Egypt. **1813 THE GOVERNOR OF ALEPPO** massacres the Janissary leaders in Syria.	**1813-1814 THE FIRST EGYPTIAN AGRICULTURAL SURVEY** is conducted under Muhammad Ali. **1814 AT THE CONGRESS OF VIENNA,** the Dutch permanently cede the Cape Province to Britain.	**1813 EGYPTIAN FORCES** retake Mecca from the Wahhabis.
1811 THE BRITISH conquer Java in the East Indies. **1818 THE MARATHA** are defeated by the British, who become in effect the rulers of India. **1819 THE BRITISH FOUND SINGAPORE** as a free-trade port, permanently breaking the Dutch trading monopoly in the region.	**1815 SUMBAWA VOLCANO ERUPTS** in Indonesia, killing more than 50,000 people.	**1812 KING POMARE II OF TAHITI** converts to Christianity. **1813 NGUYEN DU** writes the Vietnamese epic *The Tale of Kieu*. The story's heroine must suffer to atone for sins from a past life before she can find happiness. **1814 THE FIRST BRITISH PROTESTANT MISSIONARIES** arrive in New Zealand to bring the Gospel to the Maoris. **1820 THE FIRST CHRISTIAN MISSIONARIES** arrive in the Hawaiian Islands.

Deutſche Märchen in Wort und Bild.
2
Schneeweißchen.

Widmung.

Was wärſt du ſchöne Jugendzeit
Denn ohne Märchenblüthen?
Wenn ſie nicht goldnen Sternen gleich
An deinem Himmel glühten.

Ein Jugendmorgen ohne ſie
Er wäre halbes Leben;
Du glücklich Kind, dem ſie den Lenz
Der Jugend hold umſchweben.

Gewiß man ſagt es unbewußt:
„Das Märchen ſei nur Lüge;"
Es iſt des Kindes reinſte Luſt,
Des Kindergeiſtes Wiege.

Gedeih'! du ewig grüner Baum
Streu deinen Blüthenſegen
Der goldnen Jugend in den Schooß
Wie einen Zauberregen.

Frankfurt am Main
Verlag von
E. G. May Söhne.

Title page to the Grimm fairy tale of Snow White

SCIENCE & TECHNOLOGY	PEOPLE & SOCIETY
1817 NEW YORK STATE begins construction of the Erie Canal to connect the Hudson River to the Great Lakes. **1817** BALTIMORE becomes the first U.S. city to adopt gas streetlights.	**1815** THE MARKET ECONOMY begins to transform United States society in the years after the War of 1812. **1820** THE MISSOURI COMPROMISE seeks to end the crisis concerning the extension of slavery in the U.S. Maine enters the Union as a free state, Missouri as a slave state.
1812 THE CYLINDER PRINTING PRESS is invented; it is adopted by *The Times* of London. **1814** BRITISH ENGINEER GEORGE STEPHENSON builds his first locomotive, the *Blucher*. His later innovations result in the first practical steam locomotive.	**1811** A RUSSIAN CENSUS estimates the empire's population to be more than 41 million. **1815** AFTER HIS DEFEAT AT WATERLOO, Napoleon goes into exile on the island of St. Helena.
1818-1834 WOOL MILLS, sugar refineries, glassworks, and other industries are established in Egypt.	▼ **1816** SHAKA becomes ruler of the Zulu kingdom; his disciplined and mobile army conquers many peoples of southeastern Africa.
1819 THE WHALING INDUSTRY begins in the Pacific islands.	

RISE OF THE ZULUS

SHAKA ZULU is probably the most famous southern African leader in history. A fierce and militaristic king, Shaka took a then-insignificant Zulu clan and transformed it into a powerful nation with an army of 50,000 men.

An accomplished fighter at an early age, Shaka defeated his brother to gain control over the Zulu chieftaincy upon the death of their father. With great energy, he started to build a mighty army of Zulu warriors. He is credited with teaching his men to use the shield as an offensive weapon, hooking the enemy's shield to the side to expose his ribs. He also introduced a shorter version of the spear, which they brandished as a stabbing weapon. Scorning European firearms because they took so long to reload, he believed that man was the ultimate weapon. From each of his fighters he demanded total loyalty and obedience, punishing with death those who hesitated to follow his commands. But Shaka shared his army's hardships, drilling with his men and forsaking the comforts of a Zulu king.

Shaka scored victory after victory against neighboring people, uniting the tribes while averting conflict with the newly arrived white settlers. Under his rule, Zulu territory expanded rapidly. By 1820 he had won control of most of southeast Africa and Natal. Zulu empire building, however, devastated huge areas and depopulated many regions as tribes migrated away from Zulu war bands. The period of turmoil came to be known as the *mfecane* or *difaqane*—the time of troubles.

Shaka's rule came to an end in 1828 when he was assassinated by his two half brothers, who stabbed him to death with their spears and threw his body in an empty grain pit that was then filled with stones.

Shaka Zulu with his weapons of choice—the shield and the spear

POLITICS & POWER

1821 PERU declares independence from Spain.

1822 DOM PEDRO declares Brazil independent from Portugal.

1822 AFTER SAN MARTÍN'S DEPARTURE from Peru, Simón Bolívar leads a rebel force into the Andes. His lieutenant Antonio José de Sucre conquers the last Spanish stronghold.

1824 MEXICO becomes a republic, three years after declaring independence from Spain.

1828 URUGUAY becomes an independent state.

1830 REVOLUTIONS ERUPT in France, Germany, Poland, Italy, Belgium, Switzerland, and Portugal.

1821 EGYPTIANS invade the Sudan.

1830 THE FRENCH begin their conquest of Algeria, still nominally part of the Ottoman Empire.

1824 THE BRITISH begin their conquest of Burma in Southeast Asia.

1825-1830 IN THE JAVA WAR, Indonesians revolt against Dutch rule.

GEOGRAPHY & ENVIRONMENT

1821 SPAIN CEDES FLORIDA to the United States in exchange for a $5 million settlement of claims.

1828 WESTERN CHEROKEE INDIANS cede to the U.S. their lands in Arkansas in exchange for a tract of seven million acres that includes what is now northern Oklahoma.

Leading French Romantic artist Eugène Delacroix painted "Greece on the Ruins of Missolonghi" to commemorate the plight of the Greeks under the Ottoman Empire, a popular cause among European intellectuals.

1820s AUSTRALIAN WOOL EXPORTS replace earlier, less successful trade commodities, such as sealskins, seal oil, and sandalwood.

CULTURE & RELIGION

1820-1830 JOSEPH SMITH, JR., reports a series of visions in New York State that will lead to the founding of the Church of Jesus Christ of Latter-day Saints (Mormons).

◀ **1820s ROMANTICISM** in European literature and art features the works of Byron, Chateaubriand, Heine, Turner, and Delacroix.

1828 NOAH WEBSTER PUBLISHES *An American Dictionary of the English Language,* the first American unabridged dictionary.

1820s AFTER AN INITIALLY POSITIVE RECEPTION, American Protestant missionaries in Lebanon meet resistance among the Maronite hierarchy.

1829 AN OTTOMAN CLOTHING LAW substitutes the fez for the turban.

1825 QUEEN KAAHUMANU OF HAWAII converts to Christianity.

1828 THE BRAHMO SAMAJ modern Hindu reform movement is founded in India.

1829 SUTTEE, the practice of self-immolation by Hindu widows, is abolished in British India.

SCIENCE & TECHNOLOGY

1820s U.S. MANUFACTURERS develop interchangeable parts, which are originally used to produce weapons for the U.S. Army.

1825 THE ERIE CANAL opens, allowing boats to travel from the Great Lakes to the Atlantic Ocean.

1828 WORK BEGINS on the first steam-powered railroad in the U.S., the Baltimore and Ohio Railroad (B&O).

1821 MICHAEL FARADAY demonstrates electromagnetic rotation, the principle of the electric motor.

1824 LOUIS BRAILLE of Paris invents a reading system for the blind.

1825 THE FIRST PASSENGER STEAM RAILWAY opens, between Stockton and Darlington, England.

1826 JOSEPH-NICÉPHORE NIEPCE produces the first photographic image.

1820s ZULU KING SHAKA, founder of a powerful and feared military in southern Africa, ridicules European firearms, favoring instead the assegai (a slender iron-tipped wooden spear or javelin).

1830s SUGAR CULTIVATION begins in Hawaii.

PEOPLE & SOCIETY

1820s IN THE AFTERMATH of successful independence revolts, most Latin American countries drift into rule by caudillos (military strongmen), rather than rule by republic.

1830 THE U.S. CONGRESS passes the Indian Removal Act.

1824 THE REPEAL OF COMBINATIONS ACTS allows British workers to form unions.

1824 ST. PETERSBURG, RUSSIA, experiences the most destructive flood in its history.

1829 SIR ROBERT PEEL founds a new British police force in London.

1822 AMERICAN ABOLITIONISTS found Monrovia, future capital of Liberia.

1828 ZULU KING SHAKA is assassinated by his half brothers.

FREEDOM FOR SOUTH AMERICA

THE FIGHT FOR SOUTH AMERICAN independence from Spain was led by Simón Bolívar, a wealthy Creole born in Venezuela but educated in Spain. It was in Europe that Bolívar came under the influence of Enlightenment ideas. Revolutions in France and North America at the end of the 18th century showed him that the people of South America could also take control of their own destinies. He was soon calling for independence for the continent of his birth. "I will not rest body or soul," declared Bolívar, "until I have broken the chains binding us to the will of Spanish might!"

At one time, Spain's control of its colonies was total, in both political and mercantile terms. But when Napoleon's armies invaded the Iberian Peninsula, Spain's colonial grip loosened, and revolutionary juntas began to set themselves up in South America. Bolívar led the revolutionary forces in his native Venezuela. In 1819, the rebels gained power in the country, then turned toward Colombia and Ecuador.

Meanwhile, in the south of the continent, José de San Martin rallied revolutionary elements in Argentina. After freeing that country, he led 5,000 men across the Andes to Chile, where they charged down upon panicked Spanish defenders. San Martin and Bolívar eventually met in Peru, the bastion of Spanish South America. Led by San Martin, Peru gained partial independence in 1821. Under Bolívar, it achieved complete independence from Spain in 1824. (Brazil had peacefully gained its freedom from Portugal two years earlier.)

Bolívar had hoped to unite all South Americans into a single nation. In this he was unsuccessful. Nevertheless, for all of his achievements throughout the continent, he is known as El Libertador—the Liberator.

Map showing the dates when South American colonies won their independence

POLITICS & POWER

1833 GENERAL ANTONIO LOPEZ DE SANTA ANNA begins his first term as president of Mexico.

1835 JUAN MANUEL ROSAS, the tyrannical caudillo of Argentina, returns to the post of governor of Buenos Aires under the condition he receive dictatorial powers.

1836 TEXANS ARE DEFEATED by the Mexican army at the Alamo; Texas gains independence later that same year after winning the Battle of San Jacinto.

1831 GIUSEPPE MAZZINI founds Young Italy, an organization dedicated to the creation of an Italian republic.

1832 GREECE WINS its independence from the Turks.

1833 THE ZOLLVEREIN is formed, a German customs union under the leadership of Prussia.

1830 THE FRENCH invade Algeria.

1831-1839 MUHAMMAD ALI'S SON, Ibrahim Pasha, conquers Syria and threatens to overthrow Ottoman centralized power. His introduction of equal taxation and conscription provokes revolts in Syria, Palestine, and Mount Lebanon.

1832-1847 MUSLIM LEADER ABDELKADER resists the French invasion of Algeria.

1835 OTTOMANS reassert control over Tripoli and Benghazi in North Africa.

1839-1842 THE OPIUM WAR between Britain and China occurs. China is forced to open ports to Western trade and cede Hong Kong to Great Britain.

1840 IN NEW ZEALAND, the Treaty of Waitangi between the Maoris and Britain guarantees the Maori possession of certain tracts of lands and full rights of British subjects.

GEOGRAPHY & ENVIRONMENT

1831-1842 THE FIVE CIVILIZED TRIBES—Cherokee, Chickasaw, Choctaw, Creek, and Seminole—are removed from their native lands and forced west.

1830s THE SHIFTING ECOLOGY OF WEST AFRICA brings drier conditions and leads to widespread drought and dislocation.

1837 WHITE VOORTREKKERS (BOER PIONEERS) migrating from the British Cape Colony kill some 3,000 Zulus at the Battle of Blood River and push the Zulu north of the Limpopo River.

1833-1837 POOR HARVESTS lead to the Tenpo famine in Japan.

CULTURE & RELIGION

1837 CHRISTIAN EVANGELIST DWIGHT L. MOODY is born in East Northfield, Massachusetts.

1831 FRENCH AUTHOR VICTOR HUGO publishes *Notre-Dame de Paris (The Hunchback of Notre Dame).*

1835 GAETANO DONIZETTI'S OPERA *Lucia di Lammermoor* premieres in Naples.

1835 SYNAGOGUES IN JERUSALEM are rebuilt under Egyptian governor Ibrahim Pasha.

1839 SULTAN ABDULMECID I ushers in the Ottoman reform period known as Tanzimat. Ultimately, the reform effort will be in vain.

1830s OPIUM IMPORTS outstrip Chinese exports of tea and silk.

1831 KING TAUFA'AHAU OF TONGA converts to Christianity.

1833-1834 JAPANESE PAINTER AND PRINTMAKER HIROSHIGE produces his most famous work, "Fifty-three Stations of the Tokaido."

CONNECTIONS

British Opium and the Chinese

In the 1830s, British traders shipped tons of Indian-grown opium to Canton, where it was traded for silk, spices, porcelain, and tea. The trade produced serious social and economic problems because of drug addiction. For decades, the Chinese government had officially banned opium imports, a ban that British traders had ignored. But when Chinese junks attempted to turn back English merchant vessels in 1839, war erupted. Chinese old-style weaponry was no match for the British gunships, which prowled the coast, or the firepower of British land forces. In 1842, the Chinese were forced to accept the Treaty of Nanjing, which opened coastal treaty ports to foreign trade and ceded the island of Hong Kong to Britain.

SCIENCE & TECHNOLOGY

1830s **BRITISH MATHEMATICIAN CHARLES BABBAGE** expands on his "Difference Engine" calculating machine and develops a plan for the "analytical engine," the forerunner of the modern computer.

1833 **THE FIRST MECHANICAL REAPER** is patented.

1830s **BELGIUM** begins building state-owned railroads.

1840 **THE FIRST POSTAGE STAMP,** called the "penny black," is issued in England, bearing the image of Queen Victoria.

1835-1836 **NATURALIST CHARLES DARWIN** visits New Zealand and Australia on the *Beagle*.

PEOPLE & SOCIETY

1830s **NEW DICTATORSHIPS** and occasional republics in South America and Latin America leave indigenous people in exploitative relationships with Creole elites.

1830s **FEMALE TEXTILE WORKERS** in New England begin to take labor actions over wages, working conditions, and hours.

1833 **MEXICO** suffers from a cholera epidemic.

1836 **DAVY CROCKETT** and 182 others die fighting for Texas's independence from Mexico at the Alamo.

1832 **GERMAN POET** Johann Wolfgang von Goethe dies.

1832 **A CHOLERA EPIDEMIC** kills 31,000 people in Britain.

1833 **THE FACTORY ACT OF 1833** sets age, schooling, and work-hour requirements for children in Britain.

ca 1840 **ZANZIBAR** becomes the commercial center of East Africa, exporting cloves and other spices across the Indian Ocean.

THE TRAIL OF TEARS

WHEN THE U.S. CONGRESS passed the Indian Removal Act, the Creek, Chickasaw, Choctaw, Cherokee, and Seminole Indians were evicted from their lands, although the Cherokee nation attempted to fight the law's constitutionality in the Supreme Court. The effort failed, and in 1838 the federal government began the removal of Cherokees from east of the Mississippi River. In exchange, they were given land in the Indian Territory, in what is present-day Oklahoma, as well as the promise of money and provisions.

Under orders from the president, Andrew Jackson, General Winfield Scott and 7,000 of his troops were given the task of removing the Indians. Thus began one of the saddest episodes in American history. Some Cherokees ran off and took refuge in the mountains, the swamps, and other places too inhospitable for whites. Others agreed to accept United States citizenship and were allowed to remain. But in the winter of 1838-1839, some 15,000 Indians were marched more than a thousand miles through Tennessee, Kentucky, Illinois, Missouri, and Arkansas into the forbidding Indian Territory.

Many Indians walked the entire distance without footwear and barely clothed. Human losses were extremely high—about 4,000 died, from hunger, disease, exposure, and exhaustion. The Indians' forced journey westward became known as the Trail of Tears or, as a more direct translation from the Cherokee puts it, the "Trail Where They Cried."

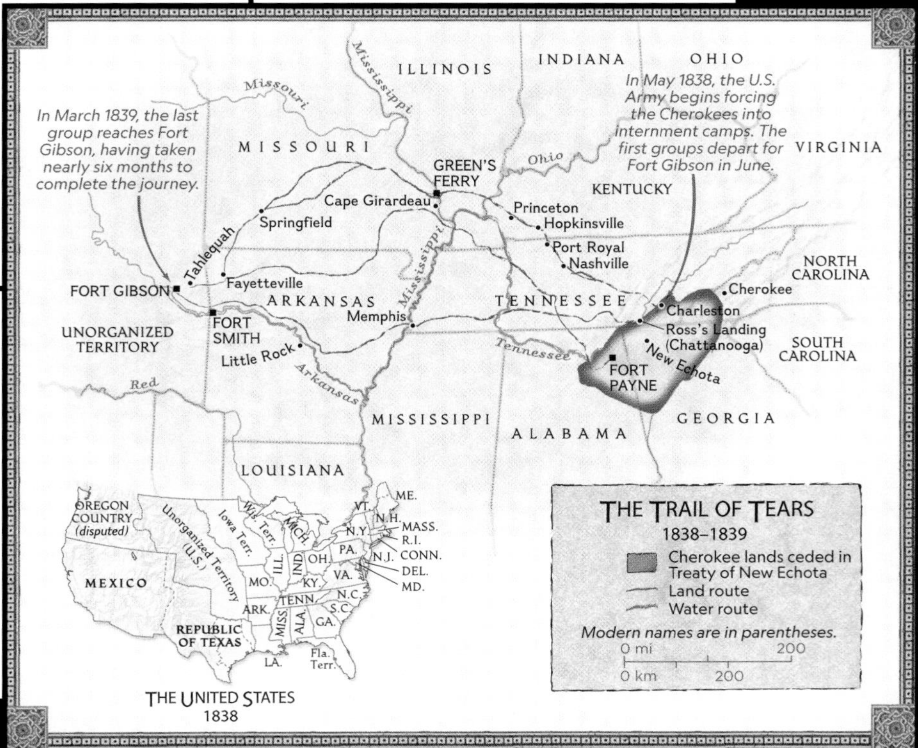

When the Cherokee, among other Native American nations, were evicted from their homes east of the Mississippi River, they began a forced march west known as the Trail of Tears.

POLITICS & POWER

1844 SANTO DOMINGO proclaims its independence from the state of Haiti and becomes the Dominican Republic.

1845 TEXAS IS ANNEXED by the United States.

1846-1848 THE MEXICAN WAR between the U.S. and Mexico results in the U.S. possession of California and much of the Southwest, which had been Mexican territory.

1841 TO STUNT RUSSIAN IMPERIAL AMBITIONS in the eastern Mediterranean, an international Straits Convention closes the Bosporus to all non-Turkish warships.

1846 BRITAIN repeals the Corn Laws that had attempted to regulate the price of grain and moves toward free trade.

1848 REVOLUTIONS BREAK OUT across much of Europe; the Second Republic is proclaimed in France.

1840 THE LEBANESE rebel against Egyptian occupation.

1844 THE BRITISH ESTABLISH an informal protectorate over the Gold Coast in West Africa.

1847 LIBERIA becomes a fully independent republic.

1848 ALGERIA is declared a part of France.

1842 THE TREATY OF NANJING ends the first Opium War between Britain and China.

1843-1849 THE BRITISH conquer Kashmir and Punjab in India.

1850-1864 MILLIONS OF PEOPLE DIE in the Taiping Rebellion, China's—and the world's—bloodiest civil war.

GEOGRAPHY & ENVIRONMENT

1841 THE FIRST OVERLAND WAGON TRAINS of settlers depart Missouri for California.

1848 AFTER DELINEATING THE CANADIAN-U.S. BOUNDARY with the British, Congress creates the Oregon Territory that will become the states Oregon, Washington, and Idaho.

1849 THE CALIFORNIA GOLD RUSH begins; more than 100,000 people rush to California to seek their fortunes after gold is found there in 1848.

1849 SCOTTISH MISSIONARY and explorer David Livingstone reaches Lake Ngami in the African interior.

1840s THE FRENCH acquire various islands in the Pacific, among them Tahiti.

CULTURE & RELIGION

1845 DOMINGO SARMIENTO publishes *Facundo: Civilization and Barbarism,* which examines the Argentine character and prescribes a modernization of Latin America.

1846 THE FIRST PROFESSIONAL BASEBALL GAME is played, in Hoboken, New Jersey.

1847 THE FIRST U.S. POSTAGE STAMPS are issued.

1848 KARL MARX AND FRIEDRICH ENGELS publish *The Communist Manifesto,* which asserts that revolution by the working classes will ultimately destroy capitalism.

1840s BOSNIAN RABBI JUDAH BEN SOLOMON HAI ALKALAI publishes books that offer a precursor to Zionism, a movement for a Jewish homeland.

1844 IN CHINA, an imperial edict relaxes a ban on the Catholic Church.

WHAT LIFE WAS LIKE

Traveling by Covered Wagon

Beginning in the 1840s, pioneers from the eastern United States began crossing the Oregon Trail from Missouri to the frontier lands of Oregon and California. They followed a route long established by fur traders, military scouts, and missionaries but used a unique form of transportation—the covered wagon. Family members traveled aboard a wagon topped with a white canvas that was stretched over big wooden hoops and rubbed with oil to make it waterproof. They closed both ends of the canvas to keep out the rain and the wind, or when it grew hot they rolled it up to get the benefit of the breeze. They feared attacks from hostile Indian nations though weather, exposure, and disease proved to be greater threats. Between 1843 and the Civil War about half a million pioneers journey across the west.

SCIENCE & TECHNOLOGY

Harriet Tubman (far left, holding a pan) photographed with a group of slaves whose escape she assisted via the Underground Railroad.

1847 IN GERMANY, Alfred Krupp's Essen Works produces the first all-steel guns; in 1867 Alfred Krupp presents the king of Prussia with a 50-ton steel cannon.

1845 BRITISH ARCHAEOLOGIST HENRY LAYARD, in his first month of digging in Iraq, discovers the Assyrian city of Nimrud.

1841 PIERRE BOITARD, a French naturalist, scientifically identifies the Tasmanian devil, an Australian marsupial, as *Sarcophilus harrisii*.

PEOPLE & SOCIETY

1848 THE PRAIEIRA REVOLUTION breaks out in Pernambuco, Brazil.

◀ **1849** HARRIET TUBMAN escapes from slavery and goes on to lead more than 300 slaves to freedom via the Underground Railroad.

1849 ABRAHAM LINCOLN, Whig congressman from Illinois and critic of the Mexican War, retires from politics after one term in office to practice law. He reemerges the following decade as a moderate opponent of slavery in the new Republican Party.

1842 AFTER INVESTIGATIONS INTO WORKING CONDITIONS, women are forbidden to work underground in British mines.

1845 THE IRISH POTATO FAMINE begins, one of the century's worst natural disasters. Between 1.1 and 1.5 million citizens die from starvation and disease, and as many as two million others immigrate, mostly to the U.S.

1849 A DEADLY CHOLERA EPIDEMIC kills about 14,000 in London, England.

1841 AN OTTOMAN POSTAL SERVICE is established.

1846 THE ISTANBUL SLAVE MARKET is abolished.

1848 THE GREAT MAHELE permits division and sale of land as private property in Hawaii.

1850 THE CHINESE POPULATION reaches 420 million.

THE IRISH POTATO FAMINE

DURING THE SUMMER of 1845, a "blight of unusual character" devastated Ireland's potato crop. Grown for more than 200 years in Ireland, the potato was the basic staple in the people's diet. Most Irish peasants rented small plots of land from absentee British landlords, and because a single acre of potatoes could support a family for a year, the Irish came to depend on the potato as their chief source of food. Potatoes were nutritious and easy to grow, requiring a minimum of labor, training, and equipment; a spade was the only tool needed. But when the blight struck, the potatoes began to turn slimy, black, and rotten just days after they were dug from the earth.

Theories abounded about the cause of the blight. Some investigators said it was the result of "static electricity" or the smoke that billowed from railroad locomotives. Or even the "mortiferous vapours" rising from underground volcanoes. The actual cause was a fungus—*Phytophthora infestans*—that had traveled from North America to Ireland.

"Famine fever"—cholera, dysentery, scurvy, typhus, and infestations of lice—soon spread through the Irish countryside. Observers reported seeing children crying with pain and looking "like skeletons, their features sharpened with hunger and their limbs wasted, so that there was little left but bones." Masses of bodies were buried without coffins, a few inches below the soil.

The government did little to help the people, merely forcing hundreds of thousands into workhouses. Over the next 10 years, one million died and as many as two million left their homeland for Great Britain, Canada, and the United States. Within five years, the Irish Potato Famine, also known as the Great Hunger, had reduced the Irish population by a quarter. The blight struck other northern European countries, such as Norway, leading to famine and increased immigration there as well.

POLITICS & POWER

1857 **OTTAWA** becomes Canada's capital by royal decree.

1857 **THE DRED SCOTT DECISION** makes the Missouri Compromise unconstitutional and increases tension between North and South over slavery in the U.S.

1858 to 1861 **CONSERVATIVES AND LIBERALS** struggle for power in Mexico in the Three Year War.

1851 **RUSSIANS** invade Turkey's Danubian provinces and, by sinking the Turkish fleet, gain control of the Black Sea.

1852 **THE FRENCH REPUBLIC** falls; Louis Napoleon (Napoleon III) is crowned emperor.

1856 **RUSSIA** is defeated by Britain, France, and the Ottoman Turks in the Crimean War. Under the Treaty of Paris, Russia accepts humiliating terms, agreeing to keep no navy on the Black Sea and to maintain no bases on its shores.

1850-1855 **FORMER BANDIT CHIEFTAIN KASSA** unifies Ethiopia's numerous small states into one empire. He has himself crowned king of kings and takes the throne name Tewodros II.

1857 **THE FRENCH** complete their conquest of Algeria.

1858 **THE FRENCH** expand their presence in West Africa by advancing up the Senegal River.

1860 **THE SPANISH** invade Morocco, just across the Strait of Gibraltar.

1855 **THE KURIL ISLANDS** are partitioned between Japan and Russia.

1856 **NEW ZEALAND AND TASMANIA** win self-government from Britain.

1856-1860 **THE SECOND OPIUM WAR** between Britain and China leads to further incursions on Chinese sovereignty.

1857 **THE INDIAN MUTINY** breaks out in opposition to British rule.

1859 **THE FRENCH** occupy Saigon in Indochina.

GEOGRAPHY & ENVIRONMENT

Demonstration of an early elevator model by Elisha Graves Otis in New York City

1854-1856 **SCOTTISH MISSIONARY** and explorer David Livingstone crosses Africa from the west coast to the east coast.

1857 **IRAN** recognizes Afghan independence.

1851 **GOLD IS DISCOVERED** in New South Wales and Victoria, accelerating immigration to Australia.

1858-1860 **IN THE TREATIES OF AIGUN AND BEIJING** a weakened China surrenders much territory to Russia.

1860-1861 **ROBERT O'HARA BURKE AND WILLIAM JOHN WILLS** complete the first north-south overland crossing of Australia; both die on the return journey.

CULTURE & RELIGION

1850 **BECAUSE BRAZIL REFUSES** to end the slave trade, the British Royal Navy begins seizing suspected slave ships and effectively blockading Brazilian ports.

1852 **HARRIET BEECHER STOWE** publishes her antislavery novel *Uncle Tom's Cabin.*

1856 **THE MEXICAN GOVERNMENT** publishes Ley Lerdo (Lerdo Law), which requires all corporations, including the Catholic Church, to sell much of their property at public auctions.

1850s **THE ROMANTIC PERIOD,** featuring the works of Berlioz, Liszt, Wagner, Brahms, and Verdi, reaches its apogee.

1853 **GEORGES-EUGÈNE,** Baron Haussmann begins rebuilding Paris, which comes to be characterized by broad boulevards.

ca 1860 **EUROPEAN LITERATURE** flourishes, with works by Dickens, Dumas, Flaubert, Turgenev, Dostoyevsky, and Tolstoy.

CONNECTIONS

Commodore Perry and Japanese Expansion

When Commodore Matthew Perry sailed into Edo Bay in 1853, he found a mysterious island kingdom that had been closed to all but a few Dutch and Chinese merchants. To the shocked onlookers, the modern American ships were like "giant dragons puffing smoke." The Japanese realized how technologically far behind their country had fallen. On March 31, 1854, they signed a historic treaty agreeing to trade with the United States. The barrier between Japan and the rest of the world started to come down; the country began to industrialize and modernize rapidly. In less than a century, Japan would transform itself from a feudal nation to an international power ready to challenge the United States for dominance in the Pacific.

SCIENCE & TECHNOLOGY

1851 **ISAAC SINGER** patents the continuous-stitch sewing machine.

1852 **THE BROWN PAPER BAG** is created.

◀ **1852** **ELISHA OTIS** designs the first elevator with an automatic safety device to prevent falls. It facilitates the future development of skyscrapers.

1853 **POTATO CHIPS** are invented.

1851 **THE GREAT EXHIBITION,** the world's first industrial fair, opens in London. More than 100,000 exhibits are housed in the Crystal Palace.

1858 **ENGLAND'S QUEEN VICTORIA** sends the first message over transatlantic cable to U.S. President James Buchanan.

1856 **THE RAILWAY** between Cairo and Alexandria in Egypt is inaugurated.

1859 **JAMES AFRICANUS BEALE HORTON** of Sierra Leone becomes the first African graduate of the University of Edinburgh, where he earns a medical degree. He writes a dissertation entitled *The Medical Topography of the West Coast of Africa.*

1859 **CONSTRUCTION OF THE SUEZ CANAL** proceeds after the death of Egyptian leader Muhammad Ali, who had refused to sanction it.

1853 **THE FIRST RAILROAD AND TELEGRAPH LINES** are laid in India.

PEOPLE & SOCIETY

1858 **ABRAHAM LINCOLN,** running for the U.S. Senate, declares, "A house divided against itself cannot stand." He loses the race to Stephen Douglas, but his performance in their now-legendary debates leads to his Republican nomination for president in 1860.

1860 **THE PONY EXPRESS** begins cross-country mail delivery.

1855-1881 **ALEXANDER II,** the "Tsar Liberator," tries to remedy the backwardness of Russia in the wake of its defeat in the Crimean War.

1859 **CHARLES DARWIN'S** *On the Origin of Species by Means of Natural Selection* is published.

1860 **ITALIAN PATRIOT GIUSEPPE GARIBALDI** leads a rebellion in southern Italy; unification of the country begins.

1857 **THE AFRICAN SLAVE TRADE** is prohibited in the Ottoman Empire.

1858 **THE OTTOMAN LAND CODE** and Egyptian land laws introduce private property; land is supposed to belong to peasant cultivators but often goes to local notables.

1860 **THE MASSACRE OF CHRISTIANS** in Damascus in the first Lebanese Civil War results in international outrage and the arrival of French and Ottoman troops to restore order.

1853 **COMMODORE MATTHEW PERRY** sails into Edo Bay, urging Japan to open trade policies with the U.S.

1854 **THE FIRST CHINESE STUDENT** to graduate from an American university is Yung Wing, a graduate of Yale.

THE TAIPING REBELLION

DURING THE MID-19TH CENTURY, China was rocked by a series of natural calamities of unprecedented proportions, including droughts, famines, and floods. The ruling Manchu dynasty did little to relieve the widespread misery caused by these events, which inflamed popular resentment against the government into the largest uprising in modern Chinese history, and the bloodiest civil war the world has known—the Taiping Rebellion.

The Taiping rebels were led by Hong Xiuquan, a failed civil service examination candidate who claimed he was the younger brother of Jesus Christ. In 1851 Hong launched an uprising in Guizhou Province in southern China, where he proclaimed the Heavenly Kingdom of Great Peace (or Taiping) with himself as king. Two years later the rebels captured the old imperial capital of Nanjing.

Hong's new order was founded on a mixture of some Christian beliefs along with a utopian tradition drawn from Chinese sources in which the peasantry owned and tilled the land in common. This vision won Hong many supporters among China's poorest classes.

The revolt held sway across a large swath of southern and central China. Soon, however, the movement's leaders found themselves in a net of internal feuds, defections, and corruption. British and French forces came to the assistance of the Manchu government once they realized that the rebellion might affect foreign trade, but the suppression of the Taipings ultimately depended on the Chinese provincial officials, whose armies rallied to the government's aid.

Well over 20 million people were reportedly killed as a result of the Taiping Rebellion. Like the savagely suppressed revolutions of 1848 that had recently swept across the continent of Europe, the Taiping Rebellion resulted in a surge of immigration to the United States.

POLITICS & POWER

▼ **1861-1865 THE U.S. CIVIL WAR** begins with the secession of southern states.

1862-1867 THE FRENCH attempt to erect a puppet empire in Mexico.

1865 ARGENTINA, BRAZIL, AND URUGUAY declare war on Paraguay, launching the War of the Triple Alliance.

1867 THE DOMINION OF CANADA is established.

1866 PRUSSIA defeats Austria at the Battle of Königgrätz.

1867 THE DUAL MONARCHY of Austria-Hungary is formed.

1870-1871 THE FRANCO-PRUSSIAN WAR leads to the formation of the German empire.

1861 LAGOS IN WEST AFRICA comes under British control.

1864 TUNISIA'S ECONOMY FALTERS, leading to increased taxes and the revolt of tribal and urban people.

1867 THE BRITISH conduct a military expedition to Ethiopia to free hostages taken by Emperor Tewodros II.

1860s LAND WARS IN NEW ZEALAND enable British settlers to seize 3.25 million acres on the North Island.

1862 A MUSLIM REVOLT breaks out in China's northwest.

1863 FRANCE establishes a protectorate over Cambodia; other protectorates follow for Cochin China, Annam, Tonkin, and Laos.

▶ **1868 THE MEIJI RESTORATION** in Japan overthrows the Tokugawa shogunate and lays the foundations of Japan's modern nation-state.

GEOGRAPHY & ENVIRONMENT

1867 THE U.S. BUYS ALASKA from Russia for $7.2 million—about two cents per acre.

1870 THE RAILROAD cuts in two the buffalo herd of the plains, breaking the economic base of Native Americans.

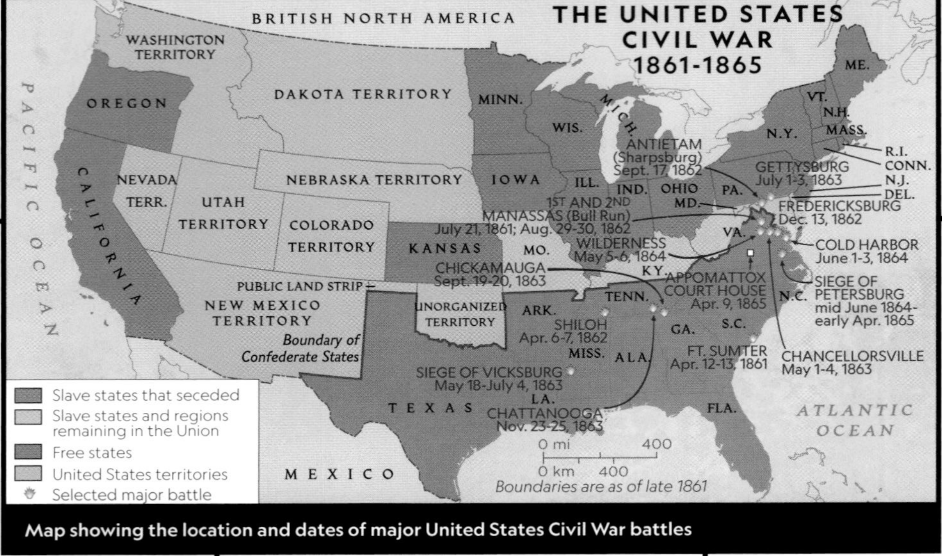

Map showing the location and dates of major United States Civil War battles

1860-1861 FAMINE leads to bread riots in Iran; women lead popular protests.

1863 COTTON CULTIVATION booms in Egypt during the American Civil War.

1863 THE BEIRUT-DAMASCUS ROAD, managed by the French, opens the interior of Syria to the port at Beirut and enables access to the West.

1867 DIAMONDS are discovered in southern Africa.

1860s SUGAR CULTIVATION begins in Fiji.

1869 JAPAN colonizes Hokkaido as part of its new nation-state.

CULTURE & RELIGION

1868-1869 LOUISA MAY ALCOTT publishes *Little Women* in two installments.

1868 DOMINGO FAUSTINO SARMIENTO, the great intellectual, educator, and liberal leader, becomes president of Argentina.

1869 PAIUTE prophet-dreamers develop the Ghost Dance.

1867 JOHAN STRAUSS II'S *On the Beautiful Blue Danube* is first performed.

1865-1868 LEO TOLSTOY publishes *War and Peace.*

1870 THE ROMAN CATHOLIC CHURCH proclaims the dogma of the infallibility of the pope.

1865 AN ARABIC TRANSLATION OF THE BIBLE is published.

1866 SYRIAN PROTESTANT COLLEGE (now the American University of Beirut) is founded in Beirut by Protestant missionaries; it contributes to the Arabic literary revival among Syrian Christians.

1870 ANTI-MISSIONARY SENTIMENTS lead to the Tianjin massacre in China.

SCIENCE & TECHNOLOGY	PEOPLE & SOCIETY
1869 THE TRANSCONTINENTAL RAILROAD is completed. By the following year, the United States has 53,000 miles of railroad.	**1865** SLAVERY IS ABOLISHED in the U.S. with the Thirteenth Amendment to the Constitution. **1865** JOHN WILKES BOOTH assassinates President Abraham Lincoln.
1861 LOUIS PASTEUR evolves the germ theory of disease. **1863** THE FIRST UNDERGROUND RAILWAY is built in London. **1870** EUROPE possesses some 64,000 miles of railroads.	**1861** RUSSIAN SERFS are emancipated, gaining liberty from their landlords but facing many obstacles to gaining promised land of their own. **1862** OTTO VON BISMARCK is appointed Prime Minister of Prussia. **1864** HENRI DUNANT founds the International Red Cross, in Switzerland.
1869 THE SUEZ CANAL OPENS, linking Egypt's Port Said on the Mediterranean coast to the Red Sea. At 101 miles long, it reduces the voyage from Britain to India by 4,000 miles. **1870** THE SUEZ CANAL carries some 437,000 tons of cargo.	**1865** THE YOUNG OTTOMANS, a secret Turkish nationalist organization, is founded in Istanbul. **1870** THE TRANSATLANTIC SLAVE TRADE between Africa and the Americas comes to an end.
	1869 MOHANDAS GANDHI, hero of India's independence struggle, is born.

Reforms under Japan's Emperor Meiji include universal education, geographic organization by prefecture, a new capital in Tokyo, mandatory military service, and the revocation of feudal class privileges.

DARWINISM

IN THE EARLY 1830S Charles Darwin had served as a naturalist aboard the H.M.S. *Beagle* on a round-the-world science expedition. In South America, he found fossils of extinct animals that were similar to modern species. And on the Galapagos Islands in the Pacific Ocean, he noticed many variations among plants and animals of the same general type as those on the South American mainland. Darwin observed that isolated populations adapt and evolve in diverse ways. For example, several species of finch had evolved on the various islands, each with a beak adapted to a different way of feeding. Unless each tiny species was the product of a miracle, populations separated by isolation on the islands had each evolved in their own way.

Drawing on the work of earlier scholars, Darwin eventually developed the theory of natural selection. The theory held that the survival or extinction of an organism was determined by that organism's ability to adapt to its environment. Successful adaptation was based on randomly occurring variations within species that proved useful in their struggle for survival and thus increased the likelihood of reproduction. Favorable variations would then be transmitted to subsequent generations of offspring. (Darwin never actually used the expression "survival of the fittest," which was coined by a contemporary admirer of Darwin, the philosopher and sociologist Herbert Spencer.)

Darwin set these theories forth in his book *On the Origin of Species by Means of Natural Selection, or the Preservation of Favoured Races in the Struggle for Life.* It is known better by its shorter title, *The Origin of Species.* Darwin's writings had a tremendous impact on society and religion during the 1860s. The theory of evolution challenged contemporary beliefs about the creation of life on Earth and set off heated debates about the theory's implications—discussions that continue to this day.

BROTHER AGAINST BROTHER

When Abraham Lincoln—the man who had called slavery "a moral, social, and political evil"—was elected president of the United States in 1860, alarmed southern states, one by one, began to secede from the Union. The breakaway states, citing their right to self rule, decided to form a new country, the Confederate States of America, and chose as its leader Jefferson Davis. President Lincoln declared the secession a rebellion, and on April 12, 1861, when Confederate troops fired on Fort Sumter, a federal post in Charleston, South Carolina, war between the Union and the Confederacy began.

Both sides in this "war between brothers" believed the conflict would be a short one. The North had more than five times as many factories as the South; it had more money and it had over 22 million people. The South had only nine million people, and three and a half million of them were slaves. Yet the Confederacy felt confident. Confederate soldiers would be fighting on familiar ground. And the South had many fine generals, including Robert E. Lee, the brilliant commander who took charge of Confederate forces. In July 1861, when a Union army marched on the Confederate capital of Richmond, Virginia, southern troops sent them scampering back toward Washington. It would be four long years before the war was over.

In the end, the North's superior numbers were decisive. Eventually, too, the Union found a general the match of Lee—Ulysses S. Grant. After a daring Confederate invasion of U.S. territory was repulsed at Gettysburg, Pennsylvania, the Confederate armies were driven deep into Virginia. Grant pursued Lee relentlessly, finally forcing his surrender at Appomattox Courthouse on April 9, 1865. The American Civil War was over.

Early works of photojournalism drove home the savagery of war, such as the dead at Gettysburg (right), and captured moments in history such as Lincoln meeting his generals after the Battle of Antietam (above).

POLITICS & POWER	GEOGRAPHY & ENVIRONMENT	CULTURE & RELIGION
1876 LIEUTENANT COLONEL GEORGE A. CUSTER and his men are killed by the Sioux and Cheyenne at the Battle of Little Bighorn. **1877 PORFIRIO DÍAZ** becomes president of Mexico. He ushers in spectacular economic progress, but the new wealth is not equally distributed throughout the country. **1879-1883 THE WAR OF THE PACIFIC** between Chile, Peru, and Bolivia breaks out over control of important Atacama mineral deposits. Chile's victory positions it as the strongest nation on South America's Pacific coast.	**1870-1900 MORE THAN 11 MILLION IMMIGRANTS** arrive in the United States. **1871 THE CHICAGO FIRE** results in about 300 deaths and millions in property damage. **1879-1880 THE ARGENTINE GOVERNMENT** begins the conquest of the desert. Indigenous peoples are driven out of the Pampas, which are converted into grazing lands for cattle.	**1870s POSITIVISM** supports intellectual movements toward dictatorship across Latin America. **1873 DICTATOR GABRIEL GARCÍA MORENO** dedicates Ecuador to the Sacred Heart of Jesus. **1876 MARK TWAIN** publishes *The Adventures of Tom Sawyer.*
1877 RUSSIANS INVADE THE BALKANS after the Turks repress revolts by its Slav peoples. **1878 THE CONGRESS OF BERLIN** grants independence from Turkey to Romania, Montenegro, and Serbia. **1879 GERMANY AND AUSTRIA-HUNGARY** form the Dual Alliance to protect against attack by Russia and pledge neutrality in aggression by other countries.	**1870s CITIES** improve their water and sewer systems for better public health.	**1870s WORKS BY MONET, RENOIR, AND DEGAS** represent the height of the Impressionist school of painting. **1878 FORMER METHODIST MINISTER** William Booth and his wife expand their Christian mission in the East End of London and rename it The Salvation Army.
1879 ZULU WARRIORS defeat the British at the Battle of Isandhlwana in southern Africa.	▶ **1871 HENRY MORTON STANLEY,** British-American journalist, finds David Livingstone in Africa, greeting the Scotsman with the famous words "Dr. Livingstone, I presume?"	**1870s EMPEROR YOHANNES IV** forces his subjects to convert to the Ethiopian Orthodox Church. **1870 THE CRÉMIEUX DECREE** grants citizenship to Algerian Jews. **1875 THE *AL-AHRAM* NEWSPAPER** is founded, which is still published in Egypt today.
1876 THE TREATY OF KANGHWA between Japan and Korea recognizes Korea as an independent state. **1876 QUEEN VICTORIA** is proclaimed empress of India. **1879 THE SECOND AFGHAN WAR** gives Britain control of Afghanistan. **1879 JAPAN** claims the nearby islands of the Ryuku archipelago, despite Chinese protests.	**1874 FIJI** becomes a British colony.	**1871-1873 JAPAN** sends the Iwakura Mission to the West to study Western ideas and institutions.

SCIENCE & TECHNOLOGY

1876 ALEXANDER GRAHAM BELL patents the telephone.

1876 THE FIRST SHIPLOAD of chilled steer carcasses arrives in France from Buenos Aires, introducing the great increase in demand for Argentine beef in Europe.

1879 THOMAS EDISON invents the incandescent light bulb.

1871 THE *OCEANIC*, a 3,800-ton transatlantic liner, is launched.

1878 LONDON INSTALLS electric streetlights.

1878 THE WORLD'S FIRST OIL TANKER is launched, in the Caspian Sea; it plies the waters between Baku and Astrakhan.

PEOPLE & SOCIETY

1879 F. W. WOOLWORTH opens his first "5 and 10 cent store."

1878 THE FIRST INTERNATIONAL CONGRESS ON WOMEN'S RIGHTS takes place in Paris.

THE SCRAMBLE FOR AFRICA

FOR MUCH OF THE 19TH century, European involvement in Africa centered on the continent's periphery—the Cape Colony to the south and the Mediterranean coast in the north. However, popular interest in the interior of the continent was sparked by a host of European explorers who trekked across Africa and left behind a trail of myths and misunderstandings.

The most famous of these was the Scottish missionary David Livingstone, who became the first European to travel the width of the continent, from coast to coast, and the British-American journalist Henry M. Stanley, whose revelations of commercial possibilities in the Congo led to increased atrocities and ruthless exploitation.

Where missionaries and explorers led, the colonial powers followed. In 1876, King Leopold II of Belgium created the International Association for the Exploration and Civilization of Central Africa and engaged Henry Stanley to establish Belgian settlements in the Congo. Alarmed by Leopold's actions, the French moved into the territory north of the Congo River. And so the race to claim Africa began.

Englishman Cecil Rhodes conquered a vast region to the south and dreamed of a British Empire that sprawled from South Africa all the way to Egypt, or as he put it, "from the Cape to Cairo." To the east, the Portuguese carved out a colony along the coast. German traders were busy in East Africa and in the coastal territory bordering the northwest Cape. The French had completed their conquest of Algeria by 1847.

In the end, colonial borders were formally established among the European powers at the Berlin Conference of 1884. By the end of the century, the scramble for Africa was over. The European powers had carved up nearly the entire continent, and only Liberia in the west and Ethiopia in the east remained nominally free of their control.

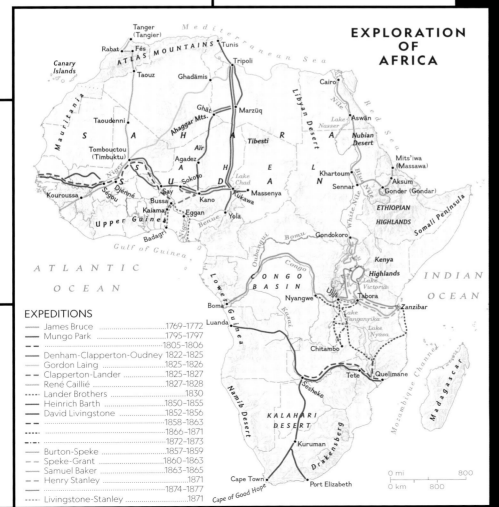

EXPLORATION OF AFRICA

EXPEDITIONS

- James Bruce 1769–1772
- Mungo Park 1795–1797
- 1805–1806
- Denham-Clapperton-Oudney 1822–1825
- Gordon Laing 1825–1826
- Clapperton-Lander 1825–1827
- René Caillié 1827–1828
- Lander Brothers 1830
- Heinrich Barth 1850–1855
- David Livingstone 1852–1856
- 1858–1863
- 1866–1871
- 1872–1873
- Burton-Speke 1857–1859
- Speke-Grant 1860–1863
- Samuel Baker 1863–1865
- Henry Stanley 1871
- 1874–1877
- Livingstone-Stanley 1871

0 mi 800
0 km 800

Map showing the routes of the major European explorers of Africa during the 19th century

BROS.

MANHATTAN MELTING POT

American cities grew quickly in the years after the Civil War, as rapid industrial development fueled the dreams of those in search of better pay and a better life. So great was the movement of people to urban areas that the newspaper editor Horace Greeley declared, "We cannot all live in cities, yet nearly all seem determined to do so." Bold and dynamic, the greatest of these growing American cities was New York.

During the 19th century, New York's expanding industries attracted job seekers from the surrounding countryside, just as had happened in London, Berlin, and other great cities of Europe. But New York was also swollen by another population source—the tide of European immigrants that was then flooding into the United States. Some of these new arrivals pressed farther afield after arriving in America. But many remained in the chief port of entry, New York City.

By the 1890s, immigrants and their children made up 80 percent or more of the city's population. New York had more Italians than the Italian cities of Florence, Genoa, and Venice put together. It was home to more Irish than Dublin, Ireland, and to more Germans than Hamburg, Germany. The city became famous for its ethnic diversity, with communities like Little Italy and Chinatown dating from this period. But providing adequate accommodation for all of these newcomers became a major problem.

People poured into New York faster than proper housing could be built for them. The population of New York and its suburbs grew from one million in 1860 to almost three and a half million in 1900. The poorest residents lived in tenements, rundown buildings in which several families rented rooms. New York's distinct neighborhoods soon included such notorious slums as Hell's Kitchen, Five Points, and the Bowery.

As these millions of people huddled in its tenements, New York's population density climbed to amazing levels. An average of 143 people per acre lived in the city, making it more crowded than the densest urban areas of Europe. Berlin, for example, had 101 inhabitants per acre. Population density in New York reached its highest level in a small area near the tip of Manhattan, where there were as many as 700 people per acre. New Yorkers were, literally, living on top of each other.

Immigrants like these on Mulberry Street on Manhattan's Lower East Side came to America for economic opportunity and a chance at the American dream.

POLITICS & POWER

1885 THE STATUE OF LIBERTY arrives in New York from France.

▶ **1886 APACHE LEADER GERONIMO** surrenders to the U.S. Army after years as a fugitive. Upon his release from prison, he becomes a national celebrity.

1887 A TREATY grants the U.S. exclusive rights to Pearl Harbor, Hawaii, as a coaling station and future naval base.

1889 A MILITARY REVOLT under Benjamin Constant Botelho de Magalhães effectively ends the Brazilian monarchy.

1882 GERMANY, AUSTRIA-HUNGARY, AND ITALY form the Triple Alliance, a secret agreement pledging to aid each other in case of war.

1890 OTTO VON BISMARCK is forced to resign as German chancellor.

1881 MUHAMMAD AHMAD, an Islamic religious leader known as a mahdī, launches a rebellion in Sudan against Egyptian rule.

1881 THE FRENCH invade Tunisia.

1882 REVOLT IN EGYPT leads to the appointment of Evelyn Baring, 1st earl of Cromer, as consul-general.

1880s CHULALONGKORN (known posthumously as King Rama V) implements reforms to modernize Siam and resist European imperialism.

1883-85 THE FRENCH AND THE CHINESE go to war over Vietnam.

1885 THE INDIAN NATIONAL CONGRESS is formed, which pursues a moderate policy of constitutional reform.

1887 THE FRENCH establish the Indochinese Union.

GEOGRAPHY & ENVIRONMENT

1883 BOLIVIA loses its entire coastline after the so-called Saltpeter War with Chile.

1889 THE FLOOD AT JOHNSTOWN, Pennsylvania, kills 2,209 people.

Geronimo (Goyathlay) was a resistance leader of the Chiricahua Apache in the American Southwest.

1884 GOLD IS DISCOVERED in South Africa, luring 44,000 outsiders to seek riches there in the 1890s.

1884-1885 THE BERLIN CONFERENCE formalizes the partitioning of Africa into European-controlled colonies.

1886 GOLD is found in the Transvaal; gold and coal mines there employ 100,000 workers by 1899.

1884 THE QING EMPIRE creates a new Xinjiang Province (Chinese Turkestan) in the northwest of China.

1884 GERMAN COLONIAL EXPANSION begins in the Pacific islands.

1886 THE BRITISH annex Burma as a province of India.

CULTURE & RELIGION

1890 THE U.S. ARMY massacres more than 300 largely unarmed Sioux at Wounded Knee in South Dakota, ending the Indian wars of resistance.

1880 RUSSIAN NOVELIST Fyodor Dostoevsky pulishes his final novel, *The Brothers Karamazov.*

1883-1885 GERMAN PHILOSOPHER Friedrich Nietzsche publishes his treatise *Thus Spoke Zarathustra.*

1881-82 URABI PASHA becomes a nationalist hero, championing the slogan "Egypt for Egyptians" and leading a revolt against the domination of Turkish and Circassian officers in the upper ranks of the Egyptian military. The British defeat his uprising and exile him to Ceylon (Sri Lanka).

1882 JAPAN begins to introduce legal codes based on French and German models.

SCIENCE & TECHNOLOGY

1882 THE FIRST HYDRO-ELECTRIC PLANT opens, in Wisconsin.

1883 THE BROOKLYN BRIDGE is completed, at that time the longest suspension bridge in the world.

1884-85 THE WORLD'S FIRST SKYSCRAPER, the Home Insurance Company Building, is erected in Chicago.

1890 THE U.S. becomes the world's leading industrial power, having tripled factory output over the previous quarter century.

▶ **1883 GERMAN ENGINEER GOTTLIEB DAIMLER** creates a portable engine that leads to the age of the automobile.

1887 JOHN BOYD DUNLOP invents the pneumatic tire.

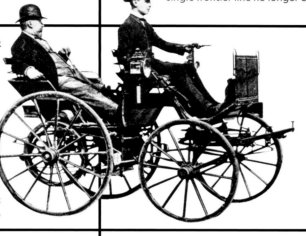

Gottlieb Daimler rides in the back of his first automobile.

1888 GERMANS get concessions to build the Anatolian Railroad, later renamed the Berlin-Baghdad Railway.

1881 CHINA'S FIRST SUCCESSFUL COMMERCIAL RAILWAY is built to service mines in Tangshan.

PEOPLE & SOCIETY

1880 PORFIRIO DÍAZ grants lucrative contracts to British and North American railroad companies to expand Mexico's rail system.

1881 CLARA BARTON founds the American Red Cross.

1888 SLAVERY IS ABOLISHED in Brazil, the last country in the Americas to do so. Blacks and mixed-race peoples remain at the foot of the economic ladder.

1890 THE SUPERINTENDENT of the U.S. census observes that for the first time a single frontier line no longer exists.

1882 THE FIRST MIGRATION of European Jews to Palestine occurs.

1888 THE PORT OF ISTANBUL is visited by 46,531 sailing ships and 1,548 steamships.

BUILDING THE BROOKLYN BRIDGE

IN 1869, with the approval of President Ulysses S. Grant and the U.S. Congress, work on the construction of the Brooklyn Bridge began. The project was plagued with problems, though, and it would take 14 years to complete.

The driving force behind the project, John Roebling, died from tetanus during the construction. His son, Washington Roebling, took over, but he developed a crippling illness called caisson disease, now known as the bends. Bedridden but determined to stay in charge, Roebling used a telescope to keep watch over the bridge's progress from his apartment. He dictated instructions to his wife, Emily, who passed them on to the workers, thereby guiding the completion of the bridge. Roebling was on his death bed during the inauguration on May 24, 1883, during which some 150,000 people crossed the bridge at a charge of one cent apiece. The bridge opened to vehicles later that day, and 1,800 made the crossing at five cents a vehicle.

The Brooklyn Bridge ranks as one of the greatest engineering feats of the 19th century and remains among New York's most popular and well-known landmarks. At the time it was built, the 1,596-foot span was also declared the longest suspension bridge in the world.

The Brooklyn Bridge connected Manhattan with the borough of Brooklyn.

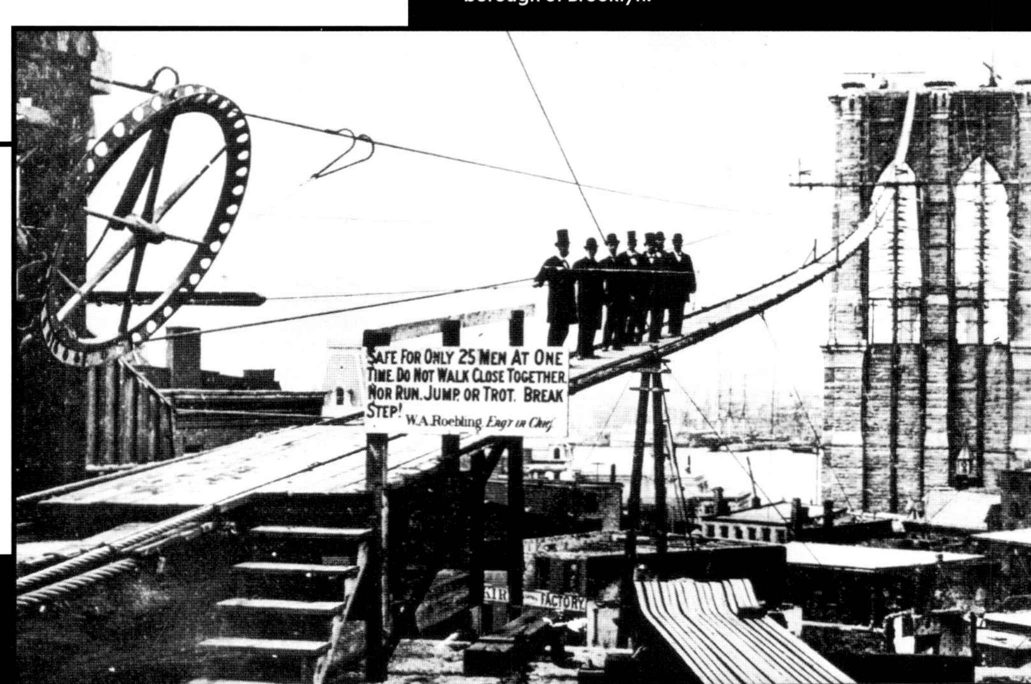

SAFE FOR ONLY 25 MEN AT ONE TIME. DO NOT WALK CLOSE TOGETHER NOR RUN, JUMP OR TROT. BREAK STEP!
W.A. Roebling Engr in Chief

POLITICS & POWER	GEOGRAPHY & ENVIRONMENT	CULTURE & RELIGION
1891 THE CONSTITUTION of the new republic of Brazil is passed. **1896 *PLESSY V. FERGUSON*** declares legalized segregation in the U.S. (in particular, the South's Jim Crow laws) constitutional. **1898 THE UNITED STATES** invades Cuba and defeats Spain in the Spanish-American War; as a consequence, Spain cedes the Philippines, Puerto Rico, and Guam.	▼ **1896 THE GOLD RUSH** to the Klondike begins. **1900 THE POPULATIONS OF BRAZIL AND ARGENTINS** swell with massive migration from Europe.	**1890s JOSÉ GUADALUPE POSADA** draws his famous calaveras political cartoons, mocking the elite Mexican classes. **1892 THE FIRST PUBLIC BASKETBALL GAME** is played, in Springfield, Massachusetts. **1894 THE FIRST COLOR SUNDAY** newspaper comics appear. **1895-1899 NEWSPAPER MAGNATES JOSEPH PULITZER AND WILLIAM RANDOLPH HEARST** engage in a bitter circulation war; their sensationalized news accounts become known as yellow journalism.
1894 NICHOLAS II, last of the Russian tsars, ascends the throne; France and Russia form the Dual Alliance, a secret military pact.		**1896 THE FIRST MODERN OLYMPIC GAMES** are held in Athens, Greece. **1898 CHRISTIAN NOVELIST,** apologist, and scholar C. S. Lewis is born in Belfast, Ireland. **1899 SIGMUND FREUD PUBLISHES** *The Interpretation of Dreams.*
1896 ETHIOPIA'S EMPEROR MENELIK II defeats the Italians at the Battle of Adowa, securing the country's survival as an independent kingdom in Africa. **1899 SAYYID MUHAMMED** launches a two-decade armed Somali resistance against British, Italian, and Ethiopian colonial forces. **1899 THE BOER WAR** breaks out between Afrikaners and the British in southern Africa. **1900 FRENCH AND BRITISH TROOPS** face each other at Fashoda on the White Nile, narrowly averting war.	**1892 A FRENCH EXPEDITION** reaches the ancient kingdom of Dahomey in West Africa and establishes a protectorate.	**1896 *SERVET-I FÜNUN*** *(The Wealth of Knowledge),* an Ottoman avant-garde journal, is founded.
1893 AMERICAN PLANTERS and businessmen depose Queen Liliuokalani of Hawaii. **1895 THE SINO-JAPANESE WAR** ends and Japan gains dominance over Taiwan. **1895 JAPANESE COLONIAL EXPANSION** begins in the Pacific islands. **1899 THE UNITED STATES AND GERMANY** divide Samoa. **1900 THE UNITED STATES** annexes Hawaii as a territory.	**1898 CHINA LEASES PORT ARTHUR** in the Yellow Sea to Russia, providing it a warm-water port unimpeded by winter ice.	**1900 AN INTERNATIONAL ALLIANCE** of Western nations puts down the Boxer Rebellion, a violent peasant uprising against foreign influence in Chinese affairs.

Prospectors in the Klondike gold rush in Alaska

SCIENCE & TECHNOLOGY

1891 **AMERICA'S FIRST GAS-POWERED AUTOMOBILE,** the Lambert (invented by John W. Lambert), is built.

1894 **THOMAS EDISON** introduces the first motion pictures.

1897 **AMERICA'S FIRST SUBWAY** opens in Boston.

1898 **WILLIAM KELLOGG** discovers a process for making toasted corn into flakes in Battle Creek, Michigan.

▼ **1895** **WILHELM CONRAD RÖNTGEN** discovers x-rays.

1895 **A MOTION PICTURE** is first shown in public, in France.

1896 **GUGLIELMO MARCONI** invents wireless telegraph.

1898 **MARIE AND PIERRE CURIE** discover radium and polonium, in France.

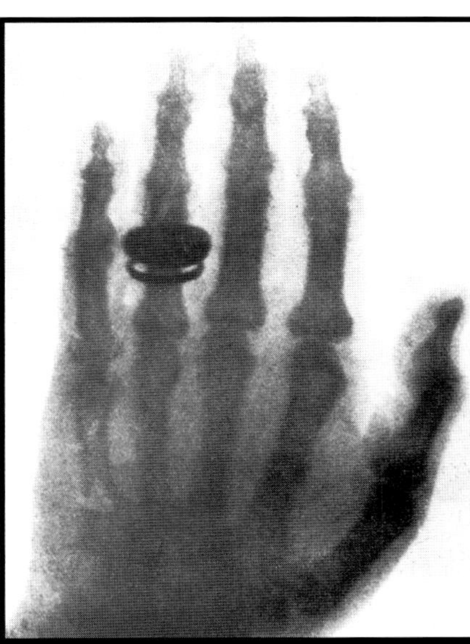

One of the first x-ray photographs, taken by Röntgen, shows his wife's hand.

1891 **CONSTRUCTION** of the Trans-Siberian Railroad begins.

1895 **HEAVY INDUSTRY** begins to develop in Japan on a considerable scale.

PEOPLE & SOCIETY

1892 **THE AMALGAMATED ASSOCIATION OF IRON AND STEELWORKERS** engages in a field battle with Carnegie Steel over wage cuts.

1898 **TEDDY ROOSEVELT** sails to Cuba to fight in the Spanish-American War with his Rough Riders, a collection of cowboys, land speculators, Native Americans, Mexicans, African Americans, and Ivy League athletes.

1891 **THOUSANDS OF JEWS** are forced into Russian ghettos.

1895 **ALFRED NOBEL'S WILL** establishes annual prizes for physics, chemistry, physiology or medicine, literature, and peace.

1896 **AUSTRIAN JEWISH LEADER THEODOR HERZL,** convinced Jews cannot assimilate in Europe, publishes *The Jewish State*, a call for a Jewish homeland. He becomes the father of Zionism.

1900 **THE LABOUR REPRESENTATION COMMITTEE** (later the Labour Party) is formed in Britain.

1890s **ARAB SLAVE TRADE** on the east coast of Africa is at last stamped out.

1897 **ZIONIST ACTIVITY** begins in the Middle East and North Africa, under the First Zionist Congress called by Theodor Herzl.

1890s **JAPANESE FOREIGN TRADE** rises sharply; cotton textiles to China and silk to the United States are primary exports.

1893 **NEW ZEALAND** becomes the first country to allow women to vote.

1895 **SUN YAT-SEN** plots the Canton uprising, a failed rebellion against the Qing dynasty. He will later lead a successful rebellion and be elected first provisional president of the Republic of China.

THE PERSECUTION OF RUSSIA'S JEWS

EVER SINCE THE EARLY Middle Ages, Jewish merchants had traveled through the Russian lands on their way to India and China. And later, as Jews began to face expulsion from the countries of western Europe, they began to move east—into Poland, Lithuania, Ukraine, and other regions that eventually came under the control of the expanding Russian Empire.

In the 1790s, Catherine the Great established a Pale of Settlement, border regions of the empire where Jews were required to remain unless they had special permission to move to other parts of Russia. During the next century, restrictions on where Jews could live, work, and be educated were alternately eased and tightened. However, after the assassination of Tsar Alexander II—which some blamed on the Jews—these restrictions were reimposed, and in 1891 any Jews living in Moscow were systematically expelled and forced into ghettos. About 20,000 had to give up their homes and livelihoods and move to the already overcrowded Pale of Settlement.

During this period, Jews were beaten and killed and their property destroyed in a wave of government-tolerated (if not government-sponsored) pogroms, a Russian term originally meaning "riot" but which soon came to refer to violent attacks on Jews in Russia. Some in the government even tried to blame the pogroms on the Jews themselves, while the media engaged in unbridled anti-Semitic propaganda.

Despite these repressive conditions and high levels of immigration to the United States, the Jewish population in Russia continued to grow rapidly in the 19th century; by the beginning of World War I, there were an estimated 5.2 million Jews living in Russia. Only in 1917, after the outbreak of the Bolshevik Revolution, were the laws against Russia's Jews overturned, though persecution would continue during the Soviet regime.

CHAPTER 7

GLOBAL CONFLICT

1900-1950

A crewman aboard the American aircraft carrier *Enterprise* directs a fighter pilot in the Pacific during World War II, the first major conflict in which air power played a commanding role.

By the early 20th century, countries around the globe were closely linked by recent advances such as radio and diesel-powered ships. With the introduction of aircraft, armored vehicles, and guided missiles, the world became an even smaller place, where hostile nations could swiftly project power far beyond their borders and wreak havoc. But not until humanity suffered through two world wars would pressure build for international organizations strong enough to prevent crises from developing into catastrophes. And even then, the possibility of a third world war involving nuclear weapons threatened humans with an apocalypse of their own making and clouded the future of this uniquely inventive and destructive species.

A GATHERING STORM

In the early 1900s rivalries between imperial powers resulted in regional struggles that foreshadowed larger conflicts to come. In Asia, Russia and Japan clashed over Manchuria, once firmly in China's grasp but now up for grabs. The Russian Empire had expanded southward in the 1800s to embrace places such as Chechnya in the Caucasus and the strategic port of Vladivostok on the Pacific. Now Tsar Nicholas II sought fresh conquests to distract Russia's disaffected populace. What the tsar got instead was a crushing defeat by the Japanese, who challenged the Russians in 1904 and destroyed their navy. Russians rebelled in 1905, and Nicholas responded by establishing a parliament called the Duma. That failed to appease radicals, who formed workers' councils called soviets and seized power in some areas, keeping up their struggle until troops put down the uprising in 1907.

Japan, emboldened by victory, continued its imperial expansion, colonizing Korea and stationing troops in Manchuria. The presence of Japanese forces in the ancestral home of China's Manchu rulers further embarrassed the beleaguered Qing dynasty. In 1912 revolutionaries led by Sun Yat-sen forced the boy emperor Puyi to abdicate and established the Chinese Republic, which was plagued by dissension and lost control of much of the country to warlords.

Two other troubled imperial powers—the Ottoman Turks and the Habsburg dynasty that ruled Austria-Hungary—figured prominently in events leading to world war. In 1908 liberals called Young Turks forced Sultan Abd al Hamid to restore a constitution drawn up in 1876 and recall parliament. Those reforms gave Turks a stronger national identity but did not appease other groups under Turkish rule striving for independence. Turks maintained their grip on the Middle East but lost control of the Balkans, where Macedonia and Albania joined Greece, Romania, and Serbia as independent states.

In 1908 Austria-Hungary annexed Bosnia, which had broken away from the Ottoman Empire and was torn by strife between Serbs, Croats, and other ethnic groups. Bosnian Serbs resented Austro-Hungarian domination and were incited to rebel by neighboring Serbia and its ally Russia, which had designs on the Balkans. In June 1914 Archduke Franz Ferdinand, heir to the Austro-Hungarian throne, was assassinated by a South Slav nationalist while visiting the Bosnian capital of Sarajevo. Austria-Hungary blamed Serbia, and Russia pledged to defend Serbia.

War between Russia and Austria-Hungary would have been bad enough, but entangling alliances on both sides made things far worse. Austria-Hungary and Germany had joined with Italy to form the Triple Alliance—a partnership strained recently when Italy sided with Balkan states against the Turks while Germany and Austria-Hungary encouraged Ottoman rulers to join them in opposing Russia. Allied with Russia in a pact called the Triple Entente were France and Great Britain. Thus a seemingly minor flare-up in the Balkans threatened to engulf all the major imperial powers in Europe and their far-flung colonies. Diplomats had little time to avert disaster, for German generals hoped to avoid war on two fronts by delivering a knockout blow to France as soon as Russia mobilized for war. In late July of 1914, Austria-Hungary declared war on Serbia, and Russia mobilized to defend Serbia. In early August, German troops invaded Belgium on their way to France, and a catastrophic conflict was under way.

THE GREAT WAR

Many Europeans who enlisted in the struggle they called the Great War assumed it would be swift and decisive.

American troops in France during World War I wear gas masks before going into action against German forces, who introduced the use of poisonous gas to the battlefield in 1915.

During World War I, France, the United Kingdom of Great Britain and Ireland, Russia, Italy, and other Allied nations opposed the Central Powers of Germany, Austria-Hungary, and the Ottoman Empire. The Central Powers advanced on the Eastern Front and forced Russia out of the conflict but lost the war on the Western Front (inset), where the entry of the U.S. on the Allied side in 1917 helped break the deadlock.

German hopes for a quick victory were dashed, however, when they encountered strong resistance along the Marne River in northern France. The opposing armies entrenched along lines that moved little for years to come. Both sides tried to break the stalemate by launching offensives, but attackers suffered terrible losses struggling through minefields and barbed wire under murderous machine-gun fire. German and Austro-Hungarian forces fared better against the Russians to the east and pushed them back, but only by forcing Russia out of the war could they hope to alter the balance on the Western Front and achieve victory.

By 1915 it was clear this would be a long and exhausting struggle, a total war that would strain the military and economic resources of both sides. Italy abandoned the Triple Alliance and cast its lot with the Allies, led by Britain, France, and Russia. The Ottoman Empire joined with Germany and Austria-Hungary to form the Central Powers. Turks repulsed Allied invasion forces, many of them from the British dominions of Australia and New Zealand, at Gallipoli in 1915 and captured a British army from India in Mesopotamia in 1916. But the Allies later made headway in the Middle East by enlisting Arabs, who were promised independence, to help drive the Turks out of the Arabian Peninsula and Palestine. Some Armenians opposed to Turkish rule joined the Russians to fight against the Turks, who retaliated by rounding up Armenians and deporting them to Syria and Mesopotamia. More than a half million Armenians starved to death in transit or were killed by Turkish guards, setting a grim precedent for ethnic cleansing in later times.

French and British colonial forces played a significant role in the Great War, invading German colonies in Africa and serving in other theaters as well. Blacks from South Africa, for example, fought for the British in German East Africa and in France. The British Indian Army contributed more than 300,000 soldiers to the Allied cause in 1914, and many in India expected to be rewarded afterward with independence or dominion status. Japan joined the Allies to pursue its own imperial aims, seizing the Marshall Islands and other German possessions in the Pacific. Only in the Americas did the war have little immediate impact. Mexico was caught up in a tumultuous revolution and remained neutral, as did many other Latin American countries. In the United States, isolationism gave way to support for the Allies as German U-boats attacked ships supplying Britain and France, claiming American lives in the process.

In April 1917 the U.S. entered the war, boosting Allied strength at a critical time. With the Russian army near collapse, the tsar abdicated. In late 1917 Bolsheviks espousing communism seized power in Moscow and withdrew from the war. Russia's capitulation came too late to save the exhausted Central Powers. Fresh American forces—and tanks impervious to machine-gun fire—helped the Allies thwart a final German offensive in 1918 and turn the tide. On November 11, Germany and its partners yielded and signed an armistice.

This ruinous conflict, which cost the lives of 8.5 to 10 million soldiers and untold millions of civilians, was not the war to end all wars, as some hoped. Instead, it set the stage for an even deadlier war a generation later, despite efforts by delegates to the Versailles Peace Conference in 1919 to impose order and stability. The defeated powers lost their imperial possessions and became the nations of Germany, Austria, Hungary, and Turkey (the core of the former Ottoman Empire). From old imperial domains came new nations such as Yugoslavia and Czechoslovakia and rehabilitated nations such as Poland. But many of them were prey to ethnic rivalries and were politically weak, making them tempting targets for future aggressors.

To discourage aggression, diplomats at Versailles created the League of Nations, but it lacked enforcement powers and lost crucial support when the U.S. Senate voted against joining the organization. Imperial ambitions that set the war in motion endured. Britain and France were drained by the carnage but retained their colonies and acquired new mandates, or dependencies, in the Middle East, which served to strengthen the determination of rival nations to build or restore their own empires.

AN UNEASY PEACE

Despite the persistence of old international tensions, the postwar world differed dramatically from what came before. Women had contributed greatly to war efforts and won the right to vote in many nations. Radio broadcasts, phonographs, and films proliferated and created an international popular culture that drew much of its energy from the U.S. Jazz music of African-American origin gained such wide appeal that some referred to the postwar era as the Jazz Age.

Hopes for the future faded when an economic panic hit the U.S. in late 1929 and spread quickly to Europe—where many nations relied on American investments—and to other regions dependent on trade with Europe and the U.S. American President Franklin Roosevelt responded to the Great Depression by working within the democratic system to implement his New Deal, which greatly increased federal aid to the poor and unemployed. In Germany, by contrast, the economic crisis destabilized the democratic Weimar Republic and helped bring Adolf Hitler to power. Hitler drew lessons from the fascist dictatorship of Italy's Benito Mussolini—who invaded Ethiopia in 1935—and sought to revive national pride and prosperity through rearmament and plans for a new German empire he called the Third Reich. France and Britain, fearful of renewed hostilities, allowed Hitler to defy the Treaty of Versailles in 1936 and reoccupy the demilitarized Rhineland, bordering France. Hitler and his Nazi Party practiced aggression both at home and abroad by persecuting Jews and terrorizing political opponents.

Another menacing dictatorship took hold in Moscow, where Bolshevik leader Vladimir Lenin had crushed resistance and preserved much of the old Russian Empire under a new title, the Soviet Union. Lenin's successor, Joseph Stalin, silenced dissent in the 1930s by carrying out purges in which millions were executed or sent to labor camps. Intent on collectivizing agriculture and making the Soviet Union an industrial power, Stalin imposed Five-Year Plans that caused turmoil and suffering but increased the war-making capacity of the Soviet economy.

In Asia, Japan remained committed to imperial expansion and sent more troops to Manchuria, taking control there in the early 1930s. That brought Japan into conflict with China, where Chiang Kai-shek, who had succeeded Sun Yat-sen as leader of the Kuomintang, or Nationalist People's Party, was vying with warlords and with communist insurgents led by Mao Zedong. Communists and Nationalists briefly set aside their differences in order to oppose Japanese forces who invaded China in 1937 and launched devastating air raids on Shanghai and other cities. An even worse fate befell the Nationalist capital of Nanjing, where Japanese troops raped and slaughtered civilians on a massive scale. By 1938 Japan controlled much of eastern China.

In Europe, meanwhile, Italy and Germany became Axis partners and intervened militarily in the Spanish Civil War to help General Francisco Franco defeat forces loyal to the republican government, backed by the Soviet Union. That conflict demonstrated the might of Germany's Luftwaffe, or air force, and left Britain and France with a dilemma—to challenge Hitler and risk a war for which they were ill-prepared or to appease him diplomatically. They chose appeasement and allowed Germany to annex Austria in 1938 and seize the Sudetenland, an ethnically German area within Czechoslovakia. When Hitler went on to occupy most of Czechoslovakia, Britain and France drew the line and backed Poland against German aggression. The pattern of alliances in Europe was similar to the alliances before the First World War with one crucial exception: The Allied powers of Britain and France could not count on Russian support. In 1939 Hitler signed a nonaggression pact with Stalin and sent his troops into Poland on September 1.

THE SECOND WORLD WAR

The conquest of Poland took less than a month, proving the efficiency of the German blitzkrieg, or lightning war, which combined air strikes with rapid advances by armored divisions. The same tactics allowed German forces to overrun Belgium and the Netherlands and defeat France in less than six weeks in the spring of 1940. Hitler expected Britain to come to terms, but newly appointed Prime Minister Winston Churchill vowed never to surrender. Aided by radar, British pilots countered onslaughts by the numerically superior Luftwaffe and forced Hitler to scrub a planned invasion that fall. Britain remained subject to air raids and devastating attacks on its maritime supply lines by German U-boats, which might have won the pivotal Battle of the Atlantic had not cryptanalysts broken German codes that revealed their location to Allied destroyers.

Events in 1941 greatly broadened the scope of the war. German forces invaded North Africa, the Balkans, and the Soviet Union as Hitler broke his pact with Stalin and pursued conquests of Napoleonic proportions. Unlike Napoleon, however, Hitler was not content to defeat opposing armies and targeted entire populations. His fateful thrust into Russia, launched in June, led to murderous attacks on Jews, Romany (Gypsies), and Slavs, groups Nazis considered less than human. Nazi officials went on to impose their "final solution" by forcing Jews into murderous prison camps where nearly six million died by war's end.

In December 1941 Soviet forces counterattacked the Germans, whose advance toward Moscow had stalled as winter closed in. Among the forces assailing the Germans were Siberian troops who had been guarding against a Japanese invasion. They were redeployed when Stalin learned that Japan—which was not obliged to join its Axis partners Germany and Italy in offensive operations—would instead

In the opening phase of World War II, between 1939 and 1941, Germany occupied much of Europe and North Africa with little help from its Axis partner Italy but failed to conquer Britain and Russia, which joined with the U.S. as Allied powers. Allied forces prevailed in North Africa in late 1942, invaded Italy in 1943, ousted Axis troops from France and eastern Europe in 1944, and defeated Germany in 1945.

German troops evict Jews from Warsaw, Poland, in 1943 after a fiery uprising in which occupants of the Jewish ghetto resisted removal. Many Jews here and elsewhere were sent to death camps, where they were murdered in gas chambers after a few months. Others were killed or died of mistreatment in concentration camps after toiling as slaves for years.

attack American and Allied bases in Southeast Asia and the Pacific. Japanese leaders settled on that course in response to an American oil embargo that forced them to choose between making peace or widening their offensive to include American targets. On December 7, Japan attacked the U.S. Pacific Fleet at Pearl Harbor in Honolulu and went on to seize the Philippines from the Americans; Indonesia from the Dutch; and Burma, Singapore, Malaya, and other colonies from the British.

The German and Japanese offensives of 1941 brought the Soviet Union and the U.S., two nations with huge populations and industrial potential, into the conflict on the side of the beleaguered Allies. This proved decisive when Germany and Japan failed to win quick victories as planned and faced prolonged struggles against foes with far greater military and economic reserves. The Allies drew support in the form of troops or raw materials from colonies in Africa and Asia and from Latin America, where many countries were economically reliant on the U.S. and followed its lead in declaring war on the Axis.

Allied triumphs at Midway in the Pacific, El Alamein in North Africa, and Stalingrad in the Soviet Union left the Axis on the defensive and gave Americans and Soviets time to bring their full might to bear. In 1943 the Soviets won an epic tank battle at Kursk and forced the Germans back toward their border, while Americans advanced on two fronts by seizing Pacific islands from the Japanese and joining with British forces in North Africa to invade Italy, where Mussolini fell from power.

Germany's fate was sealed in 1944 when Allied forces landed at Normandy on the French coast on D-Day, June 6, punched through enemy lines during the summer to liberate Paris, and repulsed a German counterattack in December. By early 1945, American and British forces were pouring into Germany from the west as Soviet troops advanced from the east. Berlin fell to the Soviets on April 30, and Hitler committed suicide, leading to Germany's unconditional surrender on May 7. The war continued in the Pacific until August when American pilots obliterated the Japanese cities of Hiroshima and Nagasaki

by dropping a single atomic bomb on each target. The 200,000 Japanese killed or wounded there were among some 60 million civilians and soldiers who perished worldwide in the most destructive war ever waged.

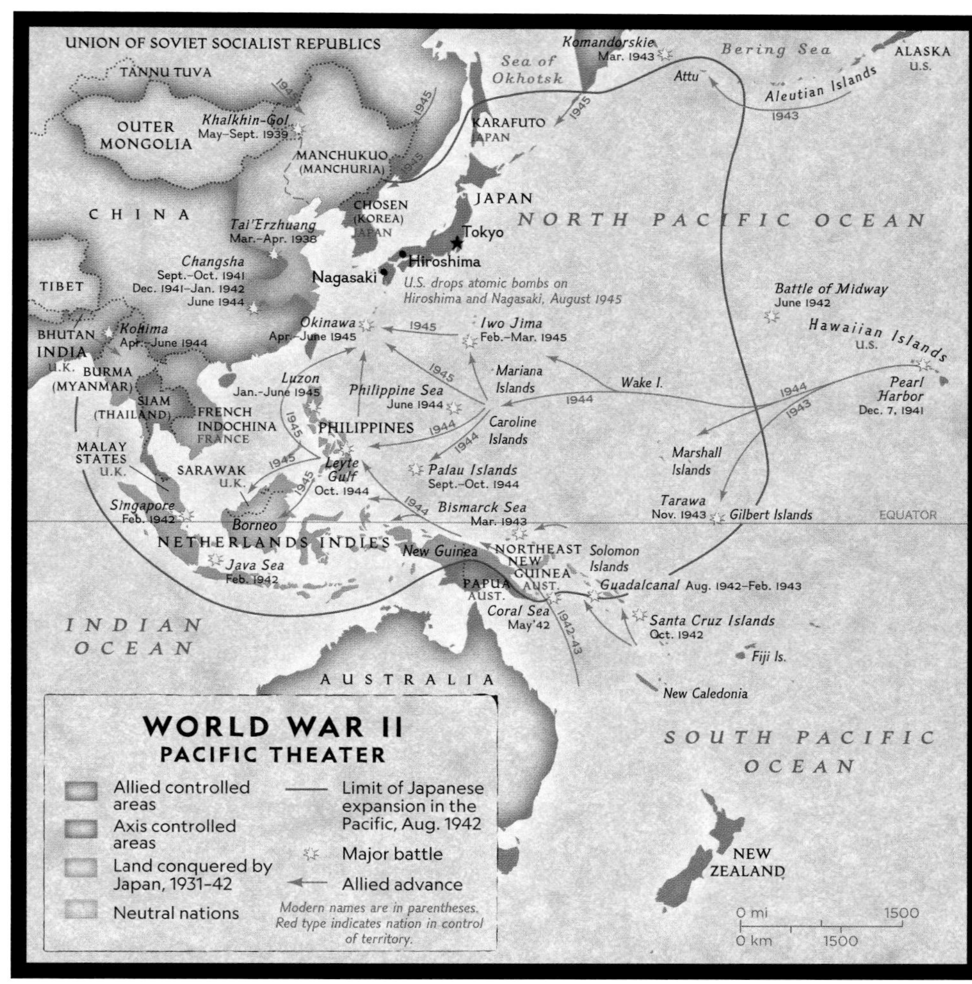

Japan, which occupied Manchuria and large parts of China before its Axis partner Germany opened hostilities in Europe, broadened the scope of World War II in December 1941 by seizing colonies in Asia and the Pacific from Britain, the Netherlands, and the U.S. Beginning in 1942, Allied forces pushed the Japanese back in brutal fighting, in the map above, epitomized by the battle for Iwo Jima, where U.S. Marines in early 1945 blasted Japanese troops, who refused to surrender and died in their bunkers, opposite.

FROM HOT WAR TO COLD WAR

Meeting at Yalta in early 1945, Allied leaders set up postwar occupation zones that gave the Soviets control of East Germany but divided Berlin, within that zone, between the Allied powers. After the fighting ended, the Soviets imposed communist regimes in East Germany, Poland, and other eastern European nations they had occupied. Churchill, who had long feared Soviet expansion, declared in 1946 that an "iron curtain has descended across the continent," words that helped define the emerging struggle called the Cold War.

Like the hot war that preceded it, the Cold War between communism and its foes engulfed much of the world. Mao Zedong, whose communists defeated Chiang Kai-shek's Nationalists in 1949 and took power in China, signed a pact with the Soviet Union and joined with the Soviets in backing a communist regime in North Korea, partitioned from South Korea in 1945. The Soviets and Chinese also aided communist forces in Vietnam led by Ho Chi Minh, who had resisted Japanese occupation during the Second World War and opposed French efforts to recolonize Vietnam afterward. The United Nations, formed in 1945, excluded China under Mao and instead recognized Chiang Kai-shek's Nationalist government, which fled to Taiwan.

The leader of the independence movement in India, Mohandas Gandhi, stood apart from the bloody power struggles of the 20th century by advocating nonviolence and a free India unbeholden to any imperial power. In 1947 Britain yielded and dropped its longstanding opposition to Indian independence. Clashes between Hindus and Muslims then forced the partition of India from Pakistan.

The end of British imperial rule also caused unrest in the Middle East. Since taking charge of Palestine in 1919, the British had allowed Jews dedicated to Zionism, or a Jewish homeland in the biblical kingdom of Israel, to settle there. After World War II, many Jewish refugees arrived in Palestine. In 1948 Jews declared an independent state of Israel, leading to fighting between Jews and Arabs and a new Arab refugee problem. Afterward, Israel remained at odds with Arab states and drew support from the U.S.

The U.S. also offered aid to Greece and Turkey in the late 1940s to fight communism there after President Harry Truman pledged to support nations "resisting attempted subjugation by armed minorities or by outside pressures." As the Cold War intensified, however, both the U.S. and the Soviet Union would pressure and subvert unfriendly governments. Tensions rose after the Soviets used nuclear secrets stolen from the U.S. to accelerate their weapons program and detonate an atom bomb in 1949. Something people had hoped for in vain earlier in the century now seemed a terrifying possibility—a war to end all wars. ■

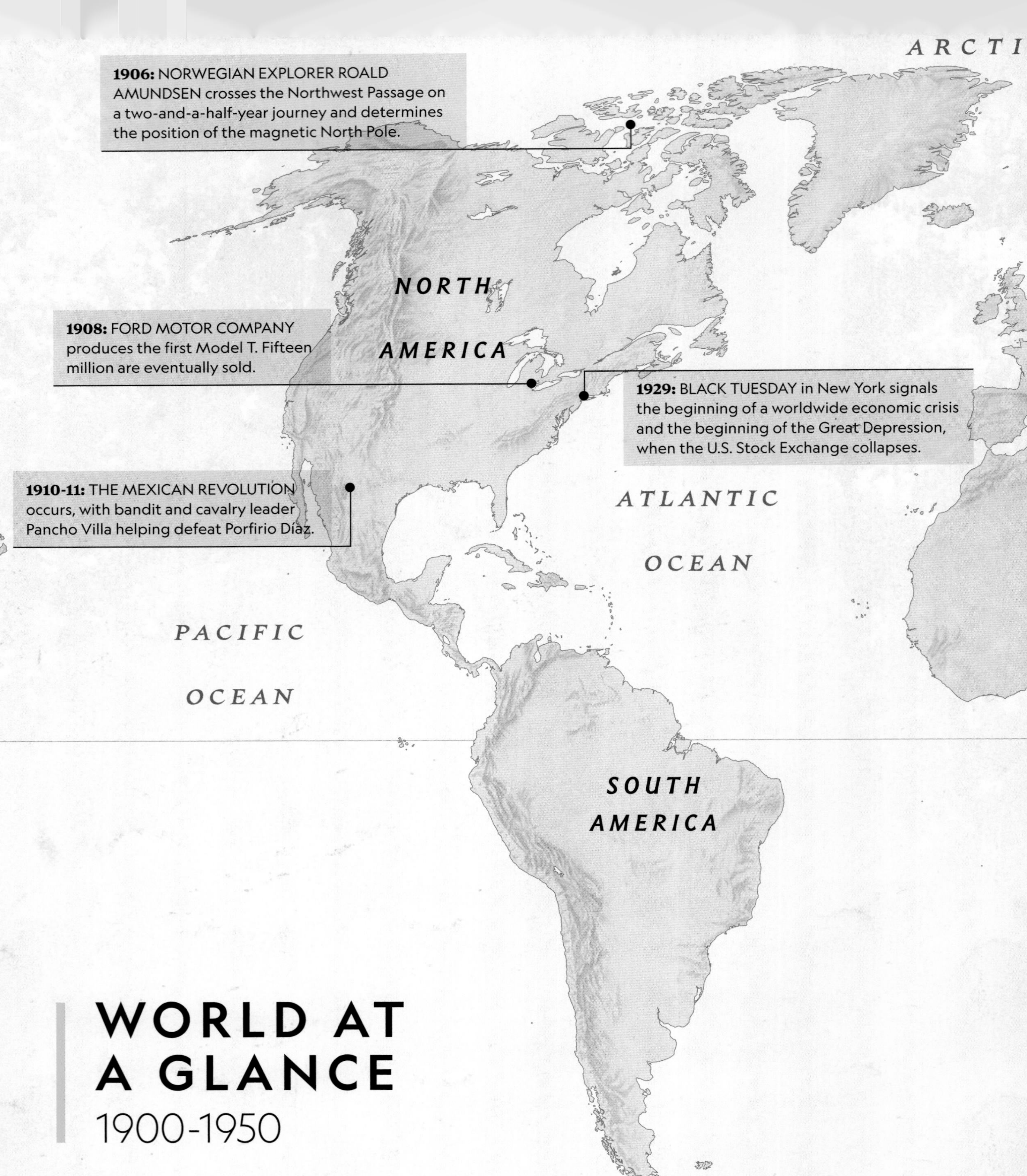
ARCTIC
1906: NORWEGIAN EXPLORER ROALD AMUNDSEN crosses the Northwest Passage on a two-and-a-half-year journey and determines the position of the magnetic North Pole.
NORTH AMERICA
1908: FORD MOTOR COMPANY produces the first Model T. Fifteen million are eventually sold.
1929: BLACK TUESDAY in New York signals the beginning of a worldwide economic crisis and the beginning of the Great Depression, when the U.S. Stock Exchange collapses.
1910-11: THE MEXICAN REVOLUTION occurs, with bandit and cavalry leader Pancho Villa helping defeat Porfirio Díaz.
ATLANTIC OCEAN
PACIFIC OCEAN
SOUTH AMERICA

WORLD AT A GLANCE

1900-1950

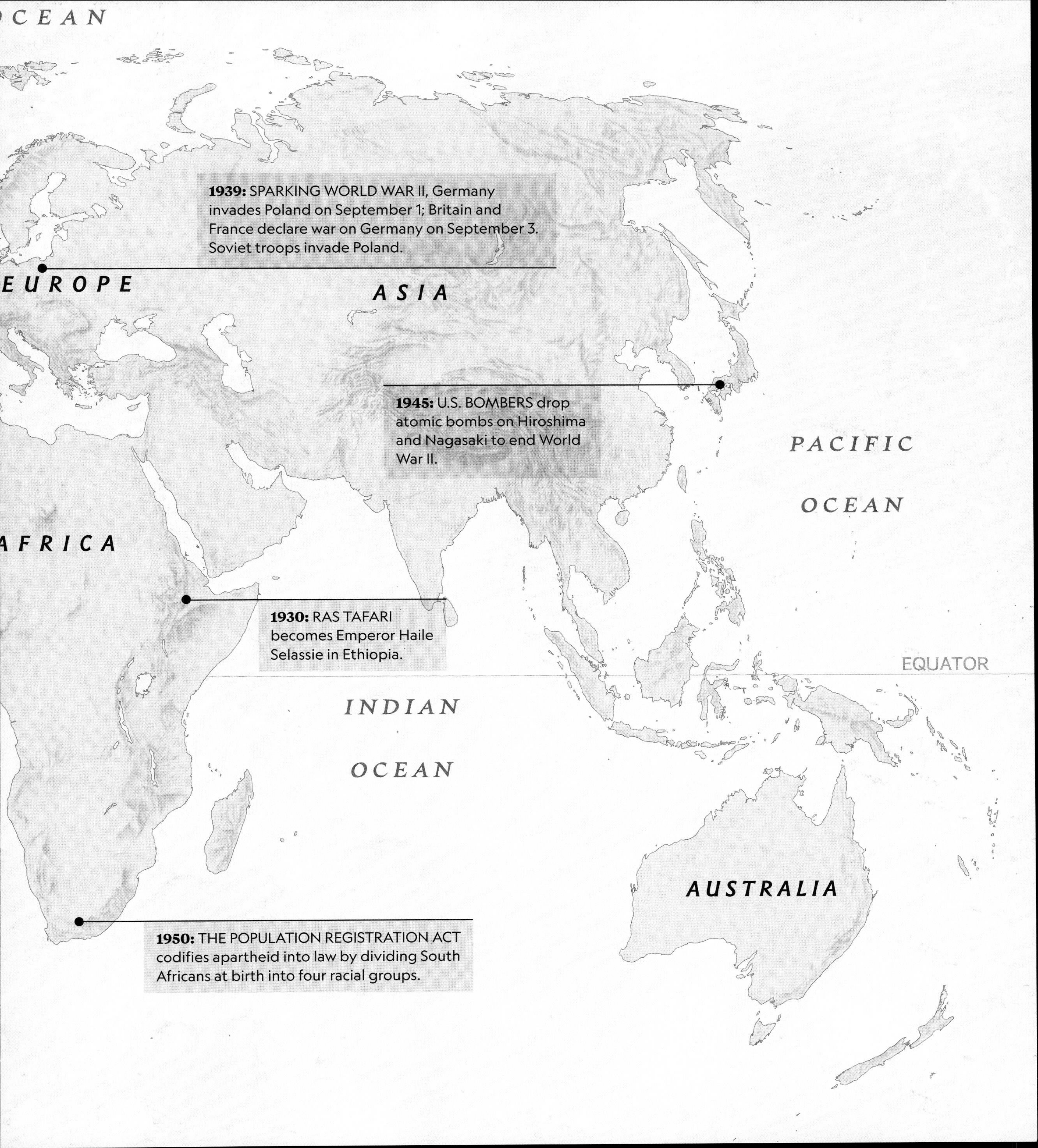

OCEAN

EUROPE

ASIA

1939: SPARKING WORLD WAR II, Germany invades Poland on September 1; Britain and France declare war on Germany on September 3. Soviet troops invade Poland.

1945: U.S. BOMBERS drop atomic bombs on Hiroshima and Nagasaki to end World War II.

PACIFIC OCEAN

AFRICA

1930: RAS TAFARI becomes Emperor Haile Selassie in Ethiopia.

EQUATOR

INDIAN OCEAN

AUSTRALIA

1950: THE POPULATION REGISTRATION ACT codifies apartheid into law by dividing South Africans at birth into four racial groups.

1900-1905

	POLITICS & POWER	GEOGRAPHY & ENVIRONMENT	CULTURE & RELIGION
THE AMERICAS	**1901 THE PLATT AMENDMENT** ends the U.S. military occupation of Cuba. **1901 U.S. PRESIDENT WILLIAM MCKINLEY** is assassinated by an anarchist. **1902 THE BUREAU OF RECLAMATION** in the U.S. becomes a powerful bureaucracy that roots out corruption in Western development. **1903 THE WAR OF THE THOUSAND DAYS** in Latin America between liberals and conservatives ends in conservative victory. **1903 A BILL** is passed in the U.S. limiting immigration and banning undesirables.	**1901 THE CONSTITUTIONAL CONVENTION IN CUBA,** under pressure from Washington, confirms Cuba's status as a U.S. protectorate. **1902 MARTINIQUE VOLCANIC FIRE** devastates the town of St. Pierre. **1904 MUCH OF CHICHÉN ITZÁ** is discovered in Mexico.	**1900 THEODORE DREISER** publishes *Sister Carrie*. **1901 RAGTIME JAZZ** develops in the U.S., led by Scott Joplin. **1903 HENRY JAMES** publishes *The Ambassadors*. **1903 THE FILM *THE GREAT TRAIN ROBBERY*** is the longest film to date at 12 minutes. **1904 MUCKRAKING U.S. JOURNALIST** Lincoln Steffens publishes *The Shame of the Cities*.
EUROPE	**1901 QUEEN VICTORIA** dies and is succeeded by her son, Edward VII. **1901 THE SOCIAL REVOLUTIONARY PARTY** is founded in Russia. **1902 AN ANGLO-JAPANESE TREATY** recognizes the independence of China and Korea. **1902 THE TRIPLE ALLIANCE** between Germany, Austria-Hungary, and Italy is renewed. **1903 THE RUSSIAN SOCIAL DEMOCRATIC PARTY** splits into Mensheviks and Bolsheviks.	**1900 ARCHAEOLOGIST SIR ARTHUR EVANS** starts excavating at Knossus, Crete, leading to the discovery of the lost Minoan civilization.	**1900 GIACOMO PUCCINI'S OPERA,** *Tosca*, is first performed. **1901 RUDYARD KIPLING** publishes *Kim*. **1901 PABLO PICASSO** is in his "blue period." **1902 BEATRIX POTTER'S *PETER RABBIT*** is published. **1903 ANTI-JEWISH POGROMS** are carried out in Russia. **1905 THE CHURCH AND STATE ARE SEPARATED** in France.
MIDDLE EAST & AFRICA	**1901 BOERS** start organized guerrilla warfare, invading Cape Colony and coming within 50 miles of Cape Town. **1903 FOLLOWING THE FALL OF KANO,** West African Frontier Force troops take Sokoto in Nigeria. The sultan flees as a result. **1904 THE HERERO** and other Africans revolt against German rule in southwest Africa.	**1900 IN THE BOER WAR** the British annex the Orange Free State and Transvaal and take Pretoria and Johannesburg. **1901 THE ASANTE KINGDOM** is annexed by Britain as part of the Gold Coast (Ghana). **1902 THE TREATY OF VEREENIGING** ends the Boer War. Orange Free State becomes British Crown Colony. **1904 MOROCCO IS DIVIDED** by the French, British, and Spanish.	**1903 THE UGANDA SCHEME** proposes a Jewish homeland in East Africa.
ASIA & OCEANIA	**1901 THE BOXER REBELLION** ends in China. **1902 THE PHILIPPINE ORGANIC ACT,** under which the nation will be controlled by the U.S., is passed. **1904 THE RUSSO-JAPANESE WAR** begins with the Japanese siege of Port Arthur in Manchuria and the occupation of Seoul. **1904 TRENCH WARFARE** begins with the Russo-Japanese War.	**1900 FAMINE** and the bubonic plague in India abate. **1901 AUSTRALIA BECOMES A COMMONWEALTH,** with Edmund Barton inaugurated as its first prime minister.	**1902 INFLUENTIAL WESTERN-TRAINED JAPANESE PAINTER** Asai Chu takes up a teaching post in France.

SCIENCE & TECHNOLOGY

1900 R. A. FESSENDEN transmits human speech via radio waves.

1900 THE BROWNIE CAMERA becomes widely available throughout the U.S.

▼ **1903 ORVILLE AND WILBUR WRIGHT** fly a powered airplane at Kitty Hawk, North Carolina.

1904 WORK BEGINS on the Panama Canal.

1901 GUGLIELMO MARCONI receives the first transatlantic radio signal, from Cornwall, England, to Newfoundland.

1901 THE METRO SUBWAY opens in Paris.

1904 SIR JOHN FLEMING uses a thermionic tube to generate radio waves.

1902 THE FIRST ASWAN DAM is completed in Egypt.

PEOPLE & SOCIETY

1901 IN NOVA SCOTIA, New Brunswick, and Prince Edward Island, Canada, 421 labor strikes occur and continue throughout 1914.

1901 J. P. MORGAN organizes the U.S. Steel Corporation.

1902 THE CADILLAC CAR COMPANY is founded in the U.S.

1903 RICHARD STEIFF designs the first teddy bears, named after President Teddy Roosevelt.

1904 HELEN KELLER, WHO IS DEAF AND BLIND, graduates from Radcliffe College.

1901 THE FIFTH ZIONIST CONGRESS begins the Jewish National Fund.

1903 EMMELINE PANKHURST founds the National Women's Social and Political Union, a women's suffrage organization in England.

1904 STEERAGE RATES for immigrants to the U.S. are cut to 10 dollars by foreign lines.

A NEW WORLD OF FLIGHT

ON DECEMBER 17, 1903, when Orville and Wilbur Wright successfully flew their motorized airplane near Kitty Hawk, North Carolina, they opened up a whole new world for flyers who had thus far succeeded in becoming airborne only in dirigibles, hot air balloons, and glider planes. By demonstrating their theory of correcting the aircraft's position with movable portions of the wing, rather than shifts in body weight, the Wright brothers made a vast leap forward in aircraft design. In addition they created useful tables of wind pressure and drift.

Becoming fascinated with aviation in the 1890s by studying the German engineer Otto Lilienthal's work with glider flights, Orville and Wilbur put their expertise as mechanics to work in their bicycle repair shop. After successfully testing their theories with glider planes, which they took to the windy beaches of Kitty Hawk every autumn, they focused next on the engine. Not able to find one that was light and powerful enough, Orville designed an engine, which the brothers built and attached to their improved glider.

On the day that changed aviation history, the brothers went up four times—Orville stayed aloft in the first flight for all of 12 seconds, and by the fourth attempt, Wilbur was able to fly 852 feet in 59 seconds. Continuing their experiments, by 1909 they had become world famous and had added a more powerful engine, a passenger seat, and more intricate controls. Now the Wright brothers could utilize their invention commercially, for governments realized how useful their planes could be in combat, and began to order them in quantity.

Orville Wright takes off at Big Kill Devil Hill, North Carolina, as brother Wilbur runs alongside to steady the wings, December 17, 1903.

POLITICS & POWER	GEOGRAPHY & ENVIRONMENT	CULTURE & RELIGION
1905 WILLIAM "BIG BILL" HAYWOOD and others found the Industrial Workers of the World (Wobblies). **1906 AFTER RECONCILIATION** following the failed liberal revolt, U.S. troops occupy Cuba. **1907 THE PANIC OF 1907** causes a bank run, which is stopped by J. P. Morgan's importation of $100 million in gold from Europe. **1909 W.E.B. DU BOIS** joins with others to found the National Association for the Advancement of Colored People (NAACP) in the U.S.	**1905 THE NATIONAL FOREST SERVICE** is established in the U.S. by Gifford Pinchot. **1906 A SAN FRANCISCO EARTHQUAKE** kills more than 3,000 people, with $400 million in property loss. **1908 TEDDY ROOSEVELT** undertakes the first inventories of public lands and their resources. **1909 U.S. EXPLORER COMMANDER ROBERT E. PEARY,** accompanied by Matthew Henson, is the first person to reach the North Pole.	**1905 THE SOCIAL GOSPEL MOVEMENT** in the U.S. embodies Christian progressive ideas about reforming capitalism. **1906 RUTH ST. DENIS** introduces modern dance. **1906 UPTON SINCLAIR** publishes *The Jungle.* **1908 THE "ASHCAN" SCHOOL OF PAINTING,** portraying common life in the U.S., is established by a group of painters known as "The Eight," led by Robert Henri. **1908 OSCAR HAMMERSTEIN** builds the Manhattan Opera House in New York.
1905 TSAR NICHOLAS II establishes reforms with his October Manifesto, hoping to quiet mounting unrest in Russia.	**1906 NORWEGIAN EXPLORER ROALD AMUNDSEN** crosses the Northwest Passage on a two-and-a-half-year journey and determines the position of the magnetic North Pole. **1906 VESUVIUS ERUPTS,** devastating the town of Ottaiano, Italy.	**1905 FRANZ LEHAR** presents *The Merry Widow*, an operetta, in Vienna. **1908 E. M. FORSTER** publishes *A Room with a View.* **1908 KENNETH GRAHAME** publishes *The Wind in the Willows.* **1908 BELA BARTOK** composes *String Quartet No. 1.*
1905 LOUIS BOTHA and his Het Volk Party ask for responsible government in the Transvaal in today's South Africa. **1905 THE IRANIAN CONSTITUTIONAL REVOLUTION** begins, spurring massive demonstrations, but is hijacked by conservatives. **1906 SELF-GOVERNMENT** is granted to the Transvaal and Orange River colonies, along with white suffrage. **1908 THE YOUNG TURK REVOLUTION** restores the constitution and parliamentary government in the Ottoman Empire.	**1905 NAIROBI** becomes the capital of British East Africa (Kenya), because it is located on the Mombasa-Uganda railroad. **1908 BELGIAN KING LEOPOLD II** makes the kingdom of the Congo part of the state. **1908 MORE THAN 6,000 DIE** during famine in the Usoga region of Uganda. **1910 THE UNION OF SOUTH AFRICA** is born.	**1909 TEL AVIV,** the first Jewish town in modern Palestine, is founded.
1905 JAPANESE sink the Russian fleet in the straits of Tsushima. **1905 PORT ARTHUR** surrenders to the Japanese in the Russo-Japanese War. The Treaty of Portsmouth ends the war. **1905 THE ANGLO-JAPANESE ALLIANCE** is renewed for 10 years. **1906 AUSTRALIA** takes control of Papua, New Guinea.	**1904-1910 FLOODS, DROUGHT, AND FAMINE** in many Chinese provinces force people into poverty. **1907 NEW ZEALAND** becomes a dominion within the British Empire.	**1905 SUN YAT-SEN** founds the revolutionary alliance known as the United League in Tokyo, dedicated to creating the Chinese Republic. **1906 AN ALL-INDIA MOSLEM LEAGUE** is founded by Aga Khan.

SCIENCE & TECHNOLOGY

1905 THE EUGENICS MOVEMENT in the U.S. advocates that certain groups such as the mentally handicapped and criminals be stopped from having children.

1906 THE U.S. PURE FOOD AND DRUGS ACT is passed.

1906 THE FIRST U.S. RADIO PROGRAM of voice and music is broadcast by R. A. Fessenden.

1909 THE PLASTIC AGE BEGINS with the first commercial manufacture of Bakelite.

▼ **1905 AN OBSCURE SWISS PATENT CLERK,** Albert Einstein, formulates the special theory of relativity and ushers in the atomic age.

1906 CLEMENS VON PIRQUET introduces the term "allergy" to medicine.

1907 LOUIS AND AUGUSTE LUMIÈRE develop a process for color photography.

1908 HANS GEIGER introduces the first successful electrical device capable of counting individual alpha rays.

1910 PAUL EHRLICH develops the Salvarsan medicine for syphilis and other diseases.

Albert Einstein in 1905

1906 THE *SATSUMA*, the world's largest battleship, is launched in Japan.

PEOPLE & SOCIETY

1910 THE FIRST NEON SIGNS appear.

1907 TYPHOID MARY (Mary Mallon) is found and incarcerated for being a carrier of typhoid in New York City.

1908 JACK JOHNSON becomes the first black world heavyweight boxing champion.

1908 GENERAL MOTORS CORPORATION is formed.

1908 FORD MOTOR COMPANY produces the first Model T. Fifteen million are eventually sold.

1906 THE FRENCH GRAND PRIX car race is run for the first time.

1906 INTERNATIONAL RESTRICTIONS are placed on night shifts for female industrial workers.

1907 ROBERT BADEN-POWELL founds the Boy Scout movement in Britain.

1909 MEN AND WOMEN OLDER THAN 70 receive their first old age pensions in London.

1910 DUTCH AND ENGLISH become the official languages of the Union of South Africa.

1907 CHINA AND BRITAIN agree to reduce opium production.

Pablo Picasso's "Les Demoiselles d'Avignon"

THE BEGINNINGS OF MODERN ART

WHEN 25-YEAR-OLD Spanish artist Pablo Picasso painted "Les Demoiselles d'Avignon" in 1907, he did not know that he would help revolutionize the art world. Picasso, in fact, was so unsure of the work's significance that he showed it only to close friends for years, and he did not exhibit it publicly until 1916.

Its subject—five nudes in various poses plus a still life—is aggressive and somewhat savage, unlike anything the art world had ever seen. The three angular figures on the left are distortions of classical ones, but the dislocated and fractured features and bodies of the two figures on the right draw inspiration from African sculpture. Organic integrity, proportions, and continuity of the human body are all ignored.

This iconic work embodied the new abstract approach to art and also signaled the birth of cubism, which represented its own world, akin to nature but constructed with different principles. Critics saw only sharp edges and angles, whereas Picasso actually combined voids and solids, giving his figures a three-dimensional quality. By the end of his long life in 1973, Picasso's numerous and varied works had made him the most revered artist of the 20th century.

POLITICS & POWER	GEOGRAPHY & ENVIRONMENT	CULTURE & RELIGION
1910-1911 THE MEXICAN REVOLUTION occurs, with bandit and cavalry leader Pancho Villa helping defeat Porfirio Díaz. **1911 THE U.S. SUPREME COURT** orders the breakup of the Standard Oil Company. **1913 THE FEDERAL INCOME TAX** is introduced in the U.S. with the 16th Amendment.	**1910 THE U.S. CONGRESS** establishes Glacier National Park.	**1912 TEXTILE WORKERS STRIKE** in Lawrence, Massachusetts, showing the power of the Wobblies. **1913 THE ARMORY SHOW** introduces Post-impressionism and cubism to New York. **1914 THE AMERICAN SOCIETY OF COMPOSERS, AUTHORS, AND PUBLISHERS** (ASCAP) is founded.
1910 MONTENEGRO is proclaimed a kingdom under Nicholas I. **1910 REVOLUTION** occurs in Portugal. **1911 WINSTON CHURCHILL** is appointed First Lord of the Admiralty. **1912 THE ALLIANCE** of Germany, Austria-Hungary, and Italy is renewed. **1914 WORLD WAR I** begins after Archduke Franz Ferdinand, heir to the Austrian throne, and his wife are assassinated in Sarajevo by Serbian nationalists.	**1911 ROALD AMUNDSEN** of Norway becomes the first person to reach the South Pole.	**1910 THE SOUTH AMERICAN TANGO** becomes wildly popular in Europe and the U.S. **1912 CARL JUNG** publishes *The Psychology of the Unconscious.* **1913 D. H. LAWRENCE** publishes *Sons and Lovers.* **1913 THOMAS MANN** publishes *Death in Venice*.
1911 LOUIS BOTHA AND JAMES HERTZOG found the South African Party. **1911 ITALY** invades Libya. **1912 THE ALLIED BALKAN ARMIES** advance on Turkey. **1912 THE SOUTH AFRICAN NATIVE NATIONAL CONGRESS** (the precursor to the African National Congress) is created. **1913 THE OTTOMANS** sign a peace treaty with the Balkan League. **1914 OTTOMAN FORCES** attack Russian ports.	**1910 THE UNION OF SOUTH AFRICA** becomes a dominion within the British Empire. **1912 MOROCCO** becomes a French protectorate. **1914 NORTHERN AND SOUTHERN NIGERIA** are united. **1914 OTTOMANS** close the Dardanelles.	**1912 OTTOMAN MINORITIES** reject multinational Ottomanism, giving rise to Turkish nationalism. Ziya Gokalp stresses Turkish language and culture, raises the position of women, and promises a rational approach to religion.
1911 MONGOLIA declares independence from China. **1912 A REPUBLICAN REVOLUTION** forces China's last emperor to abdicate the throne. **1912 THE REPUBLIC OF CHINA** is officially proclaimed with Sun Yat-sen as president. He founds the Kuomintang (Nationalist People's Party).	**1910 JAPAN** annexes Korea. **1914 NEW ZEALAND** occupies Western Samoa. **1914 JAPAN** occupies the Northern Marianas.	**1913 RABINDRANATH TAGORE** receives the Nobel Prize in literature. **1915 THE JOURNAL *NEW YOUTH*** is published in China, a sign of the new cultural movement.

SCIENCE & TECHNOLOGY

1910 THOMAS EDISON demonstrates talking motion pictures.

1910 HALLEY'S COMET is observed.

1911 CHARLES F. KETTERING develops the first practical electric self-starter for cars.

1913 H. N. RUSSELL formulates the theory of stellar evolution.

1914 ROBERT H. GODDARD receives his first patent for rocketry.

1914 THE PANAMA CANAL is opened to traffic.

1911 ERNEST RUTHERFORD publishes his theory of atomic structure.

1912 THE S.S. *TITANIC* SINKS on her maiden voyage from England to the U.S. after colliding with an iceberg in the North Atlantic.

1913 THE DIPHTHERIA IMMUNITY TEST is discovered by Bela Schick.

1913 NIELS BOHR formulates the theory of atomic structure.

1914 THE FIRST MODERN ZIPPER goes on sale.

PEOPLE & SOCIETY

1910s AFRICAN AMERICANS MIGRATE in great numbers from the rural South to the industrial North for better jobs and to escape discrimination.

1913 GRAND CENTRAL STATION, the world's largest railroad station, opens in New York.

1914 THE U.S. FEDERAL TRADE COMMISSION is established to prevent unfair or deceptive trade practices.

1914 SOME 10.1 MILLION IMMIGRANTS enter the U.S. from southern and eastern Europe between 1905 and 1914.

1912 A COAL STRIKE, London dock strikes, and a transport workers strike occur in Britain.

1912 THE ROYAL FLYING CORPS is established in Britain (later becomes the Royal Air Force, or RAF).

1912 THE INTERNATIONAL LAWN TENNIS FEDERATION is formed.

1913 RECOGNIZING RISING NATIONALISM in Egypt, British colonial rulers allow for Egyptian representation in a legislative assembly.

1913 GERMAN MEDICAL MISSIONARY ALBERT SCHWEITZER opens his hospital in Lambarene, French Congo.

1911 JAPAN'S FACTORY ACT (put into effect in 1916) limits working hours for women and prohibits the labor of young children.

CONNECTIONS

The Colonial World at War

The two world wars saw vast numbers of colonists take up arms for the countries that had subjugated them. Many were conscripted, but many volunteered, believing their mother countries would reward them with independence. Hundreds of thousands of Africans fought with the Allies in the First World War. In World War II, South Africa sent 200,000 volunteers to fight the Germans, at least a third of them black. The British, Belgians, and French mined troops from sub-Saharan Africa, while the Dutch used Asian colonists to fight the Japanese. India, denied self-government after uniting behind the British in World War I, splintered. Some fought for the Allies, but an Indian "national army" fought in Burma in support of the Japanese, a symptom of the nationalistic fervor brewing under Hindu leaders Gandhi and Nehru and Muslim League leader Muhammad Ali Jinnah.

BUILDING THE PANAMA CANAL

AMERICANS HAD LONG had their mind's eye on a proposed passageway through the narrowest part of Central America. Such a corridor would connect the region's east and west coasts and eliminate the 7,000 additional miles needed to sail around the southern tip of South America. When large numbers of pioneers began settling in Oregon and California, the desire for this seafaring shortcut intensified, which resulted in President Teddy Roosevelt's use of aggressive tactics to make construction of the Panama Canal possible.

It was not the first time such an ambitious attempt had been made. A French company had obtained a concession to construct a sea level canal across Panama in 1878. But because of disease, poor planning, and lack of funds, the project was abandoned, but not before 20,000 French lives were lost.

In 1901 the British agreed to allow the U.S. to build and fortify a canal, and the United States' choice was to cut across Nicaragua. A volcanic eruption at the site, however, made building through that country impossible, so Roosevelt turned his attention to Panama, which was a province of Colombia. After petitioning Bogotá and being rebuffed, Roosevelt encouraged a group of Colombians to start their own country. Before trouble had time to erupt, he accepted a sea-to-sea right-of-way in perpetuity from the new Republic of Panama, and after several years of developing construction facilities, disease control, and surveys, construction got under way. In 1906 Roosevelt himself visited the site, becoming the first sitting president to travel outside the U.S.

In August of 1914 the Panama Canal was informally opened. Some 5,600 American lives had been lost, mostly to tropical diseases. At 40 miles long, 500 feet wide, and 40 feet deep, the channel was the most ambitious construction project undertaken in modern times and would bring the world closer together.

DEATH IN THE TRENCHES

The First World War shocked many with its brutality and unprecedented loss of life. Mechanized weaponry, such as the magazine rifle, the machine gun, and quick-firing artillery, had enhanced every soldier's killing power, especially at a distance, compelling European armies to literally dig in to protect themselves on the open battlefield. Called trench warfare, it was first seen in the Russo-Japanese War but was elevated to a way of life here.

By the spring of 1915, with the Allies and the Central Powers stalemated, both sides began constructing more and more elaborate trench systems. Trench linings consisted of whatever material might be available, and included wattle, planking, and sandbags. The German trenches, often going quite deep, were superior to those of the British and French. The British system contained three lines of trenches: the front, which was composed of command-and-fire trenches; the support; and the reserve, behind which the artillery was positioned. Communication trenches ran at right angles, connecting the lines. No Man's Land, with barbed-wire entanglements running the length between opposing lines, could be as short as 50 yards or as much as half a mile wide. Wired telephone lines, semaphores, dogs, and pigeons were all used to transmit messages.

Trench warfare created a battlefield situation almost like siege warfare. Armies could not withdraw or pause. Soldiers lived in the fortified ditches. An individual's most essential weapons were his shovel and his machine gun. Grenades also came in handy in answer to machine-gun fire. Bayonets proved unsatisfactory, so most infantrymen had a fighting knife and a homemade trench club used for raiding. Gas masks and breathing apparatuses for tunneling were also supplied. Periscopes were useful for keeping watch, and wire cutters were vital when parties were sent out under cover of darkness to cut the barbed wire before an attack.

Life in the trenches took a severe toll. Rain could turn ditches into a sea of mud up to one's waist, and many men, standing in freezing water for days at a time, developed trench foot. Lack of sleep and proper nourishment, exhaustion, and shell shock—not to mention lack of sanitation—were common problems. Lice thrived everywhere, spreading trench fever, and huge rats, some as big as cats from feeding on corpses, would brazenly gnaw a hole in a man's haversack pocket to obtain a morsel of food. Often to break the boredom of "wait and see," soldiers would shoot rats as target practice. After a few months of this life, a man was beyond his prime as an efficient soldier. The initial horror gave way to indifference, his main defense against insanity.

ABOVE: The skeleton of a German soldier left in the trenches at Beaumont Hamel north of the River Somme in late 1916. **RIGHT:** German soldiers read the newspaper while lying in a trench in Belgium.

POLITICS & POWER

1917 THE U.S. CONGRESS grants citizenship to Puerto Ricans.

1917 THE U.S. ENTERS WORLD WAR I; General Pershing goes to Paris to lead American forces.

1918 U.S. PRESIDENT WOODROW WILSON states his Fourteen Points outlining a peace settlement for World War I.

1916 IRISH REBELS in Dublin revolt against British rule in the Easter Rising.

1917 THE OCTOBER REVOLUTION occurs in Russia, followed by the Russian Civil War in 1918.

1918 THE ARMISTICE ENDING WORLD WAR I is signed between the Allies and Germany on November 11.

1919 BENITO MUSSOLINI founds the Fasci di Combattimento.

1915 COMPULSORY MILITARY SERVICE in British East Africa (later known as Kenya) forces thousands of African males to join World War I.

1915 MUSTAFA KEMAL commands Ottoman troops at Gallipoli, brilliantly resisting the Allied invasion.

1918 TURKISH RESISTANCE COLLAPSES in Palestine; Ottomans surrender to the Allies.

1915 JAPAN makes "21 demands," which threaten Chinese sovereignty.

1917 CHINA declares war on Germany and Austria.

1919 AMANULLAH becomes amir of Afghanistan.

1919 THE CHINESE demonstrate against the signing of the Treaty of Versailles.

GEOGRAPHY & ENVIRONMENT

1917 THE MEXICAN CONSTITUTION calls for land reform and national rights to minerals and oil.

1917 THE U.S. agrees to purchase the Danish West Indies (Virgin Islands) for $25 million.

1917 STEPHEN MATHER organizes and directs the National Park Service. As a Sierra Club member, he advocates preservation and economic use of lands.

1918 VILHJALMUR STEFANSSON, Canadian explorer, returns from a five-year voyage north of the Arctic Circle.

1919 ERNEST SHACKLETON publishes *South,* an account of his 1914-1916 expedition to the Antarctic.

CULTURE & RELIGION

1915 EDGAR LEE MASTERS publishes *A Spoon River Anthology.*

1916 MARIANO AZUEL publishes *The Under Dogs.*

1916 JOHN DEWEY publishes *Democracy and Education.*

1917 GEORGE M. COHAN composes the American war song "Over There."

1919 HENRY ADAMS wins the Pulitzer Prize for *The Education of Henry Adams.*

1917 CHRISTIAN PILGRIMS visit Fatima, Portugal, where visions of the Virgin Mary have been seen.

1918 JOAN MIRÓ first exhibits his works.

1919 THE BAUHAUS MOVEMENT is founded by Walter Gropius in Germany.

1917 THE BALFOUR DECLARATION on Palestine occurs, pledging British support to the creation of a Jewish homeland, provided the civil and religious rights of non-Jewish Palestinians are respected.

1916 THE NEW CULTURE MOVEMENT gets under way in China, while Western-educated Chinese scholars argue the need for modernizing reform.

1918 INCREASINGLY DISCONTENTED MUSLIMS riot in Calcutta and Madras.

WHAT LIFE WAS LIKE

The 1918 Influenza Pandemic

Toward the end of World War I, a highly contagious virus swept the world. Often called the Spanish flu, as it was incorrectly thought to have begun in that country, the pestilence spread like wildfire among the troops as they moved about, and quickly became a pandemic. Doctors and nurses were short in number, hospitals overflowed, businesses closed down, and people were afraid to emerge from their homes. Laws were passed to prevent spitting and sneezing in public places, and many people donned face masks to try and protect themselves from the airborne germ, which was so virulent it could bring people down in an instant with a sudden fever, followed by respiratory ills. If they were lucky, the illness would eventually subside, but if not, pneumonia, "the captain of the men of death," set in and survival was less likely. Not since the bubonic, or black, plague swept Europe and Asia in the 14th century had so many victims been claimed by a single disease. Like the plague, as quickly as it came the influenza virus of 1918 disappeared, leaving millions dead.

SCIENCE & TECHNOLOGY

1915 THE FIRST TRANSCONTINENTAL TELEPHONE CALL is placed by Alexander Graham Bell in New York to Dr. Thomas A. Watson in San Francisco.

1915 WIRELESS SERVICE begins between the U.S. and Japan.

1916 BLOOD FOR TRANSFUSIONS is first refrigerated.

1918 HARLOW SHAPLEY discovers the true dimensions of the Milky Way.

1915 ALBERT EINSTEIN postulates his general theory of relativity.

1915 HUGO JUNKERS builds the first all-metal fighter plane.

1916 THE TRANS-SIBERIAN RAILROAD is completed.

1918 MAX PLANCK receives the Nobel Prize in physics for introducing the quantum theory.

1915 COTTON PRICES lead to a soaring economic boom in Egypt as resources are devoted to war. Light industry expands and an Egyptian business class develops.

1916 JAPANESE SCIENTIST KOTARO HONDA develops the first cobalt steel for permanent magnets, a material far more effective than previous metals.

PEOPLE & SOCIETY

1915 HENRY FORD produces his one-millionth car.

1916 MARGARET SANGER helps open the first birth control clinic in the U.S.

1917 WARTIME FUEL AND FOOD CONTROLS are enacted in the U.S.

1918 DAYLIGHT SAVING TIME is introduced in the U.S.

1918 THE FIRST AIRMAIL POSTAGE is created in the U.S.

1916 THE BRITISH MILITARY SERVICE ACT is put in force.

1916 DAYLIGHT SAVING TIME is introduced in Britain.

1917 THE FOOD SHORTAGE IN BRITAIN leads to the establishment of national food kitchens.

1918 WOMEN OLDER THAN 30 YEARS OF AGE get the vote in Britain.

1919 LADY ASTOR becomes the first female Member of Parliament in England.

THE RUSSIAN REVOLUTION

TSAR NICHOLAS, with his aristocratic heritage, had not realized the extent of the crisis that his country was undergoing. As early as 1905 in the Bloody Sunday uprising against his tsarist government, the proletariat, starving and desperate, rose up in anger against the current regime. Nicholas's inability to deal with the crisis facing his country inflamed the peasants to the extent that he was forced to abdicate on March 15, 1917.

A provisional government was organized in April of 1917, which quickly initiated such reforms as universal suffrage and other liberal innovations. By October of 1917, Lenin and his Bolshevik followers had mushroomed into a force powerful enough to take over the government. Lenin immediately abolished private property, granting land to the peasants, reallocating church lands to village soviets, and nationalizing industry and finance. Resistance from anti-Bolsheviks, however, led to a civil war that would cause another two years of strife and great loss of life.

In the meantime, the imperial Romanov family of Tsar Nicholas, who had surrendered to the Bolsheviks, was imprisoned on an estate in the Ural mountains, where they were shot, bayoneted, and tossed into an unmarked grave. In 1991, bodies exhumed from the grave were identified through DNA analysis as those of Nicholas, his wife Alexandra, and their three daughters. The remains of their other two children were discovered in 2007.

Survivors fleeing along the Nevsky Prospekt in Petrograd, or St. Petersburg, are fired on by machine gunners as the Bolshevik takeover falters briefly on July 4, 1917.

POLITICS & POWER	GEOGRAPHY & ENVIRONMENT	CULTURE & RELIGION
1920 THE U.S. SENATE votes against joining the League of Nations for the second and final time. **1920 THE 18TH AMENDMENT** goes into effect, enacting Prohibition, and the 19th Amendment gives American women the vote. **1923 PRESIDENT WARREN G. HARDING** dies as the Teapot Dome scandal comes to a boil. It becomes a synonym for government corruption.	**1920 THE U.S. CONGRESS** passes the Mineral Land Leasing Act. **1922 ANIAKCHAK,** one of the world's greatest volcanoes, is discovered on the Alaskan coast. **1924 A U.S. BILL LIMITS IMMIGRATION** and excludes all Asians. **1924 DANISH POLAR EXPLORER** Knud Rasmussen finishes the longest dog sled journey ever undertaken across the North American Arctic.	**1920 DIEGO RIVERA,** David Alfaro Siguieros, and José Clemente Orozco lead the politico-social school of painting, perfecting the form of Mexican muralism through the 1930s. **1920 EDITH WHARTON** publishes *The Age of Innocence;* Sinclair Lewis publishes *Main Street*. **1921 RUDOLF VALENTINO** stars in *Sheik,* establishing himself as the first Latin lover in silent films.
1920 THE LEAGUE OF NATIONS is formed in Paris and opens in Geneva. **1920 THE HAGUE** is chosen as the seat of the Permanent Court of International Justice, the precursor to the International Court of Justice. **1920 ENGLISH "BLACK AND TAN"** arrive in Ireland to put down republican revolt. **1922 BENITO MUSSOLINI** marches on Rome, then forms a fascist government. **1923 ADOLF HITLER'S COUP D'ETAT** (the Beer Hall Putsch) in Munich fails. Hitler is imprisoned for nine months.	**1922 THE IRISH FREE STATE** is officially proclaimed. **1922 SOVIET RUSSIA** is renamed the Union of Soviet Socialist Republics (U.S.S.R.). **1923 THE U.S.S.R.** opens the Matochkin Star station for meteorological and geophysical polar observations.	**1922 JAMES JOYCE** publishes *Ulysses* and T. S. Eliot publishes "The Waste Land," two significant works in the new literary movement called modernism. **1922 A. E. HOUSMAN** publishes *Last Poems*. **1923 P. G. WODEHOUSE** publishes *The Inimitable Jeeves*. **1923 VASSILY KANDINSKY** paints "Circles in the Circle."
1922 EGYPT declares independence under King Fuad. Wafd becomes the main nationalist political party. **1922 THE LEAGUE OF NATIONS** approves a mandate for the British government to control Palestine. **1922 AFTER DEFEATING A GREEK INVASION,** Mustapha Kemal declares Turkey a republic. Kemal is elected president in 1923. **1924 THE SHAH OF PERSIA,** Ahmed, is dethroned, and Reza Khan is appointed shah the following year.	**1922 PHARAOH TUTANKHAMUN'S TOMB** near Luxor is discovered by Britain's Howard Carter and the Earl of Carnarvon. **1923 RHODESIA (ZIMBABWE)** becomes a self-governing British colony. **1923 ANKARA REPLACES ISTANBUL** as the capital of Turkey, and Turkey reorganizes around the Anatolian peasants and their culture.	**1924 A MONUMENT IS ERECTED** in Reims, France, to commemorate the African soldiers who died defending France against the Germans.
1921 HARA TAKASHI, prime minister of Japan, is assassinated. **1921 THE FIRST CONGRESS** of the Chinese Communist Party takes place in Shanghai. **1921 CROWN PRINCE HIROHITO** becomes regent of Japan. **1924 A UNITED FRONT** between Chinese nationalists and communists is announced.	**1923 THE CENTERS OF TOKYO AND YOKOHAMA** are destroyed by an earthquake, leaving 120,000 people dead. **1923 R. C. ANDREWS** discovers the first known dinosaur eggs, from the late Cretaceous period in the Flaming Cliffs of Mongolia.	**1920 MOHANDAS GANDHI** becomes India's leader in its struggle for independence. His approach is one of nonviolent noncooperation with the Indian government. **1922 GANDHI** is sentenced to six years' imprisonment for civil disobedience. **1923 LU XUN** publishes *Nahan,* a powerful collection of short stories that call his countrymen to unite and save China. **1924 TSUKIJI LITTLE THEATRE** opens in Tokyo, signaling the start of the modern theater.

SCIENCE & TECHNOLOGY

1920 JOHN T. THOMPSON patents his submachine gun, nicknamed the "Tommy gun."

1923 CANADIAN PHYSICIAN FREDERICK BANTING shares the Nobel Prize for physiology or medicine for his isolation of insulin in a form effective for treating humans with diabetes.

1921 HERMANN RORSCHACH publishes *Psychodiagnostics,* which summarizes his studies using an inkblot test to diagnose mental disorders.

1921 THE B-C-G TUBERCULOSIS VACCINE is given to a human patient for the first time.

1921 FELIX D'HERELLE publishes his work on bacteriophages, viruses that infect bacteria. He coined the term, which means "bacteria eater."

1921 MARIE STOPES opens Britain's first birth control clinic in London.

PEOPLE & SOCIETY

1920s THE HARLEM RENAISSANCE sees a flourishing of social thought and artistic achievement in dance, music, literature, and theater among African Americans in Harlem, New York City.

1921 THE UNKNOWN SOLDIER is interred at Arlington National Cemetery.

1923 MEXICAN BANDIT PANCHO VILLA is killed by gunmen, ending his long career as a revolutionary and adversary of both the Mexican and U.S. governments.

1920s GERTRUDE STEIN coins the term "lost generation" to describe American expatriots Hemingway, Fitzgerald, Sherwood Anderson, and others living in Paris after World War I. The group was generally disillusioned by the war and disdainful of Victorian morality.

1920 OXFORD enrolls its first female students.

1921 LENIN'S NEW ECONOMIC POLICY goes into effect in the Soviet Union.

1922 THE BRITISH BROADCASTING COMPANY is founded.

THE JAZZ AGE

ALSO KNOWN AS THE ROARING TWENTIES, the era of wonderful nonsense, and the flapper era, the 1920s was a decade of indulgence in the United States, as a booming postwar economy led to greater prosperity and a general increase in the pursuit of happiness. Exciting new consumer products like cars and radios, flashy new styles of clothing, and crazy dances like the Charleston held great attraction for those with a flair for individualism and improvisation, as epitomized in the hot new music of the day.

Developing from music brought by African slaves to the New World, jazz traveled up the Mississippi River from New Orleans to Memphis, Kansas City, Chicago, and New York. Louis Armstrong, or "Satchmo," his very name synonymous with jazz, mesmerized audiences with trumpet improvisations that connected the blues and ragtime to swing. Nightclubs such as the Cotton Club attracted white New Yorkers to Harlem in droves to see Armstrong and other all-black acts while drinking high-priced illegal liquor.

Prohibition, enacted in 1920, defined this era as much as the new music. Delivering a password to be admitted to an illegal speakeasy where you could drink bootleg liquor became a craze for those who could afford it. Adding to the excitement was the likelihood that the liquor had been provided by some big business mobster like Chicago's Al Capone. Despite attempts by the federal government to stem the flow of John Barleycorn, "bathtub gin" flowed freely.

As with F. Scott Fitzgerald's Jay Gatsby, the epitome of the jazz age playboy, the good times couldn't last. The stock market crash of 1929 ushered out the roaring twenties and brought on the Great Depression.

A kneeling Louis Armstrong plays the slide trumpet in Joe "King" Oliver's Creole Jazz

POLITICS & POWER

1926 LIBERAL AUGUSTO CÉSAR SANDINO and his guerrillas begin a fight in Nicaragua against conservatives. He is assassinated in 1934 and inspires a modern revolutionary movement.

1927 CANADA is voted into the League of Nations Council.

1929 ALBERT B. FALL, secretary of the Interior under former president Harding, is convicted for his role in the Teapot Dome scandal.

1929 THE PARTIDO NACIONAL REVOLUCIONÁRIO begins one-party rule and controls Mexican politics until the late 1990s.

1925 HITLER reorganizes the Nazi Party and publishes Volume 1 of *Mein Kampf.*

1925 THE PACT OF LOCARNO commits its signatories—Germany, France, Belgium, Great Britain, and Italy—to terms for a mutually guaranteed peace in western Europe.

1927 AN ECONOMIC CONFERENCE in Geneva is attended by 50 nations.

1929 JOSEPH STALIN'S first Five-Year Plan begins in the U.S.S.R.

1929 LEON TROTSKY is expelled from the U.S.S.R.

1928 WAHABI TRIBESMEN from Saudi Arabia launch attacks aimed at Kuwait and the Iraqi frontier, and are strafed by British planes.

1926 A NORTHERN EXPEDITION is begun by nationalists in an effort to reunify China.

▶ **1926 HIROHITO** takes over the Japanese throne upon the death of his father, Hoshihito.

1927 MAO ZEDONG'S AUTUMN HARVEST UPRISING is defeated, but Mao begins to see potential for peasant revolution in China.

1928 NATIONALISTS take Beijing, having set up a government in Nanjing.

GEOGRAPHY & ENVIRONMENT

1925 AN INTERNATIONAL GROUP OF FLYERS makes the first successful crossing over the North Pole in an airship.

1925 THE TRI-STATE TORNADO, the deadliest in U.S. history, kills 695 people across Missouri, Illinois, and Indiana.

1929 U.S. AVIATOR RICHARD E. BYRD and three companions fly over the South Pole.

1925 NORWAY'S CAPITAL, Kristiana, is renamed Oslo.

1928 NORWEGIAN EXPLORER ROALD AMUNDSEN dies while attempting to rescue Italian explorer Umberto Nobile, whose airship had crashed in the Arctic.

1929 THE VATICAN STATE is established.

1926 THE REPUBLIC OF LEBANON is proclaimed.

CULTURE & RELIGION

1925 F. SCOTT FITZGERALD publishes *The Great Gatsby*.

1926 ARGENTINIAN RICARDO GÜIRALDES publishes *Don Segundo Sombra*, considered an exemplary work of gaucho literature.

1929 WILLIAM FAULKNER publishes *The Sound and the Fury*.

1929 GEORGIA O'KEEFFE paints "Black Hollyhock, Blue Larkspur."

1929 THE MUSEUM OF MODERN ART (MOMA) opens in New York.

1925 THE INCREASING POPULARITY OF ART DECO is reflected in the Exposition Internationale des Arts Décoratifs et Industriels Modernes.

1925 FRANZ KAFKA'S *The Trial* is published posthumously.

1925 THE FIRST SURREALIST EXHIBITION opens in Paris.

1926 A. A. MILNE publishes *Winnie the Pooh*.

1927 VIRGINIA WOOLF publishes *To the Lighthouse*.

1928 THE MUSLIM BROTHERHOOD is founded.

Official portrait of Emperor Hirohito in his kimono coronation robe

SCIENCE & TECHNOLOGY

1927 CHARLES A. LINDBERGH flies the *Spirit of St. Louis* nonstop from New York to Paris.

1930 CONSTRUCTION starts on the Empire State Building in New York City.

1926 THE PASTEUR INSTITUTE in Paris announces the discovery of an anti-tetanus serum.

1927 I. P. PAVLOV publishes *Conditioned Reflexes.*

1928 HANS GEIGER AND WALTHER MUELLER construct the improved Geiger counter.

1928 ALEXANDER FLEMING discovers penicillin.

1926 KENYAN ANTHROPOLOGIST LOUIS LEAKEY discovers a Neolithic settlement at Hyrax Hill in the Rift Valley of Kenya.

1926 OPERATING ON AN INFANT in Sydney, Australia, Dr. Mark Lidwill carries out the first successful heart pacing procedure.

PEOPLE & SOCIETY

1925 THE FIRST MOTEL in the U.S. opens its doors in San Luis Obispo, California.

1926 FRIDA KAHLO of Mexico turns to painting after a crippling bus accident.

1929 BRAZIL'S ECONOMY collapses due to plunging coffee prices and a drop in foreign investment.

1929 BLACK TUESDAY in New York signals the beginning of a worldwide economic crisis and the beginning of the Great Depression, when the U.S. Stock Exchange collapses.

1927 THE ECONOMIC SYSTEM OF GERMANY collapses on Black Friday. By 1930 three million Germans are out of work.

1928 WOMEN'S VOTING AGE IN BRITAIN is reduced from 30 to 21.

1925-1926 ATATURK secularizes the Turkish state. Reforms include the abolition of polygamy, prohibition of the fez, modernization of female attire, and the adoption of the Latin alphabet.

1927 IRAQ'S FIRST OIL STRIKE occurs at Kirkuk.

1925 JAPAN introduces general suffrage for men.

1927 THE SHANGHAI MASSACRE occurs when nationalist troops betray their communist allies and slaughter them.

BLACK TUESDAY ON WALL STREET

WALL STREET BIG SHOTS were reveling in the glory of a surging bull market. As stock prices climbed higher and higher in 1927 and 1928, investors bought wildly, many using borrowed money. By September 1929 the world of finance had lent $8.5 billion for such margin trades. Warning signs were overlooked, such as falling car sales and layoffs in automobile plants. Peaking in early September, the market bubble finally burst October 24, on what became known as Black Thursday, the first of several consecutive black days on Wall Street.

Although prices rallied briefly, by October 25, aka Black Friday, people had heard the bad news and started to panic. On Monday prices went into a free fall, and on Black Tuesday, a record number of shares were sold. In less than a week stocks lost a quarter of their value. Numerous margin buyers went bust, as their shares of stock were no longer valuable enough to allow them to repay the money they had borrowed to buy them.

Some who were completely ruined jumped from office windows to their deaths or otherwise committed suicide. Not just stockholders, but the entire American economy felt the force of the crash. Soon, the whole country entered the Great Depression, a period of severe economic hardship that was to last throughout the 1930s, with repercussions felt worldwide.

For the next decade Americans suffered massive unemployment, food shortages for millions, and numerous business foreclosures. President Franklin Roosevelt's New Deal enterprises such as the Works Progress Administration (WPA) and the Civilian Conservation Corps (CCC) provided jobs, but it was not until the early 1940s, when the government began to spend heavily on defense, that the Depression finally came to an end.

POLITICS & POWER

1930 REVOLUTIONS IN ARGENTINA AND BRAZIL bring José Uriburu and Getulio Vargas to power.

1930 THE SMOOT-HAWLEY TARIFF ACT is signed by U.S. President Hoover. It is blamed for worsening the Depression.

1933 FULGENCIO BATISTA Y ZALDÍVAR begins a dictatorship in Cuba.

1933 FRANKLIN DELANO ROOSEVELT announces his Good Neighbor Policy curtailing American intervention in Central America and the Caribbean.

1930 THE LAST ALLIED TROOPS leave the Rhineland.

1930 THE NAZIS gain 107 seats in the German Reichstag from the center parties.

1933 THE SECOND FIVE-YEAR PLAN starts in the U.S.S.R.

1933 ADOLF HITLER is appointed German Chancellor; later the same year he is granted dictatorial powers.

1934 HITLER AND MUSSOLINI meet in Venice.

1932 IRAQ joins the League of Nations as an independent state.

1933 AFTER THE DEATH OF HIS FATHER, King Faisal, Ghazi I becomes king of Iraq.

1934 THE TREATY OF TAIF ends the Saudi-Yemeni War.

1936 THE EGYPTIAN CONSTITUTION is restored; Egypt signs the Anglo-Egyptian treaty granting a 20-year military alliance.

1931 MAO ZEDONG is named chairman of the central executive committee of the new Chinese Soviet Republic.

1931 JAPAN invades Manchuria.

1932 THE SIAMESE ARMY takes power in a coup against the monarchy.

1933 ZAHIR SHAH becomes king of Afghanistan after his father's assassination.

1934 THE RED ARMY begins the Long March, their strategic retreat to China's northwest.

GEOGRAPHY & ENVIRONMENT

Construction workers relax on a steel beam 800 feet aboveground at the building site of the RCA Building at 30 Rockefeller Plaza.

1930 THE DEFENSIVE MAGINOT LINE arises on the French-German border.

1932 THE GREAT FAMINE spreads in the U.S.S.R., the result of government seizure of grain stores. More than half of the estimated six to eight million deaths occur in Ukraine.

1934 BRITISH ARCHAEOLOGIST LEONARD WOOLLEY concludes his 12 years of groundbreaking excavations at the site of Ur in ancient Sumer.

1931 AUSTRALIAN EXPLORER G. H. WILKINS captains the *Nautilus* submarine, taking it under the Arctic Ocean.

CULTURE & RELIGION

1930 DASHIELL HAMMETT publishes *The Maltese Falcon*.

1930 GRANT WOOD paints "American Gothic."

1931 ALEXANDER CALDER creates the first of his trademark abstract kinetic sculptures, which fellow artist Marcel Duchamp dubs "mobiles."

1931 SALVADOR DALÍ paints "Persistence of Memory."

1932 ALDOUS HUXLEY publishes *Brave New World*.

1933 CARL JUNG publishes *Modern Man in Search of a Soul*.

1933 LEON TROTSKY publishes *History of the Russian Revolution*.

1933 IN GERMANY, modernism in art is suppressed in favor of superficial realism.

1933 OTTOMAN UNIVERSITY becomes Istanbul University and gains an influx of German refugee professors.

1933 ASSYRIAN CHRISTIANS are massacred in Iraq.

1932 THE POONA PACT is signed, giving the untouchables voting rights in India.

1934 HU SHIH publishes *Chinese Renaissance*.

SCIENCE & TECHNOLOGY

1930 THE PLANET PLUTO is discovered by astronomer Clyde Tombaugh.

1931 HERBERT HOOVER opens the 1,250-foot, 102-story Empire State Building.

◀ **1932 CONSTRUCTION** begins on 30 Rockefeller Plaza, one of many skyscrapers constructed in New York City at this time.

1933 WORK BEGINS on the San Francisco-Oakland Bay Bridge (Golden Gate Bridge).

1932 THE NOBEL PRIZE FOR PHYSICS goes to Werner Heisenberg for the creation of the matrix theory of quantum mechanics.

1932 THE ZUIDERZEE DRAINAGE PROJECT, begun in 1906, is completed in Holland.

1933 NEW NAZI REGULATIONS hamper German scientific research.

1934 PORTUGUESE RULERS in Mozambique complete construction of a bridge crossing the Zambezi River to Malawi. It is the longest railway bridge in Africa.

1930 THE NOBEL PRIZE goes to Indian Sir C. Raman for his work on light diffusion.

1930 TWO HALVES OF THE NEW SYDNEY HARBOR BRIDGE are joined in Australia.

PEOPLE & SOCIETY

1930 THE FIRST WORLD CUP TOURNAMENT of the national soccer federations is played in Uruguay.

1931 CHICAGO GANGSTER AL CAPONE is jailed for income tax evasion.

1932 ROOSEVELT uses the expression "New Deal" for the first time in a speech accepting the Democratic nomination for president.

1933 PROHIBITION is repealed in the U.S.

1934 CANADA establishes a central bank.

1933 BOYCOTTS OF JEWISH BUSINESSES start in Germany.

1933 ALL BOOKS written by non-Nazi and Jewish authors are burned in Germany.

1933 THE FIRST CONCENTRATION CAMPS are erected by the Nazis in Germany.

1934 HITLER PROMOTES A BLOOD BATH in Germany by purging Nazi paramilitary leaders and other opponents in the Night of Long Knives.

1930 RAS TAFARI becomes Emperor Haile Selassie in Ethiopia.

1934 TURKEY'S FIRST FIVE-YEAR PLAN aims at developing chemical and textile industries and banks.

1934 TURKISH WOMEN get the vote.

1930 GANDHI launches the Salt March, one of his most successful nonviolent campaigns against British rule in India.

1932 JAPAN begins its conquest of world markets by undercutting prices.

HITLER'S RISE TO POWER

ADOLF HITLER'S RISE from undistinguished World War I veteran to chancellor and president of the German Nazi Party was unlikely indeed. Fanatical in his views concerning Jews and Marxists, he succeeded by 1921 in becoming chairman of the National Socialist German Workers', or Nazi, Party, molding the political association into a paramilitary group of storm troopers with the support of powerful men like Field Marshal Ludendorff.

Hitler's 1923 coup attempt, the Beer Hall Putsch, failed, but it made him famous throughout Germany. His brief imprisonment also gave him time to write *Mein Kampf,* which in time became the Nazi bible. With the backing of Paul Goebbels and Hermann Goering, the Nazis began to grow. Delivering frenzied hours-long harangues to large crowds, Hitler promised the economically depressed that he would despoil "Jew financiers" and restore security.

In 1933, after the Nazis became the largest party in the Reichstag, Hitler took advantage of government upheaval to make his move. Paul von Hindenburg appointed Hitler as chancellor, and by that summer, his takeover was complete.

Adolf Hitler raises a defiant, clenched fist during one of his haranguing speeches.

POLITICS & POWER	GEOGRAPHY & ENVIRONMENT	CULTURE & RELIGION
1935 PRESIDENT ROOSEVELT signs the U.S. Social Security Act. **1936 PARAGUAY** installs the Americas' first fascist regime. **1939 IN A LETTER** to Mussolini and Hitler, Roosevelt demands assurance that they will not attack 31 named states in Europe and the Middle East. **1939 ROOSEVELT** announces the Neutrality Act, which will permit Britain and France to purchase arms from the U.S.	**1935 A SERIES OF DUST STORMS** roars over the U.S. plains. **1936 FLOODS** wash through Johnstown, Pennsylvania. **1936 LAKE MEAD RECREATION AREA** is established, encompassing the largest reservoir in the United States. **1938 MEXICAN PRESIDENT LÁZARO CÁRDENAS** nationalizes private oil company properties of British and U.S. businessmen.	**1935 GEORGE GERSHWIN** presents *Porgy and Bess*, a folk opera, in New York. **1936 DALE CARNEGIE** publishes *How to Win Friends and Influence People*. **1936 MARGARET MITCHELL** publishes *Gone with the Wind*. **1939 JOHN STEINBECK** publishes *The Grapes of Wrath*. **1940 ARTIST GRANDMA MOSES** (Anna M. Robinson) finds fame after her first solo exhibition.
1936 GERMAN TROOPS occupy the Rhineland. **1936-1939 THE SPANISH CIVIL WAR** is fought. **1938 BRITISH PRIME MINISTER CHAMBERLAIN** signs the Munich Agreement, allowing Germany to occupy the Czech Sudetenland. ▶ **1939 GERMANY** invades Poland on September 1; Britain and France declare war on Germany on September 3. Soviet troops invade Poland.	**1936 GERMANY** starts building the Siegfried Line along the border with France.	**1936 BBC LONDON** inaugurates television service. **1937 PABLO PICASSO** paints "Guernica," a mural depicting the Spanish Civil War. **1938 KRISTALLNACHT** (Night of Broken Glass) occurs in Germany. Nazis vandalize Jewish homes, synagogues, and stores, breaking many windows. Jews are arrested and beaten; at least 91 are killed.
1936 THE REPRESENTATION OF NATIVES ACT further restricts blacks' voting rights in South Africa. **1936 ADDIS ABABA,** capital of Ethiopia, is seized by Italians. **1936 UPON PRINCE FUAD I'S DEATH,** 16-year-old Prince Farouk takes over Egypt. **1937 IRAQ'S DICTATOR,** General Bakr Sidqi Pasha, is assassinated.	**1935 PERSIA** changes its name to Iran. **1939 AN EARTHQUAKE IN TURKEY** kills at least 30,000 people.	**1936 PALESTINIANS** revolt against Zionist settlement. **1936 ALGERIAN MUSLIMS** are denied French citizenship. **1937 THE PEEL COMMISSION,** in full Royal Commission of Inquiry to Palestine, recommends the establishment of Arab and Jewish states.
1935 MANUEL LUIS QUEZON becomes president of the Philippines. **1935 UNDER THE GOVERNMENT OF INDIA ACT OF 1935,** the Indian constitution is drawn up. **1937 THE JAPANESE** occupy Peking, Tientsin, Nanjing, and Shanghai.	**1935 THE RED ARMY** ends the strategic Long March in Yan'an, their wartime headquarters in north-central China. **1937 THE KUOMINTANG GOVERNMENT (NATIONALIST PEOPLE'S PARTY)** retreats to Chongqing, in southwest-central China.	**1935 AN ANGLO-INDIAN TRADE PACT** is signed. **1936 AUTHOR LAO SHE,** writing under the pseudonym Shu Sheyu, publishes *Luotuo Xiangzi (Rickshaw)*. **1937-1938 INVADING JAPANESE** slaughter Chinese civilians and POWs during their occupation of Nanjing. The death toll is estimated from 100,000 to more than 300,000.

A squadron of German dive-bombing Stukas flies in tight formation.

SCIENCE & TECHNOLOGY

1936 THE HOOVER DAM is completed.

1937 WALLACE H. CAROTHERS patents nylon for the Du Pont Company in Delaware.

1937 FRANK WHITTLE tests his design of the first jet engine.

1938 ALBERT EINSTEIN AND LEOPOLD INFELD publish *The Evolution of Physics.*

1939 A HUGE CYCLOTRON is built at the University of California to produce neutrons from atomic nuclei.

1935 ROBERT WATSON-WATT of Scotland builds radar equipment to detect aircraft.

1935 THE MOSCOW SUBWAY is opened.

1937 THE DIRIGIBLE *HINDENBURG* bursts into flames while trying to dock at Lakehurst, New Jersey, after a transatlantic flight by one of the largest aircraft ever built.

1939 FRÉDÈRIC AND IRÈNE JOLIOT-CURIE demonstrate the possibility of splitting the atom.

PEOPLE & SOCIETY

1935 ALCOHOLICS ANONYMOUS is founded in Akron, Ohio.

1936 JESSE OWENS wins four gold medals at the Berlin Olympics.

1937 AMELIA EARHART is lost on her Pacific flight.

1938 THE 40-HOUR WORKWEEK is established in the U.S.

1939 THE U.S. ECONOMY begins to recover after the recession of 1937-1938.

1935 THE NAZIS repudiate the Treaty of Versailles and reintroduce compulsory military service.

1935 THE NUREMBERG LAWS go into effect, restricting Jewish rights in Germany.

1936 MEMBERSHIP IN NAZI YOUTH GROUPS becomes mandatory for German children between ages 10 and 17.

1936 THE DUKE OF WINDSOR abdicates the throne in order to marry Mrs. Wallis Simpson, an American socialite.

THE SINO-JAPANESE WAR

WHEN THE TREATY OF VERSAILLES in 1919 granted Germany's possessions in the Shandong Province to Japan, many Chinese felt this was the final blow to their wounded pride. Student protests roared through the cities, ending in a strike at Shanghai. Known as the May Fourth Movement, it marked a true cultural revolution inspired by nationalism and the desire to create a more modern society.

Using the Mukden Incident of 1931 as a pretext, the Japanese Kwantung army occupied Manchuria and established the puppet state of Manchukuo, home to the last of the Chinese warlords. In 1936 Chiang Kai-shek, Nationalist leader of China, was kidnapped by the warlord, Zhang Xueliang, and pressed to agree to a united anti-Japanese front with the Communists. In 1937, the Japanese used a confrontation at the Marco Polo Bridge to occupy Beijing and Tianjin.

Japanese troops eventually moved on the Nationalist capital of Nanjing. On December 13, 1937, they launched a horrific rampage that has come to be known as the Rape of Nanjing. Chiang Kai-shek's army, plus millions of peasants, trekked westward in an epic retreat that would go down as one of history's most torturous experiences.

For the next seven years fighting continued, further weakening the Nationalist army. After Pearl Harbor, the Sino-Japanese War became a part of World War II. China declared war on Japan, Germany, and Italy, and warred on against the Japanese. The Japanese surrender in 1945 was bittersweet for the battered Nationalists. A growing Communist Party would soon have complete control of the mainland, and Chiang Kai-shek would set up a Nationalist government-in-exile on the island of Taiwan.

An injured baby squalls amid the wreckage of Shanghai's South Station after a Japanese bombing attack in 1937.

POLITICS & POWER	GEOGRAPHY & ENVIRONMENT	CULTURE & RELIGION
September 16 CONGRESS institutes the Selective Training and Service Act to mobilize the U.S. military. **November 5** PRESIDENT FRANKLIN D. ROOSEVELT is elected to an unprecedented third term.	**"GALLOPING GERTIE,"** a suspension bridge over the narrows of Puget Sound in Tacoma, Washington, breaks up in the wind and drops almost 200 feet.	**ERNEST HEMINGWAY** publishes *For Whom the Bell Tolls.* **RAYMOND CHANDLER** publishes *Farewell, My Lovely.* **THOMAS WOLFE** writes *You Can't Go Home Again*, which is published posthumously. **EDMUND WILSON** publishes *To the Finland Station.*
April 9 GERMANS begin a full-scale invasion of Norway; Denmark has already been overrun. **June 10** ITALY declares war on Britain and France. **June 14** GERMAN TROOPS enter Paris. **July 21** SOVIET-OCCUPIED LITHUANIA, Latvia, and Estonia are issued an ultimatum to become part of the U.S.S.R. **September 7** HITLER'S BLITZ of London begins.	**THE LASCAUX CAVES** are discovered in France. On their walls are prehistoric paintings that are estimated to be around 17,000 years old.	**IN WARSAW, POLAND, MORE THAN 350,000 JEWS** are confined to a ghetto. **BRITISH ECONOMIST JOHN MAYNARD KEYNES** publishes *How to Pay for the War.* **WASSILY KANDINSKY** paints "Sky Blue." **ARTHUR KOESTLER** publishes *Darkness at Noon.* **BRITISH COMPOSER BENJAMIN BRITTEN** composes *Sinfonia de Requiem.*

June BRITAIN opens an offensive in North Africa.

July 3 THE ROYAL NAVY destroys much of the French fleet off Algeria to prevent its falling into German hands.

September 9 ITALIANS bomb Palestine.

December 9 BRITISH TROOPS launch an attack on Italians in the Western Desert of Egypt.

September 22 JAPANESE FORCES advance from China into northern Indochina, becoming the leading imperial power in the Far East and vowing to free the region from Western interference.

▶ **September 27** JAPAN, GERMANY, AND ITALY sign a military and economic pact.

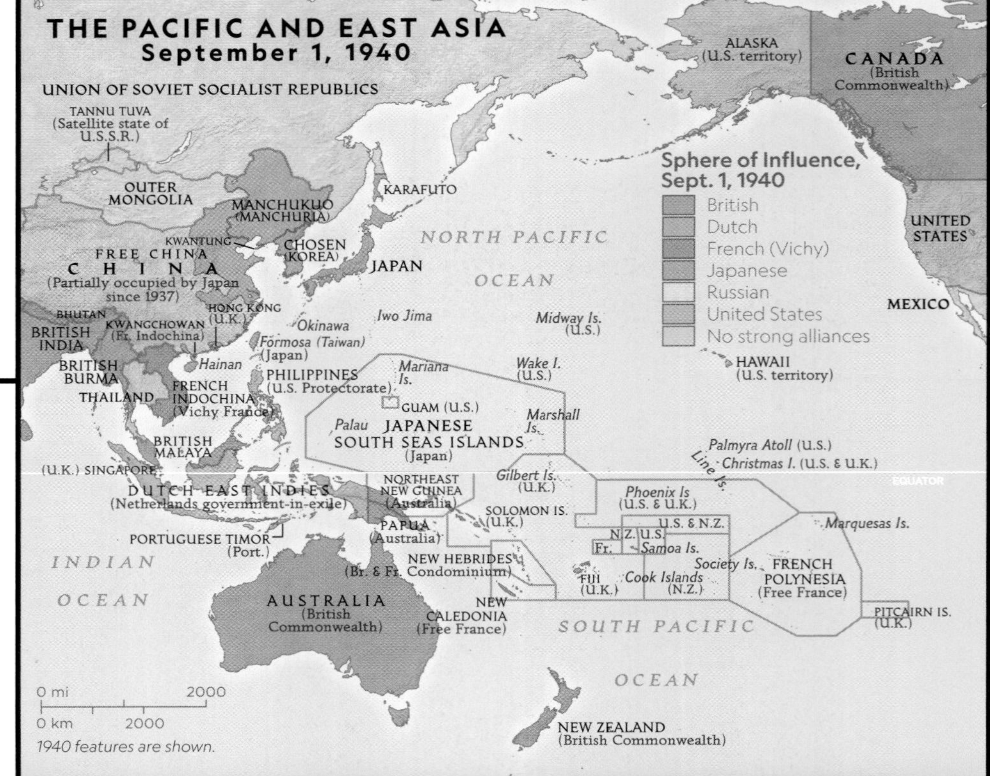

SCIENCE & TECHNOLOGY

THE FIRST SUCCESSFUL HELICOPTER FLIGHT is made in the U.S. by the Vought-Sikorsky Corporation.

EDWARD MCMILLAN AND PHILIP ABELSON discover neptunium, the first transuranic element.

THE BRITISH SCIENTIFIC ADVISORY COMMITTEE TO THE WAR CABINET is appointed.

ERNST CHAIN AND HOWARD FLOREY develop penicillin for clinical use.

BRITISH ENGINEER DONALD BAILEY invents the portable military bridge.

PEOPLE & SOCIETY

EDWARD R. MURROW broadcasts from London during the German blitz. He reports to Americans how much suffering the German bombings are inflicting on the British people.

TROTSKY is assassinated in Mexico on Stalin's orders.

CANADA institutes a national unemployment insurance program, to which the government, employers, and employees contribute.

April 27 **HEINRICH HIMMLER** starts construction of a concentration camp at Auschwitz, near Krakow, Poland.

June 4 **DUNKIRK** falls to the Germans but more than 330,000 Allied soldiers evacuate in time.

▼ **November 14** **COVENTRY CATHEDRAL** in England is devastated by aerial bombings and becomes a symbol of the barbarity of modern warfare.

THE BATTLE OF BRITAIN

BY THE SUMMER OF 1940, after Hitler's success on the Continent, he turned his attention to his biggest enemy, Great Britain. As a prelude to a planned invasion, the Nazi leader turned to one of his major assets—the mighty Luftwaffe. Knowing that the Royal Air Force (RAF) was much smaller, Hitler was confident his bombers could overwhelm the British with brute force, knocking out coastal defenses and shipping and eventually giving the Germans air control over the whole of southern England.

When this initial mission failed to destroy the RAF, the Nazis launched a nighttime bombing campaign, or blitz, of London. From September 7 through October of 1940, the Germans raided English cities as well as coastal installations. But the British, united under new Prime Minister Winston Churchill to defend their country at all costs, refused to cave, even as their cities continued to be pounded into the winter. Radar systems, in use for the first time, helped the British prepare for attacks, and the outmanned RAF fought bravely against Hitler's air force.

Gradually, realizing that their efforts to quash the RAF were in vain, the Germans gave up any hopes of invading the country. The Battle of Britain, as the various air battles were called, was the first major failure of the war for Germany. They lost about 2,300 aircraft, while the British lost some 900. And although thousands of civilians were killed, the British would fight on, determined that there would be many more losses to come for the dictator who had severely underestimated their resolve.

Winston Churchill visits Coventry Cathedral after the blitz in 1940.

POLITICS & POWER	GEOGRAPHY & ENVIRONMENT	CULTURE & RELIGION
December 7 **THE JAPANESE BOMB** the American naval base at Pearl Harbor in Hawaii. **December 8** **THE U.S. DECLARES WAR ON JAPAN.** Representative Jeannette Rankin casts the only dissenting vote in Congress to the declaration. **THE U.S. OFFICE OF THE COORDINATOR OF INFORMATION** opens, shortly to be renamed the Office of Strategic Services (OSS).	**THE GRAND COULEE DAM** in Washington State begins operation. **THE RAINBOW BRIDGE** overlooking Niagara Falls, New York, opens.	**AMONG THE LEADING FILMS** are Orson Welles's *Citizen Kane* and John Ford's *How Green Was My Valley*. **GLENN MILLER'S "CHATTANOOGA CHOO-CHOO"** is the year's top song on the Billboard chart. **AMERICAN JOURNALIST WILLIAM L. SHIRER** publishes *Berlin Diary*. **AMERICAN THEOLOGIAN REINHOLD NIEBUHR** publishes the first volume of *The Nature and Destiny of Man*.
April 13 **JOSEPH STALIN** signs a neutrality pact with Japan. **July 12** **BRITAIN AND THE U.S.S.R.** agree to the Anglo-Soviet agreement, a mutual assistance pact. **December 5-6** **SOVIET TROOPS** around Moscow counterattack and drive the Germans back. **December 11** **HITLER AND MUSSOLINI** declare war on the U.S.	**June 22** **GERMANY** invades the U.S.S.R. **BRITISH HEROINE AMY JOHNSON'S PLANE** disappears over the Thames estuary. Her body is never found.	**NOEL COWARD** writes *Blithe Spirit*. **JOHN MASEFIELD** publishes *The Nine Days Wonder* about the evacuation at Dunkirk. **DMITRI SHOSTAKOVICH** composes Symphony No. 7, during the siege of Leningrad.
February 14 **ERWIN ROMMEL'S AFRIKA KORPS** arrives in Tripoli, North Africa. **June 21** **BRITISH IMPERIAL FORCES AND FREE FRENCH FORCES** take Damascus.	**ZIMBABWE'S NATURAL RESOURCES ACT** establishes a successful community-based conservation movement.	**June 1-2** **A PRO-GERMAN COUP IN IRAQ,** known as the Farhud, leads to massacres of Jews after the British-Jewish attack on Baghdad.
July **JAPANESE FORCES** move into Cambodia. **October 18** **TOJO HIDEKI,** a pro-Axis war minister, is appointed prime minister of Japan after the resignation of Prince Fumimaro Konoe. **December 25** **HONG KONG** surrenders to Japan.	**DROUGHT** strikes Sichuan Province, China, leading to 2.5 million deaths.	**AUSTRALIAN WRITER PATRICK WHITE** wins the Australian Literature Society's gold medal for his 1939 novel *Happy Valley*.

SCIENCE & TECHNOLOGY

AMERICAN CHEMISTS Glenn Seaborg, Arthur Wahl, and Joseph Kennedy discover plutonium.

PIONEERING AMERICAN SURGEON CHARLES DREW designs a system for the mass collection and distribution of blood plasma. His experimental program ships more than 5,000 liters of plasma from America to England to treat wounded soldiers.

BRITISH CHEMISTS John Whinfield and James Dickson invent terylene, also known as Dacron.

PRIME MINISTER WINSTON CHURCHILL orders that the cryptanalysts at Bletchley Park, the British government code and cypher school, will have "all they want on extreme priority."

PEOPLE & SOCIETY

March 8 **U.S. CONGRESS** passes the Lend-Lease Act to aid the Allies with military equipment as well as food and clothing for civilians. Most of the resources go to Great Britain and the Soviet Union.

February 5 **THE AIR TRAINING CORPS** is established in Britain.

July 31 **NAZI LEADER HERMANN GOERING** authorizes SS Gen. Reinhard Heydrich to prepare the implementation of a "complete solution to the Jewish question."

August 30 **THE "SHETLAND BUS,"** a clandestine operation by Britain's Special Operations Executive (SOE) and the Military Intelligence Service of Norway's government-in-exile, begins shipping agents and equipment from the Scottish Islands to resistance fighters in Norway.

PEARL HARBOR

SUNDAY, DECEMBER 7, 1941, an unforgettable date in the memory of U.S. citizens, began as a glorious morning, a supposed day of rest and relaxation for Navy personnel. Based on Oahu, the Pacific Fleet was unaware of what was soon to befall them. At 7:55 a.m. local time, Japanese carrier planes zoomed in without warning and attacked the bulk of the U.S. Pacific fleet, moored helplessly in the harbor. Nineteen naval vessels, including eight battleships, were sunk or damaged; 188 U.S. aircraft were destroyed. Military casualties mounted to 2,335 killed and 1,109 wounded. Sixty-eight civilians also lost their lives.

President Franklin Delano Roosevelt, after hearing the news, said to a shocked country that it would be "a day which will live in infamy." Ironically, at the time of the bombing, Japanese diplomats were meeting in Washington to negotiate. Americans watched through locked gates at the Japanese Embassy as officials burned piles of U.S. papers describing the attack.

The next day the United States declared war on Japan, and Americans rallied wholeheartedly behind the cause. The Pacific Fleet quickly regrouped, aided by aircraft carriers that were at sea when the attack occurred, and the distressed country joined the rest of the world in World War II.

The view from Hickam Field as the Japanese bomb Pearl Harbor

POLITICS & POWER

GEOGRAPHY & ENVIRONMENT

CULTURE & RELIGION

May 22 **MEXICO** declares war on the Axis powers.

June 15 **MAJ. GEN. DWIGHT EISENHOWER** receives command of all U.S. forces in Europe.

August 22 **BRAZIL** declares war on Germany and Italy.

February **VIDKUN QUISLING** is appointed Minister President in Norway by the Germans.

May 27 **CZECH PARTISANS** mortally wound Gestapo leader Reinhard Heydrich by bombing his car. He dies eight days later.

June 29 **GERMANS** launch an offensive at Kursk, then advance on to Stalingrad.

November 11 **GERMANY** invades Vichy France.

May 7 **250,000 AXIS TROOPS** surrender in North Africa.

▶ **June 21** **GERMAN FIELD MARSHAL ERWIN ROMMEL'S PANZER DIVISIONS** seize Tobruk, Libya, a port that will serve as a supply base.

August 30 **ROMMEL** starts a new offensive in British-ruled Egypt.

November 4 **BRITISH GENERAL BERNARD MONTGOMERY** wins a key victory at El Alamein.

November 8 **IN OPERATION TOUCH, ALLIED TROOPS** land in Vichy-French North Africa. Rommel retreats into Tunisia.

January 2 **JAPANESE TROOPS** take Manila in the Philippines.

April 18 **U.S. PLANES** bomb Tokyo, led by Maj. Gen. Jimmy Doolittle.

May 8 **AMERICANS** win the Battle of the Coral Sea.

June 7 **THE JAPANESE WITHDRAW** after heavy fighting around Midway Island.

August 7 **U.S. MARINES** land in the Solomon Islands.

September 25 **THE JAPANESE** pull back in New Guinea in the face of advancing Allies.

WHAT LIFE WAS LIKE

Japanese Internment in the U.S.

On February 19, 1942, with fear and suspicion of the Japanese growing since the attack on Pearl Harbor, President Roosevelt ordered the forced evacuation of approximately 120,000 people of Japanese descent, 77,000 of whom were U.S. citizens. Given just days to dispose of their homes, possessions, and businesses, they were transported under military guard by train to internment camps, often remote desert camps enclosed with barbed wire. Families lived in a small room furnished only with cots and a pot-bellied stove. In 1943 the U.S. Army began to accept Japanese-American recruits, even while maintaining the internment camps. The internees were finally released in 1944, and in 1990 the U.S. government began paying $1.25 billion in reparations for this shameful incarceration.

Field Marshal Erwin Rommel, the "Desert Fox," commander of German forces in North Africa

AMONG LEADING FILMS are Disney's *Bambi* and *Holiday Inn*, starring Bing Crosby.

NAVAJO MARINES use their language to code-talk to one another in the Pacific, to ensure that the Japanese do not intercept important messages.

LANGSTON HUGHES, a central figure in the former Harlem Renaissance, publishes *Shakespeare in Harlem.*

EDWARD HOPPER paints "Nighthawks."

ALBERT CAMUS publishes *L'Étranger*.

G. M. TREVELYAN publishes *English Social History*.

RICHARD STRAUSS presents *Capriccio*, an opera, in Munich.

ARNOLD SCHOENBERG composes *Ode to Napoleon.*

SCIENCE & TECHNOLOGY	PEOPLE & SOCIETY
ENRICO FERMI splits the atom, the first controlled nuclear reaction. **BELL AIRCRAFT CORPORATION** tests the first U.S. jet airplane. **U.S. AUTOMAKERS** stop production on new passenger cars and trucks for civilian use, and tire and gas rationing is introduced.	**RATIONING** begins in the U.S. on such everyday food staples as sugar, coffee, meat, fish, flour, and canned goods. **FIVE SULLIVAN BROTHERS** serving in the U.S. Navy on the U.S.S. *Juneau* are killed when their ship is sunk. Their remaining sibling joins the WAVES the following year. **THE WOMEN'S AUXILIARY ARMY CORPS (WACS)** is established.
THE WARTIME NATIONAL LOAF is introduced in Britain, bread made with fortified whole meal flour to compensate for rationing.	**March 27** **GERMAN AUTHORITIES** begin systematic deportations of Jews from France to the Auschwitz-Birkenau concentration camp. **July 22–September 12** **GERMAN SS, POLICE AUTHORITIES, AND AUXILIARIES** deport approximately 265,000 Jews from the Warsaw ghetto to Treblinka concentration camp. Another 35,000 Jews are killed during the deportation operation. **GILBERT MURRAY** founds Oxfam.
LOUIS AND MARY LEAKEY discover ancient stone hand axes at Olorgesailie near Nairobi, Kenya.	**AFRICAN TROOPS** from the Gold Coast, Kenya, British East Africa, and British West Africa fight in Burma against the Japanese. **JEWISH WOMEN** in Palestine join the Auxiliary Territorial Service (ATS), the women's branch of the British army during World War II.
THE JAPANESE NI-GO PROJECT begins work on separating uranium-235 by thermal fusion in a quest to develop atomic weapons.	**GANDHI** appoints Jawaharlal Nehru as his successor. **AT A SERIES OF MEETINGS,** known as the Cripps Mission, the British present a plan for Indian independence after the war's end. **GANDHI** and other All-India Congress Party leaders are arrested. **THE BATAAN DEATH MARCH** takes place in the Philippines after the Japanese occupy Bataan and force-march American and Philippine prisoners to a POW camp. Many die.

THE SIEGE OF STALINGRAD

HITLER'S PLAN for the summer of 1942 was to capture Sevastopol on the Black Sea and press southward through the Caucasus to meet up with Field Marshal Erwin Rommel, who was advancing across North Africa toward Egypt with the intention of subduing the Middle East, granting Hitler control of its oil supplies. Almost as a second thought Hitler decided that the heavily defended city of Stalingrad might need to be subdued, in order to preempt a Soviet counterattack.

German forces took Sevastopol but were stalled by rough terrain and fuel shortages in the Caucasus when Hitler's fateful Stalingrad notion took hold. He ordered Friedrich Paulus's Sixth Army to attack, and the siege of Stalingrad was on, with German troops ordered to hold their ground even as their losses mounted and their position weakened.

In November the Soviets counterattacked, encircling more than 250,000 German troops. The man-to-man fighting was vicious. By January the starving survivors were ready to surrender, and Hitler knew that he had sacrificed an entire army to the Allies. Some 300,000 Germans died in the fighting. Of the almost 100,000 Germans taken prisoner, only 5,000 returned home.

German prisoners of war captured by Soviets in Stalingrad

POLITICS & POWER

June 4 **A MILITARY JUNTA IN ARGENTINA** is formed under President Arturo Rawson after he overthrows President Ramón Castillo. The new head of the National Labor Department is Juan Perón.

June 9 **A PAY-AS-YOU-GO INCOME TAX SYSTEM** is instituted in the U.S.

August 11-24 **THE FIRST OF TWO QUEBEC CONFERENCES** takes place with British Prime Minister Winston Churchill and U.S. President Franklin Roosevelt.

January 31 **THE GERMANS** surrender Stalingrad.

July 5-August 23 **GERMANY** loses the mightiest tank battle in history to the Russians near Kursk.

July 25 **MUSSOLINI** falls from power.

August 17 **SICILY** is under Allied control.

October 13 **ITALY** declares war on Germany.

January 14 **ROOSEVELT AND CHURCHILL** meet in Casablanca to orchestrate a strategy for ending the war.

January 23 **THE ALLIES SEIZE TRIPOLI,** Italy's last stronghold in North Africa.

May 7 **ALLIED TROOPS** capture Tunis, the last Axis bastion in Tunisia.

January 1-7 **JAPANESE TROOPS** are evacuated from Guadalcanal in the Solomon Islands.

March 2-4 **A JAPANESE CONVOY** is sunk in the Battle of the Bismarck Sea by U.S. and Australian planes.

▶ **June 21** **THE U.S. ARMY AND NAVY** launch the joint Operation Cartwheel to advance up the Solomon Islands to New Guinea.

November 22 **CHIANG KAI-SHEK** agrees to liberate Korea when the Japanese are defeated.

GEOGRAPHY & ENVIRONMENT

THE MAJORITY OF THE U.S. POPULATION is planting victory gardens, which supplement the rations imposed on the public food supply during World War II.

THE U.S. RECAPTURES the Aleutian Islands.

MILITARY AIRCRAFT change the ecology of isolated Pacific islands by bringing in invasive species.

CULTURE & RELIGION

BETTY SMITH publishes *A Tree Grows in Brooklyn*.

TED LAWSON publishes *Thirty Seconds Over Tokyo*.

THE FIRST ALL-AMERICAN GIRLS PROFESSIONAL BASEBALL LEAGUE begins.

JACKSON POLLOCK has his first one-man show.

RODGERS AND HAMMERSTEIN present the musical *Oklahoma!* in New York.

T. S. ELIOT publishes *Four Quartets*.

PIET MONDRIAN finishes "Broadway Boogie-Woogie."

FRANCIS POULENC composes *Les Animaux Modeles*, a ballet.

JEAN-PAUL SARTRE publishes *Les Mouches*.

SONETOS, a poetry collection by the influential Mozambican poet Rui de Noronha, is published posthumously.

August 31 **AN ALLIED SPECIAL OPERATIONS UNIT** recruits indigenous Kachin warriors to serve as guerrillas behind Japanese lines in Burma.

WHAT LIFE WAS LIKE

The Warsaw Ghetto Uprising

From the time Germans invaded and occupied Poland at the beginning of the war, Jews were herded into ghettos in Warsaw, Krakow, Lodz, and Lvov and subjected to systematic humiliation and death. After thousands had starved, the half-million Jews left in the Warsaw ghetto mounted a heroic uprising in February of 1943. Germans killed some 7,000 Jews during the fighting, which continued street by street for several months. At the end about 70 Jewish fighters had escaped through the sewers. But more than 50,000 others were transported to work camps, or even worse, to the death camps at Treblinka or Majdanek. By the time of the Allied liberation there were scarcely 200 Jews left in the entire Warsaw ghetto.

SCIENCE & TECHNOLOGY

SELMAN WAKSMAN, ALBERT SCHATZ, AND ELIZABETH BUGIE discover streptomycin, an antibiotic used to treat infection.

A 1,300-MILE-LONG OIL PIPELINE from Texas to Pennsylvania starts operating.

OTTO STERN wins the Nobel Prize for his discoveries in molecular beam theory and proton movement.

POLISH CONCENTRATION CAMP INMATES are being used for medical experiments.

HENRIK DAM (DENMARK) AND E. A. DOISY (U.S.) win the Nobel Prize for the discovery and analysis of vitamin K.

PEOPLE & SOCIETY

CALIFORNIA SHIPYARDS rely on 280,000 workers to meet the huge federal orders for ships.

AIRCRAFT MANUFACTURERS in southern California recruit 243,000 workers to build planes for the war.

THE U.S. ARMY recruits Japanese Americans.

January 28 **A DECREE IN GERMANY** institutes compulsory labor for all German men ages 16 to 65 and all women from 17 to 45.

April 13 **THE UNEARTHING OF A MASS GRAVE** of 4,443 Polish officers in the Katyń forest causes diplomatic friction. Germany accuses Russia of the murders.

June 21 **FRENCH RESISTANCE FIGHTER JEAN MOULIN** is arrested in Lyon and severely tortured by the Gestapo chief there, Klaus Barbie.

Lieutenant Walter Chewning climbs to the cockpit of an F6F Hellcat that has crash-landed on the flight deck of the U.S.S. *Enterprise* operating in the Pacific Theater in November 1943. The pilot, Ensign Byron Johnson, escaped with minor injuries.

THE ITALIAN CAMPAIGN

IN JULY OF 1943, with airborne troops preceding them by three hours, 3,000 Allied ships transporting 80,000 troops from North Africa landed on the beaches of Sicily in the first step of a major offensive to wrest Italy from the hands of Mussolini. Planning the campaign had not been easy. U.S. Army Chief George Marshall had wanted to ignore Italy and focus on the quickest route to Germany via France. Churchill, however, had convinced Roosevelt that more planning time was needed for such a huge conquest. If all went well in Sicily, the Allies there could then create a major diversion on the mainland, drawing German troops away from France to defend Italy.

Sicily's hilly and rugged terrain made hard fighting against the Germans, which was relieved somewhat by the war-weary Italian soldiers' lack of heart in battle. When Palermo fell to George Patton's Seventh Army on July 23, Mussolini was deposed and his successor surrendered to the Allies, which left Hitler on his own to defend Italy. In September, Allied forces landed at Naples, where they faced a grueling battle up the backbone of Italy. The Germans set up two lines of defense—the Gothic Line in the north and the Winter Line at Monte Cassino, just south of Rome. They also blew up communications and anything else the Allies might find usable.

Finally, in 1944, the Allies broke through the Winter Line and took Rome, shortly before D-Day on June 6. The "major diversion" had succeeded, though at a terrific loss of life and limb in some of the bloodiest fighting of the war.

POLITICS & POWER	GEOGRAPHY & ENVIRONMENT	CULTURE & RELIGION
THE DUMBARTON OAKS CONFERENCE takes place in Washington, D.C., to draft proposals for what will become the United Nations. **WILLIAM J. DONOVAN** heads approximately 12,000 employees at the Office of Strategic Services (OSS), which later becomes the Central Intelligence Agency (CIA).	**DR. NORMAN BORLAUG** launches the agricultural Green Revolution with his work in the wheat fields of Mexico.	**JOHN HERSEY** publishes *A Bell for Adano.* **TENNESSEE WILLIAMS** writes *The Glass Menagerie.* **JORGE LUIS BORGES** of Argentina publishes *Ficciones.* **AARON COPLAND** composes *Appalachian Spring.* **MORE THAN 168 PEOPLE** are killed and hundreds of others injured as a result of a fire at a Ringling Brothers and Barnum & Bailey Circus performance in Hartford, Connecticut.
January 27 **THE SOVIETS** crush the German siege of Leningrad. **June 6** **D-DAY:** Allied forces start landing in Normandy, beginning the invasion of Europe. **July 3** **SOVIETS** capture the city of Minsk. **August 25** **FREE FRENCH SOLDIERS** liberate Paris following a partisan uprising there. **December 16** **THE BATTLE OF THE BULGE** begins in Belgium, Germany's final counterattack.	**A SEVERE WINTER,** combined with a food blockade, leads to famine and the deaths of approximately 20,000 people in the Netherlands.	**STEFAN ZWEIG'S** *The World of Yesterday,* his autobiography, is published posthumously. **SERGEI PROKOFIEV** presents the opera *War and Peace* in Moscow. **THE KEYNES PLAN** for postwar economic recovery is published.
GLOBAL WAR EFFORTS rely on African rubber and minerals. **THE JEWISH BRIGADE GROUP** is formed, which serves in Egypt and Europe under British auspices.		**THE IRGUN UNDER MENACHEM BEGIN** proclaims a revolt against British rule in order to carry out the Biltmore Program of establishing a Jewish state in Palestine.
March 5 **IN OPERATION THURSDAY,** U.S. troops are landed by glider 200 miles behind Japanese lines. **May 12-15** **AT THE TRIDENT CONFERENCE,** Allied leaders approve new campaigns in Burma and China. **June 15** **U.S. PLANES** bomb the Japanese mainland. **October 20** **GENERAL MACARTHUR** lands on the Philippine island of Leyte.		**VO NGUYEN GIAP** institutes the Vietnamese People's Army.

WHAT LIFE WAS LIKE

On the Homefront

The Second World War engulfed civilian and soldier alike as men, women, and even children were called upon to contribute to or make sacrifices for the war effort. In both Allied and Axis countries, food and critical supplies were rationed, curfews were enforced, and women were suddenly deemed worthy of "men's work" in factories. Japan had a long-term strategy for replenishing their forces, asking women to help create future "cannon fodder," while in Germany, the Nazis were trying to rid themselves of an entire segment of the population, the Jews. Propaganda was a major occupation on the homefronts as well, as art and media were used to encourage loyalty or to pump up flagging morale, such as the Westinghouse "We Can Do It!" poster featuring the woman who came to be called Rosie the Riveter.

SCIENCE & TECHNOLOGY

THE WORLD'S LARGEST WARSHIP, the U.S.S. *Missouri,* is launched.

QUININE is synthesized.

GERMANS INTRODUCE the Messerschmitt Me 262 jet fighter, the fastest fighting aircraft in the war. Produced mainly with forced labor, it comes too late to alter the course of the conflict.

PEOPLE & SOCIETY

IN THE CASE OF *EX PARTE ENDO,* the U.S. Supreme Court rules to forbid the detainment of a U.S. citizen whose loyalty is recognized by the U.S. government, effectively ending the policy of internment of Japanese Americans.

SOME 17,000 U.S. CITIZENS of Mexican descent work in Los Angeles shipyards.

BLACKOUT RESTRICTIONS are relaxed in Britain.

GLENN MILLER'S ORCHESTRA performs up to 10 programs a week over the Allied Expeditionary Forces Program broadcasts.

ISLAND FIGHTING

ON AUGUST 7, 1942, U.S. Marines attacking Guadalcanal and Tulagi in the Solomon Islands caught the Japanese completely by surprise. Encountering little resistance, by the next day they had seized the airfield on Guadalcanal. But the Japanese quickly regrouped, and ultimate victory by the Allies in the Pacific would only be won at a terrible cost.

After weathering the initial attacks, the Japanese on Tulagi held out for 31 hours of hard fighting before most were killed or committed suicide. And it was not until February 1943 that the Marines could claim a victory on Guadalcanal, having learned the indelible lesson that Japanese soldiers preferred a valiant death to living with the eternal dishonor of defeat.

On Papua New Guinea, the Japanese stronghold at Buna finally fell, along with the entire island, to the forces of Gen. Douglas MacArthur, clearing the way for an Allied invasion of the Philippines. With the retaking of the Philippines in October 1944, followed by the November capture of Guam and Saipan in the Mariana Islands, the war in the Pacific was reaching its final phase.

On February 19, 1945, the Marines attacked the Japanese island of Iwo Jima, site of a key air base. Though Marines famously raised the American flag there, the victory was costly, and a hint of what was to come at Okinawa. Landing there on April 1, army and marine forces encountered Japanese soldiers fortified in the hills, while kamikaze pilots inflicted heavy damage on the ships offshore charged with supporting the landing. Not until late June was Okinawa won, after more than 12,000 Americans and 100,000 Japanese had been killed. At last, though, the landing strips that prepared the way for American bombers to island-hop to Japan were secured.

U.S. tank and infantrymen on the attack in the jungle of Bougainville, the largest of the Solomon Islands, in March 1944.

D-DAY

Dwight D. Eisenhower, the Allied Supreme Commander, began planning Operation Overlord on May 8, almost a month before his proposed D-Day, or launch date, of June 5, 1944. Wary of loose lips and German code breakers, Eisenhower kept the plan shrouded in intense secrecy; as a result, the Germans knew little of the Allied plan to break through a portion of the 2,400-mile-long Atlantic Wall along the coast of France.

Weather, though, proved to be a formidable foe. The worst front the area had experienced in 40 years threatened to scuttle the whole operation, but Eisenhower, after postponing the invasion for a day, decided to take advantage of a small opening June 6. Even when the first airborne troops parachuted down, the Germans did not believe a major invasion was under way. The night before, Field Marshal von Rundstedt failed to pass on a warning to the sleeping Hitler, believing that bad weather would make an attack impossible. As a result, Erwin Rommel, in charge of Nazi troops, had no idea the Allied invasion was imminent. This mistake made all the difference.

The first Allied troops came ashore at Normandy. The Americans landed at Omaha and Utah Beaches and the British and Canadians at Gold, Juno, and Sword Beaches. The worst of the fighting was at Omaha Beach, where approximately 2,200 Americans lost their lives before securing the beachhead. The Germans, still thinking the invasion was a diversion and that the real assault would come at Calais, did not yet send reinforcements. In spite of heavy casualties, the Allies continued to receive reinforcements while destroyers pummeled the heavy German guns on shore beyond the sea walls.

For the Allies, the day would end with a huge victory. They had breached the Atlantic Wall and secured ground beyond it. While the battle for Caen, heavily defended by the Germans, would continue until July, the Germans had already begun their retreat to the Fatherland. Allied airborne troops, who had either parachuted inland or landed in an amazing fleet of glider planes, held their ground, backing up the land troops.

On D-Day plus one, and for a number of days following, the battle inward would continue with further loss of life. In the meantime, U.S. and British forces expanded their beachheads, connecting them, allowing them to funnel in more troops and materiel. A pair of artificial harbors were built in order to dock and unload ships, while sailors disgorged cargo directly onto the beaches from their large landing craft. Three weeks after D-Day, one million Allies, 500,000 tons of supplies, and 175,000 vehicles had come ashore to lend support to the D-Day invaders.

The only question now was how long it would take to reach Berlin.

American GIs wade toward Omaha Beach on D-Day, as Germans on the bluffs beyond hit them with heavy machine-gun and mortar fire. Omaha Beach saw the most casualties in the Normandy invasion.

POLITICS & POWER

April 12 FRANKLIN DELANO ROOSEVELT dies; Harry S. Truman is sworn in as U.S. president.

July 28 THE EMPIRE STATE BUILDING is accidentally hit at the 78-79 floors by a B-25 bomber.

October 24 THE UNITED NATIONS is established to keep world peace.

▶ **February 4-11** FRANKLIN ROOSEVELT, WINSTON CHURCHILL, AND JOSEPH STALIN attend the Yalta Conference.

May 8 VICTORY IN EUROPE DAY (V-E DAY) is celebrated as Field Marshal Keitel signs Germany's final act of capitulation.

July/August THE POTSDAM CONFERENCE, led by Truman, Churchill, and Stalin, determines the intended administration of Germany.

February 23 TURKEY declares war on the Axis powers.

February 24 PRIME MINISTER AHMAD MAHIR PASHA is shot dead after reading Egypt's declaration of war on Germany and Japan.

March 22 THE ARAB LEAGUE is founded.

February 19 MARINES land on Iwo Jima.

▶ **August 6 & 9** U.S. BOMBERS drop atomic bombs on Hiroshima and Nagasaki. Japan surrenders August 15.

September 2 JAPANESE REPRESENTATIVES formally surrender aboard the battleship U.S.S. *Missouri* in Tokyo Bay.

GEOGRAPHY & ENVIRONMENT

The three Allied giants, Churchill, Roosevelt, and Stalin, meet at Yalta.

April 25 AMERICAN AND SOVIET FORCES meet along the Elbe River in Germany.

WHAT LIFE WAS LIKE

Above Hiroshima

A column of smoke rising fast. It has a fiery red core. A bubbling mass, purple-gray in color, with that red core. It's all turbulent. Fires are springing up everywhere, like flames shooting out of a huge bed of coals . . . Here it comes, the mushroom shape that Captain Parsons spoke about. It's like a mass of bubbling molasses . . . It's nearly level with us and climbing. . . .

Sgt. George Caron,
tail gunner on the *Enola Gay*

August THE U.S. AND THE U.S.S.R. divide Korea.

March 9 MORE THAN 80,000 JAPANESE, most of them civilians, perish as U.S. B-29s firebomb Tokyo, turning the city into an inferno.

CULTURE & RELIGION

AMONG LEADING FILMS is Billy Wilder's *The Lost Weekend*.

CHILEAN POET GABRIELA MISTRAL wins the Nobel Prize in literature.

U.S. WAR CORRESPONDENT ERNIE PYLE is killed in the Pacific, less than a year after winning a Pulitzer Prize for his work.

GEORGE ORWELL publishes *Animal Farm*.

EVELYN WAUGH publishes *Brideshead Revisited*.

SERGEI PROKOFIEV presents the ballet *Cinderella* in Moscow.

WOMEN vote for the first time in France.

ALBERT CAMUS publishes *Caligula*.

A GENERAL STRIKE IN NIGERIA reveals postwar discontent.

August 28 MAO ZEDONG discusses democracy, peace, and unity with Chiang Kai-shek, the anti-communist head of the National People's Party.

SCIENCE & TECHNOLOGY

July 16 THE FIRST ATOMIC BOMB is detonated near Alamogordo, New Mexico.

THE COMPANY OF BROWN AND ROOT buys pipelines financed at $142 million by the U.S. government during the war. The company becomes Texas Eastern, a Fortune 500 firm.

THE NOBEL PRIZE is won by Fleming, Florey, and Chain for the discovery of penicillin.

SOUTH AFRICA establishes the Council for Scientific and Industrial Research (CSIR).

PEOPLE & SOCIETY

THE WAR STIMULATES TREMENDOUS GROWTH in California, which overwhelms the infrastructure of its cities.

BY WAR'S END U.S. citizens have purchased some $185.7 billion worth of war bonds.

THE SEVENTH WAR LOAN DRIVE is kicked off in Washington, D.C.

CANADA INSTITUTES THE FAMILY ALLOWANCE ACT, which marks the arrival of the welfare state.

April ALLIED TROOPS liberate the concentration camps at Bergen-Belsen, Buchenwald, and Dachau.

April 28 & 30 MUSSOLINI is executed by Italians; Hitler shoots himself.

BLACK MARKETS for food, clothing, and cigarettes occur throughout Europe.

ATOMIC BOMBS FALL ON JAPAN

HARRY S. TRUMAN first learned of his nation's big secret after becoming president, upon the death of Franklin D. Roosevelt on April 12, 1945, barely a month before V-E Day was announced with the fall of Germany. The United States, he was informed, had succeeded in building an atomic bomb, which was capable of wrecking a vast, but yet unknown havoc upon the enemy.

Japan, in spite of its losses and its starving population, had thus far shown no inclination to surrender to the Allies. The next step had to be a massive invasion of Japan, with at least 500,000 troops. Weighing the death toll of such a large operation against a bombing which all hoped would cause Japan to capitulate, Truman decided on the latter.

The Allies gave Emperor Hirohito another chance to surrender, which he refused. On August 6, the first bomb, Little Boy, was dropped from the *Enola Gay* on Hiroshima, followed by *Bockscar's* Fat Man, detonated at Nagasaki three days later. The damage was horrendous—some 78,000 died at Hiroshima and some 25,000 died at Nagasaki, though the exact count will never be certain. Massive numbers of people died years afterward from radiation poisoning.

Emperor Hirohito, who was warned after the first bomb that more would fall if he didn't surrender, buckled after the destruction of Nagasaki. On September 2, Gen. Douglas MacArthur formally accepted Hirohito's signed surrender papers aboard the battleship U.S.S. *Missouri*. But the world had changed forever with the invention and deployment of the atomic bomb. Nuclear winters would be an ever-present threat of the developing Cold War.

A mushroom cloud rises above Nagasaki, Japan, on August 9, 1945, following a second nuclear attack by the U.S.

THE HOLOCAUST

The Nazis began to persecute German Jews in 1933 when Adolf Hitler rose to power. In April they enacted a law that ordered compulsory retirement of all "non-Aryans"—meaning Jews—from the civil service.

Little by little Jews suffered more indignities—the removal of telephone service or the compulsory wearing of a yellow Star of David in public. But the intent to humiliate soon became an attempt to destroy. Jews were beaten and killed in the streets, women were assaulted, store windows were smashed, and property was confiscated. Some Jews left their homeland for safe havens, but most stayed, hoping and praying the Nazi terror would soon be over.

Hitler and his leaders considered the idea of deporting Jews to Africa or Madagascar, but quickly realized it would be impossible to accomplish such a feat involving so many individuals. In January 1942, Nazi officials convened at the Wannsee Conference to coordinate the so-called final solution: extermination of the entire Jewish population of Europe. In addition to Jews, captured Slavs, Gypsies, the mentally ill, and the deformed—in other words, all human beings considered inferior to the Aryan ideal— were included in this horrific undertaking.

The ghettos, where Jews had originally been confined, were sealed off in Warsaw, Lvov, Lodz, and Krakow. Those who had survived starvation, cruel punishment, or burning were packed into boxcars and sent to concentration camps, where many were worked to death after a few months, or to death camps, where Jews were herded into "showers" and gassed. Others were randomly gathered up, shot, and pushed into mass graves, which they sometimes had been forced to dig themselves. Early on, the mentally ill and deformed had been subjected to medical experimentation. In the camps Jews became guinea pigs, too.

In 1945, when the concentration camps were finally liberated, German citizens and Allies alike saw the emaciated survivors and the dead bodies piled up for the crematoriums—a glimpse of the savagery that had been taking place. In the end, more than six million Jews had died. But ever resilient, the Jewish population, many of them Holocaust survivors, carried on in America, in other parts of Europe, and in their newly formed postwar state of Israel, rebuilding, but never forgetting their past.

Survivors at the Buchenwald concentration camp peer through a barbed wire fence at their American liberators in April 1945.

1946-1950

THE AMERICAS

POLITICS & POWER

1946 JUAN PERÓN is elected president of Argentina.

1947 THE TRUMAN DOCTRINE draws battle lines in the Cold War.

1948 THE MARSHALL PLAN goes into effect, providing more than $13 billion in aid to reconstruct western Europe.

1949 THE NORTH ATLANTIC TREATY ORGANIZATION (NATO) is founded to counter the threat of Soviet aggression.

GEOGRAPHY & ENVIRONMENT

1946 RICHARD E. BYRD leads an expedition to the South Pole.

CULTURE & RELIGION

1947 TENNESSEE WILLIAMS writes *A Streetcar Named Desire.*

1947 THE HOUSE UN-AMERICAN ACTIVITIES COMMITTEE holds hearings to determine if communist propaganda is infiltrating U.S. movies.

1948 JACKSON POLLOCK paints "Number 1A, 1948."

1948 ARTHUR MILLER writes *Death of a Salesman.*

1949 GUATEMALAN MIGUEL A. ASTURIAS publishes *Men of Maze.*

EUROPE

POLITICS & POWER

1946 A REPUBLIC is proclaimed in Italy.

1949 GERMANY IS DIVIDED into the Federal Republic (West Germany) and the Democratic Republic (East Germany).

1948 THE WESTERN ALLIES begin an 11-month airlift to provide supplies to West Berlin in opposition to the Soviet blockade.

1949 THE SOVIET UNION establishes the Council for Mutual Economic Assistance (COMECON) as an alternative to the Marshall Plan.

GEOGRAPHY & ENVIRONMENT

1947 THE UN votes to partition Palestine.

1949 THE REPUBLIC OF IRELAND is created.

CULTURE & RELIGION

1947 *THE DIARY OF ANNE FRANK* is published.

1947 H. R. TREVOR-ROPER publishes *The Last Days of Hitler.*

1948 WINSTON CHURCHILL publishes *The Gathering Storm.*

1948 THE WORLD COUNCIL OF CHURCHES is founded in Amsterdam.

1949 GEORGE ORWELL publishes *Nineteen Eighty-Four.*

MIDDLE EAST & AFRICA

POLITICS & POWER

1948 THE STATE OF ISRAEL is born. Fighting ensues with Arab Palestinians.

1949 THE WAR BETWEEN ISRAEL AND THE ARAB LEAGUE ends with an armistice agreement.

1950 THE POPULATION REGISTRATION ACT codifies apartheid into law by dividing South Africans at birth into four racial groups.

CULTURE & RELIGION

1947 THE BA'TH PARTY, founded in Syria four years earlier, adopts its first constitution.

1947 THE DEAD SEA SCROLLS, the oldest extant Hebrew documents, are discovered in Khirbat Qumrān.

1947 THE SHIP *EXODUS 1947* is denied landing in Palestine by a British blockade, forcing the more than 4,500 Jewish Holocaust survivors on board to return to Europe. The event sways public opinion toward establishmet of a Jewish National Home in Palestine.

ASIA & OCEANIA

POLITICS & POWER

1946 THE PHILIPPINES gain independence.

1948 CHINESE NATIONALISTS form a government-in-exile in Formosa (Taiwan).

1949 MAO ZEDONG defeats the Kuomintang with his peasant army in a civil war and reunifies mainland China. He declares his country the People's Republic of China, creating a communist bloc to rival American power.

GEOGRAPHY & ENVIRONMENT

1946 THE BATTLE OF HANOI is the opening salvo in the First Indochina War between French and Viet Minh forces.

1947 INDIA AND PAKISTAN become independent nations.

1948 THE UNION OF BURMA becomes an independent republic.

CULTURE & RELIGION

▶ **1948 MOHANDAS GANDHI** is assassinated.

1948 SOUTH KOREA proclaims itself a republic; North Korea proclaims itself an independent socialist republic.

CONNECTIONS

The Birth of Israel

The state of Israel was formed on May 14, 1948, after 60 years of Zionism on the part of the Jewish people. Their longtime leader, David Ben-Gurion, announced that "by virtue of the national and historic right of the Jewish people and the resolution of the United Nations: [We] hereby proclaim the establishment of the Jewish State in Palestine—to be called Israel." After World War I, Great Britain had received Palestine from the League of Nations as a mandate. Jews in Palestine, however, had been struggling for a Jewish state there since the late 19th century. The Arabs, long settled there, opposed such a state, and the British were unable to negotiate a settlement, so they turned their mandate over to the United Nations, which partitioned Palestine. Fighting ensued, with Israel increasing its land holdings and sending some 600,000 Palestinian Arabs into refugee camps in Lebanon, Gaza, Jordan, and Syria.

SCIENCE & TECHNOLOGY

1946 ENIAC, the first programmable electronic digital computer, is developed in the U.S.

1947 THE BELL X-1, piloted by Chuck Yeager, breaks the sound barrier.

1947 BELL LABORATORIES SCIENTISTS invent the transistor.

1948 ALFRED C. KINSEY publishes *Sexual Behavior in the Human Male*.

1949 A U.S. GUIDED MISSILE is launched to 250 miles, the highest altitude ever reached.

1947 THE BRITISH start operations at their first atomic pile at Harwell.

1948 THE FIRST PORT RADAR SYSTEM starts operation in Liverpool, England.

1949 SOVIET PHYSICISTS under Stalin explode their first atom bomb.

1947 RESEARCHERS studying yellow fever isolate the Zika virus from a rhesus monkey in the Zika Forest of Uganda.

1946 THE U.S. MILITARY carries out the first of several atomic tests over the Bikini Atoll in the Pacific.

PEOPLE & SOCIETY

1946 HOUSING SHORTAGES IN U.S. are a problem for returning soldiers.

1946 THE BABY BOOM begins with 3.4 million births, the largest number per year to date.

1946 JACKIE ROBINSON becomes the first African American to sign a contract with a major baseball club, the Dodgers.

1947 THANKS TO THE G.I. BILL, veterans account for 49 percent of college admissions, their peak enrollment.

1947 THE TAFT-HARTLEY ACT is passed, restricting the rights of U.S. labor unions.

1946 THE NATIONAL HEALTH SERVICE is organized in Britain.

1948 THE FIRST WORLD HEALTH ASSEMBLY convenes in Geneva.

1948 THE BRITISH GAS INDUSTRY is nationalized.

1948-1949 FLOUR AND CLOTHES RATIONING in Britain ends.

1949 NINETEEN OUT OF 22 NAZIS on trial in Nuremberg for crimes against humanity are found guilty, and 12 are sentenced to death by hanging.

1947 KENYAN WOMEN lead a revolt against forced labor in the British colony.

1948 DAVID BEN-GURION becomes prime minister of the new state of Israel. Head of the Labor Party, he encourages Jewish immigration through the Jewish Agency, which helped administer Palestine under the British mandate.

MOHANDAS GANDHI

AS A YOUNG LAWYER in South Africa in the late 1890s, British-educated Mohandas Gandhi got his first taste of the fight for independence, involving himself in efforts to end discrimination against Indians. He also began to develop a new philosophy that eschewed Western materialism in favor of Hindu ascetic ideals. He held his first *satyagraha* ("holding to the truth"), a nonviolent approach to civil disobedience in reaction to unjust laws. The South African government responded by alleviating anti-Indian discrimination, and Gandhi used this approach throughout the rest of his life.

Returning to his native land, Gandhi pushed for India's freedom from Britain, supporting them in World War I in hopes that Britain would reward India with independence. He also led labor and agrarian reform demonstrations in support of the poor, worked to eliminate the caste designation "untouchables," and pressed to develop cottage industries. After a bloody British massacre at Amritsar, Gandhi led several campaigns, becoming so well known and revered that the title Mahatma ("great soul") was given to him.

In 1930 Gandhi led a 240-mile march to the sea to protest the British salt tax. He and other Indian National Congress leaders were jailed, but upon his release less than a year later Gandhi continued his fasts and nonviolent protests. At last, in 1947, he became a major figure in negotiations with British Lord Mountbatten and Muslim League leader Muhammad Ali Jinnah, which brought about Indian's independence and the separate Muslim state of Pakistan.

On January 30, 1948, while leading a prayer meeting in New Delhi, Gandhi was assassinated by a Hindu fanatic, who believed Gandhi had been too considerate to the Muslims. Thus came a violent end to the peaceful man cherished by Indians as the father of their country.

Mohandas Gandhi reads at home next to his spinning wheel, a symbol of his nonviolent approach to India's struggle for independence.

CHAPTER 8

TOWARD A NEW WORLD ORDER

1950-2000

The Brandenburg Gate looms behind the joyful mob of demonstrators who helped demolish the Berlin Wall dividing East and West Germany in November 1989. In 1990, East Germany elects a pro-unification parliament and the two states are unified in a federal republic.

Following the Second World War, the global economy and population boomed. Human numbers climbed from 2.5 billion in 1950 to more than 6 billion by 2000, a biological success unprecedented in the history of humanity and probably in the history of large mammals. Meanwhile, the size of the world economy grew almost tenfold. On average, people were richer than ever before by the 21st century, but the average concealed vast and growing inequalities. Rapid shifts in the global balance of power ensued, ultimately resulting from the different pace of economic growth in different countries. After 1950, the world's economic production found new life in Europe and Japan and then, increasingly, in China.

OPPOSITE: Communism reached the peak of its influence in the 1970s, when communists gained control of Vietnam, Laos, Cambodia, and several African countries. By then, however, a rift had developed between the two largest communist nations, the Soviet Union and China, countering predictions that a monolithic communist bloc might one day dominate the world. Soviet Premier Nikita Khrushchev (below) pounds the lectern during a speech to the United Nations General Assembly in 1960.

The United States and the Soviet Union emerged from the 1940s as nuclear superpowers and led opposing blocs of nations in a global power struggle that became known as the Cold War. Soviet leaders blamed the upheavals of the 20th century on capitalist imperialism, and promised that the spread of communism would bring peace and justice. American leaders argued that democracy and free enterprise would achieve the same goals, and blamed communist oppression for strife in the world.

These ideological differences helped make the Cold War a hot conflict in several places, such as Korea, Vietnam, Angola, and Mozambique, which often served as proxy wars while the U.S. and the U.S.S.R. avoided a direct clash. The balance of power seemed to swing in the direction of Moscow in 1949, when the Soviets tested their first nuclear weapon and the Chinese revolution under Mao Zedong brought China into the Soviet bloc. But in the long run China and the U.S.S.R. could not remain allied, and by the 1980s the Soviet economy could no longer keep pace. The Soviets gave up trying to keep their restive bloc intact, and in short order even the Soviet Union itself ceased to exist.

The end of the Cold War did not bring peace and tranquility. International politics had become more complex in the 1950s and 1960s with the wave of decolonization that swept through Africa and Asia. More than 100 new countries came into existence between 1956 and 1991, and a few more in the 1990s with the collapse of Yugoslavia. Many of these nations were born in wars fought against European nations. Independence sometimes brought peace, but often the cycle of warfare and exploitation persisted, fueled by ethnic or religious grievance or the ambitions of a single leader, such as Saddam Hussein in Iraq.

By the end of the 20th century, the strongest trend in world politics was the rise of China. Mao's 1949 revolution had unified the country, but his economic policies brought massive famine in 1958–1960, and his political policy known as the Cultural Revolution (1966–1976) yielded economic chaos. Soon after Mao's death in 1976, China's leaders abandoned most of his economic doctrines and permitted a measure of private property and capitalism, unleashing the economic ambitions of a large part of a very large population. They also permitted economic links, both investment and trade, with the capitalist world, and by the 1990s China presided over one of the world's fastest-growing economies. In the decades thereafter, China's growth was the world's most notable economic miracle. Like every booming economy before it, the Chinese government set about translating economic strength into political and military power.

The end of the 20th century also saw rapid technological innovation, particularly in the digital realm. Personal computers appeared on desks around the world in the 1980s. By the 1990s the World Wide Web had spread across borders and was bringing e-mail, websites, and Google to the masses.

The heady economic and demographic growth of the decades after 1950 brought deepening environmental problems around the world. By the late 20th century the problem that seemed potentially the most dangerous, rapidly changing climate, proved resistant to political action.

BALANCE OF TERROR

In June 1950 North Korea, backed by the Soviet Union and China, launched an invasion of South Korea, seeking to

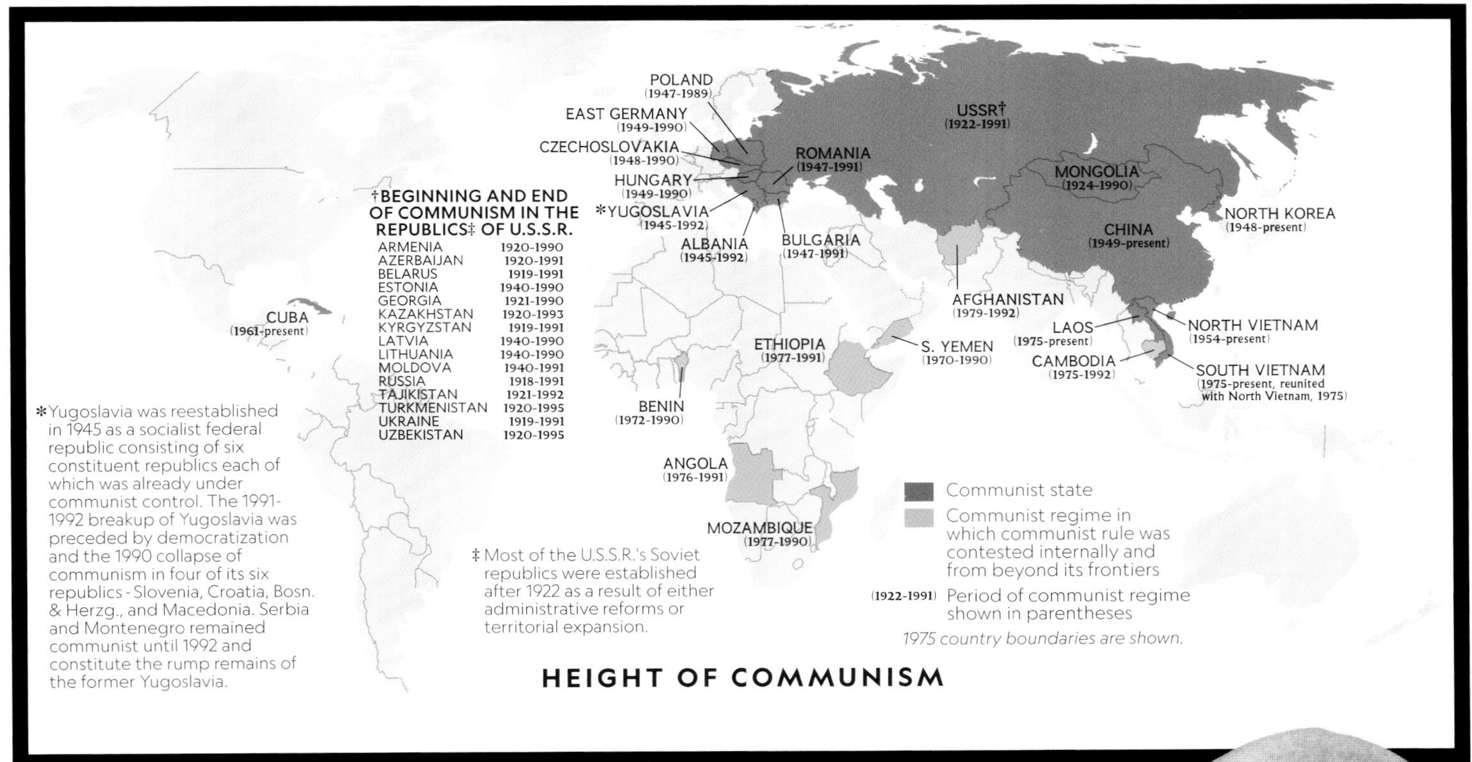

HEIGHT OF COMMUNISM

unify the country under communist leadership. The U.S. responded by obtaining a UN resolution approving the use of force against North Korea. Officially, U.S. troops fought as part of a UN force, but Americans called the shots and approached this conflict as a more traditional war, seeking not simply to repel the aggressors and restore the status quo but to defeat them. When hundreds of thousands of Chinese troops entered the contest to prevent American-led forces from conquering North Korea, President Truman placed limits on the war effort to avoid a wider conflict with China and the Soviet Union. A cease-fire arranged in 1953 fulfilled the U.S. goal of containing communism by restoring the prewar boundary between North and South Korea but fell short of the outright victory Americans had hoped for.

The Korean War provided an economic boost to Japan, where the American occupation that began in 1945 ended in 1952. Japan regained sovereignty but still housed American bases and produced more than three billion dollars' worth of supplies for American and allied troops in Korea. Those orders helped revive struggling Japanese firms such as Toyota and set the stage for an industrial boom in the years following.

U.S. soldiers dig bunkers during the Korean War.

Decolonization proved traumatic for countries such as Vietnam where colonial powers fought to retain or regain control. The French kept up their battle for Vietnam until 1954, when they were defeated at Dien Bien Phu by forces loyal to Ho Chi Minh, a communist who led the fight for independence with Soviet and Chinese aid. At peace talks, Vietnam was partitioned between the communist north and noncommunist south, pending elections intended to unite the country under one leader. That partition became permanent when South Vietnam, fearing a victory for Ho Chi Minh, withheld its approval for unity, with U.S. backing. In years to come, the U.S. grew increasingly committed to preventing communists from gaining control of South Vietnam.

In much of Africa, the end of colonial rule came slowly and painfully. Ethiopia and Libya gained independence quickly because they had been occupied by a defeated power, Italy, but other European nations were reluctant to part with African colonies, particularly those with large numbers of white settlers. In Kenya, British settlers had confiscated much of the best land from native Kenyans and now faced retribution by the Mau Mau, a secret society whose attacks led the British to crack down on Kikuyu rebels in 1952. Among those jailed were foes of colonial rule who had nothing to do with the attacks, including Jomo Kenyatta, who later led the movement that won independence for Kenya in 1963. Other African nationalists who faced jail terms before achieving their goals included Kwame Nkrumah of Ghana, which gained independence from Britain in 1957; and Nelson Mandela of South Africa, sentenced to life in prison for sabotage, conspiracy, and treason to the white government, which withdrew from the British Commonwealth in 1961 but continued its racist policy of apartheid. One of the fiercest anticolonial struggles took place in Algeria, where guerrillas clashed with French troops and settlers for eight years before winning independence in 1962.

In the Middle East, nationalism collided with the economic interests of western Europe and the U.S., which were increasingly dependent on Middle Eastern oil. In 1953 British and American agents engineered a coup against Iranian premier Mohammad Mosaddeq—who had been instrumental in nationalizing the Anglo-Iranian Oil Company—and restored to power Shah Mohammad Reza Pahlavi. The shah rewarded the U.S. and Britain by protecting their oil interests and opposing communism, but his corrupt government and his efforts to westernize Iran and crush dissent made him increasingly unpopular and led to a revolution in 1978.

Economic interests also contributed to a crisis in Egypt in 1956 when President Gamal Abdel Nasser nationalized the Suez Canal, a vital conduit for oil shipments from the Persian Gulf. Britain and France then asked Israel to ignite hostilities with Egypt, which gave them a pretext for seizing the canal. The U.S. condemned their intervention, and it collapsed. Afterward, Nasser moved closer to the Soviets and the U.S. moved closer to Israel. The deepening Arab-Israeli dispute threatened to bring the superpowers into direct conflict.

Efforts to subvert popular foreign leaders and thwart independence movements ran counter to the claims of the Western powers that they were fighting for a free world. At the same time, however, Soviet domination of eastern Europe served as a warning to developing nations that communist imperialism had its own dark side. Nikita Khrushchev, who became Soviet premier after Joseph Stalin's death in 1953, encouraged reform by disclosing details of Stalin's murderous purges and releasing political prisoners from dreaded Soviet gulags, or labor camps. Yet Khrushchev responded in Stalinist fashion when Hungary was swept by anti-Soviet demonstrations in 1956 and pulled out of the Warsaw Pact, which bound the eastern European countries to Moscow. Soviet tanks rolled into Budapest, and many demonstrators were shot. The assault reinforced the view that eastern Europe was trapped behind an Iron Curtain, and the Soviets only strengthened that impression by erecting the Berlin Wall in 1961 to stop East Germans from fleeing to the West.

In the U.S., the Cold War shattered the sense of security people had long enjoyed knowing they were oceans away from hostile powers. The American public had long harbored fears of communism, although as a political movement it had never had a major influence on U.S. politics. In 1950, Congress passed the McCarran Act, overriding a veto from President Truman. The act required supposedly communist organizations to register a list of their members with the U.S. attorney general's office. On this list of "red fronts" were such diverse groups as the National Negro Congress, the Ku Klux Klan, and the Washington Bookshop Association. Senator Joseph McCarthy, Republican of Wisconsin, took red-baiting to a new level in the '50s. Claiming, without basis, to have a list of communists working in the State Department, McCarthy launched a series of investigations into supposed communist infiltration in the Voice of America broadcasting network, the U.S. Army, and other organizations. McCarthy's ugly tactics, televised in 1954's Army-McCarthy hearings, turned the tide of public opinion against the senator and his investigations. Even so, anticommunist fears remained a powerful current in U.S. politics in the next decades, influencing both domestic and foreign policy.

In October 1957 the Soviet Union launched the satellite Sputnik I into orbit. The steady *beep-beep-beep* from on high stoked Cold War fears worldwide while launching the so-called space race between the Soviet Union and the United States. In April of 1961, Soviet cosmonaut Yuri Gagarin became the first human to orbit the Earth. In May, U.S. president John F. Kennedy responded by asking Congress to fund an ambitious space exploration program, with the aim of landing a human on the moon (and returning safely to Earth) before the decade was out. The resulting U.S.-Soviet competition saw several piloted launches a year, including the first woman in space, cosmonaut Valentina Tereshkova. The two nations rapidly progressed from short, single-person spacecraft to larger crewed vehicles, spacewalks, and finally, the moon. On July 20, 1969, U.S. astronaut Neil Armstrong became the first human to set booted foot on another world.

The same rocket technology that put Sputnik in space also allowed countries to hit distant targets with missiles carrying nuclear warheads. A ballistic missile fired at short range left commanders so little time to respond that the superpowers considered missile bases near their borders to be grave threats to their security. The installation of U.S. missiles in Turkey came as an affront to Khrushchev, and he responded in 1962 by shipping Soviet missiles to Cuba, where the revolutionary leader Fidel Castro had seized power three years earlier by toppling a regime friendly to U.S. economic interests. When spy planes detected the missiles, President Kennedy demanded their removal and blockaded Cuba. After nearly two weeks of agonizing suspense, Khrushchev ended the nuclear confrontation by agreeing to remove the missiles in exchange for private assurances that the U.S. would withdraw its missiles from Turkey and cease efforts to overthrow Castro.

At the time of the Cuban Missile Crisis, the United States had a greater nuclear deterrent than the Soviet Union, but Moscow was rapidly building their arsenal. Many believed that a balance of power—or a balance of terror—reduced the likelihood of nuclear war between the superpowers because both sides faced certain annihilation. Mutually assured destruction (MAD) did not apply to conventional conflicts pitting one superpower against forces backed by the other, and it was in such struggles that the Cold War took its heaviest toll. In the mid-1960s the U.S. sent hundreds of thousands of troops to defend an unstable regime in South Vietnam against communist insurgents, who regarded the Americans in much the same light as their former French colonizers. As casualties mounted on both sides, the war drew strong protests in the U.S. and around the world.

REMAKING SOCIETY

The American antiwar movement coincided with other social movements. The civil rights movement, which had gained hard-won victories in the 1950s, pressed forward in the '60s with protests and marches, many inspired by the civil rights leader Dr. Martin Luther King, Jr., and the Southern Christian Leadership Conference. In August 1963, the March on Washington drew more than 200,000 to the National Mall. President Kennedy had begun to push a program of reforms through Congress before his shocking assassination, by Lee Harvey Oswald, in November 1963. His successor, Lyndon B. Johnson, carried through on his efforts. Saying that he wanted to build a "Great Society" where no child would go unfed or unschooled, Johnson and his Democratic majority in Congress put into place Medicare, job training measures, and the Civil Rights Act of 1964, which guaranteed equal voting rights, banned segregation in schools and other public facilities, and prohibited discrimination in hiring. The women's liberation movement gained considerable strength in the '60s and '70s and was marked in the U.S. by advances in the rights to contraception, abortion, and equal access to credit and job opportunities. Women leaders began to gain prominence on the world stage, as well. Indian politician Indira Gandhi was elected prime minister in 1966; Golda Meir became prime minister of Israel in 1969; and Margaret Thatcher was elected to that role in England in 1979. Not until 1980, however, was an American woman elected to the U.S. Senate without following in the footsteps of her husband or father.

Growing awareness of environmental problems such as air and water pollution and species loss also spurred social action and legislation in the era. In 1970, President Richard Nixon created the Environmental Protection Agency to research and enforce environmental quality standards. In the early 1970s, the U.S. passed the Clean Air Act and the Clean Water Act and published the first list of endangered species.

The escalating war in Vietnam, and the equally escalating draft of young men, particularly African-American men, turned an otherwise fairly mellow counterculture into a more serious, and occasionally violent, movement in the U.S. Mass demonstrations in the late '60s drew hundreds of thousands of protesters to New York and Washington, D.C. Martin Luther King, Jr.'s assassination in April 1968 caused rioting that devastated urban areas. The year grew darker still with the assassination of the late President Kennedy's brother, the human rights campaigner Robert Kennedy, just two months later. Public dissatisfaction focused on the unsavory behavior of President Nixon, whose eventual extrication of the U.S. from Vietnam in 1973 was overshadowed by the Watergate scandal. The president's attempts to cover up a break-in to the Democratic Party headquarters in Washington, D.C.'s Watergate complex in June 1972 led to threats of impeachment and Nixon's resignation in 1974.

In the U.S. as in other democratic countries, however, the political system proved flexible enough to respond constructively to dissent rather than stifle it, as often happened under communist regimes. Among the many uprisings that took place around the world in 1968 was a bold effort in Czechoslovakia to reform communism and promote freedom of expression. The Soviets brought that promising Prague Spring to a bitter end by sending in tanks and toppling reform leader Alexander Dubček.

In China, poor people whose plight had long been ignored benefited from public education and health care, and women gained new rights and opportunities. But such gains were offset by ruinous social experiments such as the Great Leap Forward, an effort to ratchet up steel production and refashion agriculture in accordance with Mao Zedong's pet theories. A famine that claimed 20 million Chinese lives between 1958 and 1961 resulted. In the Cultural Revolution, launched by Mao in 1966, fervent young communists called Red Guards questioned and attacked their elders and challenged teachers, intellectuals, and others in authority. Many suspected counterrevolutionaries were placed on trial, forced to recant, and sentenced to "reeducation," which usually meant hard labor. Mao's lasting bequest to China was not communism but nationalism and self-determination. Born in 1893 when China was a decrepit empire dominated by foreign powers, he left it a strong and independent nation in 1976, no longer yoked to the Soviet Union and free to negotiate and trade with the U.S., which entered into diplomatic relations with China in 1979.

That realignment transformed the Cold War by ending fears of a monolithic communist bloc and deflating the domino theory, or the idea that if one small country such as Vietnam fell to communism many others would follow around the world. In fact, communist victories in Vietnam and in neighboring Laos and Cambodia in the 1970s had little impact beyond Indochina other than producing widespread revulsion for the mass murder of civilians by Cambodia's regime. After leaving Vietnam, the U.S. used its defense budget to rebuild its military and pursue an arms race the Soviet Union could ill afford. Despite promising results from Strategic Arms Limitation Talks (SALT) in the 1970s, the superpowers continued to spend huge sums developing and deploying nuclear weapons. (Other countries, such as the U.K. and France, also had nuclear weapons at this point, but in much smaller numbers.) The longer the buildup continued, the greater the strain on the Soviet economy.

South African police use a dog and a whip against a black man who has stepped out of line. Scenes like this one, photographed in 1967, remained all too common in South Africa until apartheid finally ended there in the 1990s.

UPHEAVAL IN THE DEVELOPING WORLD

Détente in the form of summits and SALT accords did not stop the United States and Soviet Union from intervening in developing regions subject to the economic and political influence of the superpowers. Cuba, now heavily dependent on Soviet aid, sent troops to Angola in 1975 to help communists there defeat opponents backed by South Africa. Soviet aid also fueled insurgencies in nearby Namibia, which resisted incorporation by South Africa, and in Ethiopia.

Zimbabwe won independence in 1980, overthrowing a white minority state called Rhodesia, itself recently independent from the British Empire. Many whites fled Zimbabwe, fearful of their future there, as elsewhere in Africa in the wake of independence struggles that left bitter resentments against white settlers and former colonial masters. One exception was South Africa, where Nelson Mandela, released from prison in 1990, went on to become the country's first black president and upheld his long-standing commitment to a democratic multiracial society.

Like Africa, Latin America underwent great upheaval in the late 20th century for reasons that only partly had to do with the Cold War. Efforts by Latin American nations to industrialize faltered in many cases, and grinding poverty persisted in rural areas and in shantytowns surrounding cities, where migrants pouring in from the countryside found little economic relief. Even in Argentina, one of the region's most advanced countries, glaring disparities between rich and poor caused political instability and brought to power army officers prepared to use force to impose order. Some of those strongmen were elected leaders, such as Juan Perón, a charismatic colonel who governed Argentina after the Second World War with the help of his popular and politically astute wife, Eva

Perón, and returned to power in the 1970s. Others were military dictators who formed juntas like the one that led Argentina to defeat in a war with Britain for control of the Falkland Islands, or the Malvinas, in 1982.

Latin American leaders who responded to economic ills by advocating socialism or communism risked opposition from the U.S., which was determined to keep other nations in the hemisphere from following Cuba's path. In 1954, the CIA instigated a coup that overthrew Guatemala's democratically elected president Jacobo Arbenz. Arbenz had promised to give Guatemalan peasants land, including some belonging to the American-owned United Fruit Company, but the company's allies included U.S. Secretary of State John Foster Dulles. The U.S. handed the country over to military strongmen in exchange for, theoretically, opposing communism—but also for protecting the fruit company's interests. The U.S. also backed a coup by officers in Chile in 1973 who overthrew President Salvador Allende, an avowed Marxist, and crushed political dissent. In the 1980s the U.S. aided right-wing forces called contras seeking to overthrow the left-wing government of Nicaragua. Aid to the contras was forbidden by Congress but was obtained covertly through the sale of weapons to Iran, where American citizens had been held hostage after the shah was overthrown in 1979 and where the Islamic government that succeeded him was suspected of supporting terrorism.

The Soviets had long exploited anti-American sentiments within the Islamic world, but they lost that advantage in 1979 when they invaded Afghanistan to defend a puppet regime against fundamentalists. The U.S. as well as Iran and other Islamic countries funneled weapons to mujahideen (Muslim warriors), who waged a successful guerrilla war against Soviet troops, forcing them out of Afghanistan in 1989. By then, the Soviet Union was near collapse. Mikhail Gorbachev, the last Soviet premier, recognized the signs of economic and social decay and promoted perestroika (restructuring) and glasnost (openness). Like others who had tried to reform communism, he failed, but by permitting Warsaw Pact nations to cast off Soviet restraints without retribution, he helped transform what could have been bloody uprisings into coming-out parties for the new democracies of eastern Europe.

Some in Moscow were appalled when East Germans joined with West Germans to demolish the Berlin Wall in November 1989, and when Solidarity leader Lech Walesa won a free election and became president of Poland the following year. Blaming Gorbachev for failing to stem the tide, communist hard-liners staged a coup in 1991, but their bid collapsed when Gorbachev's former aide Boris Yeltsin dissuaded troops from backing the conspirators. Under Yeltsin's leadership, the Soviet Union ceased to exist and a new Russia emerged where the seeds of democracy and free enterprise were planted in an environment long hostile to them. Before long, however, those hoping to see Russia harmoniously integrated into European society were disappointed by the establishment of an authoritarian and fiercely nationalist state, headed by the former Russian intelligence officer Vladimir Putin.

Propaganda artwork from the 1990s in Baghdad, Iraq, celebrates the military, industry, and culture under the regime of Saddam Hussein. In the first Gulf War, Hussein invaded Iraq's smaller, oil-rich neighbor Kuwait but was repulsed by an international coalition led by the United States. The invasion was thwarted, but Hussein stayed in power until American and British troops occupied Iraq in 2003.

NATION BUILDING AND GLOBALIZATION

After the Cold War, the world's wealthiest countries promoted globalization by establishing economic and political relationships that transcended national boundaries, while developing countries struggled to assert their national identity. Many of the world's trouble spots in the 1990s were born from borders drawn in the 20th century with little regard for ethnic or religious barriers to national unity. Ethnically divided Yugoslavia, forged in 1918 at the Versailles Peace Conference, was held together after the Second World War by Marshal Tito, a communist who resisted Soviet control and managed to keep Serbia, the nation's largest state, in line with his native Croatia and other smaller Yugoslav states. In 1991 Yugoslavia broke up, and Serbian troops entered Croatia and Bosnia to support Serbian minorities there. UN troops sent as peacekeepers were unable to prevent so-called ethnic cleansing by Serbian forces. More than 100,000 died and many were displaced in the ensuing violence.

Massacres on a larger scale occurred in 1994 in the young African nation of Rwanda, where militants belonging to the Hutu majority lashed out at the once dominant Tutsi. Although a minority, the Tutsi had been favored under German and Belgian colonial rule. Nearly one million Tutsi and moderate Hutu were killed in the assaults.

The legacy of colonialism also contributed to strife in the Middle East, where Iraqi dictator Saddam Hussein used deadly force at home and abroad to hold together that fragile country, formed when the Ottoman Empire broke up after the First World War. The Sunni Muslim minority to which Hussein belonged emerged from colonial rule as Iraq's dominant faction. Still, the Sunnis came under pressure from the Shiite majority in Iraq and Kurds seeking independence.

After waging a long and indecisive war against Iran, during which he used chemical weapons against Iranian troops and Kurdish civilians, Hussein invaded oil-rich Kuwait in 1990. The U.S. responded by leading an international coalition that ousted Iraqi forces from Kuwait in 1991.

Yet even as ethnic strife pulled nations apart, global trade began to draw them together. Soon after World War II, 23 nations from around the world signed the General Agreement on Tariffs and Trade (GATT), which weakened or eliminated trade barriers among the signatories. By 1995, the agreement included more than 100 countries and was succeeded by the World Trade Organization (WTO), which provides an international forum for negotiating trade agreements and resolving disputes. Other international trade treaties, including 1994's North American Free Trade Agreement (NAFTA) between the United States, Canada, and Mexico, also propelled world commerce. Between 1950 and 2000, total international trade grew more than 20-fold.

Equally dramatic, politically, was the evolution of the European Economic Community (EEC) into the European Union in 1993. In the wake of two world wars, the six founding members of the EEC—France, Italy, the Netherlands, West Germany, Belgium, and Luxembourg—established a common market in 1957 to drop tariffs and promote peaceful economic integration. In 1992, the Maastricht Treaty created the even bolder entity of the European Union (EU). The EU eliminated tariffs and border controls for goods and people among almost all of its (eventual) 28 members. Participating countries also agreed to an official currency, the euro, although not all of them went on to use it within their own states. The EU gained a headquarters in Brussels and the ability to negotiate international treaties. By the early 21st century it had become the world's largest economy.

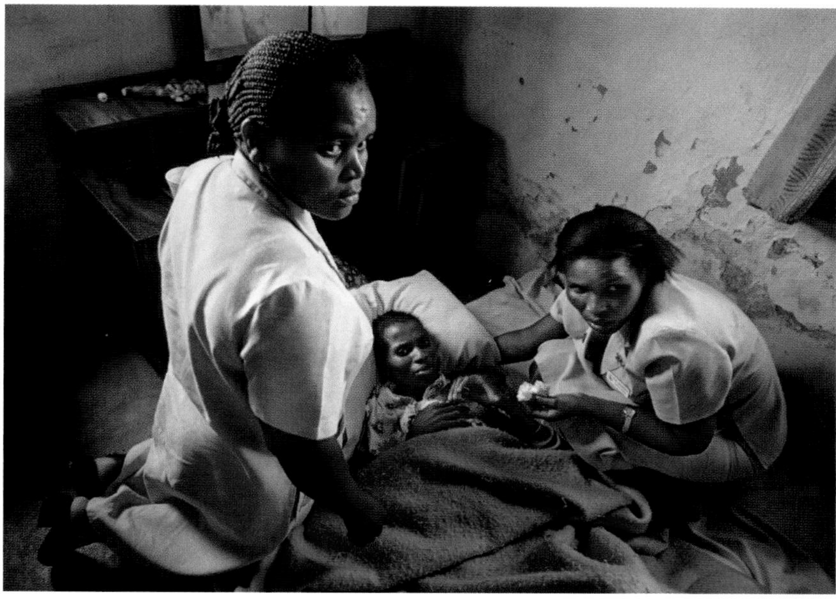

Hospice nurses care for an AIDS patient in 1999 in South Africa, where life expectancy dropped dramatically as a result of the epidemic.

Global integration and international travel marked great advances, and great threats, in public health. The last known case of smallpox, once a worldwide scourge, was registered in Somalia in 1977. On the other hand, increasingly borderless societies also eased the spread of such new and deadly pandemics as AIDS (acquired immunodeficiency syndrome). Although the disease may have had its origins in late 19th- or early 20th-century Africa, it was first officially described in California in 1981. By 1999 HIV/AIDS had become the fourth biggest killer in the world and the number one cause of death in Africa.

As the millennium ended, people around the world became anxious about an unanticipated problem: the possibility that software wouldn't recognize the date "2000" and that a worldwide computer crash would follow. The year 2000 arrived without a Y2K crisis, however, and life went on. The trends that began in the previous half century—globalization, digitization, and more—would accelerate, for good and for ill, in the next century. ■

WORLD AT A GLANCE

1950-2000

ARCTIC

NORTH AMERICA

ATLANTIC OCEAN

PACIFIC OCEAN

SOUTH AMERICA

1959: ALASKA AND HAWAII become the 49th and 50th U.S. states.

1964: THE U.S. CIVIL RIGHTS ACT of 1964 is passed. It prohibits discrimination based on race, color, religion, or national origin in public places and in employment, and provides for the integration of schools and other public facilities.

1959: FIDEL CASTRO installs the first communist regime in the West. The U.S. breaks off diplomatic relations in 1961.

1977: U.S. PRESIDENT CARTER and Panama chief Omar Torrijos sign the new Panama Canal treaties, returning the canal to Panama in 1979 but allowing the U.S. to continue managing the canal during a transition period.

1956-1961: AFRICAN COUNTRIES gain independence from European colonial rule. They include Sudan, Tunisia, Morocco, Madagascar, Somalia, Niger, Mauritania, Mali, Senegal, Chad, Ivory Coast, Togo, Benin, Upper Volta (Burkina Faso), Cameroon, Gabon, the Central African Republic, Sierra Leone, and Nigeria.

1989: TIANANMEN SQUARE in Beijing, China, is occupied by approximately one million demonstrators protesting for democracy. The government imposes martial law and uses tanks to clear the square.

1980s: SOUTHEAST ASIA'S "East Asian Tigers" emerge as Hong Kong, Singapore, Taiwan, and South Korea follow an export-driven economic model.

1990: NELSON MANDELA is released from prison after 26 years when South African president F. W. de Klerk declares amnesty for important political prisoners and lifts restrictions on the African National Congress. In 1994 the first nonracial general election in South African history results in a victory for the African National Congress and makes Nelson Mandela the first black president of South Africa.

1950-1955

	POLITICS & POWER	GEOGRAPHY & ENVIRONMENT	CULTURE & RELIGION
THE AMERICAS	**1951** THE 22ND AMENDMENT to the U.S. Constitution is ratified, limiting the president to a maximum of two terms in office. **1952** DWIGHT D. EISENHOWER is elected president of the U.S., the first Republican president in 20 years. **1954** GUATEMALAN PRESIDENT JACOBO ARBENZ is overthrown in a coup aided by the CIA.	**1951** FLOODING OF THE KANSAS RIVER in Missouri and Kansas causes damages totaling nearly $1 billion. **1954** THE UNITED STATES deports more than one million undocumented immigrants to Mexico.	**1950s** THE POSTWAR BABY BOOM dramatically increases birthrates in North America. Families increasingly move to the suburbs. **1954** THE FIRST HUMAN TRIALS of an oral contraceptive for women begin. **1955** AFL-CIO LABOR UNIONS merge.
EUROPE	**1952** KING GEORGE VI of England dies, succeeded by his daughter, Queen Elizabeth II. **1953** NIKITA KHRUSHCHEV is appointed First Secretary of the Central Committee of the Communist Party after Joseph Stalin dies. **1955** THE SOVIET UNION and its satellites form the Warsaw Pact.	**1953** HEAVY FLOODING in England, the Netherlands, and Belgium kills 2,000.	**1953** SAMUEL BECKETT'S PLAY *Waiting for Godot* (originally, *En attendant Godot*) premieres in Paris. **1955** COMMERCIAL TV begins broadcasting in Britain.
MIDDLE EAST & AFRICA	**1950** THE ARAB LEAGUE widens its economic boycott of Israel. **1951** KING ABDULLAH OF JORDAN is assassinated in Jerusalem. **1952** COL. GAMAL ABDEL NASSER seizes power in Egypt. **1953** JOMO KENYATTA and five other Kikuyu are convicted for managing Kenya's Mau Mau rebellion. **1954** A REBELLION AGAINST FRENCH RULE in Algeria begins that will last eight years.	**1952** EGYPT agrees to build a huge new dam across the Nile River in an attempt to control its annual flooding. The Aswan High Dam would be completed in 1970 at a cost of about $1 billion. **1953** SUDAN BEGINS THE TRANSITION to independence.	**1952-1956** THE MAU MAU UPRISING in Kenya consists of a core of oath-taking guerrilla warriors based on the Kikuyu Central Association. **1953** THE SHAH OF IRAN (Mohammad Reza Pahlavi) is restored to power in a coup supported by the U.S. and Great Britain. **1955** ISLAMIC COURTS are abolished in Egypt.
ASIA & OCEANIA	**1950** NORTH KOREA INVADES SOUTH KOREA and captures Seoul, initiating the Korean War. **1950** CHIANG KAI-SHEK establishes the anticommunist government of Nationalist China on the island of Taiwan (Formosa). **1953** AN ARMISTICE IS SIGNED after inconclusive fighting, ending the Korean War. **1953** CAMBODIA GAINS INDEPENDENCE from France.	**1950** DROUGHT FOLLOWED BY FLOODING kills millions in northern China. **1953** EDMUND HILLARY AND TENZING NORGAY become the first people to reach the summit of Mount Everest, the world's tallest mountain. **1954** VIETNAM SPLITS into North Vietnam and South Vietnam after the communist victory in the Indochina War.	**1950s** THE POSTWAR BABY BOOM dramatically increases birthrates in Australia and New Zealand.

SCIENCE & TECHNOLOGY

1951 UNIVAC, the first commercial computer, is introduced by Remington Rand.

1951 ELECTRIC POWER is produced from atomic energy for the first time in Arco, Idaho.

1954 CIGARETTE SMOKING is reported to cause lung cancer.

1955 THE SOVIET UNION puts ballistic missiles aboard submarines.

1952 THE BRITISH-MADE DE HAVILLAND COMET 1 becomes the first turbojet passenger plane in regular service.

1953 THE SOVIET UNION detonates its first hydrogen bomb.

1950-1953 THE KOREAN WAR is the first war to feature extensive aerial combat by jet fighters, combat use of helicopters (tactical and logistical), and synthetic bulletproof vests.

1950s THE U.S. TESTS NUCLEAR WEAPONS, including the first hydrogen bomb, at Bikini and Enewetak Atolls in the Marshall Islands.

PEOPLE & SOCIETY

1951 JULIUS AND ETHEL ROSENBERG are sentenced to death for espionage against the U.S. They are executed in 1953.

1953 JONAS SALK discovers the polio vaccine, which is approved for widespread use in 1955.

1954 THE U.S. SUPREME COURT unanimously rejects the "separate but equal" doctrine and desegregates public schools.

1955 AFRICAN AMERICAN ROSA PARKS is arrested after refusing to give up her bus seat to a white person in segregated Montgomery, Alabama.

1950s-1960s JOSIP BROZ TITO develops an independent communist state in Yugoslavia.

1953 BRITISH BIOPHYSICIST FRANCIS CRICK AND U.S. BIOLOGIST JAMES WATSON unveil the double helix model of DNA.

1954 BRITAIN'S ROGER BANNISTER breaks the 4-minute mile barrier, running a mile in 3 minutes 59.4 seconds.

THE KOREAN WAR

THE FIRST MAJOR CONFLICT of the Cold War played out on the tiny Korean Peninsula, where Soviet and U.S. forces had been occupying either side of the 38th parallel since the end of World War II. The establishment of rival governments in 1948 lit a fuse that finally exploded when communist North Korea invaded noncommunist South Korea on June 25, 1950.

President Harry Truman committed the U.S. military to Korea and returned a familiar face to Pacific combat—General Douglas MacArthur, who was made supreme commander of a coalition force of United Nations members. North Korean forces had overwhelmed the South with their initial invasion, capturing the capital, Seoul. But MacArthur staged a daring amphibious landing at Inch'on, cutting off North Korean supply lines and allowing UN forces to mount a counteroffensive. By the end of 1950 UN forces had driven their opponents all the way to the border of communist China.

The tide turned when 300,000 Chinese troops poured across the Yalu River to join the North Koreans. MacArthur wanted to take the war to China and even use nuclear weapons, but Truman believed this would only make matters worse. Unable to resolve their differences, Truman relieved MacArthur of his command in 1951. The war became what one general called a "meat grinder"—with brutal infantry battles with names like Heartbreak Ridge and Pork Chop Hill that accomplished little more than a stalemate.

When the new U.S. president Dwight Eisenhower finally wangled an armistice in 1953, after 54,000 U.S. casualties and at least two million Chinese and Korean casualties, the boundaries and governments of the North and South remained unchanged. Denied the outright victory it dearly wanted, the U.S. had to console itself with the fact that, for the time being anyway, its military had kept communism contained.

After repulsing North Korea's invasion of South Korea, UN forces proceeded northward toward the Chinese border, which China viewed as a grave threat to the security of its own country. By November 25 some 300,000 Chinese troops had entered the war in support of North Korea. In bitter winter weather they pushed the UN troops back well beyond the 38th parallel.

POLITICS & POWER	GEOGRAPHY & ENVIRONMENT	CULTURE & RELIGION
1956 U.S. PRESIDENT DWIGHT D. EISENHOWER is reelected. **1959 FIDEL CASTRO** installs the first communist regime in the West. The U.S. breaks off diplomatic relations in 1961. **1960 JOHN F. KENNEDY** becomes the youngest person elected U.S. president. **1961 U.S.-TRAINED CUBAN EXILES** attempt to overthrow Castro in the failed Bay of Pigs invasion.	**1956 THE GREEN REVOLUTION,** a combination of improved agricultural techniques and new plant breeds, brings wheat self-sufficiency to Mexico. Ultimately it is credited with saving a billion people from starvation in developing countries. **1959 ALASKA AND HAWAII** become the 49th and 50th U.S. states. **1959 THE SAINT LAWRENCE SEAWAY,** a joint U.S.-Canadian venture, is completed, linking the Great Lakes to the Atlantic Ocean.	**1959 THE GUGGENHEIM MUSEUM,** designed by Frank Lloyd Wright, opens in New York. **1960 THE U.S. FOOD AND DRUG ADMINISTRATION** approves Enovid (aka the Pill) as a prescription birth control pill.
1956 SOVIET PREMIER NIKITA KHRUSHCHEV begins "de-Stalinization," liberalizing Soviet politics. Soviet troops, though, invade Hungary and crush an uprising when the satellite tries to withdraw from the Warsaw Pact. **1957 THE EUROPEAN ECONOMIC COMMUNITY** (sometimes called the Common Market) comes into being, a bid to give Europe economic leverage equal to the U.S. and Soviet Union. **1960 LEONID BREZHNEV** becomes chairman of the Presidium of the Supreme Soviet: the head of the Soviet Union.	**1957 THE EUROPEAN ATOMIC ENERGY COMMUNITY** (Euratom) is formed in order to promote nuclear energy in Europe. **1960 CYPRUS** becomes an independent republic.	**1958 THE BRITISH** begin allowing women in the House of Lords. **1958 POPE PIUS XII DIES;** Cardinal Roncalli becomes Pope John XXIII.
1956 THE SECOND ARAB-ISRAELI WAR occurs after Egypt seizes the Suez Canal. Ultimately the canal remains Egyptian property. **1958 EGYPT AND SYRIA** join forces to create the United Arab Republic, with Nasser as president. **1959 THE MILITANT ARAB GROUP AL-FATAH** is established in Kuwait by Yasser Arafat. **1960 IN THE REPUBLIC OF THE CONGO,** CIA-backed Colonel Joseph Mobutu leads a successful coup against Soviet-supported prime minister Patrice Lumumba.	**1956-1961 AFRICAN COUNTRIES** gain independence from European colonial rule. They include Sudan, Tunisia, Morocco, Madagascar, Somalia, Niger, Mauritania, Mali, Senegal, Chad, Ivory Coast, Togo, Benin, Upper Volta (Burkina Faso), Cameroon, Gabon, the Central African Republic, Sierra Leone, and Nigeria. The Belgian Congo becomes the Republic of the Congo.	
1956 PAKISTAN becomes an Islamic republic. **1958 CHINA BEGINS THE GREAT LEAP FORWARD** (1958-1960), a planned, but disastrous, move toward rapid industrial development that leads to mass starvation. **1959 TIBETANS** revolt against Chinese control, but China crushes the uprising.	**1958 AN OUTBREAK** of cholera and smallpox in Southeast Asia kills more than 20,000. **1962 WESTERN SAMOA** gains independence from New Zealand.	

WHAT LIFE WAS LIKE

TV's First Golden Age

Paralleling the baby boom in America was the TV boom. Rapid technological advances and higher disposable incomes after World War II led to an explosion in television ownership. In 1950 there were perhaps 1.5 million sets in the U.S. The next year, 15 million. By 1960, 45 million. The phenomenon went global just as fast. The Soviets launched Sputnik in 1957 as a volley in the Cold War; in 1964 the U.S. was using artificial satellites to broadcast the Olympics worldwide from Japan. Television was creating a global village that connected cultures in an unprecedented way. The 1950s also saw TV shift from being an extension of radio to creating original formats that endure today: sitcoms such as *I Love Lucy* and cop dramas like *Dragnet*. Today virtually every country in the world has developed at least one TV channel.

SCIENCE & TECHNOLOGY	PEOPLE & SOCIETY
1957 FORTRAN, one of the first computer languages, is introduced. **1958 THE U.S. GOVERNMENT STARTS NASA** and begins to plan the country's manned space program. **1960 U.S. SCIENTISTS** develop a laser (light amplification by stimulated emission of radiation).	**1957 CANADIAN LEADER LESTER PEARSON** wins the Nobel Peace Prize for helping resolve the 1956 Arab-Israeli War. **1957 MARTIN LUTHER KING, JR.,** forms the Southern Christian Leadership Conference (SCLC) to promote nonviolent solutions to segregation. **1958 U.S. ENGINEER JACK KILBY** invents the integrated circuit.
1956 THE FIRST COMMERCIAL NUCLEAR POWER PLANT begins operating in Great Britain. **1957 THE SOVIET UNION** launches Sputnik I, the first artificial satellite. **1961 YURI GAGARIN** of the Soviet Union becomes the first human in space, about three weeks ahead of Alan Shepard of the U.S.	**1958 CHARLES DE GAULLE** is elected president of France, in part due to opposition to the Algerian War. **1961 THE BERLIN WALL** is constructed to prevent East Berliners from defecting to West Berlin.
1959 ANTHROPOLOGIST Mary Leakey finds the world's earliest known human in a Tanzanian gorge, establishing Africa as the cradle of humanity.	**1957 KWAME NKRUMAH** leads Ghana to independence as a member of the Commonwealth. **1959 JOMO KENYATTA,** imprisoned after the Mau Mau uprising in British Kenya, goes into exile, and is released in 1961. **1960 FORMER GESTAPO CHIEF** Adolf Eichmann is arrested in South America and taken to Israel, where he is found guilty after a Jerusalem trial in 1961 and hanged in 1962.
1956 THE FIRST CASE of Minamata disease, methylmercury poisoning, appears in the town of Minamata, Japan. **1961 THE HUGE PARKES RADIO TELESCOPE** begins operations in Australia.	**1959 CROWN PRINCE AKIHITO** of Japan marries commoner Michiko Shōda, the first time Japanese royalty has married a commoner in 1,500 years. **1960 DEMONSTRATORS** take to the streets all over Japan to oppose the renewal of the security treaty with the U.S. **1961 U THANT OF BURMA** (Myanmar) becomes the first Asian secretary-general of the UN.

Elvis Presley on the set of *Jailhouse Rock*

ROCK-AND-ROLL

SOME WOULD ARGUE that the decline o Western civilization can be traced to 1955, the year Bill Haley's "Rock Around the Clock" became rock-and-roll's first national hit. Others would say it was 1954, when Elvis Presley released "That's All Right" on Memphis, Tennessee's Sun Records.

In truth, the origin of rock-and-roll—the marching music for rebellious adolescents—is much harder to pinpoint. The term was actually coined by Cleveland disc jockey Alan Freed in 1951 to describe the black rhythm and blues records he was playing. But rock-and-roll as a commercial phenomenon was embodied in the swiveling hips of Elvis Presley, whose ability to combine the rhythms of black gospel, soul, and blues with smoldering sex appeal made him and rock-and-roll, a worldwide sensation.

Elvis recorded seven number-one hits, 2 top-10 hits, and more than 100 top-40 hits before his death in 1977, though Beatlemania had become the new counterculture sensation in the 1960s. As for those who would blame "the King" for pop culture's demise, a 195 calypso song says it all: "Don't blame it on Elvis for shakin' his pelvis / Shakin' the pelvis been in style way back since the River Nile."

POLITICS & POWER	GEOGRAPHY & ENVIRONMENT	CULTURE & RELIGION
1962 THE CUBAN MISSILE CRISIS: U.S. president John F. Kennedy wins a standoff with Soviet premier Nikita Khrushchev, who agrees to dismantle missile bases in Cuba. **1963 U.S. PRESIDENT KENNEDY** is assassinated on November 22 in Dallas, Texas. Lyndon B. Johnson is sworn in as president. **1964 THE U.S. CIVIL RIGHTS ACT OF 1964** is passed. It prohibits discrimination based on race, color, religion, or national origin in public places and in employment, and provides for the integration of schools and other public facilities.	**1962 JAMAICA** becomes independent of the United Kingdom. **1962 THE FIRST PORTION OF THE TRANS-CANADA HIGHWAY** is opened. It will become one of the longest continuous roads in the world. **1966 BRITISH GUIANA** becomes the independent nation of Guyana.	**1964 THE BEATLES** make their U.S. debut on *The Ed Sullivan Show*. **1965 MARTIN LUTHER KING, JR.,** leads 25,000 people on a march from Selma to Montgomery, Alabama. In New York, black liberation leader Malcolm X is assassinated.
1964 SOVIET PRESIDENT LEONID BREZHNEV becomes Communist Party secretary, replacing Khrushchev. **1967 COL. GEORGIOS PAPADOPOULOS** takes over Greece after a military coup.	**1963 AN UNDERSEA VOLCANO** erupts off the southern coast of Iceland, creating the new island of Surtsey (named in 1965) in a matter of months. **1964 MALTA** becomes independent of the United Kingdom.	**1962 THE SECOND VATICAN COUNCIL** (1962-1965) begins wide-ranging reforms and modernization of Roman Catholic practices, including the phasing out of the Latin Mass. **1963 POPE JOHN XXIII** dies, succeeded by Cardinal Montini as Pope Paul VI.
1963-1964 CIVIL WAR erupts in Cyprus between Greeks and Turks. **1967 THE SIX-DAY WAR,** the third Arab-Israeli war, begins. **1967 THE NIGERIAN CIVIL WAR** (1967-1970) begins following attempts by oil-rich Biafra to secede. The war leads to terrible famine in Biafra.	**1962 ALGERIA,** Uganda, Rwanda, and Burundi gain independence. **1962 YEMEN** splits into two republics, North and South Yemen. **1963-1964 KENYA** becomes an independent republic. Zanzibar and Tanganyika unite to form Tanzania. Rhodesia splits, with the north becoming the independent republic of Zambia. **1965 GAMBIA** becomes independent of Great Britain. **1966 BOTSWANA AND LESOTHO** become independent of Great Britain.	**1963 THE ORGANIZATION OF AFRICAN UNITY (OAU)** is formed. **1964 THE PALESTINE LIBERATION ORGANIZATION (PLO)** is established under the leadership of Ahmad Shukeiry.
1963 SOUTH VIETNAMESE PRESIDENT NGO DINH DIEM is assassinated in a military coup. **1964 NORTH VIETNAMESE TORPEDO BOATS** attack a U.S. destroyer in the Gulf of Tonkin, causing Congress to allow President Johnson to increase troop levels.	**1963 MALAYSIA** is formed from the federations of Malaya, Singapore, Sabah, and Sarawak. Singapore withdraws in 1965. **1965 CYCLONES** strike East Pakistan (Bangladesh), killing between 12,000 and 20,000 people.	**1966 CHAIRMAN MAO** launches China's Cultural Revolution (1966–1976), a revolutionary movement by students and workers against bureaucrats in the Chinese Communist Party. Mao's Red Guards begin purging intellectuals and so-called bourgeois elements, who are believed to be opposed to Mao's socialist vision.

SCIENCE & TECHNOLOGY	PEOPLE & SOCIETY
1962 JOHN GLENN, JR., becomes the first American to orbit Earth. **1963 THE MEASLES VACCINE** is licensed and distributed.	**1962 LABOR LEADER CESAR CHAVEZ** begins organizing California grape pickers. **1966 BETTY FRIEDAN** leads the newly founded National Organization for Women (NOW). **1967 REVOLUTIONARY LEADER CHE GUEVARA,** who helped bring Castro to power in Cuba, is caught and killed by troops in Bolivia.
1963 SOVIET COSMONAUT VALENTINA TERESHKOVA becomes the first woman in space. **1963 THE PHILIPS COMPANY** of the Netherlands develops cassette tapes. **1965 COSMONAUT ALEXEI LEONOV** is the first person to "walk" in space, spending 10 minutes outside Voskhod 2.	**1963 THE U.S. AND SOVIET UNION** set up a hotline between the White House and the Kremlin to provide quick communication should the countries seem on the brink of war. **1967 THE FIRST AUTOMATIC TELLER MACHINE (ATM)** is put in service, at Barclays Bank in London.
1964 ISRAEL BUILDS THE NATIONAL WATER CARRIER from the Sea of Galilee and the Jordan River to the coast and northern Negev in order to "make the desert bloom." **1967 DR. CHRISTIAAN N. BARNARD** leads the team that performs the world's first human heart transplant operation in Cape Town, South Africa.	**1966 FORMER FRENCH ARMY OFFICER** Jean-Bédel Bokassa takes over the Central African Republic in a military coup.
1964 CHINA explodes its first atomic bomb. **1967 CHINA** explodes its first hydrogen bomb.	**1965 FERDINAND MARCOS** is elected president of the Philippines. **1966 INDIRA GANDHI,** daughter of Jawaharlal Nehru, becomes prime minister of India.

Martin Luther King, Jr., delivers his "I Have a Dream" speech at the 1963 March on Washington.

CIVIL RIGHTS

IN THE EARLY 1960s, segregation, discrimination, and violence were a grim fact of life for African Americans, particularly in the South. Despite federal orders, few schools in the South had been integrated by 1961. Even with a growing economy, the unemployment rate in the black population was more than double the rate for white Americans in 1963. A federal policy of "redlining" prohibited African Americans from living in preferable white-only neighborhoods in cities in both the North and the South. Numerous civil rights groups campaigned for reform, often employing boycotts, voter registration drives, and nonviolent marches. In Birmingham, Alabama, in spring of 1963, demonstrators led by Dr. Martin Luther King, Jr., took to the streets. The peaceful protesters were countered with tear gas and police dogs. In August of that year, hundreds of thousands rallied in the March on Washington for Jobs and Freedom in Washington, D.C.

President John F. Kennedy was sympathetic to the cause, but a proposed civil rights bill stalled. The Civil Rights Act finally passed in 1964, banning discrimination and segregation in public places and in government employment and guaranteeing equal voting rights. Although hardly an instant solution to discrimination, the act was a major step in codifying equal rights.

AT A LOSS IN VIETNAM

The theory was that if you let one small country fall to communism, the rest of the region would follow, like dominoes. Fear of such a red tide led the United States to look past some hard lessons learned by the Japanese and the French about the tenacity of the Vietnamese. When the French tried to reoccupy Vietnam in 1946, Ho Chi Minh warned them that they could kill 10 of his men for every one French casualty and still lose. By 1954 the French military realized that he was right.

A decade later the U.S. was engaged in what would become the most unpopular war in American history to date, one that would become shorthand for military futility. Communist North Vietnam had begun guerrilla activity, through the Viet Cong, against noncommunist South Vietnam in 1957. After the deaths of U.S. noncombat advisers in Viet Cong attacks, the U.S. established a military council in South Vietnam in 1962. Then, in 1964, a naval attack against U.S. destroyers in the Gulf of Tonkin became the "remember the *Maine*" provocation for Congress to authorize military action. Two battalions of U.S. Marines landed at Da Nang in 1965; by 1968 almost half a million U.S. troops were on the ground. Ho Chi Minh had his own superpower ally in the Soviet Union, which supplied aid and armaments.

That evidence would later come to light casting doubt on whether the Gulf of Tonkin attack ever happened is emblematic of a war shrouded in secrecy and tainted with deception. In 1969 it was revealed that U.S. troops, in the previous year, had massacred at least 347 men, women, and children in the village of My Lai. In 1971 the Pentagon Papers were leaked to the press, exposing a deeper level of involvement in Southeast Asia than had been admitted. Television coverage (a first for a war) regularly broadcast shocking brutality and suffering of both soldiers and civilians.

The sense that their military had lost control and their government was lying drove demonstrators to extremes. Students refused to respond to conscription notices or evaded the draft by leaving the country. The athlete and icon Muhammad Ali declared himself a conscientious objector and refused to join the army. And antiwar protests often became violent, most notably the tragic confrontation in May 1970 at Kent State University in Ohio when four students were killed by National Guardsmen.

Despite eroding support and combat setbacks that ended the presidency of Lyndon Johnson, the U.S. did not withdraw completely until 1973, after extending the war to Cambodia, where supply lines to the Viet Cong were located. In 1975, with the North Vietnamese occupation of Saigon, the domino had officially fallen, and the U.S. had lost its first war.

A nine-year-old South Vietnamese girl (center) survived an errant napalm attack at Trang Bang by stripping off her burning clothes. Such scenes of civilian misery came to epitomize the Vietnam War.

POLITICS & POWER

1968 THE U.S. PRESIDENTIAL CAMPAIGN: President Johnson decides not to seek reelection because of Vietnam; Senator Robert F. Kennedy is assassinated in Los Angeles after winning the California Democratic primary; riots break out at the Democratic Convention in Chicago. Richard Nixon wins the election.

1972 RICHARD NIXON is reelected president of the United States.

1973 MARXIST CHILEAN PRESIDENT SALVADOR ALLENDE is ousted in a CIA-backed coup.

1968 THE SOVIET UNION invades Czechoslovakia and arrests President Dubček, crushing his Prague Spring.

1972 BRITAIN imposes direct rule on Northern Ireland because of the violence between Catholics and Protestants. Fourteen unarmed protesters are gunned down by British police in the "Bloody Sunday" incident.

1972 THE FIRST SUDANESE CIVIL WAR ends with the Addis Ababa Agreement, granting southern Sudan autonomy.

1973 THE FOURTH ARAB-ISRAELI WAR (the Yom Kippur War) occurs after Egypt and Syria launch a surprise attack on Yom Kippur but fails to regain lost territory.

1971 CIVIL WAR breaks out in Pakistan, with India supporting East Pakistan.

1971 THE UN expels Taiwan and recognizes the People's Republic of China as the sole Chinese government.

1973 THE U.S. AND SOUTH VIETNAM sign a cease-fire agreement with North Vietnam. The last U.S. troops are withdrawn on March 29, 1973.

GEOGRAPHY & ENVIRONMENT

1970 AN EARTHQUAKE AND LANDSLIDES kill 50,000 to 70,000 in Peru.

1970 THE ENVIRONMENTAL PROTECTION AGENCY (EPA) is established. The first Earth Day is celebrated. Greenpeace is founded the next year.

1968 AN EARTHQUAKE in Iran kills 12,000.

1968-1974 DROUGHT in the northern African Sahel region kills approximately 100,000.

1970 GAMBIA becomes a republic.

1970 A CYCLONE AND FLOODS kill up to 500,000 in East Pakistan (Bangladesh).

1970 FIJI AND TONGA gain independence from Britain.

1971 EAST PAKISTAN becomes the sovereign state of Bangladesh.

1972 CEYLON becomes the Democratic Socialist Republic of Sri Lanka.

CULTURE & RELIGION

1969 MORE THAN 300,000 ROCK-AND-ROLL FANS attend the Woodstock Music and Art Fair near Bethel, New York.

1971 CHILEAN POET PABLO NERUDA, known for his wide-ranging poetry, wins the Nobel Prize in literature.

1973 THE U.S. SUPREME COURT rules in *Roe* v. *Wade* that states may not prohibit abortions during the first six months of pregnancy.

1968 STUDENT REBELLIONS in Paris lead to reform of the French education system.

1972 ARAB TERRORISTS kill 11 Israeli athletes at the Summer Olympic Games in Munich.

1973 IN RETALIATION for Western support of Israel, Arab members of OPEC embargo oil supplies, precipitating a devastating energy crisis in major industrialized nations.

1970 POPE PAUL VI escapes an assassination attempt in the Philippines.

1972 THE ABORIGINAL TENT ASSEMBLY sets up on the parliament steps in Canberra, Australia, to demand sovereignty for the country's indigenous peoples.

1974 TERRA-COTTA WARRIORS are discovered by workers digging near the tomb of China's first emperor Qin Shihuangdi.

CONNECTIONS

A New Phase for the Beatles

By the time the Beatles dissolved in 1970 they had not only become the most successful recording group of all time but also changed the way the cultures of East and West could come together in pop music. Guitarist George Harrison began collaborating with Hindustani musician Ravi Shankar and playing the sitar in some recordings. The so-named White Album was written largely in India, and Indian musical influences can be heard in droning bass lines and mantra-like vocals. Many were turned off by the Beatles' interest in the East, especially as John Lennon had seemingly dismissed Christianity and quipped that the Beatles were "more popular than Jesus." Yet nothing could ultimately dim the popularity or influence of the boys from Liverpool, who to date have sold more than a billion recordings worldwide.

SCIENCE & TECHNOLOGY

1969 APOLLO 11 lands on the moon. More than 100 million people around the world watch on television as U.S. astronaut Neil Armstrong steps onto the surface.

1969 THE ADVANCED RESEARCH PROJECTS AGENCY NETWORK (ARPANET) system goes online, a predecessor of the Internet.

1971 THE MICROPROCESSOR, a miniature set of integrated circuits, is invented, making the computer revolution possible.

1970 LIQUID CRYSTAL DISPLAYS (LCD) are developed by a Swiss lab.

1971 THE SOVIET UNION launches the first crewed space station, Salyut 1.

1971 THE FIRST CT SCAN MACHINE for imaging brains is installed in a hospital in England.

1970 THE ASWAN HIGH DAM in Egypt is completed. Funded by Egyptian President Nasser in part by seizing the Suez Canal in 1956, the dam proves controversial environmentally and for submerging most of Nubia's archaeological remains, but it allows the reclamation of agricultural land and the generation of much needed electrical power.

1970 CHINA launches its first space satellite.

1971 JAPAN launches the tanker *Nisseki Maru*, the largest tanker ever built (372,400 tons).

PEOPLE & SOCIETY

1968 MARTIN LUTHER KING, JR., is assassinated at the Lorraine Motel in Memphis, Tennessee, by James Earl Ray. Riots erupt across the U.S.

1970s PABLO ESCOBAR builds the drug-smuggling organization later known as the Medellín Cartel.

1972 AMERICAN BOBBY FISCHER wins the world chess title from Soviet Boris Spassky in a politically charged match in Reykjavík, Iceland.

1969 WRITER ALEKSANDR SOLZHENITSYN is expelled from the Soviet Writers Union for political heresy. In 1970 he wins the Nobel Prize in literature.

▼ **1969 GOLDA MEIR** becomes Israel's fourth prime minister.

1969 MUAMMAR QADDAFI takes power in Libya with an Islamic socialist doctrine.

1970 ANWAR SADAT becomes president of Egypt after the death of Nasser.

1971 MAJ. GEN. IDI AMIN takes control of Uganda and soon becomes one of the world's most notorious dictators.

Israeli prime minister Golda Meir

Buzz Aldrin in the Sea of Tranquility

ONE GIANT LEAP

THE LAST SENTENCE OF A PLAQUE commemorating the Apollo 11 moon landing reads, "We Came in Peace for All Mankind." Yet this achievement was also a victory for the United States in the contest known as the space race.

When the Soviet Union launched the satellite Sputnik I in 1957, it raised the specter of space-based weapons and sent the U.S. scurrying to catch up. The U.S. was humiliated again in 1961 when cosmonaut Yuri Gagarin became the first human in space, a smiling symbol of Soviet supremacy.

Knowing the Soviets had already sent a rocket to the moon, President John F. Kennedy upped the ante in 1962 by promising to put an astronaut on the moon by the end of the decade, which seemed fantastical at the time. The Apollo program started disastrously when, in January 1967, Apollo 1 caught fire on the launch pad killing all three astronauts inside. But by 1968 Apollo 8 had gone so far as to orbit the moon.

On July 20, 1969, Neil Armstrong and Buzz Aldrin piloted the lunar module *Eagle* onto the Sea of Tranquility. Armstrong planted his left boot on the moon's surface, a feat the Soviets never duplicated. With one awe-inspiring step, the U.S. had won the space race. In 1975 the two nations took the first step toward collaborating on space exploration with a historic handshake in space when a Soviet Soyuz and a U.S. Apollo spacecraft docked in orbit.

POLITICS & POWER	GEOGRAPHY & ENVIRONMENT	CULTURE & RELIGION
1974 **U.S. PRESIDENT NIXON** resigns after additional White House tapes reveal his involvement in covering up the Watergate break-in. **1978** **U.S. PRESIDENT CARTER** brokers the Camp David Accords between Israeli prime minister Menachem Begin and Egyptian president Anwar Sadat. **1979** **SANDINISTA GUERRILLAS** overthrow the government of Nicaragua and install a socialist regime.	**1975** **SURINAME** becomes independent of the Netherlands. **1977** **U.S. PRESIDENT CARTER** and Panama chief Omar Torrijos sign the new Panama Canal treaties, returning the canal to Panama in 1979, but allowing the U.S. to continue managing the canal during a transition period. **1979** **ST. LUCIA AND ST. VINCENT AND THE GRENADINES** win independence from Great Britain.	**1976** **THE EPISCOPAL CHURCH** approves the ordination of women as priests and bishops. **1980** **ARCHBISHOP OSCAR ROMERO** of San Salvador, a champion of the poor, is shot to death during Mass.
1975 **KING JUAN CARLOS I** becomes the first king of Spain in 44 years after General Francisco Franco dies. **1975** **THIRTY-THREE EUROPEAN NATIONS,** plus the U.S. and Canada, sign the Helsinki Accords, designed to increase international cooperation. **1979** **MARGARET THATCHER** becomes prime minister of Great Britain and begins privatizing state-owned companies.	**1976** **BRITAIN** suffers its worst drought in more than 250 years. **1977** **BUCHAREST, ROMANIA,** is heavily damaged by an earthquake felt in Moscow and Rome.	**1974** **SWEDISH POP GROUP ABBA** wins the Eurovision Song Contest, launching the group to worldwide success. **1978** **CARDINAL KAROL WOJTYŁA** becomes Pope John Paul II, the first non-Italian pope in 455 years. He survives an assassination attempt in 1981.
1975 **CIVIL WAR** erupts in Lebanon between Palestinian, Muslim, and Christian militias. **1975** **THE ANGOLAN CIVIL WAR** begins among liberation factions, backed by the U.S., the Soviet Union, and other foreign powers. **1979** **THE SHAH OF IRAN** is forced into exile and replaced by the Ayatollah Khomeini.	**1973** **COMPLETION OF SYRIA'S EUPHRATES DAM** doubles the area devoted to irrigated agriculture and permits widespread electrification. **1975** **PORTUGAL** grants independence to former African colonies Angola, Mozambique, Cape Verde, and São Tomé and Príncipe. **1977** **KENYAN WANGARI MAATHAI,** a U.S.-educated biologist, founds the Green Belt Movement.	**1976** **NUMEROUS CHILDREN** are killed following a protest in Soweto, a black township of Johannesburg, South Africa, provoking international outrage at apartheid. **1977** **THE UNITED NATIONS** issues a mandatory arms embargo on South Africa.
1974 **NORTH VIETNAMESE COMMUNIST AND SOUTH VIETNAMESE FORCES** continue to fight. South Vietnam surrenders in 1975; Saigon is evacuated. **1975** **THE COMMUNIST KHMER ROUGE,** led by Pol Pot, takes over Cambodia's government. **1978** **VIETNAM** invades Cambodia, overthrowing Pol Pot's government early the following year. **1979** **THE SOVIET ARMY** invades Afghanistan.	**1974** **A SMALLPOX EPIDEMIC** in India kills an estimated 30,000. **1975** **PAPUA NEW GUINEA** declares independence from Australia. **1976** **NORTH AND SOUTH VIETNAM** are reunited after 22 years of separation as the Socialist Republic of Vietnam.	**1975-1977** **PRIME MINISTER INDIRA GANDHI** declares a state of emergency to deal with India's overpopulation and sectarian violence. She suspends democratic processes and compels birth control. **1979** **CHINA** institutes a one-child-per-family rule to help control its exploding population.

SCIENCE & TECHNOLOGY

1975 THE ALTAIR 8800 is the first commercially successful desktop microcomputer.

1976 LANDING VEHICLES VIKING 1 AND 2 transmit the first close-up photos of the surface of Mars.

1978 THE FIRST "TEST-TUBE BABY" is born in England when Lesley Brown gives birth to a girl conceived outside her body.

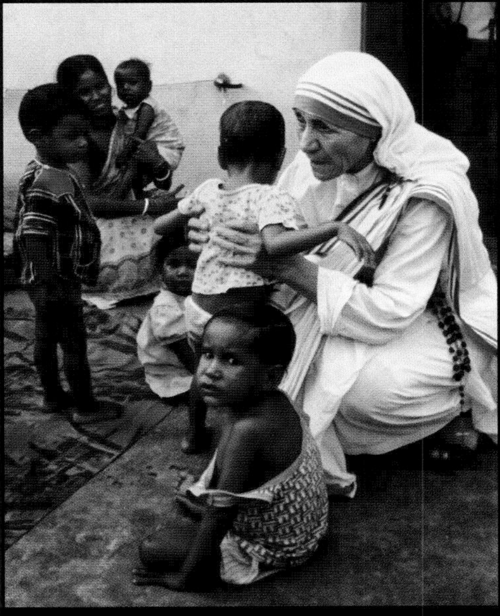

Mother Teresa ministers to children in Calcutta, India.

1974 INDIA becomes the sixth nation to explode a nuclear device. The following year it launches its first satellite.

1979 SONY introduces the Walkman portable cassette player.

PEOPLE & SOCIETY

1975 FORMER TEAMSTERS UNION PRESIDENT Jimmy Hoffa disappears.

1977 ARGENTINIAN MOTHERS *(Las Madres de Plaza de Mayo)* who gather in Buenos Aires to protest the disappearance of their children at the hands of the government attract international attention.

1978 FORMER ITALIAN PRIME MINISTER Aldo Moro is kidnapped and murdered by antigovernment Red Brigade terrorists.

1974 HAILE SELASSIE, emperor of Ethiopia since 1930, is deposed by Marxists.

1975 KING FAISAL of Saudi Arabia is assassinated by his nephew.

1979 SADDAM HUSSEIN becomes president of Iraq.

1975 JUNKO TABEI of Japan becomes the first woman to climb Mount Everest.

◀ **1979 MOTHER TERESA** wins the Nobel Peace Prize.

Skulls line a memorial to Pol Pot's reign of terror.

CAMBODIA'S KILLING FIELDS

THE VIETNAMESE CLAIM to have discovered the remains of more than two million people when Vietnam invaded neighboring Cambodia to depose the Khmer Rouge government in 1978. Other sources put the figure between one and two million. What is indisputable is that for four years, beginning in 1975, Cambodian premier Pol Pot transformed his country's rice fields and orchards into mass graves.

Cambodia was a hive of violence long before Pol Pot came to power. The country had been a battleground in both the Indochina and Vietnam Wars, and the government had been struggling against Khmer Rouge insurgents since 1970. But Pol Pot personified the monstrous dimensions of communist ideology. After leading the Khmer's successful overthrow in 1975, the Paris-educated engineer carried out a radical Maoist program of agrarianism, evacuating cities and forcing people onto collective farms. Schools and factories were shut down; skilled workers and "intellectuals" were executed. Others died during forced marches to the countryside and many more perished from starvation.

Pol Pot continued to lead guerrilla forces in Cambodia's western jungles almost until the end of his life in 1998. The thousands of skulls and bones neatly stacked and displayed at memorial sites around Cambodia are vivid reminders of his brief and terrible reign.

POLITICS & POWER

1980 RONALD REAGAN is elected president of the U.S. and reelected in 1984.

1980 A MILITARY JUNTA backed by cocaine barons takes over Bolivia.

1982 ARGENTINA attempts to seize the British-controlled Falkland Islands but is defeated, leading to an overthrow of Argentina's military junta.

1983 SHIITE MUSLIMS bomb U.S. Marine barracks in Beirut, killing 241 marines and sailors.

1980 LECH WALESA becomes chairman of a new independent trade union (Solidarity) in Poland that demands political reform from the communist government.

1981 SOCIALIST FRANÇOIS MITTERRAND is elected president of France and puts communists in his cabinet.

1983 THE U.S. DEPLOYS THE FIRST CRUISE MISSILES to Europe, at England's Greenham Common air force base, despite public protests. Pershing missiles are deployed in West Germany.

1980 A U.S. COMMANDO RAID to free American hostages held in Iran ends in disaster.

1980 IRAQ INVADES IRAN, beginning an eight-year-long war; the U.S supports Iraq.

1981 EGYPTIAN PRESIDENT ANWAR SADAT is assassinated by Islamic militants and replaced with pragmatist Hosni Mubarak.

1982 ISRAEL INVADES LEBANON in an attempt to drive out PLO terrorists.

1983 SUDANESE CIVIL WAR revives when Sudan's president imposes Islamic law on the non-Muslim south.

1984 SIKH REBELS take hold of the Golden Temple in Amritsar, India.

1983 A SOUTH KOREAN AIRLINER is shot down over the Soviet Union on its way from New York to Seoul, killing all 269 on board.

1983 TAMIL TIGER REBELS escalate their fight with the Sri Lankan government for the right to create a separate, non-Buddhist state for the ethnic minority Tamils.

GEOGRAPHY & ENVIRONMENT

1980 MORE THAN 120,000 CUBANS flee to the U.S. during the Mariel boatlift.

▼ **1980 MOUNT ST. HELENS VOLCANO** in Washington State erupts. Most people are evacuated, but 57 die. The blast is 500 times more powerful than the atomic bomb dropped on Hiroshima.

Mount St. Helens erupts.

1981 ISRAEL annexes the Golan Heights.

1982 ISRAEL returns Sinai to Egypt per the Camp David agreement but intensifies settlement in the West Bank and Gaza.

1984 THE DEATH TOLL from drought in Ethiopia approaches one million.

1984 UPPER VOLTA becomes Burkina Faso.

1980s CONCERN OVER THE LOSS OF RAINFORESTS in Asia and Brazil becomes a major environmental issue.

1980 VANUATU gains independence from Britain and France.

1982 THE POPULATION OF CHINA reaches one billion.

1984 A TOXIC GAS LEAK from the Union Carbide plant in Bhopal, India, kills approximately 2,500 and affects thousands more.

CULTURE & RELIGION

1980 CNN becomes the world's first 24-hour news station.

1981 MTV debuts on U.S. television.

1982 COLOMBIAN WRITER GABRIEL GARCÍA MÁRQUEZ, a leading exponent of magic realism, wins the Nobel Prize in literature.

1982 THE VIETNAM VETERANS MEMORIAL opens on the Mall in Washington, D.C.

1980 THE SUMMER OLYMPICS in Moscow are boycotted by 60 nations, including the U.S., to protest the Soviet invasion of Afghanistan.

1984 THE SOVIET UNION and many other communist countries boycott the Summer Olympics in Los Angeles in retaliation for the U.S. boycott in 1980.

1982 THE POLITICAL AND MILITARY ORGANIZATION HEZBOLLAH (Party of God) is founded in Lebanon, with support from Iran, to oppose the Israeli invasion and occupation of southern Lebanon.

1986 KENYAN WRITER Ngugi Wa Thiong'o publishes *Decolonising the Mind*, arguing that the adoption of colonial language carries ideological implications. He begins to write only in his native Gikuyu language.

1980s ISLAMIC WARRIORS called mujahideen take up arms against the Soviet invasion of Afghanistan with the help of U.S. ground-to-air Stinger missiles, which are used to attack Soviet helicopters.

SCIENCE & TECHNOLOGY	PEOPLE & SOCIETY
1980 THE U.S. VOYAGER 1 space probe sends back spectacular photos of Saturn, showing its rings and six new moons. **1981** THE FIRST U.S. SPACE SHUTTLE, *Columbia,* makes its maiden flight. It is the first reusable spacecraft. **1981** SCIENTISTS identify acquired immune deficiency syndrome (AIDS). **1981** IBM introduces the first home or personal computer (PC). In 1984 Apple launches its Macintosh, the first affordable PC with a graphical interface.	**1980** FORMER BEATLE JOHN LENNON is shot to death by an obsessed fan in New York City. **1981** JOHN HINCKLEY, JR., attempts to assassinate President Reagan in Washington, D.C. **1981** SANDRA DAY O'CONNOR becomes the U.S. Supreme Court's first female justice. **1981** BILL GATES devises the Microsoft Disk Operating System (MS-DOS) for IBM. **1984** GERALDINE FERRARO becomes the first woman to run for vice president on a major U.S. presidential ticket.
1980 THE WORLD HEALTH ORGANIZATION declares that smallpox is eradicated worldwide. **1981** THE WORLD'S FASTEST TRAIN, the French TGV, begins service between Paris and Lyon. **1982** SOVIET SPACECRAFTS VENERA 13 AND 14 send back the first color photos of Venus. **1985** ROBERT BALLARD OF THE U.S. and Jean-Louis Michel of France find the *Titanic* 12,000 feet deep in the North Atlantic, where it sank in 1912.	**1980** DISSIDENT PHYSICIST Andrei Sakharov is exiled by Soviet leader Leonid Brezhnev. **1984** THE LARGEST DEMONSTRATION in French history—more than a million marchers—forces the government to abandon its challenge to the independence of religious schools.
1982 ISRAELI CHEMIST Daniel Schechtman discovers symmetrical, nonrepeating crystals, or "quasicrystals."	**1984** BISHOP DESMOND TUTU, general secretary of the South African Council of Churches, wins the Nobel Peace Prize. **1984** ISRAEL successfully airlifts and relocates 10,000 Ethiopian Jews through Sudan.
1980 JAPAN becomes a leading financial center, with eight of the world's 10 largest banks. It also surpasses the U.S. as the world's largest automaker. **1982** SONY AND PHILIPS introduce the first commercial CD players.	**1980** INDIRA GANDHI returns to power in India after serving time in jail. In 1984 she is assassinated by her Sikh bodyguards, provoking anti-Sikh riots throughout the country. **1980s** DENG XIAOPING consolidates his power as leader of the Chinese Communist Party. He strives to improve relations with the West and modernize China. **1980s** SOUTHEAST ASIA'S "East Asian Tigers" emerge as Hong Kong, Singapore, Taiwan, and South Korea follow an export-driven economic model.

JAPAN'S ECONOMIC MIRACLE

IT'S HARD TO IMAGINE that the Japan towering above the industrialized world in the 1980s was the same country as the one devastated during World War II. The war blasted Japan's industrial sector and destroyed its labor force.

The land of the rising sun would see brighter days, though. The Allies provided massive relief, including food and technical assistance, and during the Korean War Japan produced billions of dollars' worth of supplies for the UN coalition. Before long the country boasted many newly rebuilt plants with state-of-the-art technology. Manufacturing could grow again. Japan embraced free enterprise with a passion and the results were staggering. The country's gross national product (GNP) more than doubled between 1955 and 1960, 1960 and 1965, and again from 1965 to 1970.

By 1971 Japan had the world's third-largest GNP after the U.S. and Soviet Union. Businesses were given healthy incentives to invest in capital expansion, and productivity among Japanese workers was high. Exports were a major key to growth, as Japan began penetrating foreign markets with quality, lower-cost products in the automotive and electronics sectors. The oil crisis of 1973 spurred demand for Japan's economy cars. By 1980 Japan had more than doubled its share of the car market in the U.S., and it surpassed the U.S. as the world's largest automaker in 1980.

Japan's recovery was the model for other free-market Asian success stories, including those of Taiwan, Hong Kong, Singapore, and South Korea. The flood of Asian imports, as well as heavy Japanese investment in U.S. businesses in the 1980s, sparked fears in the U.S. over lost jobs and foreign influence. By the late 1990s, though, bad loans and weak currencies along the Pacific Rim had led to an economic downturn referred to as the "Asian contagion."

POLITICS & POWER	GEOGRAPHY & ENVIRONMENT	CULTURE & RELIGION
1986 THE IRAN-CONTRA AFFAIR implicates Reagan aides in a secret plan to divert funds from arms sales to Iran to the anticommunist contras in Nicaragua. Congress had cut off all contra aid in 1984. **1987 COSTA RICAN PRESIDENT** Óscar Arias Sánchez brokers the Arias Peace Plan, an attempt to end political instability in Central America. **1989 U.S. TROOPS** invade Panama and arrest Manuel Noriega for authorizing hostilities against U.S. personnel.	**1987 THE LAST WILD CALIFORNIA CONDOR** is trapped and sent to a zoo for breeding. **1989 THE EXXON OIL TANKER *VALDEZ*** runs aground in Alaska, spilling 11 million gallons. **1989 MILLIONS OF TV VIEWERS** witness an earthquake strike the Bay Area during a World Series game being played in San Francisco.	**1985 *GRINGO VIEJO,*** by Carlos Fuentes, becomes (in translation) the first American best seller written by a Mexican author. **1987 AT A NEW YORK AUCTION,** Vincent van Gogh's "Irises" becomes the most expensive piece of art in history, selling for $53.9 million. Van Gogh's "Portrait of Dr. Gachet" sells for $82.5 million in 1990. **1987 CONDOM COMMERCIALS** are allowed to run on U.S. television as a result of the AIDS epidemic.
1985 NEW SOVIET GENERAL SECRETARY Mikhail Gorbachev announces his campaign for glasnost ("openness") and perestroika ("restructuring"). **1989 PROTESTERS** and Communist Party officials in Romania overthrow the government and execute president Nicolae Ceaușescu and his wife. **1989 DISSIDENT CZECH PLAYWRIGHT** Václav Havel becomes president of the new, noncommunist government of Czechoslovakia.	**1987 A YUGOSLAVIAN BABY BOY** is declared Earth's five billionth inhabitant by the UN secretary-general. **1988 AN EARTHQUAKE** in Armenia kills about 80,000. **1988 ARCHAEOLOGISTS** uncover the foundations of the original Globe Theatre in Southwark, London. **1989 EAST GERMAN LEADER** Erich Honecker resigns after thousands of refugees flee to West Germany. A reform government takes power and the Berlin Wall is demolished.	**1986 THE FINAL SUPPLEMENT (SE-Z)** of the *Oxford English Dictionary* is published, more than a century since the first edition. **1987 U.S. PRESIDENT REAGAN** visits Berlin to mark the 750th anniversary of the city's founding. Standing before the Berlin Wall, he calls on Soviet leader Gorbachev to "tear down this wall." **1988 A PAN AM 747** explodes over Lockerbie, Scotland, killing 259 aboard and 11 on the ground. Libyan-backed terrorists are thought responsible.
1986 U.S. WARPLANES bomb Libya in retaliation for Libyan terrorist actions. **1986 SOUTH AFRICAN PRESIDENT P. W. BOTHA** declares a state of emergency after 1.5 million blacks stage a massive labor strike. **1987 THE PALESTINIAN INTIFADA** begins, an organized uprising protesting Israeli rule in the West Bank and Gaza Strip. A new militant group, Hamas (Islamic Resistance Movement), is formed, dedicated to the Palestinian cause. **1987 TURKEY** is rejected for membership in the European Economic Community.	**1986 TOXIC GAS** from the volcanic Lake Nyos in Cameroon kills more than 1,700 people. **1989 KENYAN PRESIDENT** Daniel arap Moi destroys 12 tons of elephant tusks in an appeal to ban the ivory trade.	**1985-1986 AMONG ALL GIRLS AGED 12 TO 18** in Africa, only 46 percent are enrolled in school. **1986 DESMOND TUTU** becomes the first black archbishop of Cape Town, South Africa. **1989 THE ISLAMIC SALVATION FRONT,** an activist and political Islamic movement, emerges in Algeria. Its 1990 election win initiates years of political violence and repression. **1989 IRAN'S AYATOLLAH KHOMEINI** imposes a fatwa ("death sentence") on Indian-born British author Salman Rushdie for blasphemy against Islam in his novel *The Satanic Verses.*
1986 PHILIPPINES PRESIDENT FERDINAND MARCOS flees the country after his reelection is disputed. Challenger Corazon Aquino becomes the new president. **1988 SOVIET TROOPS** begin withdrawing from Afghanistan, leaving completely by 1989. **1988 BENAZIR BHUTTO** becomes prime minister of Pakistan, the first female head of an Islamic nation in modern history. **1989 HIROHITO,** emperor of Japan since 1926, dies, succeeded by Crown Prince Akihito. **1989 CHINA** imposes martial law in Lhasa, Tibet.	**1989 PAKISTAN** rejoins the Commonwealth of Nations, which it left in 1972. **1989 GREAT BRITAIN** begins forcibly repatriating Vietnamese refugees from Hong Kong to Vietnam. **1989 BURMA** is renamed Myanmar after a military takeover. The name is recognized by the UN but not by the U.S., Great Britain, or Canada. **1989 THE LAST VIETNAMESE TROOPS** leave Cambodia after 11 years of occupation.	**1985 CHINA** releases the former Roman Catholic bishop of Shanghai after nearly 30 years' imprisonment. **1988 SEOUL, SOUTH KOREA,** hosts the Summer Olympics, the first without a boycott since 1972. **1989 TIANANMEN SQUARE** in Beijing, China, is occupied by approximately one million demonstrators protesting for democracy. The government imposes martial law and uses tanks to clear the square, killing thousands and damaging Deng Xiaoping's improved relations with the West.

SCIENCE & TECHNOLOGY

1985 FIBER-OPTIC TELEPHONE TECHNOLOGY is developed, allowing for 300,000 calls to be transmitted at once.

1986 THE SPACE SHUTTLE *CHALLENGER* explodes shortly after takeoff, killing all seven crew members, including the first civilian passenger in a spaceship, teacher Christa McAuliffe.

1986 GENERAL MOTORS overtakes Exxon as the largest company in the U.S.

1987 PROZAC, a new antidepressant, hits the U.S. market.

1985 THE U.K. begins screening blood donations for the AIDS virus.

1986 THE WORLD'S WORST NUCLEAR ACCIDENT occurs at the Chernobyl Nuclear Power Station near Kiev, U.S.S.R. Fallout affects all of Europe.

1986 THE SOVIET UNION launches the Mir space station.

1986 AN ANCIENT GALILEE BOAT from the first century C.E. is discovered on the shores of the Sea of Galilee (Lake Kinneret) during a drought.

1989 AUSTRALIAN PALEONTOLOGISTS PATRICIA VICKERS-RICH and Tom Rich discover a new Cretaceous dinosaur in southern Victoria, Australia, and name it *Leaellynasaura* after their daughter, Leaellyn.

PEOPLE & SOCIETY

1986 OPRAH WINFREY'S local Chicago talk show debuts nationally. She soon becomes one of the most influential people in America.

1986 WALL STREET is rocked by numerous insider trading scandals.

1988 CHICO MENDES, a Brazilian rubber tapper who led the fight to stop logging in the Amazon rainforest, is murdered by cattle ranchers opposed to his activism.

1989 GEN. COLIN POWELL becomes the first African-American chairman of the Joint Chiefs of Staff.

1986 ANDREI SAKHAROV'S EXILE is ended by Mikhail Gorbachev, who welcomes the dissident physicist back to Moscow.

1988 BRITISH BAKER COLIN PITCHFORK becomes the first person convicted with a DNA fingerprinting technique when his DNA ties him to rape and murder victims.

1989 ETHNIC ALBANIANS begin demonstrating for independence from Serbian rule in Yugoslavia's Kosovo province.

1985 THE THIRD WORLD CONFERENCE ON WOMEN is held in Nairobi at a critical moment for developing countries, pledging links between equality for women, development, and peace.

1989 F. W. DE KLERK succeeds P. W. Botha as president of South Africa.

THE GLOBAL AIDS CRISIS

ACQUIRED IMMUNE DEFICIENCY SYNDROME (AIDS) was first identified in 1981 and quickly became the most feared and confounding disease on the planet. Caused by an insidious virus (human immunodeficiency virus, or HIV) that destroys the body's infection-fighting T-cells, AIDS leaves one helpless against infections and cancers, and can result in neurological disorders. By the new millennium more than 25 million people worldwide were infected with HIV.

The virus is transmitted through the direct exchange of body fluids (usually blood or semen) and can be contracted by anyone. Hemophiliacs and others needing transfusions were initially very vulnerable. But the prevalence of AIDS in the gay community in the 1980s made this a medical issue with explosive political dimensions. Gay-rights advocates became a vocal minority in the U.S., lobbying for more research funding and sex education. Despite notable exceptions such as NBA superstar Magic Johnson, who contracted the virus through unprotected heterosexual intercourse, homophobia created obstacles to public support and treatment of the disease.

By the early 2000s, AIDS cases were declining in the U.S. and still climbing, but leveling off, in less developed nations. Africa, where HIV is thought to have originated in chimpanzee populations, was hit particularly hard, with South Africa proving particularly intractable. Prevention and treatment have sharply reduced the number of new HIV infections worldwide since the mid-1990s.

Specialized stem cell transplants offer a glimmer of hope to those searching for a cure, but a definitive remedy has not yet been found. Antiretroviral therapy, where available, has been highly successful in reducing the viral load to undetectable levels in the body, but it does not eliminate the virus completely. In the early 21st century, deaths from AIDS were declining, but millions living with HIV await relief.

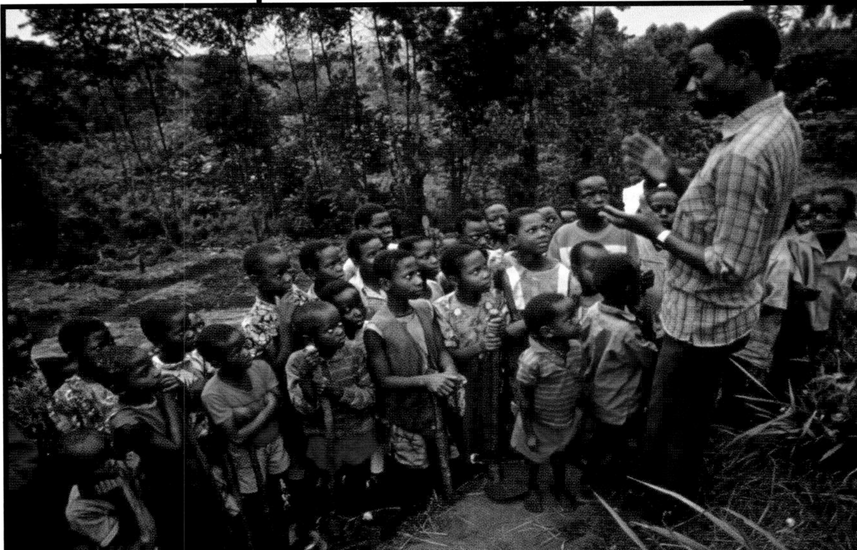

AIDS orphans in Kalagala Village, Uganda

POLITICS & POWER	GEOGRAPHY & ENVIRONMENT	CULTURE & RELIGION
1990 NICARAGUA'S COMMUNIST SANDINISTA GOVERNMENT is voted out of power with the election of Violetta Chamorro. **1991 HAITIAN PRESIDENT** Jean-Bertrand Aristide is ousted. He returns to power in 1994. **1991 THE UN** brokers an end to the 10-year-old civil war in El Salvador. **1992 WILLIAM J. CLINTON** is elected U.S. president. **1992 THE U.S., MEXICO, AND CANADA** sign the North American Free Trade Agreement (NAFTA).	**1991 A CHOLERA EPIDEMIC,** thought to be caused by contaminated seafood, breaks out in Peru, killing thousands. **1992 HURRICANE ANDREW** strikes southern Florida, Louisiana, and the Bahamas, causing $26 billion in property damage, the worst natural disaster in U.S. history.	**1990s WALMART** launches an aggressive expansion campaign. By mid-decade it is the biggest retailer in the world, with more than 2,500 stores in the U.S. and $93.6 billion in sales. **1991 MICHAEL JORDAN** leads the Chicago Bulls to the first of six NBA championships. **1992 AIDS** becomes the leading cause of death among U.S. men between 25 and 44. **1994 THE WORLD SERIES** is canceled for the first time when Major League Baseball players and management fail to settle a strike.
1991 THE BALTIC STATES of Latvia, Estonia, and Lithuania and the republics of Georgia, Azerbaijan, Armenia, and Ukraine declare independence from the Soviet Union. **1991 THE WARSAW PACT** is formally dissolved. **1991 THE SOVIET FLAG** flies over the Kremlin for the last time on December 25. **1992 THE BOSNIAN CONFLICT** begins. Serbia undertakes an ethnic cleansing program to remove Bosnian Muslims and Croats from newly independent Bosnia and Herzegovina.	**1990 EAST AND WEST GERMANY** reunify. **1991 SLOVENIA, CROATIA, AND MACEDONIA** secede from Yugoslavia. **1993 THE CZECH AND SLOVAK REPUBLICS** (formerly Czechoslovakia) become separate and sovereign countries. **1994 AN ATTEMPT BY THE CHECHNYA REGION** to break away from the Russian government is crushed by the Russian army.	**1992 THE U.S. "DREAM TEAM"**—the first Olympic U.S. basketball team featuring NBA professionals—easily wins the gold medal at the Summer Games in Barcelona, Spain. **1992 CHARLES AND DIANA,** Prince and Princess of Wales, announce their separation. **1993 THE EUROPEAN COMMUNITY** becomes the European Union (EU) with the Maastricht Treaty.
1990 CIVIL WAR ERUPTS in Rwanda, and the Hutu kill more than 800,000 Tutsi by 1994. Tutsi forces eventually regain control of the country, forcing two million Rwandans to flee. **1990-1991 IRAQ INVADES KUWAIT;** a U.S.-led coalition liberates Kuwait in the Gulf War. **1992 U.S. TROOPS** are sent to civil war–torn Somalia to ensure delivery of international food aid. **1994 KING HUSSEIN OF JORDAN** and Prime Minister Yitzhak Rabin of Israel sign a declaration ending the conflict between their countries.	**1990 NAMIBIA** becomes independent. **1990 THE ATATÜRK DAM** opens in Turkey, doubling the land area that can be cultivated. ▶**1991 IRAQ** deliberately pumps millions of barrels of Kuwaiti oil into the Persian Gulf and also sets fire to oil wells, creating an ecological disaster during the second Gulf War. **1993 ERITREA** becomes the newest African country after its long civil war with Ethiopia.	**1990 NELSON MANDELA** is released from prison after 26 years when South African president F. W. de Klerk declares amnesty for important political prisoners and lifts restrictions on the African National Congress. In 1994 the first nonracial general election in South African history results in a victory for the African National Congress and makes Nelson Mandela the first black president of South Africa.
1991 TAIWAN ends its official state of war with the People's Republic of China. **1994 KIM JONG-IL** comes to power in North Korea, replacing his long-ruling father, Kim Il-sung. **1994 NORTH KOREA AND THE U.S.** sign an agreement in which North Korea agrees to freeze its plutonium weapons programs in exchange for aid.	**1991 A CYCLONE IN BANGLADESH** kills approximately 140,000 people. **1991 MOUNT PINATUBO** in the Philippines erupts, spewing the greatest volume of sulfur dioxide ever measured.	**1992 HINDU NATIONALISTS** demolish the historic Babri Masjid mosque in Ayodhya, India.

SCIENCE & TECHNOLOGY

1990 THE HUBBLE SPACE TELESCOPE is put into operation. It orbits Earth at the edge of the atmosphere, allowing it to take the deepest space pictures ever. In 1994 Hubble finds the first conclusive evidence of black holes.

1993 THE WEB BROWSER MOSAIC, developed at the University of Illinois, is released. By combining text and images on the page, it rapidly increases the popularity of the World Wide Web.

1994 THE U.S. GLOBAL POSITIONING SYSTEM is completed.

1991 BRITISH COMPUTER SCIENTIST Tim Berners-Lee puts the World Wide Web online. Through his invention of HyperText Transfer Protocol (HTTP), Berners-Lee allows documents to be linked together on computers across the Internet.

1994 THE CHANNEL TUNNEL between Britain and France opens.

1994 THREE FRENCH CAVERS discover what will be called the Chauvet Cave in southern France. It is filled with prehistoric paintings.

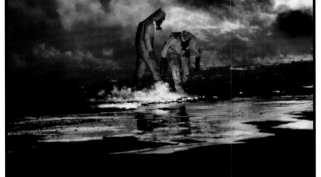

1993 CONSTRUCTION BEGINS on Three Gorges Dam in China.

PEOPLE & SOCIETY

1990 PERUVIAN MARIO VARGAS LLOSA, one of Latin America's leading novelists and essayists, runs for the presidency of Peru but loses.

1992 GUATEMALAN MAYA ACTIVIST Rigoberta Menchú wins the Nobel Peace Prize for her efforts toward social justice in the country.

1993 TONI MORRISON becomes the first African-American woman awarded the Nobel Prize in literature.

1994 ZAPATISTA REBELS in Mexico fight the country's move toward globalization.

1990 HELMUT KOHL is elected chancellor of the reunited Germany.

1990 LABOR LEADER LECH WALESA is elected president of Poland.

1991 BORIS YELTSIN is elected president of the Russian Federation.

1993 ISRAELI PRIME MINISTER YITZHAK RABIN, former prime minister Shimon Peres, and PLO leader Yasser Arafat negotiate the Oslo Accords, which grant land and authority to Palestinians (including Israel's promise to leave the Gaza Strip and West Bank).

1994 YASSER ARAFAT becomes the leader of the Palestinian National Authority, which governs the West Bank and Gaza Strip.

1992 AUSTRALIA'S HIGH COURT legally recognizes the presence of Aboriginal peoples before European settlement and later recognizes native title claims over land in Australia.

Oil fires set by Iraqis in the aftermath of the Gulf War blaze across the Persian Gulf.

THE END OF APARTHEID

WHEN NELSON MANDELA was convicted in 1964 of sabotage because of his opposition to apartheid, he expressed his wish to live to see the day when South Africa would be a "democratic and free society." Miraculously, he not only lived to see that day after 26 years in prison but became the leader of that society.

Implemented in 1948, apartheid put into law what had already been the unofficial law of the land: racial segregation and the supremacy of whites. Not only were whites to be separated from nonwhites, but nonwhites were to be separated from each other—the ten African Bantu groups were separated, for example. Large segments of the nonwhite population were forced from cities onto rural reservations. Under a euphemistic policy called separate development, each Bantu group was granted its own homeland. The reality was that about 13 percent of South Africa's land—most of it broken tracts of poor-quality land—was set aside for 75 percent of the population, while the rest of the country, including the cities and rich mineral areas, was reserved for whites.

After generations of black African resistance and decades of international pressure on South Africa, including increasing economic sanctions, the white minority's ability to keep apartheid in place finally eroded. A severe shortage of skilled labor, the fruit of segregationist labor and wage policies, also forced the government to make concessions to blacks.

By 1991 President F. W. de Klerk had completely repealed all apartheid laws, and the first democratic elections were held in 1994. The result heard round the world was a resounding victory for the African National Congress and new president Nelson Mandela. Finally, in 1996, the Constitution of the Republic of South Africa established "a society based on democratic values, social justice, and fundamental human rights."

THE LURE OF CITY LIFE

It seems almost natural for Mexico City to be the pulsating hive that it is. This was, after all, the capital of the Aztec, one of the great civilizations of the Americas. But the Mexico City of today, about 22 million strong, is a recent phenomenon. In 1950 it had only three million people. The dramatic growth of urban populations, especially in developing nations, is one of the defining trends of the post-1950 world.

The industrial revolution caused a quantum leap in urbanization in Europe and America. By 1900 about 14 percent of the world's population lived in cities, and many cities—after thousands of years as unhealthy death traps—featured birthrates in excess of their death rates. Millions more flocked to these cities in search of opportunity and excitement. By the year 2007 more than half the human population lived in towns and cities; by 2018 more than 80 percent of all North Americans did. Some cities, including Mexico City, grew so large they were dubbed "megacities"—usually defined as cities with more than 10 million inhabitants. By 2018 the world had 33 megacities, and three of them outstripped Mexico City. Tokyo topped the list, followed by New Delhi and Shanghai, evidence of the pell-mell urbanization of Asia.

On a national scale, China experienced the largest migration to cities. Hundreds of millions of villagers moved to the cities in the decades after 1980, despite official policies intended to check migration. In 1990, more than a quarter of the population lived in cities. But by 2013 China had more than 100 cities with greater than a million people, and more than half the population was urban. This process, part of a new strategy designed by the government, is the largest and fastest urbanization in any country in the history of the world.

Unfortunately, rapid urbanization has produced some of the same environmental and social problems experienced in Europe and America during the first decades of industrialization. Pollution and infectious diseases, especially waterborne ones, imperil the health of millions of city dwellers. Authorities struggle, often unsuccessfully, to provide water, electricity, sewerage, and police and firefighting services to ever growing cities. Many inhabitants continue to live in slum conditions, though their share of the urban population is dropping. Sustainable development in housing, transportation, energy, and infrastructure will be key to managing the environmental health of the city dweller, projected to be two-thirds of the global population by 2050.

Smog veils Shanghai, a manufacturing hub in China. The country's rapid growth is accompanied by illness and premature deaths caused by air pollution.

1995-2000

	POLITICS & POWER	GEOGRAPHY & ENVIRONMENT	CULTURE & RELIGION
THE AMERICAS	**1995 A BOMB EXPLODES** in front of a federal office building in Oklahoma City, killing 168 and injuring more than 500. Timothy McVeigh and Terry Nichols are arrested. **1996 BILL CLINTON** is reelected president of the United States. He is impeached by the House in 1998 for perjury and obstruction of justice but acquitted by the Senate in 1999. **1997 U.S. PRESIDENT CLINTON** and Mexican president Ernesto Zedillo pledge to devise a joint strategy to combat drug trafficking.	**1996 THE U.S. STEPS UP EFFORTS** to restrict illegal immigration from Mexico, hiring more U.S. border patrol agents and installing a 14-mile fence along the border. **1997 NEARLY TWO YEARS OF VOLCANIC ERUPTIONS** on the Caribbean island of Montserrat culminate in a violent pyroclastic flow that virtually destroys the capital of Plymouth. **1997-1998 THE WEATHER PHENOMENON EL NIÑO** is blamed for scorching temperatures, drought, and tornadoes across the U.S.	**1997 U.S. PRESIDENT CLINTON** apologizes to eight survivors of the 399 African-American men in Alabama who were left untreated for syphilis as part of a government experiment from 1932 to 1972. **1997 U.S. TOBACCO COMPANIES** agree to settle claims made against them by former smokers in the amount of $368.5 billion. **1999 A U.S. FEDERAL JUDGE** rules that software giant Microsoft is a monopoly.
EUROPE	**1997 SINN FÉIN,** the political arm of the Irish Republican Army, wins its first seat in the Irish House of Representatives. **1998 YUGOSLAVIAN PRESIDENT** Slobodan Milošević is ordered to withdraw his troops from the province of Kosovo, where Serbians have been on a campaign of ethnic cleansing. **1999 NATO** launches air strikes against Serbia. **1999 POLAND, HUNGARY, AND THE CZECH REPUBLIC** join NATO. **1999 RUSSIA** invades Chechnya.	**1996 A VOLCANO** erupts beneath Vatnajökull, a glacier that covers a tenth of Iceland, piercing the glacier and causing floods of melted ice. **1996 THE EUROPEAN COMMISSION** bans exports of beef from the U.K. because of an outbreak of mad cow disease. **1997 DNA** originally extracted from fossils in the Neander Valley in Germany in 1856 supports the theory that modern humans diverged from Neanderthals about 600,000 years ago, arising originally in Africa and replacing Neanderthals, who became extinct.	**1997 DIANA, PRINCESS OF WALES,** dies in a car accident in Paris. An estimated two billion people worldwide watch her funeral on TV. **1997 THE ROMAN CATHOLIC CHURCH** in France issues a formal apology for its silence when the French government deported Jews to Nazi death camps during World War II. **1998 GERMANY** announces the establishment of a pension fund to compensate Jewish Holocaust survivors in the former Eastern Bloc.
MIDDLE EAST & AFRICA	**1996 PLO LEADER YASSER ARAFAT** is elected president in the first Palestinian elections. **1996 ISRAEL** begins a major offensive against the Lebanese Muslim organization Hezbollah. **1998 AFTER SEVERAL YEARS** in which Iraq obstructed UN inspectors from inspecting Iraqi weapons programs, the U.S. and Great Britain send forces to the Persian Gulf. UN Secretary-General Kofi Annan eventually brokers a deal to have the inspectors return and averts a war.	**1995 ZAIRE** suffers an outbreak of the Ebola virus, which is more lethal than AIDS. **1997 ZAIRE** becomes the Democratic Republic of the Congo after Tutsi rebels from Rwanda take the capital and President Mobutu Sese Seko flees. **1998 CLIMATE CHANGE** and human activity shrink Lake Chad from 17,375 square miles in 1960 to 3,860 square miles in 1998.	**1995 NIGERIA HANGS THE WRITER KEN SARO-WIWA** and eight others for their opposition to environmental damage in the Ogoni region. **1997 REFORMIST MOHAMMAD KHATAMI** is elected president of Iran. Claiming conservatives have hijacked the revolution, he loosens restrictions and improves civil society but cannot overthrow the conservatives.
ASIA & OCEANIA	**1995 VIETNAM** resumes diplomatic relations with the U.S. and is the first communist state to be admitted to the Association of Southeast Asian Nations. **1996 THE TALIBAN** Islamic fundamentalist movement takes over the Afghan capital Kabul and imposes Islamic law. **1996 OSAMA BIN LADEN,** founder of the al Qaeda Islamic terrorist network, moves to Afghanistan after being expelled from Sudan, and forges an alliance with the Taliban.	**1997 THE BRITISH COLONY OF HONG KONG** reverts to Chinese control, becoming a Special Administrative Region. **1997-1998 PLANTATION OWNERS IN INDONESIA** cause the worst forest fires in Southeast Asian history in an attempt to clear farmland. World record levels of atmospheric pollution affect at least 20 million people with throat and respiratory problems. Almost 1.5 million acres of land are consumed. **1999 EAST TIMOR** votes for independence from Indonesia.	**1995 SARIN NERVE GAS** is released into the Tokyo subway system, killing 13 and injuring 5,500. The Aum Shinrikyo religious sect is found responsible. **1997 A STATE FUNERAL** is held in Calcutta, India, for Mother Teresa, the Catholic nun who ministered to that city's poor for nearly 70 years. **1997 THE RED CROSS** estimates that 10,000 children a month are dying in North Korea due to famine.

SCIENCE & TECHNOLOGY

1995 THE ONLINE AUCTION SITE EBAY is founded in California and becomes one of the fastest growing companies of all time.

1996 IBM'S DEEP BLUE becomes the first computer to beat a world chess champion.

1998 GOOGLE, the Internet search engine, goes online, indexing 26 million web pages.

1998 VIAGRA, a new pill to treat male impotence, becomes one of the fastest selling drugs in U.S. history.

1995 THE U.S. SPACE SHUTTLE *ATLANTIS* successfully docks with the Russian space station Mir.

1995 RUSSIAN COSMONAUT VALERY POLIAKOV returns to Earth after nearly 438 days aboard the Mir space station, the longest stay in space ever.

1995 GREAT BRITAIN establishes the world's first DNA-based crime database.

▼ **1996 BRITISH GENETICISTS** clone an adult sheep, named Dolly. The news sparks international debate on the future of human cloning.

Dolly, the first successful clone of an adult animal

1996 THE FIRST DVD PLAYERS are released, in Japan.

1996 THE PETRONAS TOWERS in Kuala Lumpur, Malaysia, become the world's tallest buildings at 1,483 feet, 33 feet higher than the Chicago Sears Tower.

1998 THE WORLD'S LONGEST SUSPENSION BRIDGE (2.4 miles long) opens in Japan, linking Kobe and Awaji Island.

1998 INDIA AND PAKISTAN begin testing nuclear weapons, sparking fears of an arms race in southern Asia.

PEOPLE & SOCIETY

1995 CAL RIPKEN, JR., of the Baltimore Orioles breaks New York Yankees star Lou Gehrig's 56-year-old record of playing 2,130 consecutive Major League Baseball games.

1995 O. J. SIMPSON, an NFL Hall of Fame running back, is acquitted of murdering his ex-wife Nicole Brown Simpson and Ronald Goldman in the "trial of the century."

1998 FORMER CHILEAN LEADER AUGUSTO PINOCHET is arrested at a London clinic for the torture and murder of Spanish citizens and others.

1995 JACQUES CHIRAC becomes president of France, succeeding François Mitterrand.

1995 THE WORLD TRADE ORGANIZATION is created to promote economic development worldwide.

1996 BORIS YELTSIN becomes the president of Russia for a second term, having defeated a communist challenger.

1997 LABOUR PARTY LEADER TONY BLAIR wins the general election in Great Britain.

1995 ISRAELI PRIME MINISTER Yitzhak Rabin is assassinated by a Jewish law student in Tel Aviv for ceding land to the Palestinians in the Oslo peace accords.

1996 NEW ISRAELI PRIME MINISTER Benjamin Netanyahu renews settlements on the east side of Jerusalem.

1995 QUEEN ELIZABETH II of Britain returns land and money to the Maori tribe of New Zealand as compensation for British aggression in the 1860s.

1995 JAPAN sets up a fund for compensation payments to an estimated 200,000 women forced to be soldiers' concubines during World War II.

1997 BAD LOANS, lower exports, and weakened currencies lead to an economic crisis, known as the "Asian contagion," in Southeast Asia.

GOOGLE

IN 1991, THE WORLD WIDE WEB consisted of a single website: http://info.cern.ch. By 1994 the number of sites had grown to a modest 700 and two Stanford grad students, Jerry Yang and David Filo, pulled together a handcompiled guide to the web that they eventually named Yahoo! The two believed, as many did in those days, that most users would not be searching for specific topics but simply browsing the wonders of the infant internet.

In 1995, with total websites now numbering some 20,000, two other Stanford graduate students took a different approach. Sergey Brin and Larry Page developed a novel search engine that they initially called BackRub. Thei algorithm, laid out in a 1998 paper titled "The Anatomy of a Large-Scale Hypertextual Web Search Engine," ranked web pages by the number and quality of pages linked to them. In tha year, they moved into a Menlo Park, California garage and incorporated as Google (a word derived from "googol," meaning "10^{100}"). With positive reviews and a lucrative advertising stream, the company rapidly came to dominate the worldwide exchange of information going into the new millennium.

Google co-founders Larry Page and Sergey Brin

CHAPTER 9

GLOBALIZATION AND DISRUPTION

2000-PRESENT

A sea of smartphones is held aloft to record an event in 2018 in the United Kingdom. New personalized communication technology is a major force shaping society, politics, and economics in the 21st century.

In the first decades of the 21st century the world became both bigger and smaller. It was certainly bigger in sheer human numbers. The global population passed the six billion mark in 1999 and hit seven billion just 12 years later, with Asian nations leading the way. However, the population growth rate had been declining since the 1980s. The lagging effects began to show up by 2011 as population increases slowed. At the same time, drastic improvements in transportation and communications shrank the world to the point where one person was no farther than a mobile phone call from any other on the globe. Connected by trade and technology, most of the world became more prosperous. The number of people living in extreme poverty plunged in the new millennium, declining by more than 200,000 a day between 2008 and 2015. Education levels and average life expectancy rose around the world in the 2000s as well. These broad trends were good news. Even so, the connected, crowded, fast-moving world was not a placid one. Moreover, in the human struggle to build and prosper, the natural environment continued to be an unintended casualty.

INTERNATIONAL CONFLICTS

The new century, like the one before it, would be roiled by violence. Unlike the battles of the 20th century, transnational terrorism and multiparty civil wars accounted for much of the damage.

On September 11, 2001, 19 hijackers belonging to the terrorist group al Qaeda commandeered four commercial airliners and flew them into both towers of New York's World Trade Center, the Pentagon outside Washington, D.C., and into a field in Pennsylvania (after courageous passengers attempted to retake the plane). Almost 3,000 people died in this, the deadliest terrorist incident in history. The horrifying attacks traumatized and angered Americans and much of the world.

In response, in October U.S. president George W. Bush sent troops into Afghanistan, which had served as a sanctuary for those organizing the attacks. Accompanied by British and other international allies, U.S. troops rapidly toppled Afghanistan's Taliban government and helped install a new government led by Hamid Karzai. By 2014 the U.S. and NATO had formally ended their military involvement, but troops remained as the wrestling match between the still-potent Taliban and outside forces dragged on. More controversial than the invasion of Afghanistan was President Bush's 2003 decision to invade Iraq, especially after it became clear that Iraq did not have weapons of mass destruction, the main justification offered for the war. The conflict, like the one in Afghanistan, dragged on for more than a decade. President Barack Obama withdrew most American forces by 2011. Continued instability inside and outside Iraq allowed the terrorist forces of al Qaeda in Iraq, which evolved into the Islamic State (ISIS or ISIL), to seize control of much of the country for several years. In addition to killing civilians, the terrorist organization deliberately destroyed priceless antiquities in museums and bulldozed ancient Assyrian cities.

As 21st-century nations learned, fighting rapidly changing terrorist organizations was tougher in some ways than conducting traditional warfare. Al Qaeda suffered a setback when U.S. Navy SEALS stormed a compound in Pakistan in 2011 and killed their leader Osama bin Laden, but the group continued to operate in areas of conflict in the Middle East. Even as ISIS gained and lost ground in war-torn Syria and Iraq, it picked up affiliate organizations in countries ranging from Nigeria to the Philippines. In Europe, individuals or small groups connected to ISIS used bombs, guns, and runaway trucks to kill and terrorize crowds in Paris, Brussels, Nice, Manchester, and elsewhere, while the Islamist group al Shabaab carried out deadly attacks in Kenya and Somalia. Many of the organizations, particularly ISIS, made canny use of videos and the internet both to publicize their killings and to recruit new members. Terrorist attacks occurred mainly in Iraq, Afghanistan, India, Pakistan, Thailand, and the Philippines, but their brutality and unpredictability spread fear across the world.

Postcolonial instability, repressive regimes, longstanding ethnic disputes, religious animosities, and oil—who had it and who wanted it—combined in the Middle East and North Africa to fuel revolution and civil war.

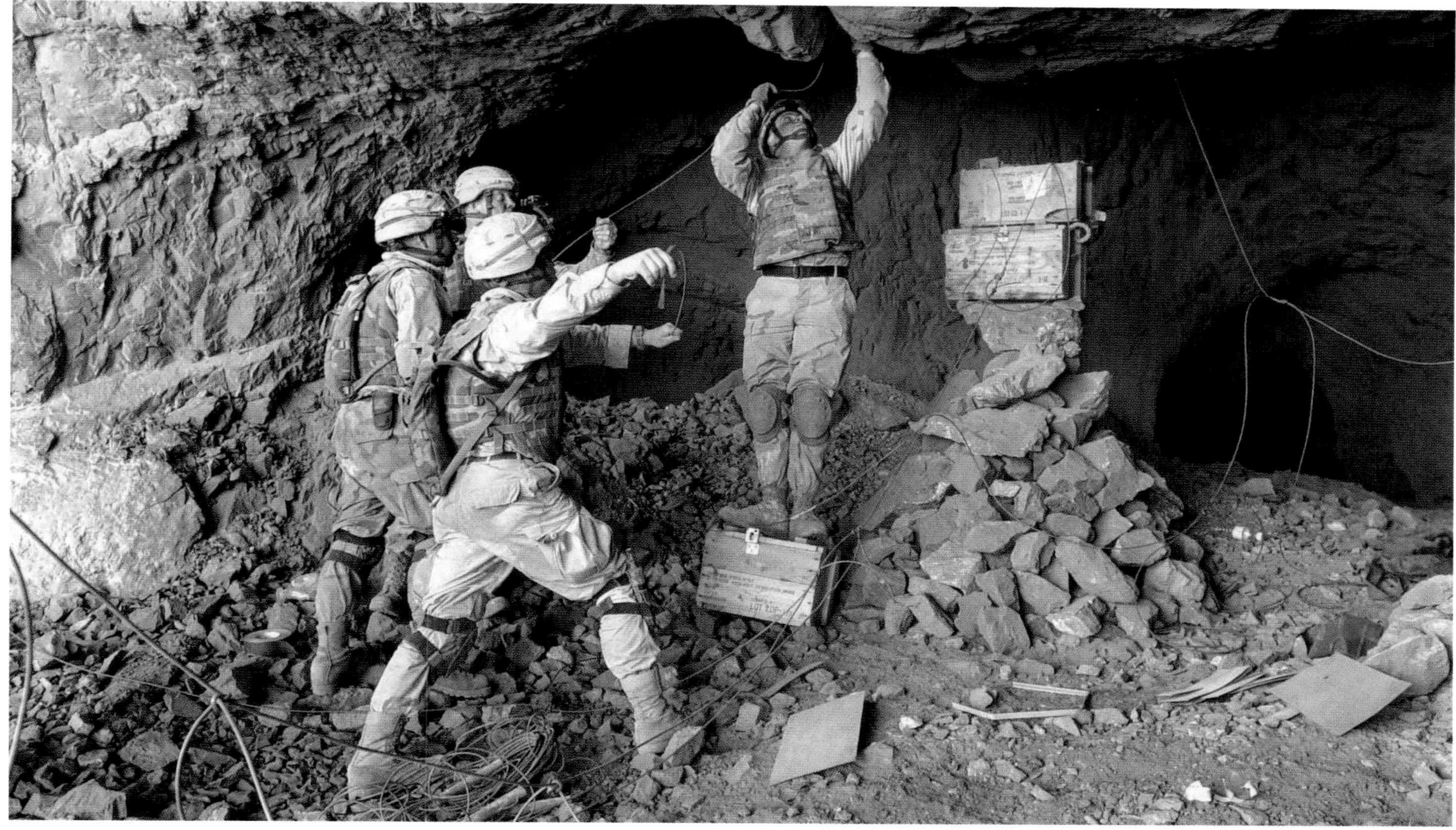

Following the terrorist attacks in New York City on September 11, 2001, the U.S. and allied forces entered Afghanistan in October 2001 and rapidly toppled the Taliban government. This photo from 2003 shows U.S. infantry setting explosives in a cave holding a suspected terrorist supply cache in Afghanistan near the border with Pakistan.

Sudan was one example. At the crossroads of the Arab north and the African south, the country had oil reserves in the south, but little else. It was embroiled in ethnic strife and civil war from 1983 to 2005, toward the end of which the government allied with Janjaweed militia groups to kill hundreds of thousands of non-Arab civilians in the Darfur region. In 2011, following a referendum, South Sudan broke away to become the world's newest nation. Infighting in the South Sudanese government promptly followed.

Meanwhile, beginning in December 2010, a series of popular revolts swept through the Middle East that promised social and political change, but in some places this led to more civil war. First, protests against the regime of Tunisian president Zine El Abidine Ben Ali led to his ouster and a more democratic new government. Encouraged by Tunisian success, Egyptians, Yemenis, Jordanians, and Algerians instigated protests in early 2011. Among their complaints were huge wealth inequalities, high unemployment, government corruption, police brutality, and authoritarian rule. Dominoes continued to fall as disturbances broke out in more than a dozen other countries including Syria, Libya, Iraq, Saudi Arabia, and Oman. These revolutions, collectively termed the "Arab Spring," saw the uprooting of authoritarian regimes throughout the Middle East.

Some uprisings were successful, others not. By mid-2012 four countries had undergone regime changes, including Egypt, with the overthrow of dictator Hosni Mubarak, who had presided over a ruthless and repressive police state since 1981. Meanwhile, rebels in Libya overthrew and killed the tyrant Muammar Qaddafi, in power since 1969. Similar events brought civil war to Syria, where in 2011 opposition forces emboldened by the Arab Spring took up arms against the repressive government of Bashar al-Assad. The government began a bombing and chemical weapons campaign against rebel-held areas and in the chaos the Islamic State (ISIS) moved in as well to capture territory. The U.S. and other nations entered the fray against ISIS, while Russia allied with the Syrian government. Multiple UN-brokered peace talks failed. Amid the fighting, hundreds of thousands were killed and cities were reduced to rubble. Millions of Syrian refugees joined others fleeing violence in Iraq, Afghanistan, Nigeria, and Pakistan to take shelter in Turkey, Lebanon, and Jordan.

Many migrants moved onward to Germany and other European nations, where their influx brought popular anxiety. Recession and a debt crisis had already stressed the alliances of the European Union, but even as economies improved in the 2010s, fractures widened in the 28-nation partnership. In 2016 the British surprised the world by voting for Brexit—a departure from the EU scheduled to take place in 2019. Across Europe, populist politicians began to win power. Right-wing parties gained ground in Germany, Austria, France, and Italy. In the Czech Republic, Hungary, and Poland, nationalist candidates won the top seats, and anti-Semitic rhetoric brought back memories of the 1930s.

Many observers believed that these conflicts and anxieties provided an opening for Russia's longtime leader Vladimir Putin to extend his country's influence. The former KGB officer first became president of Russia in 2000 and was reelected in 2004 amid a strengthening economy. Forced by constitutional rules to step down in 2008, he served as prime minister until he could run for president again, and win, in 2012. In 2014, Putin's troops quietly took over the strategically important Ukrainian region of Crimea, bringing international sanctions against his country. Putin was also believed to have directed assassinations of Russian critics around the world. In 2016, Russian hackers broke into the U.S. Democratic National Committee's computers and created thousands of phony Facebook ads as an attempt to influence the election in Donald Trump's favor. Western nations ramped up sanctions in response to both the assassinations and the election interference allegations, but these moves did little to dim Putin's immense popularity at home.

A demonstrator in London holding the Union Jack flag campaigns for Great Britain to withdraw from the European Union. The measure, popularly known as Brexit, passed in a public vote in 2016.

In the 21st century Asia remained relatively calm amid strong economic growth. The main trouble spot, as had been true for years, was North Korea. When Dear Leader Kim Jong-il died in 2011, power passed to his son, Supreme Leader Kim Jong-un. Western hopes that the son might prove more progressive than his autocratic father soon withered. North Korea's secretive government had long expressed hostility toward the world and South Korea, Japan, and the U.S. in particular, despite occasional meetings and agreements. In the new century the West's worst fears were realized when North Korea began to test long-range ballistic missiles and nuclear bombs, including what it claimed was a hydrogen bomb in 2016. In 2018, Kim met separately with South Korean president Moon Jae-in and U.S. president Donald Trump. Kim's resulting vows to ease hostilities were promising but vague.

Buffeted by recessions and political corruption, Latin American countries varied from the relatively stable and prosperous, such as Chile, to the chaotic, such as Venezuela. That country's dependence on oil exports led to economic booms and busts. In the early 2000s, leftist president Hugo Chávez nationalized the petroleum and other industries, increasing spending on social programs. By 2013 the economy had crashed, and under President Nicolás Maduro inflation skyrocketed while hungry rioters took to the streets. To the south, the state of Brazil was also struggling. Throughout most of the century, its economy had boomed, in 2012 becoming temporarily the sixth largest in the world. In the recession that followed, popular president Luiz Inácio Lula da Silva, known simply as Lula, and his successor, Dilma Rousseff, were both implicated in corruption scandals. Lula went to jail and Rousseff was impeached. In 2018, Brazilians veered to the right and elected populist Jair Bolsonaro as president.

THE GLOBAL ECONOMY

The cross-border effects of conflict and migration reflected a larger trend in the 21st century. Globalization—the worldwide integration of trade, technology, and media—reshaped everyday life from Malaysian villages to the American heartland. Countries dropped protectionist trade barriers, communication and transportation costs shrank, and new power players emerged on the world scene, notably the BRIC countries Brazil, Russia, India, and China. The components of a single product could be manufactured in countries around the world. Apple's

2018 iPhones, for instance, included parts supplied by more than 200 companies from China to Brazil, assembled in China, and sold by Apple, headquartered in Cupertino, California.

The resulting torrent of money lifted the economies of many countries, and not a few individuals, in an unequal fashion. The poorest countries and their inhabitants saw their incomes rise moderately. Already developed nations and their citizens had less to gain and were squeezed, while the richest one percent captured a lion's share of the income. Critics pointed to this income inequality as one of the negative effects of globalization, along with the growth of multinational corporations at the expense of local businesses, environment, and culture.

Propelled by market reforms that began in the 1980s, China continued to rise as an economic power in the new century. As the country moved from farming to manufacturing and introduced elements of capitalism to its markets, its gross domestic product shot up and poverty plummeted. Foreign companies vied to sell their products to the enormous Chinese populace. Taking a cue from such corporate powerhouses as Amazon, China's e-commerce company Alibaba rose to dominate 80 percent of the country's online shopping and made its debut on the New York Stock Exchange in 2014.

Its economic clout made China a force to be reckoned with, and some observers believed that the 21st century would belong to China, much as the 20th century had been America's. In the near run, however, economists predicted that the binge was largely over and that growth would level out, even as China and other industrialized countries dealt with deadly pollution and other side effects of industry.

Unplanned but inevitable consequences of globalization were also seen in the recession and European debt crisis that began in 2007. Late in 2007 a hot U.S. market in housing and land cooled off and many financial firms with risky investments in toxic mortgages crashed. Over the next two years more than eight million U.S. jobs were lost and the stock market dropped by more than half. Government bailouts and spending programs eventually pulled the U.S. economy out of recession by 2009, although unemployment and wages were slow to improve.

Meanwhile, many banks in Europe bottomed out as well and required bailouts in the 2010s. In the shaky European economic scene, it became clear that some European Union countries had built up hidden and unsustainable debt. Greece, Ireland, Portugal, Spain, and Italy were particularly hard-hit. Several required expensive support from the EU and the International Monetary Fund, whose requirements for austerity measures did not go over well with the people affected. Youth unemployment reached 50 percent in Spain and Greece. Over the next few years, most of the affected countries recovered and exited the bailout conditions, with Greece the last to climb out in 2018.

A homeless man sleeps in an alley in Athens, Greece, a nation hit hard by the economic recession and deeply in debt to its European Union partners. Greece sank into a debt crisis following the global recession of 2007, with the unemployment rate spiking above 25 percent in subsequent years. Economic recovery has been slow and hinges on bailout funds tied to austerity measures from the European Union.

The gap between rich and poor, stable and unstable countries fueled world migration. By 2018 more than 3 percent of the world's population consisted of migrants. Most had left their homes looking for work in wealthier countries. Tens of millions, however, were fleeing conflict and starvation, leading to record-high numbers of internally displaced people and refugees.

POLITICAL POLARIZATION IN THE UNITED STATES

The century in U.S. politics started with the controversial election of the Texas governor George W. Bush, who beat Vice President Al Gore in 2000. Although Bush narrowly lost the popular vote, he won in the Electoral College after a recount in Florida put him ahead by 537 votes. In December, the U.S. Supreme Court ruled against Gore's petition for another recount in four Florida counties.

President Bush soon faced a major crisis in the September 11 terrorist attacks. In addition to invading Afghanistan and Iraq, the government gained a huge new Cabinet department, Homeland Security, which incorporated 22 other agencies and grew to employ more than

Former Secretary of State Hillary Clinton (left) debates real estate and media mogul Donald Trump during the polarizing 2016 U.S. presidential race.

240,000 people. Although Bush had divided the country with his ill-informed decision to invade Iraq, he was reelected in 2004 by a wider margin than in 2000. The Iraq war, the government's lagging response to Hurricane Katrina, and the advent of the recession depressed Bush's popularity and helped pave the way for a different sort of politician in the Illinois senator Barack Obama.

Obama, a former professor of constitutional law, was a rapidly rising star in the Democratic Party who in 2008 became the first African American to reach the presidency. Elected at the height of the recession, he oversaw programs to bolster the economy, and in 2010 backed a major overhaul of the health care system when he signed into law the Affordable Care Act (ACA), often nicknamed "Obamacare." The most notable portion of the legislation required insurers to accept all applicants and charge them the same amounts regardless of preexisting conditions. In 2012 Obama was reelected. In his second term he backed the legalization of same-sex marriage, which was accomplished in 2015, and entered the United States into the Paris Agreement to combat climate change. Meanwhile, the difficult conflict in Afghanistan ground on during his time in office, as it did with presidents before—and then after—him.

Political polarization had been growing in the United States since the early 2000s. Republicans and Democrats became hardened into conservative and liberal positions and were increasingly likely to dislike the other group. These divisions were highlighted in the 2016 presidential race between Democrat Hillary Clinton, a former secretary of state, and the surprising Republican candidate Donald Trump, a real estate developer and reality TV personality who had never held public office. Trump's harsh rhetoric against immigrants, minorities, environmental regulation, the media, and foreign trade deals and treaties appealed to a Republican base anxious about the state of the country. Going into election night, polls showed Clinton winning the election, but Trump shocked pollsters, many voters, and even himself by winning the electoral vote and the presidency.

The first years of President Trump's term were marked by turmoil. Within weeks, actions by his administration were met by public protests, and many were challenged or struck down in the courts. A majority Republican Congress failed to pass most of its promised legislation, such as overturning the ACA, but it did succeed in enacting a large tax cut. Trump's business-friendly policies, on top of the long-running economic recovery from the recession, helped to keep economic growth strong and unemployment low. However, the very legitimacy of the president's position was challenged by a special counsel's investigation. By 2018 the inquiry had yielded more than 180 criminal charges and six guilty pleas from officials connected to Trump's campaign.

CONNECTIONS AND DISRUPTIONS

People in the 21st century were divided, and yet more intimately connected than ever before, thanks to the explosive growth of the internet, mobile communications, and social media. In 2000, 413 million people worldwide used the internet. By 2018 four billion plus were online: more than half the world's population. Access was unevenly distributed, though, favoring wealthier countries. Mobile phone subscriptions showed a similar vaulting profile, leaping from a minority of the population in 2000 to almost one for every person on Earth.

Early uses of the internet—email, for example—were overtaken by various forms of social media. Founded in 2004, the social networking service Facebook reached more than two billion active monthly users in 2018. Other social platforms, such as Twitter and Instagram, showed similar growth. Media and advertising companies followed the numbers, moving away from print to spread their messages online.

The ease and directness of mobile, online communication fueled the rise of disruptive companies that displaced traditional businesses. America's Amazon and China's Alibaba wiped out brick-and-mortar stores with the convenience of their e-commerce. Streaming video and music, carried on YouTube, Netflix, Spotify, and a host of other services, began to overtake physical media and traditional television. They also ate up bandwidth: by 2018 streaming consumed more than 80 percent of data traffic on the internet.

Also disruptive were the companies that took part in the sharing economy, peer-to-peer businesses that circumvented traditional company structures. Ride-sharing services such as Uber (founded in 2009) and Lyft (2012) made clever use of mobile communications to ease urban travel, at the expense of taxi businesses. Airbnb (founded in 2008) allowed travelers to book rooms or flats directly from their owners.

As the century's second decade wound to a close, governments around the world acknowledged that there was one problem they all faced together: the environmental damage that stemmed from human activity. By 2018 environmental studies had made clear that the planet's oceans and atmosphere were heating up even faster than expected. Coral die-offs, more intense storms and droughts, rising sea levels, food shortages, disease outbreaks, and mass human migration would be just some of the consequences. The displacement of coastal communities, rising temperatures, and the die-off of species were already apparent in the early 21st century. The Paris Agreement, negotiated in 2015, brought together 195 countries in a pact to reduce carbon emissions and limit temperature rise to 1.5°C, but scientists warned that holding to that limit would require a radical transition of the world's energy production toward renewable sources.

Climate change, habitat loss, hunting, and other human activities contributed to a continuing loss of biodiversity. From the 1970s to the 2010s, vertebrate species declined by 60 percent in their average populations, with freshwater animals, such as frogs, and Central American and South American creatures particularly hard-hit. Slowing the decline would take international cooperation not only to fight climate change but to conserve land and ocean habitats around the world—to leave room for all species amid a growing human presence. The 21st century's information age has given the world the tools to communicate and educate. Now the world needs to learn to use them for the common good. ■

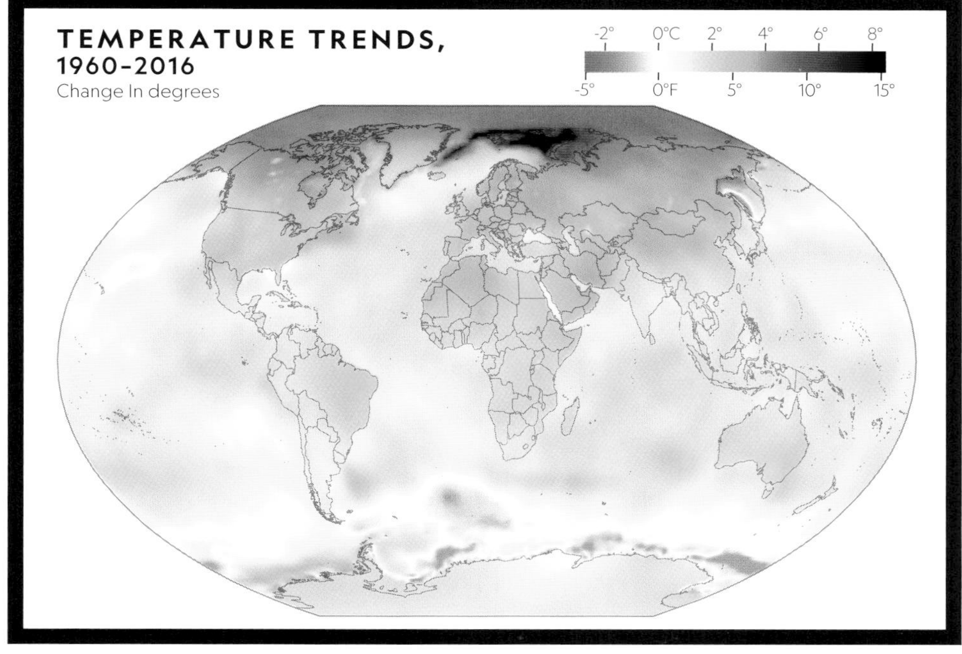

Beginning with the industrial revolution, human activity has released heat-trapping gases—most notably, carbon dioxide—into the air. As a result of this "greenhouse effect" global temperatures are rising. The effects include sea-level rise, droughts, wildfires, hurricanes, coral reef die-off, and species extinctions, which all contribute to environmental degradation, food shortages, and human displacement.

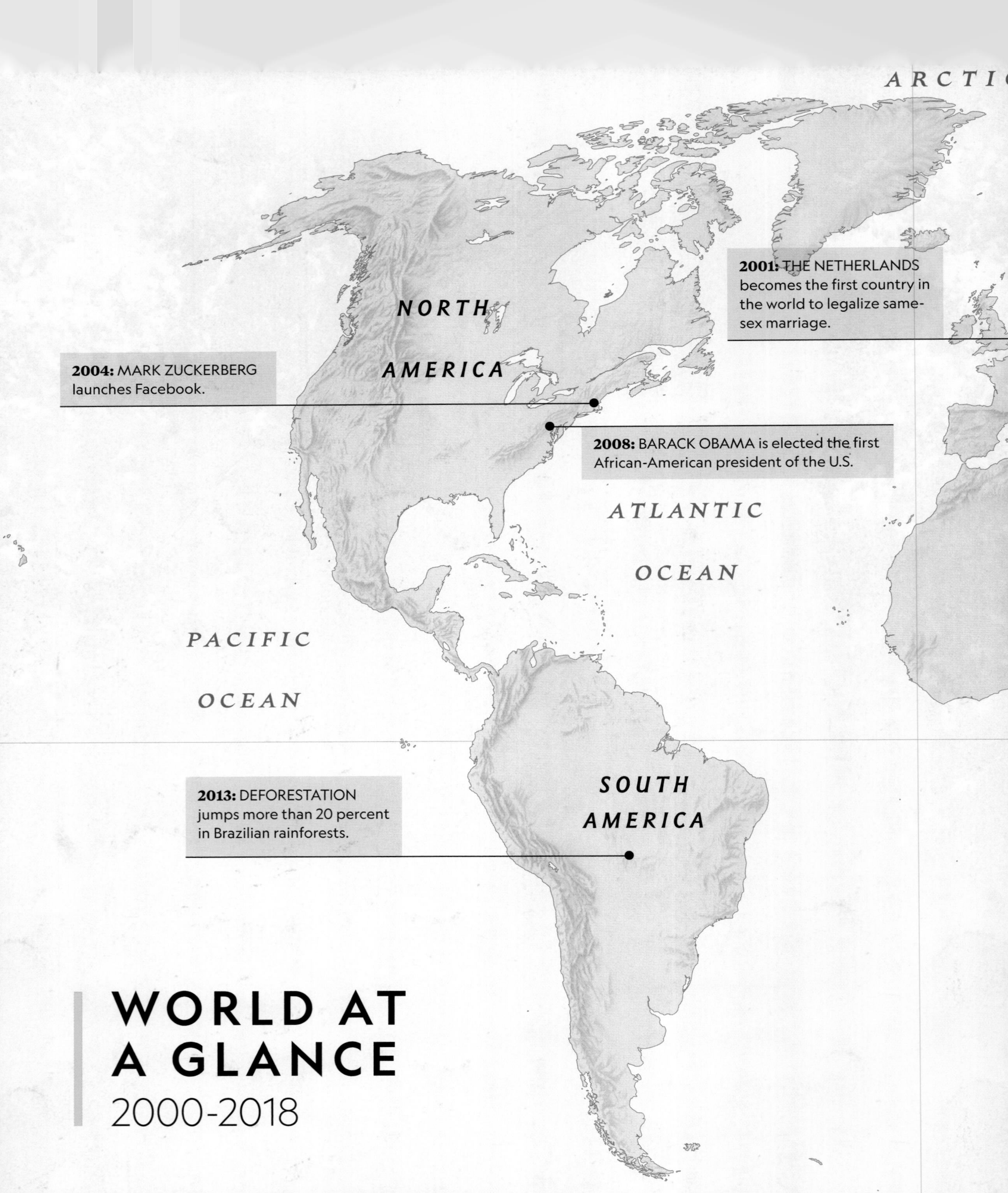
ARCTIC
NORTH AMERICA
2001: THE NETHERLANDS becomes the first country in the world to legalize same-sex marriage.
2004: MARK ZUCKERBERG launches Facebook.
2008: BARACK OBAMA is elected the first African-American president of the U.S.
ATLANTIC OCEAN
PACIFIC OCEAN
SOUTH AMERICA
2013: DEFORESTATION jumps more than 20 percent in Brazilian rainforests.
WORLD AT A GLANCE
2000-2018

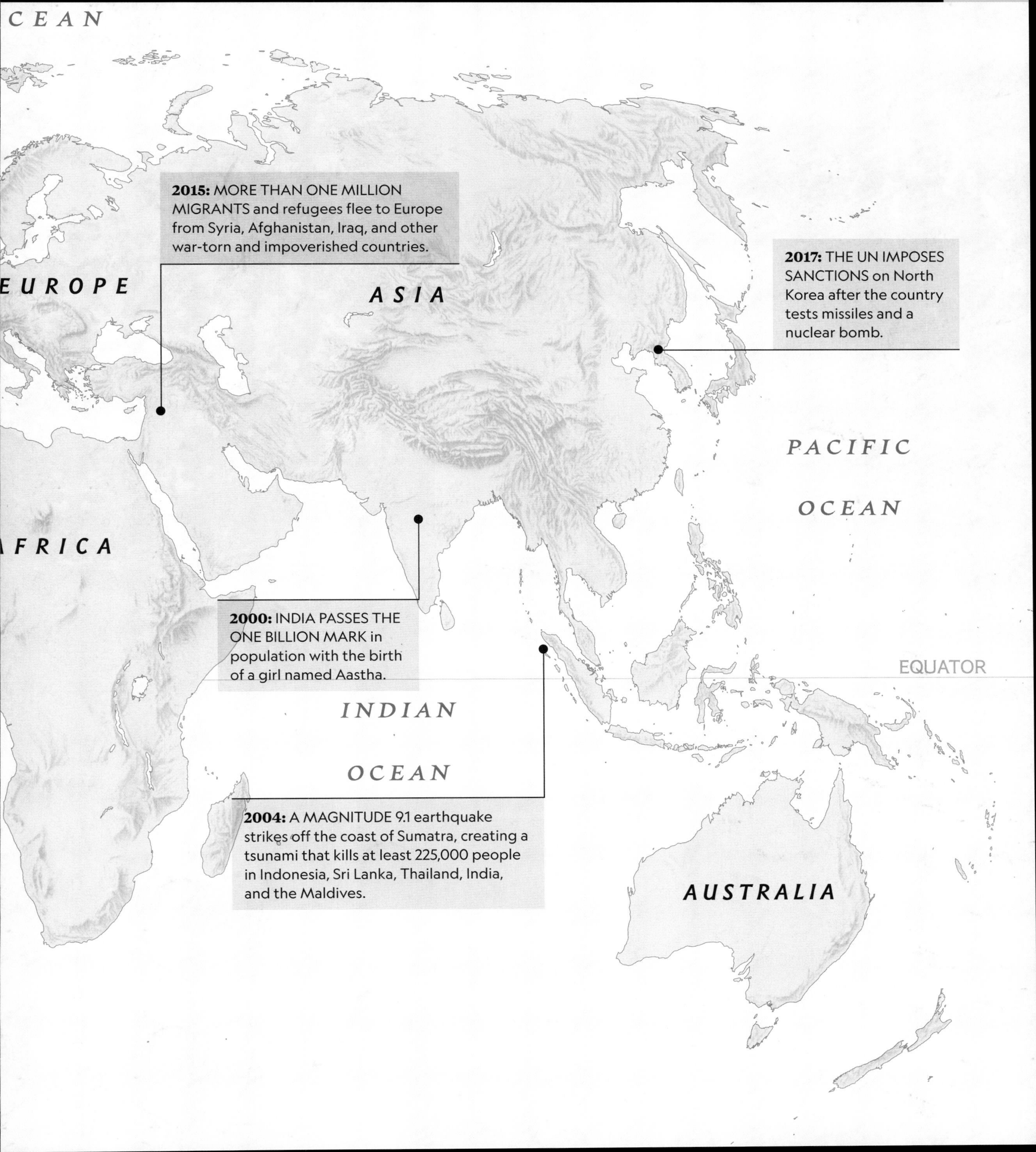

CEAN

EUROPE

ASIA

AFRICA

PACIFIC

OCEAN

INDIAN

OCEAN

EQUATOR

AUSTRALIA

2015: MORE THAN ONE MILLION MIGRANTS and refugees flee to Europe from Syria, Afghanistan, Iraq, and other war-torn and impoverished countries.

2017: THE UN IMPOSES SANCTIONS on North Korea after the country tests missiles and a nuclear bomb.

2000: INDIA PASSES THE ONE BILLION MARK in population with the birth of a girl named Aastha.

2004: A MAGNITUDE 9.1 earthquake strikes off the coast of Sumatra, creating a tsunami that kills at least 225,000 people in Indonesia, Sri Lanka, Thailand, India, and the Maldives.

2000-2004

	POLITICS & POWER	GEOGRAPHY & ENVIRONMENT	CULTURE & RELIGION
THE AMERICAS	**2000** **GEORGE W. BUSH,** son of the former president George H. W. Bush, is elected president of the United States. **2000** **VICENTE FOX** is elected president of Mexico, marking the fall of PRI, Mexico's "official" party since 1929. **2001** **TWO PLANES HIJACKED** by terrorists crash into New York's World Trade Center, destroying both towers and killing nearly 3,000. A third hijacked plane crashes into the Pentagon. A fourth is brought down by passengers.	**2001** **CONFLICTS ARISE** in Bolivia between security forces and coca growers after president Hugo Banzer attempts to eliminate coca production. **2003** **AN EARTHQUAKE** off the Pacific coast of Mexico kills 29 and injures 300.	**2000** **SCORES OF DOT-COM BUSINESSES** go belly-up as the 1990s technology boom goes bust. **2001** **THE WIKIPEDIA** online encyclopedia is founded by Larry Sanger and Jimmy Wales. **2002** **THE CATHOLIC CHURCH** is scandalized by revelations of child molestation by priests and cover-ups by the Church. **2003** **THE MASSACHUSETTS SUPREME COURT** permits same-sex marriage, the first U.S. state to do so.
EUROPE	**2000** **VLADIMIR PUTIN** is elected president of Russia. **2000** **YUGOSLAVIAN PRESIDENT** Slobodan Milošević is driven from office. **2002** **THE INTERNATIONAL CRIMINAL COURT** begins operations in The Hague, Netherlands.	Currency of the EU **2002** **OIL TANKER MV *PRESTIGE*** sinks off the coast of Spain, spilling more than 21 million gallons of fuel oil and polluting the beaches of Spain, Portugal, and France. **2003** **A DEVASTATING HEAT WAVE** leads to approximately 35,000 deaths in Europe, including 14,000 in France.	**2001** **THE NETHERLANDS** becomes the first country in the world to legalize same-sex marriage. ◀**2002** **EUROS,** the currency of the new European Union, begin circulating.
MIDDLE EAST & AFRICA	**2001** **ARIEL SHARON** becomes prime minister of Israel as violence with Palestinians worsens. **2003** **THE U.S. INVADES IRAQ** based on intelligence that Saddam Hussein is concealing weapons of mass destruction. Hussein is captured, but WMDs are never found. **2003** **ETHNIC CONFLICTS** boil over in Sudan as government-backed militias begin a campaign against non-Arab indigenous peoples of the Darfur region. At least 70,000 die of starvation and disease alone, and millions more are displaced.	**2001** **THE U.S. ENDORSES** the creation of a Palestinian state. **2002** **ISRAEL BEGINS CONSTRUCTION** of a massive wall called the "security fence" around its settlements in the West Bank. **2003** **AN EARTHQUAKE** devastates southeastern Iran, killing more than 40,000.	**2000** **POPE JOHN PAUL II** visits Israel and its Holocaust memorial Yad Vashem. **2001** **HUNDREDS OF SUSPECTED WITCHES** are murdered in war-ravaged northeastern Congo.
ASIA & OCEANIA	**2001** **THE U.S. BOMBS AFGHANISTAN** and topples the Taliban government after linking the World Trade Center attacks to Taliban-supported al Qaeda leader Osama bin Laden. **2002** **TERRORIST GROUP JEMAAH ISLAMIYAH** carries out three bombings on the Indonesian island of Bali, killing 202 people. **2002** **NORTH KOREA** admits to pursuing nuclear capability in violation of a 1994 pact with the U.S.	**2000** **THE TOYOTA PRIUS** becomes the first mass-produced hybrid vehicle to be sold worldwide.	

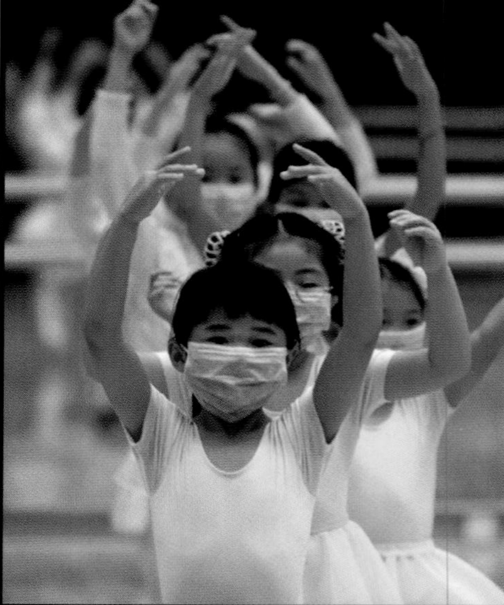

Children in Hong Kong wear masks to prevent SARS.

SCIENCE & TECHNOLOGY

2003 THE U.S. HUMAN GENOME PROJECT is completed, identifying and mapping all 20,000 to 25,000 genes in human DNA.

2003 THE *COLUMBIA* SPACE SHUTTLE explodes over north-central Texas as it returns from a mission.

2003 THE EUROPEAN SPACE AGENCY launches its first Mars mission, Mars Express.

2003 SUPERSONIC JET CONCORDE makes its final transatlantic flight.

2000s AIDS BECOMES AN EPIDEMIC in Africa, particularly in the sub-Sahara, where millions become newly infected every year.

2003 LIBYAN DICTATOR Muammar Qaddafi agrees to abandon Libya's nuclear weapons program.

◀ **2002** THE SARS VIRUS (severe acute respiratory syndrome), a lethal pneumonia-like illness, starts in China and spreads to Europe and North America.

2003 CHINA LAUNCHES Shenzhou 5, the country's first crewed space mission.

PEOPLE & SOCIETY

2000 IN THE U.S. CENSUS, citizens are able to claim for the first time more than one racial identity.

2001 HISPANICS surpass African Americans as the largest minority group in the U.S.

2001 ENERGY-TRADING COMPANY ENRON files for bankruptcy amid corporate scandal.

2002 JOURNALIST DANIEL PEARL is abducted and killed by terrorists in Pakistan.

2000 BRITISH PHYSICIAN HAROLD SHIPMAN is sentenced to life in prison for the murder of at least 15 patients. He is suspected of killing up to 250, which would make him one of the deadliest serial killers of all time.

2002 CHECHEN REBELS take Moscow theatergoers hostage, killing two. In a subsequent rescue attempt about 120 hostages are killed.

2001 SAUDI OSAMA BIN LADEN orchestrates the worst terrorist attack ever on U.S. soil.

2001 GHANAIAN KOFI ANNAN and the UN win the Nobel Peace Prize.

ROYAL MASSACRE

THE SHAH DYNASTY, which had ruled the kingdom of Nepal since 1768, had known its share of turmoil, but no one could have predicted the violence that tore it apart in 2001. On June 1 of that year, nine members of the royal family, including the king and queen, were shot and killed at the Narayanhity Royal Palace in Kathmandu. The alleged killer was Crown Prince Dipendra, who died of gunshot wounds himself three days later.

In the days after the attack a story emerged. The 29-year-old crown prince and his family had gathered for dinner at the palace. The prince became visibly drunk during the dinner, and afterward he entered the billiards room where the family was relaxing. Wearing army fatigues and carrying several guns, Dipendra opened fire. He killed his father, King Birendra, first, then shot and killed eight others, including his mother, Queen Aishwarya, his brother, and other relatives. Dipendra then shot himself. As the heir to the throne, he was crowned king while he lingered in a coma. The previous king's brother, Gyanendra, inherited the title when Dipendra died.

The motive for the killing was unclear, but the most commonly cited reason was the family's opposition to Dipendra's intended bride, Devyani Rana. Her ties to a rival family and to India were said to be a sore point. Many Nepalese continue to reject the official account of the incident, however, pointing to other suspects in the killing, including the next king, Gyanendra. The investigation into the crime was brief, and a later inquiry promised by Gyanendra never came to fruition.

The palace massacre marked an end to the royal family in more ways than one. Gyanendra's reign was short. In 2008 the Nepalese Assembly abolished the monarchy and the king went into retirement.

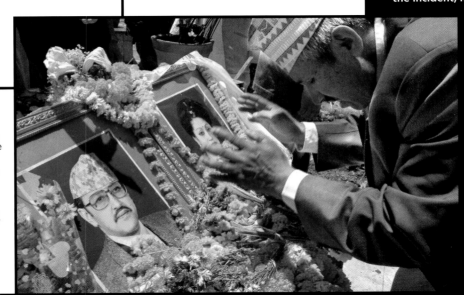

Eleven members of the Nepalese royal family are killed in 2001, including the king and queen.

THE NEW FACE OF TERRORISM

September 11, 2001, was a perfect fall day, clear and mild. People were still walking to work in Manhattan that morning when they witnessed an extraordinary sight: An American Airlines passenger jet, cruising low over the skyscrapers, smashed into the top of the World Trade Center's north tower. In the next hour and a quarter, a second jet hit the south tower, a third crashed into the Pentagon in Arlington, Virginia, and a fourth plummeted into a field near Shanksville, Pennsylvania. All had been hijacked by terrorists belonging to the Islamic extremist group al Qaeda. Almost 3,000 people died, including the 19 hijackers, in the deadliest terrorist attack in history.

The 9/11 attacks, as they came to be known, marked a new era in the old practice of terrorism. Loosely defined as violence used against civilians to influence behavior or exact revenge, terrorism in the late 20th century had been concentrated mainly in Latin America, western Europe, and Asia. However, the end of the century saw a rise in more broad-based, global terrorism springing from groups in the Middle East, Africa, and South Asia.

Long-standing instability in Afghanistan spurred the rise of the fundamentalist Islamic group al Qaeda (The Base), which initially fought the Soviet Union but then turned its attentions toward the U.S. An offshoot of the group, al Qaeda in Iraq, joined several other extremist organizations, expanded into Syria, and rebranded itself as the Islamic State (ISIS or ISIL), also known as Daesh in the Arab-speaking world.

For a time, the Islamic State gained ground in Syria, ostensibly in pursuit of a caliphate in the region. By 2018, however, it had lost most of its territory after pushback from international forces. Where it succeeded was in leveraging the power of the internet. Grisly online videos of beheadings were joined by recruitment appeals to aggrieved individuals around the world.

Similar militant groups include Boko Haram in Nigeria and the East African jihadist organization al Shabaab. Despite the groups' avowed enmity toward the West, almost all of their victims have been their Muslim neighbors. Researchers note that most modern terrorist groups rise and fall within a decade. As effective as they are in spreading fear, they typically fail at accomplishing their political goals.

As smoke blows across the skyline of New York City, the World Trade Center collapses after being struck by an airplane hijacked by terrorists on September 11, 2001.

2004-2007

THE AMERICAS

POLITICS & POWER

2004 GEORGE W. BUSH is reelected president, with Dick Cheney as vice president.

2006 DEMOCRATS take control of both houses of Congress in midterm elections.

2006 RAPHAEL CORREA is elected president of Ecuador during the peak of the Pink Tide, a wave of leftist noncommunist governments in Venezuela, Argentina, Brazil, Chile, Uruguay, Paraguay, Ecuador, and Bolivia.

GEOGRAPHY & ENVIRONMENT

2005 HURRICANE KATRINA strikes the U.S. Gulf Coast in one of the worst natural disasters in the nation's history.

2005 THE U.S. RELEASES seven billion metric tons of greenhouse gases.

2006 A MASSIVE STORM buries Buffalo under two feet of snow.

CULTURE & RELIGION

▼ **2004** THE BOSTON RED SOX overcome sports' most famous curse and win the World Series, their first title since 1918.

2005 YOUTUBE, a video-sharing website, is launched by three former PayPal employees.

2006 CHILE elects its first female president, social democrat Michelle Bachelet.

2006 TWITTER co-founder Jack Dorsey sends out the first tweet.

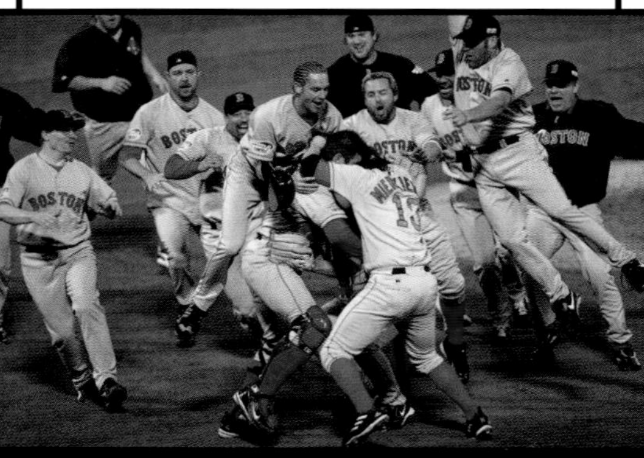

Boston Red Sox win the World Series.

EUROPE

POLITICS & POWER

2004 CHECHEN REBELS seize an elementary school in Beslan, North Ossetia, Russia; more than 330 adults and children die.

2004 CYPRUS, Czech Republic, Estonia, Hungary, Latvia, Lithuania, Malta, Poland, Slovakia, and Slovenia join the European Union.

2005 ANGELA MERKEL becomes German chancellor.

GEOGRAPHY & ENVIRONMENT

2005 THE KYOTO PROTOCOL, an international environmental treaty, comes into force following its ratification by Russia in 2004.

CULTURE & RELIGION

2004 A LAW BANNING HEAD SCARVES in public schools comes into effect in France.

2005 CARDINAL JOSEPH RATZINGER is elected Pope Benedict XVI.

2005 *HARRY POTTER AND THE HALF-BLOOD PRINCE,* the sixth book in the Harry Potter series, is published and sells nine million copies in 24 hours.

MIDDLE EAST & AFRICA

POLITICS & POWER

2004 YASSER ARAFAT DIES; in 2005 Mahmoud Abbas is elected chairman of the Palestine Liberation Organization.

▶ **2005** ELLEN JOHNSON SIRLEAF is elected president of Liberia, the first woman to lead an African country.

2006 CHARLES TAYLOR, former president of Liberia, is arrested for war crimes.

GEOGRAPHY & ENVIRONMENT

2004-2005 NINE MILLION PEOPLE across West Africa's semiarid Sahel region face famine after an invasion of locusts followed by severe drought destroys their crops and grazing land.

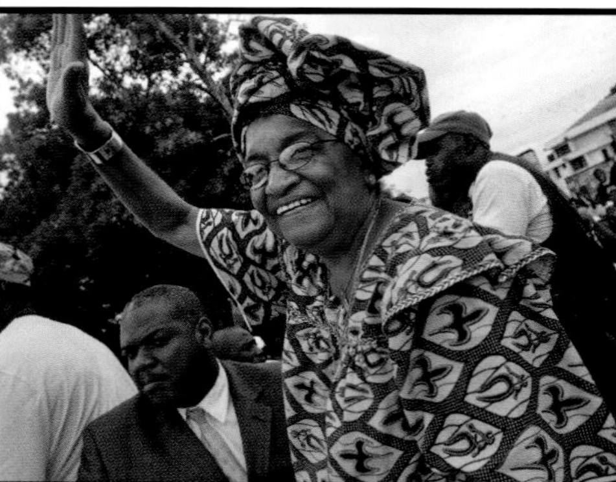

Liberian president Ellen Johnson Sirleaf

CULTURE & RELIGION

2004 IN A STAMPEDE during the hajj pilgrimage in Mecca, 251 people are trampled to death.

2004-2005 BOWING TO INTERNATIONAL PRESSURE, Saudi Arabia agrees to hold its first municipal elections in 40 years. Women, though, may not vote or run for office.

2006 TURKISH WRITER Orhan Pamuk wins the Nobel Prize in literature.

ASIA & OCEANIA

POLITICS & POWER

2004 NORODOM SIHANOUK abdicates as king of Cambodia.

2006 THE JAPANESE PARLIAMENT approves the creation of a defense ministry, the first since World War II.

GEOGRAPHY & ENVIRONMENT

2004 A LIVE GIANT SQUID is photographed in its natural habitat for the first time.

2004 A MAGNITUDE 9.1 earthquake creates a tsunami that kills at least 225,000 people in Indonesia, Sri Lanka, Thailand, India, and the Maldives.

CULTURE & RELIGION

2004 MAORI TELEVISION begins broadcasting in New Zealand.

2004 *WOLF TOTEM,* a semiautobiographical Chinese novel written under the pseudonym Jiang Rong, sells at least one million copies in its first year.

SCIENCE & TECHNOLOGY

2004 SPIRIT AND OPPORTUNITY, NASA Mars Exploration rovers, land successfully on Mars three weeks apart.

2004 MARK ZUCKERBERG launches Facebook.

2004 GOOGLE introduces its Gmail email service.

2004 THE WORLD'S HIGHEST BRIDGE, the Millau Viaduct, which crosses the River Tarn, opens in France's Massif Central region.

2003 LIFE EXPECTANCY in sub-Saharan Africa stands at 52 years, largely as a result of the AIDS epidemic.

2003 THE NUMBER OF PEOPLE with cell phone subscriptions in Africa passes 52 million.

2003 THE FOSSILIZED REMAINS of diminutive human ancestors are found on the island of Flores in Indonesia.

2004 THE HEAD OF PAKISTAN'S NUCLEAR PROGRAM is found to be selling nuclear technology to North Korea, Libya, and Iran.

2005 THE ENDANGERED STITCHBIRD is reintroduced to a sanctuary in New Zealand.

PEOPLE & SOCIETY

2004 JEAN-BERTRAND ARISTIDE of Haiti is overthrown yet again in a rebellion after becoming president for the third time in 2001.

2004 U.S. MEDIA release graphic photos of American soldiers abusing and sexually humiliating Iraqi prisoners at Abu Ghraib prison.

2006 THE U.S. POPULATION tops 300 million.

2004 UNOCAL CORPORATION of California agrees to settle landmark human rights lawsuits in Myanmar (Burma), compensating villagers who say they suffered rape, torture, and murder while working on Unocal's pipeline.

2005 ANTI-JAPANESE PROTESTS break out in China after Chinese politicians meet with Japanese ministers.

CONNECTIONS

The Rise and Fall of Blockbuster Video

There was a time when the blue-and-yellow ticket-shaped Blockbuster logo was one of the most recognizable signs in the world. Founded with a single outlet in Dallas, Texas, in 1985, the video-rental company bought out competitors and expanded to a peak of more than 9,000 stores in 2004. The outlets were a regular family destination as each weekend began, with popular movie titles quickly snapped up. Even as Blockbuster surged, however, a rival operation began to make inroads. Netflix, founded in 1997, offered consumers an even easier path to movie night with online rental and mail delivery. As Netflix transitioned to streaming video and production, Blockbuster's storefront empire waned. Unable to compete with the binge-watching convenience of Netflix and other streaming services, Blockbuster was bought out by the Dish Network in 2011. In 2018, it shuttered its last four stores in Alaska. By July of that year a single store—in Bend, Oregon—remained, a "newest releases" sign in its window.

HURRICANE KATRINA

HURRICANE KATRINA, which devastated New Orleans and its surroundings in the summer of 2005, was the costliest cyclone ever to hit the United States. Poor infrastructure, a delayed response, and confused communications contributed to a death toll over 1,800. The storm was a grim reminder that natural disasters disproportionately hurt the poorest people in their paths.

Katrina swept across Florida as a Category 1 hurricane on August 25. Over the warm waters of the Gulf of Mexico it intensified and became a Category 5 storm with winds of 175 miles an hour before making another landfall as a still powerful Category 3 in southeast Louisiana on August 28. Moving northeast, it brought with it a storm surge of close to 20 feet, overwhelming the bayous and beaches of coastal Mississippi and Alabama.

The greatest destruction, however, took place to the west in the low-lying city of New Orleans. In the heavy rain, the levees that held back Lake Pontchartrain and Lake Borgne failed. Floodwaters inundated New Orleans on August 29, and soon 80 percent of the historic city was submerged. Although most residents had evacuated, not all were able to leave. Some were lifted from rooftops but many drowned in their homes. Tens of thousands took shelter in the New Orleans Superdome, where they suffered from food shortages and filthy surroundings. At the Memorial Medical Center, trapped and desperate staff members euthanized critically ill patients.

Federal aid did not arrive for several days, but eventually survivors were rescued. Many who had fled the city never returned, and in 2016 the city was still 100,000 short of its pre-Katrina numbers. Stronger levees built in recent years are intended to protect against "100-year" storms. Residents pray that a stronger storm never comes their way.

POLITICS & POWER	GEOGRAPHY & ENVIRONMENT	CULTURE & RELIGION
2007 CRISTINA FERNÁNDEZ DE KIRCHNER becomes Argentina's first directly elected female president. ▶ **2008 BARACK OBAMA** is elected the first African-American president of the U.S. **2008 FIDEL CASTRO** retires as president of Cuba after almost 50 years in power.	**2007 THE INTERNATIONAL PANEL ON CLIMATE CHANGE** and former vice president Al Gore win the Nobel Peace Prize. **2008 THE "SUPER TUESDAY" TORNADO OUTBREAK** kills 57 across the southern U.S.	**2007 A SCHISM WITHIN THE EPISCOPAL CHURCH** over acceptance of gay clergy leads some U.S. congregations to turn to the Anglican Church. **2008 JAMAICAN SPRINTER USAIN BOLT** wins the first of his eight lifetime Olympic gold medals, shattering world records. **2009** ***AVATAR*** is released and will become the highest-grossing film in history.
2007 BULGARIA AND ROMANIA join the European Union. **2007 NICOLAS SARKOZY** becomes president of France. **2008 RUSSIAN AND GEORGIAN TROOPS** clash as the provinces of South Ossetia and Abkhazia attempt to break away from Georgia, with Russian aid.		**2008** ***MAMMA MIA!,*** the biggest success in British movie box office history to date, is released. **2009 FRANCE** fines the Church of Scientology and sentences some of its leaders for fraud.
2007 TERRORIST BOMBINGS in Iraqi Yazidi communities kill at least 500. **2008 ANGOLA** holds parliamentary elections for the first time in 16 years. **2009 JACOB ZUMA** becomes president of South Africa.	**2009 RWANDA** becomes a member of the Commonwealth of Nations. ▶ **2009 DROUGHT IN KENYA** leads to widespread starvation.	**2007 THE ANCIENT TOMB OF KING HEROD** is found in Israel, south of Jerusalem.
2007 FORMER PAKISTANI PRIME MINISTER Benazir Bhutto is assassinated by a suicide bomber. **2008 NEPAL** abolishes its monarchy and becomes the Federal Democratic Republic of Nepal. **2008 SINGAPORE, HONG KONG, AND JAPAN** slide into recession. **2009 THE SRI LANKAN GOVERNMENT** defeats the Tamil Tigers, ending a quarter century of civil war.	**2007 CYCLONE SIDR** kills thousands in Bangladesh. **2008 SMOG** makes for severe air pollution at the Beijing Summer Olympic Games. **2008 CYCLONE NARGIS** hits Myanmar and kills at least 84,000 with winds and floods. **2008 A MAGNITUDE 7.9 EARTHQUAKE** kills nearly 90,000 in Sichuan Province, China.	

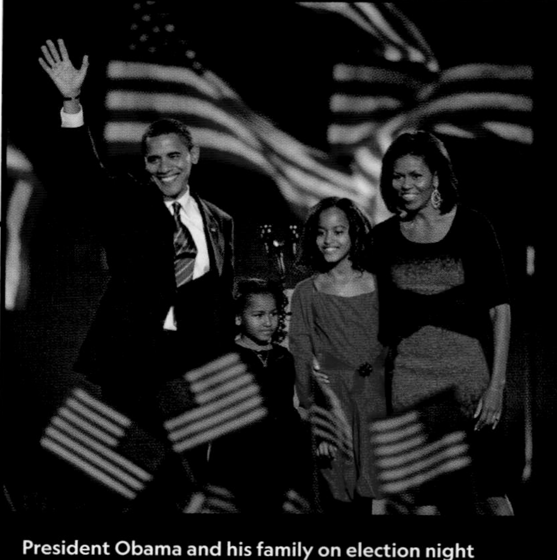

President Obama and his family on election night

Women in Kenya stand on a dry riverbed during a food and water shortage exacerbated by climate change.

SCIENCE & TECHNOLOGY

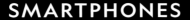

2007 APPLE releases the first iPhone smartphone.

2009 NASA launches the Lunar Reconnaissance Orbiter.

2009 A SWINE FLU EPIDEMIC breaks out in Mexico, leading to thousands of deaths worldwide.

2007 SWISS ASTRONOMER STÉPHANE UDRY and his team discover a possibly Earthlike planet, Gliese 581c, 20 light-years from Earth.

2008 THE LARGE HADRON COLLIDER, the world's largest particle accelerator, opens near Geneva.

2009 BIOCHEMIST ADA YONATH becomes the first Israeli woman to win the Nobel Prize.

2009 PALEONTOLOGISTS describe a 4.4-million-year-old skeleton found in Ethiopia as *Ardipithecus ramidus*, a primate that might be a human ancestor.

2007 CHINA sends a spacecraft, Chang'e 1, into orbit around the moon.

2007 CHINESE PALEONTOLOGIST Xing Xu and colleagues discover fossils of a huge birdlike dinosaur, *Gigantoraptor*, in Mongolia.

PEOPLE & SOCIETY

2007 HOUSING PRICES FALL, home owners start to default on risky mortgages, and investment banks develop liquidity problems as the Great Recession begins.

2008 INVESTMENT BANK Lehman Brothers files for bankruptcy.

2009 GENERAL MOTORS CORPORATION declares bankruptcy, then is reconstituted under the name General Motors Company.

2009 THE DOW JONES INDUSTRIAL AVERAGE closes at 6,547 in March, a 46 percent decrease from 2007.

2008 THE INTERNATIONAL MONETARY FUND issues a multibillion-dollar bailout package to Iceland as the country's banking system collapses.

2008 ECONOMIC DOWNTURNS in Germany and Italy push the entire Eurozone into recession.

2008 THREE AFRICAN TRADING BLOCKS announce the creation of the African Free Trade Zone, which comes to include 26 nations.

2009 U.S. DRONE STRIKES increase in frequency on CIA targets throughout the Middle East and Africa directed by Obama Administration counterterrorism advisers.

SMARTPHONES

MULTIPURPOSE MOBILE PHONES had existed since the 1990s, but for most people January 9, 2007, is the day that smartphones were born. On that morning, Apple CEO Steve Jobs unveiled the iPhone in front of an auditorium of electronics aficionados at the Macworld trade show in San Francisco. The palm-size device would change the way the world communicated.

Before the iPhone debuted, most people carried two or three devices if they wanted to make calls, listen to music, and send email. As early as 1993, IBM had produced the Simon Personal Communicator, which could make calls and send emails and faxes. It didn't catch on, perhaps because of its $1,100 price tag. By 2002 Research in Motion's BlackBerry, originally a pager, had evolved into a smartphone that could send emails and text messages and browse the web, although it couldn't display web pages as they might be seen on a computer screen.

Meanwhile, Apple had hit it out of the park with its iPod music players, and Jobs was looking toward the next big thing. He drove his engineers mercilessly for years, pressuring them to do what had never been done before: incorporate phone calls, texts, music, true web browsing, and much more into a small, streamlined package running on battery power. Mac's operating system software had to be completely rewritten. Moreover, the iPhone introduced a large multitouch, capacitive touchscreen that would allow users to navigate with just the brush of a fingertip and to zoom in and out using two fingers. The sleek, intuitive design gave it a modernistic polish unmatched by any other phone.

Jobs's presentation, which had been cloaked in secrecy, went off without a hitch. When the phone went on sale in June, customers were lined up outside the stores.

Apple CEO Steve Jobs reveals the new iPhone.

THE GREAT RECESSION

"When America sneezes, the world catches cold." The truth behind this cliché was never more apparent than in the massive recession that shook world economies beginning in 2007.

The causes of the recession were several, but they were rooted in deregulation of the U.S. banking industry around the turn of the 21st century and in the poor oversight of the speculative investments that followed. In the early 2000s the U.S. housing market was booming, and many financial institutions in the U.S. and abroad invested in subprime mortgages—money lent at high rates to borrowers with poor credit histories. Insurance companies jumped in to back up the investments. Credit-rating agencies such as Standard & Poor's, paid by the very companies they evaluated, failed to highlight the risky loans.

Then, beginning in 2007, the housing bubble burst. Housing prices dropped by about 25 percent, and by 2009 nearly 10 percent of the nation's mortgages were delinquent. Mountains of bad debt began to sink big investment banks including Bear Stearns, Merrill Lynch, and Goldman Sachs, as well as the insurance giant American International Group. The subsequent Lehman Brothers bankruptcy in 2008 was the biggest in U.S. history. U.S. government bailouts eventually saved many of the other institutions, with some huge companies deemed "too big to fail."

The U.S. stock market lost more than half its value in 17 months. Unemployment rose to 10 percent as investment dried up and businesses retrenched. The Bush and then the Obama Administrations poured trillions of dollars into stimulus packages, and the economy began a slow climb, officially moving out of the recession in June of 2009.

Meanwhile, international investors, particularly in Europe, caught the economic flu as well. Iceland's three largest banks collapsed. Wages dropped and unemployment jumped. Countries with major debt, notably Greece, Portugal, Ireland, Spain, and Italy, had to be bailed out by their northern Eurozone neighbors and the International Monetary Fund.

By 2018 most economies had largely recovered, with Greece the last to emerge from its bailout conditions. In the United States, the government once again eased rules on risky banking. Whether investors had learned their lesson would remain to be seen.

Grave miscalculations and reckless lending in the finance industry led to an economic recession in 2007 that spiked unemployment and home foreclosures.

SMITH

2010-2013

THE AMERICAS

POLITICS & POWER

2010 **SEBASTIÁN PIÑERA** becomes president of Chile.

2011 **THE ATTEMPTED ASSASSINATION** of Arizona congresswoman Gabrielle Giffords in Arizona kills six and wounds 13, including Giffords.

2012 **BARACK OBAMA** is reelected as U.S. president, defeating Mitt Romney.

GEOGRAPHY & ENVIRONMENT

2010 **AN EARTHQUAKE IN HAITI** kills approximately 100,000 and leaves millions homeless.

2010 **A CAVE-IN** traps 33 Chilean miners underground for a record 69 days.

2010 ***THE DEEPWATER HORIZON*** drilling rig explodes, killing 11, sinking the rig, and releasing a massive oil discharge into the Gulf of Mexico.

2011 **IN APRIL, 321 PEOPLE** are killed in the deadliest tornado outbreak in the southern United States since 1974. In May, an EF5 tornado hits Joplin, Missouri, killing 158 people, the single deadliest U.S. tornado in modern history.

CULTURE & RELIGION

2010 ***TOY STORY 3*** becomes the highest grossing film of the year and the first animated film to surpass $1 billion in revenue.

2012 **A RISING NUMBER** of Americans, almost 20 percent, claim "no religion" in a Pew report.

EUROPE

POLITICS & POWER

2010 **A POLISH AIR FORCE PLANE** crashes near Smolensk, Russia, killing all 96 people on board, including President Lech Kaczyński.

2012 **VLADIMIR PUTIN** is elected president of Russia, his third term under that title.

2012 **FRANÇOIS HOLLANDE** is elected the 24th president of France.

GEOGRAPHY & ENVIRONMENT

2010 **SABOTEURS** release 2.5 million liters of diesel oil into northern Italy's Lambro River.

2010 **VOLCANIC ASH** from the eruption of Eyjafjallajökull in Iceland closes airspace over most of Europe.

CULTURE & RELIGION

2010 **THE MUSLIM POPULATION OF EUROPE** reaches 44 million.

2011 **POPE JOHN PAUL II** is beatified by his successor, Pope Benedict XVI.

Burj Khalifa skyscraper

MIDDLE EAST & AFRICA

POLITICS & POWER

2011 **PROTESTERS** take to the streets in Tunisia, Egypt, Yemen, Syria, and Morocco as the "Arab Spring" begins. Egyptian president Hosni Mubarak resigns.

2011 **THE LAST U.S. TROOPS** withdraw from Iraq, formally ending the Iraq War.

2012 **CONFLICTS IN SYRIA** grow into a civil war between the government, led by President Bashar al-Assad, and rebel groups, with international allies on both sides

GEOGRAPHY & ENVIRONMENT

2011 **SOUTH SUDAN** gains independence from Sudan.

2012 **THE UN GENERAL ASSEMBLY** votes to admit the State of Palestine as a nonmember observer state.

ASIA & OCEANIA

POLITICS & POWER

2011 **TERRORIST LEADER OSAMA BIN LADEN** is killed by U.S. Navy SEALs in Abbottabad, Pakistan.

2011 **KIM JONG-UN** becomes Supreme Leader of North Korea after the death of his father, Kim Jong-il.

GEOGRAPHY & ENVIRONMENT

2011 **AN EARTHQUAKE** measuring 6.3 in magnitude strikes Christchurch, New Zealand, killing 181 people.

2011 **A TSUNAMI CAUSES** a nuclear disaster at Fukushima, Japan.

CULTURE & RELIGION

2010 **CHINESE ARTIST** and activist Ai Weiwei is placed under arrest.

2012 **"GANGNAM STYLE"** becomes the most viewed YouTube video with one billion views.

SCIENCE & TECHNOLOGY

2011 SPACE SHUTTLE *ATLANTIS* makes the final flight of the space shuttle program.

▼**2012** JAMES CAMERON becomes first solo adventurer to visit the Challenger Deep in the Mariana Trench, the deepest known point on the seabed.

2012 GENE EDITING technology Crispr is successfully demonstrated by biochemists Jennifer Doudna and Emmanuelle Charpentier. Similar research continues in labs around the world.

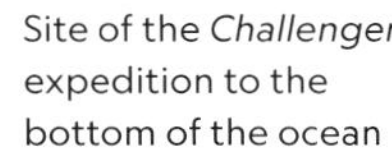

Site of the *Challenger* expedition to the bottom of the ocean

2011 GERMANY ANNOUNCES it will phase out nuclear energy.

2012 CERN'S LARGE HADRON COLLIDER provides the first evidence of the elementary particle called the Higgs boson.

◀**2010** THE BURJ KHALIFA, the world's tallest building at 2,717 feet, opens in Dubai.

2011 IRAN'S FIRST NUCLEAR POWER PLANT, Bushehr 1, officially opens.

2011 CHINA'S THREE GORGES DAM, the biggest power plant ever built, becomes operational.

2012 CHINESE PALEONTOLOGISTS discover a tyrannosaur fossil with clear evidence of feathers.

PEOPLE & SOCIETY

2011 U.S. UNEMPLOYMENT reaches 9 percent.

2011 THE OCCUPY WALL STREET movement begins in Zuccotti Park, New York City.

2012 TWENTY CHILDREN and six adults are shot and killed by 20-year-old Adam Lanza at Sandy Hook Elementary School in Newtown, Connecticut.

2011 ANDERS BREIVIK perpetrates a mass shooting and bombing in Norway, killing 77, including many teenagers.

2012 U.K. UNEMPLOYMENT reaches 8.4 percent.

2010 MUSLIM-CHRISTIAN RELIGIOUS RIOTING in central Nigeria kills more than 300.

2010 SOUTH AFRICA becomes the first African country to host the soccer FIFA World Cup.

2011 MUAMMAR QADDAFI, deposed leader of Libya, is killed by rebel fighters.

2012 SAUDI WOMEN compete on the national Olympics team for the first time.

2010 JAPAN'S POPULATION GROWTH RATE falls to zero.

2012 JAPAN'S STOCK MARKET hits its lowest point in 28 years.

2012 WOMEN'S RIGHTS ACTIVIST and youth leader Malala Yousafzai is shot and seriously injured by a Taliban gunman in Pakistan.

SOCIAL MEDIA AND THE ARAB SPRING

WHEN A TUNISIAN STREET VENDOR, Mohamed Bouazizi, set himself on fire in the town of Sidi Bouzid in 2010, he probably didn't expect to start a revolution. Born Tarek al-Tayeb Mohamed Bouazizi, he was simply a young man who struggled to support his mother and siblings by selling fruit and vegetables from a street cart. He'd had to drop out of high school, and his job prospects were poor in a time of high unemployment. Police harassed him. Inspectors demanded bribes. On December 17, 2010, after authorities confiscated his wares, he protested and was slapped by a police officer. The local governor refused him a hearing. That afternoon, he doused himself with paint thinner and lit himself on fire in front of the governor's offices.

Bouazizi's self-immolation became an immediate symbol to young Tunisians. Protests, publicized by social media, began that day in Sidi Bouzid. By the time Bouazizi died, on January 4, 2011, the outrage had spread around the country. Social media and cell phones allowed protesters to circumvent government censorship and organize quickly. Their videos and reporting could also broadcast the government's brutal repression to an international audience. When neighboring Egypt erupted in revolution, a key platform for dissent was the Facebook group called We Are All Khaled Said, named for a young man murdered in police custody.

On January 14, Tunisian president Zine El Abidine Ben Ali himself resigned and fled to Saudi Arabia. After a brief period of political turnover, Tunisians elected a constituent assembly, followed by peaceful democratic elections and a new prime minister. The effectiveness of the Tunisian protests gave hope to democracy movements, but this relatively peaceful transition proved to be the exception, not the rule. Egypt toppled long-standing dictator Hosni Mubarak, but a military regime rose in his place leaving an unstable nation prone to terrorist attacks. Similar movements for political freedom in Libya, Yemen, Syria, Morocco, Algeria, and other Middle Eastern counties also resulted in economic instability and displacement.

2013-2016

THE AMERICAS

POLITICS & POWER

2013 NSA CONTRACTOR Edward Snowden releases secret documents revealing National Security Agency data collection on U.S. citizens and then flees to Russia.

2014 THE U.S. GOVERNMENT normalizes relations with Cuba.

2014 THE AFFORDABLE CARE ACT, expanding public access to health insurance, comes into effect.

GEOGRAPHY & ENVIRONMENT

2013 ATMOSPHERIC CO_2 hits 400 parts per million, as measured on top of Hawaii's Mauna Loa volcano.

2013 DEFORESTATION jumps more than 20 percent in Brazilian rainforests.

2014 THE WORST DROUGHT in more than a thousand years blasts California.

CULTURE & RELIGION

2013 CARDINAL JORGE MARIO BERGOGLIO of Argentina becomes Pope Francis, the first pontiff from Latin America.

▼ **2015 THE U.S. SUPREME COURT** rules in favor of same-sex marriage nationwide.

The White House celebrated with rainbow lights on the night same-sex couples earned the legal right to marry in the U.S.

EUROPE

POLITICS & POWER

2014 FOLLOWING PROTESTS IN UKRAINE, President Viktor Yanukovych flees Kiev. Russia sends in troops and annexes the Ukrainian region of Crimea.

2014 SCOTTISH VOTERS defeat an independence referendum and vote to remain part of the United Kingdom.

2015 MORE THAN ONE MILLION MIGRANTS and refugees flee to Europe from Syria, Afghanistan, Iraq, and other war-torn and impoverished countries.

GEOGRAPHY & ENVIRONMENT

2015 VOLKSWAGEN admits to cheating on automotive emissions standards in diesel automobiles, releasing up to 40 times the permitted amount of pollutants.

2015 AS GLOBAL TEMPERATURES reach a record high, 195 countries agree in Paris to adopt a plan to combat climate change.

MIDDLE EAST & AFRICA

POLITICS & POWER

2013 MILLIONS IN EGYPT demonstrate against the government of President Mohammed Morsi.

2013 THE SYRIAN GOVERNMENT attacks rebel areas with sarin gas weapons, killing as many as 1,700 people.

2014 THE MILITANT GROUP ISIS takes over the cities of Fallujah, Ramadi, and Mosul in Iraq.

2014 TERRORIST GROUP BOKO HARAM kidnaps more than 200 girls from a school in the town of Chibok, Nigeria.

GEOGRAPHY & ENVIRONMENT

2014 RHINO POACHING reaches new levels in African countries, with more than 1,200 poached in South Africa alone.

ASIA & OCEANIA

POLITICS & POWER

2013 XI JINPING becomes president of the People's Republic of China.

2013 NORTH KOREA claims to have detonated its third nuclear bomb. The UN Security Council announces sanctions against the country.

2014 A COUP IN THAILAND brings in a military-backed government headed by Prime Minister Prayuth Chan-ocha.

GEOGRAPHY & ENVIRONMENT

2013 THE AIR QUALITY INDEX, measuring air pollution, hits a record-high hazardous level of 993 in January in Beijing, China.

2013 TYPHOON HAIYAN hits the Philippines with winds of 195 mph, the strongest storm on record ever to hit land.

2014 CHINA AND THE U.S. reach a mutual agreement to curb greenhouse gases by 2030.

WHAT LIFE WAS LIKE

Pope Francis

When Argentinian cardinal Jorge Mario Bergoglio became Pope Francis on March 13, 2013, he brought with him a number of firsts. He was the first pope from the Americas—indeed, the first from either the Southern or the Western Hemisphere—the first non-European pope in more than 1,000 years, and the first Jesuit. His public addresses often focused on the plight of the poor or environmental pollution and global warming. Discussing gay clergy, he said, "Who am I to judge?" though he did not change the Church's opposition to same-sex marriage or to the ordination of women. He advocated greater acceptance of divorced Catholics and those who had had abortions. Along with his modest lifestyle, his more forgiving positions earned him great affection among the world's millions of Catholics.

SCIENCE & TECHNOLOGY

2015 NASA'S NEW HORIZONS spacecraft flies past Pluto and reveals details of the dwarf planet's surface.

2015 HACKERS, possibly Chinese, steal more than 20 million records from the U.S. government's Office of Personnel Management in a massive cybersecurity breach.

2013 SCIENTISTS describe a new species of raccoon-like mammal, the olinguito, found in the forests of Colombia and Ecuador.

2013 A METEOR blows up over the Russian city of Chelyabinsk with a force greater than a nuclear explosion, shattering windows and injuring approximately 1,200 people.

2013 SCIENTISTS extract mitochondrial DNA from a 400,000-year-old bone found in Spain.

2014 THE EUROPEAN SPACE AGENCY'S Rosetta spacecraft drops a probe onto the surface of comet 67P/Churyumov–Gerasimenko, the first touchdown ever on a comet.

2014 A RECORD OUTBREAK OF EBOLA spreads from Guinea through Sierra Leone and Liberia, eventually killing more than 11,000.

2015 ANTHROPOLOGISTS discover fossils of a new human ancestor, *Homo naledi,* in a cave in South Africa. These hominins may have coexisted with *Homo sapiens.*

2013 CHINA'S TIANHE-2 becomes the world's most powerful supercomputer, with a speed of 33.86 petaflops (33.86×10^{15} floating point operations per second).

2014 SCIENTISTS CLAIM THAT CARVINGS found on shells on the Indonesian island of Java show that the human ancestor *Homo erectus* was capable of symbolic thought.

2015 RESEARCHERS IN CHINA use Crispr gene-editing technology to edit nonviable human embryos.

PEOPLE & SOCIETY

2013 TWO BOMBS kill three and injure 260 at the Boston Marathon.

2013 THE CITY OF DETROIT files for bankruptcy.

2014 ACTIVIST GROUP Black Lives Matter leads protests in Ferguson, Missouri, following the police shooting of unarmed teenager Michael Brown.

▼ **2013** CATHERINE, DUCHESS OF CAMBRIDGE, gives birth to George Alexander Louis, third in line to the British throne.

Announcement of the birth of Prince George of Cambridge

2013 CHINESE AUTHORITIES ANNOUNCE the decision to relax China's one-child family policy, in place since 1979.

2013 AUSTRALIA adopts a new policy of intercepting migrant boats and sending them back to the country of origin.

2014 MALAYSIA AIRLINES FLIGHT MH370 vanishes with 239 passengers and crew over the Indian Ocean.

2015 POPE FRANCIS draws a record crowd of six million in Manila, Philippines.

THE ANNEXATION OF CRIMEA

THE CRIMEAN PENINSULA, dangling below Ukraine into the waters of the Black Sea, has long been an object of desire for Russians, Ukrainians, and Europeans alike. The beautiful city of Sevastopol contains a strategically important naval base, and the Mediterranean climate of its southern coasts draws tourists from around the world.

After World War II, Crimea became part of Ukraine, which was then part of the U.S.S.R., and it remained so after Ukraine gained its independence following the fall of the Soviet Union. Russia, however, was allowed to keep its Black Sea fleet at Sevastopol. Relations between Crimeans, who were mostly ethnic Russians, and other Ukrainians remained uneasy.

In 2010, Viktor Yanukovych was elected president of Ukraine. Although he initially promised to strengthen Ukraine's ties with the European Union, in 2013 he changed course and steered toward a stronger alliance with Russia. Popular protests against his rule blew up in the streets, and in February 2014 Yanukovych fled, eventually turning up in Russia. Meanwhile, a quiet invasion was under way. Troops in unmarked uniforms set up roadblocks between mainland Ukraine and Crimea. Similarly, unidentified gunmen took over Crimea's parliament building. By March it was clear that these soldiers were in fact Russian, and that Russia under President Vladimir Putin had annexed the peninsula for its own.

Putin's government claimed that the Russian population of Crimea wanted to merge with their Russian neighbors. Skeptical outsiders believed that Russia feared to lose the region to European influences. Crimea voted in a referendum to join Russia, and despite sanctions imposed on Russia by the United States and the European Union it is today a part of the Russian Federation.

2016-2018

THE AMERICAS

POLITICS & POWER

2016 DONALD TRUMP defeats Hillary Clinton to become the 45th president of the United States, winning the Electoral College but losing the popular vote.

2016 DILMA ROUSSEFF, the president of Brazil, is impeached during an ongoing wave of corruption scandals.

2016 COLOMBIAN PRESIDENT Juan Santos works out a peace deal to end the country's more-than-50-year struggle with the guerrilla group FARC.

GEOGRAPHY & ENVIRONMENT

2016 PRESIDENT OBAMA expands a national marine reserve in Hawaii, passing all other U.S. presidents in the amount of land and water protected.

2017 HURRICANES HARVEY, IRMA, AND MARIA bring record flooding and destruction to Texas and the Caribbean.

CULTURE & RELIGION

2016 THE CHICAGO CUBS win the baseball World Series for the first time since 1908.

2016 SONGWRITER BOB DYLAN wins the Nobel Prize in literature.

2018 A MASS SHOOTING at the Tree of Life synagogue in Pittsburgh, Pennsylvania, kills 11 in the worst anti-Semitic attack in American history.

2018 ARCHAEOLOGISTS ANNOUNCE THE DISCOVERY of an ancient Maya metropolis below the Guatemalan jungle.

EUROPE

POLITICS & POWER

2016 A FAILED COUP in Turkey spurs President Recep Erdogan to launch a purge of government critics.

2016 THE UNITED KINGDOM votes for "Brexit," a departure from the European Union, scheduled for 2019.

GEOGRAPHY & ENVIRONMENT

2017 CATALONIA declares independence from Spain. Spain enforces direct rule over the Catalan government and imprisons some of the region's ministers.

2018 AMPLIFIED BY CLIMATE CHANGE, a Europe-wide heat wave brings record high temperatures, wildfires, and crop failures to countries from Portugal to Sweden.

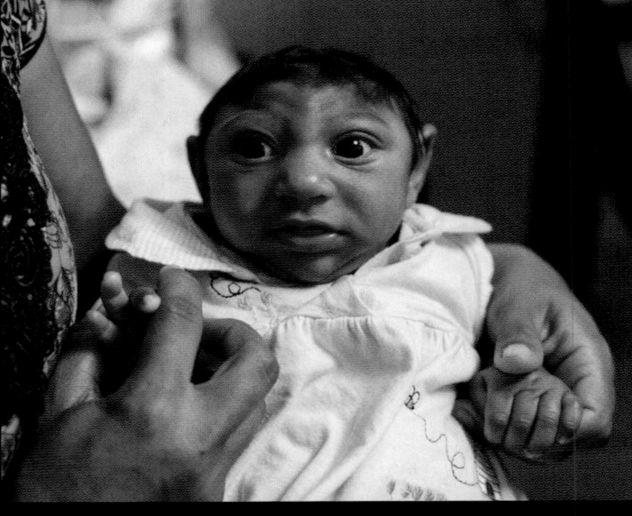

A baby in Brazil born with microcephaly

MIDDLE EAST & AFRICA

POLITICS & POWER

2016 FORCES OF SYRIAN PRESIDENT Bashar al-Assad seize the rebel-held portions of the city of Aleppo during the ongoing civil war.

2017 IRAQI FORCES drive the last ISIS fighters from Iraq. The Islamic State is down to 2 percent of its former territory.

2018 ETHIOPIA AND ERITREA end their 20-year-long conflict.

GEOGRAPHY & ENVIRONMENT

2017 KURDISTAN declares independence from Iraq. The Iraqi government reacts by taking over the city of Kirkuk, claimed by the Kurds.

2017 THE UN WARNS of a severe food crisis in the countries Yemen, Somalia, South Sudan, and Nigeria, owing to internal fighting and poor governance.

2018 THE LAST MALE NORTHERN WHITE RHINO dies in Kenya.

CULTURE & RELIGION

2017 SAUDI PRINCE Badr bin Abdullah bin Mohammed bin Farhan Al Saud buys Leonardo da Vinci's painting "Salvator Mundi" for a record $450.3 million.

2017 GUNMEN KILL 305 in an attack on a Sufi mosque in the Sinai area of Egypt.

ASIA & OCEANIA

POLITICS & POWER

2017 NORTH KOREA is sanctioned by the UN for testing missiles and a nuclear bomb.

2017 THE GOVERNMENT OF MYANMAR escalates attacks on its mostly Muslim Rohingya population, killing thousands and driving more than 600,000 into exile.

2017 INDIA PASSES FRANCE to become the world's sixth largest economy.

GEOGRAPHY & ENVIRONMENT

2018 AN EARTHQUAKE AND TSUNAMI hit Sulawesi, Indonesia, killing more than 2,100.

CULTURE & RELIGION

2016 MOTHER TERESA, Catholic nun and missionary in India who died in 1997, is canonized.

2016 FILIPINO PRESIDENT RODRIGO DUTERTE unleashes an anticrime crackdown based on vigilante justice for suspected drug traffickers.

2018 THE SUPREME COURT of India decriminalizes homosexuality.

SCIENCE & TECHNOLOGY

◀ **2016** MORE THAN 700,000 CASES of the Zika virus are reported in the Americas, some leading to microcephaly in infants.

2016 SCIENTISTS ANNOUNCE that LIGO gravitational wave detectors in Louisiana and Washington State have registered the first gravitational waves ever detected.

2017 MORE THAN 72,000 PEOPLE in the United States die from drug overdoses, the majority from opioids, a threefold increase over the previous 15 years.

2017 A BELGIAN ASTROPHYSICIST and his team discover seven Earth-size extrasolar planets around the star TRAPPIST-1.

2018 THE EUROPEAN SPACE AGENCY'S Mars Express spacecraft detects a subglacial lake on Mars.

2016 RESEARCHERS using muon detectors find a previously unknown void within the Great Pyramid of Giza, near Cairo, Egypt.

2017 *HOMO SAPIENS* FOSSILS found in North Africa date back 300,000 years, making modern humans 100,000 years older than previously thought.

PEOPLE & SOCIETY

2016 A MASS SHOOTING at the Pulse nightclub in Orlando, Florida, kills 49.

2017 WHITE SUPREMACISTS rally in Charlottesville, Virginia, and kill one protester.

2017 MASS SHOOTER Stephen Paddock kills 58 at a music festival in Las Vegas.

2017 FOLLOWING SEXUAL ASSAULT ALLEGATIONS against the film producer Harvey Weinstein, the #MeToo movement exposing sexual harassment spreads around the world.

2016 A TUNISIAN-BORN FRENCH RESIDENT drives a cargo truck into crowds in Nice, France, killing 86.

2017 A MASSIVE FIRE in the Grenfell Tower, a London high-rise, kills 72.

2017 AN AL SHABAAB TRUCK BOMB kills more than 500 in Mogadishu, Somalia.

2017 ZIMBABWEAN PRESIDENT Robert Mugabe is arrested and resigns after ruling 37 years.

THE WOMEN'S MARCH

ON JANUARY 21, 2017, the day after Donald Trump was inaugurated as president of the United States, millions of women took to the streets worldwide to demonstrate for women's rights. In the United States, approximately four million protesters marched in cities and towns across the country in the largest single-day protest in U.S. history. Washington, D.C., saw between 500,000 and a million marchers, who thronged the Metro and the wide avenues with signs and pink knitted hats. Protesters in Fairbanks, Alaska, braved temperatures of 19 below zero. Marches also took place in Paris and London and on every continent, including Antarctica, where one participant held a sign reading "Penguins for Peace."

The proximate cause of the protests was the figure of Donald Trump himself, a divisive personality who entered office with a reputation for misogyny and sexual harassment. On the day after Trump's surprising defeat of candidate Hillary Clinton, a woman in Hawaii created a Facebook event inviting friends to march in Washington. Other women started similar events using the social media platform, and the individual protests quickly merged into a national, and then an international, movement. Although Donald Trump's election was the immediate impetus for the march, long-simmering concern over many social justice issues stoked the energy for the gatherings. Speakers of diverse backgrounds addressed the crowds on a range of matters including reproductive rights, LGBTQ rights, access to health care, gender equality, and even environmental protection and immigration reform—expanding the narrow concept of "women's issues."

Despite the immense crowds, the marches were peaceful and upbeat. Upheld signs lambasted President Trump, urged politicians to keep their hands off women's rights, and spoke up in favor of science. One read, simply, "There Is So Much Wrong It Cannot Fit on This Sign."

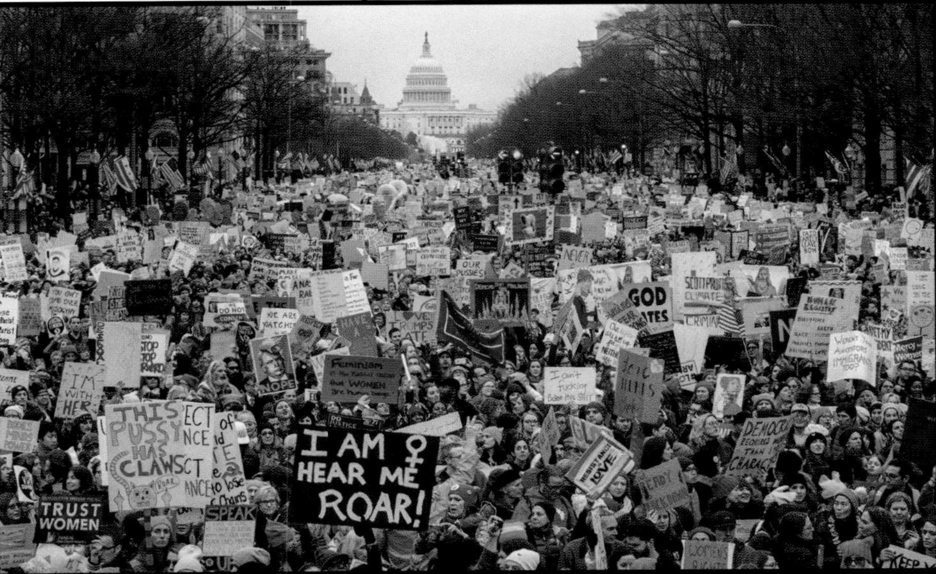

Women's March demonstrators pack the streets of Washington, D.C., on the day after President Trump's Inauguration.

CLIMATE CHANGE

In 2016 human-caused climate change claimed its first mammalian extinction. The humble Bramble Cay melomys, a long-tailed rodent that lived only on a single small island off the Australian coast, vanished as rising seas washed over its habitat.

The small downtick in the world's biodiversity was just one among a host of warnings that climate change is an urgent, worldwide problem. Beginning with the industrial revolution, human activity has released heat-trapping gases—most notably, carbon dioxide—into the air. In 1880, atmospheric CO_2 stood at 288 parts per million. In 2016 it had reached 404 parts per million and was still climbing. As a result of this greenhouse effect, global temperatures are rising. In 2018 they reached a record 1.8°F over the 20th century's average temperature.

The effects are widespread. Animals are disappearing from the warmest parts of their previous ranges. Arctic ice cover is shrinking drastically. Glaciers and other land-based ice sheets are melting as well, contributing to a sea level rise of eight or nine inches over the previous century. The warmer air pulls moisture from the ground, bringing droughts to already dry areas and floods elsewhere. The combination of moisture and heat increases the intensity and frequency of hurricanes and attendant floods and landslides. The number of climate-related disasters has more than tripled since 1980. In the 2010s alone, Hurricanes Irma, Maria, and Michael and Typhoons Haiyan and Yutu ranked among the strongest cyclones in history.

In 2018 the United Nations Intergovernmental Panel on Climate Change produced a comprehensive report that showed world temperatures could rise from preindustrial levels by 2.7°F as soon as 2040. The results include a massive die-off of coral reefs, more devastating wildfires, food shortages, and worldwide migration as the inhabitants of hot and low-lying areas flee to zones of safety.

There is good news among the frightening statistics. It is perfectly possible to avoid the worst effects of climate change if human societies turn away from carbon-emitting sources, particularly coal, toward renewable energy. Affordable technology already exists to do so. Carbon pricing programs are effective. What has been lacking, so far, is a collective political will.

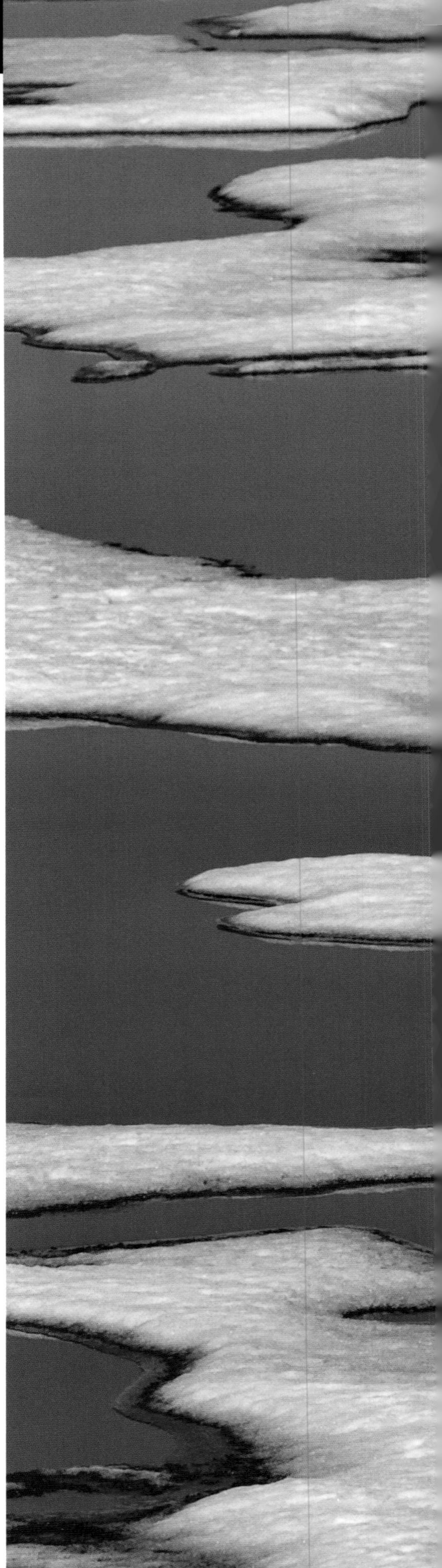

Polar bears are the only species designated for protection under the U.S. Endangered Species Act due to global warming. The bears need their Arctic sea ice habitat and the algae it grows to hunt for seals. Shrinking sea ice, tracked in satellite data, has many consequences including sea level rise, thawed permafrost, and the release of methane gas, which all intensify additional warming.

ILLUSTRATIONS CREDITS

COVER

(UP LE), Ira Block; (UP CTR), Bob Sacha; (UP RT), NASA/Neil A. Armstrong; (CTR LE), John Springer Collection/Corbis via Getty Images; (CTR RT), Mona Lisa, ca 1503-1506 (oil on panel), Vinci, Leonardo da (1452-1519)/Louvre, Paris, France/Bridgeman Images; (LO LE), O. Louis Mazzatenta/National Geographic Image Collection; (LO RT), CSP_raduang/age fotostock. Back cover: (LE), Kenneth Garrett/National Geographic Image Collection; (CTR), Matthew Horwood/Getty Images; (RT), Paul Chesley/National Geographic Image Collection.

FRONT MATTER

2-3, Andia/UIG via Getty Images; 5, REZA; 6, Peter Stackpole/The LIFE Picture Collection/Getty Images; 9, Art by Dylan Cole. Sources: Instituto Nacional de Cultura, Peru; Center for Advanced Spatial Technologies, University of Arkansas; Cotsen Institute of Archaeology, UCLA; Vincent R. Lee.

CHAPTER 1: THE FIRST SOCIETIES PREHISTORY-500 B.C.E.

10-11, Richard Nowitz/National Geographic Image Collection; 12, Kenneth Garrett/National Geographic Image Collection; 13, Kenneth Garrett/National Geographic Image Collection; 14, Steve McCurry/National Geographic Image Collection; 16, Kenneth Garrett/National Geographic Image Collection; 19, Patrick Frilet/Shutterstock; 23 (UP), Sisse Brimberg/National Geographic Image Collection; 23 (LO), Grant Dixon/Getty Images; 25, The Venus of Willendorf, fertility symbol, prehistoric sculpture, 30,000-25,000 B.C.E. (front view)/Naturhistorisches Museum, Vienna, Austria/Ali Meyer/Bridgeman Images; 26, Richard Nowitz/National Geographic Image Collection; 27, DEA/G. Dagli Orti/Getty Images; 28-9, Victor Boswell/National Geographic Image Collection; 29, Georg Gerster/Science Source; 30, DEA/G. Dagli Orti/Getty Images; 31, James P. Blair/National Geographic Image Collection; 33, Kevin Schafer/Getty Images; 34, Kenneth Garrett/National Geographic Image Collection; 35, Kenneth Garrett/National Geographic Image Collection; 37, Historical Views/age fotostock/Alamy Stock Photo; 39, Kenneth Garrett/National Geographic Image Collection; 41, DEA/G. Dagli Orti/Getty Images; 42, Bettmann/Getty Images; 43, Richard T. Nowitz/Getty Images; 45, (UP), Classic Vision/age fotostock; 45 (LO), Map artwork by Richard Schlecht; 48, Archive Photos/Getty Images; 49, DEA/G. Dagli Orti/Getty Images; 50 (UP), DEA/G. Dagli Orti/Getty Images; 50 (LO), Zev Radovan/BibleLandPictures/Alamy Stock Photo; 53 (LE), Gianni Dagli Orti/Shutterstock; 53 (RT), Map relief by Tibor Tóth; 55, Araldo de Luca/Getty Images; 56, Sisse Brimberg/National Geographic Image Collection; 57, Map artwork by John Burgoyne.

CHAPTER 2: THE CLASSICAL AGE 500 B.C.E.-500 C.E.

58-9, O. Louis Mazzatenta/National Geographic Image Collection; 61, Bettmann/Getty Images; 62, DEA/G. Nimatallah/Getty Images; 63, Hulton Archive/Getty Images; 67, Gianfranco Vivi/Shutterstock; 70, Vanni Archive/Getty Images; 71 (UP), Todd Gipstein/National Geographic Image Collection; 71 (LO), Vodjani/ullstein bild via Getty Images; 72, B. Anthony Stewart/National Geographic Image Collection; 73, kostasgr/Shutterstock; 74-5, Georg Gerster/Science Source; 77, Werner Forman/Universal Images Group/Getty Images; 78, Eye Ubiquitous/Shutterstock; 81, Peter V. Bianchi/National Geographic Image Collection; 82-3, Michael Yamashita; 84, Leemage/Getty Images; 87, Bettmann/Getty Images; 89, Araldo de Luca/Getty Images; 90, North Wind Picture Archives via AP Images; 91, David Silverman/Getty Images; 92, James L. Stanfield/National Geographic Image Collection; 92-3, Roger Ressmeyer/Corbis/VCG/Getty Images; 94, W. Langdon Kihn/National Geographic Image Collection; 95, Ira Block/National Geographic Image Collection; 98, Gianni Dagli Orti/Shutterstock; 99, William Albert Allard/National Geographic Image Collection; 100, Vanni Archive/Getty Images; 101, Vincenzo Fontana/© Arte & Immagini srl/Corbis via Getty Images; 103, Benoy K. Behl.

CHAPTER 3: FAITH AND POWER 500-1000

106-107, REZA; 108, Map artwork by Jean-Leon Huens/National Geographic Image Collection; 109, Tim Laman/National Geographic Image Collection; 113, Stefano Bianchetti/Getty Images; 115, Paul Chesley/National Geographic Image Collection; 118, N/Shutterstock; 119 (UP), Ira Block/National Geographic Image Collection; 119 (LO), Peter Noyce/imageBROKER/REX/Shutterstock; 120, Martha Avery/© Asian Art & Archaeology, Inc./Corbis via Getty Images; 121, Michael Yamashita/National Geographic Image Collection; 122-3, Bruce Dale/National Geographic Image Collection; 123, Map artwork by Ned Seidler/National Geographic Image Collection; 124, Kenneth Garrett/National Geographic Image Collection; 125, James L. Stanfield/National Geographic Image Collection; 127 (UP), Gianni Dagli Orti/Shutterstock; 127 (LO), Sarah Leen/National Geographic Image Collection; 129, Mansell/The LIFE Picture Collection/Getty Images; 130, Otis Imboden/National Geographic Image Collection; 131, George H.H. Huey/Alamy Stock Photo; 133, Kenneth Garrett/National Geographic Image Collection; 135, Leemage/Getty Images; 136 (UP), Photo by Enrico Ferorelli, art enhancement by Doug Stern; 136 (LO), Paul Chesley/National Geographic Image Collection; 138, Gianni Dagli Orti/Shutterstock; 141, W. Langdon Kihn/National Geographic Image Collection; 143, Bettmann/Getty Images; 145, The History Collection/Alamy Stock Photo; 147 (UP), George Steinmetz/National Geographic Image Collection; 147 (LO), Richard Schlecht/National Geographic Image Collection; 150-51, John and Lisa Merrill/Getty Images; 153, Martha Avery/© Asian Art & Archaeology, Inc./Corbis via Getty Images.

CHAPTER 4: INVASIONS AND ADVANCES 1000-1500

154-5, Chronicle of World History/Alamy Stock Photo; 157, DEA/M. Seemuller/Getty Images; 158, Map artwork by Christopher A. Klein; 159, CPA Media—Pictures from History/GRANGER—All rights reserved; 161, Bettmann/Getty Images; 167, Jed Share/Getty Images; 169, ©BeBa/Iberfoto/The Image Works; 171, Slim Aarons/Getty Images; 172, Bettmann/Getty Images; 174-5, Paul Chesley/National Geographic Image Collection; 176, Bettmann/Getty Images; 177, Bettmann/Getty Images; 178-9, Ira Block; 181, Richard Alexander Cooke III; 183, Ira Block/National Geographic Image Collection; 184, Peter Guttman/Getty Images; 185, Michael Yamashita/National Geographic Image Collection; 187, Bruce Dale/National Geographic Image Collection; 188-9, Mint Images/Art Wolfe/Getty Images; 189, James L. Stanfield/National Geographic Image Collection; 191, DEA/G. Dagli Orti/Getty Images; 193, Bettmann/Getty Images; 194, Leemage/Getty Images;

195, Tor Eigeland; 198, DEA/G. Nimatallah/Getty Images; 199 (UP), Bettmann/Getty Images; 199 (LO), Bob Sacha.

CHAPTER 5: CONVERGING WORLDS 1500-1750

200-201, Mark R. Godfrey; 202, Hulton Archive/Getty Images; 205, Bettmann/Getty Images; 206, Library of Congress Prints and Photographs Division, LC-USZ62-33994; 207, Hulton Archive/Getty Images; 210, "Mona Lisa," ca 1503-1506 (oil on panel), Vinci, Leonardo da (1452-1519)/ Louvre, Paris, France/Bridgeman Images; 211, Map artwork by Kinuko Y. Craft; 212-13, Victor Boswell/National Geographic Image Collection; 214, Hulton Archive/Getty Images; 215, Leemage/Corbis via Getty Images; 216, Stefano Bianchetti/Getty Images; 217, Bettmann/Getty Images; 220, Universal History Archive/ UIG/Shutterstock; 221, James L. Stanfield/National Geographic Image Collection; 222, Bettmann/Getty Images; 226, Roger Wood/Corbis/VCG via Getty Images; 228, Stock Montage/Getty Images; 229, Gordon Wiltsie/National Geographic Image Collection; 232, Bettmann/Getty Images; 233, The Picture Art Collection/Alamy Stock Photo; 235 (UP), Hulton Archive/Getty Images; 235 (LO), Universal History Archive/ UIG/Shutterstock; 236-7, Mlenny/Getty Images; 238, Dennis Frates/Alamy Stock Photo; 239, Maxim Grebeshkov/Shutterstock; 241, Courtesy Carnegie Institution for Science; 243, William Albert Allard/ National Geographic Image Collection; 244, Bettmann/Getty Images.

CHAPTER 6: EMPIRES AND REVOLUTIONS 1750-1900

246-7, Herbert Tauss/National Geographic Image Collection; 249, Library of Congress Prints and Photographs Division; 250, Corbis/Getty Images; 253, W. and D. Downey/Getty Images; 259 (UP), Hulton Archive/Getty Images; 259 (LO), Bettmann/Getty Images; 260-61, Hulton Deutsch/Getty Images; 263, Library of Congress Prints and Photographs Division, LC-USZ62-24644; 265 (UP), Historical Picture Archive/Getty Images; 265 (LO), Fine Art Images/Heritage Images/Getty Images; 267 (UP), Cci/Shutterstock; 267 (LO), Bettmann/Getty Images; 268 (UP), Bettmann/Getty Images; 268 (LO), Hulton Archive/Getty Images; 269, Fine Art/Getty Images; 270, Hulton Archive/Getty Images; 271, From Nathaniel Isaacs's *Travels and Adventures in Eastern Africa,* 1836; 272, Heritage Images/Getty Images; 277, MPI/Getty Images; 278, Bettmann/Getty Images; 281, Bettmann/Getty Images; 282, Alexander Gardner/U.S. National Archives, 165-SB-23; 282-3, Civil War photographs, 1861-65, Library of Congress, Prints and Photographs Division/ Timothy H. O'Sullivan; 286-7, Library of Congress Prints and Photographs Division, LC-USZC4-4637; 288, Ben Wittick/U.S. National Archives, 111-sC-83726; 289 (UP), Hulton Archive/Getty Images; 289 (LO), Museum of the City of New York/Getty Images; 290, Hulton Archive/Getty Images; 291, Hulton Archive/Getty Images.

CHAPTER 7: GLOBAL CONFLICT 1900-1950

292-3, Peter Stackpole/The LIFE Picture Collection/Getty Images; 295, Bettmann/Getty Images; 299, U.S. National Archives, 238-NT-282; 300, W. Eugene Smith/The LIFE Picture Collection/Getty Images; 305, Fox Photos/Getty Images; 307 (UP), © 2019 Estate of Pablo Picasso/Artists Rights Society (ARS), New York. Digital Image © The Museum of Modern Art/ Licensed by SCALA/Art Resource, NY; 307 (LO), Universal History Archive/ UIG/Shutterstock; 310, Imperial War Museum, Neg. #Q2041; 310-11, Paul Thompson/FPG/Stringer/Getty Images; 313, Corbis Historical/Getty Images; 315, Gilles Petard/Getty Images; 316, Time Life Pictures/Mansell/The LIFE Picture Collection/Getty Images; 318, Bettmann/Getty Images; 319, Bettmann/Getty Images; 320, AP Photo; 321, H. S. Wong/U.S. National Archives; 323, Imperial War Museum, Neg. #H 14250; 325, Official U.S. Navy photograph/U.S. National Archives; 326, U.S. National Archives; 327, Sovfoto/ Universal Images Group/Shutterstock; 329, Official U.S. Navy photograph/U.S. National Archives; 331, U.S. National Archives; 332-3, U.S. Coast Guard Collection/U.S. National Archives; 334, Keystone/Getty Images; 335, U.S. National Archives; 336-7, Margaret Bourke-White/Time Life Pictures/Getty Images; 339, Margaret Bourke-White/Time Life Pictures/ Getty Images.

CHAPTER 8: TOWARD A NEW WORLD ORDER 1950-2000

340-41, Shutterstock; 343, Bettmann/Getty Images; 344, Bettmann/Getty Images; 347, Peter Magubane; 348, Antonio Ribeiro/Gamma-Rapho via Getty Images; 349, Per-Anders Pettersson/Getty Images; 355, John Springer Collection/Corbis via Getty Images; 357, CNP/Getty Images; 358-9, AP Images/ Nick Ut; 361 (UP), NASA/Neil A. Armstrong; 361 (LO), Keystone-France/ Gamma-Rapho via Getty Images; 363 (UP), Gina Martin/National Geographic Image Collection; 363 (LO), Jean-Claude Francolon/Gamma-Rapho via Getty Images; 364, Historical/Getty Images; 367, Karen Kasmauski; 369, Steve McCurry; 370-71, chuyu/Getty Images; 373 (LE), Karen Kasmauski/ Getty Images; 373 (RT), Kim Kulish/Corbis via Getty Images.

CHAPTER 9: GLOBALIZATION AND DISRUPTION 2000-PRESENT

374-5, Matthew Horwood/Getty Images; 377, Eugene Hoshiko-Pool/Getty Images; 378, Luke MacGregor/Bloomberg via Getty Images; 379, Matt Cardy/ Getty Images; 380, Jim Bourg/AFP/Getty Images; 384 (UP), M Panchenko/ Shutterstock; 384 (LO), Vincent Yu/AP/Shutterstock; 385, Narendra Shrestha/EPA/Shutterstock; 386-7, Russell Kord ARCHIVE/Alamy Stock Photo; 388 (UP), Stephen Dunn/Getty Images; 388 (LO), Chris Hondros/Getty Images; 390 (UP), Nikki Kahn/The Washington Post via Getty Images; 390 (LO), Christopher Furlong/Getty Images; 391, Paul Sakuma/AP/Shutterstock; 392-3, John Gress/Corbis via Getty Images; 394, Sophie James/ Shutterstock.com; 396, Michael Reynolds/EPA/Shutterstock; 397, Lefteris Pitarakis/AP/Shutterstock; 398, Clara Gouvêa/Barcroft Media via Getty Images; 399, Michael Reynolds/EPA/Shutterstock; 400-401, Ralph Lee Hopkins/National Geographic Image Collection.

MAP CREDITS

PAGE 57:

Sources: Geoff Irwin, University of Auckland; Patrick Kirch, University of California, Berkeley; Patrick Nunn, University of the South Pacific; Matthew Spriggs, Australian National University.

PAGE 381:

Sources: Steven Mosher and Robert Rohde, Berkeley Earth.

All other maps were prepared by National Geographic Partners Cartographic Division.

INDEX

Boldface indicates illustrations.

C

D

E

F

G

H

K

L

M

N

X

Y

Z

Since 1888, the National Geographic Society has funded more than 13,000 research, exploration, and preservation projects around the world. National Geographic Partners distributes a portion of the funds it receives from your purchase to National Geographic Society to support programs including the conservation of animals and their habitats.

National Geographic Partners
1145 17th Street NW
Washington, DC 20036-4688 USA

Get closer to National Geographic explorers and photographers, and connect with our global community. Join us today at nationalgeographic.com/join

For information about special discounts for bulk purchases, please contact National Geographic Books Special Sales: specialsales@natgeo.com

For rights or permissions inquiries, please contact National Geographic Books Subsidiary Rights: bookrights@natgeo.com

ISBN: 978-1-4262-2064-7

Contributors to this volume include Neil Kagan, Patricia Daniels, Kristin Baird Rattini, Mary Stephanos, Sharon Moore, Elizabeth Allin, Timothy Wright, Kristin Sladen, Bridget E. Hamilton, Moriah Petty, Katie Olsen, Susan Blair, Melissa Farris, and Nicole Miller.

Printed in the United States of America
19/LSCK-CG/1

THE BIGGEST. THE BEST.

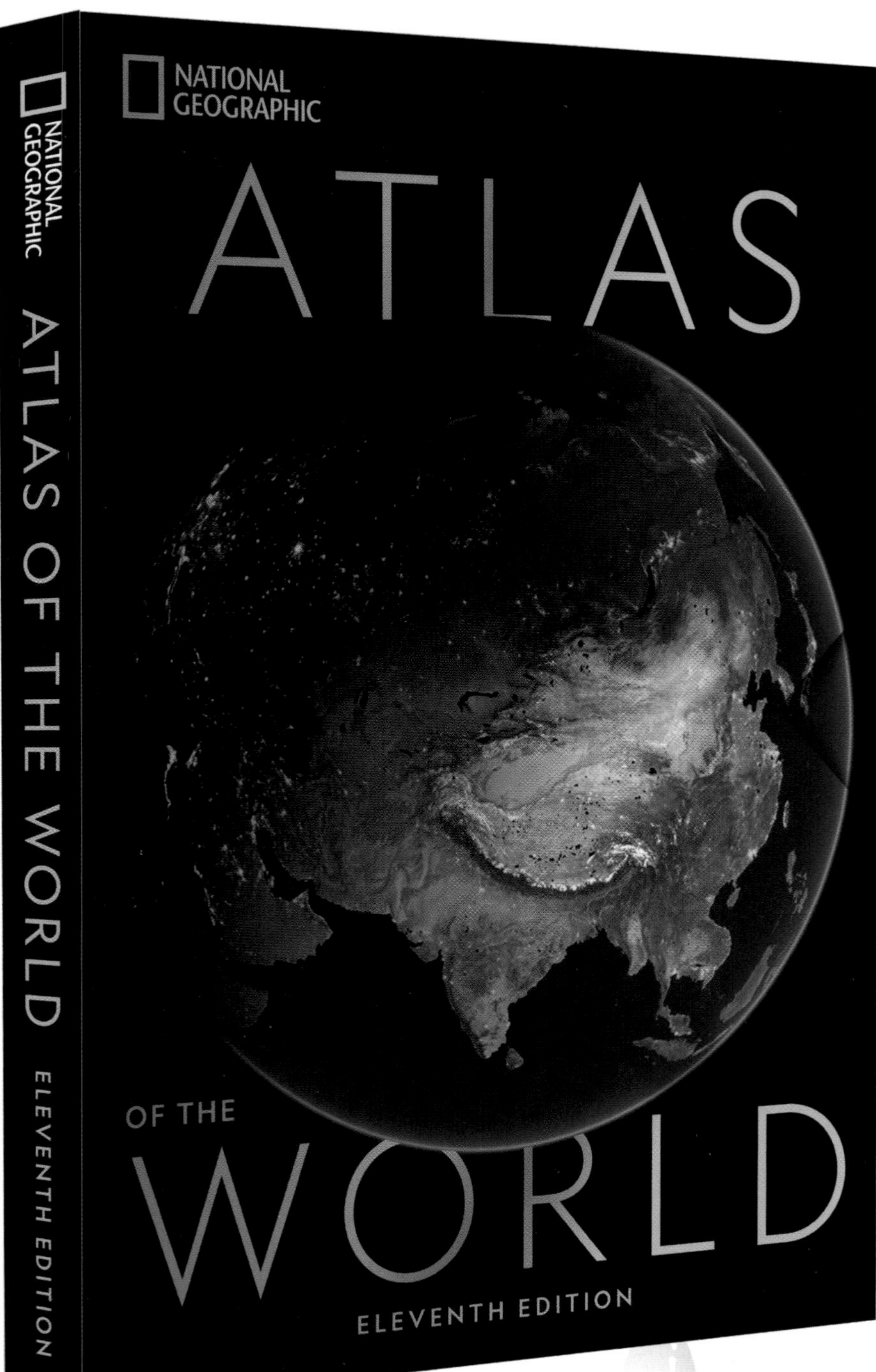

We live in the GPS era, the age of digital mapping and Google Earth. So why is it important to have printed atlases? Because a large-format printed book of maps is critical for understanding the world today. Gather around with family and friends to see the big picture and the little details.

Discover how the natural world connects to humanity. Explore hot topics like climate change, freshwater availability, human migration, and refugee movement. Maps cover not only continents and countries, but also the ocean floor, the solar system, and the universe.

Crafted by the expert hands of National Geographic's world-class cartographers, this epic atlas is in its eleventh edition, illuminating the vital role of a printed atlas even in the digital age.